Adolescent Psychopathology and the Developing Brain

Adolescent Psychopathology and the Developing Brain

Integrating Brain and Prevention Science

Edited by

Daniel Romer
and
Elaine F. Walker

A project of the Adolescent Risk Communication Institute
of the Annenberg Public Policy Center and
The Annenberg Foundation Trust at Sunnylands

2007

OXFORD

UNIVERSITY PRESS

Oxford University Press, Inc., publishes works that further
Oxford University's objective of excellence
in research, scholarship, and education.

Oxford   New York
Auckland   Cape Town   Dar es Salaam   Hong Kong   Karachi
Kuala Lumpur   Madrid   Melbourne   Mexico City   Nairobi
New Delhi   Shanghai   Taipei   Toronto

With offices in
Argentina   Austria   Brazil   Chile   Czech Republic   France   Greece
Guatemala   Hungary   Italy   Japan   Poland   Portugal   Singapore
South Korea   Switzerland   Thailand   Turkey   Ukraine   Vietnam

Published by Oxford University Press, Inc.
198 Madison Avenue, New York, New York 10016

www.oup.com

Oxford is a registered trademark of Oxford University Press.

Library of Congress Cataloging-in-Publication Data
Adolescent psychopathology and the developing brain: integrating brain
and prevention science / edited by Daniel Romer and Elaine Walker.
   p. ; cm.
Includes bibliographical references and index.
ISBN 978-0-19-530625-5
ISBN 978-0-19-530626-2 (pbk.)
1. Adolescent psychopathlogy—Congresses.   2. Brain—Growth
—Congresses.   3. Developmental neurobiology—Congresses.
I. Romer, Daniel, 1945–   II. Walker, Elaine F.
[DNLM: 1. Adolescent Development—Congresses.   2. Brain—growth
& development—Congresses.   3. Adolescent Behavior—Congresses.
4. Adolescent.   5. Mental Disorders—Congresses   WS 450 A2452
2007]
RJ499.A36 2007
616.8900835—dc22   2006015754

9 8 7 6 5 4 3 2 1

Printed in the United States of America
on acid-free paper

Preface

This book is the result of a conference held at the University of Pennsylvania on June 17–18, 2005, that brought together a distinguished group of researchers interested in brain development and mental health. The meeting was organized by the editors of this volume and Joan Bossert of Oxford University Press to provide an overview of the dramatic developments that have taken place in neuroscience, especially in regard to our understanding of normal and abnormal brain development and its implications for interventions to prevent psychopathology. The organizers felt, however, that a successful meeting would require the participation of not only neuroscientists but also those who study influences on adolescent development from both an educational and a social perspective. Hence, the meeting was as interdisciplinary as possible with developmental and educational psychologists as well as researchers who mainly study animal models of brain development.

The conference and this book are the result of many persons and organizations that are not represented in the chapters that follow. In the early stages of the project, we drew on the wisdom and guidance of Dante Cicchetti of the University of Minnesota. His work in creating the new journal *Development and Psychopathology* and the work represented therein was a major source of inspiration to us. He also gave us a great deal of advice about fruitful directions in which the meeting could go. We also have been greatly inspired by the thought-provoking insights of Eric Kandel of Columbia University, whose writings on the prospects for a new biological psychiatry rooted in brain science and the new understanding of genetics provided us with considerable direction. Finally, Kathleen Hall Jamieson, the director of the Annenberg Public Policy Center and the Annenberg Foundation Trust at Sunnylands, first suggested the merits of having the conference. She headed the important work done by the Sunnylands Commissions on Adolescent Mental Health that resulted in the award-winning volume *Treating and Preventing Adolescent Mental Health Disorders,* published by Oxford University Press. The work of the commissions that produced the book led her to recognize that we are at the threshold of a newly emerging understanding of brain development that would have important implications for prevention of mental disorders.

We also thank the Annenberg Trust at Sunnylands for providing funding for the meeting and the Annenberg Foundation for supporting the Adolescent Risk Communication Institute (ARCI) that sponsored the meeting. We owe a special debt to the Penn Mahoney Institute of Neurological Sciences, headed by Irwin Levitan and Charles O'Brien. They provided valuable suggestions for the meeting program and cheered us on as we pursued them.

We also owe debts of gratitude to the many outside reviewers who commented on the chapters in this volume and provided us with many helpful suggestions to make the material as complete and understandable as possible. This group includes Joseph Cubells, Denny Fishbein, Thomas Kosten, Marc Lewis, Chris Monk, Robert Post, Marisa Silveri, Brent Vogt, and Zuoxin Wang. Many of the authors in the volume also provided helpful suggestions to their fellow contributors in order to make the papers as useful as possible. Finally, Eian More of the ARCI staff and Annette Price of the Sunnylands staff provided invaluable assistance in the execution of the conference and this book.

This project would not have been possible without the participation of Elaine Walker, who joined Dan Romer as an organizer of the meeting and editor of this volume. Despite her heavy responsibilities as teacher, researcher, and psychology department head at Emory University, she entered the project shortly after its inception and left her mark on every phase of its implementation. Her wisdom and insights are amply evident in both the conference program and her contributions to this volume.

Daniel Romer
Director, Adolescent Risk Communication Institute
Annenberg Public Policy Center
University of Pennsylvania

Contents

Introduction

Daniel Romer and Elaine F. Walker

The Annenberg Foundation Trust at Sunnylands, under the direction of Kathleen Hall Jamieson, sponsored the Adolescent Mental Health Initiative in 2003 culminating in *Treating and Preventing Adolescent Mental Health Disorders* (Evans et al., 2005, Oxford University Press). This project synthesized the current state of knowledge about the emergence and course of major mental disorders in adolescence and what can be done to treat and prevent these illnesses. As part of this effort, it became clear that our knowledge of the brain and its development from childhood through adolescence has increased dramatically in the last decade and that this greater understanding opened new opportunities to prevent the mental disorders that often emerge during adolescence.

One of the most exciting prospects was the increasing realization that the brain remains highly plastic throughout development. However, during adolescence major forms of brain reorganization take place that make this period particularly sensitive to preventative interventions. Much of the reorganization and maturation that appears to occur during this period has been characterized as a source of maladaptive behavior, such as heightened risk taking, rather than an opportunity for growth. The extensive pruning, especially in the prefrontal cortex, that continues throughout adolescence suggested to scientists, as well as the press, that the adolescent brain was a work in progress that was not prepared for the debut of so many of the behaviors that are first attempted in this age period, such as drinking, driving, and sex.

From the perspective of the prevention researcher, however, this window of plasticity during adolescence suggests that there is still time to have a major influence on the brain's development and hence on the building of adaptive behavior patterns that can prevent disorder and instill resilience for the future. Many mental disorders have deleterious effects on brain structure with lasting consequences for subsequent adaptive behavior. If these changes can be identified and understood, it may be possible to introduce therapeutic experiences that permit the brain to return to its normal course of development and hence to resume a life free of mental disorder. This possibility is an exciting alternative to the present status of interventions that merely treat symptoms without lasting changes in the brain that can maintain adaptive function in the absence of continued intervention.

Another discovery with major implications concerned the role of genetic determinants of brain development. Genetics alone do not control how the brain develops. The environment and experience are as important to the expression of genetic influences as the genes themselves. As a result, a host of potential interventions that were not considered possible just years ago now become feasible. Experiences such as stress and trauma can have large adverse effects on brain development, often in interaction with genetic influences. But therapeutic experience (e.g., skills training, appropriate parenting, talk therapy) and pharmacotherapy may also influence brain development and make it possible to reverse adverse effects of genes and environment and to encourage healthier development. Having a genotype that predisposes one to mental illness should no longer be seen as a life sentence for disorder.

These realizations led us to collaborate with Joan Bossert of Oxford University Press in the present project that brought together experts in this newly emerging field of neurodevelopment and prevention. The resulting conference, held at the University of Pennsylvania in June 2005, asked researchers to consider two questions regarding their work: (1) What neurodevelopmental processes in children and adolescents could be altered so that mental disorders might be prevented? (2) What interventions or life experiences might be able to introduce such changes? These were challenging questions, but we feel that our participants grappled with them well.

In bringing our participants together, we attempted to merge fields that have not seen much interaction. At one extreme, we invited specialists in brain development who may not study effects on human behavior, such as adolescent development and risk for mental disorder. In some of this work, animal models of mental disorder are the primary focus. Nevertheless, much has been learned in recent years from these approaches that would never have been possible from studying humans alone. At the other extreme, we invited researchers who study human adolescents from the perspective of educational or psychological interventions. We hoped that researchers from both traditions would be better able to bring about a synthesis of the implications of the new knowledge about brain development to the problem of designing preventative interventions for mental disorder. Here again we feel we succeeded, and to this we owe a great deal of gratitude to the researchers who participated in the meeting and to the creation of this book. This volume is the culmination of this effort. We hope that readers with a background in neuroscience will find it as useful as those with an interest only in the healthy development of children.

In part I of the volume, we focus on the universals of biology and behavior that make adolescence a unique period in our lives. Linda Spear reviews what we know about the adolescent period from the perspective of evolutionary biology and the study of mammals, including humans. She highlights the universal characteristics of adolescence that make it both an exciting, as well as potentially trying, period in development. She also presents hypotheses about the role of specific areas of the brain that might influence adolescent development. In the second chapter, Ann Masten reviews the vast literature that has accumulated in recent decades on the characteristics of resilient youth and the factors that enable young people to face both external and internal challenges to their healthy development. She highlights the importance of external supports and experiences that can carry adolescents through the rough periods and confer resilience to subsequent challenges. Any attempt to understand healthy development would need to accommodate this body of knowledge.

In part II on characteristics of brain and behavior in development, we turn to the important changes that occur in brain development from birth through adolescence that have implications for the prevention of mental disorder. Elizabeth R. Sowell, Paul M. Thompson, and Arthur W. Toga review the exciting work that they and others have been conducting to identify the structural changes in the human brain during adolescence. This research shows how brain changes may be linked to disorders such as ADHD and to the debilitating effects of early alcohol exposure. It also suggests that variation in brain structure is linked to cognitive performance such as measured by intelligence tests. Don Tucker and Lyda Moller present a novel synthesis of what is known about brain development as it pertains to the formation of identity and attachments to peers during adolescence. They highlight the potential influence of differences in right- and left-hemispheric development that may underlie these changes. Finally, Scott Hemby and Joann O'Connor review the role that genetic influences play in the development of neurobiological systems that can influence the expression of such disorders as schizophrenia.

In part III, we focus on the effects of maltreatment and stress during early development and the consequences for the developing brain and later susceptibility to mental disorder. In the first chapter in this section, Megan Gunnar provides an overview of the brain's stress response system and how early stressors can influence this system as the child develops. She also reviews research suggesting that adverse effects on the stress response system produced by neglectful parenting can be reversed by subsequent more responsive care. Her work with human infants and children merges nicely with that of Michael Meaney, who has been studying the powerful role of maternal behavior in the development of mammals. His work suggests that stress experienced by the mother during both the prenatal and postnatal period can influence her behavior toward the newborn. This early maternal treatment can then influence the expression of genes that regulate the infant's stress response with life-long implications for subsequent mental disorder. A particularly intriguing aspect of this work is the transmission of these effects to the next generation. Karen Bales and C. Sue Carter then discuss the newly emerging study of two hormones, oxytocin and arginine vasopressin, that appear to influence mating and social behavior. Although our understanding of these hormones is just beginning, it appears that they may be affected by early parental behavior and play a role in the ability to form pair bonds. They may also influence the stress response and emergence of depression in adolescents. Finally, Charles A. Nelson, Charles H. Zeanah and Nathan A. Fox describe the work that they have been doing to understand the effects of early social deprivation in the institutional rearing of infants in Romania and how subsequent adoption into normal families can reverse some of the adverse effects of this early traumatic experience on brain development and behavior.

In part IV, we turn to the effects of stress and other environmental hazards experienced during adolescence. Erin McClure and Daniel Pine outline a model of brain development that can explain many of the social sources of anxiety in adolescents and ways to study these forces as they affect both normal and anxious youth. Anthony Grace presents a model for the development of schizophrenia that focuses on the combined effects of both genetic predispositions and stress experienced during adolescence that can lead to abnormal brain development and psychotic symptoms. His work suggests that intervention with antianxiety medications may short-circuit this process and prevent the emergence of psychosis. Elaine F. Walker, Amanda McMillan, and Vijay Mittal discuss the influence of stress hormones on brain development and the potential influence of these hormones on the development of psychotic symptoms during adolescence. They also discuss the potential role of drug treatments for mental disorders that might affect the expression of these symptoms. Lauren Alloy and Lyn Abramson describe a model for the emergence of depression in adolescence that combines the effects of both social stressors and normative brain development processes to explain the early rise of depression in female youth. They also suggest some strategies to reverse these processes.

In part V, we move to a discussion of potentially reversible abnormalities in brain development and strategies that have been proposed to reverse these processes. Kiki Chang, Kim Gallelli, and Meghan Howe review the work that has been undertaken to explore the brain mechanisms involved in the development of bipolar disorder. They present an overview of the wide range of interventions that the new science of brain development presents for the eventual prevention of this and other disorders. Nicole S. Cooper, Adriana Feder, Steven M. Southwick, and Dennis S. Charney discuss the deleterious effects of traumatic experience and its effects on brain development. They also review the many interventions that have evidence of efficacy for promoting resilience to subsequent traumatic events. Martha Farah, Kimberly G. Noble, and Hallam Hurt describe research they have conducted to characterize the areas of the brain that are affected by chronic poverty conditions experienced by poor urban youth. With these more precise neurological measures, they are able to identify the experiences that might be needed to reverse the adverse effects of chronic poverty conditions. Finally, Charles B. O'Brien reviews the deleterious effects of addictive drugs on brain development and what is known about ways to reverse these effects.

In the final section, part VI, we include three chapters on the newly emerging field of educational interventions for enhanced neurodevelopment. M. Rosario Rueda, Mary K. Rothbart, Lisa Saccomanno, and Michael I. Posner discuss potential computer-based interventions for young children that in interaction with genetic predispositions can increase attentional capacities but if left untreated are implicated in poor behavioral control and in several disorders, including attention deficit hyperactivity disorder, personality disorder, and schizophrenia. Patricia Gorman Barry and Marilyn Welsh have been developing a program for grades K–12 that teaches emotional and cognitive control of behavior and general problem solving skills. The program, called BrainWise, uses metaphors taken from neuroscience to help children understand how their brains work and how they can control stressful situations in which they might otherwise make hasty and maladaptive choices. Mark T. Greenberg, Nathaniel R. Riggs, and Clancy Blair have been developing similar programs for preadolescents to learn neurocognitive skills that can enable them to better control their behavior and make good decisions in risky situations. All three of these chapters provide evidence that these programs can influence the development of areas of the brain that control impulses and executive function.

In the conclusion, we provide a review of the major themes of the chapters and their implications for future research in this new and exciting field. We also discuss policy implications of the findings that subsequent research might help to validate and refine. In Appendix A, we include a glossary of terms for those new to the science of brain structure and development. We are indebted to Shivali Dhruv of Emory University for this very helpful summary. We also provide two human brain diagrams designed by Eian More to help readers locate the important brain centers discussed in this volume (see Appendix B).

Part I

Biological and Social Universals in Development

Chapter 1

The Developing Brain and Adolescent-
Typical Behavior Patterns

An Evolutionary Approach

Linda Spear

Brain development is a lifelong process. The massive growth and differentiation of the nervous system occurring prior to birth and during the early postnatal period is just one phase in its gradual elaboration and sculpting. During toddler- and child-hood, developmental changes in brain continue to be elaborated (see Ornitz, 1996, for review), even in forebrain regions including the prefrontal cortex (see Happaney et al., 2004), whose ontogeny is relatively protracted, with significant remodeling during adolescence and into adulthood (e.g., Sowell et al., 2003). It is now known that myelination and associated developmental shifts in gray/white matter volume continue in neocortical regions well into adulthood (Sowell et al., 2003) and that modest numbers of new neurons are generated in certain locations in brain throughout life (Eriksson et al., 1998), potentially providing continued opportunities for some remodeling and plasticity. Within this framework of a developmentally dynamic brain throughout life, it has gradually become recognized that the adolescent period is a time of particularly dramatic developmental change. These adolescent-associated brain changes include a considerable loss of synaptic connections in certain brain regions, and ultimately transform the more energy utilizing, seemingly less efficient brain of the child into a more rapidly communicative and more energy efficient brain of the adult (for review, see Spear, 2000).

This adolescent-associated sculpting of brain is highly conserved, with alterations similar to those seen in human adolescents also evident during the adolescent transition in mammalian species ranging from rodents to nonhuman primates. Adolescent-related brain transformations may have been highly conserved evolutionarily for a variety of reasons, perhaps not only because they serve to adaptively sculpt the brain of the juvenile into that of the mature adult. Some of these alterations are associated with the hormonal reawakening of puberty, a critical event of adolescence that leads to sexual maturation and is characterized by increased release of a cascade of hormones, including gonadotrophin-releasing hormone (GnRH) from the hypothalamus, follicle-stimulating hormone (FSH) and lutenizing hormone (LH) from the pituitary, and culminating in gonadal release of estrogen and progesterone in females and testosterone in males (see Worthman, 1999). This hormonal activation is precipitated in part by developmental changes in hypothalamus and other brain regions, although many of the details of the neural alterations involved are still unknown (e.g., Grumbach, 2002, for review). Rising hormone levels not only may be precipitated neurally but also in turn may serve to trigger some adolescent-associated brain transformations (see Steinberg, 2004).

Some alterations occurring in adolescent brain may be critical for facilitating behavioral predispositions that benefit the adolescent at this time of transition from dependence to independence. Indeed, human adolescents and their counterparts in a variety of mammalian species exhibit certain behavioral commonalities of potential adaptive significance during our evolutionary past. To set the stage for review of the adolescent brain and its highly conserved developmental sculpting, we first turn to consideration of the potential adaptive significance of adolescence and its associated neurobehavioral transformations.

Adolescence, Evolution, and Behavior

The period of adolescence subsumes the gradual transformation from immaturity/dependency to maturity/independency. Hence, by definition, adolescence is a developmental phase that can be identified across mammalian species. Among the numerous transitions occurring within the broad adolescent period is the temporally restricted interval of puberty, with the timing of puberty within adolescence of significance for both male and female adolescents, although correlates of early versus late pubertal timing often differ between boys and girls (see Steinberg & Belsky, 1996, for review). With no single event signaling the onset or termination of adolescence in any given species and a developmental pacing that varies across individuals, boundaries of adolescence are imprecise. Prototypic adolescent periods include the interval from approximately 10–20 years in humans, 2–4 years in nonhuman primates (depending on the species), and the 2-week interval from 28–42 days in rats. However, signs of impending or residual adolescence may well be seen outside these inexact boundaries, with females of a variety of species often entering adolescence sooner and males tending to lag somewhat behind (see Spear, 2000, for discussion and references).

Although ontogenetic periods corresponding to adolescence can be identified in nonhuman animals, these other species of course do not demonstrate the full complexity of brain, behavior, or psychopathology evident during human adolescence (or at any other time of life). Nevertheless, there are notable commonalities between human adolescents and their counterparts in other mammalian species in terms of developmental history and genetic constraints, as well as in their behavioral predispositions and neural and hormonal characteristics. Such similarities may have been driven in part by common evolutionary pressures.

Among the behavioral proclivities characteristic of adolescents of a variety of species are an increasing focus on peer-directed social interactions, increased interactions with peers, and occasionally increased fighting with parents relative to younger and older individuals (Csikszentmihalyi et al., 1977; Primus & Kellogg, 1989; Steinberg, 1989). Also common among mammalian adolescents are increases in behaviors termed novelty seeking, sensation seeking, risk taking, and impulsivity (Adriani et al., 1998; Trimpop et al., 1999). Behavioral commonalities seen among adolescents from a variety of species presumably are rewarding and highly conserved because of their ultimate adaptive significance. For instance, peer-directed interactions have been shown to be particularly rewarding during adolescence in research using an animal model (Douglas et al., 2004) and have been shown to support development of new social skills and social support (Galef, 1977; Harris, 1995). Novelty, likewise, appears especially rewarding for adolescents (Douglas et al., 2003), with risk taking postulated to serve a number of adaptive functions, such as increasing the probability of reproductive success in males of a variety of species, including humans (Wilson & Daly, 1985). Risk taking may also be adaptive for the adolescent by providing opportunities to explore adult behaviors and privileges (Silbereisen & Reitzle, 1992) and to face and conquer challenges (Csikszentmihalyi & Larson, 1978).

Increased affiliation with peers and elevated risk taking may also supply the impetus for maturing male and female adolescents to explore new areas away from the home. Emigrating with peers away from the home area around the time of sexual maturation to territory far from genetic relatives is a common strategy used among mammalian species to avoid inbreeding and the lower viability of resulting offspring due to greater expression of recessive genes (Bixler, 1992; Moore, 1992). Indeed, in virtually all species of mammals (including our human ancestors, e.g., Schlegel & Barry, 1991), male adolescents, female adolescents, or both emigrate away from the home territory prior to sexual maturation, a journey often taken with peers (e.g., Keane, 1990). Even in modern human societies, in which cultural traditions largely protect against inbreeding and hence reduce emigration pressure, adolescent risk taking still persists, not only because such traits may be retained for quite some time under relaxed selection pressure but also because of other potential adaptive consequences of these behaviors. Indeed, engaging in some risk taking becomes normative during adolescence, with >50% of human adolescents engaging in drunk driving, sex without contraception, use of illegal drugs, fighting, or other risk-taking behaviors (Irwin, 1989).

Although adolescent-associated increases in risk-taking behaviors may have been highly conserved in part because they served to facilitate emigration or otherwise enhance adaptive fitness during evolution, such risk taking bears considerable cost for some adolescents. There are elevated mortality rates during adolescence in virtually all species, including humans (e.g., Crockett & Pope, 1993; Irwin & Millstein, 1992). This increase, during the otherwise relatively healthy age period of adolescence, is attributable largely to risk-taking behaviors per se (e.g., Muuss & Porton, 1998), with the three highest sources of mortality among modern human adolescents being accidents, homicides, and suicides (Irwin et al., 2002). Although it is likely that those adolescents who exhibit the most risk taking are at the greatest risk of adverse outcome, for even those adolescents engaging in moderate amounts of risk taking, there is a chance for harm.

Adolescent Brain Sculpting: Pruning of Synapses, Declines in Energy Utilization, and Changes in White/Gray Matter

Development of the neocortex during adolescence is characterized more by a loss of connections rather than creation of substantial new connectivity, with an almost 50% loss of the synaptic connections between neurons estimated in some cortical regions during adolescence in the brain of nonhuman primates (Bourgeois et al., 1994; Rakic et al., 1994). A similar decline in synaptic density is seen in human neocortex between 7 and 16 years (Huttenlocher, 1979), with limitations in the amount of human autopsy material restricting more precise delineation of the time course of this decline.

The functional implications of the synaptic pruning during adolescence have yet to be determined. More synapses are not necessarily better, with some forms of mental retardation associated with elevated numbers of synapses (Goldman-Rakic et al., 1983). Indeed, "overproduction followed by pruning" is a well-known characteristic of brain ontogeny during the prenatal and early postnatal periods (see Rakic et al., 1994). Yet, an adolescent-associated synaptic decline would seemingly reflect more than the elimination of nonfunctional synapses, given the costliness of maintaining synapses with no functional role throughout infancy and the juvenile period prior to their belated demise during adolescence. Some support for this notion is seen in data from Lewis (2005) showing that properties of synapses eliminated during adolescence are similar to those that were maintained, and hence eliminated synapses presumably were functional prior to their removal. The probability of a synapse being pruned during adolescence, however, varies with type of synapse and its circuitry. For instance, excitatory input to the neocortex is particularly targeted (Bourgeois et al., 1994) and pruning is more pronounced in prefrontal cortex (PFC) and other neocortical regions than in subcortical areas (Rakic et al., 1994). Even within cortex, pruning more commonly involves circuitry intrinsic to a particular cortical region than associational circuitry that connects different cortical regions (Woo et al., 1997). Circuitry intrinsic to particular regions of cortex is important for expression of reverberating circuits, and pruning within these intrinsic circuits has been suggested to reflect a fine-tuning of neural connectivity in these cortical regions (see Woo et al., 1997). Thus, the evidence to date supports the conclusion that the often dramatic pruning of synapses during adolescence largely does not reflect elimination of nonfunctional synapses but rather involves targeted pruning that helps to sculpt the adolescent brain into its mature form. Although empirical data linking particular aspects of this neuronal sculpting to specific functional consequences is limited, this adolescent-associated synaptic elimination has been suggested to be a form of developmental plasticity by which the adolescent brain may be sculpted to match the environmental demands and opportunities that emerge during this transition (Rakic et al., 1994).

A culling of excitatory cortical synapses during adolescence, along with a decline in synaptic connections supporting reverberating circuitry in certain cortex regions, could also support a reduction or refinement in brain effort at this time. Indeed, it is interesting that during adolescence in humans (see Chugani, 1996) and other species (e.g., rats: Tyler & van Harreveld, 1942), there is an overall decline in brain energy utilization, with the high rates of glucose metabolism, blood flow, or oxygen utilization seen during childhood gradually declining to reach the more moderate utilization rates typical of the adult.

Levels of oxygen utilization have been used to index neural activation, given that activity of neurons and their associated support cells (glia) requires oxygen. Blood oxygen level dependent (BOLD) imaging can be used to noninvasively identify regions of enhanced oxygen utilization, and hence presumably enhanced neuronal activation, under various stimulus conditions. Developmental studies using functional magnetic resonance imaging (fMRI) have revealed ontogenetic changes during the transition from childhood to adolescence in patterns of BOLD signals during performance of cognitive tasks thought to index various (and sometimes overlapping) components of executive function (e.g., attention, response inhibition, working memory, and performance on delay tasks). In some instances, children have been reported to show activation in PFC that is less specific to the type of information, as well as less efficient, with children recruiting prefrontal territory more diffusely during performance on a working memory task than adolescents (Casey et al., 2000) or adults (Casey et al., 1998). In other studies, ontogenetic increases in focal activation of certain regions of PFC have been observed in adolescence during performance of working memory and response inhibition tasks (see Paus, 2005, for review), with adolescents sometimes showing greater PFC activation than children or adults during task performance (Luna et al., 2001). Ontogenetic differences have also been observed in terms of subcortical activation patterns, with evidence for developmental declines in subcortical activation between adolescence and adulthood that are converse of the increases in activation seen in certain frontal regions (Rubia et al., 2000). Such changes were observed not only on a task in which performance improved with age (delay task), but on a task in which performance was similar across age (stop task), suggesting that adolescents and adults may differ in patterns of brain activation even when they are performing similarly on a task (Rubia et al., 2000). A like conclusion was reached in work using electrophysiological measures (e.g., event-related potentials; contingent negative variation), with evidence emerging that under circumstances in which both children and adults show sustained attention, this task is accomplished by children using neural mechanisms that differ from those of adults, with continued maturation of prefrontal regions through late adolescence (Segalowitz & Davies, 2004).

This rapidly evolving literature on microstructural (e.g., synaptic) and functional ontogeny of the brain during adolescence is embedded within a literature documenting maturation of structural components of the brain from childhood through adolescence and well into adulthood, with generally more rostral (frontal) regions maturing more slowly (e.g., Gogtay et al., 2004; Sowell et al., 2003). Prominent among the changes observed are highly consistent developmental increases in cortical white matter through adolescence into adulthood in humans (Paus et al., 1999; Pfefferbaum et al., 1994; Sowell et al., 2003) and other species (Villablanca et al., 2000). Ontogenetic increases in white matter reflect axon myelination, a process by which glial processes form protective sheaths of lipid (whose appearance is white in unstained tissue) around axons. The insulation provided by myelin speeds information flow down axons, and hence is presumed to result in faster and more efficient processing of information. In the peripheral nervous system, the increase in conduction velocity provided by the development of myelin generally compensates for the increase in axonal length necessitated by growth of the body, hence the time taken for an impulse to transverse the entire length of an axon in the periphery remains roughly constant during development despite sometimes dramatic increases in motoneuron length necessitated by limb growth (see Jacobson, 1991). This seems unlikely to be the case in the brain, given that dramatic developmental increases in myelin are seen even when correcting for brain size (weight; Benes et al., 1994), suggesting that the consequence of central myelination would be to decrease the time taken for transfer of information from the cell body, down the axon to the axon terminal. The implications of this may not have been fully considered to date. Speed isn't everything, with many axonal systems in brain (e.g., intrinsic circuitry interconnecting neurons within a given brain region) never becoming myelinated. Moreover, neurons are exquisitely sensitive to the timing of input (with, for example, glutaminergic activation of NMDA receptors requiring co-occurring depolarization-dependent changes induced by other ligand/receptor interactions; e.g., see Nestler et al., 2001, for review). Consequently, if converging input pathways vary in whether they become myelinated or in when that occurs developmentally, the relative speed at which each provides input to a given common target would vary accordingly during development, potentially influencing the nature of the information being conveyed. Hence, one could imagine that substantial orchestration of myelination activities might be required within the context of other ontogenetic changes to permit selective maturational increases in speed of information flow while still preserving appropriate timing of converging inputs.

Although less prominent than developmental increases in white matter, ontogenetic declines in the relative size of cellular (gray matter) components during adolescence have been reported in some regions, particularly frontal regions such as dorsal frontal and parietal areas (Giedd et al., 1999; Rapoport et al., 1999). This decline in gray matter relative to overall volume of particular brain regions is likely attributable not only to the synaptic pruning seen in these regions during adolescence but also to ontogenetic increases in white matter (Sowell et al., 1999), with overall cerebral volume remaining approximately the same from about the age of 5 years onward (see Giedd et al., 1996). A decline in gray matter volume is not ubiquitous during adolescence, with developmental increases in gray matter volume seen in certain subcortical regions of the adolescent including the amygdala and hippocampus (Giedd et al., 1997), as well as in the posterior temporal cortex (see Sowell, this volume).

Adolescent-Associated Transformations in Forebrain: Mesocorticolimbic Circuitry, Dopamine, and Stress

Adolescent Ontogeny of PFC

As reviewed above and detailed in other chapters in this volume, studies using structural and functional MRI have revealed evidence for continued development and organization of this brain region during adolescence, along with developmental improvements in cognitive capabilities (Casey et al., 2000; Luna et al., 2001; Pine et al., 2002), and affect regulation (see Dahl, 2001, for review). The scope of PFC microstructure and function that can be dissected using imaging techniques in humans is still limited, however, although technology is improving rapidly. Thus, to the extent that certain adolescent neural changes and their functional consequences can be modeled in part in other species, studies in laboratory animals may provide clues as to specific alterations in circuitry within the PFC and associated networks during adolescence. When using such animal models, however, it is important to consider potential species differences in the homology of particular brain regions and the comparability of their organization (Preuss, 2000).

Several adolescent-associated alterations in PFC characterized in human adolescents have been observed in adolescents of other mammalian species as well. For instance, volumetric declines in PFC gray matter have been reported not only in humans (e.g., Sowell et al., 1999) but also in rats (van Eden et al., 1990). Likewise, synaptic pruning of presumed glutaminergic excitatory input is observed during adolescence in humans (Huttenlocker, 1984) and nonhuman primates (Zecevic et al., 1989), with decreases in number of glutamate receptors of the NMDA receptor subtype observed in the cortex of rats during adolescence as well (Insel et al., 1990). Complementary to the decline in excitatory glutaminergic drive to cortex (Zecevic et al., 1989), dopaminergic (DA) input to certain portions of the PFC increases during adolescence in nonhuman primates to peak at levels considerably higher than those seen earlier or later in life (e.g., Rosenberg & Lewis, 1995). Studies in rats also have revealed developmental increases through adolescence in a number of measures of DA input to PFC, including DA fiber density (Benes et al., 2000) and DA concentrations (Leslie et al., 1991). Recent rodent studies have also linked adolescence with important changes in DA modulation within PFC. For instance, there is a loss of "buffering capacity" among DA terminals in PFC during adolescence that is associated with the disappearance of DA autoreceptors, which in the juvenile had formed part of a negative feedback system to regulate rates of DA synthesis (Dumont et al., 2004). Also, PFC slices from adolescent rats do not show adult-typical depolarization in response to coactivation of DA D1 receptors and NMDA receptors, even though this depolarized "up state" is thought to be critical for information processing and plasticity (Tseng & O'Donnell, 2005). Functional implications of these ontogenetic alterations in DA activity and modulatory capacities in the PFC have yet to be characterized and may need to be interpreted within a broader context of adolescent-associated alterations in DA activity in other brain regions, as discussed next.

The Adolescent DA System and Developmental Shifts in the Balance Between Mesocortical and Mesolimbic/Striatal DA Systems

Alterations in DA activity in forebrain regions during adolescence are not restricted to the mesocortical DA system projecting to PFC but are also evident in DA projections to the striatum as well as the mesolimbic DA system (i.e., DA projections to limbic areas such as the nucleus accumbens and amygdala). One notable and well-substantiated change is the decline in DA receptors seen during adolescence in striatum, with declines of ⅓ to ½ of the striatal D1 and D2 receptors seen in human adolescents, as well as adolescents of other species (Seeman et al., 1987; Tarazi & Baldessarini, 2000; Teicher et al., 1995). Developmental declines in striatum may be sex dependent, with effects in rats generally limited to males (Andersen et al., 1997), although the presence or absence of gonadal steroids had no effect on the pruning process (Andersen et al., 2002; nor was this decline affected by blockade of NMDA receptors; Teicher et al., 2003).

Data are more mixed with regard to the ontogenetic course of DA binding in the nucleus accumbens (n.Acc), with work reporting early adolescent peaks in D1, D2, and D4 receptors that are about ⅓ greater than those seen in early adulthood (Tarazi et al., 1998, 1999) contrasting with other data reporting no notable overproduction and pruning in this region (Teicher et al., 1995). D1 and D2 receptor overproduction and pruning is also seen in the PFC, although the timing of the decline is relatively delayed, not occurring until postadolescence (Andersen et al., 2000).

Studies in laboratory animals have revealed complementary alterations in the rates of DA synthesis and turnover in mesolimbic/striatal (e.g., n.Acc and striatal) and mesocortical (e.g., PFC) brain regions during adolescence (Andersen et al., 1997; Teicher et al., 1993). Early in adolescence, estimates of basal rates of DA synthesis and turnover in PFC are high, declining to lower levels by late adolescence and adulthood, whereas DA synthesis and turnover estimates in n.Acc and DA turnover estimates in striatum conversely are lower early than late in adolescence (Anderson et al., 1997; Teicher et al., 1993; but see also Leslie et al., 1991). These data are consistent with typical reciprocal relationships often seen among forebrain DA terminal regions, with levels of DA activity in PFC generally being inversely related to DA release in subcortical regions in studies conducted in both rats (Deutsch, 1992) and nonhuman primates (Wilkinson, 1997).

These developmental alterations in DA synthesis and turnover have led to the suggestion that there is a developmental shift in the balance between mesolimbic/ striatal and mesocortical DA systems during adolescence (Andersen, 2003; Spear, 2000), with mesocortical DA influences peaking early in adolescence, followed later by a gradual shift toward enhanced activity in mesolimbic/striatal DA terminal regions (see Spear, 2000, for review). This relative shift toward mesocortical DA predominance early in adolescence likely would be even further exacerbated by stressors, given the greater sensitivity of mesocortical DA projections than mesolimbic or striatal terminal regions to activation by stressors (Dunn, 1988). Such developmental alterations in DA balance across these brain regions may be of functional significance for the adolescent, given that DA projections to n.Acc and other mesolimbic regions form part of the circuitry critical for labeling incentive stimuli with motivational relevance (Robinson & Berridge, 2003). Indeed, as discussed later, relatively low levels of mesolimbic DA activity early in adolescence may contribute to the emergence of adolescent risk taking, given that attenuated DA activity in mesolimbic regions has been linked to increased motivation for seeking out novelty, alcohol and other drugs, as well as other potentially rewarding stimuli (e.g., Gardner, 1999).

The Adolescent Amygdala

There are hints from research conducted both in laboratory animals and in humans that the adolescent amygdala may be a particularly intriguing and important area for ontogenetic investigation. This region is of particular interest for study during the highly emotionally laden and peer-driven period of adolescence given the importance of the amygdala in processing of emotional stimuli (Baxter & Murray, 2002), modulating social behavior (Amaral et al., 2003), attributing affect, and establishing reward expectancies (Bechara et al., 1999; Holland & Gallagher, 2004). The amygdala also has bidirectional and functional connectivity with the orbitofrontal cortex (OFC; Zald et al., 1998), a brain region likewise critical for the expression of social behavior (Kolb et al., 2004), and reward circuitry related to addiction (Volkow & Fowler, 2000).

Excitatory input from the amygdala (basolateral nucleus) to the PFC continues to be elaborated through adolescence (Cunningham et al., 2002). The adolescent amygdala is more prone to induction of seizures by electrical stimuli than that of younger or older animals (Teresawa & Timiras, 1968) and exhibits a different pattern of stress-induced activation of the immediate early gene c-Fos than seen in mature animals (Kellogg et al., 1998). Particularly intriguingly, the amygdala is one of the few forebrain regions where damage has been shown in animal studies to markedly influence the timing of puberty, with reports of both precocious and delayed puberty following lesions involving this brain region (see Moltz, 1975, for review of this relatively old literature). These contrary findings may be easier to reconcile when it is recognized that the amygdala consists of numerous specific subregions (nuclei) with different, and sometimes opposing, functional influences (e.g., Swanson & Petrovich, 1998).

The emerging literature in human adolescents likewise is suggestive of developmental alterations in amygdala function during adolescence, although the findings are similarly mixed. A number of studies have used fMRI to examine amygdalar activation during exposure to emotional faces through childhood and adolescence and into adulthood, with activation patterns sometimes reported to decrease developmentally (Killgore et al., 2001) whereas other studies have reported developmental increases (Thomas et al., 2001) or no change in activation patterns between adolescence and adulthood (Pine et al., 2001). Adding further to these inconsistencies are instances of ontogenetic differences in amygdalar activation that are sex-specific (e.g., McClure et al., 2004) or lateralized (e.g., Killgore & Yurgelun-Todd, 2004). Among the factors that may contribute to these varying findings is the rapid habituation of this activation, making the timing of assessment critical, as well as the lack of spatial resolution necessary to establish foci in specific amygdala nuclei (Zald, 2003). The latter point is particularly critical given the differing—and sometimes opposing—functional effects among specific subunits (nuclei) of the amygdala (Swanson & Petrovich, 1998).

Thus, although intriguing, the amygdala data are highly inconsistent at present. While it has been proposed that the development of emotional control during adolescence may be related to progressively greater PFC modulation over emotional processing within the amygdala (see Killgore et al., 2001), only limited support for this appealing hypothesis has been obtained to date. Judicious use of studies using animal models and increasing availability of higher field strength magnetic resonance scanners with their greater spatial resolution should ultimately help resolve frustrating inconsistencies in this literature.

Summary and Other Emerging Areas of Interest

The evidence to date suggests that during adolescence the brain is sculpted to transform the brain of the child into a more energy efficient brain of the adult. Some of these alterations are regressive, with a loss of a notable proportion of excitatory (glutaminergic) synapses and binding sites for both glutamate (NMDA-R) and DA in certain sites within the mesocorticolimbic system. Other alterations may involve possible ontogenetic shifts in the balance of activity among various cortical vs. subcortical forebrain regions. To the extent that the data are available, there are considerable similarities across species in the nature of these alterations in adolescent brain. Although the evidence to date suggests that this adolescent sculpting is particularly dramatic in forebrain mesocorticolimbic systems, adolescent-related neuronal changes are seen elsewhere as well. Generally speaking, though, considerably less attention has been paid to adolescent brain ontogeny outside the forebrain. One exception to this generality has been the extensive literature on hypothalamic function during the pubertal portion of adolescence, with evidence for alterations in both excitatory and inhibitory tone in the hypothalamus contributing to the reactivation of the hypothalamo-pituitary-gonadal (HPG) axis at puberty (see Grumbach, 2002; and Romeo et al., 2002; Spear, 2000, for reviews of this extensive literature). In contrast, evidence for adolescent-associated alterations in cerebellum and their potential contribution to cognitive and emotional development has begun to emerge more recently. The adolescent cerebellum is of particular interest given data showing cerebellar influences on cognition and affect in both humans (Kim et al., 1994; Schmahmann & Sherman, 1997) and rodents (Bobee et al., 2000), and anatomical data detailing cerebellar projections to the PFC, along with other circuitry relating these regions (Middleton & Strick, 2000, 2001). Some support for the involvement of the cerebellum in cognitive development has emerged using fMRI, with the cerebellum showing age-related increases in activation into or through adolescence during performance of a virtual reality spatial navigation task (Pine et al., 2002) and an oculomotor response-suppression task (Luna et al., 2001).

Implications of Adolescent-Associated Neural Transformations for Normal and Atypical Adolescent Behaviors

Adolescent sculpting in PFC and interconnected regions such as the cerebellum is seemingly related to the gradual emergence of mature cognitive capacities, including improvements observed during adolescence in aspects of executive function, response inhibition, attentional capacities, memory function (Casey et al., 2000; Luna et al., 2001; Pine et al., 2002), as well as emotional self-control (e.g., Dahl, 2001). Mesocorticolimbic brain regions undergoing particularly dramatic change during adolescence also form critical parts of the stress-sensitive neural circuitry implicated in modulating risk taking, novelty seeking, and social behaviors (e.g., Le Moal & Simon, 1991), and in assigning hedonic affect (e.g., Volkow et al., 2002) and attaching incentive motivation (Robinson & Berridge, 2003) to natural rewards (including social stimuli and novelty), drugs of abuse, and cues associated with these rewards. The postulated attenuation in mesolimbic DA activity associated with a shift towards greater mesocortical activation early in adolescence likewise may be motivationally significant, given that functional insufficiencies in mesolimbic DA terminal regions have been linked to a reward deficiency syndrome characterized by actively seeking out drugs of abuse as well as "environmental novelty and sensation as a type of behavioral remediation of reward deficiency" (Gardner, 1999, p. 82). To the extent that a mild version of this syndrome is fostered by normal developmental transitions occurring early in adolescence, young adolescents likewise might pursue novelty, drugs, and other stimuli to counter a mild and partial anhedonia. Indeed, reports of feeling "very happy" drop by 50% between childhood and early adolescence, with adolescents also experiencing positive situations as less pleasurable than adults (Larson & Richards, 1994). This possibility is highly speculative, however, with others arguing that activity in mesolimbic DA systems is positively associated with drug seeking (e.g., Spanagel & Weiss, 1999). Moreover, most of the work suggesting a shift in balance among mesocorticolimbic DA terminal regions has been derived from work with laboratory animals, and it remains to be determined how well these findings represent developmental events occurring in human adolescents. Nevertheless, given the developmental transformations that occur in mesocorticolimbic circuitry, it would be surprising if adolescents did not differ from mature animals in their motivated behavior and the way that they respond to natural rewards and drugs of abuse. And they do.

As discussed previously, adolescents of a variety of mammalian species differ considerably from younger juveniles and older adults in the ways they seek out and interact with stimuli in their environment, including notable elevations in peer-directed social interactions and novelty seeking/risk taking behaviors (see Spear, 2000, for review) and the reward value they attribute to those stimuli (e.g., Douglas et al., 2003, 2004). It is also during adolescence that drug and alcohol use is typically initiated, with use of alcohol becoming normative among human adolescents (e.g., Shedler & Block, 1990). Adolescents of other species such as the rat likewise often drink notably more alcohol than their mature counterparts (e.g., Brunell & Spear, 2005; Doremus et al., 2005), presumably in part due to their insensitivity to aversive ethanol effects that serve as cues to limit intake (see Spear & Varlinskaya, 2005, for review and references), an insensitivity seemingly related in part to immaturity in GABAergic systems (Silveri & Spear, 2002). Conversely, early adolescents are more sensitive than their more mature peers to several alcohol consequences, including ethanol-induced social facilitation (Varlinskaya & Spear, 2002) and impairments in brain plasticity and memory (Acheson et al., 1998; Swartzwelder et al., 1995a), with the latter enhanced sensitivity related in part to overexpression of hippocampal glutaminergic systems early in adolescence (Swartzwelder et al., 1995b). Studies in laboratory animals and using fMRI techniques in humans are just beginning to relate specific components of the neural circuitry undergoing change during adolescence to expression of typical behaviors of adolescents as well as their cognitive/emotional maturation.

When contemplating the relationship between cognitive/behavioral function of adolescence and the sculpting of adolescent brain, it may be important to consider the complicating variable of stress. The PFC and certain other mesocortico-limbic brain regions undergoing transformation during adolescence are highly sensitive to stressors (e.g., Dunn, 1988), and there is some evidence that adolescence may be a particularly stressful stage, with reports that adolescents not only are exposed to more life stressors (e.g., Buchanan et al., 1992), but also respond differently to stressors than at other ages (see Spear, 2000, for review). Adolescents often appear particularly sensitive to stressors, a phenomenon that can be modeled in laboratory animals, with rodents at this age showing more stress-induced behavioral disruption (e.g., Stone & Quartermain, 1998; Walker et al., 1995) and different patterns of stress-induced neural activation (Choi & Kellogg, 1996) than adults.

Normal developmental alterations in brain occurring during adolescence may influence expression of psychopathology in vulnerable individuals. Along with well-known examples of adolescent-associated emergence of overt symptomatology such as schizophrenia are examples where considerable reductions in symptomatology are often observed during adolescence (e.g., Tourette's syndrome: Kurlan, 1992; childhood epilepsy: Saugstad, 1994). In research with laboratory animals as well, various examples of alleviation or emergence of symptomatology during adolescence have been observed. For instance, an adolescent-associated decline in outcome following early orbital frontal lesions in Rhesus monkeys contrasts with evidence for the emergence of more pronounced effects of dorsolateral lesions of the PFC (Rhesus monkeys: Goldman, 1971; rats: Flores et al., 1996) or ventral hippocampus (Lipska & Weinberger, 1993) as animals reach maturity.

A number of factors may contribute to the delayed emergence or decline in symptomatology during the adolescent period. In some instances, manifestation of some early appearing deficits may decline developmentally as the brain is restructured and refined to permit the emergence of functional compensations for those deficits. Conversely, impaired neural regions may not become functionally mature until adolescence, and hence consequences of damage to that region may not surface until that time. It is also possible that the sculpting of adolescent brain may unveil early developmental compromises, plasticity-induced concessions that may effectively have masked adverse consequences of suboptimal genetic expression and environmental conditions early in life.

One potential contributor to the later unmaking of early neural compensations is stress. Increased sensitivity to stressors and environmental demands has been observed in studies in laboratory animals following a variety of early developmental perturbations, including perinatal stress (Cabib et al., 1993; Takahishi et al., 1992; Weinstock, 1997) and prenatal exposure to drugs including cocaine, ethanol, or diazepam (Kellogg, 1991; Mayes et al., 1998; Riley, 1990; Spear et al., 1998). Such stressor vulnerability may be particularly pronounced during adolescence, given evidence discussed earlier that this developmental transition may be unusually stressful for the adolescent.

Over the past decade there has been increasing recognition that highly conserved neural alterations during adolescence may contribute to cognitive and behavioral function of adolescents, their sensitivity to environmental demands, and the emergence of psychopathology among the most vulnerable. With the increasing focus on research during adolescence and ongoing improvements in MRI technology, continued rapid progress in this area is likely, progress that will be critical for designing strategies to enable adolescents to meet environment challenges, channel their proclivities, and conquer this developmental transition while avoiding long-term cost to themselves.

References

Acheson, S. K., Stein, R. M., & Swartzwelder, H. S. (1998). Impairment of semantic and figural memory by acute ethanol: Age-dependent effects. *Alcoholism: Clinical and Experimental Research*, 22(7), 1437–1442.

Adriani, W., Chiarotti, F., & Laviola, G. (1998). Elevated novelty seeking and peculiar d-amphetamine sensitization in periadolescent mice compared with adult mice. *Behavioral Neuroscience, 112*(5), 1152–1166.

Amaral, D. G., Capitanio, J. P., Jourdain, M., Mason, W. A., Mendoza, S. P., & Prather, M. (2003). The amygdala: Is it an essential component of the neural network for social cognition? *Neuropsychologia, 41,* 235–240.

Andersen, S. L. (2003). Trajectories of brain development: Point of vulnerability or window of opportunity? *Neuroscience and Biobehavioral Reviews, 27*(1–2), 3–18.

Andersen, S. L., Dumont, N. L., & Teicher, M. H. (1997). Developmental differences in dopamine synthesis inhibition by (+/-)-7-OH-DPAT. *Naunyn-Schmiedeberg's Archives of Pharmacology, 356*(2), 173–181.

Andersen, S. L., Thompson, A. P., Krenzel, E., & Teicher, M. H. (2002). Pubertal changes in gonadal hormones do not underlie adolescent dopamine receptor overproduction. *Psychoneuroendocrinology, 27,* 683–691.

Andersen, S. L., Thompson, A. T., Rutstein, M., Hostetter, J. C., & Teicher, M. H. (2000). Dopamine receptor pruning in prefrontal cortex during the periadolescent period in rats. *Synapse, 37*(2), 167–169.

Baxter, M. G., & Murray, E. A. (2002). The amygdala and reward. *Nature Reviews Neuroscience, 3*(7), 563–573.

Bechara, A., Damasio, H., Damasio, A. R., & Lee, G. P. (1999). Different contributions of the human amygdala and ventromedial prefrontal cortex to decision-making. *The Journal of Neuroscience, 19*(13), 5473–5481.

Benes, F. M., Taylor, J. B., & Cunningham, M. C. (2000). Convergence and plasticity of monoaminergic systems in the medial prefrontal cortex during the postnatal period: Implications for the development of psychopathology. *Cerebral Cortex, 10*(10), 1014–1027.

Benes, F. M., Turtle, M., Khan, Y., & Farol, P. (1994). Myelination of a key relay zone in the hippocampal formation occurs in the human brain during childhood, adolescence, and adulthood. *Archives of General Psychiatry, 51*(6), 477–484.

Bixler, R. H. (1992). Why littermates don't: The avoidance of inbreeding depression. *Annual Review of Sex Research, 3,* 291–328.

Bobee, S., Mariette, E., Tremblay-Leveau, H., & Caston, J. (2000). Effects of early midline cerebellar lesion on cognitive and emotional functions in the rat. *Behavioural Brain Research, 112,* 107–117.

Bourgeois, J.-P., Goldman-Rakic, P. S., & Rakic, P. (1994). Synaptogenesis in the prefrontal cortex of rhesus monkeys. *Cerebral Cortex, 4*(1), 78–96.

Brunell, S. C., & Spear, L. P. (2005). Effect of stress on the voluntary intake of a sweetened ethanol solution in pair-housed adolescent and adult rats. *Alcoholism: Clinical and Experimental Research, 29,* 1641–1653.

Buchanan, C. M., Eccles, J. S., & Becker, J. B. (1992). Are adolescents the victims of raging hormones: Evidence for activational effects of hormones on moods and behavior at adolescence. *Psychological Bulletin, 111*(1), 62–107.

Cabib, S., Puglisi-Allegra, S., & D'Amato, F. R. (1993). Effects of postnatal stress on dopamine mesolimbic system responses to aversive experiences in adult life. *Brain Research, 604,* 232–239.

Casey, B. J., Cohen, J. D., O'Craven, K., Davidson, R. J., Irwin, W., Nelson, C. A., Noll, D. C., Hu, X., Lowe, M. J., Rosen, B. R., Truwitt, C. L., & Turski, P. A. (1998). Reproducibility of fMRI results across four institutions using a spatial working memory task. *NeuroImage, 8*(3), 249–261.

Casey, B. J., Giedd, J. N., & Thomas, K. M. (2000). Structural and functional brain development and its relation to cognitive development. *Biological Psychology, 54*(1–3), 241–257.

Choi, S., & Kellogg, C. K. (1996). Adolescent development influences functional responsiveness of noradrenergic projections to the hypothalamus in male rats. *Developmental Brain Research, 94,* 144–151.

Chugani, H. T. (1996). Neuroimaging of developmental nonlinearity and developmental pathologies. In R. W. Thatcher, G. R. Lyon, J. Rumsey, & N. Krasnegor (Eds.), *Developmental neuroimaging: Mapping the development of brain and behavior* (pp. 187–195). San Diego, CA: Academic Press.

Crockett, C. M., & Pope, T. R. (1993). Consequences of sex differences in dispersal for juvenile red howler monkeys. In M. E. Pereira & L. A. Fairbanks (Eds.), *Juvenile primates* (pp. 104–118, 367–415). New York: Oxford University Press.

Csikszentmihalyi, M., & Larson, R. (1978). Intrinsic rewards in school crime. *Crime and Delinquency, 24,* 322–335.

Csikszentmihalyi, M., Larson, R., & Prescott, S. (1977). The ecology of adolescent activity and experience. *Journal of Youth and Adolescence, 6,* 281–294.

Cunningham, M. G., Bhattacharyya, S., & Benes, F. M. (2002). Amygdalo-cortical sprouting continues into early adulthood: Implications for the development of normal and abnormal function during adolescence. *The Journal of Comparative Neurology, 453,* 116–130.

Dahl, R. E. (2001). Affect regulation, brain development, and behavioral/emotional health in adolescence. *CNS Spectrums, 6*(1), 60–72.

Deutch, A. Y. (1992). The regulation of subcortical dopamine systems by the prefrontal cortex: Interactions of central dopamine systems and the pathogenesis of schizophrenia. *Journal of Neural Transmission, 36,* 61–89.

Doremus, T. L., Brunell, S. C., Pottayil, R., & Spear, L. P. (2005). Factors influencing elevated ethanol consumption in adolescent relative adult rats. *Alcoholism: Clinical and Experimental Research, 29,* 1796–1808.

Douglas, L. A., Varlinskaya, E. I., & Spear, L. P. (2003). Novel object place conditioning in adolescent and adult male and female rats: Effects of social isolation. *Physiology & Behavior, 80,* 317–325.

Douglas, L. A., Varlinskaya, E. I., & Spear, L. P. (2004). Rewarding properties of social interactions in adolescent and adult male and female rats: Impact of social vs. isolate housing of subjects and partners. *Developmental Psychobiology, 45,* 153–162.

Dumont, N. L., Andersen, S. L., Thompson, A. P., & Teicher, M. H. (2004). Transient dopamine synthesis modulation in prefrontal cortex: In vitro studies. *Developmental Brain Research, 150*(2), 163–166.

Dunn, A. J. (1988). Stress-related activation of cerebral dopaminergic systems. *Annals of the New York Academy of Sciences, 537,* 188–205.

Eriksson, P. S., Perfilieva, E., Bjork-Eriksson, T., Alborn, A.-M., Nordborg, C., Peterson, D. A., & Gage, F. H. (1998). Neurogenesis in the adult human hippocampus. *Nature Medicine, 4*(11), 1313–1317.

Flores, G., Wood, G. K., Liang, J.-J., Quirion, R., & Srivastava, L. K. (1996). Enhanced amphetamine sensitivity and increased expression of dopamine D2 receptors in postpubertal rats after neonatal excitotoxic lesions of the medial prefrontal cortex. *Journal of Neurosicence, 16,* 7366–7375.

Galef, B. G., Jr. (1977). Mechanisms for the social transmission of food preferences from adult to weanling rats. In L. M. Barker, M. Best, & M. Domjan (Eds.), *Learning mechanisms in food selection* (pp. 123–148). Waco, TX: Baylor University Press.

Gardner, E. L. (1999). The neurobiology and genetics of addiction: Implications of the reward deficiency syndrome for therapeutic strategies in chemical dependency. In J. Elster (Ed.), *Addiction: Entries and exits* (pp. 57–119). New York: Russell Sage Foundation.

Giedd, J. N., Blumenthal, J., Jeffries, N. O., Castellanos, F. X., Liu, H., Zijdenbos, A., Paus, T., Evans, A. C., & Rapoport, J. L. (1999). Brain development during childhood and adolescence: A longitudinal MRI study. *Nature Neuroscience, 2*(10), 861–863.

Giedd, J. N., Castellanos, F. X., Rajapakse, J. C., Vaituzis, A. C., & Rapoport, J. L. (1997). Sexual dimorphism of the developing human brain. *Progress in Neuro-Psychopharmacology & Biological Psychiatry, 21,* 1185–1201.

Giedd, J. N., Snell, J. W., Lange, N. Rajapakse, J. C., Casey, B. J., Kozuch, P. L., Viatuzis, A. C., Vauss, Y. C. Hamburger, S. D., Kaysen, D., & Rappoport, J. L. (1996). Quantitative magnetic resonance imaging of human brain development: ages 4–18. *Cerebral Cortex, 6,* 551–560.

Gogtay, N., Giedd, J. N., Lusk, L., Hayashi, K. M., Greenstein, D., Vaituzis, A. C., Nugent, T. F., III, Herman, D. H., Clasen, L. S., Toga, A. W., Rapoport, J. L., & Thompson, P. M. (2004). Dynamic mapping of human cortical development during childhood through early adulthood. *Proceedings of the National Academy of Sciences of the United States of America, 101*(21), 8174–8179.

Goldman, P. S. (1971). Functional development of the prefrontal cortex in early life and the problem of neuronal plasticity. *Experimental Neurology, 32,* 366–387.

Goldman-Rakic, P. S., Isseroff, A., Schwartz, M. L., & Bugbee, N. M. (1983). The neurobiology of cognitive development. In P. H. Mussen (Vol. Ed.), *Handbook of child psychology: Vol. II. Infancy and developmental psychobiology* (pp. 281–344). New York: Wiley.

Grumbach, M.M. (2002). The neuroendocrinology of human puberty revisited. *Hormone Research, 57*(Suppl. 2), 2–14.

Happaney, K., Zelazo, P. D., & Stuss, D. T. (2004). Development of orbitofrontal function: Current themes and future directions. *Brain and Cognition, 55*(1), 1–10.

Harris, J. R. (1995). Where is the child's environment? A group socialization theory of development. *Psychological Review, 102*(3), 458–489.

Holland, P. C., & Gallagher, M. (2004). Amygdala-frontal interactions and reward expectancy. *Current Opinion in Neurobiology, 14,* 148–155.

Huttenlocher, P. R. (1979). Synaptic density of human frontal cortex–developmental changes and effects of aging. *Brain Research, 163,* 195–205.

Huttenlocher, P. R. (1984). Synapse elimination and plasticity in developing human cerebral cortex. *American Journal of Mental Deficiency, 88,* 488–496.

Insel, T. R., Miller, L. P., & Gelhard, R. E. (1990). The ontogeny of excitatory amino acid receptors in rat forebrain: I. *N*-methyl-D-aspartate and quisqualate receptors. *Neuroscience, 35*(1), 31–43.

Irwin, C. E., Jr. (1989). Risk taking behaviors in the adolescent patient: Are they impulsive? *Pediatric Annals, 18,* 122–133.

Irwin, C. E., Jr., & Millstein, S. G. (1992). Correlates and predictors of risk-taking behavior during adolescence. In L. P. Lipsitt & L. L. Mitnick (Eds.), *Self-regulatory behavior and risk taking: Causes and consequences* (pp. 3–21). Norwood, NJ: Ablex.

Irwin, C. E., Jr., Burg, S. J., & Uhler Cart, C. (2002). America's adolescents: Where have we been, where are we going? *Journal of Adolescent Health, 2002, 31*(Suppl.6) 91–121.

Jacobson, M. (1991). *Developmental neurobiology.* New York: Plenum Press.

Keane, B. (1990). Dispersal and inbreeding avoidance in the white-footed mouse, *Peromyscus leucopus. Animal Behavior, 40,* 143–152.

Kellogg, C. K. (1991). Postnatal effects of prenatal exposure to psychoactive drugs. *Pre- and Peri-Natal Psychology, 5,* 233–251.

Kellogg, C. K., Awatramani, G. B., & Piekut, D. T. (1998). Adolescent development alters stressor-induced Fos immunoreactivity in rat brain. *Neuroscience, 83*(3), 681–689.

Killgore W. D. S., Oki, M., & Yurgelun-Todd, D. A. (2001). Sex-specific developmental changes in amygdala responses to affective faces. *Neuroreport, 12*(2), 427–433.

Killgore, W. D., & Yurgelun-Todd, D. A. (2004). Sex-related developmental differences in the lateralized activation of the prefrontal cortex and amygdala during perception of facial affect. *Perceptual and Motor Skills, 99*(2), 371–391.

Kim, S.-G., Ugurbil, K., & Strick, P. L. (1994). Activation of a cerebellar output nucleus during cognitive processing. *Science, 265,* 949–951.

Kolb, B., Pellis, S., & Robinson, T. E. (2004). Plasticity and functions of the orbital frontal cortex. *Brain and Cognition, 55*(1), 104–115.

Kurlan, R. (1992). The pathogenesis of Tourette's syndrome: A possible role for hormonal and excitatory neurotransmitter influences in brain development. *Archives of Neurology, 49,* 874–876.

Larson, R., & Richards, M. H. (1994). Divergent realities: The emotional lives of mothers, fathers, and adolescents. New York: Basic Books.

Le Moal, M. & Simon, H. (1991). Mesocorticolimbic dopaminergic network: Functional and regulatory roles. *Physiological Reviews, 71* (1), 155–234.

Leslie, C. A., Robertson, M. W., Cutler, A. J., & Bennett, J. P., Jr. (1991). Postnatal development of D1 dopamine receptors in the medial prefrontal cortex, striatum and nucleus accumbens of normal and neonatal 6–hydroxydopamine treated rats: A quantitative autoradiographic analysis. *Developmental Brain Research, 62*(1), 109–114.

Lewis, D. A. (2005, May). Postnatal development of local circuits and dopaminergic inputs to the primate prefrontal cortex. Presented at Society of Biological Psychiatry, Atlanta, GA.

Lipska, B. K., & Weinberger, D. R. (1993). Delayed effects of neonatal hippocampal damage on haloperidol-induced catalepsy and apomorphine-induced stereotypic behaviors in the rat. *Developmental Brain Research, 75,* 213–222.

Luna, B., Thulborn, K. R., Munoz, D. P., Merriam, E. P., Garver, K. E., Minshew, N. J., Keshavan, M. S., Genovese, C. R., Eddy, W. F., & Sweeney, J. A. (2001). Maturation of widely distributed brain function subserves cognitive development. *NeuroImage, 13*(5), 786–793.

Mayes, L. C., Grillon, C., Granger, R., & Schottenfeld, R. (1998). Regulation of arousal and attention in preschool children exposed to cocaine prenatally. *Annals of the New York Academy of Sciences, 846,* 126–143.

McClure, E. B., Monk, C. S., Nelson, E. E., Zarahn E., Leibenluft, E., Bilder, R. M., Charney, D. S., Ernst, M., & Pine, D. S. (2004). A developmental examination of gender differences in brain engagement during evaluation of threat. *Biological Psychiatry, 55,* 1047–1055.

Middleton, F. A., & Strick, P. L. (2000). Basal ganglia and cerebellar loops: Motor and cognitive circuits. *Brain Research Interactive, 31,* 236–250.

Middleton, F. A., & Strick, P. L. (2001). Cerebellar projections to the prefrontal cortex of the primate. *The Journal of Neuroscience, 21*(2), 700–712.

Moltz, H. (1975). The search for the determinants of puberty in the rat. In B. E. Eleftheriou & R. L. Sprott (Eds.), *Hormonal correlates of behavior: A lifespan view, vol. 1* (pp. 35–154). New York: Plenum Press.

Moore, J. (1992). Dispersal, nepotism, and primate social behavior. *International Journal of Primatology, 13,* 361–378.

Muuss, R. E., & Porton, H. D. (1998). Increasing risk behavior among adolescents. In R. E. Muuss & H. D. Porton (Eds.), *Adolescent behavior and society: A book of readings* (pp. 422–431). Boston: McGraw-Hill College.

Nestler, E. J., Barrot, M., & Self, D. W. (2001). Delta-Fos-B: A sustained molecular switch for addiction. *Proceedings of the National Academy of Sciences of the United States of America, 98*(20), 11042–11046.

Ornitz, E. M. (1996). Developmental aspects of neurophysiology. In M. Lewis (Ed.), *Child and adolescent psychiatry: A comprehensive textbook* (pp. 39–51). Baltimore: Williams & Wilkins.

Paus, T. (2005). Mapping brain maturation and cognitive development during adolescence. *Trends in Cognitive Sciences, 9*(2), 60–68.

Paus, T., Zijdenbos, A., Worsley, K., Collins, D. L., Blumenthal, J., Giedd, J. N., Rapoport, J. L., & Evans, A. C. (1999). Structural maturation of neural pathways in children and adolescents: In vivo study. *Science, 283*(5409), 1908–1911.

Pfefferbaum, A., Mathalon, D. H., Sullivan, E. V., Rawles, J. M., Zipursky, R. B., & Lim, K. O. (1994). A quantitative magnetic resonance imaging study of changes in brain morphology from infancy to late adulthood. *Archives of Neurology, 51,* 874–887.

Pine, D. S., Grun, J., Maguire, E. A., Burgess, N., Zarahn, E., Koda, V., Fyer, A., Szeszko, P. R., & Bilder, R. M. (2002). Neurodevelopmental aspects of spatial navigation: A virtual reality fMRI study. *NeuroImage, 15*(2), 396–406.

Pine, D. S., Grun J., Zarahn, E., Fyer, A., Koda, V., Li, W., Szeszko, P. R., Ardekani, B., & Bilder R. M. (2001). Cortical brain regions engaged by masked emotional faces in adolescents and adults: An fMRI study. *Emotion, 1*(2), 137–147.

Preuss, T. M. (2000). Taking the measure of diversity: Comparative alternatives to the model-animal paradigm in cortical neuroscience. *Brain, Behavior and Evolution, 55,* 287–299.

Primus, R. J., & Kellogg, C. K. (1989). Pubertal-related changes influence the development of environment-related social interaction in the male rat. *Developmental Psychobiology, 22*(6), 633–643.

Rakic, P., Bourgeois, J.-P., & Goldman-Rakic, P. S. (1994). Synaptic development of the cerebral cortex: Implications for learning, memory, and mental illness. In J. van Pelt, M. A. Corner, H. B. M. Uylings, & F. H. Lopes da Silva (Vol. Eds.), *Progress in brain research: Vol. 102. The self-organizing brain: From growth cones to functional networks* (pp. 227–243). Amsterdam: Elsevier.

Rapoport, J. L., Giedd, J. N., Blumenthal, J., Hamburger, S., Jeffries, N., Fernandez, T., Nicolson, R., Bedwell, J., Lenane, M., Zijdenbos, A., Paus, T., & Evans, A. (1999). Progressive cortical change during adolescence in childhood-onset schizophrenia. *Archives of General Psychiatry, 56,* 649–654.

Riley, E. P. (1990). The long-term behavioral effects of prenatal alcohol exposure in rats. *Alcoholism: Clinical and Experimental Research, 14,* 670–673.

Robinson, T. E., & Berridge, K. C. (2003). Addiction. *Annual Review of Psychology, 54,* 25–53.

Romeo, R. D., Richardson, H. N., & Sisk, C. L. (2002). Puberty and the maturation of the male brain and sexual behavior: Recasting a behavioral potential. *Neuroscience and Biobehavioral Reviews, 26*(3), 381–391.

Rosenberg, D. R., & Lewis, D. A. (1995). Postnatal maturation of the dopaminergic innervation of monkey prefrontal and motor cortices: A tyrosine hydroxlase immunohistochemical analysis. *Journal of Comparative Neurology, 358,* 383–400.

Rubia, K., Overmeyer, S., Taylor, E., Brammer, M., Williams, S. C. R., Simmons, A., Andrew, C., & Bullmore, E. T. (2000). Functional frontalisation with age: Mapping neurodevelopmental trajectories with fMRI. *Neuroscience and Biobehavioral Reviews, 24,* 13–19.

Saugstad, L. F. (1994). The maturational theory of brain development and cerebral excitability in the multifactorially inherited manic-depressive psychosis and schizophrenia. *International Journal of Psychophysiology, 18,* 189–203.

Schlegel, A., & Barry, H., III. (1991). *Adolescence: An anthropological inquiry.* New York: The Free Press, Maxwell Macmillan International.

Schmahmann, J. D., & Sherman, J. C. (1997). Cerebellar cognitive affective syndrome. *International Review of Neurobiology, 41,* 433–440.

Seeman, P., Bzowej, N. H., Guan, H.-C., Bergeron, C., Becker, L. E., Reynolds, G. P., Bird, E. D., Riederer, P., Jellinger, K., Wananabe, S., & Tourtellotte, W. W. (1987). Human brain dopamine receptors in children and aging adults. *Synapse, 1,* 399–404.

Segalowitz, S. J., & Davies, P. L. (2004). Charting the maturation of the frontal lobe: An electrophysiological strategy. *Brain and Cognition, 55*(1), 116–133.

Shedler, J., & Block, J. (1990). Adolescent drug use and psychological health: A longitudinal inquiry. *American Psychologist, 45*(5), 612–630.

Silbereisen, R. K., & Reitzle, M. (1992). On the constructive role of problem behavior in adolescence: Further evidence on alcohol use. In L. P. Lipsitt & L. L. Mitnick (Eds.), *Self-regulatory behavior and risk taking: Causes and consequences* (pp. 199–217). Norwood, NJ: Ablex.

Silveri, M. M., & Spear, L. P. (2002). The effects of NMDA and GABA$_A$ pharmacological manipulations on ethanol sensitivity in immature and mature animals. *Alcoholism: Clinical and Experimental Research, 26,* 449–456.

Sowell, E. R., Peterson, B. S., Thompson, P. M., Welcome, S. E., Henkenius, A. L., & Toga, A. W. (2003). Mapping cortical change across the human life span. *Nature Neuroscience, 6*(3), 309–315.

Sowell, E. R., Thompson, P. M., Holmes, C. J., Batth, R., Jernigan, T. L., & Toga, A. W. (1999). Localizing age-related changes in brain structure between childhood and adolescence using statistical parametric mapping. *NeuroImage, 9,* 587–597.

Spanagel, R., & Weiss, F. (1999). The dopamine hypothesis of reward: Past and current status. *Trends in Neuroscience, 22*(11), 521–527.

Spear, L. P. (2000). The adolescent brain and age-related behavioral manifestations. *Neuroscience and Biobehavioral Reviews, 24,* 417–463.

Spear, L. P., Campbell, J., Snyder, K., Silveri, M., & Katovic, N. (1998). Animal behavior models: Increased sensitivity to stressors and other environmental experiences after prenatal cocaine exposure. *Annals of the New York Academy of Sciences, 846,* 76–88.

Spear, L. P., & Varlinskaya, E. I. (2005). Adolescence: Alcohol sensitivity, tolerance, and intake. In M. Galanter (Ed.), *Recent developments in alcoholism: Vol. 17. Alcohol problems in adolescents and young adults* (pp. 143–159). Hingham, MA: Kluwer Academic.

Steinberg, L. (1989). Pubertal maturation and parent-adolescent distance: An evolutionary perspective. In G. R. Adams, R. Montemayor, & T. P. Gullotta (Eds.), *Advances in adolescent behavior and development* (pp. 71–97). Newbury Park, CA: Sage.

Steinberg, L. (2004). Risk taking in adolescence: what changes, and why? (2004). *Annals of the New York Academy of Sciences, 1021,* 51–58.

Steinberg, L., & Belsky, J. (1996). An evolutionary perspective on psychopathology in adolescence. In D. Cicchetti & S. L. Toth (Eds.), *Adolescence: Opportunities and challenges* (pp. 93–24). Rochester, NY: University of Rochester Press.

Stone, E. A., & Quartermain, D. (1998). Greater behavioral effects of stress in immature as compared to mature male mice. *Physiology and Behavior, 63,* 143–145.

Swanson, L. W., & Petrovich, G. D. (1998). What is the amygdala? *Trends in Neuroscience, 21*(8), 323–331.

Swartzwelder, H. S., Wilson, W. A., & Tayyeb, M. I. (1995a). Differential sensitivity of NMDA receptor-mediated synaptic potentials to ethanol in immature versus mature hippocampus. *Alcoholism: Clinical and Experimental Research, 19*(2), 320–323.

Swartzwelder, H. S., Wilson, W. A., & Tayyeb, M. I. (1995b). Age-dependent inhibition of long-term potentiation by ethanol in immature versus mature hippocampus. *Alcoholism: Clinical and Experimental Research, 19*(6), 1480–1485.

Takahashi, L. K., Turner, J. G., & Kalin, N. H. (1992). Prenatal stress alters brain catecholaminergic activity and potentiates stress-induced behavior in adult rats. *Brain Research, 574,* 131–137.

Tarazi, F. I., & Baldessarini, R. J. (2000). Comparative postnatal development of dopamine D1, D2, and D4 receptors in rat forebrain. *International Journal of Developmental Neuroscience, 18,* 29–37.

Tarazi, F. I., Tomasini, E. C., & Baldessarini, R. J. (1998). Postnatal development of dopamine D_4-like receptors in rat forebrain regions: Comparison with D_2-like receptors. *Developmental Brain Research, 110,* 227–233.

Tarazi, F. I., Tomasini, E. C., & Baldessarini, R. J. (1999). Postnatal development of Dopamine D_1-like receptors in rat cortical and striatolimbic brain regions: An autoradiographic study. *Developmental Neuroscience, 21,* 43–49.

Teicher, M. H., Andersen, S. L., & Hostetter, J. C., Jr. (1995). Evidence for dopamine receptor pruning between adolescence and adulthood in striatum but not nucleus accumbens. *Developmental Brain Research, 89,* 167–172.

Teicher, M. H., Barber, N. I., Gelbard, H. A., Gallitano, A. L., Campbell, A., Marsh, E., & Baldessarini, R. J. (1993). Developmental differences in acute nigrostriatal and mesocorticolimbic system response to haloperidol. *Neuropsychopharmacology, 9*(2), 147–156.

Teicher, M. H., Krenzel, E., Thompson, A. P., & Andersen, S. L. (2003). Dopamine receptor pruning during the peripubertal period is not attenuated by NMDA receptor antagonism in rat. *Neuroscience Letters, 339*(1), 169–171.

Terasawa, E. & Timiras, P. S. (1968). Electrophysiological study of the limbic system in the rat at onset of puberty. *American Journal of Physiology, 215*(6), 1462–1467.

Thomas, K. M., Drevets, W. C., Whalen, P. J., Eccard, C. H., Dahl, R. E., Ryan, N. D., & Casey, B. J. (2001). Amygdala response to facial expressions in children and adults. *Society of Biological Psychiatry, 49,* 309–316.

Trimpop, R. M., Kerr, J. H., & Kircaldy, B. (1999). Comparing personality constructs of risk-taking behavior. *Personality and Individual Differences, 26*(2), 237–254.

Tseng, K. Y., & O' Donnell, P. (2005). Post-pubertal emergence of prefrontal cortical up states induced by D_1-NMDA co-activation. *Cerebral Cortex, 15*(1), 49–57.

Tyler, D. B., & van Harreveld, A. (1942). The respiration of the developing brain. *American Journal of Physiology, 136,* 600–603.

van Eden, C. G., Kros, J. M., & Uylings, H. B. M. (1990). The development of the rat prefrontal cortex: Its size and development of connections with thalamus, spinal cord and other cortical areas. In H. B. M. Uylings, C. G. van Eden, J. P. C. De Bruin, M. A. Corner, & M. G. P. Feenstra (Eds.), *Progress in brain research, the prefrontal cortex: Its structure, function and pathology* (Vol. 85, pp. 169–183). Amsterdam: Elsevier.

Varlinskaya, E. I., & Spear, L. P. (2002). Acute effects of ethanol on social behavior of adolescent and adult rats: Role of familiarity of the test situation. *Alcoholism: Clinical and Experimental Research, 26,* 1502–1511.

Villablanca, J. R., Schmanke, T. D., Lekht, V., & Crutcher, H. A. (2000). The growth of the feline brain from late fetal into adult life, I. A morphometric study of the neocortex and white matter. *Developmental Brain Research, 122*(1), 11–20.

Volkow, N. D., & Fowler, J. S. (2000). Addiction, a disease of compulsion and drive: Involvement of the orbitofrontal cortex. *Cerebral Cortex, 10*(3), 318–325.

Volkow, N. D., Fowler, J. S., Wang, G.-J., & Goldstein, R. Z. (2002). Role of dopamine, the frontal cortex and memory circuits in drug addiction: Insight from imaging studies. *Neurobiology of Learning and Memory, 78*(3), 610–624.

Walker, C.-D., Trottier, G., Rochford, J., & Lavallée, D. (1995). Dissociation between behavioral and hormonal responses to the forced swim stress in lactating rats. *Journal of Neuroendocrinology, 7*(8), 615–622.

Weinstock, M. (1997). Does prenatal stress impair coping and regulation of hypothalamic-pituitary-adrenal axis? *Neuroscience and Biobehavioral Reviews, 21,* 1–10.

Wilkinson, L. S. (1997). The nature of interactions involving prefrontal and striatal dopamine systems. *Journal of Psychopharmacology, 11,* 143–150.

Wilson, M., & Daly, M. (1985). Competitiveness, risk taking, and violence: The young male syndrome. *Ethology and Sociobiology, 6,* 59–73.

Woo, T.-U., Pucak, M. L., Kye, C. H., Matus, C. V., & Lewis, D. A. (1997). Peripubertal refinement of the intrinsic and associational circuitry in monkey prefrontal cortex. *Neuroscience, 80*(4), 1149–1158.

Worthman, C. M. (1999). Epidemiology of human development. In C. Panter-Brick & C. M. Worthman (Eds.), *Hormones, health and behavior: A socio-ecological and lifespan perspective* (pp. 47–104), New York: Cambridge University Press.

Zald, D. H. (2003). The human amygdala and the emotional evaluation of sensory stimuli. *Brain Research Reviews, 41,* 88–123.

Zald, D. H., Donndelinger, M. J., & Pardo, J. V. (1998). Elucidating dynamic brain interactions with across-subjects correlational analyses of positron emission tomographic data: The functional connectivity of the amygdala and orbitofrontal cortex during olfactory tasks. *Journal of Cerebral Blood Flow and Metabolism, 18,* 896–905.

Zecevic, N., Bourgeois, J.-P., & Rakic, P. (1989). Changes in synaptic density in motor cortex of rhesus monkey during fetal and postnatal life. *Developmental Brain Research, 50*(1), 11–32.

Chapter 2

Competence, Resilience, and
Development in Adolescence

Clues for Prevention Science

Ann S. Masten

During the past 30 years, a dramatic transformation has occurred in research concerned with the origins and prevention of mental health problems as *developmental
psychopathology* emerged. Developmental psychopathology (DP) can be defined
as *the study of behavior problems and related disorders in the full context of human
development.* This multidisciplinary perspective emphasizes developmental principles, multiple causes and outcomes, the value of integrating theory or knowledge
about normal and nonnormal development (competence and psychopathology, resilience and maladaptive behavior), the importance of multiple levels of analysis
(molecules to media), and longitudinal studies (Masten, 2006a). From the perspective of developmental psychopathology, if one seeks to understand or alter the mental
health of adolescents, it is essential to consider normal and deviant development
before, during, and after this period of the life span. This chapter considers clues to
preventing adolescent psychopathology deduced from research on risk, competence,
and resilience in developmental psychopathology.

The search for understanding the etiology of mental illnesses and problems gave
rise to research on resilience, as well as the integrative science of developmental
psychopathology in the late 20th century (Masten, 1989, 2001, 2006a). It was
recognized decades ago that some children and adolescents were at greater risk
for developing mental disorders and problems, including those with biological
parents who had serious mental disorders (e.g., schizophrenia, bipolar disorder),

young people who grew up in very adverse circumstances, or children showing early signs of difficulty controlling their behavior or learning (Garmezy, 1984; Kopp, 1983; Masten & Gewirtz, 2006).

Investigators who wanted to study the origins of mental health problems began to study "high-risk" cohorts of children and youth, in hopes of learning enough about the causes and consequences of mental disorders and problems to inform practice and policy aimed at preventing or ameliorating them. Clinical scientists and experts on psychopathology began to collaborate with colleagues who studied normal human development in research teams and consortia, seeking help from each other in the design and interpretation of longitudinal studies of children and adolescents that would encompass normal and abnormal development (Cicchetti, 1990; Masten, 1989, 2006a). From longitudinal data, risk researchers soon began to note that individuals with the same kind of risks had very different outcomes, and that some children from disastrous backgrounds grew up to be highly competent and healthy adults, that many disorders had origins in childhood or adolescence, and that the same mental health problem could have different beginnings. Perhaps most important, however, these investigators became convinced of the necessity for a developmental approach to science, practice, and policy concerned with the causes, prevention, or treatment of mental health problems.

It was not long before a pioneering group of these scholars and their students began to lay the foundations of DP (Achenbach, 1974, 1990; Cicchetti, 1984, 1989, 1990, 1993; Cicchetti & Cohen, 1995; Gottesman, 1974; Masten & Braswell, 1991; Rutter, 1981; Rutter & Garmezy, 1983; Sroufe 1997; Sroufe & Rutter, 1984). DP, which spans multiple disciplines and levels of analysis, has roots deep in the history of science and medicine. However, it was not until recent decades that conditions were ripe for this cross-cutting approach to take hold as the prevailing framework for the sciences focused on mental health in childhood, adolescence, and, increasingly, across the life span (see Cicchetti, 1990, 2006),

In addition to generally anchoring the study of mental health and illness in development, DP underscored the importance of studying positive life patterns along with the negative ones. Among the early developmental psychopathologists, several leading scientists, including Norman Garmezy, Michael Rutter, and Emmy Werner (Masten, 1989; Masten & Gewirtz, 2006), were intrigued with the phenomenon of resilience in the lives of the people they were observing. Resilience in human development generally refers to positive adjustment among individuals exposed to serious threats to adaptation or development; in other words, doing well in spite of adversity. Developmental psychopathologists recognized that understanding the processes involved in competence and resilience, as well as those in psychopathology, held the promise of informing interventions to promote better development among high-risk children, to prevent mental illness, and to promote earlier or better recovery from psychopathology.

In the following discussion of competence, resilience, and psychopathology, this chapter highlights ideas and findings pertinent to prevention and adolescence. The first section is focused on competence and the developmental tasks of adolescence. The next section describes the kind of theory and evidence linking competence and symptoms of psychopathology in adolescence. The third section draws on findings from studies of risk and resilience to identify clues about what matters for adolescents at risk and the implications of these clues for resilience-focused theory and intervention. The concluding section highlights the transitions into and out of adolescence as windows of opportunity for prevention and strategic intervention, with some hints at future directions integrating the study of brain and behavioral development.

Competence and Adolescent Development

The concepts of competence, psychopathology, and resilience, though distinct, all involve judgments about how well a person is doing in life. Competence is a popular concept in many fields, as well as in conversational language, but in developmental science, it has been defined as follows:

> Competence refers to a family of constructs related to the capacity or motivation for, process of, or outcomes of effective adaptation in the environment, often inferred from a track record of effectiveness in age-salient developmental tasks and always embedded in developmental, cultural, and historical context. (Masten, Burt, & Coatsworth, 2006)

Competence develops and has a normative course, as well as multiple dimensions and individual differences. Normatively in the human population, competence would be expected to improve over the course of adolescence, as young people mature and learn, despite increases in specific problems and detours along the roads to adulthood. During the second decade of life, there are major gains across multiple domains of adaptation in basic capabilities and coordinated execution of actions, over the short and long term. There are also huge variations in the timing, pace, and nature of these changes, and in the attendant competence of adolescents as they move through these years (Steinberg et al., 2006).

Competence is multidimensional, and across domains of competence, individuals may be advanced in one key domain (e.g., doing well in academic subjects at school) and less advanced in another (e.g., making friends with peers). Individual competence, even in the same domain, may falter, then recover, or get off track for long periods of time. In other words, there is continuity and change or synchronized development and uneven development, across the broad areas encompassed by the concept of competence.

Judgments about competence of individuals or groups can be based on formal tests (e.g., school exams, driving tests) or informal expectations widely shared in a community. Scholars long have noted that there are developmentally based standards for behavior and achievement that serve as broad benchmarks for whether life is proceeding well or not (Masten, 2006b; Masten et al., 2006). *Developmental tasks* can be universal (e.g., learning to communicate in early childhood) or limited to a particular culture, gender, or time in history (e.g., learning to hunt buffalo). In many societies and cultures around the world at this time, adolescents are expected to do well in school, prepare for their roles in society, obey the laws of the society, commit themselves to the religion of the family or community, make friends, and get along with people in the community. In the United States, most adolescents are expected to begin working, driving, and socializing with potential romantic partners. At some point, young people are expected to become competent with respect to adult roles such as supporting a family, rearing children, and contributing to the community. As youth develop, the standards for meeting developmental tasks also increase. This is not an accident, but most likely the result of many generations of adults observing development and learning what young people need to be doing at any particular point in development to succeed later on in that environment and culture. Individuals are judged against age-salient developmental task expectations that reflect a general growth of competence. Perceived or actual failure in these developmental task domains may have important consequences for future competence, opportunities, self-esteem, reputation with others and symptoms of psychopathology (Masten et al., 2006).

Competence in age-salient developmental tasks is assumed to be the integrated result of many processes and interactions at multiple levels of potential analysis, from the molecular to the macro-system level. Extensive research over the course of decades in multiple fields and disciplines has been directed at understanding the developmental processes involved in the achievement of competence or its failures (brain development, cognitive development, social development, intelligence, mental retardation, personality, criminology, learning, academic achievement, motivation, self efficacy, attachment, parenting, education, school climate, etc.). Some have focused on individual differences, including giftedness and negative deviance, and others on normative patterns. Some have focused on change itself and the transitions from one context or level of competence to another.

Scaffolding is an important concept in the history of competence, capturing the idea that there are times in development when support is needed to bridge a developmental transition from one level to the next, when the child is not quite ready to function independently in a new context or new level of achievement. Thus, for example, just as a toddler can use a helping hand until he or she is a skilled walker, an adolescent may need the support of parents, peers, or teachers in navigating the new demands of developmental tasks during adolescence or the transition to adulthood. Scaffolding can be helpful, for example, when adolescents learn to drive, move into highly demanding high school classes, live away from home for the first time, or learn to handle new sexual feelings.

Competence and Psychopathology

The study of competence and psychopathology has been connected in many ways, historically, theoretically, and empirically. These connections have great significance for interventions to promote mental health before, during, and subsequent to adolescence, as well as for the basic science of how mental health and illness develop (Masten, 2004; Masten et al., 2006; Steinberg et al., 2006). A detailed discussion of these connections is well beyond the scope of this chapter (see Masten et al., 2006); however, it is important to consider briefly how competence and psychopathology may be related and how attention to these possibilities could illuminate key issues for prevention and policy design.

Evaluating competence and symptoms are both ways of judging adaptation, with overlapping histories in ancient medicine and philosophy, as well as more recent shared histories in the study of psychiatry, psychology, and related social sciences and neurosciences (Masten & Curtis, 2000; Masten et al., 2006). Some of the connections observed between competence and symptoms in research reflect artifacts of overlapping concepts, measurement, or informants with response bias, but some of the links are likely to reflect true causal connections. Causal models have taken several basic forms—common cause models, symptoms of disorders undermining competence, failures in major competence domains leading to symptoms—and more complex combinations and indirect variations of these basic models (see Masten et al., 2006, for a more detailed discussion of these models). A few examples can illustrate some of the intriguing possibilities now being considered in research on adolescent psychopathology.

Common Cause Models
Common antecedents, risk factors, genetically influenced vulnerabilities, and other shared mediating influences could account for the co-occurrence of competence problems and psychopathology in the same adolescent. Parental neglect or maltreatment, bad neighborhoods, negative emotionality, poor impulse control, poor attention control, and stressful life events have been implicated in multiple problems of adolescence, including depression, antisocial behavior, substance abuse, anxiety disorders, as well as difficulties in social and academic competence (Evans et al., 2005; Masten & Gewirtz, 2006; Masten et al., 2006; see also multiple chapters in this volume). The pathways to these problems are undoubtedly complex and highly variable from person to person, but it is certainly possible that multiple difficulties arise in the same individuals and across individuals from dysfunctions or breakdowns in fundamental adaptive systems.

Those systems could be located within the organism (e.g., dysfunctions of attention in the central nervous system), in relationships (e.g., disturbed attachment relationships or poor parenting in the family system), or in community/society (e.g., poor education or health-care system). It is also possible for extremely adverse environments or major disasters to radically alter available resources, affecting many systems at many levels. Competence in multiple domains, and the quality of functioning along symptom dimensions (e.g., internalizing or externalizing symptoms), may co-occur in people because of common underlying risks and assets, vulnerabilities and protective factors, or the powerful and broad mediating impact of key relationships, as found in the role of parenting or romantic partners. (The topic of adversity and competence is discussed further in the later section on resilience.)

Symptoms of Mental Disorders Undermine Competence

It is also possible that the symptoms of a disorder, such as bipolar disorder, schizophrenia, or autism, are so impairing that they undermine effective behavior in multiple competence domains. Developmental tasks, by definition, require coordinated use of multiple capabilities to direct behavior in context over time (Masten et al., 2006). Adolescents who are too distracted, confused, or anxious to socialize with peers, go to school, or participate in activities due to a mental illness are likely to have problems making friends, achieving at school, and succeeding on the baseball team, and may miss out on many opportunities for normal socialization of competence as a result. Adolescents with significant issues of impulse control or aggression may alienate mainstream peers or get themselves moved into special education classrooms that are not conducive to optimal academic progress.

Competence Failures Contribute to Symptoms and Disorders

Some models also propose that failure in age-salient developmental tasks, which are highly valued by parents, self, and society, can undermine well-being or exacerbate symptoms (Chen, Li, Li, Li, & Liu, 2000; Cole, Martin, Powers, & Truglio, 1996; Kiesner, 2002; Nangle, Erdley, Newman, Mason, & Carpenter, 2003). Perceived failure could lead to feelings of distress or sadness. Cole and colleagues (Cole, Martin, & Powers, 1997; Jacquez, Cole, & Searle, 2004) have proposed such a failure model for depression, and have demonstrated that social competence predicted changes in depressed affect over time, whereas the reverse was not found. Cole et al. (1997) suggest that this effect is mediated by perceived competence. There is also evidence that academic failure (often leading to school dropout) contributes to externalizing symptoms, possibly by increasing affiliation with deviant peers or increasing exposure to violence (Deater-Deckard, 2001; Dishion, Patterson, Stoolmiller, & Skinner, 1991; Masten, Roisman, et al., 2005; Patterson, Forgatch, Yoerger, & Stoolmiller, 1998). Congruent findings also indicate that academic success among adolescents predicts desistance from antisocial behavior (Maguin & Loeber, 1996; Thornberry, Lizotte, Krohn, Smith, & Porter, 2003).

Transactional and Progressive Cascade Models

It is also possible for the processes represented by the basic causal models to happen simultaneously or in sequence, so that effects are bidirectional or sequential. For example, peers could be turned off by the behavior of a sad or aggressive youth, excluding or rejecting this person, who in reaction to the rejection becomes more distressed or hostile, which further irritates or alienates peers, and so on. Individuals in deviant peer groups can escalate each other's bad behavior (Dishion, Andrews, & Crosby, 1995; Dishion & Piehler, in press). Such bidirectional or *transactional* effects are a common feature of developmental systems theory and developmental psychopathology perspectives (Sameroff, 2000). It is also possible that externalizing behavior contributes to peer rejection, which then contributes to internalizing symptoms in what has been termed a developmental cascade (Masten, Roisman, et al., 2005). Data on antisocial behavior strongly suggest that initial problems of conduct and self-control early in development lead to academic or social problems or both, either of which then contribute to worsening antisocial behavior and/or internalizing symptoms (for reviews of this evidence, see Deater-Deckard, 2001; Dodge & Pettit, 2003; Hinshaw, 2002; Hinshaw & Anderson, 1996; Masten et al., 2006). Such developmental cascades or progressions, sometimes referred to as "snowballing effects," would account for the broad predictive significance of antisocial behavior for multiple problem outcomes later in development that was observed decades ago (Kohlberg, LaCrosse, & Ricks, 1972). Such cascades also corroborate coercion theory models, initially proposed by investigators from the Oregon Social Learning Center, in which problems arising in the family context, such as noncompliance and aggression in preschoolers, lead to dual failures in the spheres of academic achievement and peer acceptance after children enter the school context (Capaldi, 1992; Patterson, Reid, & Dishion, 1992).

Implications for Preventive Interventions

Understanding how and why competence and psychopathology are linked in individual development has important implications for mental health intervention and also for the broad societal agenda of promoting positive youth development (see Masten et al., 2006). If there are common causes underlying multiple disorders and competence problems in the same individuals, preventive interventions that address the common causes should have multiple benefits. If competence failures contribute to psychopathology, then one strategy for intervention would be to promote competence in order to prevent or reduce the related psychopathology. Evidence on effective prevention programs and interventions is consistent with the possibility that promoting competence has preventive effects on a variety of mental health problems (Cicchetti, Rappaport, Sandler, & Weissberg, 2000; Greenberg, Riggs, & Blair, this volume; Masten, 2001; Masten & Coatsworth, 1998; Masten et al., 2006; Weissberg, Kumpfer, & Seligman, 2003).

Similarly, it would be possible to design an intervention strategically to interrupt a developmental cascade or progression before the initial problem undermines development in other domains. Late in a progression, even "curing" the original problem may not produce improvements in the other domains that have been affected. Thus, late interventions to help young people regulate affect, attention, or behavior more effectively cannot be expected to undue all the damage to social relationships, cumulative academic achievement, financial ruin, or one's record in the legal system. Accurately delineating a progressive or cascade causal chain of effects could make it possible to act early in a sequence, treating one problem to prevent a different problem further along a developmental cascade. The timing and nature of preventive interventions would benefit from knowledge about cascades and consideration of spreading effects over time, as well as the developmental level and contexts of the young people involved.

Resilience in Development: Competence in the Context of High Risk or Adversity

More than 3 decades ago, resilience research pioneers were inspired by the possibility that studying resilience would inform prevention and intervention efforts, arguing that we had lessons to learn from understanding how young people overcame adversity or high cumulative risk conditions to succeed in life or how good mental health outcomes are achieved among youth who start down unhealthy roads (Luthar & Cicchetti, 2000; Masten, 1989, 2001, 2004; Masten, Best, & Garmezy, 1990). This section briefly describes progress to date in reaching that goal, with a focus on implications for prevention science and the future integration of neuroscience with behavior in the study of resilience.

Inferring Resilience: Judging Risk and Positive Adaptation

If one is asked to think of a real adolescent who is "resilient," two judgments would need to be made: (1) that the adolescent is doing okay by some criteria and (2) that the adolescent has overcome significant threat to adaptation or development (Luthar, 2006; Masten, 2001; Masten & Coatsworth, 1998). Similarly, before an investigator can study resilience, that scientist must define resilience in terms of risks and positive outcomes. Resilience is inferential because it refers to good functioning during or following conditions that would be expected to disrupt or, in fact, have already disrupted the lives of typical individuals. This means defining the criteria for *risk* and *positive adaptation*.

Defining Risk in Resilience Research

Risk generally refers to an elevated probability of an undesirable outcome, although there is discussion of more precise definitions (see Kraemer et al., 1997). In the case of resilience, the threat to adaptation or development must be significant or substantial: though often unstated, the assumption is that this negative influence could alter the course of development or have serious repercussions on adaptive functioning. Many types of risk factors, including genetic risk, have been studied in resilience research. In risk and resilience studies to date, genetic risk has been measured most often by status markers, such as having a parent with a heritable disorder or biological markers of some kind associated with pathological outcomes, rather than a specific gene or set of genes, because the genes associated with vulnerability had not been identified. That is rapidly changing as gene mapping becomes more feasible, and there is likely to be a surge in research on gene-environment interaction, with a focus on both vulnerability and resilience processes (Gottesman & Hanson, 2005; Rutter, 2007; Rutter, Moffitt, & Caspi, 2006). There is extensive research on resilience in relation to risks posed by common negative life events (e.g., divorce, maltreatment), disadvantage (e.g., poverty), and disasters involving large numbers of victims, both natural (e.g., earthquakes, hurricanes) and unnatural (e.g., war, terrorism). Early in the history of risk research, investigators learned that risks often co-occur or pile up in the lives of youth, and they began to consider *cumulative risk* effects in various ways (Masten, 2001). It has been persuasively argued that cumulative risk conditions call for "cumulative protections" (see Wyman, Sandler, Wolchik, & Nelson, 2000; Yoshikawa, 1994).

Defining Positive Adaptation in Resilience Research

Resilience requires judgments about positive outcomes, which require criteria about positive adaptation or development. Developmental investigators often define those outcomes in terms of competence as defined earlier in this chapter, particularly in relation to success on age-salient developmental tasks. For example a group of adolescents might be judged as competent when they are doing well across multiple domains, including academic achievement in school, social relationships with friends, and following the law in the community and the rules at home (Masten, Coatsworth, et al., 1995; Masten, Hubbard, et al., 1999). Psychiatric researchers also have defined resilience in terms of mental health, such as youth at risk for a mental disorder who remain healthy, or youth who had mental health problems before and now show recovery. Some research includes competence and mental health criteria, defining resilience in terms of doing well socially and academically combined with the absence of mental illness or distress. One of the controversies in this literature has been whether one should be judged to show resilience even when there is internal distress or unhappiness (Luthar, 2006; Masten, 2001;

Masten & Gewirtz, 2006). Clearly it is possible to be effective in developmental tasks, even with internalizing symptoms, although significant depression or anxiety can interfere with adaptive functioning in the environment. Some would argue that particularly in cases of severe or long-term adversity, with residual suffering as a result of that adversity, observable competence across key developmental tasks constitutes resilience, even with periodic experiences of internal distress. Thus a teenage war survivor who moves to a new country, goes to school, makes friends, participates in the community, and later gets a job, marries, and raises a family successfully, would be considered resilient, even with long-lasting symptoms related to war experiences, such as nightmares, depressed mood, anxiety or panic, and so on. On the other hand, no matter how well a person feels and sleeps, if the adolescent is failing in all domains valued by society as developmental milestones, very few observers would infer resilience.

Patterns and Models of Resilience

Resilience is a broad umbrella that includes a variety of life experiences and patterns of adaptation over time. This umbrella covers observed good functioning under challenging circumstances, observed short- or long-term recovery to normal functioning or development following trauma or disaster, and also improvement from poor adaptation to good adaptation following changes in chronic conditions from terrible to favorable. In the last kind of resilience, good adaptation emerges following normalization of the environment; for example, when children are adopted from orphanages into good homes or moved with their families out of famine regions or war zones.

Nonetheless, in all cases, resilience refers to *manifested* positive functioning or outcomes (not probabilistic ones) and success by some set of criteria that is sustained over time, at least for a while (i.e., the positive functioning is not just momentary or manifested on a single occasion). Moreover, it is widely assumed that resilience results from many processes and transactions that are occurring within an individual and between an individual and the environment. Resilience, reflecting system interactions and myriad processes of adaptation, must be understood as a life pattern based on many dynamic processes. In human individuals, who are always developing, and particularly during periods of rapid development such as occur over the years of adolescence, understanding resilience requires a developmental perspective. To understand resilience in adolescence requires consideration of changing capacities for adaptation, vulnerabilities, resources, contexts, and opportunities.

Models of resilience include various ingredients, in addition to the risks and outcomes under consideration. Of particular interest, of course, are the potential assets and moderators that make a difference for adaptive success under difficult circumstances. Studies have tested models of resilience that include a wide variety of *assets* and *protective factors,* including qualities of individuals and their environments or relationships that might account for better adaptation in hazardous situations. General assets are associated with good outcomes in youth under most conditions; outcomes are generally better when a youth has two parents, better parenting, lives in a decent neighborhood and attends a good school, and has normal cognitive abilities. Protective factors refer to influences that play a special role under risky conditions. Parental monitoring, for example, may be generally a good idea, but it can be crucial in a dangerous neighborhood. Some protective factors, more like automobile airbags, are important *only* during emergencies, such as emergency shelters for teenagers.

There are also different models of how all the components involved in resilience may work to produce resilience (Masten, 2001). Some models focus on people: Some investigators have identified resilient versus maladaptive youth and then compared them with each other and with low-risk youth, to try to figure out what makes a difference. In contrast to these person-focused approaches, investigators have also used variable-focused approaches with multivariate statistics to study the relation among the measured qualities of people, their relationships, and their environments. Investigators have tested models with additive effects and with interactions. They have proposed mediating effects to try to identify when and where key processes are occurring. Investigators have asked, for example: Has the Midwestern farm crisis (Elder & Conger, 2000) or the Great Depression (Elder, 1999) affected adolescents primarily through its effects on their parents (e.g., depression, irritability, or marital conflict undermine parenting quality, which leads to problems in children), more directly (e.g., not enough food, changing jobs or educational opportunities), or in some combination of these ways, as often observed with such profound historical events?

The Short List and Its Implications for Resilience

Despite the diversity of risks and populations studied, the varying definitions of positive adaptation, and the inconsistencies and controversies in the resilience literature, the findings have been remarkably consistent in implicating a set of correlates and predictors of resilience in young people (Luthar, 2003, 2006; Masten, 2001, 2004; Masten & Coatsworth, 1998; Masten & Powell, 2003). Thus, it is possible to comprise a reasonably stable "short list" of assets and protective factors associated with resilience (Masten, 2001, 2004; Masten & Coatsworth, 1998; Masten & Reed, 2002; Wright & Masten, 2004). This list in various forms typically includes the following correlates of resilience: decent parents or effective parenting, connections to other competent and caring adults, problem-solving skills, self-regulation skills, positive self-perceptions, beliefs that life has meaning or hopefulness, spirituality or religious affiliations, talents valued by self or society, socioeconomic advantages, community effectiveness and safety, and, for adolescents, connections to prosocial and competent peers.

This list of consistently observed correlates of resilience under diverse conditions suggests the operation of fundamental adaptive systems in human development that operate to foster adaptation under high-risk and adverse conditions, as well as serving many other adaptive functions over the course of development (Masten, 2001, 2004; Masten & Coatsworth, 1998; Masten & Reed, 2002; Wright & Masten, 2004; Yates & Masten, 2004). These adaptive systems have been extensively investigated for many years in the social sciences and other fields, and more recently, have gained the attention of neuroscience researchers. Examples include the following: attachment systems and relationships that provide emotional security and a host of regulatory functions in development; a functional family that serves many roles in the caregiving, socialization, emotional or physical security, and regulation of family members; a central nervous system in good working order that is operating to process information, learn and solve problems, regulate stress, and perform many other roles; a mastery motivational system that motivates efforts to adapt and rewards success; meaning-making systems of belief that provide emotional security, hope, and a sense of coherence in life; community and school organizations that provide opportunities for learning, socialization, contexts for mastery experiences, and so on; and many other cultural and societal systems that nurture and support basic adaptive systems for development. Presumably, these systems have evolved in biological evolution and human cultural evolution because of their adaptive value. Moreover, the development of these systems is itself adaptive in ontogeny, with individual development influenced at multiple levels by experience, including the central nervous system and all the systems regulated by the brain, such as stress regulation. Many chapters in this volume illustrate the burgeoning interest in developmental neuroscience and brain plasticity and the profound implications for preventive interventions of the adaptability of primary adaptive systems during development, discussed further at later points in this chapter.

Prevention and Intervention to Promote Positive Development and to Test Resilience Theory

The significance of the short list and potential adaptive systems that this list may represent are still largely matters of speculation in regard to the causes and processes of resilience. However, randomized experiments to prevent and ameliorate problems among children and youth at risk afford one of the best strategies for testing causal models of resilience (Luthar & Cicchetti, 2000; Masten, 1994; Masten & Coatsworth, 1998; Masten & Powell, 2003). Youth cannot be randomly assigned to the hazards of life, but it is possible to provide assets and protective resources designed to promote better development or to mobilize adaptive systems on their behalf, and study whether and how these interventions work. Resilience-based models offer guidance for designing and evaluating interventions (Luthar & Cicchetti, 2000; Masten, 2001, 2006b; Masten & Gewirtz, 2006; Masten & Powell, 2003; Yates & Masten, 2004).

A compelling case can be made for the transformative influence of resilience studies on practice and the prevention field (Masten, 2001; Masten & Gewirtz,

2006; Masten & Powell, 2003; Masten et al., 2006; Yates & Masten, 2004). Research findings suggest a resilience framework for practice that has shifted away from deficit- or disease-based approaches to more strength- and competence-focused models, infusing more positive goals, measures, methods, and targets of intervention into interventions and systems of care (see Masten, 2006b; Masten & Gewirtz, 2006; Masten & Powell, 2003; or Yates & Masten, 2004). Prevention studies designed on the basis of resilience models have the potential to test mediating and moderating effects hypothesized to make a difference, as well as to improve outcomes. And it is noteworthy that the evidence from the experimental prevention field to date appears to be highly congruent with the findings that have emerged from studies of naturally occurring resilience (see Greenberg et al., this volume; Masten et al., 2006).

As research on brain plasticity and gene expression advances, it is also becoming clear that a new kind of intervention is conceivable. It may be possible to promote resilience by "reprogramming" adaptive systems that have not developed well for various reasons. Investigators are beginning to consider the possibilities of intervening to modify systems that regulate affect, attention, stress, or behavior that are crucial to learning, adaptation to stress, and appropriate social behavior (see Buonomano & Merzenich, 1998; Dahl & Spear, 2004; Greenberg et al., this volume; Rueda, Rothbart, Saccomanno, & Posner, this volume; and other papers in this volume). It may also be possible to prevent the development of mental disorders through preventive interventions with genetically vulnerable individuals, in effect promoting resilience by altering the course of epigenesis or brain development (e.g., Chang, Gallelli, & Howe, this volume). As gene-environment interactions become better explicated in the mental health field, it may also be possible to prevent maladaptive gene expression through favorable changes in the moderating environment, such as by improving parenting or education and reducing maltreatment. Research on gene-environment interactions involving specific genes and particular life experiences (e.g., Caspi et al., 2002) may provide additional evidence supporting the protective strategies already emerging from interventions designed on the basis of resilience.

Resilience and Adolescent Development: Two Key Transitional Windows

In addition to the broad models and findings emerging from resilience research with implications for prevention, this research domain has often included adolescents in longitudinal studies, and thus investigators have focused attention on patterns of risk, competence, psychopathology, and protective influences in adolescence, as well as the changes in behavior, context, and relationships that may play a role in risk, vulnerability, protection, and adaptation. Two major transition periods stand out for consideration from this work, characterized by concentrated change in individual adolescents, their contexts, relationships, and life experiences: early adolescence and the transition to adulthood (which is referred to here as emerging adulthood).

Early adolescence is a time when there are many biological and brain changes, accompanied by changes in appearance, interest and motivation, risk-seeking behavior, schools context, peer interaction, mobility, and relationships with parents (Dahl & Spear, 2004; Steinberg et al., 2006). All of the major aspects of a resilience model are changing: age-salient developmental tasks and what is required to succeed at school or with friends or behave responsibly; risks and adversities change as challenging new experiences pile up from biological, cognitive, and environmental changes and their interaction, and new conflicts emerge with parents or peers; vulnerability appears to increase in a variety of ways, with increasing sleep deprivation, sensitivity to stress, less support or scaffolding from adults, greater exposure to and understanding of negative events and trauma presented on TV or in the community, and even possibly the activation of genetically based vulnerabilities to specific disorders; resources and protection shift as parents avoid or increase monitoring, peers become better friends or more deviant, and opportunities for activities and cultural rites of passage become available. Clearly there is a shifting of challenges, capacity for adaptation, and opportunities at many levels of analysis. For young people who enter this period with a track record of poor adaptation and few resources or protection, the road can be very rocky and there are sharp increases over these years in emotional distress or depression, the risk for substance use and dependence or other risky behaviors, and criminal behavior, particularly among high-risk youth. Young people who were already showing resilience often continue to do well, though some flounder in early adolescence; it is uncommon to see newly emerging resilience during this period. Most of the evidence tracing the course of problem behaviors, such as serious offending, underage drinking, depression, or other internalizing symptoms, over time show generally rising arcs of problems or mental health issues during this period of development, although there are many youth who continue to have low rates of any kind of problems during early adolescence (Dahl & Spear, 2004; Ge, Natsuaki, & Conger, 2006; National Institute on Alcohol Abuse and Alcoholism, 2004/2005; Steinberg et al., 2006; Thornberry & Krohn, 2003). The evidence on this transition suggests that contemporary societies may not be providing adequate scaffolding for many young people in this period of development, though Spear (this volume) has noted that this period in other species also may be fraught with hazard. It is interesting to note that for centuries, this is also a time period when cultures have provided structured support and immersion in the culture through rites of passage, apprenticeships, religious training, and so on.

In contrast, the ending of adolescence and transition to adulthood, or *emerging adulthood* period (Arnett & Tanner, 2006), which is also characterized by concentrated change in individuals, contexts, and their interaction, looks promising as a time of improving prospects and emerging resilience (Masten et al., 2006). Some of the problem behaviors that spiked upward early in adolescence begin to arc downward during emerging adulthood, which is characterized by considerable normative desistance in multiple problem domains of external and internal behavior, including crime (the "age-crime" curve heads downward), party-based drinking, and self-reported symptoms of depression (e.g., Ge et al., 2006; National Institute on Alcohol Abuse and Alcoholism, 2004/2005; Thornberry & Krohn, 2003). There are some bumps upward in problems related to contextual changes (entering military service or college), but these very broad patterns suggest that there must be significant influences at work directing the behavior of young people toward acceptable mainstream adult behavior. Again, youth who enter the years from 18 to 25 with a solid foundation of competence and resources typically navigate this transition well, but additionally, some of the youth who were off track in adolescence begin to get back on track. New resilience emerges (Masten et al., 2004; Masten et al., 2006).

Emergent resilience has been reported for many years in anecdotal accounts or small studies and the qualities associated with "late blooming" are interesting: planfulness, increasing motivation to achieve future goals, connections to adult mentors outside the family, military service, marriage/romantic commitment to prosocial partners, and religious conversion (Masten et al, 2006). This may be a window in human development in modern societies when there is a positive convergence of strategic executive control and future orientation (facilitated by brain development and new capacity for executive functioning), opportunities (to leave home, join transformative new contexts such as the military, college, religious organizations, or the work world), and new adult support beyond the family (e.g., adult mentors, romantic partners) that together spur positive change. It is probably not a coincidence that many cultures around the world provide socially approved contexts and opportunities for young people around this age to move into new environments through work, education, or travel, nor that the legal age of adulthood for various activities often falls around the age of 20 (often 18 to 21).

Conclusion

Normative and individual inflection points in pathways to competence or psychopathology across adolescence may arise from a confluence of changes in adaptive capacity or motivation, contextual demands or supports, and opportunities. Turning points may also result from life-altering experiences that jolt development down a new path, as might happen after traumatic experiences, unplanned pregnancy, religious conversion, or other events.

Transitions into and out of adolescence are periods in which there are marked changes in individuals, relationships, contexts, experiences, developmental task demands, and opportunities for young people, that alter the risks and assets, vulnerabilities and protections, capacity and nature of adaptive systems. The best individual protections for negotiating the psychosocial hazards of early adolescent transitions are the human and social capital accrued in childhood, typically reflected in success in earlier age-salient developmental tasks and well-functioning adaptive systems for learning and regulating behavior, and positive relationships with parents and peers. Additionally, effective cultures and communities provide scaffolding in many forms to support successful transitions during early adolescence. Children who enter the challenges of adolescence and secondary schooling protected by good self-regulation skills, good relationships with prosocial and caring adults and prosocial peer friends, positive reputations with parents, peers and teachers, and positive beliefs about themselves have a far lower risk for psychopathology and disability than children who enter this transition already struggling and unprotected. Already maladaptive youth often face the challenges of this transition with very little scaffolding or protection. Moreover, for children who already have behavioral and emotional problems, the kinds of trouble that ensue may further weaken the protection afforded by human and social capital and the regulatory capacity they provide, while at the same time increasing the intensity of adversity youth experience, accelerating psychopathology or disability, and leading to lifelong consequences.

Similarly, the accomplishments and skills of adolescence set the stage for successful transitions to adulthood. In addition, however, there appears to be a window of opportunity in the transition to adulthood that opens as a result of converging developmental influences that alter the individual, the context, and the opportunities and motivation for changing the life course. These changes not only generate a general positive trend away from deviant behavior among normative young people in their late teens and early twenties, but also afford second chances for some of the youth who have gotten off the expected competence pathways during adolescence to turn their lives around. This window appears to reflect in part the brain development (connectivity, efficiency, etc.) underlying the improvements in a spectrum of executive functioning skills around this time, as well as growing knowledge, experience, physical prowess, and attractiveness, reaching the age of majority with its attending freedoms of action, the growing competence of friends and romantic partners, and the opportunities provided by supportive adults and society at large to promote the development of adult success and civic engagement.

The findings to date across a broad array of studies of competence, resilience, and psychopathology suggest that effective and well-timed prevention efforts could be strategically directed in several key ways: (a) intervening early in well-described progressions to prevent cascades in development that result in snowballing disabilities and comorbidity; (b) promoting competence and regulatory capacity (both self-regulation and social regulation); (c) reducing trauma exposure and boosting protection for children in risky environments; (d) strengthening the scaffolds during periods of marked change, such as early adolescence; or (e) providing opportunities, mentors, and second chances for adolescents in the transition to adulthood. Specific and coordinated efforts could take many forms.

The current explosion of research on the human genome, gene-environment interaction, and brain plasticity throughout the life course heralds a new era of research on vulnerability and resilience, with the potential to revolutionize preventive interventions for mental health throughout the life span. It is now conceivable that the vulnerabilities and adaptive systems implicated in the development of competence and psychopathology in youth might themselves be targeted for change with the aim of redirecting development. It may be possible to improve the odds for competence or recovery and reduce the risks for psychopathology and the attendant burden of suffering it imposes on youth, their families, and society. Much work lies ahead, but there are clear and compelling signs of benefits to prevention science from integrating what is known about competence, resilience, and plasticity across disciplines and systems of human functioning through a developmental approach.

References

Achenbach, T. M. (1974). *Developmental psychopathology*. Oxford, England: Ronald Press.

Achenbach, T. M. (1990). What is "developmental" about developmental psychopathology? In J. Rolf, A. S. Masten, K. Nuechterlein, & S. Weintraub (Eds.), *Risk and protective factors in the development of psychopathology*. New York: Cambridge University Press.

Arnett, J. J., & Tanner, J. (Eds.) (2006). *Emerging adults in America: Coming of age in the 21st century*. Washington, DC: American Psychological Association Press.

Buonomano, D. V., & Merzenich, M. M. (1998). Net interaction between different forms of short-term synaptic plasticity and slow IPSP's in the hippocampus and auditory cortex. *Journal of Neurophysiology, 80*, 1765–1774.

Capaldi, D. M. (1992). Co-occurrence of conduct problems and depressive symptoms in early adolescent boys: Pt. II. A 2-year follow-up at grade 8. *Development and Psychopathology, 4*, 125–144.

Caspi, A., McClay, J., Moffitt, T. E., Mill, J., Martin, J., Craig, I. W., et al. (2002). Role of genotype in the cycle of violence in maltreated children. *Science, 297*, 851–854.

Chang, K., Gallelli, K., & Howe, M. (2007). Early identification and prevention of early-onset bipolar disorder. In D. Romer & E. Walker (Eds.), *Adolescent psychopathology and the developing brain: Integrating brain and prevention science*. New York: Oxford University Press.

Chen, X., Li, D., Li, Z.-Y., Li, B.-S., & Liu, M. (2000). Sociable and prosocial dimensions of social competence in Chinese children: Common and unique contributions to social, academic, and psychological adjustment. *Developmental Psychology, 36*, 302–314.

Chen, X., Rubin, K. H., & Li, B. (1995). Depressed mood in Chinese children: Relations with school performance and family environment. *Journal of Consulting and Clinical Psychology, 63,* 938–947.

Cicchetti, D. (1984). The emergence of developmental psychopathology. *Child Development, 55,* 1–7.

Cicchetti, D. (Ed.). (1989). *The emergence of a discipline: Rochester symposium on developmental psychopathology.* Hillsdale, NJ: Erlbaum.

Cicchetti, D. (1990). An historical perspective on the discipline of developmental psychopathology. In J. Rolf, A. S. Masten, D. Cicchetti, K. H. Nuechterlein, & S. Weintraub (Eds.), *Risk and protective factors in the development of psychopathology* (pp. 2–28). New York: Cambridge University Press.

Cicchetti, D. (1993). Developmental psychopathology: Reactions, reflections, and projections. *Developmental Review, 13,* 471–502.

Cicchetti, D. (2006). Development and pscyhopathology. In D. Cicchetti & D. Cohen (Eds.), *Development and psychopathology: Vol. 1. Theory and methods* (2nd ed., pp. 1–23). New York: Wiley.

Cicchetti, D., & Cohen, D. J. (Eds.). (1995). *Developmental psychopathology: Vol. 1. Theory and methods.* New York: Wiley.

Cicchetti, D., Rappaport, J., Sandler, I., & Weissberg, R. P. (Eds.). (2000). *The promotion of wellness in children and adolescents.* Washington, DC: CWLA Press.

Cole, D. A., Martin, J. M., & Powers, B. (1997). A competency-based model of child depression: A longitudinal study of peer, parent, teacher, and self-evaluations. *Journal of Child Psychology and Psychiatry, 38,* 505–514.

Cole, D. A., Martin, J. M., Powers, B., & Truglio, R. (1996). Modeling causal relations between academic and social competence and depression: A multitrait-multimethod longitudinal study of children. *Journal of Abnormal Psychology, 105,* 258–270.

Dahl, R. E., & Spear, L. P. (Eds.). (2004). *Adolescent brain development: Vulnerabilities and opportunities* (Vol. 1021). New York: New York Academy of Sciences.

Deater-Deckard, K. (2001). Annotation: Recent research examining the role of peer relationships in the development of psychopathology. *Journal of Child Psychology and Psychiatry, 42,* 565–579.

Dishion, T. J., Andrews, D. W., & Crosby, L. (1995). Antisocial boys and their friends in early adolescence: Relationship characteristics, quality, and interactional process. *Child Development, 66,* 139–151.

Dishion, T. J., Patterson, G. R., Stoolmiller, M., & Skinner, M. L. (1991). Family, school, and behavioral antecedents to early adolescent involvement with antisocial peers. *Developmental Psychology, 27,* 172–180.

Dishion, D. J., & Piehler, T. F. (in press). Peer dynamics in the development and change of child and adolescent problem behavior. In A. S. Masten (Eds.), *Multilevel dynamics in developmental psychopathology: 34th Minnesota Symposium on Child Psychology.* Mahwah, NJ: Erlbaum.

Dodge, K. A., & Pettit, G. S. (2003). A biopsychosocial model of the development of chronic conduct problems in adolescence. *Developmental Psychology, 39,* 349–371.

Elder, G. H., Jr. (1999). *Children of the Great Depression: Social change in life experience. 25th Anniversary Edition, Enlarged.* Boulder, CO: Westview Press. [Original work published in 1974 by the University of Chicago Press]

Elder, G. H., Jr., & Conger, R. D. (2000). *Children of the land: Adversity and success in rural America.* Chicago: University of Chicago Press.

Evans, D. L., Foa, E. B., Gur, R. E., Hendin, H., O'Brien, C. P., Seligman, M. E. P., et al. (Eds.). (2005). *Treating and preventing adolescent mental health disorders: What we know and what we don't know: A research agenda for improving the mental health of our youth.* New York: Oxford University Press.

Garmezy, N. (1984). Risk and protective factors in children vulnerable to major mental disorders. In L. Grinspoon (Ed.), *Psychiatry 1983* (Vol. III, pp. 99–104, 159–161). Washington, DC: American Psychiatric Press.

Ge, X., Natsuaki, M. N., & Conger, R. D. (2006). Trajectories of depressive symptoms and stressful life events among male and female adolescents in divorced and non-divorced families. *Development and Psychopathology, 18,* 253–273.

Gottesman, I. I. (1974). Developmental genetics and ontogenetic psychology: Overdue détente and propositions from a matchmaker. In A. D. Pick (Ed.), *Minnesota symposium on child psychology* (Vol. 8, pp. 55–80). Minneapolis: University of Minnesota Press.

Gottesman, I. I., & Hanson, D. R. (2005). Human development: Biological and genetic processes. *Annual Review of Psychology, 56,* 10.11–10.24.

Greenberg, M. T., Riggs, N. R., & Blair, C. (2007). The role of preventive interventions in enhancing neurocognitive functioning and promoting competence in adolescence. In D. Romer & E. Walker (Eds.), *Adolescent psychopathology and the developing brain: Integrating brain and prevention science.* New York: Oxford University Press.

Hinshaw, S. P. (2002). Process, mechanism, and explanation related to externalizing behavior in developmental psychopathology. *Journal of Abnormal Child Psychology, 30,* 431–446.

Hinshaw, S. P., & Anderson, C. A. (1996). Conduct and oppositional defiant disorders. In E. J. Mash & R. A. Barkley (Eds.), *Child psychopathology* (pp. 113–149). New York: Guilford Press.

Jacquez, F., Cole, D. A., & Searle, B. (2004). Self-perceived competence as a mediator between maternal feedback and depressive symptoms in adolescents. *Journal of Abnormal Child Psychology, 32,* 355–367.

Kiesner, J. (2002). Depressive symptoms in early adolescence: Their relations with classroom problem behavior and peer status. *Journal of Research on Adolescence, 12,* 463–478.

Kohlberg, L., LaCrosse, J., & Ricks, D. (1972). The predictability of adult mental health from childhood behavior. In B. B. Wolman (Ed.), *Manual of child psychopathology* (pp. 1217–1284). New York: McGraw-Hill.

Kopp, C. B. (1983). Risk factors in development. In M. M. Haith & J. J. Campos (Eds.), *Handbook of child psychology, Vol. 2: Infancy and developmental psychobiology* (4th ed., pp. 1081–1188). New York: Wiley.

Kraemer, H. C., Kazdin, A. E., Offord, D., Kessler, R. C., Jensen, P. S., & Kupfer, D. (1997). Coming to terms with the terms of risk. *Archives of General Psychiatry, 54,* 337–343.

Luthar, S. S. (Ed.). (2003). *Resilience and vulnerability: Adaptation in the context of childhood adversities.* New York: Cambridge University Press.

Luthar, S. S. (2006). Resilience in development: A synthesis of research across five decades. In D. Cicchetti, & D. J. Cohen (Eds.), *Developmental psychopathology: Risk, disorder, and adaptation, Volume 3* (2nd ed., pp. 739–795). New York: Wiley.

Luthar, S. S., & Cicchetti, D. (2000). The construct of resilience: Implications for interventions and social policies. *Development and Psychopathology, 12,* 857–885.

Maguin, E., & Loeber, R. (1996). Academic performance and delinquency. *Crime and Justice: A Review of Research, 20,* 145–264.

Masten, A. S. (1989). Resilience in development: Implications of the study of successful adaptation for developmental psychopathology. In D. Cicchetti (Ed.), *The emergence of a discipline: Rochester Symposium on Developmental Psychopathology* (Vol. 1, pp. 261–294). Hillsdale, NJ: Erlbaum.

Masten, A. S. (1994). Resilience in individual development: Successful adaptation despite risk and adversity. In M. C. Wang & E. W. Gordon (Eds.), *Educational resilience in inner-city America: Challenges and prospects* (pp. 3–25). Hillsdale, NJ: Erlbaum.

Masten, A. S. (2001). Ordinary magic: Resilience processes in development. *American Psychologist, 56,* 227–238.

Masten, A. S. (2004). Regulatory processes, risk and resilience in adolescent development. *Annals of the New York Academy of Sciences, 1021*(1–11), 1–25.

Masten, A. S. (2006a). Developmental psychopathology: Pathways to the future. *International Journal of Behavioral Development, 30,* 47–54.

Masten, A. S. (2006b). Promoting resilience in development: A general framework for systems of care. In R. J. Flynn, P. M. Dudding, & J. G. Barber (Eds.), *Promoting resilience in child welfare* (pp. 3–17). Ottawa: University of Ottawa Press.

Masten, A. S., Best, K. M., & Garmezy, N. (1990). Resilience and development: Contributions from the study of children who overcome adversity. *Development and Psychopathology, 2,* 425–444.

Masten, A. S., & Braswell, L. (1991). Developmental psychopathology: An integrative framework. In P. R. Martin (Ed.), *Handbook of behavior therapy and psychological science: An integrative approach* (pp. 35–56). Elmsford, NY: Pergamon Press.

Masten, A. S., Burt, K., & Coatsworth, J. D. (2006). Competence and psychopathology in development. In D. Cicchetti & D. Cohen (Eds.), *Developmental psychopathology: Vol. 3. Risk, disorder and psychopathology* (2nd ed., pp. 710–741) New York: Wiley.

Masten, A. S., Burt, K., Roisman, G. I., Obradović, J., Long, J. D., & Tellegen, A. (2004). Resources and resilience in the transition to adulthood: Continuity and change. *Development and Psychopathology, 16,* 1071–1094.

Masten, A. S., & Coatsworth, J. D. (1995). Competence, resilience, and psychopathology. In D. Cicchetti & D. J. Cohen (Eds.), *Developmental psychopathology: Vol. 2. Risk, disorder, and adaptation* (Vol. 2, pp. 715–752). New York: Wiley.

Masten, A. S., & Coatsworth, J. D. (1998). The development of competence in favorable and unfavorable environments: Lessons from research on successful children. *American Psychologist, 53,* 205–220.

Masten, A. S., Coatsworth, J. D., Neemann, J., Gest, S. D., Tellegen, A., & Garmezy, N. (1995). The structure and coherence of competence from childhood through adolescence. *Child Development, 66,* 1635–1659.

Masten, A. S., & Curtis, W. J. (2000). Integrating competence and psychopathology: Pathways toward a comprehensive science of adaptation in development. *Development and Psychopathology, 12,* 529–550.

Masten, A. S., & Gewirtz, A. H. (2006). Vulnerability and resilience in early child development. In K. McCartney & D. Phillips (Eds.), *Handbook of early child development* (pp. 22–43). New York: Blackwell.

Masten, A. S., Hubbard, J., Gest, S. D., Tellegen, A., Garmezy, N., & Ramirez, M. (1999). Adversity, resources and resilience: Pathways to competence from childhood to late adolescence. *Development and Psychopathology, 11,* 143–169.

Masten, A. S., Obradović, J., & Burt, K. (2006). Resilience in emerging adulthood: Developmental perspectives on continuity and transformation. In J. J. Arnett & J. Tanner (Eds.), *Emerging adults in America: Coming of age in the 21st century* (pp. 173–190). Washington, DC: American Psychological Association Press.

Masten, A. S., & Powell, J. L. (2003). A resilience framework for research, policy, and practice. In S. S. Luthar (Ed.), *Resilience and vulnerability: Adaptation in the context of childhood adversities* (pp. 1–25). New York: Cambridge University Press.

Masten, A. S., & Reed, M.-G. J. (2002). Resilience in development. In C. R. Snyder & S. J. Lopez (Eds.), *Handbook of positive psychology* (pp. 74–88). London: Oxford University Press.

Masten, A. S., Roisman, G. I., Long, J. D., Burt, K. B., Obradović, J., Riley, J. R., Boelcke-Stennes, K., & Tellegen, A. (2005). Developmental cascades: Linking academic achievement, externalizing and internalizing symptoms over 20 years. *Developmental Psychology, 41,* 733–746.

Nangle, D. W., Erdley, C. A., Newman, J. E., Mason, C. A., & Carpenter, E. M. (2003). Popularity, friendship quantity, and friendship quality: Interactive influences on children's loneliness and depression. *Journal of Clinical Child and Adolescent Psychology, 32,* 546–555.

National Institute on Alcohol Abuse and Alcoholism. (2004/5). Alcohol and development in youth: An interdisciplinary overview. *Alcohol Research and Health, 28*(3).

Patterson, G. R., Forgatch, M. S., Yoerger, K. L., & Stoolmiller, M. (1998). Variables that initiate and maintain an early-onset trajectory for juvenile offending. *Development and Psychopathology, 10,* 531–547.

Patterson, G. R., Reid, J. B., & Dishion, T. J. (1992). *A social interactional approach: Vol. 4. Antisocial boys.* Eugene, OR: Castalia.

Rueda, M. R., Rothbart, M. K., Saccomanno, L., & Posner, M. I. (2007). Modifying brain networks underlying self-regulation. In D. Romer & E. Walker (Eds.), *Adolescent psychopathology and the developing brain: Integrating brain and prevention science.* New York: Oxford University Press.

Rutter, M. (1981). *Scientific foundations of developmental psychiatry.* Baltimore, MD: University Park Press.

Rutter, M. (1986). Child psychiatry: The interface between clinical and developmental research. *Psychological Medicine, 16,* 151–169.

Rutter, M. (2007). Gene-environment interplay and developmental psychopathology. In A. S. Masten (Ed.), Multilevel dynamics in developmental psychopathology: Pathways to the future. *The Minnesota Symposia on Child Psychology* (Vol. 34). Mahwah, NJ: Erlbaum.

Rutter, M., & Garmezy, N. (1983). Developmental psychopathology. In E. M. Hetherington (Vol. Ed.), P. H. Mussen (Editor), *Carmichael's manual of child psychology: Vol. 4. Social and personality development* (pp. 775–911). New York: Wiley.

Rutter, M., Moffitt, T. E., & Caspi, A. (2006). Gene-environment interplay and psychopathology: Multiple varieties but real effects. *Journal of Child Psychology and Psychiatry, 47,* 226–261.

Rutter, M., & Sroufe, L. A. (2000). Developmental psychopathology: Concepts and challenges. *Developmental Psychopathology, 12,* 265–296.

Sameroff, A. J. (2000). Developmental systems, and psychopathology. *Development and Psychopathology, 12,* 297–312.

Spear, L. (2007). The developing brain and adolescent-typical behavior patterns: An evolutionary approach. In D. Romer & E. Walker (Eds.), *Adolescent psychopathology and the developing brain: Integrating brain and prevention science.* New York: Oxford University Press.

Sroufe, L. A. (1997). Psychopathology as an outcome of development. *Development and Psychopathology, 9,* 251–268.

Sroufe, L. A., & Rutter, M. (1984). The domain of developmental psychopathology. *Child Development, 55,* 17–29.

Steinberg, L., Dahl, R., Keating, D., Kupfer, D. J., Masten, A. S. , & Pine, D. (2006). The study of developmental psychopathology in adolescence: Integrating affective neuroscience with the study of context. In D. Cicchetti, & D. Cohen (Ed.), *Developmental psychopathology* (2nd ed., pp. 710–741). New York: Wiley.

Thornberry, T. P., & Krohn, M. S. (Eds.) (2003). *Taking stock of delinquency: An overview of findings from contemporary longitudinal studies.* New York: Kluwer Academic/Plenum Press.

Thornberry, T. P., Lizotte, A. J., Krohn, M. D., Smith, C. A., & Porter, P. K. (2003). Causes and consequences of delinquency: Findings from the Rochester Youth Development Study. In T. P. Thornberry & M. D. Krohn (Eds.), *Taking stock of delinquency: An overview of findings from contemporary longitudinal studies* (pp. 11–46). New York: Kluwer Academic/Plenum Press.

Weissberg, R. P., Kumpfer, K. L., & Seligman, M. E. P. (2003). Prevention that works for children and youth. *American Psychologist, 58,* 425–432.

Wright, M. O'D., & Masten, A. S. (2004). Resilience processes in development: Fostering positive adaptation in the context of adversity. In S. Goldstein & R. Brooks (Eds.), *Handbook of Resilience in Children* (pp. 17–37). New York: Kluwer Academic/Plenum.

Wyman, P. A., Sandler, I., Wolchik, S., & Nelson, K. (2000). Resilience as cumulative competence promotion and stress protection: Theory and intervention. In D. Cicchetti, J. Rappaport, I. Sandler & R. P. Weissberg (Eds.), *The promotion of wellness in children and adolescents* (pp. 133–184). Thousand Oaks, CA: Sage.

Yates, T. M., & Masten, A. S. (2004). Fostering the future: Resilience theory and the practice of positive psychology. In P. A. Linley & S. Joseph (Eds.), *Positive psychology in practice* (pp. 521–539). Hoboken, NJ: Wiley.

Yoshikawa, H. (1994). Prevention as cumulative protection: Effects of early family support and education on chronic delinquency and its risks. *Psychological Bulletin, 115,* 28–54.

Part II

Characteristics of Brain and
Behavior in Development

Chapter 3

Mapping Adolescent Brain Maturation
Using Structural Magnetic
Resonance Imaging

Elizabeth R. Sowell, Paul M. Thompson,
and Arthur W. Toga

Adolescent brain development is one of the most compelling neuroscience research fields to emerge in the last decade. The more troublesome aspects of adolescent behavior in our society have long been difficult to explain, and they have largely been attributed to fluctuating hormones. However, recent brain imaging research showing continued brain maturation in normally developing adolescents may hold some new explanatory power in this area. Subsequent to the newest research, public interest in adolescent brain development has exploded as the media struggles to use recent neuroimaging research to help explain everything from teen-driving mishaps to recent school shooting incidents. Brain imaging research even played a prominent role in a recent United States Supreme Court hearing regarding the use of capital punishment in minors. Unfortunately, our current state of knowledge regarding adolescent brain development is not sufficient to help explain such complex behavior within individuals. Nonetheless, individuals outside the scientific community are intensely interested in applying this research, which further supports the importance of continued investigations in this area.

Continued brain development during adolescence had been demonstrated several decades prior to the most recent brain mapping studies. For example, postmortem studies revealed a protracted cycle of myelination, particularly in frontal and parietal regions (Yakovlev & Lecours, 1967) continuing well into the 3rd decade of life. Additionally, reductions in synaptic density have been reported to occur throughout adolescence (Huttenlocher, 1979). Findings from these postmortem studies went largely ignored in the literature on adolescent behavior. Perhaps this was because these cellular changes (i.e., myelination and synaptic pruning) were relatively subtle during the adolescent years relative to the dramatic changes earlier in development and it may not have seemed likely that such subtle changes in brain structure could impact behavior on such a gross level.

Although we cannot directly measure structural changes at the cellular level with MRI, the spatial and temporal patterns of maturational change observed in the recent imaging studies reflects the patterns observed postmortem. Some clear advantages of the imaging studies are that larger samples of normally developing individuals can be studied, they can be studied at multiple time points, and brain and behavioral changes can be correlated. The available imaging technology may never be adequate or appropriate for assessing such issues as individual culpability for societal extremes in troublesome adolescent behavior, but the developmental neuroscience community is clearly better poised to address questions regarding relationships between the brain and behavior than at any previous time.

The main focus of this review will be on the exciting new studies of normative brain development during childhood and adolescence that have been performed with sophisticated new brain mapping techniques, including cortical pattern matching (CPM). With these studies, we have been able to map structural changes over the entire cortical surface, advancing our understanding of the timing and localization of these alterations that occur as part of the sculpting of the human brain at various ages. We will briefly review the earliest quantitative imaging studies of child and adolescent brain development that used methods designed to calculate regional brain volumes (i.e., volumetrics). These studies continue to be the "gold standard" for assessing changes in brain morphology because they involve manual designation of cortical and subcortical structures based on visually identifiable anatomical landmarks.

More recent techniques rely on state-of-the-art computer algorithms that allow assessment of changes throughout the entire brain at once. Voxel-based morphometry (VBM), for example, involves spatially standardizing brain image volumes three-dimensionally and assessing gray or white matter change in a completely automated way. CPM is also relatively automated but provides some advantage over VBM because sulcal patterns on the cortical surface are delineated, and cortical structures are matched across subjects based on these landmarks. Both VBM and CPM provide an advantage because they allow three-dimensional visualization of changes occurring within the brain and at the cortical surface, unbiased by observable sulcal cortical boundaries necessary for making anatomical delineations in the volumetric studies. These newer brain mapping studies will be discussed in detail in this chapter, and we will concentrate on changes in the cerebral cortex during childhood and adolescence, because these have been among the most exciting findings. Because the focus of this collection of work is on adolescent psychopathology and the developing brain, we will also discuss some of our recent work describing brain morphological abnormalities in children with developmental disorders such as fetal alcohol syndrome and attention deficit/hyperactivity disorder. We relate these studies to the normative studies to help illustrate how we may learn more by integrating normative and disabled populations than from either alone.

Volumetric Image Analysis Findings

Brain developmental changes in childhood and adolescence have been the focus of numerous volumetric MRI studies in the last decade (Caviness et al., 1996; Courchesne et al., 2000; Giedd et al., 1996a; Giedd et al., 1996b; Giedd et al., 1999; Jernigan et al., 1991; Pfefferbaum et al., 1994; Reiss et al., 1996; Sowell & Jernigan, 1998; Sowell et al., 2002c). Various methods have been used to assess age effects on the volumes of various brain regions and tissues. Researchers have used tissue segmentation, which involves classification of brain tissue into distinct categories, to assess age-effects on volumes of gray matter, white matter and cerebrospinal fluid (CSF). Stereotaxic region definition schemes were most characteristic of the earlier studies (Giedd et al., 1996a; Jernigan et al., 1991; Reiss et al., 1996), frequently because the image spatial resolution was low (i.e., 4- to 5-mm MRI slice thickness), making cortical anatomical landmarks difficult to identify and follow through successive image slices. In some early volumetric studies, whole brain tissue volumes were assessed for age effects (Caviness et al., 1996; Courchesne et al., 2000), but others employed manual region definition on a slice by slice basis using cortical anatomical landmarks (where observable) as boundaries (Giedd et al., 1996b; Lange et al., 1997; Sowell & Jernigan, 1998; Sowell et al., 2002c). Finally, automated lobar region definition schemes have been used (Giedd et al., 1999), in which image warping algorithms are used to automatically, three-dimensional map brain lobe regions from one subject to another.

In the earliest report of volumetric brain differences between childhood and young adulthood, Jernigan and Tallal (1990) reported that children aged 8 to 10 years had significantly *more* cortical gray matter as a proportion of cerebral size than did young adults. These authors followed this preliminary report with a larger sample size and stereotaxic subdivision of cortical regions, and found evidence for an increase in size of the dorsal-most brain region between childhood and young adulthood (Jernigan et al., 1991), particularly in the frontal lobes. Within the dorsal brain region, the cortical gray matter appeared to decrease with age while CSF in this region increased. The inferior cortical gray matter volumes did not appear to change across the age range. The authors proposed that their observation of a "thinning" cortex in superior cortical regions could be related to reductions in synaptic density reported earlier in postmortem material (Huttenlocher, 1979).

Since these early imaging reports, cortical gray matter volume decreases have been confirmed by other groups (Pfefferbaum et al., 1994; Reiss et al., 1996). Regionally, the most notable changes during childhood and adolescence occur in the more dorsal cortices, as described by Jernigan and colleagues (1991). During adolescence, frontal and parietal lobes show highly significant increases in white matter, along with concomitant decreases in gray matter (Giedd et al., 1999; Sowell et al., 2002c). Cortex in the more ventral temporal lobes appear to change less dramatically between childhood and adolescence (Giedd et al., 1999; Jernigan et al., 1991; Sowell et al., 2002c). Notably, gray matter thinning in the frontal cortex is related to changing cognitive ability in normal children and adolescents. We found significant correlations between gray matter volume in the frontal lobe and children's performance on a verbal learning task (Sowell et al., 2001a).

From postmortem studies, we know that myelination begins near the end of the 2nd trimester of fetal development and extends beyond the 2nd decade of life (Yakovlev & Lecours, 1967). Autopsy studies consistently reveal that myelination occurs in a systematic sequence progressing from inferior to superior brain regions and from posterior to anterior. In addition to continuing myelination, a regionally variable reduction in synaptic density also occurs during the adolescent age range (Huttenlocher, 1979; Huttenlocher & de Courten, 1987). These processes are thought to reflect the regional pattern of functional maturation of the brain. Findings from the volumetric MRI studies described above have tended to concur with the postmortem studies given that cortical gray matter volume reductions appear to be somewhat specific to the superior cortices of the frontal and parietal lobes relatively late in development (i.e., between childhood and adolescence; (Jernigan et al., 1991; Sowell & Jernigan, 1998)). One volumetric study with a large sample and longitudinal data points has confirmed these results (Giedd et al., 1999), showing subtle increases in gray matter during childhood followed by significant declines during adolescence.

Voxel-Based Morphometry of Adolescent Brain Development

The volumetric studies described above have provided invaluable information about continued brain development and are still thought to be a "gold standard" in quantitative brain imaging. This is largely because the method is quite easy to understand and to replicate, provided detailed protocols for defining anatomical landmarks are established. However, they are limited because, typically, only gross lobar structures can be reliably identified visually and manually defined. Newer methods have recently been employed to assess structural age effects during normal development on a voxel-by-voxel basis (Paus et al., 1999; Sowell et al., 1999a; Sowell et al., 1999b). This method allows assessment of anatomical change within the entire brain at once, independent of explicit visualization of anatomical landmarks.

We used VBM (Ashburner & Friston, 2000) to localize age-related gray matter density reductions between childhood and adolescence in 18 normally developing individuals between 7 and 16 years of age (Sowell et al., 1999a). Essentially, VBM entails automated spatial normalization of volumes into a standard coordinate space. Images are then scaled so that each voxel coordinate is thought to be anatomically comparable across subjects. Tissue segmentation is used to assess localized differences in gray matter or white matter. Using these methods, we reported that the gray matter volume reductions observed in frontal and parietal lobes in the volumetric studies resulted mostly from gray matter density reductions in diffuse dorsal regions of these cortices (Sowell et al., 1999a). Parietal cortex changed the most in both the volumetric and VBM assessments of gray matter change during adolescence, and relatively little change occurred in the more ventral cortices of the temporal and occipital lobes (See figure 3-1).

Paus and colleagues used VBM to assess white matter changes in subjects 4 to 17 years and found prominent white matter density increases in the posterior limb of the internal capsule and in the arcuate fasciculus in the temporo-parietal region (Paus et al., 1999). Cortical change more prominent in the parietal relative to the frontal cortex was not expected during the late childhood age range given that postmortem studies have shown a posterior to anterior progression of cellular change. We would have expected age-related changes to be more prominent in the frontal lobes this late in development.

The observation of preadolescent gray matter loss in the parietal cortices prompted us to assess postadolescent gray matter change in frontal cortex. In a VBM study focusing on the adolescent (12 to 16 years) to adult age range (23 to 30 years), we observed a strikingly different pattern of change localized to large regions of dorsal, mesial, and orbital frontal cortex with relatively little gray matter density reduction in the parietal lobes (Sowell et al., 1999a). These results were consistent with our a priori predictions and made sense in light of studies showing that the frontal lobes are essential for such functions as response inhibition, emotional regulation, planning, and organization (Fuster, 1997), which may not be fully developed in adolescents. Results from this study were among the first in the brain imaging literature to suggest that troublesome adolescent behavior may not be solely hormonally related.

Adolescent Brain Development Assessed With CPM

Cortical pattern matching (CPM) techniques provide distinct advantages over the VBM methods described above. VBM typically relies on automated methods for matching cortical anatomy across subjects, but cortical anatomy varies considerably

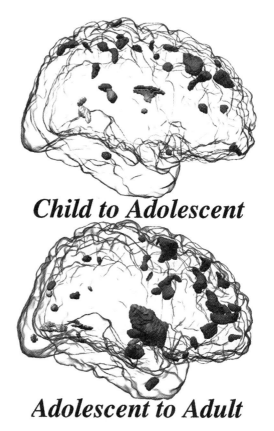

Child to Adolescent

Adolescent to Adult

Figure 3-1 *Top,* child to adolescent statistical map for the negative age effects representing gray matter density reductions observed between childhood and adolescence; *bottom,* adolescence and adulthood. These maps are three-dimensional renderings of the traditional statistical maps shown inside the transparent cortical surface rendering of one representative subject's brain. Lobes and the subcortical region were defined anatomically on the same subject's brain. Color coding is applied to each cluster based on its location within the representative brain. Clusters are shown in the frontal lobes (purple), parietal lobes (red), occipital lobes (yellow), temporal lobes (blue), and subcortical region (green). See color insert. (Sowell et al., 1999b; Sowell et al., 1999a.)

between individuals and during development. When brain volume data sets are spatially registered without taking this variability into account, cortical anatomical regions are not well matched across subjects, particularly where sulcal pattern variability is highest. CPM methods, on the other hand, can be used to assess group differences in cortical anatomy while accounting for the differences in sulcal location across subjects and also can be used to measure cortical asymmetries (Sowell et al., 2002b; Thompson, Moussai, et al., 1998). Briefly, a 3-D geometric model of the cortical surface is extracted from the MRI scan of each subject (MacDonald et al., 1994) and then flattened to a 2-D planar format (Thompson & Toga, 1997; Thompson & Toga, 2002). A complex deformation, or warping transform, is then applied that aligns the sulcal anatomy of each subject with an average sulcal pattern derived for the group (see figure 3-2). To improve sulcal alignment across subjects, all sulci that occur consistently can be manually defined on the surface rendering (see figure 3-3), and used to constrain this transformation. Cortical measures, such as gray matter thickness or local brain size, can then be compared across subjects and groups to assess age, gender, or group effects. More details on these methods can be found in other reports (Thompson, Hayashi, et al., 2004).

Mapping Sulcal Asymmetries Using CPM

Left-right asymmetries in sulcal patterns are particularly interesting in the perisylvian cortices given the functional lateralization of language in this region (reviewed in Geschwind & Galaburda, 1985). Postmortem studies have shown that in adults, the Sylvian fissure is longer in the left hemisphere than the right (Galaburda et al., 1978; Ide et al., 1996), and in vivo vascular imaging studies have shown that the Sylvian fissure angles up more dramatically at its posterior end in the right hemisphere than the left (LeMay & Culebras, 1972). Left greater than right hemisphere perisylvian asymmetries (planum temporale length) have also been observed in postmortem studies of infants (Witelson & Pallie, 1973), indicating that these asymmetry patterns may be independent of maturational change and the acquisition of language abilities throughout infancy and childhood. Until our recent in vivo imaging studies, little was known about the emergence of cortical surface gyral and sulcal asymmetries in normal adolescent development.

In a recent study, we mapped sulcal pattern asymmetry in groups of normally developing children (7 to 11 years), adolescents (12 to 16 years), and young adults (23 to 30 years) using the surface-based cortical pattern matching image analytic methods described above. Asymmetries in perisylvian cortices continued to develop between childhood and young adulthood (Sowell et al., 2002b). Although the normal left longer than right Sylvian fissure asymmetry was present in the children, adolescents, and adults, it was much more pronounced in adulthood, on average twice the magnitude of the asymmetry observed in children. The asymmetry in the slope of the Sylvian fissure also changed with age such that the normal pattern of right more sloped than left occurred without exception in the young adults studied and significantly less frequently in the children. These findings were consistent with the earlier postmortem literature, and we observed similar asymmetry patterns in an independent group of children and adolescents (Blanton et al., 2001). The functional significance of these changes in asymmetry is currently not well understood, and their relevance to adolescence is even less clear. Maturational cellular events such as continued myelination (Yakovlev & Lecours, 1967) and perhaps even new neurons (Gould et al., 1999) in perisylvian regions could contribute to the dynamic changes in sulcal asymmetry observed

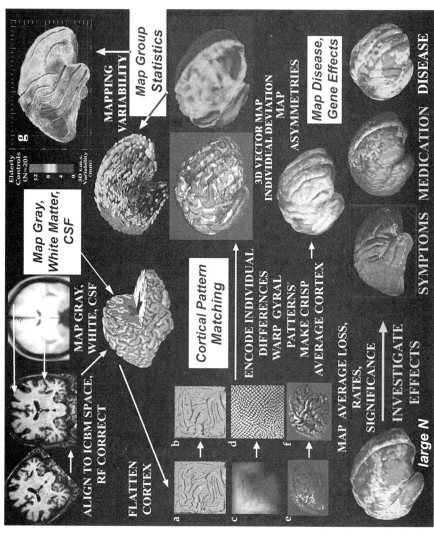

Figure 3-2 Analyzing cortical data. The schematic shows a sequence of image processing steps that can be used to map how aging affects the cortex. The steps include aligning MRI data to a standard space, tissue classification, cortical pattern matching, as well as averaging and comparing local measures of cortical gray matter volumes across subjects. To help compare cortical features from subjects whose anatomy differs, individual gyral patterns are flattened and aligned with a group average gyral pattern (a to f). Group variability (g) and cortical asymmetry can also be computed. Correlations can also be mapped between age-related gray matter deficits and genetic risk factors. Maps may also be generated visualizing linkages between deficits and clinical symptoms, cognitive scores, and medication effects. The only steps here that are currently not automated are the tracing of sulci on the cortex. Some manual editing may also be required to assist algorithms that delete dura and scalp from images, especially if there is very little CSF in the subdural space. See color insert. (Thompson et al., 2003.)

Figure 3-3 *Top left*, three representative brain image data sets with the original MRI, tissue segmented images, and surface renderings with sulcal contours shown in pink; *top right*, surface rendering of one representative subject with cutout showing tissue segmented within the surface. Sulcal lines are shown where they would lie on the surface in the cutout region. Note the sample spheres over the right hemisphere inferior frontal sulcus (lower sphere) and on the middle region of the precentral sulcus (upper sphere) that illustrate varying degrees of gray matter density. In the blown-up panel, note the upper sphere has a higher gray matter density than the lower sphere, as it contains only blue pixels (gray matter) within the brain. The lower sphere also contains green pixels (white matter) that would lower the gray matter proportion within it. In the actual analysis, the gray matter proportion was measured within 15mm spheres centered across every point over the cortical surface. *Bottom*, sulcal anatomical delineations are defined according to color. These are the contours drawn on each individual's surface rendering according to a reliable, written protocol. See color insert. (Sowell et al., 2002b.)

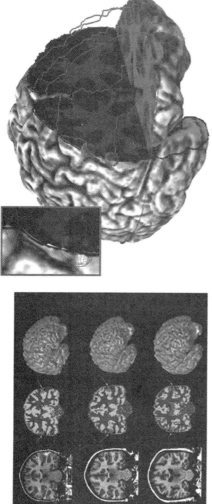

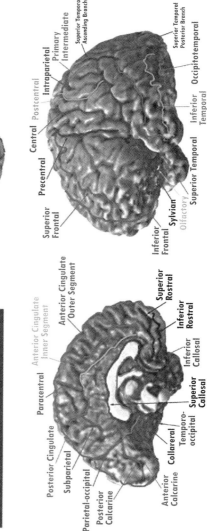

Superior Temporal Ascending Branch
Intermediate
Primary
Intraparietal
Central Postcentral
Precentral
Superior Temporal Posterior Branch
Occipitotemporal
Inferior Temporal
Superior Temporal
Superior Frontal
Inferior Frontal
Sylvian
Olfactory

Anterior Cingulate Inner Segment
Anterior Cingulate Outer Segment
Superior Rostral
Inferior Rostral
Paracentral
Inferior Callosal
Superior Callosal
Posterior Cingulate
Subparietal
Parietal-occipital
Posterior Calcarine
Anterior Calcarine
Collareal
Temporo-occipital

between childhood and young adulthood. Gender differences are observed in cognitive functions of perisylvian cortices, and sexual maturity also occurs during the age range studied, so it may be that hormonal factors are influencing the changes in brain morphology (for a discussion see Witelson, 1991).

Mapping Adolescent Gray Matter Change Using CPM

The VBM studies described above were helpful in our initial efforts to map adolescent changes in brain gray matter, but interpretation of the results may be limited due to the potentially poor matching of cortical anatomy across subjects. Thus, we conducted CPM studies of gray matter change (Sowell et al., 2001b) on the same children studied with VBM earlier described above. In addition to assessing gray matter age-effects, we were able to assess localized changes in brain size. CPM statistical maps for gray matter density differences (figure 3-4) between children and adolescents and between adolescents and adults revealed distinct patterns as expected given earlier VBM results (Sowell et al., 1999b; Sowell et al., 1999c). Between childhood and adolescence, local gray matter density loss was distributed primarily over the dorsal frontal and parietal lobes. Between adolescence and adulthood, a dramatic increase in local gray matter density loss was observed in the frontal lobes, parietal gray matter loss was reduced relative to the earlier years, and a relatively small, circumscribed region of local gray matter density increase was observed in the left perisylvian region. Unlike our previous studies using VBM, we were able to statistically map the significance of differences between child-to-adolescent, and adolescent-to-adult contrasts, finally confirming that there are regions of *accelerated* gray matter loss in the post adolescent age range, mostly in the dorsal frontal cortices (see figure 3-4). These findings suggested that changes in gray matter density between childhood and young adulthood were not linear in nature.

Mapping Adolescent Brain Growth Using CPM

In the same group of subjects described above in the VBM and CPM studies of gray matter change, we assessed localized brain growth using our "distance from center" (DFC) measure (Sowell et al., 2001c). It measures radial expansion from the center of each subject's brain—which is roughly at the midline decussation of the anterior commissure (i.e., $x = 0$, $y = 0$, $z = 0$) to each of the 65,536 matched brain surface points. Differences in the length of the DFC line at each brain surface point between groups (i.e., children and adolescents) suggest local growth in that location, and statistical analyses at each point can be conducted, as for with gray matter density. We found statistically significant spatial and temporal patterns of brain growth and surface contraction between childhood, adolescence, and young adulthood. Because the brain surfaces were scaled to remove global size differences for these analyses, local brain growth and contraction observed in these results must be considered *relative* to global differences in brain size

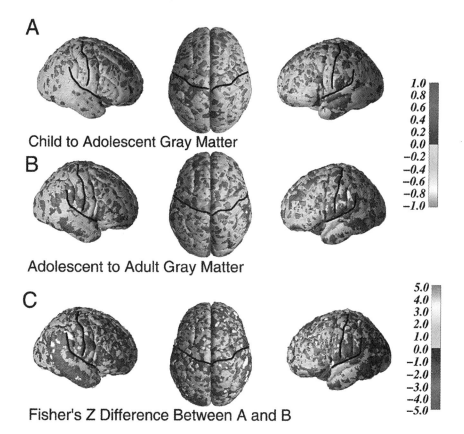

Figure 3-4 Gray matter density age-effect statistical maps (*left, right,* and *top views*) showing gray matter density changes between childhood and adolescence (A) and between adolescence and adulthood (B). Anatomically, the central sulcus (CS), Sylvian fissure (SF), and interhemispheric fissure (IF) are highlighted. In both images, shades of green to yellow represent negative Pearson's correlation coefficients (gray matter loss with increasing age) and shades of blue, purple, and pink represent positive Pearson's correlation coefficients (gray matter gain with age) according to the color bar on the right (range of Pearson correlation coefficients from −1 to +1). Regions shown in red correspond to correlation coefficients that have significant negative age effects at a threshold of $p = 0.05$ (gray matter loss), and regions shown in white correspond to significant positive age effects at a threshold of $p = 0.05$ (gray matter density gain). The images on the bottom (C) display a statistical map of the Fisher's Z transformation of the difference between Pearson correlation coefficients for the child-to-adolescent and the adolescent-to-adult contrasts (see color bar on far right representing Z-scores from −5 to +5). Shades of green to yellow represent regions where the age effects are more significant in the adolescent-to-adult contrast (*middle*) than in the child-to-adolescent contrast (*left*). Highlighted in red are the regions where the difference between Pearson correlation coefficients is statistically significant ($p = 0.05$). Shades of blue, purple, and pink represent regions where the age effects are more significant in the child-to-adolescent contrast than the adolescent-to-adult contrast. Highlighted in white are regions where these effects are significant at a threshold of $p = 0.05$. See color insert. (Sowell et al., 2001c.)

between groups. Notably, the relative maps revealed little local growth (increased DFC) occurring between childhood and adolescence (figure 3-5) once overall brain size differences were controlled.

When comparing the adolescents to the adults, there was some regional specificity with prominent local growth or increased DFC occurring in the dorsal aspects of the frontal lobes bilaterally in the same general region where we observed accelerated gray matter density reduction described above. Lateral growth also appeared in the inferior, lateral temporo-occipital junction bilaterally where the brain surface was also significantly further from the center of the brain in the adults than in the adolescents. Finally, some growth was also observed in the orbital frontal cortex, more prominent in the left hemisphere. The difference between correlation coefficients for the child to adolescent and adolescent to adult comparisons shown in figure 3-5 confirmed the *accelerated* local growth in dorsal frontal regions in the older age range and accelerated local growth in the posterior temporo-occipital junction as well.

Notably, when comparing the adolescents to the adults, significant gray matter density loss in the frontal lobes was seen almost exclusively in locations where positive age effects for DFC (i.e., brain growth) were observed, with very little gray matter loss observed in frontal regions that were not growing in this age range. The strong correspondence in the age effects for gray matter density reduction and increased brain growth in frontal cortex may provide new insight for making inferences about the cellular processes contributing to postadolescent brain maturation. Possible etiologies for these apparently counterintuitive findings (i.e., brain growth with gray matter loss) will be discussed later in this chapter (see "A Note About Cortical Thickness and Gray Matter Density" on page 78).

Mapping Nonlinear Gray Matter Change Using CPM

In a recent report (Sowell et al., 2003a), we used CPM to create three-dimensional, nonlinear statistical maps of gray matter density change on the lateral and interhemispheric brain surfaces across 9 decades (7 to 87 years) in 176 normal individuals. Significant, nonlinear age effects were observed over large areas of the most dorsal aspects of the frontal and parietal regions on both the lateral and interhemispheric surfaces and in the orbitofrontal cortex (figure 3-6). Scatterplots of these effects revealed a dramatic decline in gray matter density between the ages of 7 and 60 years with little or no decline thereafter. A sample scatterplot of the quadratic effect of age on gray matter density at one brain surface point on the superior frontal sulcus is also shown in figure 3-6 and is similar to others in the dorsal frontal and parietal regions (see figure 3-7). Notably, the most lateral aspects of the brain in the posterior temporal and inferior parietal lobes bilaterally showed a distinct pattern of gray matter change, one in which the nonlinear age effects were inverted relative to the age effects seen in more dorsal cortices. A subtle increase in gray matter density was observed until approximately age 30,

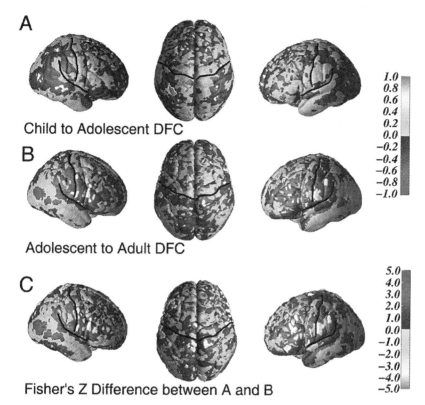

Figure 3-5 DFC age-effect statistical maps (*left, right,* and *top views*) showing changes in DFC between childhood and adolescence (*A*) and between adolescence and adulthood (*B*). Anatomically, the central sulcus (CS), Sylvian fissure (SF), and interhemispheric fissure (IF) are highlighted. In both images, shades of green to yellow represent positive Pearson's correlation coefficients (increased DFC or brain growth) and shades of blue, purple, and pink represent negative Pearson's correlation coefficients (decreased DFC or shrinkage) according to the color bar on the right (range of Pearson correlation coefficients from −1 to +1). Regions shown in red correspond to correlation coefficients that have significant positive age effects at a threshold of $p = 0.05$ (brain growth), and regions shown in white correspond to significant negative age effects at a threshold of $p = 0.05$ (brain shrinkage). The images on the bottom (*C*) display a statistical map of the Fisher's *Z* transformation of the difference between Pearson correlation coefficients for the child-to-adolescent and the adolescent-to-adult contrasts (see color bar on far right representing *Z*-scores from −5 to +5). Shades of green to yellow represent regions where the age effects are more significant in the adolescent-to-adult contrast (middle image) than in the child-to-adolescent contrast (left image). Highlighted in red are the regions where the difference between Pearson correlation coefficients is statistically significant ($p = 0.05$). Shades of blue, purple, and pink represent regions where the age effects are more significant in the child-to-adolescent contrast than the adolescent-to-adult contrast. Highlighted in white are regions where these effects are significant at a threshold of $p = 0.05$. Note the sign of the differences between contrasts is opposite to that in the difference map for the gray matter density contrasts because of the inverse relationship between gray matter density (negative effects) and late brain growth (positive effects). See color insert. (Sowell et al., 2001b.)

after which gray matter density remained stable until a precipitous decline was seen in later decades (figures 3-6 and 3-7).

Overall, the maps of nonlinear age effects show an intriguing pattern in which the association cortices of the frontal and parietal lobes show the most robust gray matter density loss during adolescence (and beyond), and primary auditory (lateral surface) and visual cortices show a much shallower decline over the life span. Further, the primary language regions of the posterior perisylvian region show continued gray matter increases into young adulthood before their later decline. Our previous studies of adolescent brain change did not allow assessment of the trajectory of gray matter changes beyond young adulthood given the restricted age range and relatively small samples. Only with this large sample and extended age range were we able to more definitively measure the nonlinear pattern of gray matter change that occurs throughout adolescence and into adulthood.

Longitudinal Assessment of Gray Matter Thickness and Cognitive Correlates

Most studies of normative brain maturation to date have been open to the criticism that they are not longitudinal. Cross-sectional samples are not sufficient to validate "change" in brain structure during maturation because of the difficulty of assembling comparable cohorts at different ages. A few recent reports have utilized longitudinal samples of children and adolescents and CPM allowing accurate mapping of anatomical changes within individuals (Gogtay et al., 2004; Sowell et al., 2004a). In one of these studies, we used our newly developed methods for measuring cortical thickness change (in millimeters; Sowell et al., 2004a). To quantify cortical gray matter thickness, we use the 3-D distance measured from the cortical white–gray matter boundary to the cortical surface (gray–CSF boundary in the tissue classified images; see figure 3-8) in each subject. As with gray matter density described above, gray matter thickness is measured at thousands of homologous cortical locations in each subject and is then compared across subjects to assess age effects or averaged to assess local thickness measures within groups of subjects. The regional variations in these average maps agree nicely with those found in the classical cortical thickness maps derived postmortem by von Economo (1929) as shown in figure 3-8. Measures of cortical thickness provide an advantage over our earlier gray matter "density" measures, in part because results may be more directly comparable across studies.

With these newly developed methods, we measured changes in cortical thickness and local brain size in a sample of 45 children studied longitudinally between the ages of 5 and 11 years with approximately 2 years between imaging sessions. Our cross-sectional studies described above revealed changes in gray matter and brain size between childhood, adolescence, and young adulthood. Results from those earlier studies, however, did not allow us to determine whether change across a 2-year age span would be detectable and statistically significant.

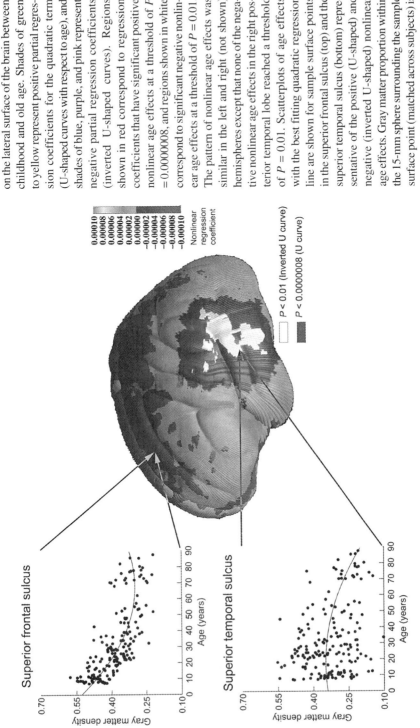

Figure 3-6 This map (left frontal view) shows age effects on gray matter density on the lateral surface of the brain between childhood and old age. Shades of green to yellow represent positive partial regression coefficients for the quadratic term (U-shaped curves with respect to age), and shades of blue, purple, and pink represent negative partial regression coefficients (inverted U-shaped curves). Regions shown in red correspond to regression coefficients that have significant positive nonlinear age effects at a threshold of $P = 0.0000008$, and regions shown in white correspond to significant negative nonlinear age effects at a threshold of $P = 0.01$. The pattern of nonlinear age effects was similar in the left and right (not shown) hemispheres except that none of the negative nonlinear age effects in the right posterior temporal lobe reached a threshold of $P = 0.01$. Scatterplots of age effects with the best fitting quadratic regression line are shown for sample surface points in the superior frontal sulcus (top) and the superior temporal sulcus (bottom) representative of the positive (U-shaped) and negative (inverted U-shaped) nonlinear age effects. Gray matter proportion within the 15-mm sphere surrounding the sample surface point (matched across subjects) is shown on the Y-axis. See color insert. (Sowell et al., 2003a.)

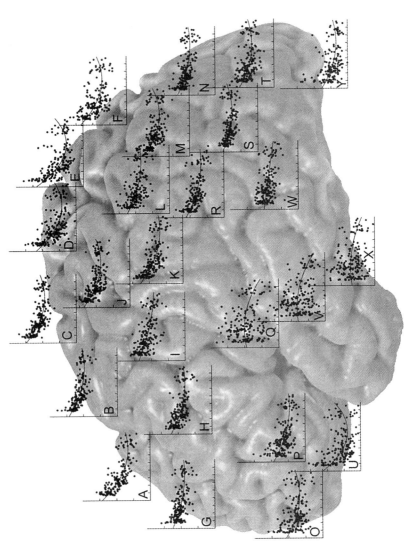

Figure 3-7 Shown is a surface rendering of a human brain (left hemisphere; left is anterior, right is posterior) with scatterplots for gray matter density at various points over the brain surface. The graphs are laid over the brain surface. The graphs are laid over the brain approximately where the measurements were taken. The axes for every graph are identical, and they are identical to the axes on graphs shown in figure 3-6. See color insert. (Sowell et al., 2003a.)

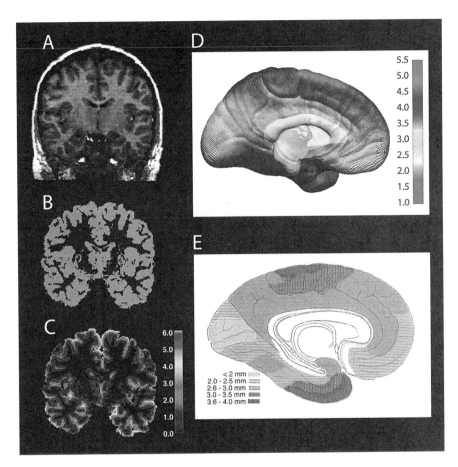

Figure 3-8 Cortical thickness maps: *A*, original T1-weighted image for one representative subject; *B*, tissue segmented image; *C*, gray matter thickness image where thickness is progressively coded in mm from inner to outer layers of cortex using the 3-D Eikonal Fire equation. Note the images were resampled to a voxel size of 0.33 mm cubed, so the thickness measures are at a submillimeter level of precision, according to the color bar on the right (mm). Figures *A* through *C* are sliced at the same level in all three image volumes from the same subject. Shown in *D* is an *in vivo* average cortical thickness map created from our 45 subjects at their first scan. The brain surface is color coded according to the color bar, where thickness is shown in mm. Our average thickness map can be compared to an adapted version of the 1929 cortical thickness map of von Economo (1929; *E*). Color coding has been applied over his original stippling pattern, respecting the boundaries of his original work, to highlight the similarities between the two maps. See color insert. (Sowell et al., 2004a.)

Notably, however, results from the longitudinal analyses revealed prominent gray matter thinning in right frontal and bilateral parieto-occipital regions, where subjects lost approximately 0.1 to 0.2 mm of cortical gray matter thickness per year. Gray matter thickness increased only in perisylvian language regions bilaterally (Wernicke's area in the left) and in the left inferior frontal gyrus (Broca's area; see figure 3-9) at a rate of approximately 0.05 to 0.15 mm per year. Statistical maps of local brain size changes revealed prominent growth in prefrontal cortices, as well as in temporal and occipital regions bilaterally (see figure 3-10). Maps of the average rate of change revealed brain growth at a rate of 0.4 to 1.0 millimeter per year in these regions. Patterns of brain growth and gray matter thinning in frontal and parieto-occipital brain regions, along with gray matter thickness increases virtually exclusive to language regions are likely related to the acquisition of new cognitive skills, such as reading, and fine tuning of previously acquired skills that tend to occur between 5 and 12 years of age. These results have prompted new investigations of cognitive and functional correlates of cortical thickness increases in language cortices in normally developing children, and these studies are currently under way.

In order to assess behavioral correlates of gray matter thickness change, we conducted analyses to correlate change in gray matter thickness with change in children's performance on the WISC-III Vocabulary subtest (raw scores) (Wechsler, 1991). Maps of the correlation between these two change measures are shown in figure 3-11, highlighting the predominant left hemisphere relationship. Permutation tests (conducted to correct for multiple comparisons) were conducted within lobar regions of interest, revealing significant relationships only in the left dorsal frontal ($p = 0.045$) and left parietal region ($p = 0.030$). In these regions, cortical thinning was associated with improvement on the cognitive test.

CPM Studies in Children With Fetal Alcohol Syndrome

Recent volumetric and VBM studies have confirmed brain morphologic abnormalities in children prenatally exposed to alcohol and have allowed a more detailed account of some of the subtler structural dysmorphology previously observed in these subjects in postmortem studies. Volumetric studies have revealed prominent reduction of parietal lobe volume that is above and beyond the generalized microcephaly observed in these subjects. They have also shown that white matter hypoplasia was more significant than gray matter hypoplasia, and relative sparing of hippocampal volume was noted (Archibald et al., 2001). In another study of the same alcohol-exposed (ALC) subjects assessed in the volumetric studies, VBM analyses were conducted in which brain tissue abnormalities in the whole brain were analyzed at once on a voxel-by-voxel basis. Results from this study (Sowell et al., 2001c) complemented findings from the volumetric studies revealing abnormalities most prominently in the

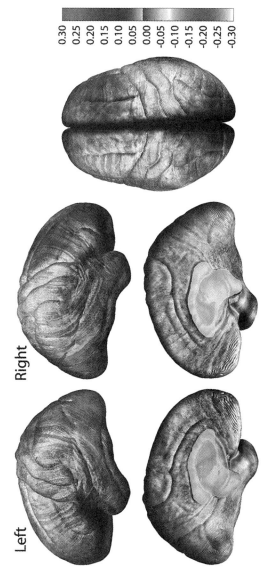

Figure 3-9 Annualized rate of change in cortical thickness: Shown in this figure is the average rate of change in cortical thickness in mm according to the color bar on the right. Maximum gray matter loss is shown in shades of red, and maximum gray matter gain is shown in shades of blue. See color insert. (Sowell et al., 2004a.)

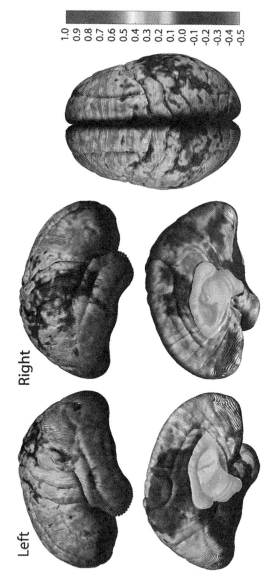

Figure 3-10 Annualized rate of change in DFC (lateral surface) and DFC-H (medial surface): These brain maps show the annualized rate of change in DFC in millimeters according to the color bar. Corpus callosum and brain stem regions have been masked out of the midline views. Note the most prominent growth shown in red, where brain size increases on average 0.5 to 1.0 mm per year. See color insert. (Sowell et al., 2004a.)

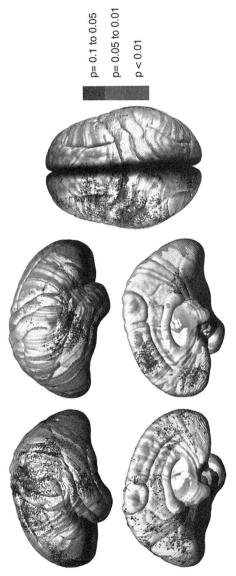

p= 0.1 to 0.05

p= 0.05 to 0.01

p < 0.01

Figure 3-11 Brain-behavior maps for vocabulary and cortical thickness: These maps show the *p*-value for negative correlations between change in cortical thickness (time 2 minus time 1) and change in vocabulary raw scores (time 2 minus time 1). Negative *p*-values (i.e., regions where greater thinning was associated with greater vocabulary improvement) are represented in color according to the color bar, and regions in white were not significant. Positive correlations were not significant in the permutation analyses for any of the ROIs and are not shown here. See color insert. (Sowell et al., 2004a.)

perisylvian cortices of the temporal and parietal lobes where the ALC subjects tended to have increased gray matter density and decreased white matter density.

Although the volumetric and voxel-based image analyses described above tended to localize cortical tissue abnormalities to parietal lobe regions, we became interested in abnormalities on the overlying cortical surface of the brain. Thus, in another study (Sowell et al., 2002a) we analyzed brain surface shape abnormalities in the same group of children, adolescents, and young adults with prenatal alcohol exposure and assessed relationships between cortical gray matter density on the brain surface and brain shape (Sowell et al., 2002a). We carefully matched brain surface anatomy across individuals using CPM techniques. Understanding spatial and temporal relationships between brain shape on the one hand, and tissue density changes on the other hand, could help shed light on the biological processes contributing most to the brain dysmorphology in the individuals observed in earlier structural MRI studies.

Results from this study revealed highly significant decreased brain surface extent or reduced brain growth in the ventral aspects of the frontal lobes most prominent in the left hemisphere. Further, we found increased gray matter density in the inferior parietal lobe and posterior temporal lobe bilaterally (see figure 3-12). The results imply that brain growth continues to be adversely affected long after the prenatal insult of alcohol exposure to the developing brain. Children with severe prenatal alcohol exposure have been shown to be impaired on neurocognitive tasks of frontal lobe and perisylvian/parietal lobe functioning (Mattson & Riley, 1998). Thus, the brain regions most implicated, frontal and inferior parietal/perisylvian, may be consistent with neurocognitive deficits characteristic of individuals prenatally exposed to alcohol.

CPM Studies in Children With ADHD

Previous structural brain imaging studies of attention deficit/hyperactivity disorder (ADHD) have demonstrated subtle reductions in total brain volume and in volumes of the right frontal lobe and caudate nucleus. Various conventional volumetric and voxel-based image analytic methods have been employed in these studies, but regional brain size and gray matter abnormalities had not previously been mapped over the entire cortical surface in patients with ADHD. Thus, we conducted CPM studies in a group of 27 children and adolescents with ADHD and 46 age- and gender-matched control subjects (Sowell et al., 2003b).

As predicted, abnormal morphology was observed in the frontal cortices of ADHD subjects, with reduced regional brain size localized primarily to inferior portions of dorsal prefrontal cortices bilaterally. Brain size was also reduced in anterior temporal cortices bilaterally. Gray matter density was prominently increased in large portions of the posterior temporal and inferior parietal cortices

Figure 3-12 Gray matter density, group-difference statistical maps showing gray matter density increase (and white matter density decrease) in the ALC subjects relative to controls (in nonscaled space). Shades of green to yellow represent positive Pearson's correlation coefficients (increased gray matter density in ALC subjects) and shades of purple and pink represent negative Pearson's correlation coefficients (decreased gray matter density in ALC subjects) according to the color bar on the right (range of Pearson correlation coefficients from −1 to +1). Regions shown in red correspond to correlation coefficients that show significant increase in gray matter in the ALC subjects relative to controls at a threshold of $p = 0.01$. Regions shown in white correspond to correlation coefficients that show significant decrease in gray matter in the ALC subjects relative to controls at a threshold of $P = 0.01$. The Sylvian fissure (SF) and central sulcus (CS) are highlighted for anatomical reference. See color insert. (Sowell et al., 2002a.)

bilaterally (see figure 3-13). The prefrontal, lateral temporal, and inferior parietal cortices we have shown to be affected in ADHD are strongly interconnected with one another anatomically (Cavada & Goldman-Rakic, 1989a, 1989b; Goldman-Rakic, 1987; Pandya & Barnes, 1987; Petrides & Pandya, 2002), suggesting that this action-attentional network is anatomically disrupted in children who have ADHD.

A Note About Cortical Thickness and Gray Matter Density

As one interprets the findings described above regarding "gray" matter changes as a function of normal adolescent development, prenatal exposure to alcohol, and ADHD, some methodological issues must be taken into account. Regardless of the method used, VBM or CPM, measurement of gray matter at the cortical surface is limited by the resolution of the imaging techniques used. In normal development, for example, we speculated that cortical gray matter density reduction could in part be due to increased proliferation of myelin into the periphery of the cortical neuropil, which would change the MR signal value from gray matter in the younger subjects to white matter in the older subjects. Apparent cortical "thinning" during childhood is probably not entirely due to a reduction in the size or number of neuron cell bodies or their synaptic processes (for a discussion see Sowell et al., 2003a; Sowell et al., 2004b), but rather by an increase in the myelin coating of fibers in the lower cortical layers. The same may be true in the ALC (Sowell et al., 2002a) and ADHD (Sowell et al., 2003b) samples in which increases in perisylvian gray matter density could be due to myelination abnormalities, and not abnormalities in the gray matter itself. Thus, the changes observed in our measurements of "gray matter" may actually be due to growth, or a lack thereof, in the underlying white matter. Given this, "gray matter" thinning or changes in "gray matter" density may not be the best terms to describe the anatomical changes we observe with VBM and CPM in these developmental populations. However, with normal development, data from ourselves and others using volumetric methods suggests that gray matter is replaced by white given that white matter volumes increase, and gray matter volumes decline (Courchesne et al., 2000; Giedd et al., 1999; Jernigan et al., 1991).

Further, our CPM studies have shown brain growth in spatial and temporal concordance with gray matter thinning (Sowell et al., 2001c; Sowell et al., 2004a). One would necessarily conclude that if only regressive changes, such as synaptic pruning, were accounting for the cortical thinning, brain growth would not be observed simultaneously. Even in histological data, the boundary between gray and white matter is not always distinct (Annese et al., 2004). Of course, MRI cannot be used to measure cell packing, myelin per se, or synaptic density.

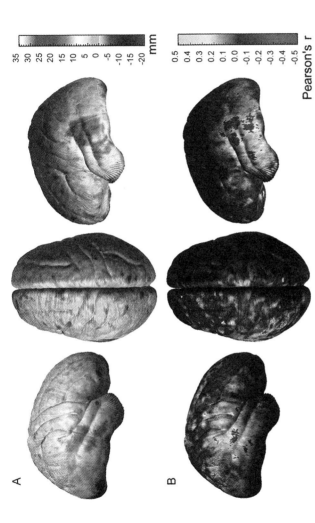

Figure 3-13 *A*, gray matter group-difference maps showing differences in gray matter density (percent difference) between the ADHD and control subjects according to the color bar on the right. Warmer colors (above 0 on the color bar) are regions where gray matter density is greater in the ADHD than control subjects, and cooler colors (below 0) are regions where the controls have greater gray matter density than the ADHD subjects. Note the approximately 20 to 30 percent increase in gray matter density in temporal and inferior parietal regions bilaterally. *B*, gray matter density group-difference statistical maps showing the significance of gray matter differences between the ADHD and control subjects according to the color bar on the right (Pearson's correlation coefficients ranging from –0.5 to 0.5). Regions overlaid in yellow correspond to correlation coefficients that show significant increase in gray matter density in ADHD subjects at a threshold of $p = 0.05$, and those in red correspond to significant increase at a threshold of $p = 0.01$. Negative correlations (i.e., decreased gray matter density in ADHD patients relative to controls) are shown in white. See color insert. (Sowell et al., 2003b.)

The cellular events that give rise to these changes may be best investigated with other in vivo and postmortem methods (separately, or even better, combined). Nonetheless, our maps of cortical thickness and gray matter density change in children and adolescents do, at least, provide evidence for localized patterns of brain developmental changes in both normal and abnormal populations.

Summary and Integration of Normative Development and Neurodevelopmental Disorders: Potential Applicability to Preventing Adolescent Psychopathology

Results from the recent brain mapping studies show dynamic changes in gray matter that occur through childhood and adolescence. Generally, the patterns suggest that in normal development, the changes in gray matter (given the caveats described above) are nonlinear in nature. Of course, our knowledge of when (and thus where) the changes occur is largely limited by the age groups we study. Thus, it is difficult to say exactly at what ages the changes take place. It seems reasonable to conclude from our studies of gray matter change across the life span (Sowell et al., 2003a) that the curve of gray matter loss during middle and late childhood is steeper in dorsal parietal cortices than it is in frontal cortices. Our earlier VBM studies (Sowell et al., 1999a; Sowell et al., 1999b) have also shown more prominent loss in parietal lobes between childhood (7 to 11 years) and adolescence (12 to 16 years). Later, after 16 years and up to age 30 (at least), gray matter loss is more prominent in larger aspects of dorsal prefrontal cortices (Sowell et al., 1999b).

Given our data looking at gray matter changes across the life span (Sowell et al., 2003a), it seems that gray matter in the more lateral cortices of the occipital, temporal and frontal lobes may have been more actively lost earlier in development, and the primary language cortices of perisylvian region undergo continued gray matter thickening to about age 30, at which point a gradual decline is then observed. Our longitudinal studies (Sowell et al., 2004a) have been consistent with this pattern of gray matter loss, and have confirmed cortical thickening in primary language cortices. Further, the longitudinal studies clearly show that we can measure changes in gray matter thickness over relatively brief time spans (i.e., 2 years) as they occur through normal development.

Our studies of prenatal alcohol exposure and ADHD have also shown patterns of brain dysmorphology that likely reflect cellular abnormalities, though again, we cannot determine with MRI which cellular processes have gone awry. Increased gray matter density was observed in perisylvian regions of both ADHD (Sowell et al., 2003b) and ALC (Sowell et al., 2002a) populations. As discussed in both of the previous reports and discussed above, cortical thickening may in fact be due to abnormalities in myelination or white matter, rather than the cellular components of the gray matter itself. An interesting, but yet unanswered, question is,

"At what point in development does the cortex of the perisylvian region become too thick in these children with neurodevelopmental disorders?" Our studies of normal development have shown cortical thinning and thickening during the adolescent period. Perhaps the trajectory of brain maturation is altered prior to the development of symptoms of ADHD, for example. Of course, insults to the brain are known to occur in utero in children with prenatal alcohol exposure, but it is possible that the cascade of cellular events that occur throughout development continue to be affected long after the exposure to alcohol. Longitudinal studies are needed to determine whether these brain abnormalities are static or dynamic in the childhood to adolescent age range.

The relevant questions in this volume are, "What neurodevelopmental processes in children and adolescents could be altered so that mental disorders might be prevented?" and "What interventions or life experiences might be able to introduce such changes?" These are difficult questions to answer given our current knowledge and technology. Although children who are normally developing, or suffer from ADHD or prenatal alcohol exposure are not the target populations in this volume, we may be able to glean information from them that is relevant to adolescent psychopathology. We know that normal developmental changes can be measured over relatively brief time intervals with longitudinal studies. It seems plausible, then, to speculate that targeting at-risk populations for inclusion in longitudinal studies may be fruitful in aiding the development of prophylactic treatments. The idea here is that children who are at risk could be assessed for abnormalities in cortical development that ultimately characterize adolescents who have the disorder. Pharmacologic, or perhaps even behavioral and educational interventions could then be developed with the brain anatomical measures as gauges for effectiveness of treatment prior to the onset of symptoms. We could also potentially use brain anatomical studies to assess departure from normal in at-risk individuals. The idea would be to conduct periodic anatomical analyses on at-risk children, and as soon as any abnormality is seen in the brain data, fast-track these children into the appropriate treatments. Clearly, we would first need to characterize cortical abnormalities in the psychopathological disorders of interest in longitudinal study designs.

References

Annese, J., Pitiot, A., Dinov, I. D., & Toga, A. W. (2004). A myelo-architectonic method for the structural classification of cortical areas. *Neuroimage, 21,* 15–26.

Archibald S. L., Fennema-Notestine, C., Gamst, A., Riley, E. P., Mattson, S. N., & Jernigan, T. L. (2001). Brain dysmorphology in individuals with severe prenatal alcohol exposure. *Developmental Medicine and Child Neurology, 43,* 148–154.

Ashburner, J., & Friston, K. J. (2000). Voxel-based morphometry—The methods. *Neuroimage, 11,* 805–821.

Blanton, R. E., Levitt, J. G., Thompson, P. M., Narr, K. L., Capetillo-Cunliffe, L., Nobel, A., Singerman, J. D., McCracken, J. T., & Toga, A. W. (2001). Mapping cortical asymmetry and complexity patterns in normal children. *Psychiatry Research, 107,* 29–43.

Cavada, C., & Goldman-Rakic, P. S. (1989a). Posterior parietal cortex in rhesus monkey: I. Parcellation of areas based on distinctive limbic and sensory corticocortical connections. *Journal of Comparative Neurology, 287,* 393–421.

Cavada, C., & Goldman-Rakic, P. S. (1989b). Posterior parietal cortex in rhesus monkey: II. Evidence for segregated corticocortical networks linking sensory and limbic areas with the frontal lobe. *Journal of Comparative Neurology, 287,* 422–445.

Caviness, V. S., Jr., Kennedy, D. N., Richelme, C., Rademacher, J., & Filipek, P. A. (1996). The human brain age 7–11 years: A volumetric analysis based on magnetic resonance images. *Cerebral Cortex, 6,* 726–736.

Courchesne, E., Chisum, H. J., Townsend, J., Cowles, A., Covington, J., Egaas, B., Harwood, M., Hinds, S., & Press, G. A. (2000). Normal brain development and aging: Quantitative analysis at in vivo MR imaging in healthy volunteers. *Radiology, 216,* 672–682.

Fuster, J. M. (1997). *The prefrontal cortex: anatomy, physiology, and neuropsychology of the frontal lobe* (3rd ed.). New York: Lippincott-Raven.

Galaburda, A. M., Sanides, F., & Geschwind, N. (1978). Human brain. Cytoarchitectonic left-right asymmetries in the temporal speech region. *Archives of Neurology, 35,* 812–817.

Geschwind, N., & Galaburda, A. M. (1985). Cerebral lateralization. Biological mechanisms, associations, and pathology: I. A hypothesis and a program for research. *Archives of Neurology, 42,* 428–459.

Giedd, J. N., Snell, J. W., Lange, N., Rajapakse, J. C., Casey, B. J., Kozuch, P. L., Vaituzis, A. C., Vauss, Y. C., Hamburger, S. D., Kaysen, D., & Rapoport, J. L. (1996a). Quantitative magnetic resonance imaging of human brain development: Ages 4–18. *Cerebral Cortex, 6,* 551–560.

Giedd, J. N., Vaituzis, A. C., Hamburger, S. D., Lange, N., Rajapakse, J. C., Kaysen, D., Vauss, Y. C., & Rapoport, J. L. (1996b). Quantitative MRI of the temporal lobe, amygdala, and hippocampus in normal human development: Ages 4–18 years. *Journal of Comparative Neurology, 366,* 223–230.

Giedd, J. N., Blumenthal, J., Jeffries, N. O., Castellanos, F. X., Liu, H., Zijdenbos, A., Paus, T., Evans, A. C., & Rapoport, J. L. (1999). Brain development during childhood and adolescence: A longitudinal MRI study. *Natural Neuroscience, 2,* 861–863.

Gogtay, N., Giedd, J., Lusk, L., Hayashi, K. M., Greenstein, D. K., Vaituzis, A. C., Nugent, T. F., Herman, D., Clasen, L. S., Toga, A. W., Rapoport, J. L., Thompson, P. M. (2004) Dynamic mapping of human cortical development during childhood through early adulthood. *Proceedings of the National Academy of Sciences (PNAS), 101,* 8174–8179.

Goldman-Rakic, P. (1987). Circuitry of primate prefronal cortex and regulation of behavior by representational memory. In V. Mountcastle, F. Plus, & S. Geiger (Eds.), *Handbook of physiology: The nervous system* (pp. 373–416). Bethesda, MD: American Physiological Society.

Gould, E., Reeves, A. J., Graziano, M. S., & Gross, C. G. (1999). Neurogenesis in the neocortex of adult primates. *Science, 286,* 548–552.

Huttenlocher, P. R. (1979). Synaptic density in human frontal cortex—developmental changes and effects of aging. *Brain Research, 163,* 195–205.

Huttenlocher, P. R., & de Courten, C. (1987). The development of synapses in striate cortex of man. *Human Neurobiology, 6,* 1–9.

Ide, A., Rodriguez, E., Zaidel, E., & Aboitiz F. (1996). Bifurcation patterns in the human sylvian fissure: hemispheric and sex differences. *Cerebral Cortex, 6,* 717–725.

Jernigan, T. L., & Tallal, P. (1990). Late childhood changes in brain morphology observable with MRI. *Developmental Medicine and Child Neurology, 32,* 379–385.

Jernigan, T. L., Trauner, D. A., Hesselink, J. R., & Tallal, P. A. (1991). Maturation of human cerebrum observed in vivo during adolescence. *Brain, 114,* 2037–2049.

Lange, N., Giedd, J. N., Castellanos, F. X., Vaituzis, A. C., & Rapoport, J. L. (1997). Variability of human brain structure size: Ages 4–20 years. *Psychiatry Research, 74,* 1–12.

LeMay, M., & Culebras, A. (1972). Human brain—morphologic differences in the hemispheres demonstrable by carotid arteriography. *New England Journal of Medicine, 287,* 168–170.

MacDonald, D., Avis, D., & Evans, A. (1994). Multiple surface identification and matching in magnetic resonance images. *Proceedings Visualization in Biomedical Computing, 2359,* 160–169.

Mattson, S. N., & Riley, E. P. (1998). A review of the neurobehavioral deficits in children with fetal alcohol syndrome or prenatal exposure to alcohol. *Alcoholism, Clinical and Experimental Research, 22,* 279–294.

Pandya, D. N., & Barnes, C. L. (1987). Architecture and connections of the frontal lobes. In E. Perecman (Ed.), The frontal lobes revisited (pp. 41–71). New York: IRBN Press.

Paus, T., Zijdenbos, A., Worsley, K., Collins, D. L., Blumenthal, J., Giedd, J. N., Rapoport, J. L., & Evans, A. C. (1999). Structural maturation of neural pathways in children and adolescents: In vivo study. *Science, 283,*1908–1911.

Petrides, M., & Pandya, D. N. (2002). Comparative cytoarchitectonic analysis of the human and the macaque ventrolateral prefrontal cortex and corticocortical connection patterns in the monkey. *European Journal of Neuroscience, 16,* 291–310.

Pfefferbaum, A., Mathalon, D. H., Sullivan, E. V., Rawles, J. M., Zipursky, R. B., & Lim, K. O. (1994). A quantitative magnetic resonance imaging study of changes in brain morphology from infancy to late adulthood. *Archives of Neurology 51,* 874–887.

Reiss, A. L., Abrams, M. T., Singer, H. S., Ross, J. L., Denckla, M. B. (1996). Brain development, gender and IQ in children. A volumetric imaging study. *Brain, 119,* 1763–1774.

Sowell, E. R., & Jernigan, T. L. (1998). Further MRI evidence of late brain maturation: Limbic volume increases and changing asymmetries during childhood and adolescence. *Developmental Neuropsychology, 14,* 599–617.

Sowell, E. R., Thompson, P. M., Holmes, C. J., Batth, R., Jernigan, T. L., & Toga, A. W. (1999a). Localizing age-related changes in brain structure between childhood and adolescence using statistical parametric mapping. *Neuroimage, 9,* 587–597.

Sowell, E. R., Thompson, P. M., Holmes, C. J., Jernigan, T. L., & Toga, A. W. (1999b). In vivo evidence for post-adolescent brain maturation in frontal and striatal regions. *Nature Neuroscience, 2,* 859–861.

Sowell, E. R., Delis, D., Stiles, J., & Jernigan, T. L. (2001a). Improved memory functioning and frontal lobe maturation between childhood and adolescence: A structural MRI study. *Journal of the International Neuropsychological Society, 7,* 312–322.

Sowell, E. R., Thompson, P. M., Mattson, S. N., Tessner, K. D., Jernigan, T. L., Riley, E. P., & Toga, A. W. (2001b). Voxel-based morphometric analyses of the brain in children and adolescents prenatally exposed to alcohol. *Neuroreport, 12,* 515–523.

Sowell, E. R., Thompson, P. M., Tessner, K. D., & Toga, A. W. (2001c). Mapping continued brain growth and gray matter density reduction in dorsal frontal cortex: Inverse relationships during postadolescent brain maturation. *Journal of Neuroscience, 21,* 8819–8829.

Sowell, E. R., Thompson, P. M., Mattson, S. N., Tessner, K. D., Jernigan, T. L., Riley, E. P., & Toga A. W. (2002a). Regional brain shape abnormalities persist into adolescence after heavy prenatal alcohol exposure. *Cerebral Cortex, 12,* 856–865.

Sowell, E. R., Thompson, P. M., Rex, D., Kornsand, D., Tessner, K. D., Jernigan, T. L., & Toga, A. W. (2002b). Mapping sulcal pattern asymmetry and local cortical surface gray matter distribution in vivo: Maturation in perisylvian cortices. *Cerebral Cortex, 12,* 17–26.

Sowell, E. R., Trauner, D. A., Gamst, A., & Jernigan, T. L. (2002c). Development of cortical and subcortical brain structures in childhood and adolescence: a structural MRI study. *Developmental Medicine and Child Neurology, 44,* 4–16.

Sowell, E. R., Peterson, B. S., Thompson, P. M., Welcome, S. E., Henkenius, A. L., & Toga, A. W, (2003a). Mapping cortical change across the human life span. *Nature Neuroscience, 6,* 309–315.

Sowell, E. R., Thompson, P. M., Welcome, S. E., Henkenius, A. L., Toga, A. W., & Peterson, B. S. (2003b). Cortical abnormalities in children and adolescents with attention deficit hyperactivity disorder. *Lancet, 362,* 1699–1707.

Sowell, E. R., Thompson, P. M., Leonard, C. M., Welcome, S. E., Kan, E., & Toga, A. W. (2004a). Longitudinal mapping of cortical thickness and brain growth in normal children. *Journal of Neuroscience, 24*(38), 8223–8231.

Sowell, E. R., Thompson, P. M., & Toga, A. W. (2004b). Mapping changes in the human cortex throughout the span of life. *Neuroscientist, 10,* 372–392.

Thompson, P. M., Hayashi, K. M., Sowell, E. R., Gogtay, N., Giedd, J. N., Rapoport, J. L., de Zubicaray, G. I., Janke, A. L., Rose, S. E., Semple, J., Doddrell, D. M., Wang, Y., van Erp, T.G., Cannon, T. D., & Toga, A. W. (2004). Mapping cortical change in Alzheimer's disease, brain development, and schizophrenia. *Neuroimage, 23*(Suppl. 1), S2–S18.

Thompson, P. M., Moussai, J., Zohoori, S., Goldkorn, A., Khan, A. A., Mega, M. S., Small, G. W., Cummings, J. L., & Toga, A. W. (1998). Cortical variability and asymmetry in normal aging and Alzheimer's disease. *Cerebral Cortex, 8,* 492–509.

Thompson, P. M., & Toga, A. W. (1997). Detection, visualization and animation of abnormal anatomic structure with a deformable probabilistic brain atlas based on random vector field transformations. *Medical Image Analysis, 1,* 271–294.

Thompson, P. M., & Toga, A. W. (2002). A framework for computational anatomy. *Computing and Visualization in Science, 5,* 1–12.

Von Economo, C. V. (1929). *The cytoarchitectonics of the human cerebral cortex.* London: Oxford Medical Publications.

Wechsler, D. (1991). *Manual for the Wechsler Intelligence Scale for Children–Third Edition.* San Antonio, TX: The Psychological Corporation.

Witelson, S. F. (1991). Neural sexual mosaicism: Sexual differentiation of the human temporo-parietal region for functional asymmetry. *Psychoneuroendocrinology, 16,* 131–153.

Witelson, S. F., & Pallie, W. (1973). Left hemisphere specialization for language in the newborn. Neuroanatomical evidence of asymmetry. *Brain, 96,* 641–646.

Yakovlev, P. I., & Lecours, A. R. (1967). The myelogenetic cycles of regional maturation of the brain. In A. Minkowski (Ed.), *Regional development of the brain in early life* (pp. 3–70). Oxford: Blackwell Scientific.

Chapter 4

The Metamorphosis

Individuation of the Adolescent Brain

Don M. Tucker and Lyda Moller

In the popular culture, parents and kids alike describe adolescence as a period of fundamental stress and change. It is a time when hearts are broken, identities prove elusive, and it sometimes seems that the only chance for forward progress is when the frequent bouts of despondence give way to undeserved and dangerous feelings of invincibility.

In the scientific and medical literature, on the other hand, the modern trend is to downplay the psychological stress and chaos of adolescence. Some textbooks, in fact, emphasize that the normal course of adolescent development can be smooth and peaceful. The implication from many experts seems to be that the popular impression of adolescent turmoil is an urban myth.

Has the popular culture fabricated the turmoil of adolescence? Or have the academics failed to observe what is obvious to everyone else? The evidence of the dramatic onset of psychopathology in adolescence is itself convincing evidence that vulnerable young people will dysfunction during adolescence in ways they did not in childhood. Strong and fortunate young people will cope well and thrive during the transformation. But they will be challenged and transformed nonetheless.

In this chapter, we outline a neuropsychological theory that views human adolescence as a fundamental reorganization of the self. The larval self that formed within the relative security of childhood must be abandoned to forge a new identity, one that is ready to face the unforgiving realities of adulthood. This is a metamorphosis, a change in neuropsychological form, a transformation of the self.

We begin with a psychological analysis of the individuation of the self in adolescence. This brief study draws on the modern psychoanalytic theory of object relations, emphasizing the importance of self-regulation in an interpersonal context. Next, we review our theoretical model of the neural mechanisms of self-regulation, emphasizing the limbic influences on motivation, and how these influences also control the process of memory consolidation. We argue that the motivational control of memory consolidation may be the central factor in the ongoing process of neuropsychological self-regulation.

Finally, we attempt a new theoretical integration of neural mechanisms of motivation with the psychoanalytic theory of self-regulation. In this approach, the motivations that awaken during the adolescent phase support not only autonomy and interpersonal individuation, but the capacity for critical thinking that underlies abstract thought. We propose that the cognitive negotiation of interpersonal relations is achieved with the same mechanisms of neural and conceptual self-regulation that are required for intellectual differentiation and critical thought. Because interpersonal orientations are the integral engines of thought in the adolescent mind, the individuation of an identity becomes an essential foundation for achieving the differentiation of abstract intelligence in the adolescent period.

The Adolescent Transition

In the United States, at least, many parents of young people would argue that adolescence is becoming less of a period of transition and more of a way of life. However vague its resolution, the onset of adolescence is definite, as gonadal hormones trigger the differentiation of secondary sex characteristics and sexual maturity. Given the powerful roles of sex hormones in regulating sexual differentiation in utero, we might expect that sex-specific differentiation of neural systems at puberty is responsible for at least some of the sex differences in cognition, affect, and perhaps even sexual preference that become apparent in adolescence. We can observe strong shifts in the young person's motivation, as the adolescent turns away from the childhood attachment to parents and toward peer affiliation and sexuality. These motive transitions suggest powerful influences of gonadal hormones on hypothalamic and limbic mechanisms (Nelson et al., 2005).

In mammals, sexual maturity is associated not only with reproductive capacity but the loss of play behavior and the assumption of species-specific adult roles. In large primates, genetic diversity has been maintained by the maturation of certain instinctual tendencies that separate individuals from the family group. In rhesus monkeys, for example, when juvenile males become sexually mature, mature females appear to become irritated with them and drive them out of the troop (Suomi,

2003). In common chimpanzees, it is females who separate from the family group and leave to find other social groups when they become sexually mature. In social mammals generally, sexual maturation requires a kind of transformation of social role marked by a radical shift from juvenile dependency toward the individuation of adult behavior. In order to avoid incestuous reproduction, the maturing offspring must separate from the birth group and establish adult roles in a new family or social context. In this general requirement to reject childhood attachments and motives and to assume adult ones, human adolescence is no different.

The difference may be one of ontogenetic complexity, in which the modern human child has traversed a decade of rich cultural exposure with a highly plastic and adaptive brain. The result is a differentiated and complex neuropsychological organization, a self. Yet the child's self is larval, one that retains a juvenile immaturity. The child has the capacity for learning through play, but only a nascent capacity for extended, focused work. He or she is oriented to the global attachment context of childhood, but not to the sex-specific attachment roles of mating and parenting. The child may gain an extensive knowledge base, but has only rudimentary capacity for abstract reasoning. He or she may engage in occasional self-reflection, and the implicit childhood self is a fundamental basis for experience and behavior. But the child is typically self-conscious only briefly, in contrast to the acute and chronic self-consciousness associated with the adolescent's emerging individuation of an adult identity.

We propose that the psychological explanation of adolescence must address two central issues. The first is the development of abstract intelligence. The second is the development of a conscious and autonomous identity. These may be related developments. Within 2 or 3 years of puberty, most adolescents show a remarkable increase in the capacity for representing events and situations with abstract and insightful concepts. This is a remarkable growth period of intelligence, one that must rival other profound cognitive transformations, such as toddler language acquisition. In addition, by the time that young adulthood is achieved, most adolescents have differentiated a representation of the self that will define many significant experiences and actions throughout life. This construct of identity is a unique representation, allowing the adolescent a reference for experience and actions that is self-organizing in a way that was largely implicit and unconscious for the child. Many of the striking psychiatric disturbances of adolescence reflect failures to achieve the coherence of an adult self, and these failures are often manifested in obsessive and distorted attempts at self-understanding.

We propose that, because of the extended neural plasticity of the human juvenile period, the transition to the adult form in humans represents a neuropsychological metamorphosis, a reorganization of the self from a juvenile form into the fundamentally different neuropsychological form of an adult identity. The increasing complexity of culture, coupled with the loss of effective guidance from rites of passage, has led modern adolescence to be challenging, extended, and, most importantly, undefined. Impending adulthood, and childhood's end, are experienced nonetheless, with the unceremonious and abrupt sexual maturation of a year or so of puberty and the corresponding hormonal differentiation of the brain.

The adolescent thus awakens as a stranger in a strange body, moving in a familiar but now strangely foreign land, and—strangest of all—for the first time acutely self-aware. Facing a vacuum where an identity should be, it is time to cast around for a new self. To transition from the globally dependent juvenile state of childhood requires mechanisms of individuation that make up perhaps the most important components of the adolescent's self-regulatory capacity. For many adolescents, autonomy is achieved not just by self-consciousness, and not just by self-direction, but by rebellion. This is a rebellion not just against parents and teachers and their restrictive role definitions. In the true sense of dialectical negation, it is a rebellion against the childhood self.

The result is a neuropsychological transformation, a new, more explicit self. A theory of adolescent identity-formation must address the critical mechanisms of individuation that achieve this transformation. The theory must then describe the new forms of attachment that are incumbent with the adult role.

We will first consider the challenge of individuation in adolescence within a psychological framework, that of developmental psychoanalytic theory. We then consider the neural foundations of these psychological processes, reasoning through a corticolimbic model of the mechanisms of attachment and individuation. In this model, the motive mechanisms of social relations include both the hedonic valuation of attachment and the anxiety and defensiveness of autonomy and individuation. The limbic networks regulating these motive mechanisms are the same networks that direct the corticolimbic operations of memory consolidation. Because of this, we can see how the exercise of autonomy and attachment provide essential foundations for the neuropsychological processes of conceptual differentiation and integration.

Interpersonal Differentiation of the Self

Among the powerful theoretical tools offered over the years by psychoanalysts, perhaps the most important was the historical, developmental analysis of personality. It was in fact the actual observation of children, beginning with Anna Freud's (1958) studies at the Hampstead War Nursery and Rene Spitz's (1945) studies of maternal deprivation in prison nurseries, that provided the interpretive basis for the modern psychoanalytic approach to the self. It is not just that adult relationships are formed on the basis of childhood relation templates; rather, the adult self is literally constructed from these internalized templates. These are the *object relations* (Guntrip, 1969; Winnicott, 1964). The key themes in this construction of self are *attachment* (Bowlby, 1969) and *separation* (Bowlby, 1973). These themes are carried from childhood experience to be woven into each of the adult's efforts at actualizing the self in current interpersonal relationships.

Infancy was the primary concern of object relations theorists because they saw—through their psychotheraputic work with disorders of the self—that the fundamental structures of interpersonal relations in infancy are internalized as the implicit expectancies that interpret each new interpersonal experience in later life. These expectancies form the implicit self, such as it is.

The inherent opposition, and thus ongoing dialectical tension, between the two infantile interpersonal orientations was articulated clearly in Mahler's (1968) intensive study of attachment and separation-individuation in toddlers. The attachment relation forms not just a supportive basis for the child's psychological development, but the enduring foundation of the self that is the context for interpreting new events. And yet this foundation is not sufficient. Forming a whole personality requires individuation from the embedding context of the attachment relation to achieve an autonomous psychological identity.

The scientific understanding of the critical role of attachment relations was given an important basis by the experimental study of primate mother-infant relations by Harlow and his associates (Harlow, 1971; Suomi, 2003). Clearly seen in these studies was the permanent damage from impaired attachment relations. Also seen was the secure base provided by attachment for the transition to peer relations. These studies with monkeys also showed the intergenerational transmission of attachment pathology that is a key factor in maintaining the prevalence of human attachment disorders. These studies also clarified the developmental progression, in which the attachment of the young infant monkey is uncomplicated by defensiveness and aggression. These motives appear at a later stage, when they form a motivational basis for separation from the mother and establishment of autonomous action (Harlow, 1971; Suomi, 2003).

Even though a large empirical literature grew up around empirical studies of attachment and its disorders, a deep theoretical understanding of the development of the self is difficult to find outside the psychoanalytic literature. Unfortunately, the psychoanalytic approach is largely anecdotal, comprising informal observations and reflections of psychotherapists dealing with disorders of the self. Adolescence was seen to represent a particularly important challenge, as the deficits in internalized object relations resulting from early childhood experience were stressed by the demand to bring the self-defining capacities for individuation and attachment into adult roles (Masterson, 1972). The stress was often sufficient to lead to disorganization and decompensation of the emerging adolescent identity.

Self-Regulation and Its Disorders

A key concept in modern psychoanalytic theory is self-regulation (Kohut, 1978). The child internalizes the attitudes and processes of early interpersonal experience as elements of the self, and these become integral to self-regulation in new relationships. The result is a personality organization around effective interpersonal patterns, the *social self* (Masterson, 1972).

In adolescence, even though the young person must reject the attachment relation of childhood and move to demand adult autonomy, the childhood attachments continue to provide an essential secure base. This base becomes increasingly less dependent on parental interaction and increasingly more internalized, forming a stable and validated representation of the self. In addition, the object relations that were established initially through parental interaction now become the templates for attachment relations with peers and potential mates.

At the same, the skills in establishing autonomy that were practiced in childhood are now put to the test of supporting a nascent adult identity. In the reasoning of object relations theory, these are not just interpersonal skills. Rather, they are now psychological capacities, integral to the representation of self as a competent, autonomous agent separate from embedding relationships. The primary task of adolescent individuation is to transition from the dependency of childhood. The primary motive for this transition is the negativism and rebellion of the young adolescent, rekindling the separation-individuation process of the toddler (Mahler, 1968; Masterson, 1972). When it is effective, the striving toward autonomy becomes a positive motivation, allowing not only independent actions but the adolescent's insightful, critical reasoning achieved from an autonomous perspective. The result is a *personal self* (Masterson, 1972).

The close integration of interpersonal orientation and psychological organization can be seen not only in the new intellectual capacities of the adolescent, but in the personality disorders that take form during this period. In modern ego analytic theory, personality disorders reflect exaggerated strategies of self-control (Shapiro, 1965). These self-regulatory patterns become lifestyles for those with enduring personality disorders. But they are often seen in more transitory forms of self-regulation in adolescence, in the young person's volatile efforts at forging roles that may eventually compose an adult identity.

In histrionic and impulsive personalities, for example, self-regulation is loose and responsive to both immediate internal urges and hedonic opportunities that appear in the environment. Both cognition and interpersonal functioning reflect a common mode of self-regulation. The hysteric or histrionic personality is easily caught up in intense, emotionally charged relationships and exhibits cognition that is not only dramatic and impressionistic, but specifically deficient in analytic reasoning (Shapiro, 1965). In the borderline personality, the self is poorly formed, such that the person attempts to self-regulate through only partially internalized object relations, and thus strives for self-control through manipulating the actions of others (Kohut, 1978; Masterson, 1972).

Quite different, and in many ways opposite, patterns of interpersonal and intrapersonal self-regulation are seen in the obsessive and schizoid personalities (Shapiro, 1965). Self-control is tight and disciplined, with little expression of personal feelings and little responsiveness to the feelings of others. Cognition is highly focused, analytic, and often preoccupied with technical detail (Shapiro, 1981). Obsessive personalities approach relationships with strong autonomy strivings, manifesting their internal self-regulatory styles in a rigid, anxious, and often hostile interpersonal orientation that is challenging at best to adult attachments. Schizoid personalities appear to withdraw from relationships completely, as if the need for autonomy negates the value of interpersonal warmth altogether.

Toward a Neuropsychological Theory of Attachment and Self-Regulation

As research with brain lesions and commissurotomy demonstrated the differing cognitive and affective characteristics of the cerebral hemispheres (Sperry, 1982), some theorists attempted to interpret hemispheric contributions to personality within a psychoanalytic framework. The right hemisphere's specialization for emotional communication through nonverbal channels seems to suggest a domain of the mind that is close to the motivationally charged psychoanalytic unconscious. In contrast, the more analytic, verbal capacities of the left hemisphere seem more relevant to the cognitive operations traditionally ascribed to the ego (Galin, 1974, 1977). An important question in this line of reasoning is the relation of cortical elaboration of cognition in each hemisphere to that hemisphere's more elemental, subcortical emotional systems. For example, the right hemisphere's skill in emotional expression and comprehension may imply a greater elaboration of subcortical processes on that side of the brain (Tucker, 1981).

The balance between cortical and subcortical networks within each hemisphere has become a key point for interpreting the nature of left and right hemisphere contributions to emotion. In an influential early study, Davidson et al. (1979) observed greater electroencephalographic (EEG) activation of the left frontal lobe when subjects reported positive emotion in response to viewing emotional material, compared to greater activation of the right frontal lobe in a negative emotional state. The interpretation advanced in many experiments in this line of work viewed the left hemisphere as underlying positive emotions and approach behavior, whereas the right hemisphere was seen as generating negative emotions and withdrawal (Davidson et al., 2000).

In contrast, Tucker et al. (1981) also observed greater right frontal EEG activation in a negative emotion (a depressed mood), but proposed that the frontal lobe activity reflected increased inhibitory control over the right hemisphere's emotional capacities in depression, rather than a general activation of the right hemisphere in negative emotion.

If the left and right hemispheres exhibit differences in positive or negative emotional bias, then this emotional bias should be found together with exaggerated cognitive characteristics of left and right hemisphere contribution, such as may be shown by an analytic or holistic conceptual style (Tucker & Frederick,

1989). The emphasis on analytic reasoning and the lack of affective color in thought and communication in obsessive and schizoid personalities suggests an exaggerated left hemisphere contribution; in addition to being flat, the emotional orientation of these personality styles is typically negative (Shapiro, 1965). In contrast, the holistic, impressionistic cognition, lack of analytic reasoning, and dramatic affective expression of the histrionic or hysteric cognitive style suggests the dominance of right hemisphere contribution; although capable of dramatic affect in several forms, the typical emotional orientation of this personality style is positive, including denial and Polyannish optimism (Shapiro, 1965).

Through a similar line of reasoning, we can infer the primary mode of interpersonal orientation biased by each cerebral hemisphere, assuming that these exaggerated personality styles are indeed reflective of a dominance of one side of the brain or the other. The facile, if superficial, attachments formed by histrionic and impulsive personalities would suggest that a cognitive style dominated by the right hemisphere is disposed to orient the self to an attachment relation. The interpersonal wariness and avoidance shown by obsessive and schizoid personalities would suggest that the left hemisphere's emotional bias is geared to maintain separation from interpersonal contact.

The confluence of social orientation and motive self-regulation in this line of reasoning is consistent with Moller's (2000) speculations on the evolution of hemispheric specialization within the group structure of early hominids. The left hemisphere's contribution to self-regulation seems to have emerged from the fight–flight system that supports individual survival. The suppression or modulation of individual motives is an essential component to support the bonding necessary for the extended juvenile period of human ancestors. With its well-developed emotional communication skills, the right hemisphere may be specialized for the attachment relation that supports the multiple-role bonds (juvenile, mating, parenting, leading) of the social group.

In humans today, the early asymmetry in the maturation of the two hemispheres supports the notion that they may play different roles in object relations that are consistent with these evolutionary speculations (Tucker, 1989). Both electrophysiological and behavioral evidence suggests that the right hemisphere matures earlier than the left, playing a dominant role in the 1st year. Accordingly, a positive emotional bias and affectively responsive communication associated with the right hemisphere may be important to supporting the establishment of a strong attachment relation in the 1st year. Within the 2nd year, several features including the remarkable onset of language capacity suggest the increasing maturation of the left cerebral hemisphere (Tucker, 1989). The emotional challenge of this developmental period is the establishment of autonomy, achieved in part through the negativistic assertiveness of the 2-year-old (Mahler, 1968). If we accept that interpersonal relations create the framework for both affective and cognitive self-regulation throughout life, the study of left and right hemisphere contributions to this process may be an important approach to clarifying the integration of the self through regulating the personal orientation to the interpersonal context (Tucker, 1989).

In more recent years, neuropsychological models building on psychoanalytic concepts have continued to examine possible roles of left and right hemispheres in personality organization. Schore (2003a, 2003b) has integrated an impressive body of literature to examine neural mechanisms of emotional self-regulation, emphasizing a primary role of the right hemisphere not only in affective response but in the support of the attachment relation. Moller (2005) has integrated classical psychoanalytic formulations of interpersonal orientations, for example, toward or away from people (Horney, 1945) with modern theoretical studies of bonding, such as mediated by oxytocin, and the relevant psychological mechanisms, such as the capacity to represent the mental states and intentions of others. The right hemisphere aim is toward social attachment, integrating emotional response with the closeness of the affectionate relationship, and it may support the empathic basis of emotional resonance that makes this possible (Tucker et al., 2005). This motivational aim becomes a defining feature for the domain of the self, represented by the right side of the brain. In contrast, the left hemisphere aim is toward autonomy and self-preservation. It is closely aligned with the primitive fight–flight response, and this motive aim is integral to even the more complex psychological structures supported by left hemisphere cognition (Moller, 2005).

Moller proposes that the analysis of human brain evolution must consider these social motives as causative processes in the primitive hominid societies that supported the neoteny and protracted development of the human brain (Moller, 2005). Whereas the right hemisphere's support of attachment and affiliation must have been the defining feature of the unusual support provided by hominid parenting, the left hemisphere's maintenance of the individual's autonomous motives appears to have been the essential counterpoint in individuating from the attachment context.

Hemispheric Contributions to Object Relations in the Adolescent Brain

With the discovery of the differing psychological capacities of the left and right hemispheres, it was perhaps inevitable that psychological theorists would attempt to relate this neuropsychological division to the psychological separation of mental functions formulated within psychoanalytic theory. Although the theorizing on hemispheric specialization in personality has not been particularly influential in today's academic cognitive neuroscience, it does offer a scope of psychological analysis that is suited to the models of self-organization in object relations theory. If we apply this approach to neuropsychological theory to the challenges faced by the adolescent brain, several considerations and questions become important to the present notion of a functional metamorphosis of the self.

If there are opposing orientations of right hemisphere attachment and left hemisphere individuation in childhood, we can expect the primitive operation of these orientations in the first years of life to have established certain motive structures (of self and object relations) that are implicit in guiding the child's experience and behavior. The normal struggles for autonomy and assertion of self-interest of the 9-year-old, for example, not only risk conflict with the current need for attachment and close relations with the parent; they inevitably recall the child's history of these relational orientations, including both the successes of coping and resolving conflict and the traumatic results of relational failures. The patterns of understanding relationships are unconscious and implicit, organized within the corticolimbic networks of each hemisphere as memory templates, implicit predictions that expect new interactions to be like old ones.

The same is true of the motive challenges of the adolescent period, except now there is a structured agenda for the reactivation of object relations. Just as biological metamorphosis is a reawakening of the morphogenetic process at the point of sexual maturation (Gilbert, 2003), human adolescence may be a reawakening of the demands of psychological self-organization through the mechanisms of object relations. This is a fixed agenda of demands. Captured by the inexorable actions of gonadal hormones, the first task is to abandon the childhood self that is inconsistent with the new maturation and the anticipation of the impending adult identity. Whereas peers naturally confirm the reality of this transition, parents hold a longstanding concept of the relationship with a child that is no longer concordant with the adolescent's emerging understanding of self. The result is a clear need to assert autonomy and correct parents on their anachronistic views.

If we frame this prototypical drama in terms of hemispheric orientations, the challenge of individuation is one of asserting left hemisphere conceptual processes to critically analyze both the family context and the childlike motives that were adapted to it. Just as the separation-individuation phase of the toddler produced an anxiety-laden challenge to the attachment relation (Mahler, 1968), the exercise of critical reasoning in the separation of the emerging self from the childhood scene must result in a precarious stage of self-definition. When it is effective, the assertion of autonomy provides confidence in self-control. But the result is indeed a negation and abandonment of the child self, with its attendant security of parental attachment. Just as the parent's provision of a secure base was essential to separation-individuation in infancy, a secure parental base (now increasingly internalized) is again essential as the adolescent enters what may be seen as the object relations void of attachment negation.

In terms of concepts of brain lateralization, what is lost in this transition is the right hemisphere's holistic, contextual embeddedness of self in the global attachment relation of the juvenile period. The nascent, individuating self is quickly alone. This is, of course, a state achieved by the adolescent's own (largely left hemisphere-mediated) critical autonomy strivings. But it has the effect of leaving the experience of self to be highly incomplete in the lack of a defining context of attachment relations. It is into this vacuum that the right hemisphere strivings for postpubertal attachment, bonding with peers and romantic interests, are engaged with both acute need and considerable enthusiasm.

Hemispheric Elaboration of Limbic Motives

A basic question in theoretical integration of the evidence on left and right hemisphere contributions to emotion and interpersonal relations has been whether there is an asymmetry in limbic regulation of the two hemispheres (Borod, 1992). The right hemisphere, with its importance to emotional expression and comprehension, would seem to elaborate limbic influences more directly than does the left hemisphere. This issue has been approached in new ways with the increasing understanding of the differentiation of limbic circuits between archicortical (hippocampus, posterior cingulate, anterior ventral thalamus, and dorsal neocortex) and paleocortical (amygdala, temporal poles, rostral anterior cingulate, mediodorsal thalamus, and ventral neocortex) networks of memory consolidation. The initial recognition of the relevance of dorsal and ventral memory circuits for hemispheric specialization was by Galaburda (1984), who considered the implications for linguistic and nonverbal, emotional communication. Liotti and Tucker (1994) also speculated that the right hemisphere may elaborate the functions of the dorsal corticolimbic pathway, and this may explain not only its skill in spatial cognition, but its facility in emotional communication. In contrast, the left hemisphere may be specialized to self-regulate through the motive controls of the ventral cortical pathway, providing not only the focusing and analytic skills associated with the object-recognition skills of the ventral cortex, but unique motive properties of the ventral limbic networks (Galaburda, 1984; Liotti & Tucker, 1994).

Through understanding hemispheric specialization in relation to specific limbic pathways, it may be possible to reason through the motivational controls of specific forms of memory consolidation in corticolimbic networks. Some mechanism of reentrant interaction between limbic cortex and neocortex is required for consolidating memory (Squire, 1986), and thus for organizing cognitive function. This must be a central question for motivated self-regulation. The ventral and dorsal corticolimbic pathways may have unique motive biases, such that the amygdala and ventral limbic circuits are important to focusing attention and actions in relation to defensive and aggressive motives. These self-regulatory influences may be integral to left hemisphere cognition.

In contrast, the hippocampus, posterior cingulate, and dorsal limbic circuits are important to maintenance of a broad contextual representation of the environment. This representation seems to engender contextual expectancies that have an inherently positive hedonic tone (Luu & Tucker, 2003a, 2003b; Tucker & Luu, in press), an affective bias that may be congruent with a right hemisphere dominance in cognition in disorders such as histrionic and impulsive personalities. In addition to clarifying how differing motives may be integral to left and right hemispheric cognition, a theoretical model of asymmetric self-regulation may help to explain how motive controls on social interaction are at the same time motive controls on the balance between left and right hemisphere contributions to cognition.

Mechanisms and Implications of the Adolescent Attitude

We can now bring this general model of asymmetric corticolimbic self-regulation to the specific challenges facing the adolescent brain. The adolescent brain self-regulates in the social context of transition from being a juvenile in a family of origin to a functioning person in an autonomous adult social role. The mechanisms of this transition, like those in the formation of the juvenile foundations of the self in the first years of life, are those that self-regulate social orientations. We have seen that these mechanisms are also multifaceted, with implications for both the mode of motive arousal and the consolidation of cognitive structure.

As the child develops in the context of the family, the attachment relation serves as the foundation of both self and social relations. The adolescent must reject this juvenile attachment orientation, individuate a separate identity, and use this new identity as the basis for adult attachment relations. The object relations with parents now recede to the unconscious background (where they continue of course to provide not only essential implicit security but the indelible templates for new relations). As a result, it is the relations with peers that must form the proving grounds for the freshly individuated self.

In considering this process, we can apply our model of neural mechanisms to developmental functions achieved by the adolescent attitude. The dorsal and ventral (right and left) corticolimbic motive regulatory systems can be seen to achieve cognitive capacities and interpersonal orientations at the same time. Just as the infant learns language not through mere exposure but through identifying and following the mother's intention (Baldwin, 1989), the adolescent learns about life, forming abstract concepts of the meaning of events, not primarily through academic instruction, but through the dialectical process of acting on individual intentions and understanding the intentional experience of others. As a result, it is no accident that there is a close parallel between Piaget's analysis of the development of formal operations (Piaget, 1992) and Kohlberg's analysis of moral reasoning (Kohlberg, 1981).

The critical experience for achieving abstract conceptual capacity may be that of individuation. The act of rebelling from parents and exercising an autonomous view of the world may be integral to the capacity for understanding the mutuality of peer relations. This mutuality is in turn the basis for the social contract in the larger context of society.

The young child is embedded in the juvenile attachment relation. The cognitive and interpersonal orientation of this relation may be maintained throughout childhood through a dominance of the dorsal limbic mode of learning and self-regulation. The metamorphosis signaled by the onset of puberty engages multiple mechanisms, but perhaps none as fundamental as the withdrawal from parental attachment through negativistic autonomy. This autonomy appears to be mediated by the ventral limbic circuits mediating defensiveness and aggression. The motive scenario of adolescent individuation not only recapitulates the infantile separation-individuation process, but forms an integral motive basis of adult individuation.

The Origins of Consciousness in Peer Relations

With peers, adolescents seem to engage other people for the first time. At least in early adolescence, parents remain identified with the anachronistic childhood context. They are thus perceived as familiar but largely inanimate instrumental objects, serving a purpose of providing a kind of dependable, inanimate support, like the living room couch. Because peers are understood to mirror their own capacities for consciousness and intentionality, adolescents discover them as separate, sentient individuals. For those adolescents who individuate fully, there is now the capacity for exercising mutuality, in which the intentions of self and other can be understood as alternative perspectives defining each event.

The object relations theorists rightly emphasize the infantile exercises of understanding mutual intentionality with an effective parent as the requisite developmental process to progress from narcissism to interpersonal mutuality. However, the progression within the family context in childhood only lays the foundation. It is in adolescent peer relations that the lessons of moving beyond egocentrism and narcissism are learned effectively. These are difficult lessons, and the tests of competence are merciless. The unfortunate adolescents who fail these lessons are quickly relegated to the underclass of the peer culture. Whether successful or traumatizing, peer relations provide the adolescent with a more structured and complex consciousness that was never possible for the child.

The mechanisms for regulating both motive and cognition in this process of understanding the abstract perspectives of interpersonal relations are the cortico-limbic pathways. The dorsal pathway provides the holistic grasp of the interpersonal context, supporting in more extreme engagements the experiential fusion with the other of the attachment relation. The ventral pathway provides the separation of the autonomous perspective in conflict with the shared context. For the adolescent who successfully individuates and explores new peer attachment relations, each social relation exercises these opposing perspectives. Successful completion of the exercise may be essential to assemble the structural elements not only of specific interpersonal relations but of abstract conceptualization in the complex interpersonal environment of adult life. Through the perspective gained by the understanding of multiple intentionalities in interpersonal interaction, the sense of self gains increasing depth, such that the young person's identity becomes articulated with a degree of differentiation that can be grasped consciously, and then used as a guide to frame the personal context of new interactions.

The psychological operations of the dorsal limbic pathway, elaborated in the right hemisphere, support not only the grasp of context but an effective fusion of self with world. Under modulation by the habituation bias and supported by the inherent positive mood, the actions of the dorsal pathway are projected directly onto the world, and the perceptions are taken directly into the syncretic matrix of the limbic representation of self. This is the fundamental psychological orientation of childhood that is lost in early adolescence. If it is not replaced by effective peer attachment relations in adolescence, and/or balanced by successful individuation and effective independence, the effect can be devastating. For many people, the adolescent individuation is limited, such that mutuality of intentional perspective is only minimally achieved, and the result is a lifelong identification with authority that precludes not only independent thought, but the full capacity for abstract reasoning (Harvey, Hunt, & Schroder, 1961).

Just as the dialectical progression of new ideas in science requires an active, painful rejection of the old paradigm (Kuhn, 1996), the adolescent's development of an adult personality may require a similar negation of the childhood self in order to achieve a full dialectical reformulation (Piaget, 1971). There must be a rejection of the assumptive matrix of childhood, not through a simple replacement by adult attitudes and values, but first through an active negation of that matrix. The new attachment relations of adulthood are then engaged with an effective mutuality that can be perceived only from an autonomous perspective. The individuation of the self allows the successful adolescent to understand the other person as individuated as well. When the juvenile orientation of fusion with authority is maintained uncritically, the individuality of the other person cannot be grasped fully, leading to a concrete and undifferentiated attitude toward others as inanimate (unintentional) objects. Such an attitude is most apparent in the bias and prejudice toward those most foreign to the local culture, in other words, to the familiar values of the juvenile assumptive matrix.

Societies of Adolescent Brains

Perhaps primarily because motives regulate memory consolidation, an analysis of brain systems may be essential to understand psychological development. Although there may be ongoing transformations in adult development, none will match the fundamental metamorphosis of self of the adolescent years. To consider the underlying basis of this transformation, we have outlined mechanisms of self-regulating the corticolimbic consolidation of cognitive representations. These are essential mechanisms for self-control, both through elementary affective states and through the formation of complex and abstract conceptualizations. Although it may be natural to think of a brain as a property of an individual, the scientific understanding of neural mechanisms requires careful study of the interpersonal ecology that shapes the self-organization of neural systems at each developmental stage (Freeman, 1995).

In adolescence, the self-regulation of orientations toward others may shape the capacity for an abstract understanding of social relations. We have argued that by examining the unique patterns taken by the self-regulatory systems of the adolescent brain, it may be possible to understand patterns of psychological development that cannot be explained by functional analysis alone.

For example, the lateral asymmetry of the dorsal and ventral limbic motive mechanisms may cause certain accidental patterns of behavior to emerge, as a result of experience with individuation and attachment. These are not easily explained by functional psychological principles, but may result from the neurocybernetic algorithms that shaped the evolution of hemispheric specialization in the human brain.

Thus, lateral orientations are seen not only in neuropsychology experiments, but in certain place preferences, such as the tendency for those who orient to the left of space (right hemisphere bias) to sit on the right of a classroom (Drake, 1991; Gur et al., 1976). In political bodies, such as the U.S. Congress, lateral orientations seem to have become ritualized components of the social dialogue. Those who occupy the right wing of the Congress hall (orienting attention toward the left) display conservative attitudes, such as identifying with authority and preferring the values and culture of the past. Could this orientation reflect the latent neural asymmetry of the motive systems of these individuals? Could it be that a dominance of the right hemisphere and dorsal limbic motive mechanisms in the cognitive consolidation of conservatives reflects a kind of default state of juvenile attachment, resulting from a more limited differentiation and individuation in the course of adolescent development?

In contrast, those who take positions on the left (reflecting the left hemisphere's orienting of attention toward the right) display more liberal political attitudes, including frequent criticism of authority and greater tolerance for social change. Could these attitudes reflect a kind of continuation of the adolescent attitude? Could it be that those on the left wing are biased to negative responses to authority, not as objective appraisals, but as a continuing effort to establish autonomy through engagement of the (left-lateralized) ventral limbic mechanisms associated with a personal history of efforts at self-organization?

If these parallels have any merit, it may be that the familiar political dialectics of current events reflect a more fundamental dialectic of self-regulation, one that is embedded in the neural operations of self-regulation in an interpersonal context. If so, then perhaps a scientific understanding of the challenges of interpersonal relations, such as those encountered by each adolescent brain, may be relevant to clarifying the vagaries of political self-regulation in societies (Freeman, 1995). The metamorphosis of individuation may not be limited to adolescents and their life changes. Similar neural dynamics may determine the balance of fundamentalist and progressive movements in societies facing the challenges of cultural change. Given the principles of abstract cognitive capacity forged through structural differentiation of cognition by limbic motive engines, we could conclude that neither right wing nor left wing orientations are adequate for establishing abstract, flexible, and complex structures of self-regulation. In societies of brains, abstract interpersonal relations—created by the dialectical balance of attachment and autonomy—may be essential to allow the appreciation of mutual intentionality and mutual perspective to allow a balanced understanding of social issues.

Of course, the laterality of attentional orientation is something of a quirk of nature. Nonetheless, our leaders line up each day on opposite sides of the political aisle, unaware of the neural or psychological basis of their lateral orientations. More generally, both leaders and followers make fundamental decisions about the fate of nations and the Earth, with little understanding of the motivational mechanisms that shape their attitudes and behavior. In this speculative overview, we have attempted to trace integral mechanisms of the adolescent brain that give form to the metamorphosis of self in the social context. The motive biases shaping the lateral orientation of attention appear to reflect an accident of neural evolution, a byproduct of lateral specialization of the bilaterally symmetric vertebrate plan. Still, as they emerge through the course of personality development, these biases apply integral motive mechanisms within the human neuraxis, shaping the capacity for balanced, abstract reasoning on social issues.

References

Baldwin, D. A. (1989). Priorities in children's expectations about object label reference: Form over color. *Child Development, 60*(6), 1291–1306.

Bowlby, J. (1969). *Attachment and loss* (Vol. 1). New York: Basic Books.

Bowlby, J. (1973). *Separation* (Vol. 2). New York: Basic Books.

Borod, J. C. (1992). Interhemispheric and intrahemispheric control of emotion: A focus on unilateral brain damage. *Journal of Consulting and Clinical Psychology, 60*, 339–348.

Davidson, R. J., Jackson, D. C., & Kalin, N. H. (2000). Emotion, plasticity, context, and regulation: Perspectives from affective neuroscience. *Psychological Bulletin, 126*(6), 890–909.

Davidson, R. J., Schwartz, G. E., Saron, C., Bennett, J., & Goleman, D. J. (1979). Frontal versus parietal EEG asymmetry during positive and negative affect. *Psychophysiology, 16*, 202–203.

Drake, R. A. (1991). Processing persuasive arguments: recall and recognition as a function of agreement and manipulated activation asymmetry. *Brain and Cognition, 15*(1), 83–94.

Freeman, W. J. (1995). *Societies of brains: A study in the neuroscience of love and hate. The spinoza lectures.* Hillsdale, NJ: Erlbaum.

Freud, A. (1937). *The ego and the mechanisms of defense.* New York: International Universities Press.

Galaburda, A. M. (1984). The anatomy of language: Lessons from comparative anatomy. In D. Caplan, A. R. Lacours, & A. Smith (Eds.), *Biological perspectives on language.* Cambridge, MA: MIT Press.

Galin, D. (1974). Implications for psychiatry of left and right cerebral specialization: A neurophysiological context for unconscious processes. *Archives of General Psychiatry, 31,* 572–583.

Galin, D. (1977). Lateral specialization and psychiatric issues: Speculations on development and the evolution of consciousness. In S. J. Dimond & D. A. Blizard (Eds.), *Evolution and lateralization of the brain* (Vol. 299, pp. 397–411). New York: New York Academy of Sciences.

Gilbert, S. F. (2003). *Developmental biology* (7th ed.). Sunderland, MA: Sinauer Associates.

Guntrip, H. (1969). *Schizoid phenomena, object relations and the self.* New York: International Universities Press.

Gur, R. C., Sackeim, H. A., & Gur, R. E. (1976). Classroom seating and psychopathology: Some initial data. *Journal of Abnormal Psychology, 85*(1), 122–124.

Harlow, H. (1971). *Learning to love.* San Francisco: Albion.

Harvey, O. J., Hunt, D. E., & Schroder, H. M. (1961). *Conceptual systems and personality organization.* New York: Wiley.

Horney, K. (1945). *Our inner conflicts.* New York: Norton.

Kohlberg, L. (1981). *The philosophy of moral development: Moral stages and the idea of justice.* New York: HarperCollins.

Kohut, H. (1978). *The search for the self.* New York: International Universities Press.

Kuhn, T. (1996). *The structure of scientific revolutions.* Chicago: University of Chicago Press.

Liotti, M., & Tucker, D. M. (1994). Emotion in asymmetric corticolimbic networks. In R. J. Davidson & K. Hugdahl (Eds.), *Human brain laterality* (pp. 389–424). New York: Oxford.

Luu, P., & Tucker, D. M. (2003a). Self-regulation and the executive functions: Electrophysiological clues. In A. Zani & A. M. Preverbio (Eds.), *The cognitive electrophysiology of mind and brain* (pp. 199–223). San Diego: Academic Press.

Luu, P., & Tucker, D. M. (2003b). Self-regulation by the medial frontal cortex: Limbic representation of motive set-points. In M. Beauregard (Ed.), *Consciousness, emotional self-regulation and the brain.* Amsterdam: John Benjamins.

Mahler, M. S. (1968). *On human symbiosis and the vicissitudes of individuation.* New York: International Universities Press.

Masterson, J. (1972). *Treatment of the borderline adolescent: A developmental approach.* New York: Wiley.

Moller, L. (2000). Have dual survival systems created the human mind? *Psychiatry, Interpersonal and Biological Processes, 63*(2), 178–201.

Moller, L. (2005). *The psychological origin of homo's sapience.* Unpublished manuscript.

Nelson, E. E., Leibenluft, E., McClure, E. B., & Pine, D. S. (2005). The social re-orientation of adolescence: A neuroscience perspective on the process and its relation to psychopathology. *Psychological Medicine, 35*(2), 163–174.

Piaget, J. (1971). *Genetic epistemology*. New York: Norton.

Piaget, J. (1992). *The origins of intelligence in children*. New York: International Universities Press.

Schore, A. (2003a). *Affect dysregulation and disorders of the self*. New York: Norton.

Schore, A. (2003b). *Affect regulation and the repair of the self*. New York: Norton.

Shapiro, D. (1965). *Neurotic styles*. New York: Basic Books.

Shapiro, D. (1981). *Autonomy and the rigid character*. New York: Basic Books.

Sperry, R. (1982). Some effects of disconnecting the cerebral hemispheres. *Science, 217*, 1223–1226.

Spitz, R. (1945). An inquiry into the genesis of psychiatric conditions in early childhood. *Biobehavioral Reviews, 27*, 33–44.

Squire, L. R. (1986). Mechanisms of memory. *Science, 232*, 1612–1619.

Suomi, S. J. (2003). Gene-environment interactions and the neurobiology of social conflict. *Annals of the New York Academy of Sciences, 1008*, 132–139.

Tucker, D. M. (1981). Lateral brain function, emotion, and conceptualization. *Psychological Bulletin, 89*(1), 19–46.

Tucker, D. M. (1989). Neural and psychological maturation in a social context. In D. Cicchetti (Ed.), *The emergence of a discipline: Rochester symposium on developmental psychopathology* (pp. 69–88). Hillsdale, NJ: Erlbaum.

Tucker, D. M., Luu, P., & Derryberry, D. (2005). Love hurts: The evolution of empathic concern through the encephalization of nociceptive capacity. *Developmental Psychopathology, 17*(3), 699–713.

Tucker, D. M., & Frederick, S. L. (1989). Emotion and brain lateralization. In H. Wagner & T. Manstead (Eds.), *Handbook of psychophysiology: Emotion and social behaviour*. New York: Wiley.

Tucker, D. M., & Luu, P. (in press). Adaptive binding. In H. Zimmer, A. Mecklinger & U. Lindenberger (Eds.), *Binding in human memory: A neurocognitive approach*. New York: Oxford University Press.

Tucker, D. M., Stenslie, C. E., Roth, R. S., & Shearer, S. L. (1981). Right frontal lobe activation and right hemisphere performance. Decrement during a depressed mood. *Archives of General Psychiatry, 38*(2), 169–174.

Winnicott, D. W. (1964). *The child, the family and the outside world*. Middlesex, England: Penguin.

Chapter 5

Transcriptional Regulation in Schizophrenia

Scott E. Hemby and Joann A. O'Connor

Transcription refers to the synthesis of messenger RNA (mRNA) from genomic DNA within the nucleus of cells. After processing in the nucleus and transport into the cytoplasm, mRNA serves as the direct template for protein synthesis, a process referred to as *translation*. Biological processes are regulated at the level of transcription throughout the course of human development. Maturational changes in transcription/gene expression are regulated in response to hormonal, behavioral, pharmacological, pathogenic, and developmental influences. Assessment of gene expression in animal models or human specimens—serum, CSF, or postmortem brain tissue—provides a biochemical window through which potential biochemical substrates or consequences of psychiatric illnesses are identified. Although this chapter is primarily focused on transcriptional regulation in schizophrenia, the processes described are also relevant to other psychiatric disorders.

Psychiatric diseases such as schizophrenia and autism spectrum disorders are generally considered to be neurodevelopmental in origin. Dysregulated gene and/ or protein expression in the brain of adult schizophrenic patients must be understood in the context of a developmental model. Do changes in gene expression occur at the time of disease vulnerability or before (i.e., in utero, childhood, adolescence)? Are they present in high-risk individuals? Current understanding of the transcriptional sequelae that occur during brain development is limited by the availability of control human brain tissue in children and adolescents. Consequently, if altered mRNA and protein expression in adult schizophrenic patients reflects altered neurodevelopmental processes occurring prior to the clinical manifestation of the disease, for instance in childhood or adolescence, these studies will provide important clues into the development and progression of the disease and, more important, identify possible targets for early intervention. This brief review covers the basic mechanisms of transcriptional regulation, current knowledge of altered gene expression in schizophrenia focusing on glutamatergic and synaptic mechanisms, relevance of these gene expression changes to neurodevelopment and other potential mechanisms of regulation in schizophrenia, and ideas about intervention to readjust dysregulated expression.

Overview of Transcriptional Regulation

To understand the contribution of gene expression in the manifestation of psychiatric disorders, a brief overview of transcriptional regulation in eukaryotes is necessary. The central dogma of molecular biology is that cells *transcribe* DNA into mRNA, and then *translate* mRNA into protein. That process, although conceptually simple, is biochemically complex and subject to regulation at several points. Within the nucleus, DNA exists in a compacted structure, termed chromatin, which is maintained through interactions with DNA binding proteins, called histones. The structure of the DNA-histone complex, as well as biochemical modification of the DNA itself (e.g., CpG methylation), affects the accessibility of chromatin to enzymes such as RNA polymerases and other proteins that regulate the transcriptional process (figure 5-1). A second point of regulation is the initiation of transcription, in which specific sequences within the DNA enhance and promote transcription. These sequences, known as enhancer sequences and promoter elements, interact with proteins called *transcription factors* to regulate the degree to which specific genes are transcribed. Other regulatory elements are sequences in the DNA that bind transcription factors (also called *trans*-acting elements) and increase the activity of RNA polymerase. These regulating elements are usually located upstream of the initiation site but might be found within the gene sequence. The interaction of regulatory elements with different combinations of transcription factors provides a means to differentially regulate transcripts based on stimulus specificity as well as cell specificity. Many second messenger systems, such as the cAMP pathway, ultimately regulate gene transcription by altering the levels or regulatory states of transcription factors (e.g., CREB).

In addition, activator and inhibitor proteins also contribute to the process to regulate the strength of transcription. After the DNA is transcribed, RNA processing and modification occur as a third level of regulation. Messenger RNA (mRNA) must be capped at the 5′ end (which protects the RNA from enzymes that degrade the RNA from the 5′ end) and polyadenylated at the 3′ end (for export to the

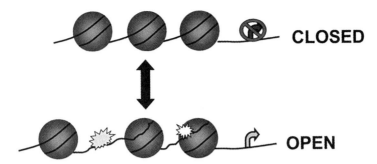

CLOSED

OPEN

Figure 5-1 Schematic of a portion of chromatin illustrating that DNA (black strand) is tightly wound around histones, which from nucleosomes (orange circles). In the cell, nucleosomes consist of eight histone proteins that form a core around which DNA is tightly wrapped and together form the fundamental structure of chromatin. In order to activate transcription, the DNA must be exposed such that transcription factors (blue and yellow stars) and enzymes can initiate and continue transcription. This is accomplished by modifying a portion of the histones, which in turn exposes regions of the DNA and also transcription factors and other proteins to bind and transcription to proceed. As the black arrow in the figure indicates, chromatin can fluctuate between the open and closed state.

cytosol) and the relevant introns must be removed. RNA editing and alternative splicing are two additional mechanisms that increase genetic diversity without increasing the overall number of genes. Once the mRNA is processed, it exits the nucleus and is translated into a protein (figure 5-2). Once outside the nucleus, the mRNA is susceptible to degradation before translation such as destruction by microRNAs.

Assuming the mRNA is not degraded or silenced and is available for translation, the process is initiated by ribosomal recognition of a methionine codon (figure 5-2). The ability of the ribosome to recognize the correct codon can affect the expression of the protein. Once the protein is synthesized, posttranslational modifications including phosphorylation, glycosylation, acetylation, and disulfide bond formations alter the functionality of the protein in response to the cellular milieu. In the nervous system, the proteins must also be actively transported to the respective site of action.

Regional Vulnerabilities and Gene Expression

Schizophrenia is a complex psychiatric disorder involving an assortment of positive (hallucinations and delusions), negative (flattened affect and social withdrawal), and cognitive (deficits in working memory and executive function) symptoms. Multiple brain regions have been implicated in schizophrenic pathology including the hippocampus, subdivisions of the prefrontal cortex, the thalamus, and the striatum. Most likely, it is the disrupted communication between these regions that leads to the manifestation of schizophrenic symptoms. Although subtle structural and anatomical irregularities within these regions have been reported, there is no gross anatomical abnormality or specific neurochemical deficit that uniquely identifies schizophrenia. More likely, molecular alterations within these

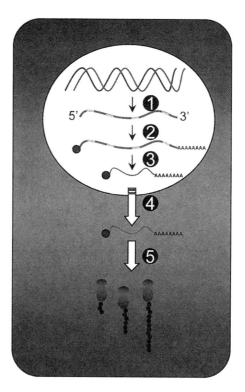

Figure 5-2 Generalized depiction of transcriptional and translational processing in nerve cells. For purposes of simplicity, the nucleus appears in white and the cytoplasm is gray.

1. DNA is transcribed into RNA. The premature RNA contains both introns (green) and exons (red). Introns are sections of the RNA that do not encode protein, whereas exons are sections of the RNA that encode protein.
2. The RNA is capped at the 5′ end and polyadenylated on the 3′ end—the first two major steps of mRNA processing. These additions protect the RNA from degradation and assist in trafficking the RNA to the cytoplasm.
3. Splicing of the primary mRNA that removes introns (noncoding regions of mRNA), resulting in messenger RNA (mRNA), is the third major step of mRNA processing.
4. mRNA is exported from the nucleus to the cytoplasm.
5. mRNA (red strand) is translated into protein by ribosomes (oblong purple objects) located in the cytoplasm. The black circles represent the nascent protein as it is translated by the ribosomes.

regions coincide to disrupt cell signaling and synaptic plasticity in a developmentally progressive manner resulting in schizophrenic symptomology.

The temporal lobe, including the hippocampus and entorhinal cortex (EC), is a primary brain region associated with schizophrenia. The EC is integral to the activity of the hippocampus, regulating the interaction of the hippocampus with other brain regions. Functionally, the EC is involved in declarative memory (Squire & Zola-Morgan, 1991; Squire & Zola, 1996). Specifically, the EC along with other regions of the temporal lobe, mediates episodic (time, place and associated emotions) and semantic (facts and concepts) memory. Bilateral lesions of the EC produce significant memory (Baxter & Murray, 2001; Leonard et al., 1995) and cognitive deficits (Chavoix et al., 2002). Moreover, functional imaging studies indicate that the EC is activated in the associative aspects of memory (Klingberg et al., 1994) and that activity modulation in the EC is involved in the encoding phase of declarative memory (Fernandez et al., 1999).

Schizophrenic patients (SCZ) exhibit diffuse cognitive impairment throughout the course of the illness that is associated with dysregulation of the temporal lobe. Neuropsychological studies attribute differential deficits in verbal and visual declarative memory to hippocampal dysfunction (Gruzelier et al., 1988; Saykin et al., 1991). Moreover, such deficits persist after more florid psychotic symptoms resolve or improve with treatment (Gur et al., 2003), perhaps indicating a neuroanatomical abnormality in the ventromedial temporal lobe.

Functional imaging studies report significant deficits in temporal lobe function in SCZ (Gur, 1995; Gur et al., 1995; Nordahl et al., 1996; Russell et al., 1997; Tamminga et al., 1992). Structural imaging studies indicate a slight, but significant, volume reduction in temporal lobe structures including the EC in SCZ (Altshuler et al., 2000; Bogerts et al., 1993; Gur et al., 2000; Lee et al., 2004; Shenton et al., 1992; B. Turetsky et al., 1995; B. I. Turetsky et al., 2003), although other studies fail to observe these differences (Buchanan et al., 1993). Normally, the human hippocampus increases in volume throughout adolescence (Saitoh et al., 2001), and this change is more pronounced in males versus females (Suzuki et al., 2005). Following young adulthood, there is a gradual decline in EC and HIPP volumes albeit at a slightly different rates (Pruessner et al., 2001; Raz et al., 2004). In contrast to individuals without schizophrenia, hippocampal volume is decreased in individuals diagnosed with childhood-onset schizophrenia (Giedd et al., 1999; Jacobsen et al., 1998) and adolescents/young adults designated as high risk show significant reductions in temporal lobe volumes (Lawrie et al., 2002). Interestingly, there is a relative paucity of neurodegeneration, cell death, or gliosis observed in the brains of SCZ (Arnold et al., 1998; Falkai et al., 1999), suggesting that there are alterations in the neural circuitry in SCZ.

The human cortex has a laminar structure consisting of six "layers." In normal human cortex, the different cell types are distributed in a specific laminar pattern.

However, in SCZ several studies show evidence of laminar displacement of neurons toward the deeper layers in various cortical regions, including EC (Arnold et al., 1995; Arnold et al., 1991; Arnold et al., 1997; Jakob & Beckmann, 1986), prefrontal and associated cortices (Akbarian et al., 1993), and the cingulate cortex (Benes et al., 1991). These findings are parsimonious with data that indicate brain volume differences in SCZ and suggest a failure of normal neuronal migration from deep to superficial cortical layers, a process known to occur during the second trimester of pregnancy (Rakic, 1988). How such deficits in neuronal wiring occur is not fully understood, but it is interesting that several studies indicate an increased association with schizophrenia in the offspring of mothers who had viral infections during the second trimester of pregnancy (Brown & Susser, 2002; Ebert & Kotler, 2005; Isohanni et al., 2004; Koenig et al., 2002; Rapoport et al., 2005). In addition, poor maternal health during pregnancy, anoxic birth injuries, low birth weight and other perinatal complications are associated with subsequent development of schizophrenia (Arnold, 1999; M. Cannon et al., 2002), suggesting developmental influences in the disease.

The existence of the primary insult in schizophrenia at birth suggests the presence of behavioral deficits before onset in late adolescence or young adulthood. Interestingly, research reveals that individuals who develop schizophrenia show deficits in childhood and early adolescence, particularly in social and cognitive realms (T. D. Cannon et al., 2000; Niemi et al., 2003; Rapoport et al., 2005; Tarrant & Jones, 1999; Venables, 1989). However, the disease does not fully manifest until late adolescence or young adulthood. From a neuroscience perspective, it is known that at birth many more synapses (neuronal connections) are present than will be retained later in life and that a significant minority of synapses are eventually removed through synaptic pruning (Luo & O'Leary, 2005). A wave of synaptic pruning occurs during late adolescence (reviewed in Arnold, 1999), which coincides with the age of onset of schizophrenic symptoms. Thus, the consequences of erroneous neuronal wiring that occurs in the early stages of brain development may not functionally manifest until the process of synaptic pruning is complete (Konradi & Heckers, 2003)—late adolescence to young adulthood.

The prefrontal cortex (PFC) is another cortical brain region whose influence in schizophrenia has been well documented. The PFC is crucial for the "top-down" direction of behavior, especially when it is guided by internal states or intentions, when behaviors are not closely linked to stimuli, or when the rules governing behavior must be changed rapidly as environmental contingencies change. To perform such functions, the PFC must maintain representations not only of goals, but of the means to achieve them (Miller & Cohen, 2001). A common approach for dividing the many fields of the prefrontal cortex into functional domains associates the dorsolateral PFC (DLPFC) with more semantic, cognitive, external sensory, and voluntary motor functions, and the orbitofrontal cortex (OFC) with more affective, internal sensory, and autonomic functions.

The DLPFC is one brain region that has been implicated in the pathophysiology of schizophrenia. Significant decreases in prefrontal cortical volume in adolescent SCZ (James et al., 2004) and in first episode SCZ (Bagary et al., 2003) have been observed. Glutamate serves as the primary chemical transmitter in cortical regions and serves to integrate and coordinate information within the DLPFC and between other cortical regions (Levitt et al., 1993). Changes in glutamate transmission in the DLPFC are believed to underlie cognitive functions that are disturbed in schizophrenia (Lewis & Gonzalez-Burgos, 2000), and pathophysiological evidence in SCZ supports this: decreased cell size of neurons that utilize glutamate as their primary transmitter (Pierri et al., 2001), decreased inputs to these neurons (Glantz & Lewis, 2000), and crowding of these glutamate neurons (Selemon et al., 1998) in the DLPFC. In addition to glutamate, studies using postmortem brain tissue from SCZ reveal changes in another important cell type in the DLPFC–GABA utilizing cells (Hashimoto et al., 2003; Lewis et al., 1999; Pierri et al., 1999; Woo et al., 1997; Woo et al., 1998). Despite evidence for the involvement of these cell populations in schizophrenia, specific molecular changes underlying this cellular dysfunction are not well characterized in SCZ.

Synaptic Proteins and Schizophrenia

Several possible mechanisms of neuronal dysfunction underlie schizophrenia, including alterations in synaptic function (Aston et al., 2004). Synapses are comprised of several types of proteins and are known to be involved in the pathogenesis of schizophrenia (Eastwood, 2004), but two groups that have received considerable attention include synaptic vesicle proteins (e.g., syntaxin, synpatophysin, synaptotagmin), which assist in neurotransmitter release, and synaptic plasma membrane proteins (e.g., SNAP23 and SNAP25), which play a critical role in synaptogenesis. Two approaches have been taken to further understand the influence of the genes encoding synaptic proteins on the manifestation of schizophrenia. Mutational/polymorphic analysis has revealed a significant association of a nonsense mutation (an alteration in sequence that results in premature cessation of translation, producing a truncated protein that is usually not functional) in synaptogyrin 1 with schizophrenia (Verma et al., 2004), whereas another study did not find an association of polymorphisms in synapsin III, even though the gene encoding the transcript maps to a schizophrenia susceptibility region (Imai et al., 2001; Ohmori et al., 2000; Ohtsuki et al., 2000; Tsai et al., 2002). A greater number of studies have examined levels of mRNA and/or protein in specific brain regions to determine their relationship to the pathophysiology of schizophrenia. For example, synaptophysin mRNA is significantly decreased in the hippocampus (Eastwood et al., 1995a; Eastwood & Harrison, 1999; Webster et al., 2001) and mRNA and protein levels are decreased in the temporal lobe of SCZ (Eastwood & Harrison, 1995). Decreases in additional synaptic proteins are reported in the temporal lobe of

SCZ, including synapsin I (Browning et al., 1993; Vawter et al., 2002b), dystrobrevin-binding protein 1 (dysbindin; Talbot et al., 2004), and synaptoso-mal-associated protein, 25kDa (SNAP25; Fatemi et al., 2001; Thompson et al., 2003; Young et al., 1998), whereas growth associated protein 43 (GAP43) is increased (Blennow et al., 1999). Similarly, mRNAs of six presynaptic proteins are decreased in the DLPFC of SCZ, including N-ethylmaleimide sensitive fac-tor (NSF), synapsin II, synaptojanin 1, synaptotagmin 5, synaptogyrin 1, and the vacuolar proton pump (Mirnics et al., 2000). Using a discrete cell gene expression analysis, we found significantly decreased mRNA levels of synapto-physin, synaptosomal-associated protein, 23kDa (SNAP23), and SNAP25, as well as decreased synaptotagmin I and IV, synaptic vesicle amine transporter, and γ-adaptin in Layer II/III stellate cells in SCZ compared to controls (Hemby et al., 2002a). Given the vast array of potential mechanisms that can regulate transcrip-tion, it is essential to note that schizophrenia-associated differences in levels of mRNA such as those just reviewed do not necessarily imply that the gene en-coding the mRNA is a "susceptibility gene" for schizophrenia.

As noted previously, RNA editing and splice variations are alternative means to regulate the expression of gene products. Although it is estimated that over 30% of human mRNA undergoes modifications after the mRNA is exported from the nucleus, only a few have been related to schizophrenia. The degree to which such regulation contributes to early symptoms in SCZ is not fully appreciated. Neural cell adhesion molecule (N-CAM) plays an important role in neurodevelopment including cell migration, axon guidance, and cell-to-cell interactions during de-velopment and synaptic stability in the adult brain. Previous studies show an in-crease in N-CAM in the cortex of schizophrenics (Gabriel et al., 1997; Honer et al., 1997), and it is hypothesized that N-CAM is associated with ventricular en-largement in schizophrenics (Vawter, 2000; Vawter et al., 2001). In addition, there is evidence for decreased synthesis of membrane phospholipids and possibly al-terations in content or the molecular environment of synaptic vesicles and/or phos-phoproteins in the prefrontal cortex of adolescents at risk for schizophrenia (Keshavan et al., 2003).

Glutamate and SCZ

Glutamatergic dysfunction is another possible mechanism underlying the neuro-pathophysiology of schizophrenia. Administration of compounds that block the actions of glutamate produces symptoms markedly similar to the schizophrenic symptoms in humans and behaviors reminiscent of such symptoms in rats and monkeys (Javitt & Zukin, 1991). In healthy human volunteers, such compounds induce both positive (hallucinations, thought disorder) and negative (blunted af-fect, social withdrawal) symptoms, as well as cognitive deficits (Malhotra et al., 1996). In addition, when administered to SCZ, such compounds induce an acute relapse in psychotic symptoms that mimic the patient's typical pattern of psychotic episodes and induce behavioral and cognitive deficits that can be attenuated by antipsychotic administration (Lahti et al., 1995; Malhotra et al., 1997).

As mentioned previously, glutamate is a major transmitter in the EC and DLPFC and is involved in the ability of the synapse to change its function and activity—making it an interesting candidate for investigation in the pathology of schizophrenia. Glutamate exerts its effects by interacting with receptors to generate a cellular response. The primary type of receptors with which glutamate interacts are ionotropic receptors: classified as N-methyl-D-aspartate (NMDA; comprised of combinations of NR1, NR2A-D, NR3A,B subunits), (±)-α-amino-3-hydroxy-5-methyl-4-isoxazolepropionic acid (AMPA; comprised of GluR1-4 subunits), and kainate (GluR5-7, KA1-2), based on their pharmacological characteristics and sequence information (Borges & Dingledine, 2002; Hollmann & Heinemann, 1994). All three receptor types are thought to play roles in long-term potentiation, a well studied form of synaptic plasticity (Bortolotto et al., 1999; Nestler, 2001; Ungless et al., 2001). NMDA, AMPA, and kainite receptors are ion channels formed from some combination of NMDA, AMPA, or kainite receptor subunits, respectively. A distinct gene encodes each of these subunits. Transcriptional regulation within the cell determines the expression level of the specific subunits available to interact and form functional receptors, and subunit composition alters the properties of the receptor.

NMDA receptors mediate slower and more long-lasting neuronal excitability by allowing more calcium ions to flow into the neuron. Subunit composition of the NMDA receptor affects how NMDA receptors interact with glutamate and subsequently how NMDA receptors mediate cellular excitability. In addition, the genes encoding certain NMDA subunits can be alternatively spliced to generate distinct variants of the subunit. These splice variants provide different degrees of control over the function of the receptor (Dingledine et al., 1999; Hollmann et al., 1993; Koltchine et al., 1996; Traynelis et al., 1995). In contrast to NMDA receptors, AMPA receptors contribute to *fast* neuronal excitation. Subunit composition of the AMPA receptor contributes to functional properties of the receptor, such as the ability of calcium to enter the neuron and increase neuronal excitability (Burnashev et al., 1992; Jonas et al., 1994). Like NMDA subunits, AMPA and kainite receptors exist in different splice-variant forms that alter the amount of time these receptors stay open (and thus change neuronal excitability; Koike et al., 2000; Mosbacher et al., 1994). Studies have found the expression of the genes encoding these splice variants differ in ratio depending on development, drug administration, and disease state (Eastwood et al., 1997a; Monyer et al., 1991). Because subunit composition determines the functional properties of ionotropic glutamate receptors (Borges & Dingledine, 2002), alterations in expression of specific subunits could have profound influences on neurotransmission underlying biochemical and behavioral effects associated with schizophrenia.

Using magnetic resonance spectroscopy, glutamate/glutamine has been found to be significantly higher in the prefrontal cortex of adolescents at high genetic risk for schizophrenia than in the low-risk offspring, as well as in nontreated adult schizophrenics (Bartha et al., 1997; Tibbo et al., 2004). Moreover, the impairment of glutamate metabolism also occurs in adult SCZ (Burbaeva et al., 2003). These data demonstrate decreased glutamatergic function in these subjects, as well as the persistence of such changes throughout the disease. In postmortem DLPFC of SCZ, NMDA subunit mRNAs are elevated, which suggests a compensatory change to possibly offset the decrease in glutamate neurotransmission (Dracheva et al., 2001). Evidence of altered AMPA and kainate subunits in the DLPFC (Dracheva et al., 2001; Meador-Woodruff et al., 2001; Mirnics et al., 2000; Vawter et al., 2002a) further implicate the dysregulation of glutamate receptors in the pathology of schizophrenia. However, expression of AMPAR subunit mRNAs are unchanged in other schizophrenic cohorts (Healy et al., 1998).

Previous studies have demonstrated decreased levels of AMPA subunit mRNAs in the temporal lobe and hippocampal subfields (Eastwood et al., 1995b; Gao et al., 2000; Harrison et al., 1991) and NMDA subunit mRNA in temporal cortex (Hemby et al., 2002b; Humphries et al., 1996). Given that NMDA subunit mRNA levels are in low abundance in neonates (Law et al., 2003), Harrison and colleagues suggest that decreased glutamate receptor levels in SCZ may be "recapitulating an 'immature' receptor phenotype." As noted earlier, NR1 mRNA is posttranscriptionally modified into various splice variants, all conferring different kinetic and pharmacological properties of the receptor.

Moreover, GluR1 immunoreactivity is decreased in the parahippocampal gyrus, and GluR2/3 imunoreactivity is decreased in the CA4 subfield (Eastwood et al., 1997b). Others have shown decreased GluR2/3 protein levels in hippocampus and no change in GluR1 or GluR5 protein levels in human postmortem tissue of SCZ (Breese et al., 1995). Extending these findings, we recently demonstrated significant down-regulation of GluR3 mRNA in a specific cell type within the EC (Hemby et al., 2002b). Similar to NMDA subunits, the AMPA subunits are posttranscriptionally modified into flip and flop variants conferring different pharmacology and biochemistry to the receptor. Eastwood and colleagues demonstrated an increase in the GluR2 flip/flop ratio in the hippocampal formation of SCZ (Eastwood et al., 1997a). On the other hand, recent data in our laboratory suggest that flip and flop variants are not altered at a regional level in the DLPFC of SCZ. Understanding the altered abundance of flip and flop variants in schizophrenics may be advantageous for the development of pharmacotherapies selective for the variants. Dysregulation of ionotropic glutamate receptors may have profound downstream effects, including alterations in excitatory neurotransmission and subsequent cognitive and behavioral sequelea believed to be driven by glutamatergic circuitry.

Additional Means of Transcriptional Regulation in Schizophrenia

RNA interference (RNAi) is a recently described phenomenon that is another means by which gene expression can be regulated. mRNA usually exists in the cytoplasm as single-stranded RNA. The unpaired nucleotides of the mRNA can then interact with the ribosomal complex to translate the message and synthesize protein. However, like DNA, mRNA can exist in double-stranded form (dsRNA). RNA interference machinery in the cell finds dsRNA, cuts it with an enzyme known as Dicer, separates the two strands of mRNA, and then proceeds to destroy other single-stranded RNA with that same sequence. Like mRNA, microRNAs (miRNA) are another type of RNA transcribed from genomic DNA. However, these smaller miRNAs fold back on themselves generating a double-stranded hairpin shape. The RNA interference machinery then detects these dsRNAs, breaks them apart, and destroys mRNAs with the same sequence as the miRNA, thus reducing the expression of many mRNAs. Recent studies have identified 66 brain specific miRNAs and identified a subset of 19 miRNAs expressed during neuronal differentiation (Sempere et al., 2004). The demonstration of a temporal expression wave of select miRNAs during mouse brain development (Miska et al., 2004) may provide new insight on our understanding of transcriptional regulation during development and may provide clues as to which transcripts may be modified in schizophrenia.

Methylation of DNA is another means by which transcription can be regulated. DNA methylation is a process by which a methyl group is added to specific base pairs of DNA after replication. Of the four types of base pairs, methylation occurs only at the cytosine-guanine pairing (CG). Once the methyl group is added to the base pair, the DNA is unrecognizable to enzymes in the nucleus, particularly enzymes that initiate transcription. Repetitive runs of CG doublets in the DNA sequence are referred to as "CpG islands" and are important sites of methylation in the genome. In general, genes are methylated in tissues in which they are not expressed and are unmethylated in tissues in which they are active. Methylation at specific sites, such as promoter elements, is likely important for suppression of transcription. Interestingly, DNA-methyltransferase 1 (DNMT1), a protein that contributes to the hypermethylation of promoter CpG islands is upregulated in the cortex of schizophrenics—preferentially expressed in interneurons secreting GABA (Veldic et al., 2004; Veldic et al., 2005). Reelin, a protein that is important to neuronal development, is decreased in the brains of schizophrenic patients. Interestingly, DNMT1–induced hypermethylation decreases reelin expression in mouse primary cortical cultures and may mediate the decreased reelin expression observed in the schizophrenic brain (Chen et al., 2002; Noh et al., 2005). Further studies are warranted to assess hypermethylation as a mechanism for transcriptional regulation in schizophrenia.

Toward Intervention

As noted previously, the cause of schizophrenia is not well understood, although evidence implicates genetic, environmental, developmental, and nutritional factors. Most pharmacotherapies have focused on particular receptors; however, the multigenetic nature of schizophrenia suggests the development of therapeutics that target multiple genes and proteins involved in signal transduction. Moreover, because conventional antipsychotics are only partially effective in attenuating psychosis, medication development should be directed at the more specific aspects of signal transduction associated with schizophrenia. A primary function of the central nervous system is cellular communication; therefore, most biochemical pathways related to neuronal function can be viewed as contributing to the process of signal transduction.

The last 10 to15 years have witnessed a significant advancement of the development and refinement of antipsychotic pharmacotherapies for schizophrenia, as well as of our understanding of the receptor and biochemical neuropathology associated with the disease. Typical and atypical antipsychotic medications are effective in attenuating negative and positive symptoms to varying degrees; however, these medications target proteins (i.e., receptors) with vast roles in cognitive and behavioral function that limit the specificity and efficacy of these compounds. Future development of antipsychotic medications should selectively target specific signaling cascade mechanisms, possibly improving efficacy and diminishing side effects of these drugs. The advancement of functional genomic (measuring mRNAs) and proteomic (measuring levels of proteins) technologies will contribute to a more comprehensive evaluation of the molecular pathology of schizophrenia and better our understanding of orchestrated alterations in signaling cascades. In the years to come, the focus of functional genomics/proteomics approaches to schizophrenia should shift from regional to targeted cell assessment to provide a more refined and detailed evaluation of molecular alterations in this disease. Evaluation of different cell populations within a given brain region may also provide insight into particular cellular vulnerabilities correlated with the disease. Finally, studies should begin to incorporate the large amounts of clinical data available about subjects used in microarray analysis. Correlating clinical data such as age, severity of illness, and type of symptoms present with molecular data may allow for identification of specific expression profiles associated with particular facets of the disease.

The description of dysregulated gene expression begs the question of how such information can be translated into meaningful intervention strategies. Although not currently available, the regulation of gene transcription at critical development periods in high-risk individuals will be an important target for the action of future pharamcotherapies. Such transcription-based strategies are likely feasible in the near future and will provide a level of specificity heretofore unattainable with pharmacological therapies. However, there are additional milestones that must be attained by the basic science community. First and foremost, we need to develop a better understanding of biochemical pathways and upstream regulatory sequence for transcripts involved in these disorders in order to discern the mechanisms by which they are regulated. The advent of high throughput genomics and proteomic strategies will accelerate the discovery process of novel transcripts, and data-mining algorithms currently under development will guide the identification of disease relevant and specific transcripts. Also, a more detailed understanding of promoters and transcription factors that regulate the transcription of disease relevant genes must be identified. Given that schizophrenia appears to preferentially affect defined brain regions and particular cell populations within those regions, the identification of region and cell-specific promoters would provide the means to selectively direct transcript-based pharmacotherapies to the intended sight of action. A critical caveat to reaching the aforementioned milestones is the use of primate tissue—either human postmortem or nonhuman primate that recapitulates the diversity and complexity of the human cortex.

References

Akbarian, S., Bunney, W. E., Jr., Potkin, S. G., Wigal, S. B., Hagman, J. O., Sandman, C. A., et al. (1993). Altered distribution of nicotinamide-adenine dinucleotide phosphate-diaphorase cells in frontal lobe of schizophrenics implies disturbances of cortical development. *Archives of General Psychiatry, 50*(3), 169–177.

Altshuler, L. L., Bartzokis, G., Grieder, T., Curran, J., Jimenez, T., Leight, K., et al. (2000). An MRI study of temporal lobe structures in men with bipolar disorder or schizophrenia. *Biological Psychiatry, 48*(2), 147–162.

Arnold, S. E. (1999). Neurodevelopmental abnormalities in schizophrenia: Insights from neuropathology. *Development and Psychopathology, 11*(3), 439–456.

Arnold, S. E., Franz, B. R., Gur, R. C., Gur, R. E., Shapiro, R. M., Moberg, P. J., et al. (1995). Smaller neuron size in schizophrenia in hippocampal subfields that mediate cortical-hippocampal interactions. *American Journal of Psychiatry, 152*(5), 738–748.

Arnold, S. E., Hyman, B. T., Van Hoesen, G. W., & Damasio, A. R. (1991). Some cytoarchitectural abnormalities of the entorhinal cortex in schizophrenia. *Archives of General Psychiatry, 48*(7), 625–632.

Arnold, S. E., Ruscheinsky, D. D., & Han, L. Y. (1997). Further evidence of abnormal cytoarchitecture of the entorhinal cortex in schizophrenia using spatial point pattern analyses. *Biological Psychiatry, 42*(8), 639–647.

Arnold, S. E., Trojanowski, J. Q., Gur, R. E., Blackwell, P., Han, L. Y., & Choi, C. (1998). Absence of neurodegeneration and neural injury in the cerebral cortex in a sample of elderly patients with schizophrenia. *Archives of General Psychiatry, 55*(3), 225–232.

Aston, C., Jiang, L., & Sokolov, B. P. (2004). Transcriptional profiling reveals evidence for signaling and oligodendroglial abnormalities in the temporal cortex from patients with major depressive disorder. *Molecular Psychiatry, 10,* 309–322.

Bagary, M. S., Symms, M. R., Barker, G. J., Mutsatsa, S. H., Joyce, E. M., & Ron, M. A. (2003). Gray and white matter brain abnormalities in first-episode schizophrenia inferred from magnetization transfer imaging. *Archives of General Psychiatry, 60*(8), 779–788.

Bartha, R., Williamson, P. C., Drost, D. J., Malla, A., Carr, T. J., Cortese, L., et al. (1997). Measurement of glutamate and glutamine in the medial prefrontal cortex of never-treated schizophrenic patients and healthy controls by proton magnetic resonance spectroscopy. *Archives of General Psychiatry, 54*(10), 959–965.

Baxter, M. G., & Murray, E. A. (2001). Impairments in visual discrimination learning and recognition memory produced by neurotoxic lesions of rhinal cortex in rhesus monkeys. *European Journal of Neuroscience, 13*(6), 1228–1238.

Benes, F. M., McSparren, J., Bird, E. D., SanGiovanni, J. P., & Vincent, S. L. (1991). Deficits in small interneurons in prefrontal and cingulate cortices of schizophrenic and schizoaffective patients. *Archives of General Psychiatry, 48*(11), 996–1001.

Blennow, K., Bogdanovic, N., Gottfries, C. G., & Davidsson, P. (1999). The growth-associated protein GAP-43 is increased in the hippocampus and in the gyrus cinguli in schizophrenia. *Journal of Molecular Neuroscience, 13*(1–2), 101–109.

Bogerts, B., Lieberman, J. A., Ashtari, M., Bilder, R. M., Degreef, G., Lerner, G., et al. (1993). Hippocampus-amygdala volumes and psychopathology in chronic schizophrenia. *Biological Psychiatry, 33*(4), 236–246.

Borges, K., & Dingledine, R. (2002). Molecular pharmacology and physiology of glutamate receptors. In B. H. Herman, J. Frankenheim, R. Z. Litten, P. H. Sheridan, F. F. Weight & S. R. Zukin (Eds.), *Glutamate and addiction* (pp. 3–22). Totowa, NJ: Humana Press.

Bortolotto, Z. A., Clarke, V. R., Delany, C. M., Parry, M. C., Smolders, I., Vignes, M., et al. (1999). Kainate receptors are involved in synaptic plasticity. *Nature, 402*(6759), 297–301.

Breese, C. R., Freedman, R., & Leonard, S. S. (1995). Glutamate receptor subtype expression in human postmortem brain tissue from schizophrenics and alcohol abusers. *Brain Research, 674*(1), 82–90.

Brown, A. S., & Susser, E. S. (2002). In utero infection and adult schizophrenia. *Mental Retardation and Developmental Disabilities Research Reviews, 8*(1), 51–57.

Browning, M. D., Dudek, E. M., Rapier, J. L., Leonard, S., & Freedman, R. (1993). Significant reductions in synapsin but not synaptophysin specific activity in the brains of some schizophrenics. *Biological Psychiatry, 34*(8), 529–535.

Buchanan, R. W., Breier, A., Kirkpatrick, B., Elkashef, A., Munson, R. C., Gellad, F., et al. (1993). Structural abnormalities in deficit and nondeficit schizophrenia. *American Journal of Psychiatry, 150*(1), 59–65.

Burbaeva, G., Boksha, I. S., Turishcheva, M. S., Vorobyeva, E. A., Savushkina, O. K., & Tereshkina, E. B. (2003). Glutamine synthetase and glutamate dehydrogenase in the prefrontal cortex of patients with schizophrenia. *Progress in Neuropsychopharmacology and Biological Psychiatry, 27*(4), 675–680.

Burnashev, N., Monyer, H., Seeburg, P. H., & Sakmann, B. (1992). Divalent ion permeability of AMPA receptor channels is dominated by the edited form of a single subunit. *Neuron, 8*(1), 189–198.

Cannon, M., Jones, P. B., & Murray, R. M. (2002). Obstetric complications and schizophrenia: Historical and meta-analytic review. *American Journal of Psychiatry, 159*(7), 1080–1092.

Cannon, T. D., Bearden, C. E., Hollister, J. M., Rosso, I. M., Sanchez, L. E., & Hadley, T. (2000). Childhood cognitive functioning in schizophrenia patients and their unaffected siblings: A prospective cohort study. *Schizophrenia Bulletin, 26*(2), 379–393.

Chavoix, C., Blaizot, X., Meguro, K., Landeau, B., & Baron, J. C. (2002). Excitotoxic lesions of the rhinal cortex in the baboon differentially affect visual recognition memory, habit memory and spatial executive functions. *European Journal of Neuroscience, 15*(7), 1225–1236.

Chen, Y., Sharma, R. P., Costa, R. H., Costa, E., & Grayson, D. R. (2002). On the epigenetic regulation of the human reelin promoter. *Nucleic Acids Research, 30*(13), 2930–2939.

Dingledine, R., Borges, K., Bowie, D., & Traynelis, S. F. (1999). The glutamate receptor ion channels. *Pharmacological Reviews, 51*(1), 7–61.

Dracheva, S., Marras, S. A., Elhakem, S. L., Kramer, F. R., Davis, K. L., & Haroutunian, V. (2001). N-methyl-D-aspartic acid receptor expression in the dorsolateral prefrontal cortex of elderly patients with schizophrenia. *American Journal of Psychiatry, 158*(9), 1400–1410.

Eastwood, S. L. (2004). The synaptic pathology of schizophrenia: Is aberrant neurodevelopment and plasticity to blame? *International Review of Neurobiology, 59*, 47–72.

Eastwood, S. L., Burnet, P. W., & Harrison, P. J. (1995a). Altered synaptophysin expression as a marker of synaptic pathology in schizophrenia. *Neuroscience, 66*(2), 309–319.

Eastwood, S. L., Burnet, P. W., & Harrison, P. J. (1997a). GluR2 glutamate receptor subunit flip and flop isoforms are decreased in the hippocampal formation in schizophrenia: A reverse transcriptase-polymerase chain reaction (RT-PCR) study. *Brain Research Molecular Brain Research, 44*(1), 92–98.

Eastwood, S. L., & Harrison, P. J. (1995). Decreased synaptophysin in the medial temporal lobe in schizophrenia demonstrated using immunoautoradiography. *Neuroscience, 69*(2), 339–343.

Eastwood, S. L., & Harrison, P. J. (1999). Detection and quantification of hippocampal synaptophysin messenger RNA in schizophrenia using autoclaved, formalin-fixed, paraffin wax-embedded sections. *Neuroscience, 93*(1), 99–106.

Eastwood, S. L., Kerwin, R. W., & Harrison, P. J. (1997b). Immunoautoradiographic evidence for a loss of alpha-amino-3-hydroxy-5-methyl-4-isoxazole propionate-preferring non-N-methyl-D-aspartate glutamate receptors within the medial temporal lobe in schizophrenia. *Biological Psychiatry, 41*(6), 636–643.

Eastwood, S. L., McDonald, B., Burnet, P. W., Beckwith, J. P., Kerwin, R. W., & Harrison, P. J. (1995b). Decreased expression of mRNAs encoding non-NMDA glutamate receptors GluR1 and GluR2 in medial temporal lobe neurons in schizophrenia. *Brain Research Molecular Brain Research, 29*(2), 211–223.

Ebert, T., & Kotler, M. (2005). Prenatal exposure to influenza and the risk of subsequent development of schizophrenia. *The Israeli Medical Association Journal, 7*(1), 35–38.

Falkai, P., Honer, W. G., David, S., Bogerts, B., Majtenyi, C., & Bayer, T. A. (1999). No evidence for astrogliosis in brains of schizophrenic patients. A post-mortem study. *Neuropathology and Applied Neurobiology, 25*(1), 48–53.

Fatemi, S. H., Earle, J. A., Stary, J. M., Lee, S., & Sedgewick, J. (2001). Altered levels of the synaptosomal associated protein SNAP-25 in hippocampus of subjects with mood disorders and schizophrenia. *Neuroreport, 12*(15), 3257–3262.

Fernandez, G., Brewer, J. B., Zhao, Z., Glover, G. H., & Gabrieli, J. D. (1999). Level of sustained entorhinal activity at study correlates with subsequent cued-recall performance: A functional magnetic resonance imaging study with high acquisition rate. *Hippocampus, 9*(1), 35–44.

Gabriel, S. M., Haroutunian, V., Powchik, P., Honer, W. G., Davidson, M., Davies, P., et al. (1997). Increased concentrations of presynaptic proteins in the cingulate cortex of subjects with schizophrenia. *Archives of General Psychiatry, 54*(6), 559–566. [Erratum appears in *Archives of General Psychiatry* (1997, October), *54*(10), 912.]

Gao, X. M., Sakai, K., Roberts, R. C., Conley, R. R., Dean, B., & Tamminga, C. A. (2000). Ionotropic glutamate receptors and expression of N-methyl-D-aspartate receptor subunits in subregions of human hippocampus: Effects of schizophrenia. *American Journal of Psychiatry, 157*(7), 1141–1149.

Giedd, J. N., Jeffries, N. O., Blumenthal, J., Castellanos, F. X., Vaituzis, A. C., Fernandez, T., et al. (1999). Childhood-onset schizophrenia: Progressive brain changes during adolescence. *Biological Psychiatry, 46*(7), 892–898.

Glantz, L. A., & Lewis, D. A. (2000). Decreased dendritic spine density on prefrontal cortical pyramidal neurons in schizophrenia. *Archives of General Psychiatry, 57*(1), 65–73.

Gruzelier, J., Seymour, K., Wilson, L., Jolley, A., & Hirsch, S. (1988). Impairments on neuropsychologic tests of temporohippocampal and frontohippocampal functions and word fluency in remitting schizophrenia and affective disorders. *Archives of General Psychiatry, 45*(7), 623–629.

Gur, R. E. (1995). Functional brain-imaging studies in schizophrenia. In F. E. Bloom & D. J. Kupfer (Eds.), *Psychopharmacology: The fourth generation of progress* (4th ed., pp. 1185–1192). New York: Raven Press.

Gur, R. E., Kohler, C., Ragland, J. D., Siegel, S. J., Bilker, W. B., Loughead, J., et al. (2003). Neurocognitive performance and clinical changes in olanzapine-treated patients with schizophrenia. *Neuropsychopharmacology, 28*(11), 2029–2036.

Gur, R. E., Mozley, P. D., Resnick, S. M., Mozley, L. H., Shtasel, D. L., Gallacher, F., et al. (1995). Resting cerebral glucose metabolism in first-episode and previously treated patients with schizophrenia relates to clinical features. *Archives of General Psychiatry, 52*(8), 657–667.

Gur, R. E., Turetsky, B. I., Cowell, P. E., Finkelman, C., Maany, V., Grossman, R. I., et al. (2000). Temporolimbic volume reductions in schizophrenia. *Archives of General Psychiatry, 57*(8), 76–775.

Harrison, P. J., McLaughlin, D., & Kerwin, R. W. (1991). Decreased hippocampal expression of a glutamate receptor gene in schizophrenia. *Lancet, 337*(8739), 450–452.

Hashimoto, T., Volk, D. W., Eggan, S. M., Mirnics, K., Pierri, J. N., Sun, Z., et al. (2003). Gene expression deficits in a subclass of GABA neurons in the prefrontal cortex of subjects with schizophrenia. *Journal of Neuroscience, 23*(15), 6315–6326.

Healy, D. J., Haroutunian, V., Powchik, P., Davidson, M., Davis, K. L., Watson, S. J., et al. (1998). AMPA receptor binding and subunit mRNA expression in prefrontal cortex and striatum of elderly schizophrenics. *Neuropsychopharmacology., 19*(4), 278–286.

Hemby, S. E., Ginsberg, S. D., Brunk, B., Arnold, S. E., Trojanowski, J. Q., & Eberwine, J. H. (2002a). Gene expression profile for schizophrenia: Discrete neuron transcription patterns in the entorhinal cortex. *Archives of General Psychiatry, 59*(7), 631–640.

Hemby, S. E., Ginsberg, S. D., Brunk, B., Trojanowski, J. Q., & Eberwine, J. H. (2002b). Gene expression profile for schizophrenia: Discrete neuron transcription patterns in the entorhinal cortex. *Archives of General Psychiatry, 59*(7), 631–640.

Hollmann, M., Boulter, J., Maron, C., Beasley, L., Sullivan, J., Pecht, G., et al. (1993). Zinc potentiates agonist-induced currents at certain splice variants of the NMDA receptor. *Neuron, 10*(5), 943–954.

Hollmann, M., & Heinemann, S. (1994). Cloned glutamate receptors. *Annual Review of Neuroscience, 17*, 31–108.

Honer, W. G., Falkai, P., Young, C., Wang, T., Xie, J., Bonner, J., et al. (1997). Cingulate cortex synaptic terminal proteins and neural cell adhesion molecule in schizophrenia. *Neuroscience, 78*(1), 99–110.

Humphries, C., Mortimer, A., Hirsch, S., & de Belleroche, J. (1996). NMDA receptor mRNA correlation with antemortem cognitive impairment in schizophrenia. *Neuroreport, 7*(12), 2051–2055.

Imai, K., Harada, S., Kawanishi, Y., Tachikawa, H., Okubo, T., & Suzuki, T. (2001). Polymorphisms in the promoter and coding regions of the synapsin III gene. A lack of association with schizophrenia. *Neuropsychobiology, 43*(4), 237–241.

Isohanni, M., Isohanni, I., Koponen, H., Koskinen, J., Laine, P., Lauronen, E., et al. (2004). Developmental precursors of psychosis. *Current Psychiatry Report, 6*(3), 168–175.

Jacobsen, L. K., Giedd, J. N., Castellanos, F. X., Vaituzis, A. C., Hamburger, S. D., Kumra, S., et al. (1998). Progressive reduction of temporal lobe structures in childhood-onset schizophrenia. *American Journal of Psychiatry, 155*(5), 678–685.

Jakob, H., & Beckmann, H. (1986). Prenatal developmental disturbances in the limbic allocortex in schizophrenics. *Journal of Neural Transmission, 65*(3–4), 303–326.

James, A. C., James, S., Smith, D. M., & Javaloyes, A. (2004). Cerebellar, prefrontal cortex, and thalamic volumes over two time points in adolescent-onset schizophrenia. *American Journal of Psychiatry, 161*(6), 1023–1029.

Javitt, D. C., & Zukin, S. R. (1991). Recent advances in the phencyclidine model of schizophrenia. *American Journal of Psychiatry, 148*(10), 1301–1308.

Jonas, P., Racca, C., Sakmann, B., Seeburg, P. H., & Monyer, H. (1994). Differences in Ca2+ permeability of AMPA-type glutamate receptor channels in neocortical neurons caused by differential Glur-B subunit expression. *Neuron, 12*(6), 1281–1289.

Keshavan, M. S., Stanley, J. A., Montrose, D. M., Minshew, N. J., & Pettegrew, J. W. (2003). Prefrontal membrane phospholipid metabolism of child and adolescent offspring at risk for schizophrenia or schizoaffective disorder: An in vivo 31P MRS study. *Molecular Psychiatry, 8*(3), 316–323, 251.

Klingberg, T., Roland, P. E., & Kawashima, R. (1994). The human entorhinal cortex participates in associative memory. *Neuroreport, 6*(1), 57–60.

Koenig, J. I., Kirkpatrick, B., & Lee, P. (2002). Glucocorticoid hormones and early brain development in schizophrenia. *Neuropsychopharmacology, 27*(2), 309–318.

Koike, M., Tsukada, S., Tsuzuki, K., Kijima, H., & Ozawa, S. (2000). Regulation of kinetic properties of GluR2 AMPA receptor channels by alternative splicing. *Journal of Neuroscience, 20*(6), 2166–2174.

Koltchine, V. V., Anantharam, V., Bayley, H., & Treistman, S. N. (1996). Alternative splicing of the NMDAR1 subunit affects modulation by calcium. *Brain Research Molecular Brain Research, 39*(1–2), 99–108.

Konradi, C., & Heckers, S. (2003). Molecular aspects of glutamate dysregulation: Implications for schizophrenia and its treatment. *Pharmacology and Therapeutics, 97*(2), 153–179.

Lahti, A. C., Koffel, B., LaPorte, D., & Tamminga, C. A. (1995). Subanesthetic doses of ketamine stimulate psychosis in schizophrenia. *Neuropsychopharmacology, 13*(1), 9–19.

Law, A. J., Weickert, C. S., Webster, M. J., Herman, M. M., Kleinman, J. E., & Harrison, P. J. (2003). Expression of NMDA receptor NR1, NR2A and NR2B subunit mRNAs during development of the human hippocampal formation. *European Journal of Neuroscience, 18*(5), 1197–1205.

Lawrie, S. M., Whalley, H. C., Abukmeil, S. S., Kestelman, J. N., Miller, P., Best, J. J., et al. (2002). Temporal lobe volume changes in people at high risk of schizophrenia with psychotic symptoms. *The British Journal of Psychiatry, 181*, 138–143.

Lee, J. M., Kim, S. H., Jang, D. P., Ha, T. H., Kim, J. J., Kim, I. Y., et al. (2004). Deformable model with surface registration for hippocampal shape deformity analysis in schizophrenia. *Neuroimage, 22*(2), 831–840.

Leonard, B. W., Amaral, D. G., Squire, L. R., & Zola-Morgan, S. (1995). Transient memory impairment in monkeys with bilateral lesions of the entorhinal cortex. *Journal of Neuroscience, 15*(8), 5637–5659.

Levitt, J. B., Lewis, D. A., Yoshioka, T., & Lund, J. S. (1993). Topography of pyramidal neuron intrinsic connections in macaque monkey prefrontal cortex (areas 9 and 46). *Journal of Comparative Neurology, 338*(3), 360–376.

Lewis, D. A., & Gonzalez-Burgos, G. (2000). Intrinsic excitatory connections in the prefrontal cortex and the pathophysiology of schizophrenia. *Brain Research Bulletin, 52*(5), 309–317.

Lewis, D. A., Pierri, J. N., Volk, D. W., Melchitzky, D. S., & Woo, T. U. (1999). Altered GABA neurotransmission and prefrontal cortical dysfunction in schizophrenia. *Biological Psychiatry, 46*(5), 616–626.

Luo, L., & O'Leary, D. D. (2005). Axon retraction and degeneration in development and disease. *Annual Review of Neuroscience, 28*, 127156.

Malhotra, A. K., Pinals, D. A., Adler, C. M., Elman, I., Clifton, A., Pickar, D., et al. (1997). Ketamine-induced exacerbation of psychotic symptoms and cognitive impairment in neuroleptic-free schizophrenics. *Neuropsychopharmacology, 17*(3), 141–150.

Malhotra, A. K., Pinals, D. A., Weingartner, H., Sirocco, K., Missar, C. D., Pickar, D., et al. (1996). NMDA receptor function and human cognition: The effects of ketamine in healthy volunteers. *Neuropsychopharmacology, 14*(5), 301–307.

Meador-Woodruff, J. H., Davis, K. L., & Haroutunian, V. (2001). Abnormal kainate receptor expression in prefrontal cortex in schizophrenia. *Neuropsychopharmacology., 24*(5), 545–552.

Miller, E. K., & Cohen, J. D. (2001). An integrative theory of prefrontal cortex function. *Annual Review of Neuroscience, 24*, 167–202.

Mirnics, K., Middleton, F. A., Marquez, A., Lewis, D. A., & Levitt, P. (2000). Molecular characterization of schizophrenia viewed by microarray analysis of gene expression in prefrontal cortex. *Neuron, 28*(1), 53–67.

Miska, E. A., Alvarez-Saavedra, E., Townsend, M., Yoshii, A., Sestan, N., Rakic, P., et al. (2004). Microarray analysis of microrna expression in the developing mammalian brain. *Genome Biology, 5*(9), R68.

Monyer, H., Seeburg, P. H., & Wisden, W. (1991). Glutamate-operated channels: Developmentally early and mature forms arise by alternative splicing. *Neuron, 6*(5), 799–810.

Mosbacher, J., Schoepfer, R., Monyer, H., Burnashev, N., Seeburg, P. H., & Ruppersberg, J. P. (1994). A molecular determinant for submillisecond desensitization in glutamate receptors. *Science, 266*(5187), 1059–1062.

Nestler, E. J. (2001). Neurobiology. Total recall—the memory of addiction. *Science, 292*(5525), 22662267.

Niemi, L. T., Suvisaari, J. M., Tuulio-Henriksson, A., & Lonnqvist, J. K. (2003). Childhood developmental abnormalities in schizophrenia: Evidence from high-risk studies. *Schizophrenia Research, 60*(2–3), 239–258.

Noh, J. S., Sharma, R. P., Veldic, M., Salvacion, A. A., Jia, X., Chen, Y., et al. (2005). DNA methyltransferase 1 regulates reelin mRNA expression in mouse primary cortical cultures. *Proceedings of the National Academy of Sciences of the USA, 102*(5), 1749–1754.

Nordahl, T. E., Kusubov, N., Carter, C., Salamat, S., Cummings, A. M., O'Shora-Celaya, L., et al. (1996). Temporal lobe metabolic differences in medication-free outpatients with schizophrenia via the PET-600. *Neuropsychopharmacology, 15*(6), 541–554.

Ohmori, O., Shinkai, T., Hori, H., Kojima, H., & Nakamura, J. (2000). Synapsin III gene polymorphisms and schizophrenia. *Neuroscience Letters, 279*(2), 125–127.

Ohtsuki, T., Ichiki, R., Toru, M., & Arinami, T. (2000). Mutational analysis of the synapsin III gene on chromosome 22q12–q13 in schizophrenia. *Psychiatry Research, 94*(1), 1–7.

Pierri, J. N., Chaudry, A. S., Woo, T. U., & Lewis, D. A. (1999). Alterations in chandelier neuron axon terminals in the prefrontal cortex of schizophrenic subjects. *American Journal of Psychiatry, 156*(11), 1709–1719.

Pierri, J. N., Volk, C. L., Auh, S., Sampson, A., & Lewis, D. A. (2001). Decreased somal size of deep layer 3 pyramidal neurons in the prefrontal cortex of subjects with schizophrenia. *Archives of General Psychiatry, 58*(5), 466–473.

Pruessner, J. C., Collins, D. L., Pruessner, M., & Evans, A. C. (2001). Age and gender predict volume decline in the anterior and posterior hippocampus in early adulthood. *Journal of Neuroscience, 21*(1), 194–200.

Rakic, P. (1988). Specification of cerebral cortical areas. *Science, 241*(4862), 170–176.

Rapoport, J. L., Addington, A., & Frangou, S. (2005). The neurodevelopmental model of schizophrenia: What can very early onset cases tell us? *Current Psychiatry Report, 7*(2), 81–82.

Raz, N., Rodrigue, K. M., Head, D., Kennedy, K. M., & Acker, J. D. (2004). Differential aging of the medial temporal lobe: A study of a five-year change. *Neurology, 62*(3), 433–438.

Russell, J. M., Early, T. S., Patterson, J. C., Martin, J. L., Villanueva-Meyer, J., & McGee, M. D. (1997). Temporal lobe perfusion asymmetries in schizophrenia. *Journal of Nuclear Medicine, 38*(4), 607–612.

Saitoh, O., Karns, C. M., & Courchesne, E. (2001). Development of the hippocampal formation from 2 to 42 years: MRI evidence of smaller area dentata in autism. *Brain, 124*(Pt. 7), 1317–1324.

Saykin, A. J., Gur, R. C., Gur, R. E., Mozley, P. D., Mozley, L. H., Resnick, S. M., et al. (1991). Neuropsychological function in schizophrenia. Selective impairment in memory and learning. *Archives of General Psychiatry, 48*(7), 618–624.

Selemon, L. D., Rajkowska, G., & Goldman-Rakic, P. S. (1998). Elevated neuronal density in prefrontal area 46 in brains from schizophrenic patients: Application of a three-dimensional, stereologic counting method. *Journal of Comparative Neurology, 392*(3), 402–412.

Sempere, L. F., Freemantle, S., Pitha-Rowe, I., Moss, E., Dmitrovsky, E., & Ambros, V. (2004). Expression profiling of mammalian micrornas uncovers a subset of brain-expressed micrornas with possible roles in murine and human neuronal differentiation. *Genome Biology, 5*(3), R13.

Shenton, M. E., Kikinis, R., Jolesz, F. A., Pollak, S. D., LeMay, M., Wible, C. G., et al. (1992). Abnormalities of the left temporal lobe and thought disorder in schizophrenia. A quantitative magnetic resonance imaging study. *New England Journal of Medicine, 327*(9), 604–612.

Squire, L. R., & Zola, S. M. (1996). Structure and function of declarative and nondeclarative memory systems. *Proceedings of the National Academy of the Sciences of USA, 93*(24), 13515–13522.

Squire, L. R., & Zola-Morgan, S. (1991). The medial temporal lobe memory system. *Science, 253*(5026), 1380–1386.

Suzuki, M., Hagino, H., Nohara, S., Zhou, S. Y., Kawasaki, Y., Takahashi, T., et al. (2005). Male-specific volume expansion of the human hippocampus during adolescence. *Cerebral Cortex, 15*(2), 187–193.

Talbot, K., Eidem, W. L., Tinsley, C. L., Benson, M. A., Thompson, E. W., Smith, R. J., et al. (2004). Dysbindin-1 is reduced in intrinsic, glutamatergic terminals of the hippocampal formation in schizophrenia. *Journal of Clinical Investigation, 113*(9), 1353–1363.

Tamminga, C. A., Thaker, G. K., Buchanan, R., Kirkpatrick, B., Alphs, L. D., Chase, T. N., et al. (1992). Limbic system abnormalities identified in schizophrenia using positron emission tomography with fluorodeoxyglucose and neocortical alterations with deficit syndrome. *Archives of General Psychiatry, 49*(7), 522–530.

Tarrant, C. J., & Jones, P. B. (1999). Precursors to schizophrenia: Do biological markers have specificity? *Canadian Journal of Psychiatry, 44*(4), 335–349.

Thompson, P. M., Egbufoama, S., & Vawter, M. P. (2003). Snap-25 reduction in the hippocampus of patients with schizophrenia. *Progress in Neuropsychopharmacology and Biological Psychiatry, 27*(3), 411–417.

Tibbo, P., Hanstock, C., Valiakalayil, A., & Allen, P. (2004). 3–T proton MRS investigation of glutamate and glutamine in adolescents at high genetic risk for schizophrenia. *American Journal of Psychiatry, 161*(6), 1116–1118.

Traynelis, S. F., Hartley, M., & Heinemann, S. F. (1995). Control of proton sensitivity of the NMDA receptor by RNA splicing and polyamines. *Science, 268*(5212), 873–876.

Tsai, M. T., Hung, C. C., Tsai, C. Y., Liu, M. Y., Su, Y. C., Chen, Y. H., et al. (2002). Mutation analysis of synapsin III gene in schizophrenia. *American Journal of Medical Genetics, 114*(1), 79–83.

Turetsky, B., Cowell, P. E., Gur, R. C., Grossman, R. I., Shtasel, D. L., & Gur, R. E. (1995). Frontal and temporal lobe brain volumes in schizophrenia. Relationship to symptoms and clinical subtype. *Archives of General Psychiatry, 52*(12), 1061–1070.

Turetsky, B. I., Moberg, P. J., Roalf, D. R., Arnold, S. E., & Gur, R. E. (2003). Decrements in volume of anterior ventromedial temporal lobe and olfactory dysfunction in schizophrenia. *Archives of General Psychiatry, 60*(12), 1193–1200.

Ungless, M. A., Whistler, J. L., Malenka, R. C., & Bonci, A. (2001). Single cocaine exposure in vivo induces long-term potentiation in dopamine neurons. *Nature, 411*(6837), 583–587.

Vawter, M. P. (2000). Dysregulation of the neural cell adhesion molecule and neuropsychiatric disorders. *European Journal of Pharmacology, 405*(1–3), 385–395.

Vawter, M. P., Crook, J. M., Hyde, T. M., Kleinman, J. E., Weinberger, D. R., Becker, K. G., et al. (2002a). Microarray analysis of gene expression in the prefrontal cortex in schizophrenia: A preliminary study. *Schizophrenia Research, 58*(1), 11–20.

Vawter, M. P., Thatcher, L., Usen, N., Hyde, T. M., Kleinman, J. E., & Freed, W. J. (2002b). Reduction of synapsin in the hippocampus of patients with bipolar disorder and schizophrenia. *Molecular Psychiatry, 7*(6), 571–578.

Vawter, M. P., Usen, N., Thatcher, L., Ladenheim, B., Zhang, P., VanderPutten, D. M., et al. (2001). Characterization of human cleaved n-cam and association with schizophrenia. *Experimental Neurology, 172*(1), 29–46.

Veldic, M., Caruncho, H. J., Liu, W. S., Davis, J., Satta, R., Grayson, D. R., et al. (2004). DNA-methyltransferase 1 mRNA is selectively overexpressed in telencephalic gabaergic interneurons of schizophrenia brains. *Proceedings of the National Academy of the Sciences of USA, 101*(1), 348–353.

Veldic, M., Guidotti, A., Maloku, E., Davis, J. M., & Costa, E. (2005). In psychosis, cortical interneurons overexpress DNA-methyltransferase 1. *Proceedings of the National Academy of the Sciences of USA, 102*(6), 2152–2157.

Venables, P. H. (1989). The Emanuel Miller Memorial Lecture 1987. Childhood markers for adult disorders. *Journal of Child Psychology and Psychiatry, 30*(3), 347–364.

Verma, R., Chauhan, C., Saleem, Q., Gandhi, C., Jain, S., & Brahmachari, S. K. (2004). A nonsense mutation in the synaptogyrin 1 gene in a family with schizophrenia. *Biological Psychiatry, 55*(2), 196–199.

Webster, M. J., Shannon Weickert, C., Herman, M. M., Hyde, T. M., & Kleinman, J. E. (2001). Synaptophysin and gap-43 mRNA levels in the hippocampus of subjects with schizophrenia. *Schizophrenia Research, 49*(1–2), 89–98.

Woo, T. U., Miller, J. L., & Lewis, D. A. (1997). Schizophrenia and the parvalbumin-containing class of cortical local circuit neurons. *American Journal of Psychiatry, 154*(7), 1013–1015.

Woo, T. U., Whitehead, R. E., Melchitzky, D. S., & Lewis, D. A. (1998). A subclass of prefrontal gamma-aminobutyric acid axon terminals are selectively altered in schizophrenia. *Proceedings of the National Academy of the Sciences of USA, 95*(9), 5341–5346.

Young, C. E., Arima, K., Xie, J., Hu, L., Beach, T. G., Falkai, P., et al. (1998). SNAP-25 deficit and hippocampal connectivity in schizophrenia. *Cerebral Cortex, 8*(3), 261–268.

Part III

Effects of Early Maltreatment
and Stress on Brain Development

Chapter 6

Stress Effects on the Developing Brain

Megan R. Gunnar

Although stress is often construed as something bad (e.g., Sapolsky, 1996), we have known for a long time that it's not exposure to stressors that has ill effects, but how we react to stressors that can contribute to physical and mental problems (Lazarus & Folkman, 1984; Selye, 1977). How we respond is intimately related to the neurophysiology of stress and emotions, and to the role that the stress-emotion system has played in survival throughout our evolution (LeDoux & Phelps, 2000; Porges, 1995a). At its core, the stress-emotion system is a defense motivational system. In response to situations that pose potential threats to our well-being, it allows us to mobilize defensive responses, shunt physical resources to the mobilized target organs, shift from storing to using energy, alter priorities from preparing for the future to responding to immediate circumstances, narrow and heighten perception to threat-relevant cues, and increase the salience of threat-relevant memories.

Over the last half century, researchers have come to understand a great deal about the stress-emotion system, its impact on mental and emotional health, and the weaving of genes and experiences that shape the organization of the stress-emotion system during development (for review, see Gunnar & Vazquez, 2006). Much of this work has been based on animal models (c.f., Sanchez, Ladd, & Plotsky, 2001); however, with the new tools of neuroscience, the emergence of the field of affective neuroscience, and the modification of assays to allow measurement of one component of the stress-emotion system noninvasively through sampling saliva, significant advances are being made in translating the import of the animal work to our understanding of human children and adolescents. In this chapter, I will briefly outline the current state of our knowledge and recent attempts to merge this work with preventive intervention study designs.

The Neurobiology and Neuroendocrinology of the Stress-Emotion System

The neuroendocrine component of the emotion-stress system focuses on centers deep in the brain, in the hypothalamus and brainstem (Habib, Gold, & Chrousos, 2001). In an area of the hypothalamus called the paraventricular region lie cells that secrete corticotrophin-releasing hormone (sometimes referred to as CRH and sometimes CRF) and arginine vasopressin (AVP; see figure 6-1). These neuropeptides travel through a small vascular system to the anterior part of the pituitary gland where they stimulate the production and release of adrenocorticotropic hormone (ACTH). ACTH, in turn, is released into general circulation and is carried through the blood to the cortex (outer part) of the adrenal glands. In the adrenal cortex, ACTH triggers the production and release of glucocorticoids, critical stress hormones (note: cortisol in humans and corticosterone in rats). This whole system is called the HPA axis for its three components: hypothalamus-pituitary-adrenal cortex.

In a region of the brainstem called the locus coeruleus (LC) lie the cell bodies of the brain's norepinephrine (NE) system, the neurotransmitter system that is intimately involved in regulating vigilance and fear behavior (see figure 6-1, panel A). Also in the brainstem are regions that regulate the sympathetic and parasympathetic arms of the autonomic nervous system. The sympathetic nervous system includes a direct connection between brainstem nuclei and the inner part of the adrenal glands (the medulla) that secretes epinephrine (also called adrenaline) as part of the fight/flight response. This system is called SAM, standing for sympathetic-adrenal medullary system. Both glucocorticoids produced by the HPA system and adrenaline produced by the SAM system mobilize the body for action through liberating energy stores. Adrenaline also increases heart rate and blood pressure and orchestrates where blood is shunted, to muscles and brain over the reproductive and digestive systems. Glucocorticoids, in contrast, serve a wide range of additional functions beyond energy mobilization, which I will return to in a moment. The SAM system is a subcomponent of the sympathetic arm of the autonomic nervous system. The other arm of the autonomic nervous system, the parasympathetic arm, also plays a role in the stress-emotion system through reversing the effects of increased SAM activity and providing input to emotion-organizing regions in the brain (e.g., the amygdala; see below) that reduce reactivity to threat stimuli (see Porges, 1995b).

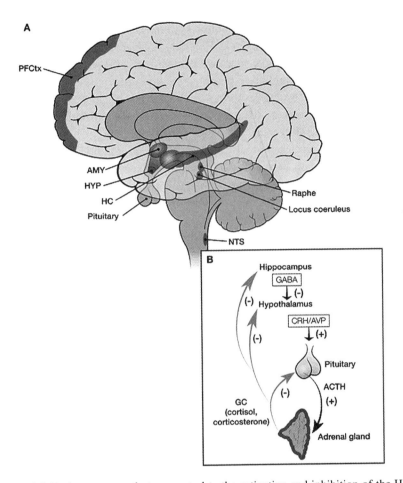

Figure 6-1 Brain structures that are central to the activation and inhibition of the HPA endocrine stress response. *A,* the main brain areas that participate in the regulation of the HPA axis; *B,* a schematic representation of the HPA endocrine stress response initiated by the release of CRH/AVP from the medial parvocellular region of the paraventricular nucleus (mpPVN) in the hypothalamus. The darkened area of the adrenal gland reflects the cortex; the lighter area, the medulla. Glucocorticoids inhibit this system acting at the level of the pituitary, hypothalamus, and hippocampus. PFCtx = prefrontal cortex, AMY = amygdala, HYP = hypothalamus, HC = hippocampus, NTS = nucleus tractus, solitarius; GABA = gamma animobutyric acid, CRH = corticotropin releasing hormone, AVP = arginine vasopressin, ACTH = adrenocorticotropic hormone. Reprinted with permission from Gunnar & Vazquez, 2006.

The emotion part of the stress-emotion system is highly complex and not fully understood (see Davidson et al., 2002; Heinrichs & Koob, 2004; LeDoux & Phelps, 2000). It seems, however, to center on the amygdala, a bilateral structure (one in the left and one in the right hemisphere), that plays critical roles in emotion processing and in orchestrating responses to threat. The amygdala is itself a highly complex structure, with its different components serving different functions in emotion processing (Pitkanen, Savander, & LeDoux, 1997). However, the central amygdala serves as an output station, relaying information that then triggers many of the behaviors associated with fear (e.g., freezing, the prickling sense of one's hair standing on edge, vigilance), and it connects with the brainstem and hypothalamic regions that produce the outflow of adrenaline by the SAM system and glucocorticoids by the HPA system.

Interestingly, CRH, the neuropeptide that coordinates the HPA system, is also produced in the central nucleus of the amygdala, and infusing CRH into this region of the brain triggers both the behavioral and physiological components of the stress-emotion response (Heinrichs, Menzaghi, Pich, Britton, & Koob, 1995). On the other hand, there are NE pathways from the brainstem LC region to the amygdala, and stimulating this pathway also results in activation of the stress-emotion system (Van Bockstaele, Bajic, Proudfit, & Valentino, 2001). Thus one way of conceptualizing the emotion component of the stress-emotion system is as a reverberating bidirectional system in which information about threat stimulates the central nucleus of the amygdala to orchestrate fear/defensive responses increasing the tone of stimulation from the LC to the amygdala. This increased LC input lowers the threshold for subsequent amygdala activation. Without mechanisms to counteract this reverberation, threatened individuals might remain in a constant state of fear and hyperstress responding. Input from the parasymethetic system, as well as from regions in the prefrontal cortex, appear to provide inputs to the amygdale and LC that disrupt this reverberation and return the individual to a calm state (Phillips, Drevets, Rauch, & Lane, 2003; Porges, 1995b).

Glucocorticoids play multiple roles in physiology, some critical to stress and some critical to survival under nonstressful conditions. Glucocorticoids produce their effects primarily through regulating gene expression (see review, deKloet, Vreugdenhil, Oitzl, & Joels, 1998). Once glucocorticoids dock with their receptors, they get carried into the nucleus of the cell, where they connect with glucocorticoids receptive elements (GREs) that typically lie in promoter regions of genes. These GREs, once activated, interact with other gene regulatory signals to increase or decrease gene transcription. There are two types of glucocorticoid receptors in the brain, mineralocorticoid receptors (MR) and glucocorticoid receptors (GR). The effects of these two types of receptors, as described below, are quite different. Notably, however, because it takes time (many minutes to hours) for these kinds of gene-mediated events to have any effect on brain or body, it has been a challenge to understand just what role glucocorticoids play in stress.

Recently, four roles for glucocorticoids have been posited that help reduce confusion over the functions of glucocorticoids in stress: permissive, stimulatory, suppressive, and preparatory (see review, Sapolsky, Romero, & Munck, 2000). The permissive role is served by the impact of glucocorticoids operating through mineralocorticoid receptors (MR) that are stimulated at basal or nonstress ranges of the hormone. These functions include helping nerve cells remain responsive to their neurotransmitters and facilitating glucose uptake by cells. Interestingly, disorders like chronic fatigue and chronic pain syndromes have been associated with remarkably low basal glucocorticoid concentrations and problems in increasing glucocorticoids to stressors. This may reflect low occupation of MR by glucocorticoids in these patients. The stimulatory role is captured by the ability of glucocorticoids to liberate energy stores, increasing the glucose available for action. Notably, adrenaline from the SAM system also serves this function but produces this glucose-liberating effect much more quickly than can stress increases in glucocorticoids. This is one reason that the SAM system is viewed as mobilizing energy resources for rapid response, whereas the HPA system is viewed as mobilizing energy resources for prolonged periods of threat.

The suppressive role of glucocorticoids involves their inhibitory impact on many of the events set into motion by the SAM system and other elements of the stress-emotion system. These suppressive effects of glucocorticoids operate through glucocorticoid receptors (GR), the receptors that become activated once glucocorticoids are in stress ranges (or at the peak of the daily basal cycle). Suppressive effects of glucocorticoids include such things as reducing the cells ability to take up glucose, increasing the production of excitatory amino acids in nerve cells, and interfering with activity of the immune system. Suppressive effects, although they would seem quite counterproductive, are argued to be highly important because they check, reverse, or contain other stress-related effects, preventing them from "overshooting." This may be seen in posttraumatic stress disorder, in which the emergence of the disorder may be related to a failure to mount a strong glucocorticoid response to the traumatic event (Yehuda, 2000). However, like any other powerful suppressive system, just enough tends to support healthy functioning, whereas too much tends to impair functioning. For example, an acute and short-lived stress response of the HPA axis may help prevent the immune system from "overshooting," but prolonged stress activation of the HPA axis may chronically suppress immune functioning, increasing susceptibility to infections. Similarly, an acute and short-lived stress response of the HPA system may allow nerve cells in the hippocampus to respond more intensely and lay down emotional memories more effectively, but a prolonged HPA stress response may produce cell death and fewer connections among nerve cells in the hippocampus (McEwen et al., 1992; Strand, 1999).

Finally, preparatory effects involve the ability of glucocorticoids to alter gene expression in ways that then alter responses to subsequent stressors. This function of stress elevations in glucocorticoids is less well studied but is likely related to evidence that frequent or chronic exposure to high levels of glucocorticoids lowers the threshold for activation of the amygdala-LC reverberating threat circuit, making it easier for milder threats to activate and maintain anxious, vigilant defensive responses (see review, Rosen & Schulkin, 1998).

In summary, the emotion-stress system likely evolved to foster survival in the face of threatening or potentially threatening events. The capacity to activate this system, thus, is essential for adaptation. Basal levels of glucocorticoids that are extremely low and stress responses that are extremely high pose risks to health and adaptive functioning because they result in failure of the HPA system to serve its permissive, stimulatory, suppressive, and preparatory roles in stress and adaptation. However, the HPA system is a powerful system that needs to be regulated such that it is activated only when needed and returned to normal basal levels of activity when threat has passed. Frequent stress activation, particularly when it produces high and prolonged glucocorticoid levels, can impair brain growth and organization (e.g., produce damage to the hippocampus, thus impairing its role in learning and memory) and chronically suppress immune functioning, thus increasing vulnerability to infectious diseases. It may also lower the threshold and increase the vigor of the neural systems underlying fear and anxiety, increasing risks of affective disorders. In sum, the relation between activity of the HPA system and adaptive functioning is typically seen as that of an inverted-U shaped function whereby both low and high levels of reactivity are associated with poor mental and emotional health, and moderate and well-timed response are associated with health and adaptive functioning (Sapolsky, 1997).

Early Experiences in the Laboratory Rat and Development of the Stress-Emotion System

Much of our understanding of the impact of early experiences on the stress-emotion system comes from rat research. The rat exhibits a curiously hyporesponsive HPA system for several weeks postbirth (Sapolsky & Meaney, 1986). This stress hyporesponsive period (SHRP) lasts from approximately day 4 to day 14 of life, during which time stimuli that would normally activate the axis produce modest, if any, responses. Other facets of the stress-emotion system (e.g., amygdala CRH system) are not hyporesponsive during this time, and the rat pup is quite capable of emitting distress vocalizations. Thus the relative stress hyporesponsive period refers only to relative hyporesponsiveness of the HPA axis (Smith, Kim, Van Oers, & Levine, 1997). Maternal behaviors, in particular licking and grooming of the pup and provision of milk into the gut, maintain the HPA axis in this relatively quiescent state (Rosenfield, Suchecki, & Levine, 1992). The SHRP roughly defines a period when disturbing the nest by separating the dam and her pups will produce long-term changes in the stress-emotion system of the pups (see review, Sanchez et al., 2001). If the disturbances induce increased maternal licking/grooming (LG), the HPA axis develops in a stress-resilient fashion, as does the emotion component of the stress-emotion system. Pups of high LG dams show less fear behavior, better containment of the HPA response to stressors, lower amygdala-CRH and LC-NE production to stressors, and a shift in the pattern of CRH receptors away from those that support fearful/anxious behavior (Liu et al., 1997). If the disturbance is repeated and prolonged and/or if maternal behavior is deficient (low LG), then pup development is shifted onto a high stress-emotion trajectory (Caldji et al., 1998). It has now been demonstrated that, in part, these shifts in the stress-emotion system reflect the influence of maternal behavior on methylation of the GR gene in the brain. Methylation is a process that permanently silences a gene, preventing it from being transcribed into RNA. Low levels of licking and grooming result in more methylation (silencing) of the GR gene in the brain, thus reducing the number of glucocorticoid receptors (GRs). This effect has been shown in the hippocampus, where GR are involved in negative feedback regulation of the HPA axis. As a consequence, offspring of low licking and grooming mothers with fewer GR in the hippocampus are unable to contain stress responses of the HPA system as effectively. They experience more prolonged elevations in glucocorticoids, thus falling more on the "too high" end of the inverted-U function described earlier (Weaver et al., 2004).

Social Regulation of the HPA Axis in Infancy and Early Childhood in Humans

This rat story is exciting because it offers a possible mechanism through which early adverse experiences in humans might shift developmental trajectories onto ones of heightened vulnerability to stress as the child develops. The question is whether it actually has implications for human development, and if so, when during human development might comparable influences on the stress-emotion system occur? The rodent is born at a much earlier stage of brain development than is the human child (Dobbing, 1981). Indeed, the end of the first postnatal week in rats is often viewed as comparable to birth in humans. This fact raises the possibility that prenatal development might be the comparable period for shaping of the stress-emotion system in humans. Indeed, there is increasing evidence that low birth weight, the result of a stressed human pregnancy, is associated with higher cortisol levels and greater cortisol reactivity among human adults (e.g., Reynolds et al., 2001). However, it seems unlikely, given what we know about the impact of early psychosocial adversity on emotional development and the risk for psychopathology (Cicchetti & Lynch, 1995), that the shaping of human stress-emotion biology stops at birth.

It is now clear that in humans, as in rodents, there is a period in our development when it is difficult to activate the HPA axis, and that this period is one during which stimuli from the caregiver maintain the axis in a relatively quiescent
state (Gunnar, 2003). As shown in figure 6-2, taking the infant to the doctor for
her well-baby checkups and childhood inoculations provokes a significant elevation in cortisol at 2 months of age. This elevation is comparable to that seen at
birth to mild pain stressors (see review, Gunnar, 1992). There is a reduction in
response at 4 and 6 months, and then at 15 months, on average, no significant
increases in cortisol are observed. Other researchers have shown a similar pattern
(c.f. Lewis & Ramsay, 1995), with work by Jacobson and colleagues (Jacobson,
Bihun, Chiodo, & Berube, 1994), who studied babies receiving their exam and
inoculations at 12 months, suggesting that this process is complete by the end of
the first year. Studies of other psychosocial stressors confirm this pattern, with
brief separations being capable of elevating cortisol among 9-month-olds but not
13-month-olds (Gunnar, Mangelsdorf, Larson, & Hertsgaard, 1989).

In all these studies, the infant has been with the parent during the stressor period,
and this appears to be critical in producing this type of hyporesponsivity (see review, Gunnar & Donzella, 2002). Furthermore, there are marked individual differences, with many babies showing no stressor-induced elevations in cortisol, whereas
some babies continue to show significant cortisol elevations. Echoing the rat research,
whether or not elevations in cortisol are provoked appears to depend, in part at least,
on the nature of the relationship between the infant and the caregiver. In relationships in which the infant has experienced sensitive and responsive care, the pres-

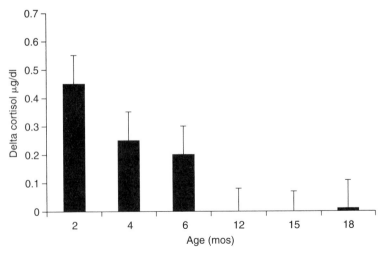

Figure 6-2 Salivary cortisol increases (posttest–pretest) studied longitudinally in response
to well-baby exams and inoculations in a sample of typically developing infants. Figure
adapted from Gunnar et al., 1996.

ence of the responsive caregiver somehow blocks activation of the HPA axis (see also Spangler & Schieche, 1998). This is true even for babies who are expressing high distress—that is, even when the emotion component of the stress-emotion system appears to be activated by the stressor. In contrast, if the infant is with someone who is insensitive, unresponsive, or intrusive, that person's presence does not block activation of the HPA axis and significant correlations between behavioral distress and cortisol elevations are observed.

Much of this information comes from laboratory experiments and thus may be difficult to generalize to life as it unfolds outside the laboratory. However, two recent studies suggest that this laboratory research has captured real-world phenomena. The first study examined children in Berlin, Germany, who were entering child care for the first time as toddlers (Ahnert, Gunnar, Lamb, & Barthel, 2004). In Berlin, women typically stay at home with the infant for the first year, and then return to work in the baby's second year. Furthermore, the child-care centers encourage mothers to spend a number of days adapting their toddlers to the child-care setting before the first real child-care day.

A month before the children started child care, Ahnert and colleagues (2004) assessed the security of the infant-mother attachment relationship using the Strange Situation assessment and collected salivary cortisol levels at home in the morning at about the same time of day as the children would soon be leaving the house for child care. They then collected salivary cortisol levels at child care during the adaptation period when the mothers accompanied the children and over the first weeks when the child attended child care in the mother's absence. Finally, samples were taken at child care after 5 months of child-care attendance. As shown in figure 6-3, infants in insecure mother-toddler attachment relationships exhibited significant elevations in cortisol during the adaptation period (left side of graph). We can speculate only that the child-care setting with new adults, new children, and exciting opportunities for exploration was a potent novelty-stressor for the toddlers, thus activating the HPA axis. Nonetheless, toddlers in secure attachment relationships did not exhibit the same cortisol elevations. The presence of the mother in a secure relationship appeared to be the critical factor, because when the mother was not present (see first separation day), her toddler's cortisol levels soared to levels previously shown by only the toddlers in insecure attachment relationships.

The second study underscores the fact that it may be the quality of nurturance or care the child receives, and not whether that care is provided by the mother or father for that matter. In this study, preschoolers in family-based child care provided cortisol sample at midmorning and midafternoon. Our research group had previously shown that cortisol levels tend to rise over the day at child care and that these increases are the most marked among toddlers (Dettling, Gunnar, & Donzella, 1999). In addition to measuring cortisol, Dettling and colleagues (Dettling, Parker, Lane, Sebanc, & Gunnar, 2000) also observed care provider–child interactions using the instrument developed by the NICHD child care study

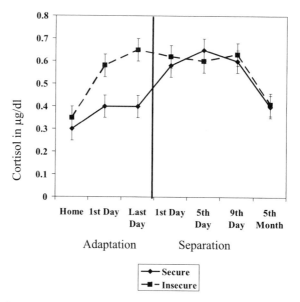

Figure 6-3 Salivary cortisol levels for toddlers in secure and insecure attachment relationships with their mothers assessed before starting child care, during an adaptation period when the mothers accompanied them in child care, and during their first weeks and months of child care. Figure adapted from Ahnert et al., 2004.

(National Institute of Child Health and Development Early Childcare Research Network, 2000). They found that care providers who were actively and positively engaged with the child prevented the child care rise in cortisol, whereas this rise was increasingly steep as these facets of caregiving were less often observed.

Taken together, the studies just reviewed indicate that in humans there is a period when the HPA axis is relatively quiescent but that this period is under strong social regulation. When the child is receiving sensitive, responsive, supportive care, the HPA axis remains quiescent, even when the child is behaviorally upset and distressed. When that care is removed and not immediately replaced by similarly high quality care from a substitute caregiver, the HPA axis becomes highly responsive to stressors.

Disturbances in the Social Regulatory System and Stress-Emotion Functioning

Although the development of the stress-emotion system may be of interest to scholars, the critical question for those who fund our research is whether any of this matters for the child's development, and if so, can we do anything to repair stress-emotion systems among children who have experienced failures of the caregiving system early in life? The answers to these questions are just beginning to emerge and are likely to be qualified by individual differences among children reflecting inherited genetic vulnerabilities. I will deal first with the emerging literature on whether it matters to human development and, if so, how. Then I will turn to the very nascent intervention research.

The does-it-matter question has two parts. Part one involves whether early experiences shape reactivity of the HPA axis and/or the functioning of the stress-emotion system. Part two involves whether these alterations predict children's physical and mental health. Unfortunately, to date, nearly all of our information about whether it matters comes from studies that have only indirectly measured the patterns of care children received early in development. Nonetheless, the results of this work are suggestive. One of the most interesting findings comes by work of Essex and colleagues (Essex, Klein, Cho, & Kalin, 2002). They followed a large cohort of families recruited during pregnancy with the goal of examining how families balanced work and family life. When the children were 4.5 years old, measures of cortisol were obtained in the late afternoon at home over several days. These researchers found that maternal stress during the child's infancy combined with her stress when the child was 4 predicted child cortisol levels. Specifically, maternal stress at age 4 did not produce elevated child cortisol levels, unless the mother was also highly stressed during the child's infancy. The authors argued that maternal stress during her child's infancy impacted her parenting and shaped an HPA system in the child that was more reactive to stress—hence, the child's response to maternal stress at age 4. Notably, among their indices of maternal stress, it was maternal depression that accounted for the child cortisol finding. This is consistent with work by Lupien and colleagues (Lupien, King, Meaney, & McEwen, 2000). They studied school-aged children when the children arrived at school in the morning. Higher cortisol levels were observed among children whose mothers reported more symptoms of depression.

Maternal depression has been the focus of a number of studies as it is associated with heightened risk for a variety of poor outcomes in children, including both anxiety/depression and delinquency/aggression (see review, Downey & Coyne, 1990). Children of depressed mothers tend to show more right-sided frontal EEG patterns, associated with withdrawal emotions (sadness, fear, anxiety), and they also exhibit higher cortisol levels at home during the preschool period (Dawson & Ashman, 2000). The higher preschool-aged cortisol levels were associated with maternal depression in the child's first year of life more so than the mother's depressive episodes after the child's infancy. This same research group, however, failed to find direct associations with early maternal depression when they saw the children for laboratory testing at age 7 (Ashman, Dawson, Panagiotides, Yamada, & Wilkinson, 2002). Instead, at 7 years, HPA axis responsivity appeared to be a joint function of the mother's earlier depressive episodes and the child's current emotional problems. Early maternal depression plus concurrent internalizing (sad, withdrawn, fearful, anxious) behavior problems predicted larger cortisol responses.

Finally, again on the issue of maternal depression and more particularly relevant to issues of adolescence, Halligan and colleagues (Halligan, Herbert, Goodyer, & Murray, 2004) recently reported that in early adolescence, children whose early morning cortisol levels vary a good deal from day to day, often spiking to higher than expected concentrations, had mothers who were clinically depressed during the child's infancy. Furthermore, maternal depression during a child's infancy was a significant factor even after taking into account maternal depression between infancy and early adolescence. The authors noted that their measure of erratic basal cortisol concentrations had previously been shown to be a risk factor for the onset of depression in studies of adolescents (Goodyer, Herbert, & Tamplin, 2003), thus raising the possibility that maternal depression in infancy impaired the mother's ability to provide sensitive, responsive care, shaping vulnerabilities in the child's HPA system that later, in adolescence, might increase the risk that the child would also experience clinical depression.

Evidence From Orphaned Children

Notably, none of the studies of maternal depression or maternal stress that have shown relations with children's cortisol levels has based their findings on measures of the caregiver-infant relationship. Thus we can only speculate that mothers who were more stressed or depressed were providing less supportive care and that it was the care the children received that mediated the association between maternal factors and child HPA axis functioning. This is also true of the next set of studies that have examined the impact of early, severe, maltreatment. However, with the maltreatment literature we can at least be assured that the care the child received fell into the grossly inadequate range. The HPA axis studies of maltreated children can be summarized as follows. If the maltreatment resulted in chronic posttraumatic stress disorder (PTSD), two studies have now shown that prepubescent children with PTSD pursuant to early, severe, and prolonged abuse have significantly elevated basal cortisol levels (Carrion et al., 2002; De Bellis et al., 1999). However, it is possible that this heightened reactivity reflects ongoing adversity in the children's home lives, possibly contributed to by their own behavior problems (Kaufman et al., 1997).

In part because of the difficulty of disentangling early versus later psychosocial adversity, my research group has chosen to focus on children adopted from institutions (i.e., postinstitutionalized, or PI, children). Conditions in orphanages vary around the world and even from room to room within the same orphanage (see review, Johnson, 2000). However, few orphanages manage to provide their charges with consistent, sensitive, and individualized care (Castle et al., 1999). Although family processes undoubtedly vary among adoptive families, care provided in these families certainly is an improvement over what the children received in their orphanages, and this conclusion is supported by the remarkable catch-up observed in behavioral, cognitive, and physical development (e.g., Rutter, 1998). Although many children seem to make a total recovery, a significant minority continue to exhibit ongoing problems in attention, impulse control, emotion regulation, and both family (attachment) and peer relationships (see, for example, Rutter, Kreppner, O'Connor, & English and Romanian Adoptees (ERA) Study Team, 2001). In several studies, my students and I have examined home baseline cortisol levels several years postadoption in these children (Gunnar, Morison, Chisholm, & Schuder, 2001; Kertes, Gunnar, Madsen & Long, 2006). Similar to the children who experienced abuse early in life, some of the PI children exhibit an increased set point in the HPA axis, meaning that they appeared to be maintaining a higher basal level of HPA activity than other children. These are the children who came from the most deprived preadoption circumstances according to parent report and/or who exhibited severe growth failure at adoption that was reversed by adoption.

Do these early adversity effects on the HPA axis have any implications for children's health and well-being? Theoretically they should, but we are far from having clear demonstrations of this in the human literature. Again, the work by Essex and colleagues (Essex et al., 2002; Smider et al., 2002) is suggestive. Recall that they found that maternal stress during the child's infancy, particularly as reflected in maternal depressive symptoms, predicted higher child cortisol levels at age 4.5 yrs if the mother was still highly stressed during the child's preschool years. These researchers have also reported that cortisol levels at 4.5 years predicted child behavior problems as rated by parent and teacher in kindergarten and first grade. Notably, they did not predict whether the child would exhibit anxious, internalizing problems or aggressive, externalizing problems. Rather they predict the severity or number of behavior problems.

Turning to PI children, so far, my students and I have not found that cortisol levels among PI children are associated with broad-band measures of internalizing or externalizing behavior problems. However, in a reanalysis of a study of 100 children who experienced at least 1 month of institutional care prior to adoption, we (Kertes & Gunnar, unpublished data) noted that wakeup but not bedtime cortisol levels at ages 7 to 9 years were correlated with higher scores on the Child Behavior Checklist scale of anxiety and depressive symptoms. In another as-yet-unpublished study (Bruce, Tarullo, & Gunnar, unpublished data), we have found that 6-year-old PI children scoring high on a combined observation and interview measure of indiscriminate friendliness exhibited higher cortisol levels in the late afternoon and evening. Indiscriminate friendliness is defined as overly intimate behavior with strangers (i.e., immediately sitting on a stranger's lap, hugging and cuddling with a stranger, being willing to go home with a stranger). Thus there are beginning to be some tantalizing suggestions that early adverse conditions that impact activity of the HPA axis may result in patterns of stress-system functioning that are associated with and may contribute to these children's behavior problems.

Although there are certainly gaps in our knowledge, one is of particular concern to the focus of this book. Specifically, we have very little prospective information about the impact of early adversity on stress reactivity and regulation as children transition into and through adolescence. This may be particularly important as there is evidence that the pubertal transition is associated with rising cortisol levels and possibly more neuroendocrine reactivity to psychosocial stressors (for review, see Gunnar & Vazquez, 2006; Spear, 2000). It is possible that impacts of early adversity on the development of the stress-emotion system may increase in its influence on health and emotional functioning with the adolescent/pubertal shift in life circumstances and biological functioning.

Intervention Studies

Not surprising, given that we are just beginning to document the impact of early psychosocial adversity on the developing stress-emotion system in human children, intervention studies in this area are scarce. Nonetheless, we can infer from studies of PI children that being placed in a family has significant impacts. Toddlers studied while they were in an orphanage in Romania failed to exhibit the normal diurnal rhythm in cortisol production over the day (Carlson & Earls, 1997). We obtained similar results in an orphanage in Russia (Kroupina, Gunnar, & Johnson, 1997). In both institutions, the children tended to have low early morning cortisol levels and slightly, but not significantly, higher noon and evening levels. There is increasing evidence that low levels of cortisol at the peak of the diurnal cycle may reflect chronic stress (Freese, Hesse, Hellhammer, & Hellhammer, 2005). Low early A.M. cortisol levels result in a flat pattern of cortisol production across the day, which among adults has been associated with chronic idiopathic pain disorders and chronic fatigue syndrome (Heim, Ehlert, & Hellhammer, 2000).

Among nonhuman primates, rhesus infants have been shown to develop similar disturbances in HPA axis rhythmicities when exposed to repeated (36), brief (30 min to 6 hr), unpredictable maternal separations between 3 and 6 months of age (Sanchez et al., 2005). Notably, in the monkey research, maternal responsivity to the infant at reunion reduced the impact of separation on diurnal cortisol production, and more disrupted cortisol rhythms predicted larger startle reactions (an index of amygdala reactivity) when the animals were 22 months of age. Thus, a disturbed diurnal HPA axis rhythm may be a biomarker of HPA axis dysregulation (see also Gunnar & Vazquez, 2001).

If so, and if most children in orphanages exhibit this form of stress system dysregulation, then adoption is an effective intervention. In all of the studies we have conducted with PI children we have yet to find a child that shows the flat diurnal cortisol pattern (Gunnar et al., 2001; Kertes et al., 2006). Unfortunately, we have not yet had the chance to examine changes in the HPA axis diurnal rhythm as they transition into the adoptive home.

There is, however, one as-yet-unpublished study by Fisher and colleagues (see Gunnar & Fisher, in press) that does not suffer this problem. Fisher and colleagues studied preschool-aged children entering a new foster placement. Approximately a month into that placement, they obtained wakeup, noon, and bedtime cortisol levels over several days. Thirty-five percent of the foster care children had a low, flat pattern of diurnal cortisol production, compared to 5% in a community sample matched for socioeconomic status. Furthermore, those foster care preschoolers with the flat, low pattern of cortisol production were more likely to have entered the foster care system as infants and to have experienced four or more placements prior to the placement studied by Fisher and colleagues.

The purpose of Fisher's study, however, was to examine the impact of a comprehensive intervention that helped train foster parents to manage the children's behavior problems, gave the foster family a case worker available for support 24 hours a day, 7 days a week, and worked with the county agencies to provide comprehensive services (Fisher, Burrasten, & Pears, 2005). Over time in the treatment foster care homes, A.M. cortisol levels were more similar to those of the community control children, whereas children in regular foster care exhibited increasingly low A.M. cortisol levels. Children in regular foster care also experienced more disruptions in care (changes from one foster home to another, reunion with their parents with a rebound back into foster care, etc.) than did children in treatment foster care, and this may help explain why regular foster care appeared to be associated with increasing evidence of low A.M. cortisol levels.

Taken together, the indirect evidence from the PI children and more direct evidence from children in treatment foster care suggest that as late as the preschool years, interventions that improve the quality of care children receive may help to normalize activity of the stress-emotion system. Much more research is needed to verify this and to indicate which aspects of the intervention experience are relevant to modifying the stress-emotion system. Critically, we also need to know whether intervening early in a child's development in ways that help reorganize the stress-emotion system will have an influence on the child's passage through the adolescent years and, if so, the pathways over which any such influence may operate.

Individual Differences

Any intervention study we might devise will likely conclude that not all children are responsive and that some children appear to do well with minimal intervention. We can anticipate this because heterogeneity is a hallmark of exposure to early adversity and to our attempts to intervene to improve children's lives.

Differential vulnerability to early neglect and maltreatment and differential responsiveness to intervention are not simply noise in our research, but are potential clues that may aid our understanding of the mechanisms of early experience effects and thus our ability to intervene more effectively with the difficult-to-help cases. It is unlikely that these individual differences can be reduced to variation in genetic vulnerabilities; on the other hand, it is also likely that genetics play a role. Recently, studies of variations (polymorphisms) in the serotonin transporter gene provide evidence that this major neurotransmitter system is involved in mediating the impact of early adverse caregiving.

Both humans and rhesus monkeys have similar functional variations in the serotonin transporter, or SERT, gene (Bennett et al., 2002). The variations involve the promoter region of the gene—that is the region that regulates gene transcription. One version of the SERT gene (short) appears to reduce the efficiency of serotonin regulation. Individuals carrying at least one short SERT allele may be at higher risk of impairments in stress-emotion system functioning under conditions of adversity, particularly perhaps, adversity during early development. Caspi and colleagues (Caspi, Sugden, & Moffit, 2003), for example, have shown that the onset of depression is associated with the short SERT allele, but only for individuals who experience more stressful life events, including being maltreated prior to puberty. Conversely, carrying two long versions of the gene seems to protect maltreated children from depression as a consequence of their maltreatment history.

In studies of rhesus monkeys, animals carrying one short copy of the SERT gene were found to be at risk for low serotonin production (Higley, Suomi, & Linnoila, 1992), high HPA axis stress responses (Fahlke et al., 2000), and an affinity for alcohol consumption if they were reared without mothers (i.e., with only other infant monkeys as attachment figures), but not if they were mother reared (Bennett et al., 2002). Conversely, monkeys with two long versions of the gene seemed relatively protected from these adverse consequences of peer-only rearing. Finally, in the repeated, unpredictable separation paradigm described earlier, it was the infants with two short SERT alleles that exhibited heightened HPA axis stress responses as a consequence of this early adversity (Sanchez et al., 2005). It is likely that the SERT–stress story is only one of many gene-environment interactions that play a role in individual differences in vulnerability to early adverse care and susceptibility to intervention. Understanding these stories should help us identify the neural systems impacted by early adverse care and may potentially help guide the selection of intervention experiences that will be most helpful for different children.

Future Directions

The work outlined above is an example of the emerging field of translational studies focused on bringing basic science to bear on clinically significant problems. When we consider young children, this work should naturally meld with intervention/ prevention research. Surprisingly, this melding of research traditions is at its earliest phase. Most intervention/prevention research designed to improve outcomes for children exposed to adverse early life histories has paid little or no attention to animal studies of the impact of early experience on the developing brain. As a consequence, there are very few intervention/prevention studies that have used preclinical research on the developing stress-emotion system to guide the measures and hypotheses of prevention/intervention studies designed to reduce the risk of psychopathology. Nonetheless, as reviewed in this chapter, there is good reason to believe that the animal work has implications for human development and that integration of this research tradition will enrich our ability to intervene effectively in children's lives.

References

Ahnert, L., Gunnar, M., Lamb, M., & Barthel, M. (2004). Transition to child care: Associations with infant-mother attachment, infant negative emotion and cortisol elevations. *Child Development, 75,* 639–650.

Ashman, S. B., Dawson, G., Panagiotides, H., Yamada, E., & Wilkinson, C. W. (2002). Stress hormone levels of children of depressed mothers. *Development & Psychopathology, 14,* 333–349.

Bennett, A. J., Lesch, K. P., Heils, A., Long, J. C., Lorenz, J. G., Shoal, S. E., et al. (2002). Early experience and serotonin transporter gene variation interact to influence primate CNS function. *Molecular Psychiatry, 7,* 118–122.

Bruce J., Tarullo, A.R., & Gunnar, M. (2006). Disinhibited social behavior among internationally adopted children (under review).

Caldji, C., Tannenbaum, B., Sharma, S., Francis, D., Plotsky, P. M., & Meaney, M. J. (1998). Maternal care during infancy regulates the development of neural systems mediating the expression of fearfulness in the rat. *Proceedings of the National Academy of Sciences of the United States of America, 95*(9), 5335–5340.

Carlson, M., & Earls, F. (1997). Psychological and neuroendocrinological sequelae of early social deprivation in institutionalized children in Romania. *Annals of the New York Academy of Sciences, 807,* 419–428.

Carrion, V. G., Weems, C. F., Ray, R. D., Glaser, B., Hessl, D., & Reiss, A. L. (2002). Diurnal salivary cortisol in pediatric posttraumatic stress disorder. *Biological Psychiatry, 51,* 575–582.

Caspi, A., Sugden, K., & Moffit, T. E. A. (2003, July 18). Influence of life stress on depression: Moderation by a polymorphism in the 5-HTT gene. *Science, 301,* 386–389.

Castle, J., Groothues, C., Bredenkamp, D., Beckett, C., O'Conner, T., & Rutter, M. (1999). Effects of qualities of early institutional care on cognitive attainment. *American Journal of Orthopsychiatry, 69,* 424–437.

Cicchetti, D., & Lynch, M. (1995). Failures in the expectable environment and their impact on individual development: the case of child maltreatment. In D. Cicchetti & D. J. Cohen (Eds.), *Developmental psychopathology* (Vol. 2, pp. 32–71). New York: Wiley.

Davidson, R. J., Lewis, M., Alloy, L. B., Amaral, D. G., Bush, G., Cohen, J., et al. (2002).

Neural and behavioral substrates of mood and mood regulation. *Biological Psychiatry, 52*(6), 478–502.

Dawson, G., & Ashman, S. B. (2000). On the origins of a vulnerability to depression: The influence of the early social environment on the development of psychobiological systems related to risk for affective disorder. In C. A. Nelson (Ed.), *The effects of adversity on neurobehavioral development: Minnesota symposia on child psychology.* (Vol. 31, pp. 245–280). Mahwah, NJ: Erlbaum.

De Bellis, M. D., Baum, A. S., Birmaher, B., Keshavan, M. S., Eccard, C. H., Boring, A. M., et al. (1999). Developmental traumatology, Part 1: Biological stress systems. *Biological Psychiatry, 9,* 1259–1270.

deKloet, R., Vreugdenhil, E., Oitzl, M., & Joels, A. (1998). Brain corticosteroid receptor balance in health and disease. *Endocrine Reviews, 19,* 269–301.

Dettling, A. C., Gunnar, M. R., & Donzella, B. (1999). Cortisol levels of young children in full-day childcare centers: Relations with age and temperament. *Psychoneuroendocrinology, 24*(5), 505–518.

Dettling, A. C., Parker, S., Lane, S. K., Sebanc, A. M., & Gunnar, M. R. (2000). Quality of care and temperament determine changes in cortisol concentrations over the day for young children in childcare. *Psychoneuroendocrinology, 25,* 819–836.

Dobbing, J. (1981). The later development of the brain and its vulnerability. In J. A. Davis & J. Dobbing (Eds.), Scientific foundations of paediatrics (pp. 766–759). London: Heinemann Medical Books.

Downey, G., & Coyne, J. C. (1990). Children of depressed parents: An integrative review. *Psychological Bulletin, 108,* 50–76.

Essex, M. J., Klein, M., Cho, E., & Kalin, N. H. (2002). Maternal stress beginning in infancy may sensitize children to later stress exposure: Effects on cortisol and behavior. *Biological Psychiatry, 52,* 776–784.

Fahlke, C., Lorenz, J. G., Long, J., Champoux, M., Suomi, S. J., & Higley, J. D. (2000). Rearing experiences and stress-induced plasma cortisol as early risk factors for excessive alcohol consumption in nonhuman primates. *Alcoholism: Clinical and Experimental Research, 24*(5), 644–650

Fisher, P. (2001). *Physical growth, cortisol, and neuropsychological functioning among maltreated preschoolers in the foster care system.* Paper presented at the Society for Research in Child Development, Minneapolis, Minnesota.

Fisher, P. A., Burraston, B., & Pears, K. (2005). The early intervention foster care program: Permanent placement outcomes from a randomized trial. *Child Maltreatment, 10,* 61–71.

Friese, E., Hesse, J., Hellhammer, J., & Hellhammer, D. (2005). A new view on hypocortisolism. *Psychoneuoendocrinology, 30,* 1010–1016.

Goodyer, I. M., Herbert, J., & Tamplin, A. (2003). Psychoendocrine antecedents of persistent first-episode major depression in adolescents: A community-based longitudinal enquiry. *Psychological Medicine, 33,* 601–610.

Gunnar, M. (2003). Integrating neuroscience and psychosocial approaches in the study of early experiences. In J. A. King, C. F. Ferris, & I. I. Lederhendler (Eds.), *Roots of mental illness in children* (Vol. 1008, pp. 238–247). New York: New York Academy of Sciences.

Gunnar, M., Brodersen, L., Krueger, K., & Rigatuso, J. (1996). Dampening of behavioral and adrenocortical reactivity during early infancy: Normative changes and individual differences. *Child Development, 67,* 877–889.

Gunnar, M., Mangelsdorf, S., Larson, M., & Hertsgaard, L. (1989). Attachment, temperament and adrenocortical activity in infancy: A study of psychoendocrine regulation. *Developmental Psychology, 25,* 355–363.

Gunnar, M., & Vazquez, D. M. (2001). Low cortisol and a flattening of the expected daytime rhythm: Potential indices of risk in human development. *Development and Psychopathology, 13*(3), 516–538.

Gunnar, M., & Vazquez, D. M. (2006). Stress neurobiology and developmental psychopathology. In D. Cicchetti & D. Cohen (Eds.), *Developmental psychopathology: Vol. 2. Developmental neuroscience* (2nd ed., pp. 533–577). New York: Wiley.

Gunnar, M. R. (1992). Reactivity of the hypothalamic-pituitary-adrenocortical system to stressors in normal infants and children. *Pediatrics, 90*(3), 491–497.

Gunnar, M. R., & Donzella, B. (2002). Social regulation of the cortisol levels in early human development. *Psychoneuroendocrinology, 27,* 199–220.

Gunnar, M. R., Morison, S. J., Chisholm, K., & Schuder, M. (2001). Salivary cortisol levels in children adopted from Romanian orphanages. *Development and Psychopathology, 13,* 611–628.

Habib, K. E., Gold, P., & Chrousos, G. (2001). Neuroendocrinology of stress. *Endocrinology and Metabolism Clinics of North America, 30*(3), 695–728.

Halligan, S., Herbert, J., Goodyer, I. M., & Murray, L. (2004). Exposure to postnatal depression predicts elevated cortisol in adolescent offspring. *Biological Psychiatry, 55,* 376–381.

Heim, C., Ehlert, U., & Hellhammer, D. K. (2000). The potential role of hypocortisolism in the pathophysiology of stress-related bodily disorders. *Psychoneuroendocrinology, 25,* 1–35.

Heinrichs, S. C., & Koob, G. F. (2004). Corticotropin-releasing factor in brain: a role in activation, arousal, and affect regulation. *The Journal of Pharmacology and Experimental Therapeutics, 311*(2), 427–440.

Heinrichs, S. C., Menzaghi, F., Pich, E. M., Britton, K. T., & Koob, G. F. (1995). The role of CRF in behavioral aspects of stress. *Annals of the New York Academy of Sciences, USA, 771,* 92–104.

Higley, J. D., Suomi, S. J., & Linnoila, M. (1992). A longitudinal study of CSF monoamine metabolite and plasma cortisol concentrations in young rhesus monkeys: Effects of early experience, age, sex, and stress on continuity of individual differences. *Biological Psychiatry, 32,* 127–145.

Jacobson, S. W., Bihun, J. T., Chiodo, L. M., & Berube, R. L. (1994). Differences in cortisol levels in infants exposed prenatally to alcohol and cocaine. *Infant Behavior and Development, 17,* 722.

Johnson, D. E. (2000). The impact of orphanage rearing on growth and development. In C. A. Nelson (Ed.), *The effects of adversity on neurobehavioral development: Minnesota symposia on child psychology* (Vol. 31, pp. 113–162). Mahwah, NJ: Erlbaum.

Kaufman, J., Birmaher, B., Perel, J., Dahl, R. E., Moreci, P., Nelson, B., et al. (1997). The corticotropin-releasing hormone challenge in depressed abused, depressed nonabused, and normal control children. *Biological Psychiatry, 42,* 669–679.

Kertes, D. A., Gunnar, M., Madsen, N. J., & Long, J. (in press). Early deprivation and home basal cortisol levels: A study of internationally-adopted children. *Development & Psychopathology.*

Kroupina, M., Gunnar, M., & Johnson, D. (1997). *Report on salivary cortisol levels in a Russian baby home.* Minneapolis, MN: Institute of Child Development, University of Minnesota.

Lazarus, R. S., & Folkman, S. (1984). *Stress, appraisal, and coping.* New York: Springer.

LeDoux, J. E., & Phelps, E. A. (2000). Emotional networks in the brain. In M. Lewis & J. M. Haviland-Jones (Eds.), *Handbook of emotions* (2nd ed., pp. 157–172). New York: Guilford.

Lewis, M., & Ramsay, D. S. (1995). Developmental change in infants' responses to stress. *Child Development, 66,* 657–670.

Liu, D., Diorio, J., Tannenbaum, B., Caldji, C., Francis, D., Freedman, A., et al. (1997). Maternal care, hippocampal glucocorticoid receptors, and hypothalamic-pituitary-adrenal responses to stress. *Science, 227,* 1659–1662.

Lupien, S. J., King, S., Meaney, M. J., & McEwen, B. S. (2000). Child's stress hormone levels correlate with mother's socioeconomic status and depressive state. *Biological Psychiatry, 48,* 976–980.

McEwen, B. S., Angulo, J., Cameron, H. A., Chao, H. M., Daniels, D., Gannon, M. N., et al. (1992). Paradoxical effects of adrenal steroids on the brain: Protection versus degeneration. *Biological Psychiatry, 31,* 177–199.

National Institute of Child Health and Human Development (NICHD) Early Child Care Research Network. (2000). Characteristics and quality of child care for toddlers and preschoolers. *Applied Developmental Science, 4*(3), 116–135.

Phillips, M. L., Drevets, W. C., Rauch, S. L., & Lane, R. (2003). Neurobiology of emotion perception II: Implications for major psychiatric disorders. *Biological Psychiatry, 54,* 515–528.

Pitkanen, A., Savander, V., & LeDoux, J. E. (1997). Organization of intra-amygdaloid circuitries in the rat: An emerging framework for understanding function of the amygdala. In J. Smith & G. Schoenwolf (Eds.), *Neurulation* (pp. 517–523). Elsevier Science.

Porges, S. W. (1995a). Orienting in a defensive world: Mammalian modifications of our evolutionary heritage. A polyvagal theory. *Psychophysiology, 32,* 301–318.

Porges, S. W. (1995b). Cardiac vagal tone: A physiological index of stress. *Neuroscience and Biobehavioral Reviews, 19*(2), 225–233.

Reynolds, R. M., Walker, B. R., Syddall, H. E., Wood, P. J., Phillips, D. I. W., & Whorwood, C. B. (2001). Altered control of cortisol secretion in adult men with low birthweight and cardiovascular risk factors. Journal of *Clinical Endocrinology & Metabolism, 86,* 245–250.

Rosen, J. B., & Schulkin, J. (1998). From normal fear to pathological anxiety. *Psychological Review, 105*(2), 325–350.

Rosenfield, P., Suchecki, D., & Levine, S. (1992). Multifactorial regulation of the hypothalamic-pituitary-adrenal axis during development. *Neuroscience and Biobehavioral Reviews, 16,* 553–568.

Rutter, M. (1998). Developmental catch-up, and deficit, following adoption after severe global early privation. English and Romanian Adoptees (ERA) Study Team. *Journal of Child Psychology and Psychiatry and Allied Disciplines, 39*(4), 465–476.

Rutter, M., Kreppner, J. M., O'Connor, T. G., & English and Romanian Adoptees (ERA) Study Team. (2001). Specificity and heterogeneity in children's responses to profound institutional privation. *British Journal of Psychiatry, 179,* 97–103.

Sanchez, M. M., Ladd, C. O., & Plotsky, P. M. (2001). Early adverse experience as a developmental risk factor for later psychopathology: Evidence from rodent and primate models. *Development and Psychopathology, 13,* 419–449.

Sanchez, M. M., Noble, P. M., Lyon, C. K., Plotsky, P., Davis, D., Nemeroff, C. B., et al. (2005). Alterations of diurnal cortisol rhythm and acoustic startle response in non-human primates with adverse rearing experience. *Biological Psychiatry, 57,* 373–381.

Sapolsky, R. M. (1996). Why stress is bad for your brain. *Science, 273*(749–750).

Sapolsky, R. M. (1997). McEwen-induced modulation of endocrine history: A partial review. *Stress, 2*(1), 1–12.

Sapolsky, R. M., & Meaney, M. J. (1986). Maturation of the adrenocortical stress response: Neuroendocrine control mechanisms and the stress hyporesponsive period. *Brain Research Reviews, 11,* 65–76.

Sapolsky, R. M., Romero, L. M., & Munck, A. U. (2000). How do glucocorticoids influence stress responses? Integrating permissive, suppressive, stimulatory, and preparative actions. *Endocrine Reviews, 21,* 55–89.

Selye, H. (1977, March 21, 1977). Secret of coping with stress. *U.S. News & World Report,* 51–53.

Smider, N. A., Essex, M. J., Kalin, N. H., Buss, K. A., Klein, M. H., Davidson, R. J., et al. (2002). Salivary cortisol as a predictor of socioemotional adjustment during kindergarten: A prospective study. *Child Development, 73*(1), 75–92.

Smith, M. A., Kim, S. Y., Van Oers, H. J., & Levine, S. (1997). Maternal deprivation and stress induce immediate early genes in the infant rat brain. *Endocrinology, 138*(11), 4622–4628.

Spangler, G., & Schieche, M. (1998). Emotional and adrenocortical responses of infants to the strange situation: The differential function of emotional expression. *International Journal of Behavioral Development, 22*(4), 681–706.

Spear, L. P. (2000). The adolescent brain and age-related behavioral manifestations. *Neuroscience and Biobehavioral Reviews, 24,* 417–463.

Strand, F. L. (1999). *Neuropeptides: Regulators of physiological processes.* Cambridge, MA: MIT Press.

Van Bockstaele, E. J., Bajic, D., Proudfit, H., & Valentino, R. J. (2001). Topographic architecture of stress-related pathways targeting the noradrenergic locus coeruleus. *Physiology and Behavior, 73,* 273–283.

Weaver, I. C., Cervoni, N., Champagne, F. A., D'Alessio, A. C., Sharma, S., Seckl, J. R., et al. (2004). Epigenetic programming by maternal behavior. *Nature Neuroscience, 7*(8), 847–854.

Yehuda, R. (2000). Biology of Posttraumatic Stress Disorder. Journal of Clinical *Psychiatry, 61*(Suppl. 7), 15–21.

Chapter 7

Maternal Programming of Defensive
Responses Through Sustained
Effects on Gene Expression

Michael J. Meaney

There are profound maternal effects on individual differences in defensive responses and reproductive strategies in species ranging literally from plants to
insects to birds. Maternal effects commonly reflect the quality of the environment and are most likely mediated by the quality of the maternal provision (egg,
propagule, etc.), which in turn determines growth rates and adult phenotype. In
this chapter we review data from studies of the rat that suggest comparable forms
of maternal effects on defensive responses to stress, which are mediated by the
effects of variations in maternal behavior on gene expression. Under conditions
of environmental adversity, maternal effects enhance the capacity for defensive
responses in the offspring. In mammals, these effects appear to "program" emotional, cognitive, and endocrine systems toward increased sensitivity to adversity. In environments with an increased level of adversity, such effects can be
considered adaptive, enhancing the probability of offspring survival to sexual
maturity; the cost is that of an increased risk for multiple forms of pathology in
later life.

We begin by providing an overview of the long-term effects of early stress on
the subsequent development of both physical and mental disorder; then we discuss the role of maternal care during the pre- and postnatal periods as an early
source of these effects, mainly examining research in our laboratory with the rat.
We then review potential mediators of the effects of maternal behavior on gene

expression and conclude with the questions that remain to be answered in regard to the effects of early stress on pathology.

The Role of Early Life Stress

Epidemiological studies reveal the importance of family function and early life events as predictors of mental health in adulthood (Repetti et al., 2002). Such studies show that the quality of family life influences the development of individual differences in vulnerability to illness throughout life. Importantly, such effects include vulnerability for obesity, metabolic disorders, and heart disease, as well as affective disorders and drug abuse (e.g., Feletti et al., 1998; Lissau & Sorenson, 1994; McCauley et al., 1997). Recent findings from epidemiological studies (e.g., Caspi et al., 2003), as well as from primate models (e.g., Bennett et al., 2002), further suggest that developmentally determined vulnerability can emerge from the interaction between genotype and early environmental events, including early life adversity. In each of these studies, the consequences associated with a genetic variant (the short variant of the serotonin transporter promoter) were defined by the quality of parent–offspring interactions. As exemplified in these wonderful studies, the critical questions for developmentalists concern the identity of the relevant genomic targets, the nature of the gene–environment interactions and their relation to specific phenotypic outcomes.

Such studies have fueled a renewed interest among neuroscientists in the effects of early environment on neural development and emotional/cognitive function. From the basic sciences, "stress diathesis" models have emerged as explanations for the effects of early life on health in adulthood and suggest that adversity in early life alters the development of neural systems in a manner that predisposes individuals to disease in adulthood. These models place considerable emphasis on the influence of early experience on the development of defensive responses and the relevance of these effects for vulnerability over the life span. Chronic illness is thought to emerge as a function of the altered responses to environmental demand (stressors) in conjunction with an increased level of prevailing adversity.

There are two critical assumptions here: first, that prolonged activation of neural and hormonal responses to stressors can promote illness, and second, that early environmental events influence the development of stress responses. There is strong evidence in favor of both ideas. In humans, physical and/or sexual abuse in early life, poor parental bonding, and family dysfunction increase endocrine and autonomic responses to stress in adulthood and adolescence (de Bellis et al., 1994; Essex et al., 2002; Heim et al., 2000, 2002; Luecken & Lemery, 2004; Pruessner et al., 2004), as well as dysfunctional cognitive processing of potentially threatening stimuli.

There is evidence for comparable developmental effects in primates (Bennett et al., 2002; Higley et al., 1991; Suomi, 1997) and rodents (e.g., Newport et al., 2002; Plotsky & Meaney, 1993; Plotsky et al., 2005), albeit with models that rely on prolonged periods of separation of parent and offspring. Moreover, sustained exposure to elevated levels of stress hormones, including corticotrophin-releasing factor (CRF), catecholamines, most notably norepinepherine, and glucocorticoids can actively promote the development of a diverse range of high-risk conditions, such as visceral obesity, hypertension, and insulin intolerance, or overt pathology, including diabetes, depression, anxiety disorders, drug addiction, and multiple forms of coronary heart disease (Arborelius et al., 1999; Chrousos & Gold, 1992; Dallman et al., 2001, 2004; McEwen, 1998; Schulkin et al., 1994).

The relation between the quality of the early environment and health in adulthood appears to be mediated by parental influences on the development of neural systems that underlie the expression of behavioral and endocrine responses to stress (Meaney, 2001). There is strong evidence for such parental mediation in developmental psychology. For example, the effects of poverty on emotional and cognitive development are mediated by variations in parent-offspring interactions: If parental care factors are statistically controlled, there no longer remains any discernible effect of poverty on child development (e.g., Conger et al., 1994; McLloyd, 1998). Such findings are not surprising. Poverty imposes considerable stress on the family unit, and stressors seriously compromise the quality of parental care (Hart & Risley, 1995; Repetti et al., 2002). In humans, high levels of maternal stress during the transition to parenthood are associated with depressed/anxious mood states and less sensitive parent-child interactions that, in turn, influence the quality of parent-child attachment (Fleming, 1988; Fleming et al., 1999; Goldstein et al., 1996). Unstable/stressful environments, such as those prevailing under conditions of poverty, are associated with greater variability in the quality of infant-mother attachments (Vaughn et al., 1979). Parents who experience poverty or other environmental stressors more frequently experience negative emotions such as irritability, depression, and anxious moods, which can then lead to more punitive forms of parenting (Belsky, 1997; Conger et al., 1984; Grolnick, 2002). Reduced education of parents, low income, multiple children, the absence of social support, and single parenthood predict forms of parenting (verbal threats, pushing or grabbing the child, emotional neglect, overt physical abuse, and more controlling attitudes toward child) that compromise cognitive development and result in more anxious and behaviorally inhibited children.

In this review, we consider environmental effects occurring during the early postnatal period. There is considerable evidence for the effects of adversity on the mother and offspring during the prenatal period (e.g., Glover & O'Connor, 2002; Matthews & Meaney, 2005; C. M. McCormick et al., 1995; Seckl, 2001; Weinstock, 1997), and thus, the influence of adversity is best seen as being continuous, with effects through development at multiple genomic targets and influences on a wide range of functional outcomes. Importantly, prenatal adversity is also associated with increased HPA and autonomic responses to stressors (Amiel-Tison et al., 2004; Chapillon et al., 2002; Maccari et al., 2003; Wadhwa et al., 2001; Weinstock, 2001).

Support for the basic elements of stress diathesis models appears compelling. Adversity during perinatal life alters development in a manner that seems likely to promote vulnerability, especially for stress-related diseases. Diathesis-stress models describe the interaction between development, including the potential influence of genomic variations and the prevailing level of stress in predicting health outcomes. Such models could identify both the origins and the nature of vulnerability. However, much of the evidence from both human and nonhuman models remains correlational. How might parental care affect the development of neural systems that regulate stress responses? Are such effects apparent only under conditions of extreme adversity (physical or sexual abuse, persistent emotional neglect, etc.), as some have suggested (Scarr, 1997)? Or, are parental effects part of normal developmental processes? We address these fundamental questions using an animal model that examines the developmental consequences of variations in mother-infant interactions.

Maternal Care in the Rat: Behavioral and Endocrine Responses to Stress

Central corticotropin-releasing factor (CRF) systems furnish the critical signal for the activation of behavioral, emotional, autonomic, and endocrine responses to stressors. There are two major CRF pathways regulating the expression of these stress responses. First, a CRF pathway extends from the periventricular nucleus of the hypothalamus (PVNh) to the anterior pituitary, which serves as the principal mechanism for the transduction of a neural signal into a pituitary-adrenal response (Antoni, 1993; Herman et al., 2003; Plotsky, 1991; Rivier & Plotsky, 1986; Whitnall, 1993). In responses to stressors, CRF, as well as co-secretagogues such as arginine vasopressin, are released from PVNh neurons into the portal blood supply of the anterior pituitary, where it stimulates the synthesis and release of adrenocorticotropin hormone (ACTH). Pituitary ACTH, in turn, causes the release of glucocorticoids from the adrenal gland. CRF synthesis and release is subsequently inhibited through a glucocorticoid negative-feedback system mediated by both mineralocorticoid and glucocorticoid receptors in a number of brain regions including, and perhaps especially, in the hippocampus (de Kloet et al., 1998; Sapolsky et al., 2000). For example, selective disruption of the glucocorticoid receptor gene in the hippocampus and cortex that is unique to adulthood results in negative feedback impairments and increased HPA activity (Boyle et al., 2005).

CRF neurons in the central nucleus of the amygdala project directly to the locus coeruleus and increase the firing rate of locus coeruleus neurons, resulting in increased noradrenaline release in the vast terminal fields of this ascending noradrenergic system. Infusion of CRF increases extracellular noradrenaline levels (Emoto et al., 1993; Lavicky & Dunn, 1993; Page & Valentino, 1994; Valentino et al., 1998). The amygdaloid (BNST) CRF projection to the locus coeruleus (Gray & Bingaman, 1996; Koegler-Muly et al., 1993; Moga & Gray, 1989; Valentino et al., 1998; Van Bockstaele et al., 1996) is also critical for the expression of behavioral responses to stress (Bakshi et al., 2000; Butler et al., 1990; Davis & Whalen, 2001; Koob et al., 1994; Liang et al., 1992; Schulkin et al., 1994; Stenzel-Poore et al., 1994; Swiergiel et al., 1993). Hence, the CRF neurons in the PVNh and the central nucleus of the amygdala serve as important mediators of both behavioral and endocrine responses to stress.

We examine the relation between maternal care and the development of behavioral and endocrine responses to stress in the Long-Evans rat using a rather simple model of naturally occurring variations in maternal behavior over the first 8 days after birth (Champagne et al., 2003). We characterize individual differences in maternal behavior through direct observation of mother-pup interactions in normally reared animals. These observations reveal considerable variation in two forms of maternal behavior—licking/grooming (LG) of pups and arched-back nursing (ABN; Stern, 1997). Licking/grooming includes both body as well as anogenital licking. Arched-back nursing, also referred to as "crouching," is characterized by a dam nursing her pups with her back conspicuously arched and legs splayed outward. Although common, it is not the only posture from which dams nurse. A blanket posture represents a more relaxed version of the arched-back position in which the mother is almost lying on the suckling pups. As you can imagine, it provides substantially less opportunity for pup movement such as nipple switching. Dams also nurse from their sides and often will move from one posture to another over the course of a nursing bout. Interestingly, the frequency of LG and ABN is correlated across animals and thus we are able to define mothers according to both behaviors, as High or Low LG-ABN mothers. For the sake of most of the studies described here, High and Low LG-ABN mothers are females whose scores on both measures were ± 1 SD above (High) or below (Low) the mean for their cohort.

Importantly, High and Low LG-ABN mothers do not differ in the amount of contact time with pups. Differences in the frequency of LG or ABN do not occur simply as a function of time in contact with pups. High and Low LG-ABN mothers raise a comparable number of pups to weaning, and there are no differences in the weaning weights of the pups, suggesting an adequate level of maternal care across the groups. These findings also suggest that we are examining the consequences of variations in maternal care that occur within a normal range. Indeed, the frequency of both LG and ABN are normally distributed across large populations of lactating female rats (Champagne et al., 2003).

One critical question concerns the potential consequences of these differences in maternal behavior for the development of behavioral and neuroendocrine responses to stress (Caldji et al., 1998; Liu et al., 1997; Weaver et al., 2004a,b). As adults, the offspring of High LG-ABN mothers show reduced plasma ACTH and corticosterone responses to acute stress by comparison to the adult offspring of Low LG-ABN mothers. As mentioned above, circulating glucocorticoids regulate HPA activity in corticolimbic structures, such as the hippocampus. High LG-ABN offspring show significantly increased expression of genes that control hippocampal glucocorticoid receptors, enhanced glucocorticoid negative feedback sensitivity and decreased hypothalamic CRH mRNA levels. Moreover, Liu et al. (1997) found that the magnitude of the corticosterone response to acute stress was significantly correlated with the frequency of both maternal LG ($r = -.61$) and ABN ($r = -0.64$) during the first week of life, as was the level of hippocampal glucocorticoid receptor mRNA and hypothalamic CRH mRNA expression (all r's > 0.70).

The offspring of the High and Low LG-ABN mothers also differ in behavioral responses to novelty (Caldji et al., 1998; Francis et al., 1999). As adults, the offspring of the High LG-ABN mothers show decreased startle responses, increased open-field exploration, and shorter latencies to eat food provided in a novel environment. The offspring of Low LG-ABN mothers also show greater burying in the defensive burying paradigm (Menard et al., 2005), which involves an *active* response to a threat. The offspring of the High LG-ABN mothers also show decreased CRF receptor levels in the locus coeruleus and increased GABA$_A$/BZ receptor levels in the basolateral and central nucleus of the amygdala, as well as in the locus coeruleus (Caldji et al., 1998, 2003) and decreased CRF mRNA expression in the central nucleus of the amygdala. Note that BZ agonists suppress CRF expression in the amygdala (Owens et al., 2001). Predictably, stress-induced increases in PVNh levels of noradrenaline that are normally stimulated by CRF were significantly higher in the offspring of the Low LG-ABN offspring (Caldji et al., 1999).

Effects of Maternal Care on Genetic Expression

Maternal care during the first week of life is associated with stable individual differences in the expression of genes in brain regions that regulate stress reactivity. The adult offspring of High LG-ABN mothers show significantly higher levels of GABA$_A$/BZ receptor binding in the basolateral and central nuclei of the amygdala as well as the locus coeruleus. These findings provide a mechanism for increased GABAergic inhibition of amygdala-locus coeruleus activity. A series of in situ hybridization studies (Caldji et al., 2003) illustrate the molecular mechanism for these differences in receptor binding and suggest that variations in maternal care might actually permanently alter the subunit composition of the GABA$_A$ receptor complex in the offspring. These studies suggest that differences in $GABA_A$/BZ receptor binding are not simply due to a deficit in genetic expression in the offspring of the Low LG-ABN mothers, but to an apparently "active" attempt to maintain a specific $GABA_A$/BZ receptor profile in selected brain regions.

The critical question concerns the relation between these "profiles" and fear-related behavior. Studies with animals bearing mutations of various $GABA_A$/BZ receptor subunits suggest that these mutations do indeed lead to decreased BZ receptor binding and increased fearfulness. Furthermore, individual differences in behavioral and neuroendocrine responses to stress in the rat are associated with naturally occurring variations in maternal care. The effects of these variations might serve as a possible mechanism by which selected traits are transmitted from one generation to another. Indeed, Low LG-ABN mothers are more fearful and show increased HPA responses to stress by comparison to High LG-ABN dams (Francis et al., 2000). Individual differences in stress reactivity are apparently transmitted across generations: Fearful mothers beget more stress reactive offspring. The obvious question is whether the transmission of these traits occurs only as a function of genomic-based inheritance. If this is the case, then the differences in maternal behavior may simply be an epiphenomenon, and not causally related to the development of individual differences in stress responses. The issue is not one of inheritance, but the mode of inheritance.

The results of cross-fostering studies provide evidence for a nongenomic transmission of individual differences in stress reactivity (Francis et al., 1999). The critical groups of interest are the biological offspring of Low LG-ABN mothers fostered onto High LG-ABN dams, and vice versa. The results are consistent with the idea that variations in maternal care are causally related to individual differences in the behavior of the offspring. The biological offspring of Low LG-ABN dams reared by High LG-ABN mothers are significantly less fearful under conditions of novelty than are the offspring reared by Low LG-ABN mothers, including the biological offspring of High LG-ABN mothers (Francis et al., 1999). Subsequent studies reveal similar findings for hippocampal glucocorticoid receptor expression and for the differences in $GABA_A$ receptor subunit expression in the amygdala (Caldji et al., 2003). These findings suggest that individual differences in patterns of gene expression and stress responses can be directly linked to maternal care over the first week of life.

Maternal Care and Development

Tactile stimulation from the mother stimulates the release of growth hormone and inhibits that of adrenal glucocorticoids in the offspring (Levine, 1994; Schanberg et al., 1984). Pups exposed to prolonged periods of maternal separation show increased levels of glucocorticoids and decreased levels of growth hormone. These effects can be reversed with "stroking" with a brush, a manipulation that mimics the tactile stimulation derived from maternal licking/grooming. Maternal deprivation also decreases the expression of brain-derived neurotrophic factor (BDNF) expression in neonates (Roceri et al., 2002; Zhang et al., 1997). The results of these studies suggest that tactile stimulation derived from maternal licking/grooming can serve to promote an endocrine or paracrine state that fosters growth and development. cDNA array analyses (Diorio et al., 2000) reveal major classes of maternal effects on hippocampal gene expression in postnatal Day 6 offspring, including (1) genes related to cellular metabolic activity (e.g., glucose transporter, cFOS, cytochrome oxidase, LDL receptor), (2) genes related to glutamate receptor function, including effects on the glycine receptor, as well as those mentioned for the NMDA receptor subunits, and (3) genes encoding for growth factors, including BDNF, bFGF, and ß-NGF. In each case, expression was greater than 3-fold higher in hippocampal samples from offspring of High compared to Low LG-ABN mothers.

Variations in maternal care are also associated with individual differences in the synaptic development of selected neural systems that mediate cognitive development. As adults, the offspring of High LG-ABN mothers show enhanced spatial learning/memory in the Morris water maze (Liu et al., 2000), as well as in object recognition (Bredy et al., 2003a,b). The performance in both tasks is dependent on hippocampal function (e.g., Morris et al., 1986; Whishaw, 1998), and maternal care alters hippocampal synaptogenesis. At either Day 18 or Day 90, there was evidence of increased synapse formation/survival in hippocampal samples from the High LG-ABN offspring. More recent studies reveal significant effects of maternal care on neuron survival in the hippocampus (Bredy et al., 2004), as well as on hippocampal LTP (Bredy et al., 2003a,b). There was increased evidence for long-term neuron survival of cells generated during the first week of postnatal life in the offspring of High compared with Low LG-ABN mothers.

Naturally occurring variations in maternal licking/grooming and arched-back nursing are associated with the development of cholinergic innervation to the hippocampus, as well as differences in the expression of NMDA receptor subunit mRNAs. These findings provide a mechanism for the differences observed in spatial learning and memory in adult animals. In the adult rat, spatial learning and memory is dependent on hippocampal integrity; lesions of the hippocampus result in profound spatial learning impairments. These results are also consistent with the idea that maternal behavior actively stimulates hippocampal synaptogenesis in offspring through systems known to mediate experience-dependent neural development (e.g., Kirkwood et al., 1993; Schatz, 1990).

These findings suggest that maternal care in the rat directly influences hippocampal development through effect on the expression of genes involved in both neuron survival and synaptic development. The group differences in performance in the Morris water maze are consistent with a maternal effect on cognitive performance in adulthood. However, the Morris water maze is a model of escape learning that, by definition, involves an aversive component, which provides the motivation for escape. The water maze is an interesting task for the current discussion because it provides an opportunity to examine cognitive performance under stressful conditions. In sequence, the animal must contend with (1) removal from the home cage, (2) transport to the testing area, (3) placement into the pool of water, murky at that, and (4) the uncertainty at each stage of testing. Initially, most animals behave in a manner similar to that of an open-field test, circling the perimeter and remaining close to the walls (i.e., thigmotaxis). There is little opportunity for learning so long as the animal refuses to enter the center area of the swim maze where the platform is located. The tendency to remain close to the walls and reluctance to enter the center area is commonly associated with a fear response to the environment. Not surprisingly, thigmotaxis is significantly more prevalent in the offspring of Low compared to High LG-ABN mothers. The difference in thigmotaxis is reversed with postweaning environmental enrichment (Bredy et al., 2003a,b). Moreover, Smythe and colleagues (Smythe et al., 1996, 1998) show that blockade of hippocampal cholinergic input results in increased fear behavior under conditions of novelty. The effect is blocked with administration of acute benzodiazepine, an anxiety reducer. The offspring of Low LG-ABN mothers show decreased hippocampal cholinergic innervation, which might well explain the increased thigmotaxis and thus the impaired performance in the Morris water maze.

The hippocampus is also implicated in processing information related to the discrimination of novelty/familiarity (Habib & Lepage, 2000), and thus the actual nature of the behavioral differences between the offspring of High and Low LG-ABN mothers in settings such as the Morris water maze become difficult to disentangle. Rather than becoming lost in the debate over whether such differences emerge due to alterations in emotional *or* cognitive function, which is clearly beyond resolution at this time, it is probably best to simply restate the findings: The offspring of High and Low LG-ABN mothers differ in hippocampal development and plasticity, behavioral responses to novelty, and performance in tests of episodic learning and memory. Although the cause-effect relations embedded within these findings remain to be determined, the important point concerns the pronounced maternal effect on cognitive performance under stressful conditions.

Maternal Programming of Attentional Systems

Performance on tests of object recognition or the Morris water maze also depends on the ability of animals to attend and process relevant stimuli. The medial prefrontal cortex (mPFC) plays a pivotal role in so-called executive functions, in which information is processed on line through working memory. Neurons within the mPFC are involved in maintaining task-relevant information "on line" for brief periods (Fuster, 1997) and subserve processes of working memory and sustained attention, both essential components for structuring goal-directed behaviors.

Dopamine plays a critical modulatory role, optimizing the activity of mPFC neurons (Murphy et al., 1996; Williams & Goldman-Rakic, 1995). These functions appear to be modified by postnatal maternal care through effects on genes that influence extracellular dopamine signals in the mPFC.

Prepulse inhibition (PPI) refers to the attenuation of an acoustic startle response (ASR) to a loud noise that is immediately preceded by a weaker acoustic stimulus (Geyer et al., 1990). PPI is sensitive to manipulations of mesocorticolimbic dopamine transmission in the nucleus accumbens (Geyer et al., 1990, 2001; Swerdlow et al., 2001; Zhang et al., 2000) and mPFC (Bubser & Koch, 1994; Ellenbroek et al., 1999). The development of the mesocortical dopamine system and sensory gating, as measured by PPI, are sensitive to postnatal environmental conditions (Brake et al., 2004; Cilia et al., 2001; Ellenbroek et al., 1998; Le Pen & Moreau, 2002; but also see Weiss et al., 2001).

The offspring of Low LG-ABN mothers exhibit decreased PPI and show more pronounced, longer-lasting dopamine stress responses in the left mPFC compared to the offspring of High LG-ABN mothers (Zhang et al., 2005). There are no differences in the right mPFC dopamine response to stress. Both the prelimbic and infralimbic areas of the mPFC are involved in the modulation of PPI. Nevertheless, the relationship between frontal dopamine activity and attention is not simple, with evidence that either deficits or excess dopamine produces attentional deficits (Arnsten, 2000). Nevertheless, the stress-induced increase in dopamine in the left mPFC is 2–3 times higher than that in the offspring of High LG-ABN mothers, which would suggest the possibility of a dopamine-induced disruption of attention and working memory.

Recent findings from the Fleming lab support this idea. Lovic and Fleming (2004) found that as adults, pups reared artificially in complete absence of maternal care show deficits in reversal learning, forming an attentional set (measured by intradimensional shifts), and shifting attention (measured by extradimensional shifts), with no deficits in simple and compound stimulus discriminations (Lovic & Fleming, 2004). In normally reared animals, this same pattern of behavior is produced through lesions of either the prefrontal cortex or the hippocampus (Birrell & Brown, 2000; Li & Shao, 1998; Murray & Riddley, 1999). The effects of artificial rearing can be at least partially reversed during the first weeks of life by additional tactile stimulation through stroking pups with an artist paintbrush, which mimics the tactile stimulation afforded through licking/grooming by the rat mother. These findings are consistent with the idea that the tactile stimulation associated with maternal licking/grooming alters the mesocortical dopamine system and performance on attentional tests.

The increased dopamine response to stress in the offspring of Low LG-ABN mothers is accompanied by decreased mPFC expression of catechol-*O*-methyl transferase (COMT) by comparison to levels observed in samples from High-LG offspring (Zhang et al., 2005). COMT is a postsynaptic enzyme that methylates dopamine in the mPFC and is the primary form of dopamine clearance in the mPFC (Matsumoto et al., 2003). COMT is highly expressed in the mPFC (Matsumoto et al., 2003), and COMT knockout mice show increases in mPFC dopamine concentrations (Gogos et al., 1998). COMT levels are significantly increased in the mPFC in adult offspring of High compared with Low LG-ABN mothers (Zhang et al., 2005), a difference that may contribute to the different cortical dopamine response to stress. However, this effect alone cannot explain the difference in stress-induced mPFC dopamine levels because the alteration in COMT expression unlike that for the dopamine stress response is apparent in both hemispheres.

Environmental Regulation of Maternal Behavior

The argument presented here is that environmental influences shape the development of defensive responses in early life, and that these environmental effects are mediated by variations in parental investment. If parental care is to serve as the mediator for the effects of environmental adversity on development, then there must be a predictable relation between the quality of the environment and parental care. There is considerable evidence for a relationship between environmental adversity and parental care in humans (Fleming, 1999; Repetti et al., 2002). Such studies are, of course, correlational. Perhaps the most compelling evidence for a direct effect of environmental adversity on parent-infant interactions emerges from the studies of Rosenblum, Coplan, and colleagues with nonhuman primates (Coplan et al., 1996, 1998; Rosenblum & Andrews, 1994). Bonnet macaque mother-infant dyads were maintained under one of three foraging conditions: Low Foraging Demand (LFD), in which food was readily available, High Foraging Demand (HFD), in which ample food was available but required long periods of searching, and Variable Foraging Demand (VFD), a mixture of the two conditions on a schedule that did not allow for predictability. At the time that these conditions were imposed, there were no differences in the nature of mother-infant interactions. However, following a number of months of these conditions, there were highly significant differences in mother-infant interactions. The VFD condition was clearly the most disruptive. Mother-infant conflict increased in the VFD condition. Infants of mothers housed under these conditions were significantly more timid and fearful. These infants showed signs of depression commonly observed in maternally separated macaque infants. Remarkably these reactions are apparent even when the infants are in contact with their mothers. As adolescents, the infants reared in the VFD conditions are more fearful, submissive, and showed less social play behavior.

More recent studies demonstrate the effects of these conditions on the development of neural systems that mediate behavioral and endocrine response to stress. As adults, monkeys reared under VFD conditions showed increased CSF levels of CRF (Coplan et al., 1996, 1998). Increased central CRF drive would suggest altered noradrenergic and serotonergic responses to stress, and this is exactly what was seen in adolescent VFD-reared animals. It will be fascinating to see whether these traits are then transmitted to the next generation.

A critical issue here is that of the effect of environmental adversity on maternal behavior. One might well wonder how variations in maternal behavior in the rat maintained in the constancy of laboratory animal housing fit within such a model. Indeed, the variations in pup licking/grooming described above occur in the presence of a rather stable environment (at least physically). We think that the explanation for this apparent paradox lies in the relation between anxiety and maternal behavior (Fleming, 1999; Francis et al., 2000; Meaney, 2001). In humans and laboratory rats, anxiety predicts maternal sensitivity to pups; indeed, Fleming (1988) argued that among human females, anxiety was the best predictor of maternal sensitivity to her infant. This idea is consistent with several clinical studies suggesting that environmental stressors alter human parental behavior through effects on mood and general emotional well-being (see above). Importantly, Low LG-ABN mothers are significantly more fearful than are High LG-ABN dams (Francis et al., 2000).

If this idea has merit, then chronic stress, which renders laboratory rats more anxious, should alter maternal behavior. Female rats exposed to stress during pregnancy show increased retrieval latencies (Fride et al., 1985; Kinsely et al., 1988; Moore & Power, 1986), a finding that would seem to reflect an effect of stress on maternal responsivity. Gestational stress in the rat decreases the frequency of pup licking/grooming during lactation (Champagne & Meaney, 2000; Smythe et al., 2004). We examined the effect of such gestational stress on maternal behavior in High and Low LG-ABN mothers (Champagne & Meaney, 2006). Females previously characterized as High or Low LG-ABN mothers with their first litter were exposed to restraint stress during the last half of gestation or to control conditions. Gestational stress decreased the frequency of maternal LG with the second litter in the High but not in Low LG-ABN mothers. Thus, a stressful environmental signal during gestation was sufficient to completely reverse the pattern of maternal behavior in High LG-ABN mothers. The maternal behavior of High LG-ABN mothers exposed to gestational stress during an earlier pregnancy was indistinguishable from that of Low LG-ABN mothers. And of course these effects on maternal behavior are apparent in the development of the offspring. As adults, the offspring of High LG-ABN/gestationally stressed mothers were comparable to those of Low LG-ABN dams on measures of behavioral and HPA responses to stress.

Effects on offspring in these studies might be associated with classic "prenatal stress" effects, because these animals were in utero during the imposition of the stressor. To address this question, we examined the offspring of a subsequent pregnancy over which time no experimental manipulations were imposed. As it turns out, the effects of gestational stress during the second pregnancy were apparent with a subsequent, third litter, even in the absence of any further stress.

This finding enabled us to examine the effects of stress-induced alterations in maternal behavior independent of the presence of the stressor during prenatal life. As with the second litter, the adult offspring of the High LG-ABN/gestationally stressed mothers were again comparable to those of Low LG-ABN dams on measures of behavioral and HPA responses to stress.

The effects of gestational stress were also apparent in the maternal behavior of the female offspring. The female offspring of High LG mothers exposed to gestational stress behave toward their pups in a manner consistent with the behavior of their mothers; as adults, these females are Low LG-ABN mothers. Hence the effects of environmental adversity are effectively transmitted from parent to offspring. Taken together with the data from studies of human and nonhuman primates, these findings suggest that environmental adversity in mammals alters maternal behavior through effects on anxiety and that such effects are then apparent as individual differences in mother-offspring interactions, with predictable consequences for development.

Adaptive Effects of Stress Reactivity in Offspring

The findings we have reviewed suggest that the offspring of Low LG mothers show increased fearfulness and enhanced HPA responses to stress. Additionally, there are affects on cognitive systems that suggest greater vulnerability for stress-induced impairments in attentional processes, as well as in learning/memory under certain conditions. It is important to appreciate the potential adaptive virtues of increased stress reactivity. Under conditions of adversity, stress hormones promote alterations in metabolism (mobilization of glucose and lipid stores) that assist in meeting the increased energy demands associated with stress, increased vigilance and alertness, and enhanced defensive responses, all of which serve to enhance survival under conditions of chronic stress. Indeed, we suggest that such effects may be considered as adaptive within certain contexts (children in extremely impoverished and violent environments). The cost of enhanced stress reactivity is likely reflected in an increased vulnerability for stress-induced disease. However, such developmental strategies have been shaped by evolutionary pressures that focus on survival and reproduction: Chronic illness is relevant only to the extent that it impinges on these fundamental outcomes. At least two studies in human populations have identified the advantages associated with increased stress reactivity (i.e., behavioral inhibition) for children living in poverty (Farrington et al., 1988; Haapasap & Tremblay, 1994).

Within evolutionary biology, maternal or parental effects are defined as sustained influences on any component of the phenotype of the offspring that is derived from either the mother or the father, apart from nuclear genes. Such parental effects have been studied across a variety of species, and the results indicate that environmentally induced modifications of the parental phenotype can be transmitted to offspring through an epigenetic mechanism. Epigenesis refers to any functional modification of the genome that does not involve a change of DNA sequence.

What is perhaps most surprising is that these developmental effects derive from variations in parental care that appear to lie within a normal range for the species. However, as Hinde (1986) suggested, this is likely due to the fact that natural selection shaped offspring to respond to subtle variations in parental care as a forecast of the environmental conditions they would ultimately face following independence from the parent. Evolution should come to favor offspring that are able to accurately "read" variations in parental behavior as forecasts of environmental conditions, and thus as useful signposts for developmental trajectories. By definition, such responses should occur in reaction to variation within the normal range: why evolve responses to forms of parental care that are unlikely to occur? Moreover, parents (or parent in some cases) are a logical source of such information since they are the one "environmentally-informed," constant experience of the offspring. Moreover, since parents are genetically invested in the development of their biological offspring, one would expect that the fidelity of signals emanating from a parent would be greater than that of adult conspecifics. Thus, to the extent that parent and offspring share a common interest in the adaptive value of such phenotypic plasticity, selection may also act on the signaling of the parent. Indeed, phenotypic plasticity in response to parental signals may also be thought of as a parental strategy (Wells, 2003). In either case, the sensitivity of the offspring to parental signals during critical phases of development may be thought of as a strategy that favors a highly predictable relation between environmental conditions, parental input and phenotypic variation in defensive responses. Hence, parents matter.

Potential Mediating Mechanisms

Maternal care alters the expression of genes in brain regions that subserve emotional, cognitive, and endocrine responses to stress. These effects are associated with tissue-specific alterations in gene expression that are sustained into adulthood. Existing evidence suggests a direct effect of maternal care, at least with respect to modifications of glucocorticoid receptor and $GABA_A$ receptor subunit expression. Studies on HPA function and performance in the Morris water maze suggest a direct link between the changes in gene expression and function. Nevertheless there are substantial gaps in the story. First, although cross-fostering studies suggest a direct link between variations in mother-pup interactions, the evidence for a causal role of pup licking/grooming or arched-back nursing remains circumstantial. More recent studies with the artificially reared pups raised under conditions that systematically vary the level of tactile stimulation represent a useful experimental approach to this problem (e.g., Lovic & Fleming, 2004). Second, evidence for the direct relation between the alteration in gene expression and function in adulthood remains to be defined for most of the effects described above, including effects on $GABA_A$ receptor and COMT. Third, the nature of the maternal effects on cognitive-emotional process remains to be defined. Most studies are merely descriptive. As discussed above in relation to performance in the Morris water maze, the mediating processes remain to be clarified, and this is also true for measures of fear-related behavior. Are differences in the behavior of the adult offspring of High and Low LG-ABN mothers in novel environments associated with differences in the perception of threat, or in the emotional response to a common perception of the environmental condition? Do differences in performance in tests of spatial learning and memory reflect differences in information processing and storage, or in the disruption of these processes by emotional reactions to the testing environment? And what of attentional/working memory systems that function at the initial phases of information processing and are subject to disruption by stressors? Do the effects of early experience on the performance of animals in tests of attentional/working memory reflect differences in stress-induced disruption of prefrontal function (animals are tested in novel testing conditions), or are there specific, independent effects on neural circuits that subserve attention?

Another intriguing possibility is that early experience creates a specific "cognitive" bias in information processing. Preliminary studies reveal that in a test of alternation in a T-maze, in which animals are rewarded for turning in the opposite direction from that which was rewarded on the previous trial, the adult offspring of Low LG-ABN animals show very significantly improved performance over that of animals reared by High LG-ABN mothers. Such findings might reveal a bias for a somewhat pessimistic "win-shift" cognitive strategy in which an animal preferentially avoids a location previously associated with food; a win-stay strategy reflects the more optimistic bias of returning to the same location. Clearly we have much to learn about exactly how early experience modifies behavior in adulthood. Our ability to meaningfully relate environmentally induced changes in gene expression to function in adulthood depends on progress at each level of analysis. And so too does our ability to use this research in the development of intervention programs for high-risk individuals. What, for example, are the clinically relevant targets for intervention? This question can be posed either at the level of neurochemistry or function.

These issues notwithstanding, the current evidence suggests that variations in mother-pup interactions program multiple neural systems in the forebrain that mediate cognitive, emotional, and endocrine responses to stress. Such effects are apparent in HPA function, fear-related behavior, attentional processes, and learning and memory under stressful conditions. These effects are associated with alterations in the gene expression that are highly tissue specific. For example, alterations in the $GABA_A/BZ$ receptors are observed in the amygdala and locus coeruleus, and almost nowhere else in the corticolimbic system (Caldji et al., 2003). Such effects may well represent a developmental strategy that permits phenotypic plasticity in response to early environmental conditions. Although such effects may be adaptive with respect to survival and reproduction, the cost of enhanced defensive responses may be reflected in an increased risk for multiple forms of chronic illness over the life span.

Conclusions

We have described what appears to be a sustained change in gene expression that reflects variation in maternal care. So the obvious biological question is, why bother? As suggested earlier, we think that maternal effects represent a developmental strategy whereby the defensive responses of the offspring are refined in response to the prevailing level of environmental demand. In mammals, the relevant signal that predicts the level of environmental demand is the behavior of the parent. Indeed, we use the term "developmental strategy" here more in a descriptive sense because the strategy may be seen as emerging from a strategy on the part of the offspring (i.e., use the signals of the parent to forecast environmental demand) or the parent (i.e., signal the offspring in a manner that influences the development of defensive responses; see Wells, 2003). These need not be considered as mutually exclusive options. The crucial assumption is that the result confers some advantage onto the offspring with respect to survival and reproduction.

Thus we propose that adversity in mammals alters parent-offspring interactions in a manner that is designed to increase endocrine, cognitive, and emotional responses to stress. In the rat, gestational stress is associated with decreased maternal licking/grooming (Champagne et al., 2001; Smith et al., 2004) and increased stress reactivity in the offspring (Champagne et al., submitted). In the macaque, stress imposed on lactating females decreases the quality of mother-infant interactions (Rosenblum & Andrews, 1994) and increases endocrine and behavioral responses to stress (Coplan et al., 1996, 1998). In the rat, decreased maternal licking/grooming is associated with increased fearfulness, enhanced HPA responses to stress, and impaired performance on attentional tasks and tests of declarative learning/memory under stressful conditions. These effects appear to be mediated by maternal effects on gene expression in relevant brain regions. We suggest that such effects produce an increased "preparedness" of defensive systems. Considering the adaptive value of behavioral and endocrine responses to stress, such a bias may be functional for an individual under conditions of increased adversity. If this is the case, then we are better to consider functional differences in developmental outcomes under conditions of adversity as reflecting alternative phenotypes, as opposed to impairments in development. Finally, although these studies certainly support efforts to consider parental care as a relevant and perhaps critical target for intervention, ultimately the issue is that of the relevant social and economic context within which development occurs.

Acknowledgment

This chapter is adapted from Zhang, T., Bagot, R., Parent, C., Nesbitt, C., Bredy, T. W., Caldji, C., Fish, E., Anisman, H., Szyf, M., & Meaney, M. J. (2006). Maternal programming of defensive responses through sustained effects on gene expression. *Biological Psychology, 73,* 72–89.

References

Amiel-Tison, C., Cabrol, D., Denver, R., Jarreau, P. H., Papiernik, E., & Piazza, P. V. (2004). Fetal adaptation to stress: Part II. Evolutionary aspects; stress-induced hippocampal damage; long-term effects on behavior; consequences on adult health. *Early Human Development, 78,* 81–94.

Antoni, F. A. (1993). Vasopressinergic control of pituitary adrenocorticotropin secretion comes of age. *Frontiers in Neuroendocrinology, 14,* 76–122.

Arborelius, L., Owens, M. J., Plotsky, P. M., & Nemeroff, C. B. (1999). The role of corticotropin-releasing factor in depression and anxiety disorders. *Journal of Endocrinology, 160,* 1–12.

Arnsten, A. F. T. (2000). Stress impairs prefrontal cortical function in rats and monkeys: Role of dopamine D1 and norepinepherine α-1 receptor mechanisms. *Progress in Brain Research., 126,* 183–192.

Bakshi, V. P., Shelton, S. E., & Kalin, N. H. (2000). Neurobiological correlates of defensive behaviors. *Progress in Brain Research, 122,* 105–115.

Belsky, J. (1997). Attachment, mating, and parenting: An evolutionary interpretation. *Human Nature, 8,* 361–381.

Bennett, A. J., Lesch, K. P., Heils, A., Long, J. C., Lorenz, J. G., Shoaf, S. E., Champoux, M., Suomi, S. J., Linnoila, M. V., & Higley, J. D. (2002). Early experience and serotonin transporter gene variation interact to influence primate CNS function. *Molecular Psychiatry, 7,* 118–122.

Birrell, J. .M, & Brown, V. J. (2000). Medial frontal cortex mediates perceptual attentional set shifting in the rat. *Journal of Neuroscience, 20,* 4320–424.

Boyle, M. P., Brewer, J. A., Funatsu, M., Wozniak, D. F., Tsien, J. Z., Izumi, Y., & Muglia, L. J. (2005). Acquired deficit of forebrain glucocorticoid receptor produces depression-like changes in adrenal axis regulation and behavior. *Proceedings of the National Academy of Science, 102,* 473–478.

Brake, W. G., Zang, T. Y., Diorio, J., Meaney, M. J., & Gratton, A. (2004). Influence of early postnatal rearing conditions on mesocorticolimbic dopamine and behavioral responses to psychostimulants and stress in adult rats. *European Journal of Neuroscience, 19,* 1863–1874.

Bredy, T. W., Diorio, J., Grant, R., & Meaney, M. J. (2003a). Maternal care influences hippocampal neuron survival in the rat. *European Journal of Neuroscience, 18,* 2903–2909.

Bredy, T. W., Humpartzoomian, R. A., Cain, D. P., & Meaney, M. J. (2003b). Partial reversal of the effect of maternal care on cognitive function through environmental enrichment. *Neuroscience, 118,* 571–576.

Bredy, T. W., Zhang T.-Y., Grant, R. J., Diorio, J., & Meaney, M. J. (2004). Peripubertal environmental enrichment reverses the effects of maternal care on hippocampal development and glutamate receptor subunit expression. *European Journal of Neuroscience, 20,* 1355–1362.

Bubser, M., & Koch, M. (1994). Prepulse inhibition of the acoustic startle response of rats is reduced by 6-hydroxydopamine lesions of the medial prefrontal cortex. *Psychopharmacology, 113,* 487–492.

Butler, P. D., Weiss, J. M., Stout, J. C., & Nemeroff, C. B. (1990). Corticotropin-releasing factor produces fear-enhancing and behavioural activating effects following infusion into the locus coeruleus. *Journal of Neuroscience, 10,* 176–183.

Caldji, C., Diorio, J., & Meaney, M. J. (2003). Variations in maternal care alter GABAA receptor subunit expression in brain regions associated with fear. *Neuropsychopharmacology, 28,* 150–159.

Caldji, C., Diorio, J., Plotsky, P. M., & Meaney, M. J. (1999). Multiple central benzodiazepine/GABAA receptor subunits regulated by maternal behavior in infancy. *Society for Neuroscience (Abstracts), 25,* 616.

Caldji, C., Tannenbaum, B., Sharma, S., Francis, D., Plotsky, P. M., & Meaney, M. J. (1998). Maternal care during infancy regulates the development of neural systems mediating the expression of behavioral fearfulness in adulthood in the rat. *Proceedings of the National Academy of Sciences of the United States of America, 95,* 5335–5340.

Caspi, A., Sugden, K., Moffitt, T. E., Taylor, A., Caraig, I. W., Harrington, H., McClay, J., Mill, J., Martin, J., Braithwaite, A., & Poulton, R. (2003). Influence of life stress on depression: Moderation by a polymorphism in the 5-HTT gene. *Science, 301,* 386–390.

Champagne, F., Diorio, J., Sharma, S., & Meaney, M. J. (2001). Naturally occurring variations in maternal behavior in the rat are associated with differences in estrogen-inducible central oxytocin receptors. *Proceedings of the National Academy of Science, 98,* 12736–12741.

Champagne, F., & Meaney, M. J. (2000). Gestational stress effects on maternal behavior. *Abstracts—Society for Neuroscience, 26,* 2035.

Champagne, F. A., Francis, D. D., Mar, A., & Meaney, M. J. (2003). Variations in maternal care in the rat as a mediating influence for the effects of environment on the development. *Physiology & Behavior, 79,* 359–371.

Champagne, F. A., Weaver, I. C. G., Diorio, J., Dymov, S., Szyf, M., & Meaney, M. J. (2006). Maternal Care Associated with Methylation of the Estrogen Receptor-α 1b Promoter and Estrogen Receptor-α Expression in the Medial Preoptic Area of Female Offspring. *Endocrinology, 147,* 2909–2915.

Champagne, F. A., & Meaney, M. J. (2006). Stress During Gestation Alters Postpartum Maternal Care and the Development of the Offspring in a Rodent Model. *Biological Psychiatry, 59,* 1227–1235.

Chapillon, P., Patin, V., Roy, V., Vincent, A., & Caston, J. (2002). Effects of pre- and postnatal stimulation on developmental, emotional, and cognitive aspects in rodents: A review. *Developmental Psychobiology, 41,* 373–387.

Chrousos, G. P., & Gold, P. W. (1992). The concepts of stress and stress system disorders. *Journal of the American Medical Association, 267,* 1244–1252.

Cilia, J., Reavill, C., Hagan, J. J., & Jones, D. N. (2001). Long-term evaluation of isolation-rearing induced prepulse inhibition deficits in rats. *Psychopharmacology 156,* 327–337.

Conger, R., Ge, X., Elder, G., Lorenz, F., & Simons, R. (1994). Economic stress, coercive family process and developmental problems of adolescents. *Child Development, 65,* 541–561.

Coplan, J. D., Andrews, M. W., Rosenblum, L. A., Owens, M. J., Friedman, S., Gorman, J. M., & Nemeroff, C. B. (1996). Persistent elevations of cerebrospinal fluid concentrations of corticotropin-releasing factor in adult nonhuman primates exposed to early-life stressors: Implications for the pathophysiology of mood and anxiety disorders. *Proceedings of the National Academy of Sciences of the United States of America, 93,* 1619–1623.

Coplan, J. D., Trost, R. C., Owens, M. J., Cooper, T. B., Gorman, J. M., Nemeroff, C. B., & Rosenblum, L. A. (1998). Cerebrospinal fluid concentrations of somatostatin and biogenic amines in grown primates reared by mothers exposed to manipulated foraging conditions. *Archives of General Psychiatry, 55,* 473–477.

Dallman, M. F., Akana, S. F., Strack, A. M., Hanson, E. S., & Sebastian, R. J. (2001). The neural network that regulates energy balance is responsive to glucocorticoids and insulin and also regulates HPA axis responsivity at a site proximal to CRF neurons. *Annals of the New York Academy of Sciences, 771,* 730–742.

Dallman, M. F., la Fleur, S. E., Pecoraro, N. C., Gomez, F., Houshyar, H., & Akana, S. F. (2004). Minireview: Glucocorticoids—food intake, abdominal obesity, and wealthy nations in 2004. *Endocrinology, 145,* 2633–2638.

Davis, M., Whalen, P. J. (2001). The amygdala: Vigilance and emotion. *Molecular Psychiatry, 6,* 13–34.

De Bellis, M. D., Chrousos, G. P., Dorn, L. D., Burke, L., Helmers, K., Kling, M. A., Trickett, P. K., & Putnam, F. W. (1994). Hypothalamic-pituitary-adrenal dysregulation in sexually abused girls. *Journal of Clinical Endocrinology and Metabolism, 78,* 249–255.

de Kloet, E. R., Vregdenhil, E., Oitzl, M. S., & Joels, M. (1998). Brain corticosteroid receptor balance in health and disease. *Endocrine Reviews, 19,* 269–301.

Diorio, J., Weaver, I. C. G., & Meaney, M. J. (2000). A DNA array study of hippocampal gene expression regulated by maternal behavior in infancy. *Abstracts—Society for Neuroscience, 26,* 1366.

Ellenbroek, B. A., van den Kroonenberg, P. T., & Cools, A. R. (1998). The effects of an early stressful life event on sensorimotor gating in adult rats. *Schizophrenia Research, 30,* 251–260.

Ellenbroek, B. A., van Luijtelaar, G., Frenken, M., & Cools, A. R. (1999). Sensory gating in rats: Lack of correlation between auditory evoked potential gating and prepulse inhibition. *Schizophrrenia Bulletin, 25,* 777–788.

Emoto, H., Yokoo, H., Yoshida, M., & Tanaka, M. (1993). Corticotropin-releasing factor enhances noradrenaline release in the rat hypothalamus assessed by intracerebral microdialysis. *Brain Research, 601,* 286–288.

Essex, M. J., Klein, M. H., Cho, E., & Kalin, N. H. (2002). Maternal stress beginning in infancy may sensitize children to later stress exposure: Effects on cortisol and behavior, *Biological Psychiatry, 52,* 776–784.

Farrington, D. A., Gallagher, B., Morley, L., St Ledger, R. J., & West, D. J. (1988). Are there any successful men from criminogenic backgrounds? *Psychiatry, 51,* 116–130.

Felitti, V. J., Anda, R. F., Nordenberg, D., Williamson, D. F., Spitz, A. M., Edwards, V., Koss, M. P., & Marks, J. S. (1998). Relationship of childhood abuse and household dysfunction to many of the leading causes of death in adults. *American Journal of Preventive Medicine, 14,* 245–258.

Fleming, A. S. (1988). Factors influencing maternal responsiveness in humans: Usefulness of an animal model. *Psychoneuroendocrinology, 13,* 189–212.

Fleming, A. S. (1999). The neurobiology of mother-infant interactions: Experience and central nervous system plasticity across development and generations. *Neuroscience and Biobehavioral Reviews., 23,* 673–685.

Francis, D. D., Champagne, F., & Meaney, M. J. (2000). Variations in maternal behaviour are associated with differences in oxytocin receptor levels in the rat. *Journal of Neuroendocrinology, 12,* 1145–1148.

Francis, D. D., Diorio, J., Liu, D., & Meaney, M. J. (1999). Nongenomic transmission across generations in maternal behavior and stress responses in the rat. *Science, 286,* 1155–1158.

Fride, E., Dan, Y., Gavish, M., & Weinstock, M. (1985). Prenatal stress impairs maternal behavior in a conflict situation and reduces hippocampal benzodiazepine receptors. *Life Sciences, 36,* 2103–2109.

Fuster, J. M. (1997). Network memory. *Trends in Neuroscience, 20,* 451–459.

Geyer, M. A., Krebs-Thomson, K., Braff, D. L., & Swerdlow, N. R. (2001). Pharmacological studies of prepulse inhibition models of sensorimotor gating deficits in schizophrenia: A decade in review. *Psychopharmacology 156,* 117–154.

Geyer, M. A., Swerdlow, N. R., Mansbach, R. S., & Braff, D. L. (1990). Startle response models of sensorimotor gating and habituation deficits in schizophrenia. *Brain Research Bulletin, 25,* 485–498.

Glover, V., & O'Connor, T. G. (2002). Effects of antenatal stress and anxiety: Implications for development and psychiatry. *British Journal of Psychiatry, 180,* 389–391.

Gogos, J. A., Morgan, M., Luine, V., Santha, M., Ogawa, S., Pfaff, D., & Karayiorgou, M. (1998). Catechol-O-methyltransferase-deficient mice exhibit sexually dimorphic changes in catecholamine levels and behavior. *Proceedings of the National Academy of Sciences of the United States of America, 95,* 9991–9996.

Goldstein, L. H., Diener, M. L., & Mangelsdorf, S. C. (1996). Maternal characteristics and social support across the transition to motherhood: Associations with maternal behavior. *Journal of Family Psychology, 10,* 60–71.

Gray, T. S., & Bingaman, E. W. (1996). The amygdala: Corticotropin-releasing factor, steroids, and stress. *Critical Reviews in Neurobiology, 10,* 155–168.

Grolnick, W. S., Gurland, S. T., DeCourcey, W., & Jacob, K (2002). Antecedents and consequences of mothers' autonomy support: An experimental investigation. *Developmental Psychology, 38,* 143–155.

Haapasap, J., & Tremblay, R. E. (1994). Physically aggressive boys from ages 6 to 12: Family background, parenting behavior, and prediction of delinquency. *Journal of Consulting and Clinical Psychology, 62,* 1044–1052.

Habib, R., & Lepage, M. (2000). Novelty assessment in the brain. In E. Tulving (Ed.), *Memory, Consciousness, and the Brain: The Tallin Conference* (pp. 265–277). Philadelphia: Psychology Press.

Hart, B., & Risley, T. R. (1995). *Meaningful differences.* Baltimore: Paul H. Brookes.

Heim, C., Newport, D. J., Heit, S., Graham, Y. P., Wilcox, M., Bonsall, R., Miller, A. H., & Nemeroff, C. B. (2000). Pituitary-adrenal and autonomic responses to stress in women after sexual and physical abuse in childhood. *Journal of the American Medical Association, 284,* 592–597.

Heim, C., Newport, D. J., Wagner, D., Wilcox, M. M., Miller, A. H., & Nemeroff, C. B. (2002). The role of early adverse experience and adulthood stress in the prediction of neuroendocrine stress reactivity in women: A multiple regression analysis. *Depression and Anxiety, 15,* 117–125.

Herman, J. P., Figueiredo, H., Mueller, N. K., Ulrich-Lai, Y., Ostrander, M. M., Choi, D. C., & Cullinan, W. E. (2003). Central mechanisms of stress integration: hierarchical circuitry controlling hypothalamo-pituitary-adrenocortical responsiveness. *Frontiers in Neuroendocrinology, 24,* 151–180.

Higley, J. D., Hasert, M. F., Suomi, S. J., & Linnoila, M (1991). Nonhuman primate model of alcohol abuse: Effects of early experience, personality and stress on alcohol consumption. *Proceedings of the National Academy of Sciences of the United States of America, 88,* 7261–7265.

Kim, J. J., & Diamond, D. M. (2002). The stressed hippocampus, synaptic plasticity and lost memories. *Nature Reviews. Neuroscience, 3,* 453–462.

Kinsley, C. H., Mann, P. E., & Bridges, R. S. (1988). Prenatal stress alters morphine-and stress induced analgesia in male and female rats. *Pharmacology, Biochemistry, and Behavior, 50,* 413–419.

Kirkwood, A., Dudek, S. M., Gold, J. T., Aizenman, C. D., & Bear, M. F. (1993). Common forms of synaptic plasticity in the hippocampus and neocortex in vitro. *Science, 260,* 1518–1521.

Koegler-Muly, S. M., Owens, M. J., Ervin, G. N., Kilts, C. D., & Nemeroff, C. B. (1993). Potential corticotropin-releasing factor pathways in the rat brain as determined by bilateral electrolytic lesions of the central amygdaloid nucleus and paraventricular nucleus of the hypothalamus. *Journal of Neuroendocrinology, 5,* 95–98.

Koob, G. F., Heinrichs, S. C., Menzaghi, F., Pich, E. M., & Britton, K. T. (1994). Corticotropin-releasing factor, stress, and behavior. *Seminars in the Neurosciences, 6,* 221–229.

Lavicky, J., & Dunn, A. J. (1993). Corticotropin-releasing factor stimulates catecholamine release in hypothalamus and prefrontal cortex in freely moving rats as assessed by microdialysis. *Journal of Neurochemistry, 60,* 602–612.

Le Pen, G., & Moreau, J. L. (2002). Disruption of prepulse inhibition of startle reflex in a neurodevelopmental model of schizophrenia: Reversal by clozapine, olanzapine and risperidone but not by haloperidol. *Neuropsychopharmacology, 27,* 1–11.

Levine, S. (1994). The ontogeny of the hypothalamic-pituitary-adrenal axis. The influence of maternal factors. *Annals of the New York Academy of Sciences, 746,* 275–288.

Li, L., & Shao, J. (1998). Restricted lesions to the ventral prefrontal subareas block reversal learning but not visual discrimination learning in rats. *Physiology & Behavior, 65,* 371–379.

Liang, K. C., Melia, K. R., Miserendino, M. J., Falls, W. A., Campeau, S., & Davis, M. (1992). Corticotropin releasing factor: Long-lasting facilitation of the acoustic startle reflex. *Journal of Neuroscience, 12,* 2303–2312.

Liu, D., Diorio, J., Day, J. C., Francis, D. D., & Meaney, M. J (2000). Maternal care, hippocampal synaptogenesis and cognitive development in rats. *Nature Neuroscience, 3,* 799–806.

Liu, D., Tannenbaum, B., Caldji, C., Francis, D., Freedman, A., Sharma, S., Pearson, D., Plotsky, P. M., & Meaney M. J. (1997). Maternal care, hippocampal glucocorticoid receptor gene expression and hypothalamic-pituitary-adrenal responses to stress. *Science, 277,* 1659–1662.

Lissau, I., & Sorensen, T. I. A. (1994). Parental neglect during childhood and increased risk of obesity in young adulthood. *Lancet, 343,* 324–327.

Lovic, V., & Fleming, A. S. (2004). Artificially reared female rats show reduced prepulse inhibition and deficits in the attentional set shifting task—reversal of effects with maternal-like licking stimulation. *Behavioural Brain Research., 148*(1–2), 209–219.

Luecken, L. J., & Lemery, K. S. (2004). Early caregiving and physiological stress responses. *Clinical Psychology Review, 24*, 171–191.

Maccari, S., Darnaudery, M., Morley-Fletcher, S., Zuena, A. R., Clinique, C., & Van Reeth, O. (2003). Prenatal stress and long-term consequences: Implications of glucocorticoid hormones. *Neuroscience & Biobehavioral Reviews, 27*, 119–127.

Matsumoto, M., Weickert, C. S., Akil, M., Lipska, B. K., Hyde, T. M., Herman, M. M., Kleinman, J. E., & Weinberger, D. R. (2003). Catechol O-methyltransferase mRNA expression in human and rat brain: Evidence for a role in cortical neuronal function. *Neuroscience, 116*, 127–137.

Matthews, S. G., & Meaney, M. J. (2005). Maternal adversity, vulnerabiity, and disease. In A. Reicher-Rossler & M. Steiner (Eds.), *Perinatal Stress, Mood and Anxiety Disorders: From Bench to Bedside (Bibliotheca Psychiatrica)* (pp. 28–49). Switzerland: S. Karger AG.

McCarty, R., & Lee, J. H. (1996). Maternal influences on adult blood pressure of SHRs: A single pup cross-fostering study. *Physiology & Behavior, 59*, 71–75.

McCauley, J., Kern, D. E., Kolodner, K., Dill, L., Schroeder, A. F., DeChant, H. K., Ryden, J., Derogatis, L. R., & Bass, E. B. (1997). Clinical characteristics of women with a history of childhood abuse: Unhealed wounds. *Journal of the American Medical Association, 277*, 1362–1368.

McCormick, C. M., Smythe, J. W., Sharma, S., & Meaney, M. J. (1995). Sex-specific effects of prenatal stress on hyppthalamic-pituitary-adrenal responses to stress and brain glucocorticoid receptor density in adult rats. *Developmental Brain Research, 84*, 55–61.

McEwen, B. S. (1998). Protective and damaging effects of stress mediators. *New England Journal of Medicine, 338*, 171–179.

McHugh, T. J., Blum, K. I., Tsien, J. Z., Tonegawa, S., & Wilson, M. A. (1996). Impaired hippocampal representation of space in CA1-specific NMDAR1 knockout mice. *Cell, 87*, 1339–1349.

McLloyd, V. C. (1998). Socioeconomic disadvantage and child development. *The American Psychologist, 53*, 185–204.

Meaney, M. J. (2001). Maternal care, gene expression, and the transmission of individual differences in stress reactivity across generations. *Annual Review of Neuroscience, 24*, 1161–1192.

Menard, J., Champagne, D., & Meaney, M. J. (2004a). Variations of maternal care differentially influence "fear" reactivity and regional patterns of cFos immunoreactivity in response to the shock-probe burying test. *Neuroscience, 129*, 297–308.

Minichiello, L., Korte, M., Wolfer, D., Kuhn, R., Unsicker, K., Cestari, V., Rossi-Arnaud, C., Lipp, H. P., Bonhoeffer, T., & Klein, R. (1999). Essential role for TrkB receptors in hippocampus-mediated learning. *Neuron, 24*, 401–414.

Moga, M. M., & Gray, T. S. (1989). Evidence for corticotropin-releasing factor, neurotensin, and somatostatin in the neural pathway from the central nucleus of the amygdala to the parabrachial nucleus. *Journal of Comparative Neurology, 241*, 275–284.

Moore, C. L., & Power, K. L. (1986). Parental stress affects mother-infant interaction in Norway rats. *Developmental Psychology, 19*, 235–245.

Morris, R. G., Anderson, E., Lynch, G. S., & Baudry, M. (1986). Selective impairment of learning and blockade of long-term potentiation by an N-methyl-D-aspartate receptor antagonist, AP5. *Nature, 319*, 774–776.

Murphy, B. L., Arnsten, A. F., Goldman-Rakic, P. S., & Roth, R. H. (1996). Increased dopamine turnover in the prefrontal cortex impairs spatial working memory performance in rats and monkeys. *Proceedings of the National Academy of Sciences of the United States of America, 93,* 1325–1329.

Murray, T. K., Ridley, R. M. (1999). The effects of excitotoxic hippocampal lesions on simple and conditioned discrimination learning in the rat. *Behavioural Brain Research, 99,* 103–113.

Newport, D. J., Stowe, Z. N., & Nemeroff, C. B. (2002). Parental depression: Animal models of an adverse life event. *American Journal of Psychiatry, 159,* 1265–1283.

Owens, M. J., Vargas, M. A., Knight, D. L., & Nemeroff, C. B. (1991). The effects of alprazolam on corticotropin-releasing factor neurons in the rat brain: acute time course, chronic treatment and abrupt withdrawal. *The Journal of Pharmacology & Experimental Therapeutics, 258,* 349–356.

Page, M. E., & Valentino, R. J. (1994). Locus coeruleus activation by physiological challenges. *Brain Research Bulletin, 35,* 557–560.

Plotsky, P. M. (1991). Pathways to the secretion of adrenocorticotropin: A view from the portal. *Journal of Neuroendocrinology, 3,* 1–9.

Plotsky, P. M., & Meaney, M. J. (1993). Early, postnatal experience alters hypothalamic corticotropin-releasing factor (CRF) mRNA, median eminence CRF content and stress-induced release in adult rats. *Molecular Brain Research, 18,* 195–200.

Plotsky, P. M., Thrivikraman, K. V., Nemeroff, C. B., Caldji, C., Sharma, S., & Meaney, M. J. (2005). Long-term consequences of neonatal rearing on central corticotropin releasing factor systems on adult male offspring. *Neuropsychopharmacology, 30,* 2192–2204.

Pruessner, J. L., Champagne, F. A., Meaney, M. J., & Dagher, A. (2004). Parental care and neuroendocrine and dopamine responses to stress in humans: A PET imaging study. *Journal of Neuroscience, 24,* 2825–2831.

Repetti, R. L., Taylor, S. E., & Seeman, T. E. (2002). Risky families: Family social environments and the mental and physical health of offspring. *Psychological Bulletin, 128,* 330–366.

Rivier, C., & Plotsky, P. M. (1986). Mediation by corticotropin-releasing factor of adenohypophysial hormone secretion. *Annual Review of Physiology, 48,* 475–489.

Roceri, M., Hendriks, W., Racagni, G., Ellenbroek, B. A., & Riva, M. A. (2002). Early maternal deprivation reduces the expression of BDNF and NMDA receptor subunits in rat hippocampus. *Molecular Psychiatry, 7,* 609–616.

Rosenblum, L. A., & Andrews, M. W. (1994). Influences of environmental demand on maternal behavior and infant development. *Acta Paediatrica Supplement, 397,* 57–63.

Sapolsky, R. M., Romero, L. M., & Munck, A. U. (2000). How do glucocorticoids influence stress responses? Integrating permissive, suppressive, stimulatory, and preparative actions. *Endocrine Reviews, 21,* 55–89.

Scarr, S. (1997). Why Child Care Has Little Impact on Most Children's Development. *Current Directions in Psychological Science, 6,* 143–148.

Schanberg, S. M., Evoniuk, G., & Kuhn, C. M. (1984). Tactile and nutritional aspects of maternal care: specific regulators of neuroendocrine function and cellular development. *Proceedings of the Society for Experimental Biology and Medicine, 175,* 135–146.

Schatz, C. J. (1990). Impulse activity and the patterning of connections during CNS development. *Neuron, 5,* 745–756.

Schulkin, J., McEwen, B. S., & Gold, P. W. (1994). Allostasis, the amygdala and anticipatory angst. *Neuroscience and Biobehavioral Reviews, 18,* 385–396.

Seckl, J. R. (2001). Glucocorticoid programming of the fetus; adult phenotypes and molecular mechanisms. *Molecular and Cellular Endocrinology, 185,* 61–71.

Smith, J. W., Seckl, J. R., Evans, A. T., Costall, B., & Smythe, J. W. (2004). Gestational stress induces post-partum depression-like behaviour and alters maternal care in rats. *Psychoneuroendocrinology, 29,* 227–244.

Smythe, J. W., Bhatnagar, S., Murphy, D., Timothy, C., & Costall, B. (1998). The effects of intrahippocampal scopolamine infusions on anxiety in rats as measured by the black-white box test. *Brain Research Bulletin, 45,* 89–93.

Smythe, J. W., Murphy, D., & Costall, B. (1996). Benzodiazepine receptor stimulation blocks scopolamine-induced learning impairments in a water maze task. *Brain Research Bulletin, 41,* 299–304.

Stenzel-Poore, M. P., Heinrichs, S. C., Rivest, S., Knob, G. F., & Vale, W. W. (1994). Overproduction of corticotropin-releasing factor in transgenic mice: A genetic model of anxiogenic behavior. *Journal of Neuroscience, 14,* 2579–2584.

Stern, J. M. (1997). Offspring-induced nurturance: Animal-human parallels. *Developmental Psychobiology, 31,* 19–37.

Suomi, S. J. (1997). Early determinants of behaviour: Evidence from primate studies. *British Medical Bulletin., 53,* 170–184.

Swerdlow, N. R., Geyer, M. A., & Braff, D. L. (2001). Neural circuit regulation of prepulse inhibition of startle in the rat: Current knowledge and future challenges. *Psychopharmacology, 156,* 194–215.

Swiergiel, A. H., Takahashi, L. K.. & Kahn, N. H. (1993). Attenuation of stress-induced by antagonism of corticotropin-releasing factor receptors in the central amygdala in the rat. *Brain Research, 623,* 229–234.

Valentino, R. J., Curtis, A. L., Page, M. E., Pavcovich, L. A., & Florin-Lechner, S. M. (1998). Activation of the locus coeruleus brain noradrenergic system during stress: Circuitry, consequences, and regulation. *Advances in Pharmacology, 42,* 781–784.

Van Bockstaele, E. J., Colago, E. E., & Valentino, R. J. (1996). Corticotropin-releasing factor-containing axon terminals synapse onto catecholamine dendrites and may presynaptically modulate other afferents in the rostral pole of the nucleus locus coeruleus in the rat brain. *Journal of Comparative Neurology, 364,* 523–534.

Vaughn, B., Egeland, B., Sroufe, L. A., & Waters, E. (1979). Individual differences in infant-mother attachment at twelve and eighteen months: Stability and change in families under stress. *Child Development, 50,* 971–975.

Wadhwa, P. D., Sandman, C. A., & Garite, T. J. (2001). The neurobiology of stress in human pregnancy: Implications for prematurity and development of the fetal central nervous system. *Progress in Brain Research, 133,* 131–142.

Weaver, I. C. G., Cervoni, N., D'Alessio, A. C., Champagne, F. A., Seckl, J. R., Szyf, M., & Meany, M. J. (2004). Epignetic programming through maternal behavior. *Nature Neuroscience, 7,* 847-854.

Weaver, I. C. G., Diorio, J., Seckl, J. R., Szyf, M., & Meaney, M. J. (2004b). Environmental regulation of hippocampal glucocorticoid receptor gene expression: Characterization of intracellular mediators and potential genomic targets. *Annals of the New York Academy of Sciences, 1024,* 182–212.

Weinstock, M. (1997). Does prenatal stress impair coping and regulation of hypothalamic-pituitary-adrenal axis. *Neuroscience and Biobehavioral Reviews, 21,* 1–10.

Weinstock, M. (2001). Alterations induced by gestational stress in brain morphology and behavior of the offspring. *Progress in Neurobiology, 65,* 427–451.

Weiss, I. C., Domeney, A. M., Moreau, J. L., Russig, H., & Feldon, J. (2001). Dissociation between the effects of pre-weaning and/or post-weaning social isolation on prepulse inhibition and latent inhibition in adult Sprague-Dawley rats. *Behavioural Brain Research, 121,* 207–218.

Wells, J. C. K. (2003). The thrifty phenotype hypothesis: Thrifty offspring or thrifty mother? *Journal of Theoretical Biology, 221*, 143–161.

Whishaw, I. Q. (1998). Place learning in hippocampal rats and the path integration hypothesis. *Neuroscience and Biobehavioral Reviews, 22*, 209–220.

Whitnall, M. H. (1993). Regulation of the hypothalamic corticotropin-releasing hormone neurosecretory system. *Progress in Neurobiology, 40*, 573–629.

Williams, G. V., & Goldman-Rakic, P. S. (1995). Modulation of memory fields by dopamine D1 receptors in prefrontal cortex. *Nature, 376*, 572–575.

Zhang, J., Forkstam C., Engel, J. A., & Svensson, L. (2000). Role of dopamine in prepulse inhibition of acoustic startle. Psychopharmacology 149, 181–188.

Zhang, L. X., Xing, G. O., Levine, S., Post, R. M., & Smith, M. A. (1997). Maternal deprivation induces neuronal death. *Society for Neuroscience (Abstract), 23*, 1113.

Zhang, T. Y., Chrétien, P., Meaney, M. J., & Gratton, A. (2005). Influence of Naturally Occurring Variations in Maternal Care on Prepulse Inhibition of Acoustic Startle and the Medial Prefrontal Cortical Dopamine Response to Stress in Adult Rats. *Neuroscience, 25*, 1493–1502.

Chapter 8

Neuropeptides and the Development of Social Behaviors

Implications for Adolescent Psychopathology

Karen L. Bales and C. Sue Carter

Adolescence is by definition a period of rapid hormonal change, and also a time in life when many individuals form new social relationships. However, the link between hormones and social bonding is difficult to study in humans, and particularly in the complex hormonal milieu associated with puberty. For this reason, much of what is known about the hormonal regulation of social behavior and social bonding has come from animal research. Specifically helpful in understanding the causes and consequences of social behaviors have been comparisons among highly social versus less social species. In particular, highly social species, capable of selective and long-lasting social relationships, have been identified as models for the analysis of the physiological basis of social bonds.

The purpose of this review is to provide an overview of the role of two mammalian neuropeptide hormones, oxytocin (OT) and arginine vasopressin (AVP), in the development and expression of social behaviors, including selective behaviors that are indicative of social bonds. Both genetic (especially species and individual differences) and epigenetic (postgenomic or experiential) processes, mediated by physiological changes and acting throughout the life span, can have immediate and long-lasting consequences for both selective and nonselective social behaviors. We begin by giving general background on social behavior in monogamous species, as well as the previously studied physiological and behavioral effects of oxytocin and vasopressin, followed by a description of animal studies describing the role of OT and AVP during development. We then will discuss current knowledge of possible developmental actions of OT and AVP, especially as these may be related to psychopathologies in later life.

Social Behaviors in the Context of Social Systems

Social behaviors by definition involve interactions between two or more individuals. These can be classified as either agonistic (aggressive or defensive) or affiliative (prosocial). Positive social behaviors are less commonly studied, but in general require at a minimum mutual willingness to congregate, remain together, and in some cases engage in selective social behaviors, indicative of social bonds.

Selective behaviors, such as the formation of a pair bond, are directed toward specific individuals and therefore require "social memory"—the ability to recognize other individual animals. These behaviors differ from nonselective or indiscriminate social behaviors, in which the exact identity of the other individual is less relevant—for instance, mating in a species in which the animals do not form a pair bond.

Selective social interactions are of particular importance to human behavior and the behavior of animals that form social bonds. Social behaviors, including social bonds and other forms of social support facilitate both the survival of the individual, as well as reproduction—necessary in turn for genetic survival. In humans, as in other species, social bonds can provide a sense of safety, reduce anxiety, and may influence physical and mental health. In addition, selective social behaviors and social bonds are often critical to long-lasting relationships.

In mammals, the best studied and most enduring relationships, defined by selective social behaviors and in some cases by emotional responses, are between mothers and infants or within breeding pairs (sometimes termed pair-bonds). However, selective social bonds are rare, especially among mammals. Adult social bonds, usually between two adults of the opposite sex, are most clearly identified in highly social species, sometimes termed "monogamous." However, the use of this term must be understood in context. In biology, one method for categorizing species is based on mating systems, which are characterized by the species-typical number of sexual partners, and often focused on male reproductive behavior. The most common mating system in mammals is polygamy (many mates) or more specifically polygyny (many female mates). The less common alternative is monogamy (one mate; Kleiman, 1977), whereas polyandry (many male mates) is rarest. Complicating this story is the fact that it is now well-established that sexual exclusivity is not necessarily a reliable trait of species that live in pairs. For this reason it has become common to use the term "social monogamy" to refer to the social system or social organization of species that form pair bonds. In the absence of other partners, or when mate guarding is successful, social monogamy can promote sexual exclusivity.

Although superficially confusing, the distinction between social systems and mating systems further highlights the overarching importance of social behavior. Even in the absence of absolute "sexual" or "genetic" monogamy, there is no doubt that pair bonds and other forms of stable social groups do exist. These relationships may endure beyond the periods of sexual interaction. In some species individuals may remain together for a lifetime. For example, among the diverse species that share the traits of social monogamy are wolves, several New World primates including tamarins and marmosets, titi monkeys, and even a few rodents, including prairie voles.

Pair bonding and the capacity to form long-lasting social relationships can lead to the formation of extended family groups. Although male parental behavior is uncommon in polygynous species, among socially monogamous mammals both parents tend to exhibit parental behavior. In addition, older reproductively naive offspring may remain with the family, helping to care for younger infants (alloparenting). The extended family groups which arise as a function of these social bonds appear remarkably similar to those seen in some traditional human cultures.

Animal Models for the Analysis of the Physiology of Social Behavior

Differences in sociality among species and individuals have proven especially useful to understanding the biological basis of sociality and the role of hormones in pair-bond formation. For example, much of the recent neuroendocrine work on social behavior has taken advantage of the fact that the genus *Microtus* includes socially monogamous prairie voles (*M. ochrogaster*) and related, nonmonogamous meadow voles (*M. pennsylvanicus*) and montane voles (*M. montanus*).

Descriptions of the proximate mechanisms responsible for different kinds of social groups are most easily understood by analyzing the behavioral responses of individual animals. The tendency toward selectivity in social responses probably relies on mechanisms (see below) that promote both general sociality, as well as specific neurophysiological processes necessary to reinforce or reward selective sociality (Insel, 2003). Animals in nonmonogamous species also may be capable of individual recognition, but may be less inclined to be selective in their social or reproductive behaviors. In addition, species that are not socially monogamous may lack or fail to activate neural mechanisms necessary to reinforce individual preferences. Finally, after a pair bond is formed, individuals may begin to show selective aggression toward strangers (Carter, DeVries, & Getz, 1995).

Oxytocin and Vasopressin Play a Central Role in Social Behavior and Social Bonding

Recent research on the mechanisms underlying selective social behaviors has tended to focus on two major mammalian neuropeptides, oxytocin (OT) and arginine vasopressin (AVP). OT and AVP consist of nine amino acids each, and are produced primarily in the hypothalamus (De Vries & Miller, 1998; Zingg, 2002). OT and AVP receptors are widespread throughout the central and peripheral nervous systems (Barberis & Tribollet, 1996; Jard, Barberis, Audigier, & Tribollet, 1987).

OT and AVP are central to sociality (Carter and Keverne, 2002) but have many other functions as well. Both of these neuropeptides have important physiological roles, including the milk ejection reflex during lactation and labor induction for OT (Russell, Douglas, & Ingram, 2001) and regulation of water balance and cardiovascular functions for AVP (Ring, 2005).

A series of studies (primarily conducted in socially monogamous species) have linked OT and AVP to sociality in general, and in particular to the formation of social bonds (Carter & Keverne, 2002; Lim, Hammock, & Young, 2004). These same peptides also have been linked to parental behavior (Pedersen, Ascher, Monroe, & Prange, 1982; Pedersen & Boccia, 2002). Research in prairie voles and other socially monogamous rodents has implicated OT in female pair bonding and parental care (Insel & Hulihan, 1995; Pedersen et al., 1982; Pedersen & Prange, 1979; Williams, Insel, Harbaugh, & Carter, 1994), whereas AVP has been more extensively studied in the context of male pair bonding and parental care (Aragona & Wang, 2004; Bester-Meredith & Marler, 2003; Lim et al., 2004; Wang, Ferris, & Devries, 1994; Winslow, Hastings, Carter, Harbaugh, & Insel, 1993). However, there is considerable potential for cross-communication between OT and AVP, which differ structurally by only two amino acids and can bind to each other's receptors (Barberis and Tribollet 1996). Pharmacological studies of pair bonding behavior have shown that in both males and females access to both OT and AVP receptors is necessary for pair bond formation (Cho, DeVries, Williams, & Carter, 1999). Blocking either set of receptors in either sex resulted in failure to form a pair bond, although these animals given additional OT or AVP still displayed indiscriminate social behavior. Interestingly, when both OT and AVP receptors were blocked, animals showed a dramatic reduction in sociality and the absence of selective social behaviors.

Both OT and AVP also may be important to male parental behavior, another form of sociality (Bales, Kim, Lewis-Reese, & Carter, 2004a). When parental care in male prairie voles was manipulated with intracerebroventricular injections of different dosages and combinations of OT, AVP, and their antagonists, the ONLY treatment which significantly reduced overall levels of male parental care was a high (10 ng) dosage of both OT antagonist and AVP antagonist. However, in contrast to pair bonding, male parental care does not appear to be selective (i.e., males will care for any pup, not just their own offspring; Lonstein & De Vries, 2000; Roberts, Miller, Taymans, & Carter, 1998).

Relevant data supporting the notion that OT is not essential for (nonselective) social behavior comes from mice with a mutation in the gene for OT (OT knock-out mice: OTKO). OTKO mice continued to mate and to express maternal behavior (Nishimori, Young, Guo, Wang, & Insel, 1996) and were as likely to show social contact as nonmutant control mice. However, the OTKO mice did fail to show selective social behaviors, as measured in a task for social recognition (Ferguson et al., 2000). A similar pattern of social behavior is also seen in mice with a null mutation in the gene for the vasopressin (V1a) receptor (AVP V1aKO mouse; Bielsky, Hu, Szegda, Westphal, & Young, 2004). These data are consistent with the hypothesis that nonselective social behavior can be achieved through the activation of either OT or AVP receptor systems in either sex, whereas *selective* social behavior requires access to both OT and AVP receptors (Cho et al., 1999).

Sociality is highly interwoven with behavioral homeostasis, and many of OT and AVP's actions on social behavior may be affected by their interactions with hormones that have been associated with stress or other forms of challenge. For example, OT or related hormones may suppress hypothalamic-pituitary-adrenal (HPA) axis activity (Altemus, Deuster, Galliven, Carter, & Gold, 1995; Amico, Johnston, & Vagnucci, 1994; Carter et al., 1997; Heinrichs, Baumgartner, Kirschbaum, & Ehlert, 2003; Legros, 2001; Thoman, Conner, & Levine, 1970). In addition, treatment with exogenous OT is associated with reductions in anxiety and a sense of safety and calm (Carter and Keverne, 2002; Uvnas-Moberg, 1998). As with other components of the HPA axis, this is not a simple story, because very recent studies suggest that chronic stress, such as that associated with social isolation, is capable of increasing the synthesis of OT (Grippo et al., 2006).

The effects of AVP also are commonly associated with periods of stress and arousal. However, in contrast to OT, which probably serves to down-regulate stress, AVP may potentiate the secretion of adrenocorticotrophin-releasing-hormone (ACTH; Levine, 2001), especially during chronic stress. AVP is associated with vigilance and defensive aggression, including mate-guarding in male prairie voles (Ferris, 2000; Ferris & Delville, 1994; Stribley & Carter, 1999; Winslow et al., 1993).

A particularly interesting feature of OT and AVP synthesis is the fact that these neuropeptides and at least some of their effects are sexually dimorphic. Exposure to stress also has sexually dimorphic effects, especially in the vole model. For example, activation of the HPA axis affects social behavior differently in male and female voles, with males forming a pair bond more quickly under stressful conditions, and females forming a heterosexual pair bond less quickly when stressed (DeVries, DeVries, Taymans, & Carter, 1996). Support for related but separable actions of OT and AVP comes from the finding that the knockout mouse for the AVP V1a receptor shows reductions in various indications of anxiety (Bielsky et al., 2004), whereas OTKO mice tend to be more anxious than normal animals (Amico, Mantella, Vollmer, & Li, 2004). It is possible that sex differences in endogenous OT and AVP may be critical components of the sexual dimorphism in the capacity of males and females to cope with stressful experiences that has been reported in humans (Taylor et al., 2000).

The functional effects of AVP are less easily summarized than those of OT, and may be dose dependent. For example, it is possible that low doses of AVP or acute exposure to this peptide may increase certain forms of social behavior (Cho et al., 1999), possibly by reducing social anxiety (Dharmadhikari, Lee, Roberts, & Carter, 1997). However, higher doses or perhaps chronic or peripheral changes in AVP might have the opposite effect, creating visceral states that are more commonly associated with higher levels of anxiety (Landgraf & Wigger, 2002; Wigger et al., 2004). The role of AVP may be especially context dependent, and probably relies on the presence or absence of other neurochemical changes, including changes in hormones of the HPA axis, which remain to be fully understood.

Recent studies in voles also have identified a role for dopamine and the reward system in many types of social behavior, including the formation of a pair bond (Aragona, Liu, Curtis, Stephan, & Wang, 2003; Gingrich, Liu, Cascio, Wang, & Insel, 2000; Liu & Wang, 2003; Wang et al., 1999) and the expression of parental care (Lonstein, 2002). Pair bonding behavior has even been compared to an "addiction" due to its use of the neural pathways implicated in substance abuse (Insel, 2003). Access to dopamine receptors is also necessary for formation of a pair bond (Aragona and Wang, 2004). However dopamine, although necessary, does not appear to be sufficient for pair bond formation. Species capable of forming social bonds may exhibit a unique co-occurrence of dopamine and OT (particularly in the nucleus accumbens) or dopamine and AVP (particularly in the ventral pallidum). Sex differences in the neurochemistry of pair bond formation may be partially explained by endogenous differences in OT (more abundant in female) and AVP (androgen dependent and centrally more abundant in males). A sexual dimorphism in these central neuropeptides could have a major impact on sex differences in social behavior and the management of reactivity to stressors (Carter, 1998).

Variation in Neonatal Experience Can Affect Peptide Levels and Later Behavior

Of importance to understanding the actions of neuropeptide hormones is the potential for these compounds to have long-lasting, epigenetic actions, including changes in neuropeptide receptors for OT or AVP (Carter, 2003). The epigenetic effects of OT may be of particular medical relevance because this peptide is commonly modified by modern obstetric practices; in these cases, OT has the potential to influence physiology and behavior in both the mother and offspring (Pedersen et al., 2002).

Pitocin (synthetic OT) is used to induce labor in approximately 30% of births in the United States, and in some hospitals the rate is much higher. For example, over 90% of the women giving birth at Northwestern University Hospital in Chicago in 2005 received pitocin to either induce or augment labor (C. Wong, personal communication, 2005). Atosiban, an oxytocin antagonist, is approved for use in 43 countries (although not in the United States) for the prevention of preterm labor (Husslein, 2002). Both pitocin and atosiban have obvious applications in the management of term and preterm labor. Atosiban has been shown to drastically reduce the risk of maternal cardiac complications in comparison to other currently available treatments for preterm labor (Cabrol et al., 2001; Husslein, 2002; Romero et al., 2000). However, it is unclear how much pitocin/atosiban crosses the placental barrier and infant blood-brain barrier. A study in baboons found that atosiban crossed the placental barrier "relatively freely" (Nathanielsz et al., 1997). Caesarian section has also been shown to alter endogenous OT in the mother, which could affect OT exposure in the infant (Nissen, Gustavsson, Widstrom, & Uvnas-Moberg, 1998).

Variations in child-rearing practices also hold the potential to influence OT synthesis. OT is present in breast milk (Leake, Wietzman, & Fisher, 1981) and is released by warmth and touch (Uvnas-Moberg, 1998) . Animal studies have shown that variation in maternal care in rats can affect OT and AVP receptor binding in offspring (Champagne, Diorio, Sharma, & Meaney, 2001; Francis, Young, Meaney, & Insel, 2000; Francis, Young, Meaney, & Insel, 2002); while handling, especially during the first week of life, in voles can also affect OT and AVP peptide levels in the hypothalamus (Carter et al., 2003). The effects of early experience are often sexually dimorphic, and again raise the possibility that sex differences in either peptides or the response of peptides to other treatment will be important in understanding their functions.

Early exposure to AVP can also have long-lasting developmental effects. In prairie voles, exposure to exogenous AVP or an AVP V1a receptor antagonist (AVPA) has long lasting, dose-dependent effects on aggression; extra AVP increased aggression, especially in males, and animals treated with the AVPA exhibited almost no aggression in later life (Stribley and Carter, 1999). Animals receiving either AVP or AVPA treatments continued to show pair bonds and did not differ in behavior in an elevated plus-maze, considered indicative of anxiety.

Children may also face varying amounts of exposure to AVP through either treatment for bed-wetting (Moffatt, 1997) or through exposure to nicotine, which releases AVP (Andersson, Siegel, Fuxe, & Eneroth, 1983; Matta, Foster, & Sharp, 1993). Almost nothing is known regarding the possible consequences of neonatal manipulations of AVP in humans. However, nicotine experienced during pregnancy or the postpartum period (via lactation) could potentially affect AVP in the off-spring. The relationship between AVP and nicotine also might have special rele-vance in adolescent or preadolescent users of tobacco.

Developmental Manipulation of OT Affects Later Behavior and Neurobiology

Developmental studies in rats have shown long-term physiological effects of neo-natal exposure to OT. Neonatal exposure to OT can lead to lower corticosterone levels in rats (Sohlstrom, Carlsson, & Uvnas-Moberg, 2000), higher body weight (Sohlstrom et al., 2000), lower blood pressure (Holst, Uvnas-Moberg, & Petersson, 2002), and alleviation of effects caused by maternal malnutrition (Olausson, Uvnas-Moberg, & Sohlstrom, 2003). Rats are not, however, an ideal model for studying the role of early exposure to OT and AVP on social behavior. In particu-lar, behaviors such as social bonding and behavioral responses to an infant that are a normal component of the behavioral repertoire of prairie voles have proven a useful model for examining the long-term consequences of developmental ex-posure to peptides. Behaviors toward an infant may be considered a measure of alloparental behavior, but also may be indicative of general sociality (Bales et al., 2004a; Kim & Kirkpatrick, 1996) or of reactivity to novelty (Carter, 1998).

A series of studies in prairie voles, modeled on manipulation of OT that may occur in humans, has analyzed the possible behavioral consequences of neonatal exposure to exogenous OT and substances that block the OT receptor (known as oxytocin antagonists or OTAs; Carter, 2003). Prenatal changes in OT also could have long-term consequences but are more difficult to study because prenatal hormonal manipulations can lead to premature labor. These studies focused on dependent variables, such as social behaviors and stress management, in which OT also has been implicated. Using the prairie vole model, OT was manipulated within the first 24 hours postpartum by injecting pups with one of the following treatments: 1 mg/kg OT, 0.1 mg/kg OTA, or a saline vehicle; or animals were handled without injection. A smaller dosage of OTA (compared to OT) was used because it is 10 to 100 times more effective in receptor binding than the natural ligand (Barberis and Tribollet, 1996). In early life, the rodent neonatal blood-brain barrier is permeable to peripherally injected peptides (Vorbrodt, 1993), and in vole pups, systemically injected OT or OTA does reach and affect the nervous system, as indicated by increased expression of the immediate early gene c-Fos, a sign of cellular activation (Cushing, Yamamoto, Hoffman, & Carter, 2003). In these ex-periments, animals with different hormonal experiences were later exposed to pups (which were not their own, hence termed "alloparental" behavior) during the immediate postweaning period (Roberts, Williams, Wang, & Carter, 1998). Animals in this study also received a series of other behavioral tests, including a second alloparental care test, a partner preference test (Williams, Catania, & Carter, 1992), plus-maze testing (to index anxiety in a novel environment; Ramos & Mormede, 1998), same-sex aggression tests and, in males, tests of mating behavior and reproductive fertility.

Alloparental behavior is measured as the time spent huddling over pups, retrieving the pup, licking and grooming, and so forth, whereas ignoring or attacking infants is considered nonalloparental. In the immediate postweaning period, a high percentage of both male and female voles are alloparental. However, whereas male alloparenting normally stays high throughout life (with 70–80% of animals responsive to pups), female alloparenting starts nearly as high, but declines with age (Bales, Pfeifer, & Carter, 2004b; Lonstein & De Vries, 1999; Lonstein and De Vries, 2000; Roberts et al., 1998). A deficit in parenting or alloparenting could be indicative of increasing anxiety or fear of the pups (Bales et al., 2004b; Fleming & Corter, 1995; Fleming & Leubke, 1981). Both OT and AVP are capable of influencing anxiety although as mentioned above, the effects, especially of AVP, may be complex and not necessarily linear. It is possible that sex differences in alloparental behavior during the postweaning period may be related to a sexual dimorphism in the actions of OT or AVP or other neuroendocrine changes that emerge during this or other periods of rapid maturation.

Sex Differences in the Developmental Effects of Neuropeptides

The developmental manipulations of OT described above tend to produce long-lasting effects that are different in male versus female prairie voles. At the comparatively low doses used in this initial study, neither neonatal OT nor OTA affected alloparental behavior in females; however, in male voles, a single exposure to OTA on the first day of life significantly reduced responsivity to an infant and significantly increased attacks in animals tested during the immediate postweaning period (Bales et al., 2004b).

In addition, males treated with exogenous OT (1 mg/kg) formed pair bonds as adults more quickly than controls (Bales & Carter, 2003b). However, when allowed to mate, males that had been exposed to OT or OTA showed atypical patterns of sexual behavior. Many OT- or OTA-treated males failed to mate. Even among those males that showed behavioral ejaculations, OT- and OTA-treated males were less likely to leave sperm in the female tract during mating (Bales, Abdelnabi, Cushing, Ottinger, & Carter, 2004). Males treated with OTA tended to be less aggressive than those treated with OT or controls (Bales & Carter, 2003a), and had higher corticosterone and dysregulated reactions to stress (Carter, 2003).

The capacity of peptide manipulations to disrupt reproduction was especially apparent in males and once more supports the general hypothesis that the developmental effects of either OT or OTA are both enduring and sexually dimorphic, with males sensitive to doses of OT or OTA that seemed to have little behavioral effect in females. In comparison, the effects of OT in females were either remarkable by their absence or suggested an enhancement of the tendency of animals of this species to show the traits of social monogamy. However, females were not totally insensitive to early manipulations of OT or OTA. For example, females exposed on postnatal Day 1 to a low dosage of OT (1 mg/kg) displayed accelerated development of same-sex aggression after exposure to a male; intrasexual aggression may be indicative of the onset of mate-guarding behavior, which also is characteristic of pair bond formation in monogamous species (Bales and Carter, 2003a). Furthermore, in response to a novel stranger, females that had been exposed to a single neonatal OTA treatment showed an elevation of c-Fos expression in the central amygdala (Kramer, Choe, Carter, & Cushing, 2006). This brain region is implicated in fear and autonomic reactivity, suggesting that although the overt behavior of females was not dramatically disrupted by these manipulations, the emotional reactivity of animals probably was affected by developmental changes in OT.

In addition, our early studies involved only a single comparatively low dose of OT. A more recent study examined the effects of neonatal exposure to higher doses of OT in female prairie voles. In this study, each female was tested for alloparenting, the capacity to form a pair bond, and performance in the elevated plus-maze. Females showed a nonlinear dose-response relationship between OT and later partner preference behavior, with a 2 mg/kg dose (twice the previous dose) associated with a strong partner preference, whereas after neonatal exposure to an even higher dosage (4 mg/kg) females tested later in life showed no partner preference (Bales et al., unpublished data, 2005b). The effects of the highest (4 mg/kg) dose of OT was probably not due to increased fear or anxiety in general, since measures of anxiety were actually reduced in females receiving the highest dose of OT (Bales et al., unpublished data). In addition, females receiving the highest dose of OT were not asocial, at least as indexed by parental behavior, because females receiving 4 mg/kg of OT were about twice as likely as the control females to show alloparental behavior toward pups.

It is possible that the capacity of a high dose of OT to disrupt the tendency to form partner preferences reflects selective actions of neonatal OT on brain areas that are essential for pair bond formation, while leaving these animals capable of showing high levels of other forms of sociality. This finding confirms the general notion that pair bonding relies on mechanisms that are separable from those responsible for general sociality or fear. Ongoing studies are examining the hypothesis that high doses of OT might disrupt receptor binding for OT or dopamine in brain regions such as the nucleus accumbens.

Are the Effects of Early Hormonal
Manipulations Permanent?

It is important to note that the results of early exposure to neuropeptides, as in the pharmacological studies described above, may be at least partially reversible. Another study investigated the possibility that injection with OT later in development could ameliorate the effects of early exposure to OTA. Male pups were injected with one treatment on Day 1 and a second treatment on Day 8; the groups, including various controls, consisted of saline/saline, OTA/saline, OTA/OTA, OTA/OT, and OTA/AVP groups. The subjects were given an alloparental care test on Day 21, and a partner preference test as adults. The results from this study showed that OT could reverse the detrimental effects of OTA. However, exposure to OTA on Day 8 also appeared to at least partially ameliorate the behavioral deficits of OTA-treated males (Bales and Carter, unpublished data, 2005c). Earlier studies had shown that both OT and OTA can have the effect of increasing later endogenous production of OT; however, this effect is more pronounced in females than males (Yamamoto et al., 2004).

Mechanisms for Sexually Dimorphic Effects
of Developmental Neuropeptides

Sex-related behavioral differences in response to early manipulations of OT are probably due at least in part to differential effects of neonatal OT or OTA on the subsequent production of hypothalamic peptides. Yamamoto et al. (2004) found that 21-day-old male prairie voles that had been treated with OTA as infants tended to have a decreased number of AVP-staining cells in the paraventricular nucleus of the hypothalamus (PVN). In contrast, as mentioned above, females treated with either OT (1 mg/kg) or OTA had increased numbers of OT cells in the PVN.

Another (nonmutually exclusive) possibility is that neonatal manipulations may affect receptor binding, either for OT or AVP. The effects of neonatal OT manipulation on peptide receptor binding have not to date been studied in juveniles, but have been measured in adult voles of approximately 60 days of age (Bales et al., 2004c). Neonatal treatment with OTA had marked effects on AVP V1a receptor binding in male prairie voles. Males treated with neonatal OTA had lower V1a binding in the lateral septum (LS) and the bed nucleus of the stria terminalis (BNST) relative to controls. These brain areas contain the AVP peptide in adult male, but not female, prairie voles (De Vries & Simerly, 2002), and these regions are implicated in reactivity to stimuli that could induce fear or anxiety. In contrast, adult males that had been treated neonatally with OT had no changes in the amygdala or BNST, but tended to have an increase in V1a receptor binding in the ventral pallidum and lateral septum (Bales et al., 2004c). The ventral pallidum contains both dopamine and V1a receptors and may be particularly important to pair bonding in males (Lim, Insel, & Young, 2001); this finding is consistent with the increased tendency to form pair bonds in neonatally OT-treated males (Bales and Carter, 2003b).

The effects of neonatal manipulations of OT on the AVP V1a receptor were sexually dimorphic; females treated with OT (rather than OTA) showed decreased V1a receptor binding in the ventral pallidum and LS. Consistent with our behavioral findings, the low doses used here did not disrupt pair bonding, OT receptors, or dopamine (D2) receptors (Bales et al., 2004c). The capacity of neonatal OT or OTA to produce regionally selective and sexually dimorphic effects on the AVP (V1a subtype) receptor system is consistent with several of the behavioral effects seen after peptide manipulations. These findings support the importance of continuing to explore the developmental actions of these and related peptides in both sexes and on specific neural targets.

Because the adolescent period is typically marked by increases in sexual dimorphism, it seems likely that neuropeptide effects also might become more apparent during adolescence. However, in voles the dramatic changes normally associated with puberty are modulated by social experience (Carter et al., 1995). Especially in female prairie voles, puberty can be delayed in animals that remain in the family and stimulated by exposure to a novel member of the opposite sex. This feature of vole reproductive biology has advantages in studies in which it is desirable to minimize the role of gonadal steroids. In addition, it has allowed the functions of neuropeptides such as OT and AVP to be understood somewhat independently of steroid hormones. However, for this same reason, studies of pubertal changes in prairie voles may not be identical to those in mammals that exhibit a spontaneous puberty.

Does Neonatal "Handling" Have Parallels to Those Observed Following Neuropeptide Manipulations?

In ongoing studies, we have observed striking differences in behavior due to apparently minor manipulations of prairie voles in the first few weeks of life. These findings, described below, are consistent with an earlier literature in rats, sometimes called "handling" paradigms, in which animals were either left undisturbed (no handling) during the first week or more of life or experienced brief (15-minute) or longer (3-hour) separations from the mother. Brief separations can be apparently advantageous, possibly through the induction of subsequent increases in maternal stimulation. Longer separations typically resulted in dysregulation of the hypothalamic-pituitary adrenal (HPA) axis and may produce animals that are particularly reactive to stressors experienced in later life (Levine, 2001; Levine, 2002; Plotsky, Sanchez, & Levine, 2001). As mentioned above, research in rats does not address the effects of early "handling" on selective social behaviors or social bonds. The research in rats and coincidental observations of our own in voles led us to explore the effects of early handling/manipulations on the features of social monogamy including pair bonding, as well as alloparenting. This work arose from an initial observation that some of the characteristics of prairie voles, generally viewed as species-typical traits, became less apparent in animals in which early manipulations were deliberately reduced, in comparison to normal husbandry procedures in our laboratory.

In our first version of an early experience paradigm in prairie voles, for 21 days after birth one group of voles underwent weekly "manipulations" (MAN). This involved lifting each parent (the father and mother are both present in prairie vole families) by the scruff of their necks during the weekly cage changes. Infants were attached by milk teeth to the mother's nipples and were usually not directly touched. Another group was "unmanipulated" (UNMAN), which involved transferring pups and parents in a clear cup rather than touching them. In the immediate postweaning period, juvenile animals received an alloparental care test as described above. The proportion of adolescent males showing alloparental behavior, over several replications, was approximately 80% of MAN, whereas between 6% and 45% of UNMAN males showed spontaneous alloparental behavior. In addition, adult UNMAN females failed to form pair bonds after 6 hours of cohabitation; this is 6 times the amount of time needed for a normal female to form a pair bond under our current colony conditions (Bales, Lewis-Reese, & Carter, 2003). Subsequent experiments have indicated that the critical period for manipulation occurs during the first week of life, but also revealed that it is possible to overdo early handling. Animals picked up on three separate times on the first day of life, like those left undisturbed, showed a significant reduction in later sociality (Boone et al., 2006). Analysis of levels of OT- and AVP-immunoreactive cells and levels of receptor binding in the brain as a function of differential amounts of manipulation in early life are currently underway. In a separate preliminary study of the effects of handling on postpartum Day 1 versus Days 1–7, we found indications that picking up animals once a day for 7 consecutive days was associated with an increase in the number of OT-immunoreactive cells in the PVN (Carter et al., 2003).

The effects seen in these paradigms are particularly interesting because of the subtle nature of the neonatal manipulation, which does not require active separation, but which nonetheless may create enduring changes in the tendency of individuals to show positive or negative social behaviors. Effects of early differential manipulations are presumably mediated, at least in part, by an observed increase in pup-directed behaviors (including sniffing, retrievals, etc.) by the parents in the MAN group (Tyler, Michel, Bales, & Carter, 2005), similar to those described in rats (Levine, 2001; Smotherman & Bell, 1980; Meaney, 2001).

Possible Epigenetic Mechanisms for Long-Lasting Changes in Brain and Behavior

The effects of early experience may be mediated in part by genetic differences. However, of particular interest are chains of epigenetic events, such as those described due to deacetylation/methylation-mediated changes in gene expression (Weaver, Diorio, Seckl, Szyf, & Meaney, 2004). The mechanisms for long-lasting changes in centrally active neuropeptides, including OT and AVP and their receptors, remain to be identified but presumably rely on related processes.

Primate Models

The large number of differences between human and rodent neurobiology limits the utility of a rodent model; yet many studies are impossible or unethical to conduct in human subjects. Nonhuman primate models offer another opportunity to examine the relationship between early experience and neuroendocrine factors, including OT and AVP, in behavioral development. The titi monkey (*Callicebus cupreus*) exhibits the traits of social monogamy, including the formation of long-term pair bonds and high levels of male parental care (Mason & Mendoza, 1998; Mendoza & Mason, 1997; Mendoza, Reeder, & Mason, 2002). Pilot studies of plasma OT and AVP levels in titi monkeys indicate individual stability in OT levels, with repeated samples from the same monkeys achieving nearly perfect correlations (Bales et al., 2005a); it is possible that OT production might be associated with individual behavioral traits. Plasma AVP, on the other hand, is more variable and may be more responsive to environmental factors, including stressors.

Additional support for a role for OT in the mediation of, or response to, differential early experience comes from a comparison of rhesus monkeys reared either by a mother or under nursery conditions (Winslow, Noble, Lyons, Sterk, & Insel, 2003). As predicted by other research on OT, the levels of this peptide measured later in life, especially in CSF, were highest in maternally reared animals.

Oxytocin and Vasopressin Have Been Linked to Human Psychopathology

The importance of parenting behavior and early stimulation has long been recognized in human psychology and psychiatry (Bowlby, 1969; Harlow, 1959). However, whether mechanisms for the lasting effects of early experience in humans parallel those in animal models is difficult to prove. Controlled "rearing" experiments on children or adolescents are of course not ethical. However, children who have experienced different degrees of deprivation in early life have been studied (O'Conner, Rutter, & English and Romanian Adoptee Study Team, 2000). At the behavioral level, it has been suggested that in humans the effect of early experience on subsequent social behavior may be mediated by the child or adolescent's ability to exert effortful control (Eisenberg et al., 2005), a relationship that holds up across more than one culture (Zhou, Eisenberg, Wang, & Reiser, 2004). This lack of effortful control over behavior, presumably due at least in part to lack of neural maturation, can lead to many externalizing problems of childhood and adolescence.

Depression and anxiety have also been linked to early social deprivation (Teicher et al., 2003). In addition, it is possible that OT and AVP may influence reactivity to stressors and anxiety (Carter & Altemus, 2004). It has been noted that an increase in depression in females may occur around adolescence when gonadal hormone levels are also rising; OT also is responsive to changes in gonadal hormones (Cyranowski, Frank, Young, & Shear, 2000). Cyranowski and colleagues propose a hypothetical model in which the rise in both gonadal hormones, and presumably OT, coincides with the transition from parental attachment to peer/ romantic attachments. In those vulnerable due to high anxiety or low coping skills, depression might develop. In normal individuals, OT, which may downregulate reactivity to stressors, could have a protective role against stress-induced depression (Carter, 1998; Carter and Altemus, 2004).

In recent experiments using intranasal OT (in comparison to saline), men, especially in the presence of a supportive friend, showed reductions in the release of cortisol following a stressor (Heinrichs et al., 2003). In addition, treatment with intranasal OT was associated with an increase in "trust," measured by the exchange of money in a computer game (Kosfeld, Heinrichs, Zak, Fischbacher, & Fehr, 2005). Intranasal OT has also been shown, measured using fMRI, to inhibit activity in the amygdala, and to reduce connectivity between the amygdala and brainstem autonomic centers (Kirsch et al., 2005). These very recent experiments leave many important questions unanswered. For example, is age or sex or hormonal status a factor in the response to neuropeptides? As suggested by research in animals, might the developmental history of an individual influence later reactivity to OT or AVP?

Of particular relevance to the animal models of early experience and the role of OT and AVP in behavior, may be studies of children who have been reared in orphanages or otherwise deprived of normal parenting (Bowlby, 1969; O'Conner et al., 2000). Some, but not all, of these children experience vulnerabilities to psychopathologies later in life (Teicher et al., 2003). A recent study measuring urinary OT and AVP revealed that orphanage-reared children, even after several years of living in normal homes, tended to have lower levels of AVP and OT measured in urine than children who had been reared by their biological parents; reductions in OT were especially obvious after a period of parental interaction (Carter, 2006; Fries, Ziegler, Kurian, Jacoris, & Pollak, 2006).

Whether or not connections between early environment and human adolescent social disorders are mediated by OT and AVP remains to be examined. However, OT and AVP have been associated with social disorders that are prominent during adolescence, including depression (Carter and Altemus, 2004) and aggressive or asocial behaviors (Ferris and Delville, 1994; King, Ferris, & Lederhendler, 2004). The literature is at best ambiguous as to the role of peptides as either causal or due to changes that might result from these disorders.

Many methodological issues remain to be resolved. Some changes in plasma and central levels of OT and AVP have been noted in depressed patients, but these are not always consistent. Findings in patients with depression include lower plasma OT (Frasch, Zetzsche, Steiger, & Jirikowski, 1995); higher CSF OT (Swedo et al., 1992); higher numbers of OT- and AVP-immunoreactive cells in the hypothalamus (Purba, Hoogendijk, Hofman, & Swaab, 1996); lower levels of AVP in cerebrospinal fluid (Gjerris, Hammer, Vendsborg, Christensen, & Rafaelson, 1985), or no differences (Heuser et al., 1998). Of particular relevance may be the observation that the use of selective serotonin reuptake inhibitors (SSRIs) is associated with both increased OT and reductions in AVP (Altemus, Cizza, & Gold, 1992; De Bellis, Gold, Geracioti, Listwak, & Kling, 1993; Uvnas-Moberg, Bjokstrand, Hillegaart, & Ahlenius, 1999). There is a paucity of descriptive research in which OT or AVP is either measured or manipulated. The history of individuals being studied must be carefully measured. Technological advances, such as the ability to use in vivo imaging technology to examine OT and AVP receptor levels, are needed for a more precise description of the role of OT and AVP in human behavior (Carter and Altemus, 2004).

Another area of adolescent psychopathology in which neuropeptides may play a role is aggression. In animal studies, AVP has been implicated in various types of defensive behavior including mating-induced aggression (Winslow et al., 1993) and resident-intruder aggression (Bester-Meredith, Martin, & Marler, 2005; Ferris, 2000; Ferris et al., 1994). The levels of aggression in rodents can vary according to previous experience and developmental exposures (Bales et al., 2003a; Ferris, 2000). In personality-disordered human subjects, CSF AVP was positively correlated with a history of aggression (Coccaro, Kavoussi, Hauger, Cooper, & Ferris, 1998),. Once more, whether these relationships are causal or not remains to be determined, and it is possible that actions of neuropeptides, including OT and AVP, on these disorders may be mediated through secondary effects on visceral states, including anxiety and arousal (Carter et al., 2004).

The adolescent period of life is characterized by constant change and challenge. Understanding—especially in a life-span context—the neuroendocrine basis of social bonding and related positive social experiences provides a window into the mechanisms through which positive social behaviors and related physiological-visceral states may buffer individuals in the face of such challenges. It is plausible that adverse early experiences, either due to pharmacological exposure, differential parenting, or a history of trauma, might create vulnerabilities to subsequent emotional and cognitive disorders, such as anxiety, depression, schizophrenia, or even autism (Teicher, et al., 2003). Repeated findings of sex differences also are of considerable relevance to adolescent psychology and probably interact with early experiences. Further knowledge of the neuroendocrine foundations of gender-based differences, including those that may be exacerbated during adolescence, may aid in understanding individual differences in both normal and atypical behaviors.

Acknowledgments

This research was funded by the National Alliance for Autism Research, IRUL #322, and NIH P01 HD 38490 to CSC, NIH R01 MH073022 to CSC and KLB, NRSA F32 HD

08702 and NSF #0437523 to KLB, and a pilot grant from the California National Primate Research Center. We thank the following people for their collaboration and research assistance: Antoniah Lewis-Reese, Nathaniel Grotte, Ericka Boone, Pamela Epperson, Julie Hazelton, Albert Kim, Shannon Darkey, Erica Smith, Sheryl Katta, Jalene Lanter, Emily Harden, Ngozi Mogekwu, Lisa Pfeifer, Uzoma Okorie, Kristin Kramer, Michael Ruscio, Carla Ferris, Jeff Stone, Matt Gordon, Titiola Iyun, Britney Allen, Maleeka Kazmi, Dan Geisler, Paul Plotsky, Larry Young, Miranda Lim, Sally Mendoza, William Mason, Carmel Stanko, Caroline Hostetler, Alison Bort, and Lorraine Smith.

References

Altemus, M., Cizza, G., & Gold, P. W. (1992). Chronic fluoxetine treatment reduces hypothalamic vasopressin secretion in vitro. *Brain Research, 593,* 311–313.

Altemus, M., Deuster, P. A., Galliven, E., Carter, C. S., & Gold, P. W. (1995). Suppression of hypothalamic-pituitary-adrenal axis responses to stress in lactating women. *Journal of Clinical Endocrinology and Metabolism, 80,* 2954–2959.

Amico, J. A., Johnston, J. M., & Vagnucci, A. H. (1994). Suckling-induced attenuation of plasma cortisol concentrations in postpartum lactating women. *Endocrine Research, 20,* 79–87.

Amico, J. A., Mantella, R. C., Vollmer, R. R., & Li, X. (2004). Anxiety and stress responses in female oxytocin deficient mice. *Journal of Neuroendocrinology, 78,* 333–339.

Andersson, K., Siegel, R., Fuxe, K., & Eneroth, P. (1983). Intravenous injections of nicotine induce very rapid and discrete reductions of hypothalamic catecholamine levels associated with increases of ACTH, vasopressin and prolactin secretion. *Acta Physiologica Scandinavica, 118,* 35–40.

Aragona, B. J., Liu, Y., Curtis, T., Stephan, F. K., & Wang, Z. X. (2003). A critical role for nucleus accumbens dopamine in partner-preference formation in male prairie voles. *Journal of Neuroscience, 23,* 3483–3490.

Aragona, B. J., & Wang, Z. X. (2004). The prairie vole (*Microtus ochrogaster*): An animal model for behavioral neuroendocrine research on pair bonding. *Ilar Journal, 45,* 35–45.

Bales, K. L., Abdelnabi, M., Cushing, B. S., Ottinger, M. A., & Carter, C. S. (2004). Effects of neonatal oxytocin manipulations on male reproductive potential in prairie voles. *Physiology & Behavior, 81,* 519–526.

Bales, K. L., & Carter, C. S. (2003a). Sex differences and developmental effects of oxytocin on aggression and social behavior in prairie voles (*Microtus ochrogaster*). *Hormones and Behavior, 44,* 178–184.

Bales, K. L., & Carter, C. S. (2003b). Developmental exposure to oxytocin facilitates partner preferences in male prairie voles (*Microtus ochrogaster*). *Behavioral Neuroscience, 117,* 854–859.

Bales, K. L., Kim, A. J., Lewis-Reese, A. D., & Carter, C. S. (2004a). Both oxytocin and vasopressin may influence alloparental behavior in male prairie voles. *Hormones and Behavior, 45,* 354–361.

Bales, K.L., Kramer, K.M., Hostetler, C.M., Capitanio, J.P., and Mendoza, S.P. (2005a) Validation of oxytocin and vasopressin plasma assays for primates: what can blood tell us? *American Journal of Primatology, 66,* 73.

Bales, K.L., Lewis-Reese, A.D., & Carter, C.S. (2005b). [Oxytocin has dose-dependent developmental effects on social behavior, anxiety, and neuroendocrine parameters in a socially monogamous rodent]. Unpublished raw data.

Bales, K.L., Lewis-Reese, A.D., & Carter, C.S. (2005c). [Remediation of exposure to developmental oxytocin antagonist by later exposure to oxytocin]. Unpublished raw data.

Bales, K. L., Lewis-Reese, A. D., & Carter, C. S. (2003). Neonatal handling affects male monogamous behaviors in prairie voles. *Developmental Psychobiology, 43,* 246.

Bales, K. L., Pfeifer, L. A., & Carter, C. S. (2004b). Sex differences and effects of manipulations of oxytocin on alloparenting and anxiety in prairie voles. *Developmental Psychobiology, 44,* 123–131.

Bales, K. L., Plotsky, P. M., Young, L. J., Lim, M. M., Grotte, N. D., Ferrer, E., and Carter, C. S. (in press). Neonatal oxytocin manipulations have long-lasting, sexually dimorphic effects on vasopressin receptors. *Neuroscience.*

Barberis, C., & Tribollet, E. (1996). Vasopressin and oxytocin receptors in the central nervous system. *Critical Reviews in Neurobiology, 10,* 119–154.

Bester-Meredith, J. K., & Marler, C. A. (2003). Vasopressin and the transmission of paternal behavior across generations in mated, cross-fostered *Peromyscus* mice. *Behavioral Neuroscience, 117,* 455–463.

Bester-Meredith, J. K., Martin, P. A., & Marler, C. A. (2005). Manipulations of vasopressin alter aggression differently across testing conditions in monogamous and non-monogamous *Peromyscus. Aggressive Behavior, 31,* 189–199.

Bielsky, I. F., Hu, S.-B., Szegda, K. L., Westphal, H., & Young, L. J. (2004). Profound impairment in social recognition and reduction in anxiety-like behavior in vasopressin V1a receptor knockout mice. *Neuropsychopharmacology, 29,* 483–493.

Boone, E., Sanzenbacher, L., Carter, C.S., and Bales, K.L. (2006) Sexually-dimorphic effects of early experience on alloparental care and adult social behavior in voles [Abstract]. *Society for Neuroscience abstracts.*

Bowlby, J. (1969). *Attachment and loss.* New York: Basic Books.

Cabrol, D., Gillet, J. Y., Madelenat, P., Lansac, J., Paniel, B., Dellenbach, P. et al. (2001). Treatment of preterm labor with the oxytocin antagonist atosiban: A double-blind, randomized, controlled comparison with salbutamol. *European Journal of Obstetrics Gynecology and Reproductive Biology, 98,* 177–185.

Carter, C. S. (1998). Neuroendocrine perspectives on social attachment and love. *Psychoneuroendocrinology, 23,* 779–818.

Carter, C. S. (2003). Developmental consequences of oxytocin. *Physiology & Behavior, 79,* 383–397.

Carter, C. S. (2006). The chemistry of child neglect: Do oxytocin and vasopressin mediate the effects of early experience? *Proceedings of the National Academy of Sciences, 102,* 18247–18248.

Carter, C. S., & Altemus, M. (2004). Oxytocin, vasopressin, and depression. In J. A. den Boer, M. S. George, & G. J. ter Horst (Eds.), *Current and future developments in psychopharmacology* (pp. 201–216). Amsterdam: Benecke.

Carter, C. S., DeVries, A. C., & Getz, L. L. (1995). Physiological substrates of mammalian monogamy: The prairie vole model. *Neuroscience and Biobehavioral Reviews, 19,* 303–314.

Carter, C. S., DeVries, A. C., Taymans, S. E., Roberts, R. L., Williams, J. R., & Getz, L. L. (1997). Peptides, steroids, and pair bonding. *Annals of the New York Academy of Sciences, 807,* 260–272.

Carter, C. S., & Keverne, E. B. (2002). The neurobiology of social affiliation and pair bonding. In D. Pfaff (Ed.), *Hormones, brain, and behavior* (Vol. 1, pp. 299–337). San Diego: Academic Press.

Carter, C. S., Yamamoto, Y., Kramer, K. M., Bales, K. L., Hoffman, G. E., & Cushing,

B. S. (2003). Early handling produces long-lasting increases in oxytocin and alters the response to separation [Abstract]. *Society for Neuroscience Abstracts, 14,* 191.

Champagne, F., Diorio, J., Sharma, S., & Meaney, M. J. (2001). Naturally occurring variations in maternal behavior in the rat are associated with differences in estrogen-inducible central oxytocin receptors. *Proceedings of the National Academy of Sciences of the United States of America, 98,* 12736–12741.

Cho, M. M., DeVries, A. C., Williams, J. R., & Carter, C. S. (1999). The effects of oxytocin and vasopressin on partner preferences in male and female prairie voles (*Microtus ochrogaster*). *Behavioral Neuroscience, 113,* 1071–1079.

Coccaro, E. F., Kavoussi, R. J., Hauger, R. L., Cooper, T. B., & Ferris, C. F. (1998). Cerebrospinal fluid vasopressin levels: Correlates with aggression and serotonin function in personality-disordered subjects. *Archives of General Psychiatry, 55,* 708–714.

Cushing, B. S., Yamamoto, Y., Hoffman, G. E., & Carter, C. S. (2003). Central expression of c-Fos in neonatal male and female prairie voles in response to treatment with oxytocin. *Developmental Brain Research, 143,* 129–136.

Cyranowski, J. M., Frank, E., Young, E., & Shear, M. K. (2000). Adolescent onset of the gender difference in lifetime rates of major depression. *Archives of General Psychiatry, 57,* 21–27.

De Bellis, M. D., Gold, P. W., Geracioti, T. D., Jr., Listwak, S. J., & Kling, M. A. (1993). Association of fluoxetine with reductions in CSF concentrations of corticotropin-releasing hormone and arginine vasopressin in patients with major depression. *American Journal of Psychiatry, 150,* 656–657.

DeVries, A. C., DeVries, M. B., Taymans, S. E., & Carter, C. S. (1996). The effects of stress on social preferences are sexually dimorphic in prairie voles. *Proceedings of the National Academy of Sciences, 93,* 11980–11984.

De Vries, G. J., & Miller, M. A. (1998). Anatomy and function of extrahypothalamic vasopressin systems in the brain. *Progress in Brain Research, 119,* 3–20.

De Vries, G. J., & Simerly, R. B. (2002). Anatomy, development, and function of sexually dimorphic neural circuits in the mammalian brain. In D. W. Pfaff (Ed.), *Hormones, brain, and behavior* (Vol. 4, pp. 137–192). San Diego: Academic Press.

Dharmadhikari, A., Lee, Y. S., Roberts, R. L., & Carter, C. S. (1997). Exploratory behavior correlates with social organization and is responsive to peptide injections in prairie voles. *Annals of the New York Academy of Sciences, 807,* 610–612.

Eisenberg, N., Zhou, Q., Spinrad, T. L., Valiente, C., Fabes, R. A., & Liew, J. (2005). Relations among positive parenting, children's effortful control, and externalizing problems: A three-wave longitudinal study. *Child Development, 76,* 1055–1071.

Ferguson, J. N., Young, L. J., Hearn, E. F., Matzuk, M. M., Insel, T. R., & Winslow, J. T. (2000). Social amnesia in mice lacking the oxytocin gene. *Nature Genetics, 25,* 284–288.

Ferris, C. F. (2000). Adolescent stress and neural plasticity in hamsters: a vasopressin-serotonin model of inappropriate aggressive behaviour. *Experimental Physiology, 85,* 85S–90S.

Ferris, C. F., & Delville, Y. (1994). Vasopressin and serotonin interactions in the control of agonistic behavior. *Psychoneuroendocrinology, 19,* 593–601.

Fleming, A. S., & Corter, C. M. (1995). Psychobiology of maternal behavior in nonhuman mammals. In M. H. Bornstein (Ed.), *Handbook of parenting: Vol. 2. Biology and ecology of parenting* (pp. 59–85). Mahwah, NJ: Erlbaum.

Fleming, A. S., & Leubke, C. (1981). Timidity prevents the virgin female rat from being a good mother: Emotionality differences between nulliparous and parturient females. *Physiology & Behavior, 27,* 863–868.

Francis, D. D., Young, L. J., Meaney, M. J., & Insel, T. R. (2000). Variations in maternal behavior are associated with differences in oxytocin receptor levels in the rat. *Journal of Neuroendocrinology, 12,* 1145–1148.

Francis, D. D., Young, L. J., Meaney, M. J., & Insel, T. R. (2002). Naturally occurring differences in maternal care are associated with the expression of oxytocin and vasopressin (V1a) receptors: Gender differences. *Journal of Neuroendocrinology, 14,* 349–353.

Frasch, A., Zetzsche, T., Steiger, A., & Jirikowski, G. F. (1995). Reduction of plasma oxytocin levels in patients suffering from major depression. *Advances in Experimental Medical Biology, 395,* 257–258.

Fries, A. B., Ziegler, T. E., Kurian, J. R., Jacoris, S., & Pollak, S. D. (2006). Early experience in humans is associated with changes in neuropeptides critical for regulating social behavior. *Proceedings of the National Academy of Sciences, 102,* 17237–17240.

Gingrich, B., Liu, Y., Cascio, C., Wang, Z. X., & Insel, T. R. (2000). Dopamine D2 receptors in the nucleus accumbens are important for social attachment in female prairie voles (*Microtus ochrogaster*). *Behavioral Neuroscience, 114,* 173–183.

Gjerris, A., Hammer, M., Vendsborg, P., Christensen, N. J., & Rafaelson, O. J. (1985). Cerebrospinal fluid vasopressin—changes in depression. *British Journal of Psychiatry, 147,* 696–701.

Harlow, H. F. (1959, June). Love in infant monkeys. *Scientific American, 200*(6), 68–74.

Heinrichs, M., Baumgartner, T., Kirschbaum, C., & Ehlert, U. (2003). Social support and oxytocin interact to suppress cortisol and subjective responses to psychosocial stress. *Biological Psychiatry, 54,* 1389–1398.

Heuser, I., Bissette, G., Dettling, M., Schweiger, U., Gotthardt, U., Schmider, J. et al. (1998). Cerebrospinal fluid concentrations of corticotropin releasing hormone, vasopressin, and somatostatin in depressed patients and healthy controls: Response to amitryptiline treatment. *Depression and Anxiety, 8,* 71–79.

Holst, S., Uvnas-Moberg, K., & Petersson, M. (2002). Postnatal oxytocin treatment and postnatal stroking of rats reduce blood pressure in adulthood. *Autonomic Neuroscience: Basic and Clinical, 99,* 85–90.

Husslein, P. (2002). Development and clinical experience with the new evidence-based tocolytic atosiban. *Acta Obstetricia et Gynecologica Scandinavica, 81,* 633–641.

Insel, T. R. (2003). Is social attachment an addictive disorder? *Physiology & Behavior, 79,* 351–357.

Insel, T. R., & Hulihan, T. J. (1995). A gender-specific mechanism for pair bonding—oxytocin and partner preference formation in monogamous voles. *Behavioral Neuroscience, 109,* 782–789.

Jard, S., Barberis, C., Audigier, S., & Tribollet, E. (1987). Neurohypophyseal hormone receptor systems in brain and periphery. *Progress in Brain Research, 72,* 173–187.

Kim, J. W., & Kirkpatrick, B. (1996). Social isolation in animals models of relevance to neuropsychiatric disorders. *Biological Psychiatry, 40,* 918–922.

King, J. A., Ferris, C. F., & Lederhendler, I. (2004). *Roots of mental illness in children.* New York: New York Academy of Sciences.

Kirsch, P., Esslinger, C., Chen, Q., Mier, D., Lis, S., Siddanthi, S., et al. (2005). Oxytocin modulates neural circuitry for social cognition and fear in humans. *Journal of Neuroscience, 25,* 11489–11493.

Kleiman, D. G. (1977). Monogamy in mammals. *Quarterly Review of Biology, 52,* 39–69.

Kosfeld, M., Heinrichs, M., Zak, P. J., Fischbacher, U., & Fehr, E. (2005). Oxytocin increases trust in humans. *Nature, 435,* 673–676.

Kramer, K. M., Choe, C., Carter, C. S., & Cushing, B. S. (2006). Developmental effects of oxytocin on neural activation and neuropeptide release in response to social stimuli. *Hormones and Behavior, 49,* 206–214.

Landgraf, R., & Wigger, A. (2002). High vs. low anxiety-related behavior rats: An animal model of extremes in trait anxiety. *Behavior Genetics, 32,* 301–314.

Leake, R. D., Wietzman, R. E., & Fisher, D. A. (1981). Oxytocin concentrations during the neonatal period. *Biology of the Neonate, 39,* 127–131.

Legros, J. J. (2001). Inhibitory effect of oxytocin on corticotrope function in humans: are vasopressin and oxytocin ying-yang neurohormones? *Psychoneuroendocrinology, 26,* 649–655.

Levine, S. (2001). Primary social relationships influence the development of the hypothalamic-pituitary-adrenal axis in the rat. *Physiology & Behavior, 73,* 255–260.

Levine, S. (2002). Enduring effects of early experience on adult behavior. In D. W. Pfaff, A. P. Arnold, A. M. Etgen, S. E. Fahrbach, & R. T. Rubin (Eds.), *Hormones, brain, and behavior* (pp. 535–542). New York: Academic Press.

Lim, M. M., Hammock, E. A. D., & Young, L. J. (2004). The role of vasopressin in the genetic and neural regulation of monogamy. *Journal of Neuroendocrinology, 16,* 325–332.

Lim, M. M., Insel, T. R., & Young, L. J. (2001). The ventral pallidum in the monogamous prairie vole: Neuroanatomy and activity during mating. *Hormones and Behavior, 39,* 336–337.

Liu, Y., & Wang, Z. X. (2003). Nucleus accumbens oxytocin and dopamine interact to regulate pair bond formation in female prairie voles. *Neuroscience, 121,* 537–544.

Lonstein, J. S. (2002). Effects of dopamine receptor antagonism with haloperidol on nurturing behavior in the biparental prairie vole. *Pharmacology, Biochemistry and Behavior, 74,* 11–19.

Lonstein, J. S., & De Vries, G. J. (1999). Sex differences in the parental behaviour of adult virgin prairie voles: Independence from gonadal hormones and vasopressin. *Journal of Neuroendocrinology, 11,* 441–449.

Lonstein, J. S., & De Vries, G. J. (2000). Sex differences in the parental behavior of rodents. *Neuroscience and Biobehavioral Reviews, 24,* 669–686.

Mason, W. A., & Mendoza, S. P. (1998). Generic aspects of primate attachments: Parents, offspring and mates. *Psychoneuroendocrinology, 23,* 765–778.

Matta, S. G., Foster, C. A., & Sharp, B. M. (1993). Nicotine stimulates the expression of cFos protein in the parvocellular paraventricular nucleus and brainstem catecholaminergic regions. *Endocrinology, 132,* 2149–2156.

Meaney, M. J. (2001). Maternal care, gene expression, and the transmission of individual differences in stress reactivity across generations. *Annual Review of Neuroscience, 24,* 1161–1192.

Mendoza, S. P., & Mason, W. A. (1997). Attachment relationships in New World primates. *Annals of the New York Academy of Sciences, 807,* 203–209.

Mendoza, S. P., Reeder, D. M., & Mason, W. A. (2002). Nature of proximate mechanisms underlying primate social systems: Simplicity and redundancy. *Evolutionary Anthropology, S1,* 112–116.

Moffatt, M. E. K. (1997). Nocturnal enuresis: A review of the efficacy of treatments and practical advice for clinicians. *Journal of Developmental and Behavioral Pediatrics, 18,* 49–56.

Nathanielsz, P. W., Honnebier, M. B., Mecenas, C., Jenkins, S. L., Holland, M. L., & Demarest, K. (1997). Effects of the OT antagonist atosiban (1–deamino-2-D-try(OET)-4–thr-8–orn-vasotocin/OT) on nocturnal myometrial contractions, maternal cardiovascular function, transplacental passage, and fetal oxygenation in the pregnant baboon during the last third of gestation. *Biology of Reproduction, 57,* 320–324.

Nishimori, K., Young, L. J., Guo, Q. X., Wang, Z. X., & Insel, T. R. (1996). Oxytocin is required for nursing, but is not essential for parturition or reproductive behavior. *Proceedings of the National Academy of Sciences of the United States of America, 93,* 11699–11704.

Nissen, E., Gustavsson, P., Widstrom, A. M., & Uvnas-Moberg, K. (1998). Oxytocin, prolactin, milk production and their relationship with personality traits in women after vaginal delivery or Cesarean section. *Journal of Psychosomatic Obstetrics and Gynecology, 19,* 49–58.

O'Conner, T. G., Rutter, M., & English and Romanian Adoptee Study Team (2000). Attachment disorder behavior following early severe deprivation: extension and longitudinal follow-up. *Journal of the American Academy of Child and Adolescent Psychiatry, 39,* 703–712.

Olausson, H., Uvnas-Moberg, K., & Sohlstrom, A. (2003). Postnatal oxytocin alleviates adverse effects in adult rat offspring caused by maternal malnutrition. *American Journal of Physiology: Endocrinology and Metabolism, 284,* E475–E480.

Pedersen, C. A., Ascher, J. A., Monroe, Y. L., & Prange, A. J., Jr. (1982). Oxytocin induces maternal behavior in virgin female rats. *Science, 216,* 648–650.

Pedersen, C. A., & Boccia, M. L. (2002). Oxytocin links mothering received, mothering bestowed, and adult stress responses. *Stress, 5,* 267.

Pedersen, C. A., & Prange, A. J., Jr. (1979). Induction of maternal behavior in virgin rats after intracerebroventricular administration of oxytocin. *Proceedings of the National Academy of Sciences of the United States of America, 76,* 6661–6665.

Plotsky, P. M., Sanchez, M. M., & Levine, S. (2001). Intrinsic and extrinsic factors modulating physiological coping systems during development. In D. M. Broom (Ed.), *Coping with challenge: Welfare in animals including humans* (pp. 169–196). Berlin: Dahlem University Press.

Purba, J. S., Hoogendijk, W. J., Hofman, M. A., & Swaab, D. F. (1996). Increased number of vasopressin and oxytocin expressing neurons in the paraventricular nucleus of the hypothalamus in depression. *Archives of General Psychiatry, 53,* 137–143.

Ramos, A., & Mormede, P. (1998). Stress and emotionality: A multidimensional and genetic approach. *Neuroscience and Biobehavioral Reviews, 22,* 33–57.

Ring, R. H. (2005). The central vasopressonergic system: Examining the opportunities for psychiatric drug development. *Current Pharmaceutical Design, 11,* 205–225.

Roberts, R. L., Miller, A. K., Taymans, S. E., & Carter, C. S. (1998). Role of social and endocrine factors in alloparental behavior of prairie voles (*Microtus ochrogaster*). *Canadian Journal of Zoology-Revue Canadienne de Zoologie, 76,* 1862–1868.

Roberts, R. L., Williams, J. R., Wang, A. K., & Carter, C. S. (1998). Cooperative breeding and monogamy in prairie voles: Influence of the sire and geographical variation. *Animal Behaviour, 55,* 1131–1140.

Romero, R., Sibai, B. M., Sanchez-Ramos, L., Valenzuela, G. J., Veille, J. C., Tabor, B., et al. (2000). An oxytocin receptor antagonist (atosiban) in the treatment of preterm labor: A randomized, double-blind, placebo-controlled trial with tocolytic rescue. *American Journal of Obstetrics and Gynecology, 182,* 1173–1183.

Russell, J. A., Douglas, A. J., & Ingram, C. D. (2001). Brain preparations for maternity-adaptive changes in behavioral and neuroendocrine systems during pregnancy and lactation: An overview. In J. A. Russell, A. J. Douglas, R. J. Windle, & C. D. Ingram (Eds.), *The maternal brain: Neurobiological and neuroendocrine adaptation and disorders in pregnancy and postpartum* (pp. 1–38). New York: Elsevier Press.

Smotherman, W. P., & Bell, R. W. (1980). Maternal mediation of early experience. In W. P. Smotherman & R. W. Bell (Eds.), *Maternal influence and early behavior*. New York: Spectrum.

Sohlstrom, A., Carlsson, C., & Uvnas-Moberg, K. (2000). Effects of oxytocin treatment in early life on body weight and corticosterone in adult offspring from ad libitum-fed and food-restricted rats. *Biology of the Neonate, 78,* 33–40.

Stribley, J. M., & Carter, C. S. (1999). Developmental exposure to vasopressin increases aggression in adult prairie voles. *Proceedings of the National Academy of Sciences, 96,* 12601–12604.

Swedo, S. E., Leonard, H. L., Kruesi, M. J., Rettew, D. C., Listwak, S. J., Berrettini, W., et al. (1992). Cerebrospinal fluid neurochemistry in children and adolescents with obsessive-compulsive disorder. *Archives of General Psychiatry, 49,* 29–36.

Taylor, S. E., Klein, L. C., Lewis, B. P., Gruenewald, T. L., Gurung, R. A. R., & Updegraff, J. A. (2000). Bio-behavioral responses to stress in females: Tend-and-befriend, not fight-or-flight. *Psychological Review, 107,* 411–429.

Teicher, M. H., Andersen, S. L., Polcari, A., Anderson, C. M., Navalta, C. P., & Kim, D. M. (2003). The neurobiological consequences of early stress and childhood maltreatment. *Neuroscience and Biobehavioral Reviews, 27,* 33–44.

Thoman, E. B., Conner, R. L., & Levine, S. (1970). Lactation suppresses adrenocorticosteroid activity and aggressiveness in rats. *Journal of Comparative Physiological Psychology, 70,* 364–369.

Tyler, A. N., Michel, G. F., Bales, K. L., & Carter, C. S. (2005). Do brief early disturbances of parents affect parental care in the bi-parental prairie vole (*Microtus ochrogaster*)? *Developmental Psychobiology, 47,* 451.

Uvnas-Moberg, K. (1998). Oxytocin may mediate the benefits of positive social interactions and emotions. *Psychoneuroendocrinology,* 819–835.

Uvnas-Moberg, K., Bjokstrand, E., Hillegaart, V., & Ahlenius, S. (1999). Oxytocin as a possible mediator of SSRI-induced antidepressant effects. *Psychopharmacology, 142,* 95–101.

Vorbrodt, A. W. (1993). Morphological evidence of the functional polarization of brain microvascular epithelium. In W. M. Pardridge (Ed.), *The blood-brain barrier* (pp. 137–164). New York: Raven Press.

Wang, Z. X., Ferris, C. F., & Devries, G. J. (1994). Role of septal vasopressin innervation in paternal behavior in prairie voles (*Microtus ochrogaster*). *Proceedings of the National Academy of Sciences, 91,* 400–404.

Wang, Z. X., Yu, G. Z., Cascio, C., Liu, Y., Gingrich, B., & Insel, T. R. (1999). Dopamine D2 receptor-mediated regulation of partner preferences in female prairie voles (*Microtus ochrogaster*): A mechanism for pair bonding? *Behavioral Neuroscience, 113,* 602–611.

Weaver, I. C. G., Diorio, J., Seckl, J. R., Szyf, M., & Meaney, M. J. (2004). Early environmental regulation of hippocampal glucocorticoid receptor gene expression—Characterization of intracellular mediators and potential genomic target sites. *Annals of the New York Academy of Sciences, 1024,* 182–212.

Wigger, A., Sanchez, M. M., Mathys, K. C., Ebner, K., Frank, E., Liu, D., et al. (2004). Alterations in central neuropeptide expression, release, and receptor binding in rats bred for high anxiety: Critical role of vasopressin. *Neuropsychopharmacology, 29,* 1–14.

Williams, J. R., Catania, K. C., & Carter, C. S. (1992). Development of partner preferences in female prairie voles (*Microtus ochrogaster*): The role of social and sexual experience. *Hormones and Behavior, 26,* 339–349.

Williams, J. R., Insel, T. R., Harbaugh, C. R., & Carter, C. S. (1994). Oxytocin centrally administered facilitates formation of a partner preference in female prairie voles (*Microtus ochrogaster*). *Journal of Neuroendocrinology, 247–250.*

Winslow, J. T., Hastings, N., Carter, C. S., Harbaugh, C. R., & Insel, T. R. (1993). A role for central vasopressin in pair bonding in monogamous prairie voles. *Nature, 365,* 545–548.

Winslow, J. T., Noble, P. L., Lyons, C. K., Sterk, S. M., & Insel, T. R. (2003). Rearing effects on cerebrospinal fluid oxytocin concentration and social buffering in rhesus monkeys. *Neuropsychopharmacology, 28,* 910–918.

Yamamoto, Y., Cushing, B. S., Kramer, K. M., Epperson, P. D., Hoffman, G. E., & Carter, C. S. (2004). Neonatal manipulations of oxytocin alter expression of oxytocin and vasopressin immunoreactive cells in the paraventricular nucleus of the hypothalamus in a gender specific manner. *Neuroscience, 125,* 947–955.

Zhou, Q., Eisenberg, N., Wang, Y., & Reiser, M. (2004). Chinese children's effortful control and dispositional anger/frustration: Relations to parenting styles and children's social functioning. *Developmental Psychology, 40,* 352–366.

Zingg, H. H. (2002). Oxytocin. In D. Pfaff, A. P. Arnold, A. M. Etgen, S. E. Fahrbach, & R. T. Rubin (Eds.), *Hormones, brain, and behavior* (pp. 779–802). New York: Academic Press.

Chapter 9

The Effects of Early Deprivation
on Brain-Behavioral Development

*The Bucharest Early
Intervention Project*

Charles A. Nelson III, Charles H. Zeanah, and Nathan A. Fox

The effects of early experience on brain and behavioral development are most frequently examined by studying the effects of early deprivation. Indeed, using both animal models and so-called "experiments of nature" with humans, extremes of early experience provide opportunities to explore the origins of typical and atypical psychological development, along with the neurobiological underpinnings that support such development. A short list of examples from this literature include the effects of (a) monocular and binocular deprivation on visual development, (b) early auditory deprivation on auditory and linguistic development, (c) poverty on cognitive development, and (d) psychosocial deprivation on psychological, mental, and physical development (for discussion of these and related topics, see Knudsen, 2003; Nelson, Thomas, & de Haan, 2006).

In nearly all cases, deprivation exerts powerful effects on the course of development. It must be underscored, however, that the specific effects and the severity of effects will vary as a function of the dose, timing, and duration of the deprivation and, as well, individual differences in the response to the deprivation (which likely have most to do with the individual's genetic makeup and experiential history). Thus, for example, being deprived of auditory or visual input during the time the auditory or visual system is developing will lead to a different developmental outcome than if such deprivation occurs later, once these systems are online and mature. Most sensory and perceptual systems generally have

197

sensitive periods that occur very early in development; less is known about cognitive and social-emotional development, although both domains clearly share features with sensory and perceptual development (e.g., the importance of early cognitive stimulation or the opportunity to form an attachment).

Not surprisingly, there is a vast literature on the effects of deprivation on rodents and nonhuman primates that extends from sensory to cognitive to social development. Such work has the advantage of being able to manipulate variables in a controlled and systematic way that permits causal or semicausal inferences to be drawn. Such is not the case when it comes to the human, as one cannot randomly assign infants and children to differing degrees of deprivation at different ages. Rather, one often takes advantage of so-called experiments of nature, by which we mean situations in which a child has been deprived of a given experience by virtue of a congenital abnormality or, sadly, by sociopolitical circumstances. Children born with cataracts or born deaf represent an example of the former, whereas children abandoned at birth and placed in institutions represent an example of the latter. In this chapter we focus specifically on children being reared in institutions.

Institutional care, which was studied with small scale and often poorly controlled studies through much of the early to mid-20th century, recently has reemerged as a focus of study as tens of thousands of "postinstitutionalized" children have been adopted into the United States and Western Europe (Zeanah, Smyke, & Settles, 2005). More recent investigations have been more rigorous and have confirmed earlier findings from descriptive studies suggesting that institutional care was associated with a variety of deleterious outcomes. Contemporary research has documented many problems in young children adopted out of institutions in Eastern Europe and Russia. Although there may be wide variability in the quality of care between and even within institutions, there are certain modal features that tend to characterize institutional care: regimented daily schedule, high child/caregiver ratio, nonindividualized care, lack of psychological investment by caregivers, lack of sensory, cognitive, and linguistic stimulation, and rotating shifts, all leading to an adverse caregiving environment (for an example of such conditions in Russian orphanages, see St. Petersburg–USA Orphanage Research Team, 2005).

Not surprisingly, young children adopted out of institutions characterized by social and material deprivation have been shown to be at risk for a variety of social (Chisholm, 1998; O'Connor et al., 2003), cognitive (Hodges & Tizard, 1989; O'Connor, Rutter, Beckett, et al., 2000a), and psychiatric sequelae (e.g., Ellis, Fisher, & Zaharie, 2004). Despite the importance of their contributions, these studies have important limitations that must be acknowledged. First, most adoption studies have not been able to assess important details of the preadoptive caregiving environment (that is, what the institutional environment is like). This is important, because there is wide variability between and within settings (Smyke, Zeanah, & Koga, 2002b; Zeanah et al., 2003). Second, children are not adopted randomly from institutions, and selection bias may limit our ability to understand developmental differences associated with institutionalization because more impaired children are less likely to be studied. Third, measures of important constructs have often been limited. For example, in the area of psychiatric symptomatology, most studies have relied on behavior problem checklists rather than structured psychiatric interviews (Fisher et al., 1997; Hoksbergen et al., 2003; Kreppner, O'Connor, & Rutter, 2001; Marcovitch et al., 1997; Roy, Rutter, & Pickles, 2000). Fourth, in the context of social development, attachment and indiscriminate sociability[1] have been studied (Chisholm, 1998; O'Connor et al., 2003; Smyke et al., 2002a; Vorria et al., 2003; Zeanah et al., 2005), but many other developmental processes vital to social adaptation have not been examined, especially social cognition. Fifth, more within-country studies of the effects of institutionalization are needed so that effects resulting from the experience of adoption into another culture (and often into a different language environment) can be disentangled from the effects of institutionalization itself. Sixth, other than a study of PET scans in 10 children adopted out of institutions (Chugani et al., 2001) and our preliminary work (Marshall, Fox, & the BEIP Core Group, 2004; Parker & Nelson, 2005; Parker, Nelson, & the BEIP Core Group, 2005), there have been no studies of brain functioning, and we know far too little about functional differences in brain development in children raised in institutions. Ultimately, behavioral plasticity and recovery from early abnormalities must involve neurobiological processes, but formidable challenges remain before we determine which ones.

The Bucharest Early Intervention Project (BEIP) was designed to address these limitations. The project itself was an outgrowth of a broader initiative aimed at understanding the role of experience in influencing brain and behavioral development. This initiative was embedded in the work of a MacArthur Foundation research network entitled Early Experience and Brain Development (www .macbrain.org). The premise of this group of researchers was to systematically examine how experience influences brain development and behavioral development across species; indeed, the BEIP has a nonhuman primate counterpart designed to examine the effects of early social bond disruption in rhesus monkeys (for a summary of this and related work in the context of developmental psychopathology, see Nelson et al., 2002). In so doing, we hope to take advantage of this comparative approach by modeling in the nonhuman primate the "experiment of nature" we are studying in Romania.

Bucharest Early Intervention Project

The Bucharest Early Intervention Project is a randomized controlled trial comparing the effects of foster care as an alternative to institutional care for young children abandoned at birth and placed in institutions (Zeanah et al., 2003). The study was collectively designed by members of the Early Experience and Brain Development network and implemented by the three authors of this chapter. This study, which is still ongoing, comprehensively assessed 136 children between the ages of 6 and 31 months who were institutionalized in all six of the institutions for young children in Bucharest, Romania, and followed them systematically though 54 months of age. The details of this assessment are described in the next section.

Study Design

Assessing children at baseline—that is, prior to randomization—increased our confidence that outcome differences would reflect true effects of the intervention and not, for example, differences in sample makeup. As discussed in Zeanah et al. (2003), randomization prior to intervention addressed the concerns about previous studies of adopted children that have the potential of selection bias with regard to who is adopted and therefore included in studies. In addition, randomization prior to intervention increased the chance that prenatal risk factors would be evenly distributed across the intervention and control groups. The inclusion of a community sample of Romanian never-institutionalized children permitted us to ascertain whether our measures would yield the same findings in a Romanian comparison sample as in a U.S. sample and to reveal potential ethnic differences. Moreover, because we predicted that foster care would serve to redress the sequelae associated with institutional care, it was imperative that we be able to compare our intervention group with an in-country comparison group.

Our study design permitted us to juxtapose length of time in the institution with months of intervention, and in so doing permitted us to assess the effects of timing of intervention on remediation.

Participants

INSTITUTIONAL GROUP (IG). We initially screened 187 children (51% boys, 49% girls) who resided in any of the six institutions in Bucharest, and who at the age of screening were 31 months of age or less. An additional eligibility criterion was that these children needed to have spent at least half of their lives living in an institution. The screening, which took place in February 2000, consisted of a pediatric/neurologic exam, growth measurements, an auditory assessment, and assessment of any physical abnormalities. Of those screened, we excluded 51 children for medical reasons, including genetic syndromes; frank signs of fetal alcohol syndrome, based in large part on facial dysmorphology; and microcephaly using standards from Tanner (1973), which then resulted in 136 children in our institutionalized group (prior to randomization to foster care).

NEVER-INSTITUTIONALIZED GROUP (NIG). These children were drawn from the same maternity hospitals as our IG, and matched on age and gender to them.[2]

Eighty children were initially recommended by their pediatricians, and after screening 72 were enrolled.

Each assessment consists of up to 14 procedures (depending on the age of the child). These assessments are divided into 3 lab assessments and 1 home/institutional observation. Additionally, physical growth measures of all children in the institutional and foster care groups are obtained monthly.

Measures

The measures we employ include a range of structured and unstructured procedures in laboratory and naturalistic settings, as well as elicited and observed behaviors in the child. Cognitive functioning, social communication and social relatedness, and attachment (Ames, 1997; Chisholm, 1998; Johnson, 2000; O'Connor et al., 2003; O'Connor et al., 2000a; O'Connor et al., 2000b; Zeanah, 2000) were all included as central measures due to the fact that these domains are all known to be compromised among previously institutionalized children. Note that although we list all the dimensions we assessed, not all of these findings will be discussed in this chapter.

CAREGIVING ENVIRONMENT. We used the Observational Record of the Caregiving Environment (ORCE) to assess qualitative and quantitative differences in caregiving environments in the institution, foster care homes, and homes of the never-institutionalized children.

PHYSICAL GROWTH. Physical growth is assessed (monthly, permitting us to construct growth curves) using standard measures of weight, length/height, occipitofrontal circumference, mid-arm circumference, triceps skin-fold, and height.

COGNITIVE FUNCTION. The Bayley Scales of Infant Development (BSID-II) are used to assess developmental level through 42 months of age, whereas the Weschler Preschool Primary Scales of Intelligence (WPPSI) is used for the 54-month assessment.

LANGUAGE. Language development is assessed with the Receptive-Expressive Emergent Language (REEL) scales (Bzoch & League, 1972) and the Reynell Developmental Language Scales III (Edwards, Garman, Hughes, Letts, & Sinka, 1997), as well as by quantitative assessments during social interaction.

SOCIAL COMMUNICATION. The Early Social Communication Scales (ESCS; Mundy, P., Delgado, C., Block, J., Venezia, M., Hogan, A., & Seibert, J., 2003) assess the child's initiation of joint attention, response to joint attention, and behavior regulation.

EMOTIONAL REACTIVITY. We selected two tasks from a standard laboratory battery for the assessment of temperament (LAB-TAB, Goldsmith, & Rothbart, 1999) to assess positive affect reactivity: the peek-a-boo and the puppet interview tasks. For peek-a-boo, the child's caregiver/mother participated; for the puppet task, a female experimenter performed the task.

INTERACTIONAL BEHAVIOR. The Crowell Procedure (Crowell & Feldman, 1988) was used to observe a variety of structured episodes of parent-child interaction, including free play, clean up, blowing bubbles, a series of teaching tasks, and a separation and reunion between the child and a caregiver who knew the child well.

ATTACHMENT. In order to assess attachment in the institutional setting, we use three different methods. First, we use classifications of the Strange Situation Procedure (Ainsworth, Blehar, Waters, & Wall, 1978), observing the child with his/her "favorite" caregiver. Second, we developed a continuous rating of the degree to which a child has formed an attachment to a parent/caregiver based on behavior in the Strange Situation. Finally, we use the Disturbances of Attachment Interview (Smyke & Zeanah, 1999) to assess attachment disorder symptomatology. This interview has been validated preliminarily in a sample of institutionalized Romanian children (Smyke et al., 2002a; Zeanah, Smyke, & Dumitrescu, 2002).

EMOTION RECOGNITION. Based on the assumption that face recognition is an experience-expectant and activity-dependent process (see Nelson, 2001), we posited that institutional care would lead to impairments in emotion recognition, possibly due to delays in the development of the amygdala and surrounding circuitry purported to be involved in this process (for review, see Nelson, 2001; Nelson & de Haan, 1996). We employed two tasks designed to examine the discrimination and recognition of facial expressions. The first involves the visual paired comparison procedure (VPC), in which infants are first presented with pairs of identical faces (e.g., the same model posing the same expression; "happy") and then tested by presenting the familiar stimulus alongside a stimulus in which the facial expression has changed ("happy" vs. "fear"). Looking time is recorded, and longer looking at the novel stimulus permits the inference that the infant has discriminated the two emotions. In our second paradigm, we record event-related potentials (ERPs) while infants are presented with happy, fear, anger, and sad faces (25% probability each). Here, the goal is to examine whether the neural correlates of emotion recognition differ across our samples. Collectively, we hope to be able to specify some of the areas of neural functioning underlying social relatedness that are impacted by early social deprivation.

ELECTROPHYSIOLOGY. Conventional neuroimaging tools such as MRI and fMRI exist in only a limited fashion in Bucharest. As well, we first studied the children when they were infants or toddlers. As a result, we focused our efforts on the recording of the brain's electrical activity, including both the resting electroencephalogram (EEG) and the event-related potential (ERP). Both measures provide detailed information about the transmission of electrical information throughout the brain (i.e., mental chronometry); in the case of the ERP, some information about the neural and mental operations the brain performs when engaged in a cognitive task is also provided. To this end we used the EEG as our metric of overall brain development and brain health and the ERP to probe the child's knowledge of facial identity and facial expressions. Each of these is described below.

We are investigating four elements of our EEG data: (1) the patterning of EEG power in different frequency bands across the scalp (a metric of the brain's general level of functioning across different domains; thus, the alpha band reflects sensory processing, the beta band reflects cognitive processing, etc.), (2) the development of EEG power spectra (a metric of the general amount of electrical activity generated by the brain), (3) intrahemispheric EEG coherence (a metric of the brain's ability to communicate from one region to another), and (4) frontal EEG asymmetry (a metric of differential activity recorded over the frontal lobe and thought to reflect individual differences in temperament or emotion). In addition to collecting EEG data during different stimulus conditions, we acquire EEG time locked to the presentation of auditory and visual stimuli. We are interested in the infants' and young children's physiological responses to novelty in the auditory modality. Inspection of ERP waveforms allows us to investigate electrophysiological reactivity to auditory novelty.

FACE RECOGNITION. Face recognition plays an important role in caregiver-infant interactions prior to the onset of language. In this context we are evaluating the child's ability to recognize his/her caregiver's face and discriminate this from the face of a stranger. Children are presented with digitized images of their primary caregiver's face and the face of a stranger while ERPs are recorded. From this project we intend to evaluate not only whether children show ERP evidence of discriminating caregiver from stranger, but as well, whether the neural processes involved in such discrimination are the same across groups.

Experimental Design
The BEIP began with comprehensive assessments of children and their caregiving environments prior to randomization, and then assessed their development serially at 9, 18, 30, 42, and 54 months. Because participants were 6–30 months of age at the beginning of the study, *all* children were seen for follow-up assessments at 30, 42, and 54 months.

DESCRIPTION OF FOSTER PARENTS. Before describing our findings, some mention should be made of our foster care intervention. A challenge entering the study was that foster care did not exist in Bucharest prior to our arrival, and for this reason we needed to develop our own system. Because of the extreme deprivation our institutionalized children experienced, we thought it essential to develop a foster care system that was high quality, but also one that was realistically replicable. To this end we actively recruited and then screened potential foster care parents. After screening, we were able to identify 56 foster care families who met our rigorous criteria, and 69 institutionalized children were randomly assigned to be placed in foster care (leaving 67 children to be randomly assigned to remain in the institutions). Of 56 foster families eventually recruited to participate, 46% were single-parent families. All foster mothers had at least a high school education, with an additional 63% having completed vocational training, possessed specialized skills, or completed college. In addition, 27% were retired, and 5% had never been employed before.

All foster care parents received a monthly stipend, and we provided essential supplies for the children (e.g., diapers, toys) and a 24-hour, on-call pediatrician for all children. Moreover, our team of social workers visited the families on a regular basis, and if the child or family required clinical services, the social workers either provided those services directly or made necessary referrals. Crucial to this model was clinical supervision provided on a weekly basis to the social workers in Bucharest by American psychologists.

In the discussion that follows, we highlight just a few of the major findings at baseline and when possible, follow-up. It is important to underscore that many of these findings are preliminary because data collection continues, but the pattern of findings is fairly clear. First, institutional environments were less adequate based on quantitative and qualitative ratings when compared to family settings at all points in time. Further, children in institutions had more developmental delays and deviance in almost every domain assessed. Foster care appears to be leading to amelioration of some of these delays and deviances, but in no domain did children in foster care catch up to children who had never been institutionalized (insofar as we have been able to look at our data thus far).

Findings

After briefly describing some general findings, we will focus most on just a few domains of functioning that we consider most germane to this volume.

GENERAL OBSERVATIONS ABOUT CAREGIVING. In the BEIP study, caregivers of never-institutionalized children were both more available and interacted more frequently with their children than did caregivers in institutional settings. Further, within the institutionalized group, quality of caregiving at baseline was strongly associated with cognitive development and with child competence. Care was assessed based on ratings of 2-hour videotaped observations. They were coded with the Observational Record of the Caregiving Environment (ORCE), which is described in Zeanah et al. (2003) and Smyke et al. (2006), explaining variance over and above what was accounted for by large between-group (institutionalized vs. never-institutionalized) differences (Smyke et al., 2004). Among institutionalized children, quality of caregiving was related to signs of attachment disorder and to a more fully developed attachment to the caregiver. Quality of caregiving also was the only significant factor associated with an institutionalized child having an organized (as opposed to disorganized or unclassifiable) attachment.[3]

At follow-up, infants and toddlers randomized into foster care were observed to use speechlike vocalizations and to exhibit more positive interactions with caregivers significantly more frequently than children who had been randomized to continued institutional care (Smyke et al., 2004). This pattern of findings, both in the NICHD child care studies (see NICHD Early Child Care Research Network, 1996, 2003, 2005) and in the findings from the infant and toddler BEIP, suggest that quality of the caregiving environment, as measured by the ORCE, is an important construct in understanding child outcome. Examples of inadequate caregiving include being less available to the child or interacting less with the child.

To illustrate differences in our institutionalized versus never-institutionalized children, we are sampling five different domains, including attachment, cognitive development (i.e., Bayley scores), EEG power, ERPs to facial recognition of emotion, and psychiatric disorders. Note that because both data collection and data analysis is ongoing, only an overview of these findings will be discussed (here the reader is encouraged to consult our existing published data).

Mental age: At baseline, there were substantial differences in the institutionalized group and the never-institutionalized group. Mean scores on the Bayley Mental Development Index (MDI) were 103 in the never-institutionalized group (virtually identical to the population mean of the US of 100) and 65 in the institutionalized group (Smyke et al., 2003). The latter score was inflated because the lowest score assigned on the Bayley is < 50. All children who received this score were assigned a score of 49. Following randomization, children in foster care demonstrated more significant gains in MDI scores than children in the institution group, although they did not attain levels of the never-institutionalized group at any follow-up point (Smyke et al., 2004).

To examine the effects of foster care on developmental status, we compared the data from our IG to our foster care group (FCG) at 42 months of age. As can be seen in figure 9-1, the Developmental Quotient (roughly comparable to full scale IQ) of the Bayley improved significantly for those placed in foster care, but only modestly for those who remained in the institution.

Attachment: At baseline, institutionalized children had substantially more disorganized (including nonattached) attachment than children raised with their parents (78% vs. 22%; for discussion, see Zeanah et al., 2005). Furthermore, 100% of never-institutionalized children were coded blindly as having fully developed attachments to their mothers, whereas only 3% of institutionalized children were

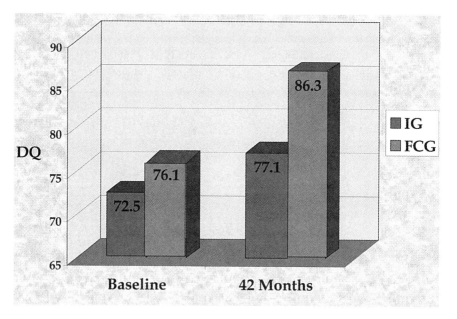

Figure 9-1 Change in developmental quotient from the Bayley exam at 42 months, IG versus FCG. Note the 10 point improvement in DQ among those placed in foster care compared to 5 points among those remaining in the institution.

coded as having fully developed attachments to their caregivers. In addition, caregivers reported significantly more signs of both emotionally withdrawn/ inhibited reactive attachment disorder (RAD)[4] and indiscriminately social/ disinhibited RAD in institutionalized compared to never-institutionalized children. At follow-up, signs of emotionally withdrawn/inhibited RAD were significantly lower in the foster care group than the institutionalized group, and indistinguish-able from the never-institutionalized group. Indiscriminate sociability/disinhibited RAD, on the other hand, was significantly lower at follow-up in the foster care group than in the institutional group, but was still significantly higher than in the never-institutionalized group (Zeanah et al, 2005).

Event-Related Potentials: Event-related potentials (ERPs) in response to four facial expressions—fear, angry, happy, and sad—were collected from institutionalized children and never-institutionalized children ranging in age from 7 to 32 months. The ERP findings are complicated by the fact that we observed several components over several regions of the scalp; moreover, previous research has revealed rather dramatic developmental changes in the ERP across this age range. As a result, we have subdivided our sample into those younger or older than 23 months of age, and have focused on one specific component, the P400. The P400 component reflects the brain's obligatory and specific response to faces and, as such, provides a metric of whether face processing has been perturbed by early institutionalization (which we expect it to be). In previous studies (e.g., de Haan & Nelson, 1997), it was reported that the latency to peak for the P400 is faster to faces than to objects, and faster in the right hemisphere than left (reflecting an adult configuration). Focusing first on the baseline data, comparing IG to NIG, we find a faster P400 for NIG compared to IG, reflecting the typical developmental pattern we would expect. At follow-up (figure 9-2), our latency effect is replaced by an amplitude effect.[5] Specifically, now we find that amplitude of the P400 is greatest among the NIG, smallest among the IG, and in-between among the FCG. Reframing these findings, the data from the FCG appear to be moving in the direction of the NIG, that is, are beginning to normalize. (Note that this same pattern of findings can be observed for the P100 component. The P100 is thought to reflect the early sensory processing of a visual stimulus.)

EEG Power: At each assessment in the original BEIP study, the EEG was recorded from 15 electrode sites during an episode designed to elicit quiet attention in infants and young children. Power in three frequency bands (3–5 Hz as theta, 6–9 Hz as alpha, 10–18 Hz as beta) was computed at each electrode site using both the absolute and relative power metrics. At the baseline assessment, the institutionalized group (IG) showed a higher level of relative theta power and a reduction in alpha and beta relative power compared with a group of never-institutionalized children (NIG; see Marshall, Fox, & the BEIP Core Group, 2004).

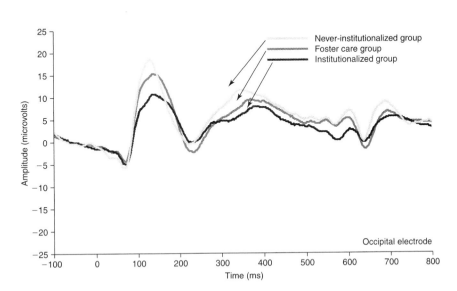

Figure 9-2 Event-related potentials (ERPs) invoked by pictures of facial expressions (collapsed to reveal a main effect of amplitude). The data illustrate the P400 component of the ERP, with the largest amplitude obtained by the NIG ($n = 13$), the smallest by the IG ($n = 29$), and the FCG ($n = 33$) between IG and NIG. See color insert.

Recent preliminary analyses of the 42-month EEG data suggest that, surprisingly, foster care is exerting little effect on the EEG—in other words, the EEG among the FCG is essentially identical to the IG. There is some hint, however, that among the FCG children who have spent the most time in foster care, the EEG is, in fact, beginning to resemble the NIG. This is encouraging, and may reflect a general principle through much of our project: that there is a dose × response × domain interaction, with some domains of function recovering with less intervention (foster care) than others.

Psychopathology

The Preschool Age Psychiatric Assessment (PAPA) is being administered to children at 54 months of age. The PAPA is a structured interview of the caregiver that covers psychiatric symptomatology and disorders, stressful life events, and impairment in functioning associated with the symptoms (see Egger & Angold, 2004; Egger, Ascher, & Angold, 1999; Egger, Erkanli, Keeler, Potts, Walter, & Angold, 2005). It permits us to examine psychiatric symptoms and disorders, specifically emotional disorders (e.g., depression, anxiety, and posttraumatic stress disorder), and behavior disorders (e.g., oppositional defiant disorder, conduct disorder, and attention deficit/hyperactivity disorder).

Preliminary findings on about two-thirds of the sample demonstrate several important preliminary trends (Egger, 2005). First, we found a substantial increase in the incidence of psychiatric disorders in institutionalized and foster care children compared to never-institutionalized children, indeed, the overall base rate of endorsing *any* disorder is approximately 50% for the IG children. Second, the incidence of disorders among our community sample of NIG children is virtually identical to a sample of 2- to 5-year-old children recruited from pediatric clinics in Durham, North Carolina. This is reassuring, as it suggests that our metric of psychopathology (the PAPA) is performing in Romania as it does in the United States; it also suggests that the general incidence of child psychopathology is comparable across countries. Third, foster care appears to be very effective in ameliorating both depression and anxiety; however, foster care does not appear to have any effect on externalizing symptoms such as ADHD and disruptive behavior disorders (i.e., oppositional defiant disorder and conduct disorder) in these two groups.

The efficacy of foster care in preventing some disorders but not others is intriguing. This may have to do with the issue of sensitive periods; for example, perhaps whatever the environment is contributing to the expression of ADHD does so very early in life, before our children are placed in foster care, and thus, our intervention comes too late. Or perhaps genetics plays a role here; indeed, this would account for why foster care is having little effect on previously institutionalized children, as perhaps the genetic loading for the disorder is overwhelming whatever effect the environment might have on ADHD symptoms. However, inattention/hyperactivity is well known to be increased in formerly institutionalized children (Kreppner, O'Connor, & Rutter, 2001; Roy, Rutter, & Pickles, 2004). The fact that roughly one quarter of both the FCG and the IG meet diagnostic criteria for ADHD, and the fact that most children in the study were placed at or near birth (before ADHD symptomatology would manifest), mean that it is unlikely that differential placement of genetically vulnerable children could account for the finding. A third interpretation may be that ADHD may be expressing itself in two distinct contexts for different reasons. In the case of institutionalized children, for example, perhaps children possess poor attentional control because (a) there is no environmental support to teach them how to acquire such skills and/ or (b) the environment is so lacking in stimulation that children engage in self-stimulatory activities (an observation confirmed by the far higher incidence of stereotypies among our IG vs. NIG children) and thus, inattention/hyperactivity results. Children in foster care, however, may show this same pattern of poor attentional control because the environment is *so* stimulating and they are having a difficult time regulating their behavior in the face of such new challenges. We are hopeful that as our study progresses we will be able to address these and other hypotheses.

Conclusions

On the whole, it is clear that institutionalization is associated with profoundly negative effects on child and brain development. As we have reported in our recently published papers and summarized in this chapter, virtually all domains of development are compromised by institutional rearing; thus, physical, brain, cognitive, linguistic, and social-emotional development are all deleteriously affected. Moreover, nearly half of institutionalized children appear to suffer from one or more forms of psychopathology. The good news is that foster care appears to be effective in diminishing some forms of psychopathology and normalizing other domains of development; the bad news is that it is not affecting all domains of development, nor has full recovery occurred in most domains assessed to date. Of course, this picture may change as our study progresses and children spend more time in foster care, especially because we already have determined that some domains demonstrate recovery only for those children who have been in foster care the longest. Unfortunately, we are only now beginning to examine our foster care data in this light, and thus, it would be premature to comment further on the related issues of how length of time in the institution or length of time in foster care relate to long-term outcome.

Of the many questions we hope to address in the coming years, one pressing issue concerns the processes or mechanisms that underlie the success or failure of foster care in ameliorating the sequelae of early institutionalization. Thus, what is it about our foster care program (e.g., what components) that makes possible the recovery we are seeing in so many domains? A second issue we hope to shed light on pertains to sensitive periods of development. Thus, is there a point after which a child placed in foster care will *not* recover because he/she was placed too late? We sincerely hope this is not the case, although from a neuroscience perspective we should anticipate a point of diminishing returns in some domains: the longer the child lives in such a deprived environment, the harder it will be to set that child back on a typical developmental course. We might predict fuller recovery in physical growth and cognitive competence, for example, but attachment behavior and linguistic function may be harder to remediate if children are reared for too long in institutions.[6]

Despite the preliminary nature of our follow-up findings, it is worth speculating about the neural bases underlying recovery, or lack of recovery. Of particular relevance is the seeming lack of recovery of a normative EEG pattern. Interestingly, although we are observing a rapid improvement in both height and weight among our FCG children, there is no discernable effect on head circumference, a finding that may be relevant to our EEG findings. Specifically, it may be the case that the failure to observe dramatic changes in head circumference or EEG could be due to an error in apoptosis (programmed cell death), which in turn will lead to too few neurons and thus a smaller, underpowered brain (which will account for smaller heads and underpowered EEG). It may therefore require a number of compensatory, plastic mechanisms to become engaged in order to redirect the brain onto a typical developmental trajectory. Thus, particularly for children who have spent the longest amount of time in the institution, the overt changes in brain function may take some time to accrue. Our behavioral data clearly suggest that such change is occurring, but it is occurring on a smaller scale and perhaps slower time frame than we had expected. This argues for the important need to study these children when they are older.

A second finding we wish to comment on concerns changes in DQ. First, as can be inferred from figure 9-1, the DQ among our currently institutionalized children has gone up about 5 points from baseline to 42 months. We attribute this to the inadvertent changes that likely took place in the institutions, once we began our intervention (e.g., a more favorable child-to-caregiver ratio). Second, there is quite a dramatic increase in DQ among those placed in foster care. This is encouraging, as it suggests that as a group (i.e., with regard to *age* at placement in foster care) children's "IQ" is benefiting from the more enriched environment of foster care.

It is difficult to say how our IG and FCG will fare as adolescents. Although the oldest children in our cohort are only now turning 7 years old, it will not be long before these children will face the challenges and opportunities that await them as adolescents. We hope to be able to track their development at that time, and to glean from our current study what preventive efforts can be implemented to minimize maladaptation these children may experience. For the moment, however, we feel it prudent to shy away from pronouncements about the implications of our findings for prevention science; still, our PAPA findings are encouraging in suggesting that at least in the domains of depression and anxiety, foster care can have a powerful effect on reducing the burden of suffering. Of course, this same intervention, implemented at the same age, appears to be having little effect on externalizing symptoms such as ADHD and oppositional deviant disorder. From the perspective of adolescent development, this is discouraging, as it suggests that even when such a powerful intervention is implemented very early in life, it is difficult to prevent such disorders from developing. On the other hand, the life circumstances our children find themselves in are hopefully far worse than the typical adolescent.

On the whole, the ideal situation would be to improve the means by which we identify adolescents at greatest risk for developing mental health problems and to intervene as early as possible. In the current context, teens who spend their early months and years living in acutely and/or chronically deprived environments would receive most attention. Here, getting these teens into solid family environments would likely prove beneficial. Of course, our success in doing so depends as much on changing public policy as it does on conducting sound scientific studies.

Acknowledgments

The writing of this chapter was made possible, in part, by the MacArthur Foundation research network on Early Experience and Brain Development. The authors wish to extend their gratitude to their colleagues involved in conducting the Bucharest Early Intervention Project, including Sebastian Koga, Susan Parker, Anna Smyke, Peter Marshall, and Dana Johnson and the staff that oversees this project in Bucharest, Romania.

Notes

1. The term *indiscriminate sociability* is typically construed to refer to a child who interacts with adults in an indiscriminate way—for example, failing to distinguish between caregivers and complete strangers. Thus, such a child is as likely to hold the hand and walk off with a stranger as they might with a caregiver.

2. By drawing on the same maternity hospitals as we drew on for our IG children, we were attempting to control for differences in SES.

3. *Organized* refers to secure, avoidant and resistant classifications and is contrasted with *not organized*, which includes both disorganized and unclassifiable (insufficient attachment behaviors evident; Zeanah et al., 2005).

4. Reactive attachment disorder is used to describe children who have experienced adverse caregiving environments (e.g., maltreatment or institutional rearing) and who develop aberrant social behaviors as a result, including absence or disturbances of attachment behaviors. Two patterns are defined: (1) an emotionally withdrawn/inhibited pattern, in which the child is minimally responsive, shows limited positive affect, expresses no

preference for any adult caregiver, and has difficulties with emotion regulation, and (2) an indiscriminately social/disinhibited pattern, in which the child fails to check back with a caregiver in unfamiliar settings, lacks reticence around strangers, and is willing to "go off" with a stranger. In the first instance, the child's social behavior is inhibited, and in the second, the social behavior is disinhibited.

5. Whereas latency to peak reflects the rate of information transmission through the brain, amplitude is typically taken to reflect the summation of synchronous neuronal activity; as such, larger amplitudes are taken to reflect a more normative response.

6. It should be noted that at the outset of our project, it was decided that any child living in an institution would be moved to state-run foster care or reunited with his/her biological family should the opportunity present itself. Indeed, as of December 2005, only 17 of our original IG children still reside in an institution.

References

Ainsworth, M. D. S., Blehar, M. C., Waters, E., & Wall, S. (1978). *Patterns of attachment: A psychological study of the strange situation procedure.* Hillsdale, NJ: Erlbaum.

Ames, E. W. (1997). *The development of Romanian orphanage children adopted into Canada: Final report to Human Resources Development Canada.* Burnaby, Canada: Simon Fraser University Press.

Bzoch, K. & League, R. (1972). Receptive–Expressive Emergent Language (REEL) Scale. Baltimore, MD: University Park Press.

Chisholm, K. (1998). A three year follow-up of attachment and indiscriminate friendliness in children adopted from Romanian orphanages. *Child Development, 69,* 1092–1106.

Chugani, H. T., Behen, M. E., Muzik, O., Juhasz, C., Nagy, F., & Chugani, D. C. (2001). Local brain functional activity following early deprivation: A study of postinstitutionalized Romanian orphans. *Neuroimage, 14,* 1290–1301.

Crowell, J. A., & Feldman, S. S. (1988). Mothers' internal models of relationships and children's behavioral and developmental status: A study of mother-child interactions. *Child Development, 59,* 1273–1285.

de Haan, M., & Nelson, C. A. (1997). Recognition of the mother's face by 6-month-old infants: A neurobehavioral study. *Child Development, 68,* 187–210.

Edwards, S., Garman, M., Hughes, A., Letts, C., & Sinka, I. (1997). Assessing the comprehension and production of language in young children: An account of the Reynell Developmental Language Scales III. *International Journal of Language and Communication Disorders, 34,* 151–171.

Egger, H. L. (April, 2005). *Psychiatric disorders at age 5 in the children participating in the Bucharest Early Intervention Project.* Paper presented at the biennial meeting of the Society for Research in Child Development, Atlanta, GA.

Egger, H. L., & Angold, A. (2004). The Preschool Age Psychiatric Assessment (PAPA): A structured parent interview for diagnosing psychiatric disorders in preschool children. In R. DelCarmen-Wiggins & A. Carter (Eds.), *Handbook of infant, toddler, and preschool mental assessment* (pp. 223–243). New York: Oxford University Press.

Egger, H. L., Ascher, B. H., & Angold, A. (1999). *The Preschool Age Psychiatric Assessment: Version 1.1.* Unpublished interview schedule, Center for Developmental Epidemiology, Department of Psychiatry and Behavioral Sciences, Duke University Medical Center, Durham, NC.

Egger, H. L., Erkanli, A., Keeler, G., Potts, E., Walter, B., & Angold, A. (2006). Test-retest reliability of the Preschool Age Psychiatric Assessment (PAPA). *Journal of the American Academy of Child and Adolescent Psychiatry, 45*, 538–549.

Ellis, B. H., Fisher, P. A., & Zaharie, S. (2004). Predictors of disruptive behavior, developmental delays, anxiety, and affective symptomatology among institutionally reared Romanian children. *Journal of the American Academy of Child and Adolescent Psychiatry, 43*, 1283–1292.

Fisher, L., Ames, E. W., Chisholm, K., & Savoie, L. (1997). Problems reported by parents of Romanian orphans adopted to British Columbia. *International Journal of Behavioral Development, 20,* 67–82.

Goldsmith, H.H., & Rothbart, M.K. (1999). *The Laboratory Temperament Assessment Battery* (Locomotor Version, Edition 3.1). Madison, WI: University of Wisconsin–Madison.

Hodges, J., & Tizard, B. (1989). Social and family relationships of ex-institutional adolescents. *Journal of Child Psychology, Psychiatry, and Allied Disciplines, 30,* 77–97.

Hoksbergen, R., ter Laak, J., van Dijkum, C., Rijk, S., Rijk, K., & Stoutjesdijk, F. (2003). Posttraumatic stress disorder in adopted children form Romania. *American Journal of Orthopsychiatry, 73,* 255–265.

Johnson, D. E. (2000). Medical and developmental sequelae of early childhood institutionalization among eastern European adoptees. In C. A. Nelson (Ed.), *Minnesota Symposium on Child Psychology: Vol. 31. The effects of early adversity on neurobehavioral development* (pp. 113–162). Mahwah, NJ: Erlbaum.

Knudsen, E. I. (2003). Early experience and critical periods. In L. R. Squire, F. E. Bloom, S. K. McConnell, J. L. Roberts, N. C. Spitzer, & M. J. Zigmond (Eds.), *Fundamental neuroscience* (2nd ed., pp. 555–573). New York: Academic Press.

Kreppner, J. M., O'Connor, T. G., & Rutter, M. (2001). Can inattention/hyperactivity be an institutional deprivation syndrome? *Journal of Abnormal Child Psychology, 29,* 513–528.

Marcovitch, S., Goldberg, S., Gold, A., Washington, J., Wasson, C., Krekewich, K., et al. (1997). Determinants of behavioral problems in Romanian children adopted in Ontario. *International Journal of Behavioral Development, 20,* 17–31.

Marshall, P. J., Fox, N. A., & the BEIP Core Group. (2004). A comparison of the electroencephalogram between institutionalized and community children in Romania. *Journal of Cognitive Neuroscience, 16,* 1327–1338.

Mundy, P., Delgado, C., Block, J., Venezia, M., Hogan, A., & Seibert, J. (2003). A Manual for the Abridged Early Social Communication Scales (ESCS). Available through the University of Miami Psychology Department, Coral Gables, Florida (pmundy@miami.edu).

Nelson, C. A. (2001). The development and neural bases of face recognition. *Infant and Child Development, 10,* 3–18.

Nelson, C. A., Bloom, F. E., Cameron, J., Amaral, D., Dahl, R., & Pine, D. (2002). An integrative, multidisciplinary approach to the study of brain-behavior relations in the context of typical and atypical development. *Development and Psychopathology, 14,* 499–520.

Nelson, C. A., & de Haan, M. (1996). A neurobehavioral approach to the recognition of facial expressions in infancy. In J.A. Russell (Ed.), *The Psychology of Facial Expression* (pp. 176–204). Cambridge University Press: Cambridge, MA.

Nelson, C. A., Thomas, K. M., & de Haan, M. (2006). Neural bases of cognitive development. To appear in W. Damon, R. Lerner, D. Kuhn, & R. Siegler (Volume Editor), *Handbook of child psychology: Vol. 2. Cognitive, perception and language* (6th. ed.). Hoboken, NJ: Wiley.

NICHD Early Child Care Research Network. (1996). Characteristics of infant child care: Factors contributing to positive caregiving. *Early Childhood Research Quarterly, 11,* 269–306.

NICHD Early Child Care Research Network. (2003). Does quality of child care affect child outcomes at age 4½? *Developmental Psychology, 39,* 451–469.

NICHD Early Child Care Research Network. (2005). Predicting individual differences in attention, memory, and planning in first graders from experiences at home, child care, and school. *Developmental Psychology, 41,* 99–114.

O'Connor, T. G., Marvin, R. S., Rutter, M., Olrick, J. T., Brittner, P. A., & the English and Romanian Adoptees. (2003). Child–parent attachment following severe early institutional deprivation. *Development and Psychopathology, 15,* 19–38.

O'Connor, T. G., Rutter, M., Beckett, C., Keaveney, L., Kreppner, J. M., & the ERA Adoptees Study Team. (2000). The effects of global severe privation on cognitive competence: Extension and longitudinal follow-up. *Child Development, 71,* 376–390.

O'Connor, T. G., Rutter, M., & the English and Romanian Adoptees Study Team. (2000). Attachment disorder behavior following early severe deprivation: Extension and longitudinal follow-up. *Journal of the American Academy of Child and Adolescent Psychiatry, 39,* 703–712.

Parker, S. W., & Nelson, C. A. (2005). The impact of institutional rearing on the ability to discriminate facial expressions of emotion: An event related potential study. *Child Development, 76,* 54–72.

Parker, S. W., Nelson, C. A., & the BEIP Core Group. (2005). An event-related potential study of the impact of institutional rearing on face recognition. *Development and Psychopathology, 17,* 621–639.

Roy, P., Rutter, M., & Pickles, A. (2000). Institutional care: Risk from family background or pattern of rearing? *Journal of Child Psychology and Psychiatry, 41,* 139–141.

Roy, P., Rutter, M., & Pickles, A. (2004). Institutional care: Associations between overactivity and lack of selectivity in social relationships. *Journal of Child Psychology and Psychiatry, 45,* 866–873.

St. Petersburg–USA Orphanage Research Team. (2005). Characteristics of children, caregivers, and orphanages for young children in St. Petersburg, Russian Federation. *Journal of Applied Developmental Psychology, 26,* 477–506.

Smyke, A. T. (2005, April). Catch-up in cognitive, language, and physical development among Romanian adopted children. Paper presented at the biennial meeting of the Society for Research in Child Development, Atlanta, GA.

Smyke, A. T., Dumitrescu, A., & Zeanah, C. H. (2002a). Disturbances of attachment in young children. I: The continuum of caretaking casualty. *Journal of the American Academy of Child and Adolescent Psychiatry, 41,* 972–982.

Smyke, A. T., Koga, S. F., Johnson, D. E., Fox, N. A., Marshall, P. J., Nelson, C. A., Zeanah, C. Z, & the BEIP Core Group. (in press). The caregiving context in institution reared and family reared infants and toddlers in Romania. *Journal of Child Psychology and Psychiatry*

Smyke, A. T., Zeanah, C. H., & Koga, S. F. M. (2002b, April). Effects of caregiving environment on the behavior of institutionalized, formerly institutionalized, and community children. Paper presented at the International Conference on Infant Studies. Toronto, CA

Tanner, J. M. (1973). Physical growth and development. In J. O. Forfar & G. C. Ameil (Eds.), *Textbook of pediatrics.* London: Churchill Livingston.

Vorria, P., Papaligoura, Z., Dunn, J., van IJzendoorn, M. H., Steele, H., Kontopoulou, A., et al. (2003). Early experiences and attachment relationships of Greek infants raised in residential group care. *Journal of Child Psychology, Psychiatry and Allied Disciplines, 44,* 1208–1220.

Zeanah, C. H. (2000). Disturbance of attachment in young children adopted from Institutions. *Journal of Developmental and Behavioral Pediatrics, 21,* 230–236.

Zeanah, C. H., Nelson, C. A., Fox, N. A., Smyke, A. T., Marshall, P., Parker, S. W., et al. (2003). Designing research to study the effects of institutionalization on brain and behavioral development: The Bucharest Early Intervention Project. *Development and Psychopathology, 15,* 885–907.

Zeanah, C. H., Smyke, A. T., Koga, S. F., Carlson, E., & the BEIP Core Group. (2005). Attachment in institutionalized and community children in Romania. *Child Development, 76,* 1015–1028.

Part IV

Effects of Stress and Other
Environmental Influences
During Adolescence

Chapter 10

Social Stress, Affect, and Neural Function in Adolescence

Erin B. McClure and Daniel S. Pine

Although its reputation as a period of inevitable "storm and stress" has recently been tempered, considerable evidence suggests that adolescence is nonetheless marked by heightened vulnerability for affective dysregulation and distress (Arnett, 1999). One way in which this vulnerability manifests is an increase in the incidence and prevalence of a specific set of anxiety disorders in the periadolescent years (Costello et al., 2003; Pine et al., 1998). Multiple factors likely converge to facilitate the emergence of this elevated risk in the period surrounding puberty; prominent among these are the potentially stressful biological and social transitions that characteristically occur during adolescence (E. E. Nelson et al., 2005).

Although they are commonly perceived as less severe than other forms of psychopathology, anxiety disorders are associated with varied adverse outcomes, including school dropout, development of other disorders such as major depression, and suicide (Katzelnick et al., 2001; Pine et al., 1998; Stein & Kean, 2000). Consequently, much research in recent years has focused on developing and evaluating treatment approaches aimed at decreasing anxiety symptoms in acutely symptomatic youth (Mancini et al., 2005; Reinblatt & Walkup, 2005; Roblek & Piacentini, 2005; RUPP, 2001). Although such research has been fruitful, the risk of symptomatic recurrence and escalation, even among successfully treated children and adolescents, is substantial (Pine et al., 1998; Weissman et al., 1999). This renders costly efforts at relapse prevention and remediation necessary. Multipronged preventive approaches aimed at ameliorating effects of social and biological pressures before they trigger psychopathology are therefore much needed.

A first step toward both the development of prevention tactics and the improvement of treatment methods is clarifying the mechanisms that underlie the onset and evolution of adolescent anxiety disorders. In particular, it is critical that we better understand the ways in which social stressors and neural development interact to precipitate symptoms. The present chapter reviews the literature on such mechanisms as they relate to the development of anxiety in youth. The chapter first examines adolescents' increased risk for anxiety disorders and the roles that social and biological, particularly neural, changes may play in its onset. Subsequently, the focus shifts to alterations in patterns of cognition that are associated with adolescent anxiety disorders, as well as their putative underlying neural mechanisms. Then, the chapter describes an approach to studying the intersections among adolescent psychopathology, emotion and cognition, and underlying neural substrates. In closing, possible prevention approaches that integrate neuroscience and clinical research are presented.

Clinical Perspectives on the Adolescent Risk for Anxiety Disorders

Anxiety disorders, although widely prevalent throughout development, have been relatively understudied until the past few decades. Studies in youth are particularly sparse, which is surprising given that clinically significant anxiety commonly affects this population. Recent epidemiological findings suggest that the median age of onset for most anxiety disorders is approximately 11 years, with some disorders (e.g., separation anxiety and specific phobias) emerging most commonly in childhood and others (e.g., social phobia, agoraphobia without panic) more likely to first appear during adolescence and early adulthood (Kessler et al., 2005). Vulnerability for anxiety disorders appears particularly marked among females, whose lifetime risk is 1.6 times that of males (Kessler et al., 2005). This pattern of incidence is consistent with the notion that developmental factors contribute heavily to risk for clinically significant anxiety, particularly for anxiety focused on interpersonal or social content. It also points to the importance of considering gender as a potential moderator of developmental influences on anxiety onset.

Barriers to the Study of Anxiety: Typical Versus Pathological Anxiety

Many issues clearly contribute to the dearth of research on anxiety; however, lingering questions concerning the boundaries between typical and pathological anxiety constitute one of the more prominent stumbling blocks. In many circumstances, anxiety and the related emotion "fear" represent adaptive responses to dangerous events or circumstances; across species, organisms that effectively recognize and react to danger tend to enjoy enhanced fitness. Among humans, typical development involves the emergence of a relatively stereotyped pattern of fears or worries that tend to serve adaptive purposes (Marks, 1987; Muris et al., 2000). For example, fears of strangers and of separation become evident in normally developing preschoolers across many cultures. Additionally, adolescents show a normative increase in concerns about scrutiny from peers or adults. Such increases in anxiety, which can be associated with marked discomfort, are a feature of healthy development at key stages of life. Consequently, it can be difficult to identify the point at which anxiety crosses the line into pathological manifestations.

Two criteria, sometimes referred to as the "impairment" and "distress" criteria, form the basis on which distinctions between normal and pathological anxiety are typically made. First, anxiety is considered pathological when it disrupts functioning and interferes with the successful completion of daily living tasks. Thus, shyness becomes pathological when it leads an adolescent to avoid social situations or events that most peers would not avoid. Second, anxiety is considered pathological when the degree of distress is extreme, in terms of intensity, frequency, and duration.

Although these criteria provide guidelines for distinguishing healthy from pathological anxiety, they remain controversial. In particular, practitioners debate whether severity of distress should serve as an index of pathology. To evaluate distress, a clinician must determine whether an adolescent's subjectively reported internal state is within the expected range for youth of similar age. Such subjective ratings are potentially fraught with bias and influenced by varying cultural or family standards, which raises questions about whether this criterion forms a valid basis for classifying youth into diagnostic groups. Moreover, although the "impairment" criterion is less likely to be affected by the biases inherent in applications of the "distress" criterion, it too is problematic. For example, relatively subtle variations in the rules for applying the impairment criterion exert profound effects on prevalence estimates, particularly for adolescent anxiety disorders (Shaffer et al., 1996).

This controversy is not surprising, given the state of psychiatric nosology. Current nosological classifications, as articulated in DSM-IV, are based on clinical assessments that rely heavily on reports of symptoms from patients and relevant informants, such as parents. Use of this classification system has led to markedly better diagnostic reliability than was possible using earlier classification schemes. This increase in reliability has, in turn, introduced much-needed standards into mental health care. Nevertheless, as the science of mental illness matures, it seems plausible and desirable that diagnosis will eventually be based on an understanding of pathophysiology. In particular, laboratory-based assessments of brain dysfunction have the potential to provide a more objective or at least a corroborative index of mental status. Unfortunately, the field is many years away from moving from a scheme based on clinical assessments to one that integrates results of clinical evaluation and laboratory tests.

Barriers to the Study of Anxiety: Distinctions Among Disorders

The limitations of current nosological schemes are also evident when clinicians must distinguish among specific anxiety disorders rather than more broadly conceptualized clinical versus normal anxiety. In particular, it is unclear whether and how adolescent anxiety disorders can be conceptualized as pathophysiologically distinct conditions. From some perspectives, current classifications for anxiety disorders distinguish artificially among conditions. Rates of comorbidity among anxiety disorders are high among both clinically referred youth (Verduin & Kendall, 2003) and in general population samples (Essau et al., 2000), although some findings indicate lower comorbidity rates among anxiety disorders than between anxiety and other disorders, such as depression (Essau, 2003). Further, the risk for developing chronic mood or anxiety disorders in adulthood is equally strong in adolescents with generalized anxiety disorder and major depressive disorder, which are currently classified as distinct types of psychopathology (Pine et al., 1998). The genetics of these two conditions in adolescence also overlap markedly, so much so that researchers consider genetic contributions to the two syndromes to be largely identical (Costello et al., 2002a). These lines of research suggest that the utility of distinguishing between the two disorders may be limited.

Other evidence, however, suggests that some distinctions among anxiety disorders are valid. For example, the longitudinal course of social anxiety disorder, which is highly prevalent among adolescents, appears to differ from that of other childhood or adolescent anxiety disorders, such as separation anxiety disorder or generalized anxiety disorder (Pine et al., 2000a; Pine et al., 1998). In particular, whereas childhood social anxiety disorder predicts later development of social anxiety disorder, separation anxiety disorder does not; rather some evidence suggests that it predicts the development of panic attacks or disorder (Aschenbrand et al., 2003; Klein & Pine, 2002). Similarly, the degree to which individuals with social versus separation anxiety disorders exhibit perturbed responses to laboratory threats such as carbon dioxide (CO_2) challenges or angry facial expressions also reliably differs (Pine et al., 2000b; Pine et al., 2005b). Specifically, youth with separation anxiety show a heightened response to CO_2 challenge and socially anxious youth show elevated sensitivity to angry faces. Thus, some findings suggest that current, relatively narrow classification schemes may be valid, if imperfect.

Impact of Anxiety Disorders on Youth

Despite its limitations, the current clinically based diagnostic scheme has proved useful for quantifying the burden of mental illness faced by adolescents. The development of reliable, standard diagnostic tools for assessing rates of mental illnesses has led to a relatively large series of studies documenting the prevalence and impact of various mental syndromes (Cohen et al., 1993a, 1993b; Costello et al., 2003). These studies have shown that psychopathology takes a high toll on youth, particularly adolescents. Moreover, during this developmental period, anxiety disorders appear to have a particularly strong impact, which is associated with potential long-term functional impairment.

For example, recent research demonstrates that pediatric anxiety predicts adult mood and anxiety disorders, in that the majority of adults who suffer from a mood or anxiety disorder will have developed initial signs of their illness, manifest as an anxiety disorder, during childhood or adolescence (Costello et al., 2002b; Pine et al., 1999; Pine et al., 2001; Pine et al., 1998). Anxiety disorders also exact a financial toll on society; they are associated with sharply elevated medical costs and utilization rates (Hunkeler et al., 2003; Martin & Leslie, 2003), as well as decreased productivity (Dewa & Lin, 2000; Kessler & Frank, 1997). Finally, anxiety disorders are severely distressing and impairing for youth (Klein & Pine, 2002; Langley et al., 2004).

Moving Beyond Clinical Perspectives: The Utility of Neuroscience for Understanding Anxiety

As noted above, the current classification scheme for anxiety disorders represents a compromise. The scheme works well, in that it facilitates reliable diagnosis and increases the likelihood that adolescents in need of treatment due to impairment and risk for chronic disability will be identified. However, it is designed to take into account only surface manifestations of underlying pathophysiologic processes that shape and perturb aspects of brain function.

Such surface manifestations are critically important for diagnosing and treating mental illness. Indeed, for all forms of illness, observable distress and impairment provide some of the strongest justification for intervention. However, in areas of medicine outside of mental health, classification and intervention are based not only on observable distress and impairment but also on underlying perturbations in pathophysiology. Thus, the adult who presents with extreme angina and dyspnea in the context of a myocardial infarction clearly merits clinical attention. However, the adult who presents for a routine checkup that reveals "silent" ischemia is also in need of care. Improvements in classification, prediction, and treatment of mental illness are likely to follow when current methods for assessing clinical signs can be augmented with methods for directly assessing perturbations in physiology.

Thus, although clinical symptoms are necessary to assess, in that they provide measure of subjectively experienced distress, they paint a limited picture of complex, likely biologically based dysfunction. Pathophysiologic models are beginning to ground current classification schemes in neuroscience. Perhaps the most important models, which draw heavily on recent advances in cognitive and affective neuroscience, emphasize examining the role of information processing functions of the brain in the manifestations of psychopathology (Pine et al., 2002).

These advances in neuroscience have led to the realization that individual differences in behavior reflect functional differentiation within brain circuits that connect distributed, but finite, collections of neural structures. In terms of ultimate pathophysiologic causes, psychiatric disorders are thought to stem from the operation of environmental and genetic factors that shape functioning in relevant circuits. For most disorders, particularly the anxiety disorders, research in the basic sciences suggests that these shaping processes occur throughout development, with key changes becoming relatively permanent during adolescence. For example, epidemiological studies following children and adolescents into adulthood suggest that anxiety disorders tend to show an episodic course relatively early in development, with the majority of disorders remitting before late adolescence. However, for children who continue to show anxiety through adolescence, risk for a chronic course into adulthood becomes considerably higher (Kim-Cohen et al., 2003; Pine et al., 1998). Such clinical findings parallels work from the basic sciences demonstrating long-term influences of either environmental or genetic influences on functional aspects of the fear circuit (Gross & Hen, 2004).

The functioning of neural circuits is thought to manifest in patterns of information processing that are observable in the laboratory. When these patterns relate strongly to both overt manifestations of a disorder and underlying genetic risk, they are typically termed *endophenotypes* (Berrettini, 2005; Gottesman & Gould, 2003). Perhaps the strongest example of such an endophenotype is a pattern of cognitive dysfunction involving perturbations in working memory; this pattern is associated both with schizophrenia and with underlying risk for the disorder (Winterer et al., 2004). In other circumstances, perturbations in information processing may relate strongly to overt manifestations of a disorder or acute symptoms but show weaker relationships with risk for the disorder. Under these circumstances, it may not be accurate to identify information-processing perturbations as endophenotypes. Other terms, such as *core psychological feature*, which implies that a perturbed information processing function represents a central characteristic of the disorder, may be more appropriate. However, the term endophenotype would not be appropriate, as this term implies a strong relationship with not only overt expression of the disorder but also risk for the disorder.

Probably the best example of the distinction between an endophenotype and a core psychological process in adolescence emerges in work on response to respiratory challenges in the anxiety disorders. Much like adult panic disorder, adolescent separation anxiety disorder is characterized by enhanced sensitivity to the effects of CO_2 (Pine et al., 2000b; Pine et al., 2005b). However, unlike adults with panic disorder, adolescents at risk for panic disorder, by virtue of parental history of the condition, exhibit a normal response to CO_2. Thus, abnormal response to CO_2 clearly can be conceptualized as a core psychological process implicated in panic disorder and separation anxiety disorder. However, the term endophenotype has less clear applicability. Regardless of the nature of a given disorder-linked information processing perturbation, however, a conceptualization that ties it clearly to patterns of brain functioning has many clear advantages.

Social Factors, Risk for Anxiety, and Perturbations in Brain Function

A growing body of evidence suggests that multiple pressures, both biological and environmental, converge during childhood and adolescence to precipitate elevated risk for psychopathology (C. A. Nelson et al., 2002; E. E. Nelson et al., 2005; Steinberg, 2005; Walker et al., 2004). Research that integrates biological and social perspectives, therefore, appears critical if we are to understand the paths along which psychological disorders emerge and the factors that increase vulnerability for these disorders at particular developmental stages. In a recent review, E. E. Nelson and colleagues (2005) proposed an integrative model that might guide such research, particularly studies aiming to elucidate why adolescence is such a risky period for the onset of anxiety and mood disorders.

This model rests on two basic tenets. First, it sets forth that adolescence is characterized by a number of potentially stressful social transitions. These social transitions have been noted to occur across cultures and throughout a relatively long historical time period. Moreover, studies in nonhuman primates suggest that stressful social transitions represent a core feature of development in groups of highly social, intelligent organisms. The nature of such social stress during human development has been delineated with some specificity.

During the adolescent transition period, youth become increasingly autonomous (Larson et al., 1996; Meeus et al., 2005) and seek different types and amounts of support and companionship from peers and family members (Furman & Buhrmester, 1992; Smetana et al., 2005). As sexual maturation progresses, opposite-sex peers progressively gain importance in adolescents' social spheres (Furman, 1989; M. H. Richards et al., 1998), and romantic and sexual relationships become more common (Kuttler & La Greca, 2004). Additionally, social stimuli and events assume growing salience for adolescents (Larson & Richards, 1994; Steinberg & Morris, 2001), who are highly attuned to social nuances and who tend to report prominent social-evaluative concerns (Weems & Costa, 2005; Weems et al., 2000; West & Sweeting, 2003). Although many youth negotiate these changes in patterns of social functioning without notable difficulty, others find them to be a source of considerable concern and discomfort.

The second tenet underlying Nelson and colleagues' (2005) model is that adolescence is a period of ongoing neural development. Several recent studies point to marked structural and functional neural changes that occur between childhood and adulthood throughout the brain (Giedd, 2004; Sowell et al., 2002). Of particular interest are developments in the regions that constitute what Nelson and coworkers (2005) have termed the social information processing network (SIPN). This network consists of three, reciprocally interactive, primary "nodes": the detection node, the affective node, and the cognitive-regulation node (see figure 10-1).

The detection node, which includes regions such as the superior temporal sulcus, fusiform face area, and inferior temporal and occipital cortices, acts to detect and decode socially salient environmental features. Available data suggest that functional aspects of this node mature relatively early, before the social transitions of adolescence. Such data include findings from electrophysiological studies in human infants demonstrating distinct neural responses to various classes of social stimuli (Halit et al., 2004; Halit et al., 2003; Johnson et al., 2005).

The affective node, which comprises regions engaged by reward or punishment cues (e.g., amygdala, orbitofrontal cortex, and ventral striatum), evaluates the

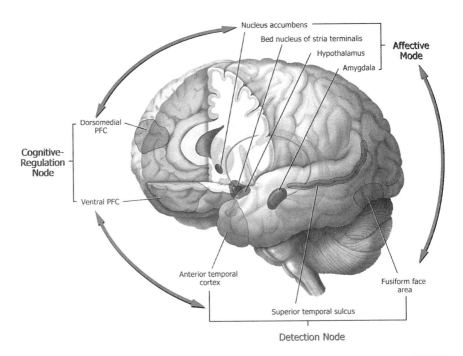

Figure 10-1 The three nodes of the neural social information processing network (SIPN) that E. E. Nelson and colleagues (2005) describe. Figure used with permission of the publisher.

emotional significance of salient stimuli (Bechara, 2004; Bechara et al., 2000; Coricelli et al., 2005; Walter et al., 2005). This node appears to undergo relatively abrupt changes in functioning with puberty and the associated abrupt changes in the hormonal milieu. Such data include findings in rodents and nonhuman primates showing pubertal changes in functions mediated by regions in this node, as well as findings in human adolescents showing changes in social cognition at puberty (E. E. Nelson et al., 2005).

The cognitive-regulation node, which consists primarily of the dorsal and medial prefrontal cortices, as well as parts of the ventral prefrontal cortex, then participates in evaluation of theory of mind, inhibition of prepotent responses, and generation of goal-directed behavior. Available data suggest that this node undergoes a late, relatively protracted development that extends well into adolescence. Such data include findings in nonhuman primates showing very late changes in prefrontal cortex (PFC) structure and function, as well as findings in human adolescents showing late maturation of the PFC (E. E. Nelson et al., 2005). Interestingly, the differences in developmental timing for structures in the affective and cognitive-regulation nodes might relate to the emergence of some adolescent patterns of behavior. Many investigators have commented on the degree to which adolescent behavior stems from emotional influences and other processes mediated by the affective node in the absence of inhibition or other regulatory influences mediated by the cognitive-regulation node (E. E. Nelson et al., 2005). Such behavioral tendencies may reflect operation of the mature affective node in concert with the immature cognitive-regulation node.

According to the Nelson et al. (2005) model, adolescence represents a period in which changes at both social and neural levels converge to form a context within which risk for affective dysregulation, particularly anxiety, is heightened. More precisely, the social shifts that occur during adolescence likely place a high level of stress on a network of neural structures that is already vulnerable as a function of its ongoing reorganization and development. Under conditions of such stress, the social information processing network is at risk for functional impairment; indeed a small, but growing, body of evidence suggests that adolescents with clinically significant anxiety show both structural and functional alterations in neural regions within the SIPN (De Bellis et al., 2002; Killgore & Yurgelun-Todd, 2005; Milham et al., 2005; Richert et al., 2005; Thomas et al., 2001).

Tests of the model proposed by Nelson et al. (2005) require implementation of laboratory-based paradigms that engage psychological processes mediated by one or another of the three nodes explicated in the model. Surprisingly little research has used cognitive neuroscience techniques to examine the neural mediators of psychological processes in children and adolescents. As a result, considerable methodological work will be required before a set of standard laboratory-based paradigms can be proposed. A review of all research in this area is beyond the scope of this chapter.

Attention, Emotion, and Adolescent Anxiety Disorders

Perhaps the most extensively explored psychological processes that are relevant to adolescent anxiety involve interactions between emotions and attention allocation/control. This chapter therefore uses research on attention and emotion to exemplify one way in which neuroscience and clinical developmental approaches can be integrated. This focused review is designed to provide a template for future work examining relationships among behavior, brain activity, and a variety of information processing functions.

Considerable research in the basic and cognitive neurosciences delineates neural circuits involved in attention, or the prioritizing of stimulus features for elaborative processing (Kastner & Ungerleider, 2000). Emotional processes play important roles in such prioritization, and considerable work focuses specifically on associations between environmental threats and attention (Vuilleumier, 2005). From the clinical and developmental perspectives, a growing body of work delineates both behavioral and neural correlates of interactions between threat content and attention regulation. In the present chapter, we focus in detail on attention to cues of social threat in the context of anxiety.

Attention to Social/Emotional Cues
and Adolescent Anxiety Disorders

In the course of a single social interaction, individuals confront a vast array of stimuli, often many at once. It is necessary to engage cognitive and neural processes that constitute "attention" to determine which stimuli merit immediate processing—particularly those with either salient rewarding or punitive properties—and which can be ignored or processed later. The term "attention" refers to the result of interactions among neural mechanisms that work to resolve competition among environmental stimuli for processing and prioritize those that warrant responses (Desimone & Duncan, 1995).

Studies of rodents and nonhuman primates have led to the development of precise models of the neural circuitry that participates in this complex prioritization process (Davis & Whalen, 2001). Subsumed under the general rubric of "prioritization" are a wide range of simpler processes, which include those related to shifts or maintenance in the orientation of attention, maintenance of arousal or an alert state, and the control of information processing resources to maximize goal attainment. Research on each of these processes demonstrates clearly that attention-related circuits encompass many of the structures in the SIPN, including the amygdala and regions of the PFC (Davis & Whalen, 2001; Miller & Cohen, 2001). Moreover, both a large body of research on rodents and an emerging literature on nonhuman primates suggest that social stressors that occur early in development can precipitate anxiety-relevant changes in the functioning of structures within this circuit (Coplan et al., 2001; Meaney, 2001).

Anxious individuals respond atypically on a number of cognitive tasks designed to measure aspects of attention, especially when the stimuli comprise emotionally salient cues. Attention interference tasks, for instance, require study participants to attend to nonemotional stimulus features while simultaneously ignoring emotional features of the same stimulus. During one such task, the emotional Stroop, individuals are asked to label the colors in which different words are printed. Some of the words are neutral in meaning, whereas others carry emotional (typically threatening, in studies of anxiety) connotations. In general, it is more difficult for people to ignore threatening words (e.g., "death") than neutral words, and thus they are slower to name the colors of threat-related stimuli (Williams et al., 1996). Adolescents who have or are at risk for developing anxiety disorders appear to be particularly prone to such interference (Moradi et al., 1999; A. Richards et al., 2000; Schwartz et al., 1996), which suggests that the effects of emotional stimulus features on attention allocation are magnified in these populations.

Studies using tasks that require individuals to orient to specified cues have also demonstrated that anxious and nonanxious individuals differ in aspects of attentional functioning. For instance, during visual search tasks that involve scanning fields of stimuli (most of which are emotionally evocative) for isolated nonemotional targets, youth who self-report high levels of anxious symptoms are slower than low-anxious controls to locate target stimuli (Hadwin et al., 2003). Research employing other types of attention orientation tasks with anxious youth has yielded similar results. For example, performance on a visual probe detection task, which requires participants to respond to nonemotional cues that are either spatially or temporally contiguous to emotional stimuli (Mogg & Bradley, 1998, 2002), has been shown to differ between youth with some anxiety disorders and their nonanxious peers (Dalgleish et al., 2001; Pine et al., 2005c).

It remains unclear whether, as several researchers have hypothesized, underlying abnormalities in attention regulation predispose individuals toward anxious behavior (Clark et al., 1990; MacLeod et al., 2002; Mogg & Bradley, 2002) or, alternatively, if changes in levels of anxiety influence the functioning of attentional processes. If the former hypothesis is true, as results of some studies suggest (Mathews & Mackintosh, 2000; Wilson et al., 2006), attention allocation tasks could be used to help identify individuals who are at high risk for anxiety. If, however, the latter hypothesis were confirmed, it would suggest that attention bias abnormalities constitute epiphenomena rather than risk factors for later anxiety.

Neural Development and Attention-Emotion Interactions in Adolescence

As noted above, results from a growing body of studies suggests that attention to threat-related information is perturbed during states of anxiety. Such findings provide an excellent foundation for translational research that integrates basic and clinical approaches. Not only have behavioral effects consistently been observed in experimental attention paradigms relevant to anxiety, but the neural structures involved in these effects have also been identified in multiple laboratories using a variety of techniques, including relatively novel brain imaging approaches. Functional magnetic resonance imaging (fMRI) permits noninvasive assessment of the neural correlates of various psychological processes, including attention to threat cues. Because this technique is noninvasive and associated with minimal risks, it can be used to examine developmental aspects of neural functioning as children pass through adolescence. fMRI provides an index of changes in blood flow that occur while study participants perform cognitive tasks. This index reflects differences in the magnetic susceptibility properties of oxygenated and deoxygenated hemoglobin, arming the brain with its own "endogenous contrast agent," such that increases in the flow of oxygenated blood are reflected in regional patterns of "activation" in fMRI scans.

Although fMRI provides a novel means for developmentally oriented translational studies, such research remains difficult to conduct. One major problem is that neuroscience studies of human fear typically employ highly aversive stimuli, including electric shocks, noxious smells, grotesque pictures, verbal prompts, and pharmacological compounds. Due to ethical restrictions, such stimuli cannot be used in research with children and adolescents. Other classes of stimuli, such as abstract verbal representations of fearful events, that are less noxious, also have inherent limitations for use with youth. Because such stimuli often require sophisticated elaborative processing, they may not evoke emotion as reliably in children and adolescents as they do in adults. One of the few stimulus classes that are both ethically permissible for use with youth and adequately simple to process consists of photographs of emotionally expressive facial displays. This class of stimuli is well suited for developmental research on emotion and information processing and thus has been employed in a wide range of studies in this area.

Facial emotion displays show a striking capacity to induce emotion in primates across a variety of developmental stages, cultures, and species (Darwin, 1998; C. A. Nelson et al., 2002). The evocative quality of such displays have led to their widespread use as stimuli in studies of emotion processing in healthy children, adolescents, and adults (Haxby et al., 2002; Monk et al., 2003). Such studies have demonstrated reliably that emotion and information processing interact in ways that mediate both task performance and neural circuitry engagement. Taken together, these findings permit the generation of hypotheses regarding relationships between psychological processes and neural circuit function. For example, findings indicate that angry faces, which signal interpersonal threat and thus constitute a salient stimulus for many anxious individuals, can engage attention and interfere with performance on nonemotional tasks (Mogg & Bradley, 2002). Moreover, angry faces have been shown to be more memorable than other types of expressive faces under some circumstances (Lundh & Ost, 1996). These effects likely reflect influences of angry faces on the engagement of specific brain regions, such as ventral components of the prefrontal cortex (PFC), and associated aspects of information processing. A growing body of data supports this contention; recent fMRI studies, for instance, report reliable activations of ventral and medial PFC regions by angry facial displays (Haxby et al., 2002). Additionally, such studies indicate that there is consistent activation of the amygdala during viewing of fearful faces, which may convey cues of indirect threat (Haxby et al., 2002; Whalen, 1998).

fMRI studies initially used face-emotion viewing paradigms in healthy adults and demonstrated reliable activation in anxiety-relevant structures, with particularly robust findings for contrasts of responses to fearful and neutral facial stimuli (Haxby et al., 2002). Based on these results, researchers began to implement comparable paradigms in psychiatric populations. In these studies, adults with social anxiety disorder, MDD, and PTSD have been shown to exhibit abnormal activation in the amygdala during the viewing of facial emotions (Rauch et al., 2000; Sheline et al., 2001). Moreover, such abnormalities have been linked to potential genetic susceptibility markers for each condition (Hariri et al., 2002).

The success of these adult fMRI studies set the stage for extensions to studies of development and developmental psychopathology. Such extensions have been greeted enthusiastically within the developmental research community, because few approaches permit the use of methods from basic science to examine brain-behavior relationships in specific neural circuits across development in humans and nonhuman primates. Initial studies have yielded evidence of both differences and similarities in patterns of activation to threat cues between children and adults.

Clear differences are evident in patterns of performance and associated neural activation on threat cue processing tasks in studies of healthy children and adults. For example, one of the more consistent findings in healthy adults is reliable amygdala activation during the viewing of fearful faces, contrasted with activation during viewing of neutral or happy faces (Haxby et al., 2002). This finding has not been consistently replicated in healthy children. In fact, some studies suggest that children show greater activation to neutral than to fearful faces (Thomas et al., 2001).

Similarities between children and adults are more strongly evident in studies of clinical populations. Children with anxiety disorders, for example, like adults with some mood or anxiety disorders, show enhanced amygdala activation during the viewing of some emotional facial displays (Thomas et al., 2001). Moreover, youth with anxiety disorders, like adults with mood and anxiety disorders, show structural abnormalities in the amygdalae, though the nature of these abnormalities varies depending on participants' diagnoses and the research methods used (De Bellis et al., 2002; Milham et al., 2005). Specifically, whereas some researchers have found enlarged amygdalae in youth with generalized anxiety disorder (De Bellis et al., 2000), others have found reduced amygdalar volume in a heterogeneous sample of youth with anxiety disorders (Milham et al., 2005).

Interpretations of imaging studies necessarily depend on the nature of psychological processes engaged during acquisition of neural response data. Psychological processes can be assessed using a range of behavioral or physiologic approaches, including measures of reaction time, autonomic fluctuation, or eye movements. In the absence of data from such measures, it is difficult to determine the precise psychological processes that an imaging study engages. In brain imaging studies, however, as in studies of patients with brain lesions (Bechara, 2004), task instructions or attention allocation can affect activation in brain structures engaged by emotionally evocative stimuli (Hariri et al., 2000). Further, such effects can differ among participants who differ in levels of cognitive development. Consequently, many developmentally oriented studies of facial emotion processing have used passive viewing tasks that require no behavioral responses or relatively easy behavioral tasks, such as gender discrimination, in which no developmental differences in associated cognitive processes are anticipated.

On the one hand, such studies have the advantage of limiting the impact of higher level cognitive processes on the more basic psychological processes engaged during face viewing. On the other hand, however, they have the disadvantage of leaving unspecified the nature of specific psychological processes that are engaged. Clearly more work is needed examining relationships among development, task performance, and fMRI activation in both healthy and psychiatrically impaired groups. Recent experimental psychology research lays the groundwork for future fMRI studies of adolescent development and anxiety disorders. We provide two relevant examples below.

Attention Orienting to Threat Cues and Anxiety

First, attention-orienting tasks measure the effects of an emotional stimulus on attention allocation. Studies using such tasks have shown that angry faces reliably capture attention when they are presented in the context of nonemotional faces (Mogg & Bradley, 1998). This effect is thought to occur because angry faces more readily engage the amygdala and key components of the PFC, including the ventral or orbital frontal cortex and the medial or cingulate aspect of the PFC, than do other emotional faces (Haxby et al., 2002). Behaviorally, individuals with anxiety disorders perform differently from nonanxious peers on attention-orienting tasks (Mogg & Bradley, 2002). These behavioral group differences are also hypothesized to result from anxiety-associated decreases in the threshold for engaging the amygdala and the ventral and medial PFC during tasks designed to elicit orienting to emotionally salient cues (Pine, 2001). Thus, tests of attention orienting provide a measure of emotional reaction that is appropriate for studies of development and psychopathology.

Results from one recent study using this attention-orienting task (see figure 10-2) suggest that adolescents with generalized anxiety disorder (GAD) differ both in patterns of neural activation and attention bias from nonanxious peers (Monk et al., 2006). Specifically, adolescents with GAD showed more activation in the ventrolateral prefrontal cortex (VLPFC) when presented with threat cues than did healthy controls. They also showed a bias to direct their attention away from threat cues; however, this bias did not relate to differential patterns of neural activation. This suggests that the enhanced VLPFC activation could be either a direct neural correlate of increased anxiety or a compensatory response aimed at regulating abnormal function in another region. The severity of anxiety symptoms correlated negatively with VLPFC activation, which lends support to the compensatory response hypothesis. However, further research aimed at elucidating the function of enhanced activation in prefrontal regions during attention orienting to threat cues will be needed to shed light on the nature of this pattern of activation that emerged in youth with GAD. Examination of VLPFC activation during threat cue orientation in both anxious and calm states or before and after successful treatment for anxiety disorders would be particularly useful for clarifying the findings described above.

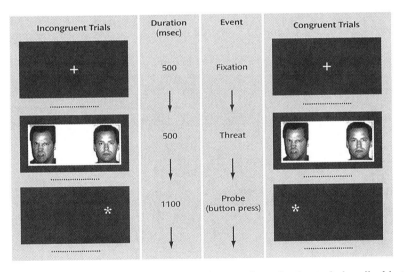

Figure 10-2 The two primary trial types in the attention orienting task described in the text. After a fixation cross is displayed, pairs of faces (neutral, angry) appear on for 500 ms, followed by a probe signal (asterisk). In some trials, as shown in the column on the far left, the angry face and the subsequent probe appear on different sides of the screen. In other trials, as shown in the column on the right, the angry face and the probe appear on the same side of the screen. When attention is oriented toward threat cues (angry faces), response time to identify the location of the probe (left or right side of the screen) should be faster when the angry face and probe appear in the same location and slower when the two are on opposite sides of the screen. Figure used with permission of the publisher.

Explicit Manipulation of Attention to Threat and Anxiety

A second type of task that has been used recently to examine attention-emotion interactions in youth with anxiety disorders involves the explicit manipulation of attention toward and away from emotionally evocative cues. Such tasks complement attention allocation paradigms by providing a window into the correlates of intentionally directed attentional processes. One recently developed task of this type (see figure 10-3) requires research participants to alternately direct their attention to their own emotional reaction to facial expressions and to either emotional or nonemotional features of faces that do not relate to their internal emotional responses (Monk et al., 2003). When this task has been administered to healthy adults in the context of the MRI scanner, the ventral and medial PFC have been shown to engage differentially in response to such manipulations of attention during the viewing of evocative photographs (Monk et al., 2003). Some controversy persists about whether such manipulations also differentially engage subcortical structures such as the amygdala during such manipulations. Certain studies lend support to the presence of differential amygdala modulation between the two states; other studies suggest that both attentional states reliably engage such structures in adults (Dolan, 2002; Pessoa et al., 2002) However, regardless of the patterns observed in healthy adults, it appears that in healthy adolescents, the amygdala and regions of the PFC show differential modulation across types of emotional

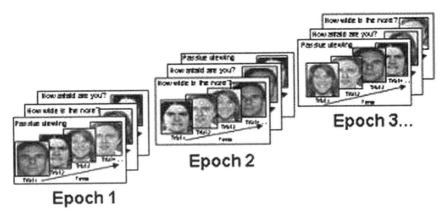

Figure 10-3 During the attention manipulation task, participants adopt a variety of attention states. Three of the states require participants to make one of three ratings while viewing a face stimulus: "How afraid are you?" "How hostile is the face?" "How wide is the nose?" During the fourth state, participants passively view a face stimulus. These four attention states alternate during repeated viewing of 32 standardized grayscale evocative faces (eight stimuli from each of four emotion categories: afraid, happy, neutral, angry) drawn from three widely used stimulus sets. At the end of the task, participants have seen all 32 faces in all four attention states. Ratings and reaction times, as well as patterns of neural response, can then be compared across attention states and stimulus facial expression types. Figure used with permission of the publisher.

stimuli rather than across attention states (Monk et al., 2003). These developmental differences in patterns of attention-modulated activation are consistent with the idea that adults can modify activity in relevant brain structures based on the attentional demands of the task at hand, whereas adolescents, whose neural structures are still immature, are less capable of such modulation and their patterns of activation are instead driven by emotional content.

Behavioral findings using this type of task indicate that youth with anxiety disorders or those at high risk for the development of anxiety disorders show different patterns of response than do low-risk youth, depending on whether their attention was directed toward or away from emotional cues associated with the face. In one recent study, for instance, ratings and response times during different attention sets were compared across adolescent offspring of adults with panic disorder (PD), major depressive disorders (MDD), or no disorder (Pine et al., 2005a). When attention was focused on participants' subjectively evaluated fear in response to the facial stimuli, the children of adults with PD reported higher fear levels and were slower to respond than were members of the other two groups. Additionally, those adolescent participants who met criteria for social phobia were slower than were other participants to rate their own fear levels. They did not, however, report more fear than did their peers.

Neural correlates of performance on this type of attention allocation task also appear to differ between adolescents with GAD and those without anxiety diagnoses (McClure et al., in press). Specifically, a group of adolescent GAD patients ($n = 15$) showed significantly greater amygdala activation to fearful faces than did healthy adolescents ($n = 20$) when attending to their own internal fear states, as contrasted with attending to a nonemotional facial feature or with passively viewing the faces in the absence of specific attentional instructions. These findings lend support to the notion that the amygdala activates atypically in youth with GAD, but suggest that this pattern of pathological amygdala activation is evident only in certain attentional states. In particular, group differences emerged only when attention was directed to participants' subjectively experienced fear. Attention and its interaction with emotion thus appear to play an important role in shaping the functional development of structures within the immature human fear circuit.

These studies of attention orientation and allocation exemplify one approach to examining links among adolescent anxiety disorders, behaviors and cognitions associated with the experience of social stress, and neural substrate. This approach is useful not only for studying the concurrent associations among functioning at multiple levels, but also for examining change over time. Such research carries considerable implications for future studies on underlying risk for and prevention and treatment of anxiety disorders. For example, currently ongoing studies using the tasks described above are focused on possible changes in patterns of behavior and neural activation associated with successful treatment in youth with anxiety disorders. Findings from these studies hold promise for providing a first step toward clarifying the mechanisms that underlie the onset and evolution of adolescent anxiety and that might ultimately point toward means for its prevention.

The Next Frontier: Neuroscience and Prevention of Anxiety Disorders

Clearly, although information from neuroscience might eventually guide prevention efforts, researchers are still laying the groundwork for such translational work. However, because both neuroscience and clinical research have advanced and will likely continue to advance at rapid paces, it may be fruitful now to consider concrete instances in which preventative interventions may be developed. It is important to note that such instances should be conceived as hypothetical. Before any intervention can be recommended for widespread use, hypotheses regarding its efficacy and effectiveness require testing in the setting of a randomized controlled trial. Prior work on debriefing emphasizes the need for such experimental evaluations (Stallard et al., 2006).

The first example in which neuroscience may offer insights for prevention efforts concerns the role of attention orienting in the genesis of anxiety. As noted above, anxiety disorders are associated with perturbed attention orienting, which in turn relates to dysfunction in a well defined set of neural structures. These perturbations are conceptualized as causally related to the onset of anxiety disorders, following exposure to stress. Clearly, this view is controversial, despite the fact that it has persisted for decades. Recent research has begun to demonstrate the manner in which orienting biases may indeed play a causal role in anxiety. Perhaps the most convincing example derives from a study by MacLeod and colleagues (2002). In a series of experiments, these researchers manipulated threat bias in a group of late-adolescent volunteers. Specifically, one group was trained to attend to threats (increased threat bias), and the other group was trained to direct their attention away from threats (decreased threat bias). This training involved implicitly instantiating a bias by consistently directing participants' attention either toward or away from threat cues during multiple exposures to attention orienting. Participants were not instructed explicitly to direct their attention in any particular direction. During training, participants also reported their mood states at regular intervals. Following training, participants were exposed to an experimental stressor. Participants who had received training that reduced threat bias reported less of a decrease in mood following exposure to the stressor than did those whose training increased their threat bias.

Thus, comparable training exercises may one day be useful in inoculating individuals at risk for adverse emotional reactions following stress exposure. Arguably, this group difference in self-reported emotional response to the stressor was mediated by subtle alterations in patterns of neural response to threat-related cues in the decreased-bias group. If researchers can more precisely identify the nature and location of such changes, it may be possible to further refine attention training exercises to provide rapid and lasting benefits to individuals who are particularly vulnerable to stress. This may be a particularly advantageous approach if implemented early in development; longitudinal study of high-risk children and adolescents who are trained to allocate attention away from threat would provide powerful evidence regarding the generalizability and duration of such learning effects.

Studies examining changes in brain function following exposure to trauma point to a second way in which neuroscience may inform prevention efforts. Recent work in the neurosciences conceptualizes posttraumatic anxiety reactions in humans as a type of aberrant memory formation. This work extends research in rodents demonstrating the role of a circuit encompassing the amygdala, hippocampus, and ventral prefrontal cortex in the formation and extinction of fear memories (Debiec et al., 2006; Milad & Quirk, 2002; Nader, 2003). This view of fear-memory formation suggests that novel preventative interventions may prove helpful in minimizing sequalae of trauma. For example, some have suggested that pharmacologic interventions that alter physiological arousal might prevent the development of posttraumatic anxiety reactions if administered immediately following trauma (Pitman & Delahanty, 2005). Like attentional retraining, such interventions might be particularly powerful if implemented in youth, when they could have marked effects on later functioning in still-developing neural structures within the SIPN. Long-term effects have yet to be studied but merit careful attention.

Both of these novel approaches to prevention are notable because they emerge from integrations of basic and clinical perspectives and represent hypotheses that must be tested experimentally. Although neither intervention may ultimately prove to be beneficial, both advance thinking along theoretical lines by integrating insights from multiple scientific perspectives. Traditionally, theories in the mental health sciences have benefited from broad support from diverse lines of scientific inquiry.

Conclusions

In this chapter, we reviewed the literature on the increased risk for anxiety disorders that emerges during adolescence, with a focus on the social and neural changes that may figure prominently in the onset of this elevated risk. We then proposed an approach to studying the interactions among social and neural mechanisms underlying risk that integrates research from clinical psychopathology, developmental psychology, and cognitive neuroscience. Studies emerging from the intersection of these fields hold promise for elucidating new prevention and treatment approaches to adolescent anxiety disorders; the literature that incorporates aspects of all three fields has grown markedly in recent years, which suggests that translational approaches are gaining credence in the research community. To this end, we close by providing examples of potential prevention approaches that are emerging from translational work.

Such translational research approaches may be particularly useful for better defining the line between normal and abnormal anxiety, which is difficult to identify. This line is particularly fuzzy at the level of behavior in which normal, transient anxiety states can closely resemble states that occur within the context of enduring and impairing disorders. If we can elucidate the distinctive pathophysiologies of specific anxiety disorders, however, it may become possible to identify more objective markers of risk and optimal pathways for treatment.

Given that the neural circuits involved in fear and anxiety have been well defined in the animal literature, anxiety disorders serve as especially good candidates for translational work bridging the gap between basic science and clinical utility. In particular, fMRI studies offer a promising means for integrating recent behavioral research on threat cue processing in humans with more basic neuroscience work on fear circuitry. By uniting these disparate areas of study, researchers increase the likelihood that we can eventually move from a reactive stance in which we treat anxiety symptoms as they emerge to a proactive, preventive approach in which we interrupt the downward spiral of anxiety disorders at, or before, its outset.

References

Arnett, J. J. (1999). Adolescent storm and stress, reconsidered. *The American Psychologist, 54*(5), 317–326.

Aschenbrand, S. G., Kendall, P. C., Webb, A., Safford, S. M., & Flannery-Schroeder, E. (2003). Is childhood separation anxiety disorder a predictor of adult panic disorder and agoraphobia? A seven-year longitudinal study. *Journal of the American Academy of Child & Adolescent Psychiatry, 42*(12), 1478.

Bechara, A. (2004). The role of emotion in decision-making: Evidence from neurological patients with orbitofrontal damage. *Brain and Cognition, 55*(1), 30–40.

Bechara, A., Damasio, H., & Damasio, A. R. (2000). Emotion, decision making and the orbitofrontal cortex. *Cerebral Cortex, 10*(3), 295.

Berrettini, W. H. (2005). Genetic bases for endophenotypes in psychiatric disorders. *Dialogues in Clinical Neuroscience, 7*(2), 95.

Clark, D. A., Beck, A. T., & Stewart, B. (1990). Cognitive specificity and positive-negative affectivity: Complementary or contradictory views on anxiety and depression? *Journal of Abnormal Psychology, 99*, 148–155.

Cohen, P., Cohen, J., & Brook, J. (1993a). An epidemiological study of disorders in late childhood and adolescence—ii. Persistence of disorders. *Journal of Child Psychology and Psychiatry, 34*(6), 869–877.

Cohen, P., Cohen, J., Kasen, S., Velez, C. N., Hartmark, C., Johnson, J., et al. (1993b). An epidemiological study of disorders in late childhood and adolescence—i. Age- and gender-specific prevalence. *Journal of Child Psychology and Psychiatry, 34*(6), 851–867.

Coplan, J. D., Smith, E. L., Altemus, M., Scharf, B. A., Owens, M. J., Nemeroff, C. B., et al. (2001). Variable foraging demand rearing: Sustained elevations in cisternal cerebrospinal fluid corticotropin-releasing factor concentrations in adult primates. *Biological Psychiatry, 50,* 200–204.

Coricelli, G., Critchley, H. D., Joffily, M., O'Doherty, J. P., Sirigu, A., & Dolan, R. J. (2005). Regret and its avoidance: A neuroimaging study of choice behavior. *Nature Neuroscience, 8*(9), 1255.

Costello, E. J., Mustillo, S., Erkanli, A., Keeler, G., & Angold, A. (2003). Prevalence and development of psychiatric disorders in childhood and adolescence. *Archives of General Psychiatry, 60*(8), 837–844.

Costello, E. J., Pine, D. S., Hammen, C., March, J. S., Plotsky, P. M., Weissman, M. M., et al. (2002a). Development and natural history of mood disorders. *Biological Psychiatry, 52*(6), 529–542.

Costello, E. J., Pine, D. S., Hammen, C., March, J. S., Plotsky, P. M., Weissman, M. M., et al. (2002b). Development and natural history of mood disorders. *Biological Psychiatry, 52*(6), 529–542.

Dalgleish, T., Moradi, A. R., Taghavi, M. R., Neshat-Doost, H. T., & Yule, W. W. (2001). An experimental investigation of hypervigilance for threat in children and adolescents with post-traumatic stress disorder. *Psychological Medicine, 31*(3), 541–547.

Darwin, C. (1998). *The expression of the emotions in man and animals* (3rd ed). New York: Oxford University Press.

Davis, M., & Whalen, P. J. (2001). The amygdala: Vigilance and emotion. *Molecular Psychiatry, 6,* 13–34.

De Bellis, M., Keshavan, M., Shifflett, H., Iyengar, S., Beers, S., Hall, J., et al. (2002). Brain structures in pediatric maltreatment-related posttraumatic stress disorder: A sociodemographically matched study. *Biological Psychiatry, 52,* 1066–1078.

Debiec, J., Doyere, V., Nader, K., & LeDoux, J. E. (2006). Directly reactivated, but not indirectly reactivated, memories undergo reconsolidation in the amygdala. *Proceedings of the National Academy of Sciences, 103*(9), 3428–3433.

Desimone, R., & Duncan, J. (1995). Neural mechanisms of selective visual attention. *Annual Review of Neuroscience, 18,* 193–222.

Dewa, C. S., & Lin, E. (2000). Chronic physical illness, psychiatric disorder and disability in the workplace. *Social Science and Medicine, 51*(1), 41–50.

Dolan, R. J. (2002). Emotion, cognition, and behavior. *Science, 298,* 1191–1194.

Essau, C. A. (2003). Comorbidity of anxiety disorders in adolescents. *Depression and Anxiety, 18*(1), 1.

Essau, C. A., Conradt, J., & Petermann, F. (2000). Frequency, comorbidity, and psychosocial impairment of anxiety disorders in German adolescents. *Journal of Anxiety Disorders, 14*(3), 263.

Furman, W. (1989). The development of children's social networks. In D. Belle (Ed.), *Children's social networks and social supports* (pp. 151–172). New York: Wiley.

Furman, W., & Buhrmester, D. (1992). Age and sex differences in perceptions of networks of personal relationships. *Child Development, 63*(1), 103–115.

Giedd, J. N. (2004). Structural magnetic resonance imaging of the adolescent brain. *Annals of the New York Academy of Sciences, 1021*(1), 77–85.

Gottesman, I. I., & Gould, T. D. (2003). The endophenotype concept in psychiatry: Etymology and strategic intentions. *American Journal of Psychiatry, 160*(4), 636–645.

Gross, C., & Hen, R. (2004). The developmental origins of anxiety. *Nature Reviews Neuroscience, 5*(7), 545–552.

Hadwin, J. A., Donnelly, N., French, C. C., Richards, A., Watts, A., & Daley, D. (2003). The influence of children's self-report trait anxiety and depression on visual search for emotional faces. *Journal of Child Psychology and Psychiatry, 44*(3), 432–444.

Halit, H., Csibra, G., Volein, A., & Johnson, M. H. (2004). Face-sensitive cortical processing in early infancy. *Journal of Child Psychology and Psychiatry, 45*(7), 1228–1234.

Halit, H., de Haan, M., & Johnson, M. H. (2003). Cortical specialisation for face processing: Face-sensitive event-related potential components in 3– and 12–month-old infants. *Neuroimage, 19*(3), 1180–1193.

Hariri, A. R., Bookheimer, S. Y., & Mazziotta, J. C. (2000). Modulating emotional responses: Effects of a neocortical network on the limbic system. *Neuroreport, 11*(1), 43–48.

Hariri, A. R., Mattay, V. S., Tessitore, A., Kolachana, B., Fera, F., Goldman, D., et al. (2002). Serotonin transporter genetic variation and the response of the human amygdala. *Science, 297*(5580), 400–403.

Haxby, J. V., Hoffman, E. A., & Gobbini, M. I. (2002). Human neural systems for face recognition and social communication. *Biological Psychiatry, 51*(1), 59–67.

Hunkeler, E. M., Spector, W. D., Fireman, B., Rice, D. P., & Weisner, C. (2003). Psychiatric symptoms, impaired function, and medical care costs in an HMO setting. *General Hospital Psychiatry, 25*(3), 178–184.

Johnson, M. H., Griffin, R., Csibra, G., Halit, H., Farroni, T., M, D. E. H., et al. (2005). The emergence of the social brain network: Evidence from typical and atypical development. *Developmental Psychopathology, 17*(3), 599–619.

Kastner, S., & Ungerleider, L. G. (2000). Mechanisms of visual attention in the human cortex. *Annual Review of Neuroscience, 23*(1), 315–341.

Katzelnick, D. J., Kobak, K. A., DeLeire, T., Henk, H. J., Greist, J. H., Davidson, J. R., et al. (2001). Impact of generalized social anxiety disorder in managed care. *American Journal of Psychiatry, 158*(12), 1999–2007.

Kessler, R. C., Berglund, P., Demler, O., Jin, R., Merikangas, K. R., & Walters, E. E. (2005). Lifetime prevalence and age-of-onset distributions of DSM-IV disorders in the national comorbidity survey replication. *Archives of General Psychiatry, 62*(6), 593–602.

Kessler, R. C., & Frank, R. G. (1997). The impact of psychiatric disorders on work loss days. *Psychological Medicine, 27*(4), 861–873.

Killgore, W. D. S., & Yurgelun-Todd, D. A. (2005). Social anxiety predicts amygdala activation in adolescents viewing fearful faces. *Neuroreport, 16*(15), 1671–1675.

Kim-Cohen, J., Caspi, A., Moffitt, T. E., Harrington, H., Milne, B. J., & Poulton, R. (2003). Prior juvenile diagnoses in adults with mental disorder: Developmental follow-back of a prospective-longitudinal cohort. *Archives of General Psychiatry, 60*(7), 709.

Klein, R. G., & Pine, D. S. (2002). Anxiety disorders. In M. Rutter, E. Taylor, & L. Hersov (Eds.), *Child and adolescent psychiatry: Modern approaches* (4th ed., pp. 486–509). London: Blackwell.

Kuttler, A. F., & La Greca, A. M. (2004). Linkages among adolescent girls' romantic relationships, best friendships, and peer networks. *Journal of Adolescence, 27*(4), 395–414.

Langley, A. K., Bergman, R. L., McCracken, J., & Piacentini, J. C. (2004). Impairment in childhood anxiety disorders: Preliminary examination of the child anxiety impact scale-parent version. *Journal of Child and Adolescent Psychopharmacology, 14*(1), 105–114.

Larson, R., Richards, M., Moneta, G., Holmbeck, G., & Duckett, E. (1996). Changes in adolescents' daily interactions with their families from ages 10–18: Disengagement and transformation. *Developmental Psychology, 32*, 744–754.

Larson, R., & Richards, M. H. (1994). *Divergent realities: The emotional lives of mothers, fathers, and adolescents.* New York: Basic Books.

Lundh, L. G., & Ost, L. G. (1996). Recognition bias for critical faces in social phobics. *Behaviour Research and Therapy, 34*, 787–794.

MacLeod, C., Rutherford, E., Campbell, L., Ebsworthy, G., & Holker, L. (2002). Selective attention and emotional vulnerability: Assessing the causal basis of their association through the experimental manipulation of attentional bias. *Journal of Abnormal Psychology, 111*, 107–123.

Mancini, C., Van Ameringen, M., Bennett, M., Patterson, B., & Watson, C. (2005). Emerging treatments for child and adolescent social phobia: A review. *Journal of Child and Adolescent Psychopharmacology, 15*(4), 589–607.

Marks, I. (1987). The development of normal fear: A review. *Journal of Child Psychology and Psychiatry and Allied Disciplines, 28*(5), 667–697.

Martin, A., & Leslie, D. (2003). Psychiatric inpatient, outpatient, and medication utilization and costs among privately insured youths, 1997–2000. *American Journal of Psychiatry, 160*(4), 757–764.

Mathews, A., & Mackintosh, B. (2000). Induced emotional interpretation bias and anxiety. *Journal of Abnormal Psychology, 109*(4), 602.

McClure, E. B., Monk, C. S., Nelson, E. E., Parrish, J. M., Adler, A., Blair, R. J. R., et al. (in press). Abnormal attention modulation of fear circuit activation in pediatric Generalized Anxiety Disorder. *Archives of General Psychiatry*.

Meaney, M. J. (2001). Nature, nurture, and the disunity of knowledge. *Annals of the New York Academy of Sciences, 935*, 50–61.

Meeus, W., Iedema, J., Maassen, G., & Engels, R. (2005). Separation-individuation revisited: On the interplay of parent-adolescent relations, identity and emotional adjustment in adolescence. *Journal of Adolescence, 28*(1), 89–106.

Milad, M. R., & Quirk, G. J. (2002). Neurons in medial prefrontal cortex signal memory for fear extinction. *Nature, 420*(6911), 70–74.

Milham, M. P., Nugent, A. C., Drevets, W. C., Dickstein, D. P., Leibenluft, E., Ernst, M., et al. (2005). Selective reduction in amygdala volume in pediatric anxiety disorders: A voxel-based morphometry investigation. *Biological Psychiatry, 57*(9), 961–966.

Miller, E. K., & Cohen, J. D. (2001). An integrative theory of prefrontal cortex function. *Annual Review of Neuroscience, 24*, 167–202.

Mogg, K., & Bradley, B. P. (1998). A cognitive-motivational analysis of anxiety. *Behaviour Research and Therapy, 36*(9), 809–848.

Mogg, K., & Bradley, B. P. (2002). Selective orienting of attention to masked threat faces in social anxiety. *Behaviour Research and Therapy, 40*(12), 1403–1414.

Monk, C. S., McClure, E. B., Nelson, E. E., Zarahn, E., Bilder, R. M., Leibenluft, E., et al. (2003). Adolescent immaturity in attention-related brain engagement to emotional facial expressions. *Neuroimage, 20*(1), 420–428.

Monk, C. S., Nelson, E. E., McClure, E. B., Mogg, K., Bradley, B., Leibenluft, E., et al. (2006). Ventrolateral prefrontal cortex activation and attentional bias in response to angry faces in adolescents with generalized anxiety disorder. *American Journal of Psychiatry, 163*, 1091–1097.

Moradi, A. R., Taghavi, M. R., Neshat Doost, H. T., Yule, W., & Dalgleish, T. (1999). Performance of children and adolescents with PTSD on the Stroop colour-naming task. *Psychological Medicine, 29*(2), 415–419.

Muris, P., Merckelbach, H., Gadet, B., & Moulaert, V. (2000). Fears, worries, and scary dreams in 4– to 12–year-old children: Their content, developmental pattern, and origins. *Journal of Clinical Child Psychology, 29*, 43–52.

Nader, K. (2003). Memory traces unbound. *Trends in Neurosciences, 26*(2), 65.

Nelson, C. A., Bloom, F. E., Cameron, J. L., Amaral, D., Dahl, R. E., & Pine, D. (2002). An integrative, multidisciplinary approach to the study of brain-behavior relations in the context of typical and atypical development. *Development and Psychopathology, 14*(3), 499.

Nelson, E. E., Leibenluft, E., McClure, E. B., & Pine, D. S. (2005). The social re-orientation of adolescence: A neuroscience perspective on the process and its relation to psychopathology. *Psychological Medicine, 35*(2), 163–174.

Pessoa, L., McKenna, M., Gutierrez, E., & Ungerleider, L. G. (2002). Neural processing of emotional faces requires attention. *Proceedings of the National Academy of Sciences, 99*(17), 11458–11463.

Pine, D. S. (2001). Affective neuroscience and the development of social anxiety disorder. *Psychiatric Clinics of North America, 24*(4), 689–705.

Pine, D. S., Alegria, M., Cook, E. H. J., Costello, E. J., Dahl, R. E., Koretz, D., et al. (2002). Advances in developmental science and DSM-V. In D. J. Kupfer, M. B. First, & D. A. Regier (Eds.), *A research agenda for DSM-V* (pp. 85–122). Washington, DC: American Psychiatric Association.

Pine, D. S., Cohen, E., Cohen, P., & Brook, J. (1999). Adolescent depressive symptoms as predictors of adult depression: Moodiness or mood disorder? *American Journal of Psychiatry, 156*(1), 133–135.

Pine, D. S., Cohen, E., Cohen, P., & Brook, J. S. (2000a). Social phobia and the persistence of conduct problems. *Journal of Child Psychology and Psychiatry, 41*(5), 657–665.

Pine, D. S., Cohen, P., & Brook, J. (2001). Adolescent fears as predictors of depression. *Biological Psychiatry, 50*(9), 721–724.

Pine, D. S., Cohen, P., Gurley, D., Brook, J., & Ma, Y. (1998). The risk for early-adulthood anxiety and depressive disorders in adolescents with anxiety and depressive disorders. *Archives of General Psychiatry, 55*(1), 56–64.

Pine, D. S., Klein, R. G., Coplan, J. D., Papp, L. A., Hoven, C. W., Martinez, J., et al. (2000b). Differential carbon dioxide sensitivity in childhood anxiety disorders and nonill comparison group. *Archives of General Psychiatry, 57*(10), 960–967.

Pine, D. S., Klein, R. G., Mannuzza, S., Moulton, J. L., III, Lissek, S., Guardino, M., et al. (2005a). Face-emotion processing in offspring at risk for panic disorder. *Journal of the American Academy of Child and Adolescent Psychiatry, 44*(7), 664–672.

Pine, D. S., Klein, R. G., Roberson-Nay, R., Mannuzza, S., Moulton, J. L., III, Woldehawariat, G., et al. (2005b). Response to 5% carbon dioxide in children and adolescents: Relationship to panic disorder in parents and anxiety disorders in subjects. *Archives of General Psychiatry, 62*(1), 73–80.

Pine, D. S., Mogg, K., Bradley, B. P., Montgomery, L., Monk, C. S., McClure, E., et al. (2005c). Attention bias to threat in maltreated children: Implications for vulnerability to stress-related psychopathology. *American Journal of Psychiatry, 162*(2), 291–296.

Pitman, R. K., & Delahanty, D. L. (2005). Conceptually driven pharmacologic approaches to acute trauma. *CNS Spectrum Disorders, 10*(2), 99–106.

Rauch, S. L., Whalen, P. J., Shin, L. M., McInerney, S. C., Macklin, M. L., Lasko, N. B., et al. (2000). Exaggerated amygdala response to masked facial stimuli in posttraumatic stress disorder: A functional MRI study. *Biological Psychiatry, 47*, 769–776.

Reinblatt, S. P., & Walkup, J. T. (2005). Psychopharmacologic treatment of pediatric anxiety disorders. *Child and Adolescent Psychiatric Clinics of North America, 14*(4), 877.

Richards, A., Richards, L. C., & McGeeney, A. (2000). Anxiety-related Stroop interference in adolescents. *Journal of General Psychology, 127*(3), 327–333.

Richards, M. H., Crowe, P. A., Larson, R., & Swarr, A. (1998). Developmental patterns and gender differences in the experience of peer companionship during adolescence. *Child Development, 69*(1), 154–163.

Richert, K. A., Carrion, V. G., Karchemskiy, A., & Reiss, A. L. (2005). Regional differences of the prefrontal cortex in pediatric PTSD: An MRI study. *Depression and Anxiety, 23*(1), 17–25.

Roblek, T. T., & Piacentini, J. J. (2005). Cognitive-behavior therapy for childhood anxiety disorders. *Child and Adolescent Psychiatric Clinics of North America, 14*(4), 863.

Research Units on Pediatric Psychopharmacology. (2001). Fluvoxamine for the treatment of anxiety disorders in children and adolescents. The research unit on pediatric psychopharmacology anxiety study group. *New England Journal of Medicine, 344*(17), 1279–1285.

Schwartz, C. E., Snidman, N., & Kagan, J. (1996). Early temperamental predictors of Stroop interference to threatening information at adolescence. *Journal of Anxiety Disorders, 10*, 89–96.

Shaffer, D. D., Fisher, P. P., Dulcan, M. M. K., Davies, M. M., Piacentini, J. J., Schwab-Stone, M. M. E., et al. (1996). The NIMH Diagnostic Interview Schedule for Children Version 2.3 (DISC-2.3): Description, acceptability, prevalence rates, and performance in the MECA study. Methods for the epidemiology of child and adolescent mental disorders study. *Journal of the American Academy of Child & Adolescent Psychiatry, 35*(7), 865.

Sheline, Y. I., Barch, D. M., Donnelly, J. M., Ollinger, J. M., Snyder, A. Z., & Mintun, M. A. (2001). Increased amygdala response to masked emotional faces in depressed subjects resolves with antidepressant treatment: An fMRI study. *Biological Psychiatry, 50*, 651–658.

Smetana, J. G., Campione-Barr, N., & Metzger, A. (2005). Adolescent development in interpersonal and societal contexts. *Annual Review of Psychology, 57*, 1–30.

Sowell, E. R., Trauner, D. A., Gamst, A., & Jernigan, T. L. (2002). Development of cortical and subcortical brain structures in childhood and adolescence: A structural MRI study. *Developmental Medicine and Child Neurology, 44*(1), 4.

Stallard, P., Velleman, R., Salter, E., Howse, I., Yule, W., & Taylor, G. (2006). A randomised controlled trial to determine the effectiveness of an early psychological intervention with children involved in road traffic accidents. *Journal of Child Psychology and Psychiatry, 47*(2), 127–134.

Stein, M. B., & Kean, Y. M. (2000). Disability and quality of life in social phobia: Epidemiologic findings. *American Journal of Psychiatry, 157*(10), 1606–1613.

Steinberg, L. (2005). Cognitive and affective development in adolescence. *Trends in Cognitive Sciences, 9*(2), 69–74.

Steinberg, L., & Morris, A. S. (2001). Adolescent development. *Annu Rev Psychol, 52*, 83–110.

Thomas, K. M., Drevets, W. C., Dahl, R. E., Ryan, N. D., Birmaher, B., Eccard, C. H., et al. (2001). Amygdala response to fearful faces in anxious and depressed children. *Archives of General Psychiatry, 58*(11), 1057–1063.

Verduin, T. L., & Kendall, P. C. (2003). Differential occurrence of comorbidity within childhood anxiety disorders. *Journal of Clinical Child and Adolescent Psychology, 32*(2), 290.

Vuilleumier, P. (2005). How brains beware: Neural mechanisms of emotional attention. *Trends in Cognitive Sciences, 9*(12), 585.

Walker, E. F., Sabuwalla, Z., & Huot, R. (2004). Pubertal neuromaturation, stress sensitivity, and psychopathology. *Development and Psychopathology, 16*(4), 807.

Walter, H., Abler, B., Ciaramidaro, A., & Erk, S. (2005). Motivating forces of human actions. Neuroimaging reward and social interaction. *Brain Research Bulletin, 67*(5), 368.

Weems, C. F., & Costa, N. M. (2005). Developmental differences in the expression of childhood anxiety symptoms and fears. *Journal of the American Academy of Child and Adolescent Psychiatry, 44*(7), 656.

Weems, C. F., Silverman, W. K., & La Greca, A. M. (2000). What do youth referred for anxiety problems worry about? Worry and its relation to anxiety and anxiety disorders in children and adolescents. *Journal of Abnormal Child Psychology, 28*(1), 63–72.

Weissman, M. M. M., Wolk, S. S., Wickramaratne, P. P., Goldstein, R. R. B., Adams, P. P., Greenwald, S. S., et al. (1999). Children with prepubertal-onset major depressive disorder and anxiety grown up. *Archives of General Psychiatry, 56*(9), 794.

West, P., & Sweeting, H. (2003). Fifteen, female and stressed: Changing patterns of psychological distress over time. *Journal of Child Psychology and Psychiatry, 44*, 399–411.

Whalen, P. J. (1998). Fear, vigilance and ambiguity: Initial neuroimaging studies of the human amygdala. *Current Directions in Psychological Science, 7*, 177–188.

Williams, J. M., Mathews, A., & MacLeod, C. (1996). The emotional Stroop task and psychopathology. *Psychological Bulletin, 120*(1), 3–24.

Wilson, E. J., Macleod, C., Mathews, A., & Rutherford, E. M. (2006). The causal role of interpretive bias in anxiety reactivity. *Journal of Abnormal Psychology, 115*(1), 103.

Winterer, G., Coppola, R., Goldberg, T. E., Egan, M. F., Jones, D. W., Sanchez, C. E., et al. (2004). Prefrontal broadband noise, working memory, and genetic risk for schizophrenia. *American Journal of Psychiatry, 161*(3), 490–500.

Chapter 11

Stress-Induced Pathophysiology
Within the Schizophrenia Patient Brain

A Model for the Delayed Onset
of Psychosis and Its Circumvention
by Anxiolytic Agents

Anthony A. Grace

With few exceptions, schizophrenia is a disorder that exhibits a genetic predisposition. However, studies have shown that the disorder is not completely genetically determined, in that even identical twins with essentially the same genetic makeup exhibit only a 40–60% concordance (Kendler et al., 1996). Moreover, despite this genetic predisposition that is believed to be present from birth, the onset of psychosis is generally delayed until late adolescence or early adulthood (Häfner et al., 1993; Kendler et al., 1987; Loranger, 1984; Pogue-Geile, 1997). This has given rise to a model whereby the onset of schizophrenia is based on a "two-hit" system—in other words, a genetic predisposition coupled with another factor that triggers the pathological processes that eventually lead to the first break. Nonetheless, even in those individuals in whom schizophrenia psychosis is not yet evident, a prodromal state has been frequently observed. This prodromal condition often presents as deficits in cognitive abilities and executive function (Parnas, 1999; Parnas & Jorgensen, 1989). Thus, although patients with prodromal symptoms do not show the full psychosis symptoms, they do show deficits such as depression, increases in anxiety, problems with concentration, altered cognition and perception, social withdrawal, anhedonia, and deterioration in functioning (an der Heiden & Hafner, 2000; Parnas, 1999). However, the factors that differ in the propensity of an individual to progress from the prodromal state to the first break are not clear.

One model that has been advanced is that stress may play a role in the transition to psychosis (Corcoran et al., 2003; Grace, 2004; Thompson et al., 2004; Walker & Diforio, 1997). Of course, not all highly stressful environments will lead to the onset of schizophrenia. What is proposed here is that the genetic predisposition may lead to deficits in the manner by which the prefrontal cortex (PFC) is capable of modulating responses to stressors, causing the individual to be particularly vulnerable to the pathological changes that eventually culminate in psychosis in adulthood. Moreover, I present a potential means to circumvent the transition to psychosis in predisposed individuals by pharmacotherapy of an already-present abnormal response to stress.

Stress as a Factor in Schizophrenia

Stress is a factor that is ever-present in the life of an organism. The reaction to stress can be adaptive, in enabling an organism to respond appropriately to a threatening environment. However, stress can also trigger pathological processes if it is extreme, maintained for extended periods of time, or if the individual is particularly vulnerable. Under such conditions, stress can lead to the onset or exacerbation of psychiatric disorders, including posttraumatic stress syndrome, schizophrenia, or affective disorders. Schizophrenia patients who are in remission show a higher level of relapse when they are returned to a high-stress environment (Birley, 1970; Norman & Malla, 1993). Moreover, there is evidence to suggest that, of those individuals who are at genetic risk for developing schizophrenia, those who show significantly higher stress reactivity are the individuals most likely to convert to schizophrenia later in life (Johnstone et al., 2005).

Stress Circuitry

Stressful stimuli elicit responses in a complex network of nuclei within the brain (e.g., see figure 11-2). There are several areas in particular that have been associated with stress responses. The locus coeruleus is a group of neurons in the brainstem that contain and release the neurotransmitter norepinephrine. Norepinephrine has been shown to increase when an animal is exposed to stress, and the primary metabolite of norepinephrine, methyl-hydroxy-phenol glycol (MHPG), shows a substantial increase in the CSF in an animal that has been exposed to stressors (Abercrombie & Jacobs, 1988; Abercrombie et al., 1988; Shanks et al., 1991; Thierry et al., 1968), The locus coeruleus will also show increased reaction to stressors in an animal that has been chronically stressed. Thus, chronically stressed animals show an increase in stress-evoked norepinephrine release (Abercrombie et al., 1992), and the noradrenergic neurons of the locus coeruleus show a significantly greater response to acute stressors following chronic stress (Jedema & Grace, 2003a; Mana & Grace, 1997). The locus coeruleus neurons themselves are po-

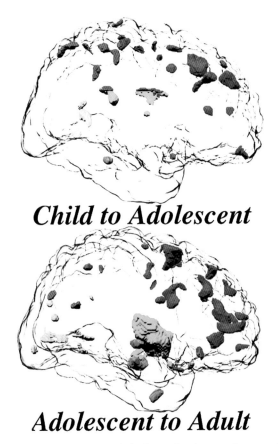

Child to Adolescent

Adolescent to Adult

Figure 3-1 *Top,* child to adolescent statistical map for the negative age effects representing gray matter density reductions observed between childhood and adolescence; *bottom,* adolescence and adulthood. These maps are three-dimensional renderings of the traditional statistical maps shown inside the transparent cortical surface rendering of one representative subject's brain. Lobes and the subcortical region were defined anatomically on the same subject's brain. Color coding is applied to each cluster based on its location within the representative brain. Clusters are shown in the frontal lobes (purple), parietal lobes (red), occipital lobes (yellow), temporal lobes (blue), and subcortical region (green). (Sowell et al., 1999b; Sowell et al., 1999a.)

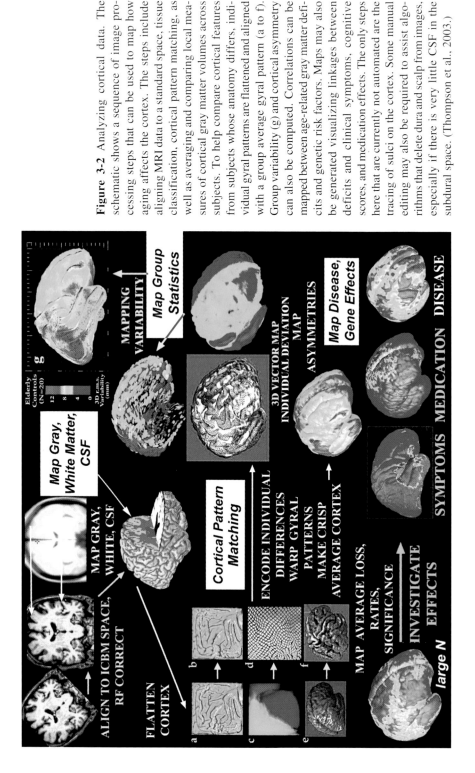

Figure 3-2 Analyzing cortical data. The schematic shows a sequence of image processing steps that can be used to map how aging affects the cortex. The steps include aligning MRI data to a standard space, tissue classification, cortical pattern matching, as well as averaging and comparing local measures of cortical gray matter volumes across subjects. To help compare cortical features from subjects whose anatomy differs, individual gyral patterns are flattened and aligned with a group average gyral pattern (a to f). Group variability (g) and cortical asymmetry can also be computed. Correlations can be mapped between age-related gray matter deficits and genetic risk factors. Maps may also be generated visualizing linkages between deficits and clinical symptoms, cognitive scores, and medication effects. The only steps here that are currently not automated are the tracing of sulci on the cortex. Some manual editing may also be required to assist algorithms that delete dura and scalp from images, especially if there is very little CSF in the subdural space. (Thompson et al., 2003.)

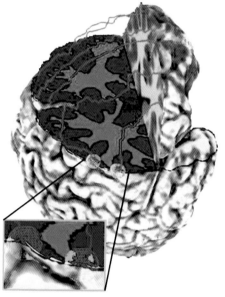

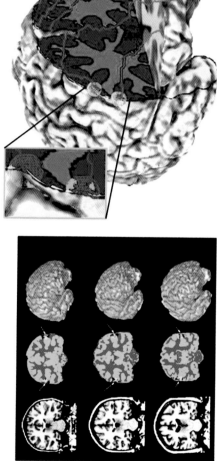

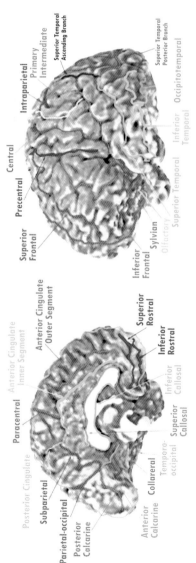

Figure 3-3 *Top left,* three representative brain image data sets with the original MRI, tissue segmented images, and surface renderings with sulcal contours shown in pink; *top right,* surface rendering of one representative subject with cutout showing tissue segmented coronal slice and axial slice superimposed within the surface. Sulcal lines are shown where they would lie on the surface in the cut-out region. Note the sample spheres over the right hemisphere inferior frontal sulcus (lower sphere) and on the middle region of the pre-central sulcus (upper sphere) that illustrate varying degrees of gray matter density. In the blown-up panel, note the upper sphere has a higher gray matter density than the lower sphere, as it contains only blue pixels (gray matter) within the brain. The lower sphere also contains green pixels (white matter) that would lower the gray matter proportion within it. In the actual analysis, the gray matter proportion was measured within 15mm spheres centered across every point over the cortical surface. *Bottom,* sulcal anatomical delineations are defined according to color. These are the contours drawn on each individual's surface rendering according to a reliable, written protocol. (Sowell et al., 2002b.)

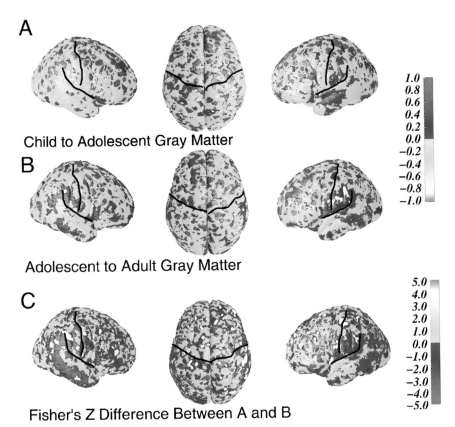

A

Child to Adolescent Gray Matter

1.0
0.8
0.6
0.4
0.2
0.0
−0.2
−0.4
−0.6
−0.8
−1.0

B

Adolescent to Adult Gray Matter

C

Fisher's Z Difference Between A and B

5.0
4.0
3.0
2.0
1.0
0.0
−1.0
−2.0
−3.0
−4.0
−5.0

Figure 3-4 Gray matter density age-effect statistical maps (*left, right,* and *top views*) showing gray matter density changes between childhood and adolescence (A) and between adolescence and adulthood (B). Anatomically, the central sulcus (CS), Sylvian fissure (SF), and interhemispheric fissure (IF) are highlighted. In both images, shades of green to yellow represent negative Pearson's correlation coefficients (gray matter loss with increasing age) and shades of blue, purple, and pink represent positive Pearson's correlation coefficients (gray matter gain with age) according to the color bar on the right (range of Pearson correlation coefficients from −1 to +1). Regions shown in red correspond to correlation coefficients that have significant negative age effects at a threshold of $p = 0.05$ (gray matter loss), and regions shown in white correspond to significant positive age effects at a threshold of $p = 0.05$ (gray matter density gain). The images on the bottom (C) display a statistical map of the Fisher's Z transformation of the difference between Pearson correlation coefficients for the child-to-adolescent and the adolescent-to-adult contrasts (see color bar on far right representing Z-scores from −5 to +5). Shades of green to yellow represent regions where the age effects are more significant in the adolescent-to-adult contrast (*middle*) than in the child-to-adolescent contrast (*left*). Highlighted in red are the regions where the difference between Pearson correlation coefficients is statistically significant ($p = 0.05$). Shades of blue, purple, and pink represent regions where the age effects are more significant in the child-to-adolescent contrast than the adolescent-to-adult contrast. Highlighted in white are regions where these effects are significant at a threshold of $p = 0.05$. (Sowell et al., 2001c.)

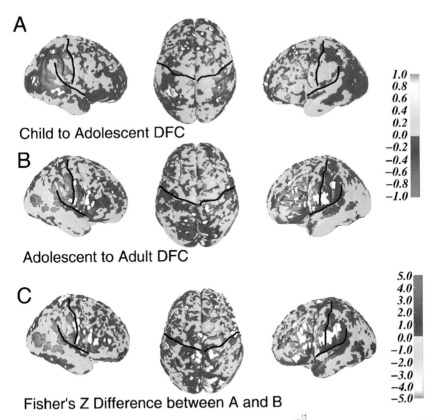

A

Child to Adolescent DFC

B

Adolescent to Adult DFC

C

Fisher's Z Difference between A and B

Figure 3-5 DFC age-effect statistical maps (*left, right,* and *top*) showing changes in DFC between childhood and adolescence (A) and between adolescence and adulthood (B). Anatomically, the central sulcus (CS), Sylvian fissure (SF), and interhemispheric fissure (IF) are highlighted. In both images, shades of green to yellow represent positive Pearson's correlation coefficients (increased DFC or brain growth) and shades of blue, purple, and pink represent negative Pearson's correlation coefficients (decreased DFC or shrinkage) according to the color bar on the right (range of Pearson correlation coefficients from −1 to +1). Regions shown in red correspond to correlation coefficients that have significant positive age effects at a threshold of $p = 0.05$ (brain growth), and regions shown in white correspond to significant negative age effects at a threshold of $p = 0.05$ (brain shrinkage). The images on the bottom (C) display a statistical map of the Fisher's Z transformation of the difference between Pearson correlation coefficients for the child-to-adolescent and the adolescent-to-adult contrasts (see color bar on far right representing Z-scores from −5 to +5). Shades of green to yellow represent regions where the age effects are more significant in the adolescent-to-adult contrast (middle image) than in the child-to-adolescent contrast (left image). Highlighted in red are the regions where the difference between Pearson correlation coefficients is statistically significant ($p = 0.05$). Shades of blue, purple, and pink represent regions where the age effects are more significant in the child-to-adolescent contrast than the adolescent-to-adult contrast. Highlighted in white are regions where these effects are significant at a threshold of $p = 0.05$. Note the sign of the differences between contrasts is opposite to that in the difference map for the gray matter density contrasts because of the inverse relationship between gray matter density (negative effects) and late brain growth (positive effects). (Sowell et al., 2001b.)

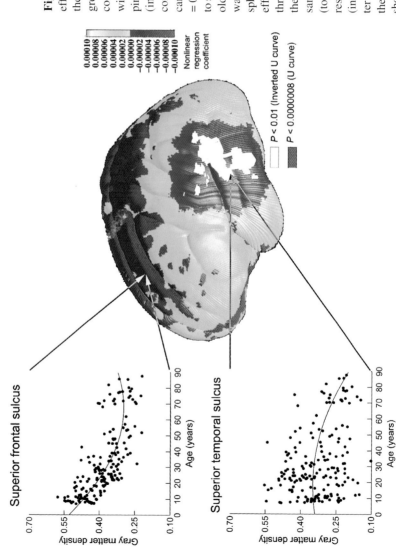

Figure 3-6 This map (left frontal view) shows age effects on gray matter density on the lateral surface of the brain between childhood and old age. Shades of green to yellow represent positive partial regression coefficients for the quadratic term (U-shaped curves with respect to age), and shades of blue, purple, and pink represent negative partial regression coefficients (inverted U-shaped curves). Regions shown in red correspond to regression coefficients that have significant positive nonlinear age effects at a threshold of $P = 0.0000008$, and regions shown in white correspond to significant negative nonlinear age effects at a threshold of $P = 0.01$. The pattern of nonlinear age effects was similar in the left and right (not shown) hemispheres except that none of the negative nonlinear age effects in the right posterior temporal lobe reached a threshold of $P = 0.01$. Scatterplots of age effects with the best fitting quadratic regression line are shown for sample surface points in the superior frontal sulcus (top) and the superior temporal sulcus (bottom) representative of the positive (U-shaped) and negative (inverted U-shaped) nonlinear age effects. Gray matter proportion within the 15-mm sphere surrounding the sample surface point (matched across subjects) is shown on the Y-axis. (Sowell et al., 2003a.)

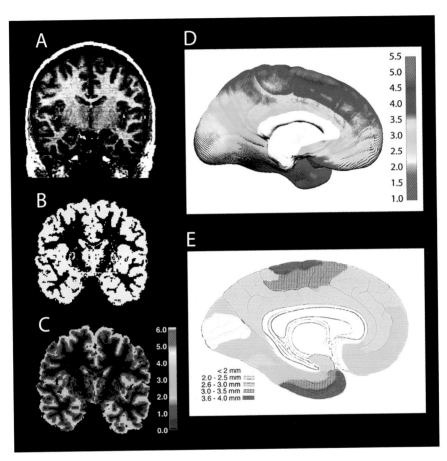

Figure 3-8 Cortical thickness maps: *A,* original T1-weighted image for one representative subject; *B,* tissue segmented image; *C,* gray matter thickness image where thickness is progressively coded in mm from inner to outer layers of cortex using the 3-D Eikonal Fire equation. Note the images were resampled to a voxel size of 0.33 mm cubed, so the thickness measures are at a submillimeter level of precision, according to the color bar on the right (mm). Figures *A* through *C* are sliced at the same level in all three image volumes from the same subject. Shown in *D* is an *in vivo* average cortical thickness map created from our 45 subjects at their first scan. The brain surface is color coded according to the color bar, where thickness is shown in mm. Our average thickness map can be compared to an adapted version of the 1929 cortical thickness map of von Economo (1929; *E*). Color coding has been applied over his original stippling pattern, respecting the boundaries of his original work, to highlight the similarities between the two maps. (Sowell et al., 2004a.)

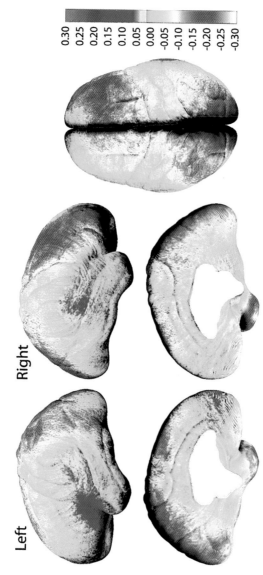

Figure 3-9 Annualized rate of change in cortical thickness: Shown in this figure is the average rate of change in cortical thickness in mm according to the color bar on the right. Maximum gray matter loss is shown in shades of red, and maximum gray matter gain is shown in shades of blue. (Sowell et al., 2004a.)

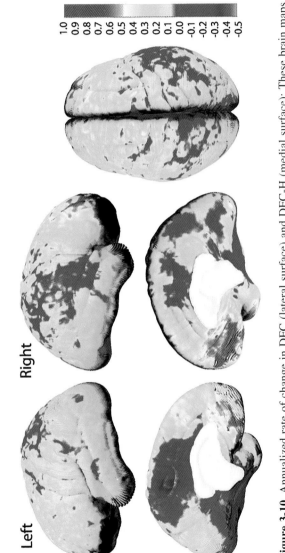

Figure 3-10 Annualized rate of change in DFC (lateral surface) and DFC-H (medial surface): These brain maps show the annualized rate of change in DFC in millimeters according to the color bar. Corpus callosum and brain stem regions have been masked out of the midline views. Note the most prominent growth shown in red, where brain size increases on average 0.5 to 1.0 mm per year. (Sowell et al., 2004a.)

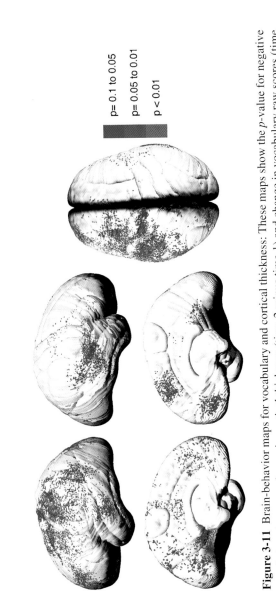

p= 0.1 to 0.05

p= 0.05 to 0.01

p < 0.01

Figure 3-11 Brain-behavior maps for vocabulary and cortical thickness: These maps show the *p*-value for negative correlations between change in cortical thickness (time 2 minus time 1) and change in vocabulary raw scores (time 2 minus time 1). Negative *p*-values (i.e., regions where greater thinning was associated with greater vocabulary improvement) are represented in color according to the color bar, and regions in white were not significant. Positive correlations were not significant in the permutation analyses for any of the ROIs and are not shown here. (Sowell et al., 2004a.)

Figure 3-12 Gray matter density, group-difference statistical maps showing gray matter density increase (and white matter density decrease) in the ALC subjects relative to controls (in nonscaled space). Shades of green to yellow represent positive Pearson's correlation coefficients (increased gray matter density in ALC subjects) and shades of purple and pink represent negative Pearson's correlation coefficients (decreased gray matter density in ALC subjects) according to the color bar on the right (range of Pearson correlation coefficients from –1 to +1). Regions shown in red correspond to correlation coefficients that show significant increase in gray matter in the ALC subjects relative to controls at a threshold of $p = 0.01$. Regions shown in white correspond to correlation coefficients that show significant decrease in gray matter in the ALC subjects relative to controls at a threshold of $P = 0.01$. The Sylvian fissure (SF) and central sulcus (CS) are highlighted for anatomical reference. (Sowell et al., 2002a.)

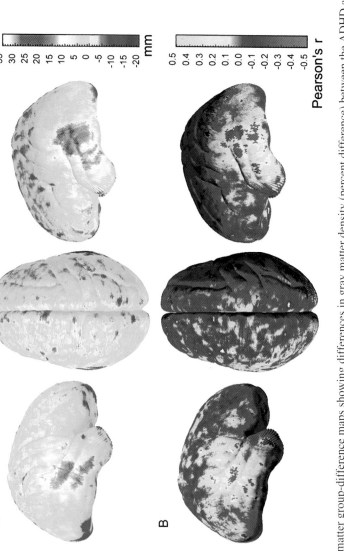

Figure 3-13 *A*, gray matter group-difference maps showing differences in gray matter density (percent difference) between the ADHD and control subjects according to the color bar on the right. Warmer colors (above 0 on the color bar) are regions where gray matter density is greater in the ADHD than control subjects, and cooler colors (below 0) are regions where the controls have greater gray matter density than the ADHD subjects. Note the approximately 20 to 30 percent increase in gray matter density in temporal and inferior parietal regions bilaterally. *B*, gray matter density group-difference statistical maps showing the significance of gray matter differences between the ADHD and control subjects according to the color bar on the right (Pearson's correlation coefficients ranging from –0.5 to 0.5). Regions overlaid in yellow correspond to correlation coefficients that show significant increase in gray matter density in ADHD subjects at a threshold of p = 0.05, and those in red correspond to significant increase at a threshold of p = 0.01. Negative correlations (i.e.. decreased gray matter density in ADHD patients relative to controls) are shown in white. (Sowell et al., 2003b.)

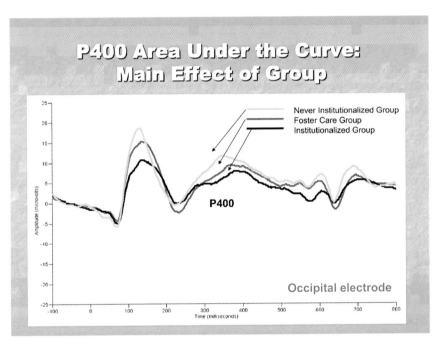

Figure 9-2 Event-related potentials (ERPs) invoked by pictures of facial expressions (collapsed to reveal a main effect of amplitude). The data illustrate the P400 component of the ERP, with the largest amplitude obtained by the NIG ($n = 13$), the smallest by the IG ($n = 29$), and the FCG ($n = 33$) between IG and NIG.

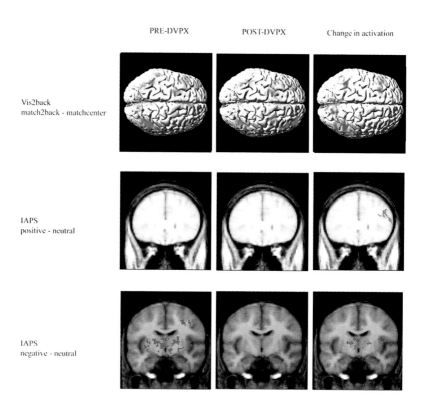

PRE-DVPX   POST-DVPX   Change in activation

Vis2back
match2back - matchcenter

IAPS
positive - neutral

IAPS
negative - neutral

Figure 14-4 Areas of activation and deactivation in pediatric patients with putative prodromal BD before and after 12 weeks of divalproex monotherapy (red = areas of activation; blue = areas of decreases in activation compared to baseline).

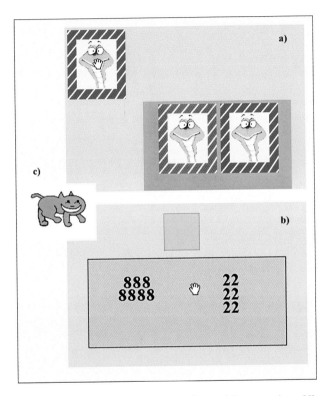

Figure 18-3 Pictures on the screen during attention training exercises. Visual attention and conflict resolution exercises. *A,* matching-to-sample exercise: The child must select the picture on the brown board that matches the sample on the upper left corner. Matching to sample difficulty is increased over the trials by making the competing pictures more similar. At advanced levels, the sample picture is removed from the screen and the child has to memorize it in order to select the correct matching picture. *B,* conflict resolution exercise: The child has to select the group with the most numbers in it. In congruent trials, like the one illustrated, the more numerous group is made up of numbers larger in value. In incongruent trials, the more numerous group is made up of numbers smaller in value. *C,* illustration of the visual feedback for completing a set of trials of equal difficulty.

tently excited by a peptide, corticotrophin releasing factor (CRF), that has also been associated with stressors (Jedema & Grace, 2003b; Valentino & Foote, 1988). When an animal is exposed to chronic stress, the levels of CRF in the locus coeruleus will increase (Valentino & Foote, 1986). Therefore, it is believed that chronic stress will sensitize the response of the locus coeruleus both directly by changes in membrane characteristics of the neurons (Jedema & Grace, 2003b), as well as via increasing the levels of CRF in this region.

One area that supplies CRF input into the locus coeruleus is the central nucleus of the amygdala. This region comprises primarily gama aminobutyric acid (GABA) containing neurons that also utilize CRF as a cotransmitter. Our recent data (Rosenkranz et al., 2006) show that, recorded in vivo, the neurons of the central nucleus of the amygdala exhibit bistable firing patterns similar to that described for the nucleus accumbens (O'Donnell & Grace, 1995), in which the neurons alternate from a hyperpolarized, inactive state and a depolarized state during which they fire spontaneously and can be driven by excitatory afferents. Such bistable states in the accumbens and the cortex are thought to provide a gating of information flow through these regions (O'Donnell & Grace, 1995). Despite the fact that the primary transmitter emanating from the central amygdala output region has long been considered to be the inhibitory GABAergic circuitry, our recent data (Ramsooksingh et al., 2004) show that stimulation of this region provides an excitatory drive onto the locus coeruleus, particularly when stimulated in bursts. Moreover, a CRF antagonist, revealing an underlying GABAergic component, can block this excitation.

The central nucleus of the amygdala receives a complex array of afferent inputs. As mentioned above, one of the primary inputs is via the glutamatergic pyramidal neurons of the basal and lateral nuclear complex of the amygdala (Kretteck & Price, 1978). However, studies that have tried to evaluate the net effect of activating this pathway are controversial. This is because the output neurons in the basal/lateral amygdala region project both directly to the central amygdala, as well as activating a group of GABAergic interneurons lying within the region known as the intercalated cell masses. This region provides a potent GABAergic inhibition of the central amygdala. In vivo extracellular studies have shown that stimulation of the basal/lateral amygdala tends to excite the central amygdala (Quirk et al., 2003). However, the central amygdala tends to show very low levels of spontaneous activity, making an inhibitory input difficult to detect. In contrast, when examined using in vivo intracellular recordings, we have demonstrated that basal and lateral amygdala activation produces primarily an inhibition of central amygdala output via activation of the intercalated cell masses (Rosenkranz et al., 2006). This finding is actually more consistent with the behavioral data concerning basal and lateral amygdala interactions than is the excitatory interaction proposed to occur as derived from extracellular recording studies (Quirk et al., 2003). The interaction of these regions is central to understanding how the prefrontal cortex will affect amygdala output, particularly after chronic stress, as outlined below.

Modulation of the Amygdala

BASAL/LATERAL COMPLEX. The amygdala is under the regulatory control of several systems that appear to exert a modulatory influence over this region and its response to stressors. In particular, the prefrontal cortex and the dopamine system have potent regulatory influences over the amygdala. Moreover, these afferent systems also show complex interactions with each other. We have shown that stimulation of sensory afferents, such as the auditory association cortex, will cause a depolarization and activation of neurons in the basal/lateral amygdala nucleus (Rosenkranz & Grace, 1999; Rosenkranz & Grace, 2001). However, stimulation of the prefrontal cortex evokes a very different response. Thus, when the prefrontal cortex is stimulated electrically, we observe an inhibitory postsynaptic potential (IPSP). When the membrane potential of the pyramidal (output) neuron is hyperpolarized by current injection, the IPSP exhibits a reversal potential of approximately –68 mV; this is consistent with a reversal potential for a chloride ion-mediated conductance, such as those activated by $GABA_A$-mediated synapses. Because the prefrontal cortical afferents to the amygdala are known to be glutamatergic and not GABAergic in nature, this response appears to be mediated by an interneuron within the amygdala that is activated by prefrontal cortical afferents. Indeed, we have shown that stimulation of the prefrontal cortical input to the amygdala will preferentially activate interneurons within this structure, whereas sensory cortical input will preferentially activate the pyramidal neurons (Rosenkranz & Grace, 2001; Rosenkranz & Grace, 2002a). Moreover, it is clear from the analysis of latencies that the evoked IPSP is due to prefrontal cortical excitation of interneurons (Rosenkranz & Grace, 2002a), and not antidromic activation of amygdalofugal neurons and activation of interneurons by local collaterals, as proposed by others (Likhtik et al., 2005).

The ability of the prefrontal cortex to activate interneurons has important functional consequences. Thus, stimulation of the auditory association cortex is capable of evoking action potentials within the lateral amygdala nucleus. However, if the prefrontal cortex is stimulated first, the resultant IPSP will block activation produced by auditory association cortex stimulation. This blockade will take place only if the interval after prefrontal cortical stimulation is brief (i.e., about 50 ms or less). Therefore, this is a type of event-related attenuation. We have proposed that this type of attenuation has important implications for prefrontal regulation of emotional responses. We believe that, via activation of interneurons, the prefrontal cortex has the capacity to attenuate responses to inappropriate stimuli. For example, a higher-level sensory input (e.g., the sound of a dog barking) may typically evoke a fear response via activation of the amygdala. However, if the barking occurs in an environment or a context that is nonthreatening (e.g., if the dog is familiar, if one is among restrained or caged animals), then the prefrontal cortex has the ability to override an inappropriate emotional response. Indeed, drawing from our example, Harari and colleagues (2003) have examined this type of interaction in humans using a functional imaging study. In this study, the subject was presented with a picture of a threatening object; as expected from other reports, this resulted in an activation of the amygdala. However, if the subject first receives verbal instructions regarding description or identification of objects in the following picture, when the threatening picture is presented, the amygdala is not activated. Instead, there is an activation of frontal cortical regions. This is consistent with what would be predicted from our study of evoked neuronal responses in anesthetized rodents.

We have found that dopamine also exerts a potent regulatory influence over the amygdala. Thus, dopamine was found to exert two effects over the responses of basal/lateral amygdala neurons to stimuli. First, we observed that dopamine acting via D1 receptors increases the excitability and via D2 receptors increases the input resistance of pyramidal neurons in vitro (Kroner et al., 2005). This is consistent with the observed increase in excitability following systemic administration of dopamine D2 agonists in vivo (Rosenkranz & Grace, 2001). This translates into a greater amplitude of evoked response produced by stimulation of sensory afferents to the basal/lateral amygdala complex (Rosenkranz & Grace, 2001; Rosenkranz & Grace, 2002a). In contrast, activation of D1 receptors decreases the amplitude of the evoked IPSP observed in vivo upon stimulation of prefrontal cortical afferents (Rosenkranz & Grace, 2002a). Therefore, in the presence of dopamine, there is an increase in response to the sensory input and an attenuation in the ability of the prefrontal cortex to downregulate this response.

In the case of normal activation of the dopamine system, as may occur during a heightened vigilance state, this would keep the organism attentive toward many stimuli that may otherwise be ignored. However, a hyperdopaminergic state may result in a pathological consequence. Thus, if there is too much dopamine stimulation, as may occur with amphetamine administration, the prefrontal cortex would lose its ability to attenuate normally benign stimuli, causing such stimuli to evoke a maximal emotional response. Therefore, even a familiar or nonthreatening stimulus may cause the individual to respond with a strong fear response. Such a condition would also be present if the prefrontal cortex is incapable of normal activation, as may occur with schizophrenia. This exaggerated fear response to stimuli known to be benign may represent a type of paranoia response in the subject.

CENTRAL MEDIAL NUCLEUS. The prefrontal cortex also exerts a potent regulatory influence over the baseline activity and responsivity of neurons within the primary autonomic output region of the amygdala, the central medial nucleus. The influence of the prefrontal cortex was examined by testing the effects of transection of the fibers that connect the prefrontal cortex with the amygdala (Correll et al., 2005). The lesion of these afferents resulted in a substantial decrease in central medial nucleus neuron activity; there was a significant decrease in both the baseline firing rate and in the population of active neurons. The neurons in the central medial nucleus typically exhibited on average a small decrease in firing rate upon presentation of a footshock. Moreover, this response showed accommodation with repeated footshocks, returning to baseline after four repetitions of the shock. However, after lesion of the prefrontal cortical afferents, there was a dramatic change in response: The neurons showed a significant footshock-evoked increase in activity, and there was no accommodation to repeated footshock presentation. Therefore, in the control rat, the prefrontal cortex provides a potent suppression of baseline activity, as well as a strong suppression in the response of this region to acute noxious stimuli.

Conditioned Responses Within the Amygdala-Prefrontal Cortical Circuit

In addition to short-term responses evoked by noxious or threatening stimuli, the amygdala circuit also shows longer-term plasticity with repeated presentation of a stimulus. Moreover, this plasticity is dependent on the nature of the stimulus presented. Thus, presentation of an odor to the nose of an anesthetized rat will cause an increase in excitatory synaptic potentials (i.e., EPSPs) within the lateral amygdala nucleus. However, if the odor is presented repeatedly, the amplitude of the EPSPs occurring during the odor presentation will progressively decrease, and after 5-8 presentations actually fall below the spontaneous nonodor baseline (Rosenkranz & Grace, 2002b). This would be a type of habituation, in which the neuron has "learned" that the odor is benign and therefore the response amplitude decreases. A footshock, even in an anesthetized rat, typically evokes a much higher amplitude response, consisting of a membrane depolarization and spike discharge. If the footshock is delivered at the same time as a novel odor, after several pairings the odor itself begins to elicit a high-amplitude evoked response when presented alone. Therefore, this would be a neuronal equivalent of a "fear conditioning" paradigm within the amygdala, in which the odor has taken on the activational properties of the footshock with which it was paired. Note that this conditioned response can take place even when the entire procedure is done in the anesthetized rat. On the other hand, if the pairing is done while the animal is awake, leading to behavioral correlates of a fear response (i.e., freezing, decreased exploration) when the odor is presented alone, subsequent electrophysiological recordings from the anesthetized rat show that the amplitude of the response to the conditioned odor versus the nonpaired odor is significantly greater as compared to when the entire procedure takes place in the anesthetized rat (Rosenkranz & Grace, 2002b; Rosenkranz et al., 2003).

This type of conditioned association is dependent on the state of the dopamine system. In order to test this, we found that two odors may be sequentially conditioned with footshock. This enables us to test the ability of a neuron to exhibit conditioning to a footshock, then perform a manipulation of the dopamine system, and examine whether the manipulation affects the pairing that has already occurred, or if it interferes with new conditioning. Using this paradigm, administration of a control solution such as a saline injection between conditioning sessions did not interfere with either the amplitude of the previous conditioned response when the odor is presented alone, or with the ability to condition a response to a new odor paired with a footshock. If a dopamine antagonist is administered systemically prior to the second odor, we found that there was also no interference with the previously conditioned response. However, there was a complete blockade in the ability to condition the second odor to the footshock. Therefore, dopamine appears to be required for conditioning to occur; on the other hand, once the conditioning is present, dopamine is no longer required to maintain the conditioned response.

The prefrontal cortex also is capable of modulating the conditioning. If the prefrontal cortex is stimulated electrically following the first conditioning procedure, there is no interference with the conditioned response when the odor is then presented alone. However, if the prefrontal cortex is stimulated during the pairing of the second odor with the footshock, there is an inability to obtain a conditioned response to the odor. Therefore, the prefrontal cortex appears to affect the system in the opposite manner as does dopamine, in that dopamine is required for new conditioning to occur, but the prefrontal cortex is capable of suppressing new conditioning. On the other hand, once a conditioned response is present, neither prefrontal cortical activation nor dopamine receptor blockade has an effect (Rosenkranz & Grace, 2002b).

Drawing from the previous results, one might expect a deficit in prefrontal cortical function to cause the system to show an abnormally high level of associations of a pathological nature. Indeed, schizophrenia patients are known to make inappropriate associations. On the other hand, it has been suggested that one of the effects of antipsychotic drugs is to prevent schizophrenia patients from making new inappropriate associations; however, the associations already present are not affected (Kapur, 2003). This could be a behavioral reflection in the human schizophrenia patient of the conditioned processes observed in the amygdala of the anesthetized rat.

Chronic Stress and Amygdala Activity

The research just reviewed further confirms the involvement of the amygdala in aversive events and its plasticity in response to these learned events (LeDoux,

2000). It is also likely that the amygdala plays a role in how an organism responds to maintained, chronic stressors. We examined this effect using chronic cold exposure (Zigmond et al., 1995), a well-characterized stress paradigm that has been employed at the University of Pittsburgh for over 25 years. In this paradigm, rats are exposed to a cold environment for a prolonged period of time (i.e., 5°C for 14 days) and then are subjected to study 24 hours following removal from the cold. Overall, this is a rather mild stressor, in that indices of stress return to baseline levels within 24–72 hours after initiation of cold exposure and do not produce as many external signs of a stress as those elicited by other procedures such as inescapable shock (see Moore et al., 2001b). Nonetheless, the rats show a sensitized response to acute stressors when tested a day or more following the cold exposure (Zigmond et al., 1995). We examined the effects of this chronic stress exposure paradigm on neuronal activity and response to acute noxious stimuli within the amygdala complex.

Recordings performed from the basolateral amygdala reveal that following chronic stress exposure, there is a small but nonsignificant increase in baseline spike discharge rate. Nonetheless, if a count is made regarding the proportion of neurons showing spontaneous activity (i.e., cells/track, as first defined by Bunney & Grace, 1978), an increase in the number of spontaneously active basolateral amygdala neurons is observed. However, the most significant change is the response of basolateral amygdala neurons to acute noxious stimuli. Thus, a footshock typically causes a small activation of neuronal firing within this brain region in control rats. However, following chronic stress exposure, the same amplitude of footshock evokes a powerful excitatory response in these neurons. Therefore, chronic cold stress causes an increase in baseline population activity and responsivity of neurons in the basolateral amygdala complex.

The basolateral amygdala also exerts modulatory control over the central amygdala, as described above. Given that the central amygdala, and the medial portion of the central amygdala in particular, is considered to be the output region of this nucleus with respect to the regulation of autonomic structures (Veening et al., 1984), we examined how neurons in the central medial amygdala are affected by chronic stress. We found that chronic stress alters the baseline activity and responsivity of the neurons in the central medial amygdala as well. Following chronic stress, there was a significant decrease in both the baseline firing rate (by 56%) and the population activity of neurons within the medial central nucleus (Correll et al., 2005). This was opposite of what was observed in the basolateral area, but consistent with our observed reciprocal relationship between these structures. This was not the case with the response to footshock, however. In control rats, a footshock causes only a minimal change in central amygdala neuron firing rate; moreover, this response accommodates after only a few exposures. However, following chronic stress, the same amplitude of footshock produces a dramatic activation of the central medial nucleus. Moreover, there is an absence of accommodation of the response with repeated presentation. The fact that both the basolateral and central amygdala respond to footshock in the same direction after chronic stress suggests that these regions both receive direct input from regions mediating this response. In summary, chronic cold stress strongly augmented the signal-to-noise ratio of central amygdala responses by causing a decrease in baseline activity but an augmentation of stimulus-evoked responses.

Prefrontal Cortical Modulatory Effects in Chronically Stressed Subjects

The studies reviewed above show that chronic stress alters the baseline population activity and responsivity of neurons within the amygdala. In particular, there was a substantial effect on the autonomic output region, the central medial nucleus. It is clear from our studies that the central medial nucleus is strongly controlled by the intercalated cell masses, and studies by Quirk et al. (2003) provide evidence suggesting that the intercalated cell masses may receive input from the prefrontal cortex. Given the evidence that the prefrontal cortex modulates responses to stress, we examined whether the responses observed in the central medial nucleus following chronic stress may be due to a regulatory influence of the prefrontal cortex.

As reviewed above, central medial amygdala neurons in chronic cold-stressed rats exhibited significantly decreased baseline activity. Following prefrontal cortical lesions, the average baseline activity exhibited a small decrease with respect to poststress baseline activity; however, the decrease was substantially less than that observed with a prefrontal cortical lesion in control rats (Correll et al., 2005). Similarly, lesion of the prefrontal cortex also revealed a substantially augmented footshock-induced activation of central medial neurons. However, as with baseline activity, the percent increase above the elevated baseline response was significantly diminished compared to that in the nonstressed rats. Therefore, the effects of chronic cold on central medial neuron activity were similar in direction as those produced by prefrontal cortical lesions. However, the effects of prefrontal lesions and cold stress were not additive. Indeed, chronically stressed rats exhibited activity and responsivity levels similar to what would be expected in a rat with decreased prefrontal cortical function.

Relevance of Stress Effects in Amygdala to the Pathophysiology of Schizophrenia

We believe that the apparent decreased prefrontal cortical function in chronically stressed rats has relevance for the onset of schizophrenia symptoms (Grace, 2004;

Thompson et al., 2004). Our studies have shown that the prefrontal cortex plays an important modulatory role over the reactivity of the amygdala to stress. Moreover, studies by others have shown that stress can lead to an exacerbation of schizophrenia symptoms, and that of the children at risk for developing schizophrenia, those that eventually convert to schizophrenia are the individuals showing a higher reactivity to stress in the premorbid state (Johnstone et al., 2005). Furthermore, the prodromal symptoms of schizophrenia are reported to include deficits in executive function (Parnas & Jorgensen, 1989; Parnas et al., 1982), which are indicative of prefrontal cortical pathology (Goldman-Rakic, 1998). Finally, studies have provided evidence that the prefrontal cortex of schizophrenia subjects exhibits pathological changes such as decreased GABAergic markers (Lewis et al., 1999) and decreased dopamine innervation (Akil et al., 1999) that may be present before the onset of symptoms. Indeed, dopamine is known to activate prefrontal cortical neuronal activity (Yang & Seamans, 1996), and stress has been shown to increase prefrontal cortical dopamine levels (Finlay & Zigmond, 1997; Finlay et al., 1995), potentially facilitating prefrontal cortical neuron modulation of subcortical stress responses. A deficit in prefrontal cortical dopamine function would therefore limit the ability of this region to properly react to acute stressors, and thereby leave subcortical systems unregulated.

This would potentially be of significant importance when one considers the subdivisions of the amygdala and their effect on target structures. The basolateral amygdala is known to innervate structures that are typically considered to be involved in cognitive or affective responses, including the striatum, prefrontal cortex, and cingulate cortex (Gray, 1999). In contrast, the central amygdala nucleus preferentially innervates regions that are more involved in autonomic response to stressors, such as the bed nucleus of the stria terminalis, the nucleus tractus solitarius, the dorsal motor nucleus of the vagus, the hypothalamus, the parabrachial nucleus, and the locus coeruleus (figure 11-1; Veening et al., 1984). Our studies show that the prefrontal cortex, potentially acting via the intercalated cell mass, limits the response of the central amygdala to stressors. This would be consistent with what one would expect for a normally functioning system. Thus, it would be beneficial for the cognitive component of the stress response to be maintained. In this way, the individual can maintain a heightened state of vigilance in a threatening environment. In contrast, it would not be beneficial to maintain a constant, heightened level of activity within the central amygdala-autonomic outflow pathway. If such a heightened level of activity is also maintained, it is likely to result in a number of pathological consequences secondary to the increase in catecholamine output, glucocorticoid levels, and so on. This attenuation of autonomic function would be dependent on the ability of the prefrontal cortex to regulate the central medial nucleus via the intercalated cell masses. However, in an individual with disrupted prefrontal cortical function, this attenuation may not be optimally functional.

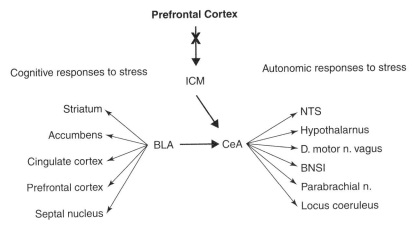

Figure 11-1 The basolateral amygdala (BLA) and central amygdala (CeA) are proposed to regulate different aspects of the stress response. The BLA exhibits ascending projections to areas involved in the cognitive responses to stress. In contrast, the CeA projects to regions that are more typically involved in the autonomic responses to stress. It is proposed that the prefrontal cortex, acting via the inhibitory intercalated cell mass (ICM), will preferentially attenuate the CeA drive of autonomic systems, thereby preventing pathological consequences from maintained increased autonomic drive.

Based on these evidences, we proposed a model to account for why deficits that are present soon after birth do not lead to schizophrenia symptomatology until late adolescence or early adulthood (Grace, 2004; Thompson et al., 2004). In this model, we proposed that an underlying deficit in prefrontal cortical function in adolescence makes the individual more susceptible to the deleterious influences of stress. Therefore, the onset of schizophrenia, as outlined above, is due to two "hits:" a potentially genetically determined pathology within the prefrontal cortex that leads to abnormal reactivity to stressors combined with a stressful environment during childhood. The central component of this model is the abnormal regulation of stress responses leading to activation of a positive feedback loop (figure 11-2). Thus, in a susceptible individual, the prefrontal cortex would be incapable of providing the normal suppressive influence over subcortical reactivity across a number of circuits. We have proposed previously that the abnormally heightened response of the dopamine system in the ventral striatum (Laruelle, 1998) occurs secondary to a deficit in prefrontal cortical modulation of this system (Grace, 1991). This uncontrolled dopaminergic reactivity in itself is likely to be highly stressful to the patient. In addition, a deficit in prefrontal cortical function would also attenuate the ability of the prefrontal cortex to modulate activation of the amygdala. The increase in amygdala responsivity, and consequently an amygdala-mediated activation of the locus coeruleus (Ramsooksingh et al., 2004), would also exacerbate the response to stress. The consequence is that there

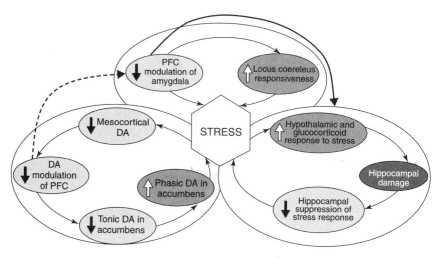

Figure 11-2 In the schizophrenia patient, a preexisting deficit in prefrontal cortical function is proposed to initiate a cascade of events that may lead to schizophrenia in late ado-
lescence/early adulthood. The pathology within the prefrontal cortex may relate to the
reported decrease in dopamine modulation of this region, given that: (1) dopamine is known
to increase output neuron excitability in the prefrontal cortex, (2) stress is known to increase dopamine levels in the prefrontal cortex, and (3) schizophrenia patients are reported
to have deficits in dopamine innervation of the prefrontal cortex. Such prefrontal cortical
dysfunction would lead to abnormal regulation of the dopamine system, as well as a decrease in control of the amygdala response to stress; each of which would be expected to
increase the response of the organism to acute stressors. This would be further exacerbated by an increased amygdala drive of the locus coeruleus, a region that has been associated with stress responses. The net effect of this would be activation of hypothalamic
glucocorticoid response and a resultant glucocorticoid-mediated degeneration of the hippocampus. Such interlocking positive feedback loops have the characteristic that the loop
may be engaged by pathological changes within any of the interconnected structures, with
the common result being abnormal augmentation of the stress response and hippocampal
damage.

would be augmentation of the autonomic outflow, and in particular increased
glucocorticoid release (Sapolsky, 1996, 1999).

   The increase in stress-induced glucocorticoid release may be of particular significance for the pathophysiology of schizophrenia. Thus, studies by Sapolsky
et al. (Sapolsky, 1996; Sapolsky et al., 1985; Sapolsky et al., 1990) show that increased glucocorticoid levels, particularly when combined with other stress factors, can lead to damage to the hippocampus. The hippocampus has been repeatedly
associated with schizophrenia pathology. Thus, Lipska et al. (1993) have shown
that a ventral hippocampal lesion in neonatal rats is an effective animal model of
the schizophrenia pathology in animals. Moreover, studies have shown that of
monozygotic schizophrenia twins discordant for schizophrenia, the afflicted twin
always had a smaller hippocampal volume (Baare et al., 2001; Weinberger et al.,

1992). Finally, Pantelis and colleagues (2000) have shown that in imaging studies of high-risk individuals, the first schizophrenic break (i.e., onset of psychotic symptoms) is associated with an increased volume of the hippocampus followed by a decrease, which may be indicative of the onset of a pathological process in this structure.

We also have evidence that in a developmental model of schizophrenia (Moore et al., 2001a, 2006), the rats are more susceptible to stress-induced disruption of synaptic plasticity within the hippocampal-prefrontal cortex (Goto & Grace, 2006). The hippocampus itself is a central component in the functioning of the limbic system, as it provides a potent contextual gating influence over the accumbens (O'Donnell & Grace, 1995). Indeed, in both the developmental model of schizophrenia (Moore et al., 2006) and in animals treated with phencyclidine (O'Donnell & Grace, 1998b), there is a disruption in the ability of the hippocampus to gate information flow within the accumbens. Therefore, pathology of the hippocampus leading to disturbances in hippocampal gating would severely disrupt the ability of the schizophrenia patient to selectively attend to salient stimuli and to effectively screen out distractions (Grace & Moore, 1998). Such a condition would leave them constantly bombarded with stimuli demanding attention.

Implications for the Onset of Schizophrenia and Its Potential Pharmacological Circumvention

Taken together, the results reviewed above suggest that a deficit in the regulation of the response to stress may be a central component in the delayed onset of schizophrenia symptomatology. It also suggests a potential means for preventing the cascade of events during adolescence that are proposed here to lead to the onset of the first psychotic break and the symptoms of schizophrenia in late adolescence/early adulthood. One method that is currently suggested and is under evaluation to prevent the onset of schizophrenia is preventive treatment with antipsychotic drugs, which appears to be effective in some but not all individuals when given during the prodrome (Cornblatt et al., 2002). In my opinion, this would not be the most effective course to circumvent the onset of psychosis. First, it is not likely advisable to treat young adolescents at risk for schizophrenia with antipsychotic drugs, because these are rather potent pharmacological interventions to be given to a population of which a large percentage are not likely to develop psychosis regardless of treatment (Cornblatt et al., 2001). But moreover, it is not evident that treatment with drugs that are primarily dopaminergic antagonists is the best pharmacotherapeutic approach. Thus, Laruelle (1998) has shown that a hyper-dopaminergic state in schizophrenia is observed in schizophrenia patients only when tested for their response to low doses of amphetamine when the amphetamine administration also results in the exacerbation of positive symptoms.

However, given that in the premorbid state psychosis is not typically evident, there is no reason to suspect the presence of a hyperdopaminergic state. Indeed, the fact that novel antipsychotic drugs can limit activation of the HPA axis and the stress-induced cortisol response (Corcoran et al., 2003) may be more of a factor in their efficacy than their antidopaminergic properties.

A more effective and benign treatment may be to pharmacologically address the effects of an exacerbated stress response. Thus, as Johnstone et al has found (2005), individuals at risk for schizophrenia who are most likely to convert to psychosis are those who are already showing a heightened stress response. Thus, factors that alleviate stress may limit the transition to psychosis (Grace, 2004; Thompson et al., 2004). There are several potential approaches to achieve such a result. Treatment of intervening life events that may lead to stress in susceptible individuals could be an effective approach (Corcoran et al., 2003), as is treatment with mood stabilizing drugs (Cornblatt et al., 2001). On the other hand, a more effective, direct, and benign treatment approach may be pharmacological intervention at this already extant abnormally high stress response using antianxiety agents.

It would be important that such interventions occur early in adolescence. Studies have shown that stressful life events that occur as early as 5 years of age can predispose an individual to schizophrenia (Howes et al., 2004). The data from animal studies (Lipska, 1993; Moore et al., 2001a, 2006) show that insults that occur very early in life have the most potent effects on circuit pathology in the adult, but that insults that occur later in adolescence or early adulthood have comparatively little impact. Therefore, to limit the damaging effects of stress, an intervention would need to be put in place at the earliest point that a susceptible individual can be identified. Such an individual may be identified by an abnormally heightened response to stress, or perhaps failure to activate the PFC while trying to suppress stress reactions. Thus, according to the model presented here, such a pharmacological intervention would be designed to circumvent the stress-induced pathological feedback loop that results in hippocampal damage and schizophrenia. In particular, given the evidence that corticotrophin releasing factor (CRF) is often associated with chronic stress, perhaps treatment with the novel CRF antagonists now in development may be the most selective and effective treatment for chronic stress-induced pathophysiology in susceptible individuals. Such an approach is proposed to not only treat the stress itself, but potentially circumvent the transition into psychosis (Grace, 2004; Thompson et al., 2004).

References

Abercrombie, E. D., & Jacobs, B. L. (1988). Systemic naloxone administration potentiates locus coeruleus noradrenergic neuronal activity under stressful but not non-stressful conditions. *Brain Research, 441,* 362–366.

Abercrombie, E. D., Keller, R. W., Jr., & Zigmond, M. J. (1988). Characterization of hippocampal norepinephrine release as measured by microdialysis perfusion: Pharmacological and behavioral studies. *Neuroscience, 27,* 897–904.

Abercrombie, E. D., Nisenbaum, L. K., & Zigmond, M. J. (1992). Impact of acute and chronic stress on the release and synthesis of norepinephrine in brain: microdialysis studies in behaving animals. In R. Kvetnansky, R. McCarty, & J. Axelrod (Eds.), *Stress: Neuroendocrine and molecular approaches* (pp. 29–42). New York: Gordon and Breach Science Publishers.

Akil, M., Pierri, J. N., Whitehead, R. E., Edgar, C. L., Mohila, C., Sampson, A. R., & Lewis, D. A. (1999). Lamina-specific alterations in the dopamine innervation of the prefrontal cortex in schizophrenic subjects. *American Journal of Psychiatry, 156,* 1580–1589.

An der Heiden, W., & Hafner, H. (2000). The epidemiology of onset and course of schizophrenia. *European Archives of Psychiatry and Clinical Neuroscience, 250,* 292–303.

Baare, W. F., van Oel, C. J., Hulshoff Pol, H. E., Schnack, H. G., Durston, S., Sitskoorn, M. M., & Kahn, R. S. (2001). Volumes of brain structures in twins discordant for schizophrenia. *Archives of General Psychiatry, 58,* 33–40.

Birley, J., & Brown, G. W. (1970). Crisis and life changes preceding the onset or relapse of acute schizophrenia: Clinical aspects. *British Journal of Psychiatry, 16,* 327–333.

Bunney, B. S., & Grace, A. A. (1978). Acute and chronic haloperidol treatment: Comparison of effects on nigral dopaminergic cell activity. *Life Sciences, 23,* 1715–1727.

Corcoran, C., Walker, E., Huot, R., Mittal, V., Tessner, K., Kestler, L., & Malaspina, D. (2003). The stress cascade and schizophrenia: Etiology and onset. *Schizophrenia Bulletin, 29,* 671–692.

Cornblatt, B. A., Lencz, T., & Kane, J. M. (2001). Treatment of the schizophrenia prodome: Is it presently ethical? *Schizophrenia Research, 51,* 331–338.

Cornblatt, B., Lencz, T., & Obuchowski, M. (2002). The schizophrenia prodrome: Treatment and high-risk perspectives. *Schizophrenia Research, 54,* 177–186.

Correll, C. M., Rosenkranz, J. A., & Grace, A.A. (2005). Chronic cold stress alters prefrontal cortical modulation of amygdala neuronal activity in rats. *Biological Psychiatry, 58,* 382–391.

Finlay, J. M., & Zigmond, M. J. (1997). The effects of stress on central dopaminergic neurons: Possible clinical implications. *Neurochemical Research, 22,* 1387–1394.

Finlay, J. M., Zigmond, M. J., & Abercrombie, E. D. (1995). Increased dopamine and norepinephrine release in medial prefrontal cortex induced by acute and chronic stress: Effects of diazepam. *Neuroscience, 64,* 619–628.

Goldman-Rakic, P. S. (1998). The cortical dopamine system: Role in memory and cognition. *Advances in Pharmacology, 42,* 707–711.

Grace, A. A. (1991). Phasic versus tonic dopamine release and the modulation of dopamine system responsivity: A hypothesis for the etiology of schizophrenia. *Neuroscience, 41,* 1–24.

Grace, A. A. (2000). Gating of information flow within the limbic system and the pathophysiology of schizophrenia. *Brain Research Reviews, 31,* 330–341.

Grace, A. A. (2004). Developmental dysregulation of the dopamine system and the pathophysiology of schizophrenia. In M. S. Keshavan, J. L. Kennedy, & R. M. Murray (Eds.), *Neurodevelopment and schizophrenia* (pp. 273–294). Cambridge, UK: Cambridge University Press.

Grace, A. A., & Moore, H. (1998). Regulation of information flow in the nucleus accumbens: A model for the pathophysiology of schizophrenia. In M. F. Lenzenweger

& R. H. Dworkin (Eds.), *Origins and development of schizophrenia: Advances in experimental psychopathology* (pp. 123–157)., Washington, DC: American Psychological Association Press.

Gray, T. S. (1999). Functional and anatomical relationships among the amygdala, basal forebrain, ventral striatum, and cortex: An integrative discussion. *Annals of the New York Academy of Sciences, 877,* 439–444.

Häfner, H., Maurer, K., Löffler, W., & Riecher-Rössler, A. (1993). The influence of age and sex on the onset and early course of schizophrenia. *British Journal of Psychiatry, 162,* 80–86.

Hariri, A. R., Mattay, V. S., Tessitore, A., Fera, F., and Weinberger, D. R. (2003). Neocortical modulation of the amygdala response to fearful stimuli. *Biological Psychiatry, 53,* 494–501.

Howes, O. D., McDonald, C., Cannon, M., Arseneault, L., Boydell, J., & Murray, R. M. (2004). Pathways to schizophrenia: The impact of environmental factors. *International Journal of Neuropsychopharmacology, 7*(Suppl. 1), S7–S13.

Jedema, H. P., & Grace, A. A. (2003a). Chronic exposure to cold stress alters electrophysiological properties of locus coeruleus neurons recorded *in vitro. Neuropsychopharmacology, 28,* 63–72.

Jedema, H. P., & Grace, A. A. (2003b). The effect of corticotropin-releasing hormone on noradrenergic neurons of the locus coeruleus recorded *in vitro. Journal of Neuroscience, 24,* 9703–9713.

Johnstone, E.C., Ebmeier, K.P., Miller, P., Owens, D.G., & Lawrie, S.M. (2005). Predicting schizophrenia: findings from the Edinburgh High-Risk Study. *British Journal of Psychiatry, 186*:18–25.

Kapur, S. (2003). Psychosis as a state of aberrant salience: a framework linking biology, phenomenology, and pharmacology in schizophrenia. *American Journal of Psychiatry, 160,* 13–23.

Kendler, K. S., Gallagher, T. J., Abelson, J. M., & Kessler, R. C. (1996). Lifetime prevalence, demographic risk factors, and diagnostic validity of nonaffective psychosis as assessed in a U.S. community sample: The National Comorbidity Survey. *Archives of General Psychiatry, 53,* 1022–1031.

Kendler, K. S., Tsuang, M. T., & Hays, P. (1987). Age at onset in schizophrenia: A familial perspective. *Archives of General Psychiatry, 44,* 881–890.

Kirkpatrick, B., Buchanan, R. W. , Ross, D. E., & Carpenter, W. T., Jr. (2001). A separate disease within the syndrome of schizophrenia. *Archives of General Psychiatry, 58,* 165–171.

Kretteck, J. E., & Price, J. L. (1978). A description of the amygdaloid complex in the rat and cat with observations on intra-amygdaloid axonal connections. *Journal of Comparative Neurology, 178,* 255–280.

Kroner, S., Rosenkranz, J. A., Grace, A. A., & Barrionuevo, G. (2005). Dopamine modulates excitability of basolateral amygdala neurons in vitro. *Journal of Neurophysiology, 93,* 1598–1610.

Laruelle, M. (1998). Imaging dopamine transmission in schizophrenia. A review and meta-analysis. *Quarterly Journal of Nuclear Medicine, 42,* 211–221.

LeDoux, J. E. (2000). Emotion circuits in the brain. *Annual Review of Neuroscience, 23,* 155–184.

Lewis, D. A., Pierri, J. N., Volk, D. W., Melchitzky, D. S., & Woo, T. U. (1999). Altered GABA neurotransmission and prefrontal cortical dysfunction in schizophrenia. *Biological Psychiatry, 46,* 616–626.

Likhtik, E., Pelletier, J. G., Paz, R., & Paré, D. (2005). Prefrontal control of the amygdala. *Journal of Neuroscience, 25,* 7429–7437.

Lipska, B. K., Jaskiw, G. E., & Weinberger, D. R. (1993). Postpubertal emergence of hyperresponsiveness to stress and to amphetamine after neonatal excitotoxic hippocampal damage: A potential animal model of schizophrenia. *Neuropsychopharmacology, 9,* 67–75.

Loranger, A. W. (1984). Sex difference in age at onset of schizophrenia. *Archives of General Psychiatry, 41,* 157–161.

Mana, M. J., & Grace, A. A. (1997). Chronic cold stress alters the basal and evoked electrophysiological activity of rat locus coeruleus neurons. *Neuroscience, 81,* 1055–1064.

Moore, H., Ghajarnia, M., Geyer, M., Jentsch, J. D., & Grace, A. A. (2001a). Selective disruption of prefrontal and limbic corticostriatal circuits by prenatal exposure to the DNA methylating agent methylazoxymethanol acetate: Anatomical, neurophysiological and behavioral studies. *Schizophrenia Research, 49*(Suppl.), 48.

Moore, H., Ghajarnia, M. E., Jentsch, J. D., Geyer, M. A., & Grace, A. A. (2006). A Neurobehavioral Systems Analysis of Adult Rats Exposed to Methylazoxymethanol Acetate on E17: Implications for the Neuropathology of Schizophrenia *Biological Psychiatry, 60,* 253–264.

Moore, H., Rose, H. J., & Grace, A. A. (2001b). Chronic cold stress reduces the spontaneous activity of ventral tegmental dopamine neurons. *Neuropsychopharmacology, 24,* 410–419.

Norman, R. M. G., & Malla, A. K. (1993). Stressful life events and schizophrenia. I: A review of research. *British Journal of Psychiatry, 162,* 161–166.

O'Donnell, P., & Grace, A. A. (1995). Synaptic interactions among excitatory afferents to nucleus accumbens neurons: Hippocampal gating of prefrontal cortical input. *Journal of Neuroscience, 15,* 3622–3639.

O'Donnell, P., & Grace, A. A. (1998b). Phencyclidine interferes with the hippocampal gating of nucleus accumbens neuronal activity in vivo. *Neuroscience, 87,* 823–830.

Pantelis, C., Velakoulis, D., Suckling, J., McGorry, P. D., Phillips, L., Yung, A., Wood, S., Bullmore, E., Brewer, W., Soulsby, B., & McGuire, P. (2000). Left medial temporal volume reduction occurs during the transition from high-risk to first-episode psychosis. *Schizophrenia Research, 41,* 35.

Parnas, J. (1999). From predisposition to psychosis: Progression of symptoms in schizophrenia. *Acta Psychiatrica Scandinavica, Supplementum, 99,* 20–29.

Parnas, J., & Jorgensen, A. (1989). Pre-morbid psychopathology in schizophrenia spectrum. *British Journal of Psychiatry, 155,* 623–627.

Parnas, J., Schulsinger, F., Schulsinger, H., Mednick, S. A., & Teasdale, T. W. (1982). Behavioral precursors of schizophrenia spectrum. *Archives of General Psychiatry, 39,* 658–664.

Pogue-Geile, M. F. (1997). Developmental aspects of schizophrenia. In M. S. Keshavan & R. M. Murray (Eds.), *Neurodevelopment and adult psychopathology* (pp. 137–154). New York, Cambridge University Press.

Quirk, G. J., Likhtik, E., Pelletier, J. G., & Pare, D. (2003). Stimulation of medial prefrontal cortex decreases the responsiveness of central amygdala output neurons. *Journal of Neuroscience, 23,* 8800–8807.

Ramsooksingh, M. D., Jedema, H.P., & Grace, A. A. (2004). Stimulation of the central nucleus of the amygdala increases single unit activity of locus coeruleus neurons. *Society for Neurosciences Abstract, 29,* Program No. 282.210.

Rosenkranz, J. A., Buffalari, D. M. & Grace, A. A. (2006). Opposing influence of basolateral amygdala and footshock stimulation on neurons of the central amygdala. *Biological Psychiatry, 59: 801–811.*

Rosenkranz, J. A., & Grace, A. A. (1999). Modulation of basolateral amygdala neuronal firing and afferent drive by dopamine receptor activation in vivo. *Journal of Neuroscience, 19,* 11027–11039.

Rosenkranz, J. A., & Grace, A. A. (2001). Dopamine attenuates prefrontal cortical suppression of sensory inputs to the basolateral amygdala of rats. *Journal of Neuroscience, 21,* 4090–4103.

Rosenkranz, J. A., & Grace, A. A. (2002a). Cellular mechanisms of infralimbic and prelimbic prefrontal cortical inhibition and dopaminergic modulation of basolateral amygdala neurons in vivo. *Journal of Neuroscience, 22,* 324–337.

Rosenkranz, J. A., & Grace, A. A. (2002b). Dopamine-mediated modulation of odour-evoked amygdala potentials during Pavlovian conditioning. *Nature, 417,* 282–287.

Rosenkranz, J. A., Moore, H., & Grace, A. A. (2003). The prefrontal cortex regulates lateral amygdala neuronal plasticity and responses to previously conditioned stimuli. *Journal of Neuroscience, 23,* 11054–11064.

Sapolsky, R. M. (1996). Stress, glucocorticoids, and damage to the nervous system: The current state of confusion. *Stress, 1,* 1–19.

Sapolsky, R. M. (1999). Glucocorticoids, stress, and their adverse neurological effects: Relevance to aging. *Experimental Gerontology, 34,* 721–732.

Sapolsky, R. M., Krey, L. C., & McEwen, B. S. (1985). Prolonged glucocorticoid exposure reduces hippocampal neuron number: Implications for aging. *The Journal of Neuroscience, 5,* 1222–1227.

Sapolsky, R. M., Uno, H., Rebert, C. S., & Finch, C. E. (1990). Hippocampal damage associated with prolonged glucocorticoid exposure in primates. *Journal of Neuroscience, 10,* 2897–2902.

Shanks, N., Zalcman, S., Zacharko, R. M., & Anisman, H. (1991). Alterations of central norepinephrine, dopamine and serotonin in several strains of mice following acute stressor exposure. *Pharmacology, Biochemistry & Behavior, 38,* 69–75.

Thierry, A. M., Javoy, F., Glowinski, J., & Kety, S. S. (1968). Effects of stress on the metabolism of norepinephrine, dopamine and serotonin in the central nervous system of the rat. I. Modifications of norepinephrine turnover. *Journal of Pharmacology & Experimental Therapeutics, 163,* 163–171.

Thompson, J. L., Pogue-Geile, M. F., & Grace, A. A. (2004). The interactions among developmental pathology, dopamine, and stress as a model for the age of onset of schizophrenia symptomatology. *Schizophrenia Bulletin, 30,* 875–900.

Valentino, R. J., & Foote, S. L. (1986). Brain noradrenergic neurons, corticotropin-releasing factor, and stress. In T. W. Moody (Ed.), *Neural and endocrine peptides and receptors* (pp. 101–120). New York: Plenum Press.

Valentino, R. J., & Foote, S. L. (1988). Corticotropin-releasing hormone increases tonic but not sensory-evoked activity of noradrenergic locus coeruleus neurons in unanesthetized rats. *Journal of Neuroscience, 8,* 1016–1025.

Veening, J. G., Swanson, L. W., & Sawchenko, P. E. (1984). The organization of projections from the central nucleus of the amygdala to brainstem sites involved in central autonomic regulation: A combined retrograde transport-immunohistochemical study. *Brain Research 303*(2), 337–357.

Walker, E. F., & Diforio, D. (1997). Schizophrenia: A neural diathesis-stress model. *Psychological Review, 104,* 667–685.

Weinberger, D. R., Zigun, J. R., Bartley, A. J., Jones, D. W., & Torrey, E. F. (1992).

Anatomical abnormalities in the brains of monozygotic twins discordant and concordant for schizophrenia. *Clinical Neuropharmacology, 15,* 122A–123A.

Yang, C. R., & Seamans, J. K. (1996). Dopamine D1 receptor actions in layers V-VI rat prefrontal cortex neurons in vitro: Modulation of dendritic-somatic signal integration. *Journal of Neuroscience, 16,* 1922–1935.

Zigmond, M. J., Finlay, J. M., & Sved, A. F. (1995). Neurochemical studies of central noradrenergic responses to acute and chronic stress. In M. J. Friedman, D. S. Charney, & A. Y. Deutsch (Eds.), *Neurobiological and clinical consequences of stress: From normal adaptation to PTSD* (pp. 45–60). Philadelpia: Lippincott-Raven.

Chapter 12

Neurohormones, Neurodevelopment, and the Prodrome of Psychosis in Adolescence

Elaine F. Walker, Amanda McMillan, and Vijay Mittal

The transition from childhood into adulthood is marked by significant improvements in cognitive function, yet the adolescent capacity to inhibit responses is not mature (Luna & Sweeney, 2004), mortality rises due to risk-taking behaviors (Irwin, Burg, & Uhler Cart, 2002), and there is a gradual increase in the risk for mood disorders and psychosis (Walker, 2002). At the biological level, these behavioral changes co-occur with dramatic increases in steroid hormone secretion, and, more recently, researchers have also documented significant postpubertal maturation of the brain.

With the advent of new and noninvasive technologies for in vivo study of brain structure and function, a window has opened on the maturation of the human brain. As a result, the biological bases for normative postpubertal behavioral changes have come into clearer focus. At the same time, our conceptualizations of the neural mechanisms that might subserve abnormal brain function have become more sophisticated. Contemporary research is yielding a picture of diverse and complex neuropathological processes that might give rise to the genesis of psychopathology during adolescence and young adulthood.

It is widely recognized that there are dramatic developmental changes in clinical expression of vulnerability to psychosis. Most notable among these is the marked rise in risk of clinical onset in adolescence and early adulthood (Walker, 2002). Numerous studies have documented that individuals who are diagnosed with schizophrenia during the modal risk period, early adulthood, manifest a gradual deterioration in function that begins in early adolescence (Neumann & Walker, 1995). These findings suggest that postpubertal neurodevelopmental processes interact with the expression of vulnerability.

Research on diagnosed patients has shown that a variety of both structural and functional brain abnormalities are linked with psychotic disorders, indicating that multiple neural systems are affected. One or more of these neural abnormalities may be critical for the emergence of psychotic symptoms in adolescence/young adulthood, whereas other neural systems are likely to play a modulating role in the expression of dysfunction in key systems. Further, as stated above, there is strong evidence that maturational changes are playing a role in the expression of the basic neuropathology and, as a consequence, the clinical manifestations.

It has been suggested that the neural systems governing the response to stress, especially the hypothalamic-pituitary-adrenal (HPA) axis, may function to augment the expression of the core vulnerability to psychosis (Cunningham, Bhattacharayya, & Benes, 2002; Walker & Diforio, 1997). In this chapter, we briefly review research findings that bear on adolescent vulnerability for psychosis and neurodevelopment of the HPA-hippocampal system, with an emphasis on implications for preventive intervention. (We use the general term *psychosis,* rather than *schizophrenia,* because of evidence that the same neural mechanisms are implicated in most forms of psychosis). The working model posits that the HPA-hippocampal system moderates the expression of constitutional vulnerability for psychosis, and assumes that adolescence is a critical period for this effect because postpubertal neurodevelopment of the HPA axis and hippocampus increases susceptibility to the adverse effects of stress-induced glucocorticoid secretion, and because hormonal changes during this period can trigger latent genetic vulnerabilities.

Finally, because the rate of psychotropic medication of adolescents has risen sharply in recent years, it is now possible to examine their biobehavioral consequences for development (Zito et al., 2003). We present preliminary data from our recent research that suggests how psychopharmacologic interventions might alter HPA function, and thereby modify the transition to psychosis in at-risk adolescents.

The HPA Axis

The HPA axis is a neural system that is sensitive to environmental challenges and is activated in response to physical and psychological factors that threaten homeostasis (Charmandari, Kino, Souvatzoglou, & Chrousos, 2003; Dorn & Chrousos, 1997). The initial step in the neurohormonal cascade of the HPA axis is the release of the hypothalamic hormone, corticotropin releasing hormone (CRH). This, in turn, triggers the release of adrenocorticotropin (ACTH) from the anterior pituitary. ACTH then acts on the adrenal glands, leading to the release of glucocorticoids (cortisol in primates) from the adrenal cortex into circulation. An acute rise in cortisol levels can be adaptive, because it serves to increase the availability of energy substrates, but persistent elevations can be maladaptive.

The actions of cortisol are mediated by two types of receptors: mineralocorticoid receptors (MRs) and glucocorticoid receptors (GRs), also referred to as Type I and Type II receptors, respectively. MRs and GRs are two closely related members of the steroid nuclear receptor family of transcription factors that bind cortisol. These receptors are present on many cells throughout the body, including the brain, and they are pivotal in the self-modulation of the HPA axis. Thus glucocorticoids act to suppress their own release through activation of MRs and GRs, which initiate both fast and slow acting negative feedback systems that inhibit ACTH release. These feedback systems act through the hypothalamus and pituitary, although other regions are also implicated.

The HPA-Hippocampal System

The hippocampus is relevant to functioning of the HPA axis for two reasons. First, as noted, it plays a role in modulation of the HPA system. This is presumed to be a consequence of steroid receptors on hippocampal neurons (Watzka et al., 2000). Second, the hippocampus may be uniquely sensitive to the adverse effects of sustained, high levels of glucocorticoid secretion (Charmandari et al., 2003; Dorn & Chrousos, 1997). Thus, heightened levels may have neurotoxic effects that structurally compromise the hippocampus. For both of these reasons, an inverse relation between glucocorticoid levels and hippocampal volume would be predicted.

Consistent with the hypothesized modulating role of the hippocampus, studies using rodent models have revealed an inverse relation between glucocorticoid levels and hippocampal volume (Hibberd, Yau, & Seckl, 2000; Meaney et al., 1995; Meaney et al., 1996). Similar findings have been reported in the rhesus (Coe et al., 2003) and tree shrew (Ohl, Michaelis, Vollmann-Honsdorf, Kirschbaum, & Fuchs, 2000). A recent study suggests that the relation can be measured on the cellular level; in pigs exposed to chronic stress, basal cortisol is negatively correlated with hippocampal neuron number, as well as volume (van der Beek et al., 2004). These relations were most pronounced in the dentate gyrus.

Subsequent neuroimaging studies of human subjects have also revealed a relation between glucocorticoid secretion and hippocampal volume. Consistent with the notion of hippocampal negative feedback, the findings show an inverse relation. In patients with dementia, higher serum cortisol concentrations are associated with the reduction of cerebral volume in both the hippocampus and temporal lobes (Ferrari, Fioravanti, Magri, & Solerte, 2000). Similarly, a longitudinal study revealed that in aged humans a measure of hippocampal atrophy was positively correlated with both basal cortisol and the magnitude of cortisol elevation over time (Lupien et al., 1998). Further, prolonged cortisol elevation was linked with hippocampus-dependent memory deficits. The link between hippocampal volume and cortisol levels is not restricted to clinical populations. A study of both young (19-30 years) and older (59-76 years) healthy male subjects showed that hippocampal volume was inversely associated with urinary cortisol and corticotropin (ACTH) levels, after controlling for cerebral vault size (Wolf, Convit, de Leon, Caraos, & Qadri, 2002).

Extending these findings, we recently conducted an investigation of salivary cortisol and hippocampal volume in a group of healthy young males (mean age 25 years; Tessner et al., unpublished paper). The study employed a double-blind crossover design. There were two experimental conditions: placebo and hydrocortisone (cortisol) administration. Each subject was assessed under both conditions, with half randomly assigned to each of the two condition orders. The placebo or drug (100 mg) was administered approximately 2 hours prior to MRI scanning. Saliva was sampled 12 times at regular intervals, prior to scanning. The average of all cortisol samples was computed for each subject within condition. As expected, the administration of hydrocortisone resulted in a significant increase in cortisol secretion above placebo levels. Controlling for whole brain volume, there was a trend toward a significant inverse correlation between total hippocampal volume and mean cortisol in the placebo condition. In the hydrocortisone condition, the inverse correlation was larger, and statistically significant ($r = -.59$, $p < .05$). These findings lend further support to the link between hippocampal volume and cortisol secretion, and suggest that the relation is more pronounced when cortisol secretion is elevated. Thus the hippocampus may play a greater role in modulating HPA activity when it is elevated above baseline in response to challenge.

As noted, the relation between cortisol levels and hippocampal volume appears to be partially due to an adverse effect of elevated cortisol on hippocampal morphology. When compared to age-matched controls, patients receiving chronic corticosteroid therapy have smaller hippocampal volumes and declarative memory deficits (E. S. Brown et al., 2004). Also, functional neuroimaging of human subjects has revealed that acute administration of cortisol selectively reduces hippocampal glucose utilization, suggesting that cortisol elevation has direct and acute effects on hippocampal function (de Leon et al., 1997).

From the standpoint of preventive intervention, it is noteworthy that the adverse effects of elevated cortisol on hippocampal structure and function may be reversible, under some circumstances. Sapolsky (1994) found reversible morphological changes in animals exposed to moderate stress. This suggests hippocampal plasticity in animals, and recent findings suggest this is also the case in humans. For example, after cortisol levels decline to normal concentrations in treated Cushing's patients, there is an increase in hippocampal volume that is accompanied by cognitive improvements (Starkman et al., 1999; Starkman, Giordani, Gebarski, Berent, & Schork & Berent, 2003). At this point, there is no data base for drawing inferences about the temporal course of plasticity; the hippocampal change may occur shortly after reductions in cortisol levels or extend over long time periods.

In summary, it appears that there is a dynamic relation between circulating glu-cocorticoids and hippocampal morphology. The specific neural mechanisms have not been elucidated, nor do we know the time course for these events. But, as described below, there may be critical developmental periods for these processes.

The HPA-Hippocampal System and Psychosis

Four general lines of investigation provide support for the hypothesis that dys-regulation of the HPA axis is involved in the expression of vulnerability for psy-chosis (Walker & Diforio, 1997). First, behavioral studies have shown that clinical symptoms can be exacerbated by exposure to stress. Second, medical disorders (e.g., Cushing's) that involve elevated levels of the "stress" hormone, cortisol, are associated with increased risk for psychosis. Third, unmedicated psychotic patients manifest abnormalities in several aspects of the neural system that gov-erns cortisol release; namely, the hypothalamic-pituitary-adrenal (HPA) axis. These include an elevated rate of nonsuppression in response to dexamethasone challenge, heightened baseline cortisol (Muck-Seler et al., 2004; Ritsner et al., 2004), and a positive correlation between cortisol levels and symptom severity (Shirayama, Hashimoto, Suzuki, & Higuchi, 2002; Walder, Walker, & Lewine, 2000). Also, the fact that baseline cortisol is elevated in never-medicated, first-episode patients indicates that elevated HPA activity precedes clinical onset (Ryan, Collins, & Thakore, 2003; Ryan, Sharifi, Condren, & Thakore, 2004). Lastly, among the most compelling evidence that the HPA system is implicated in schizophrenia are data showing significant hippocampal volume reduction and structural abnormalities (Harrison, 2004). This is relevant to HPA function because, as described below, the hippocampus appears to play an important role in regulating the activity of the HPA axis (Altamura, Boin, & Maes, 1999).

As noted, numerous studies of diagnosed schizophrenia patients have revealed significantly smaller hippocampal volumes when patients are compared to matched controls (Harrison, 2004; Shenton, Dickey, Frumin, & McCarley, 2001). When effect sizes are compared across brain regions, hippocampal volume is characterized by the largest diagnostic group difference. Other research suggests that reductions in hippocampal volume are present early in the illness, such that studies of young, first-onset schizophrenia patients reveal hippocampal volume reductions (Seidman et al., 2003). These results parallel the evidence that memory deficits, a well-documented consequence of hippocampal impairment, are present in schizophrenia and spec-trum disorders (Antonova, Sharma, Morris, & Kumari, 2004).

Further, twin studies indicate that both environmental and genetic factors con-tribute to hippocampal reductions in schizophrenia. The NIMH studies of discor-dant monozygotic (MZ) twins revealed that the affected twins showed smaller brain volumes than their healthy co-twins, but the hippocampal/amygdala complex was most markedly reduced in volume (Suddath, Christison, Torrey, Casanova, & Weinberger, 1990). Subsequent studies of discordant MZ twins have replicated these findings. One investigation showed that schizophrenic twins, whether from concordant or discordant MZ pairs, had smaller whole brain volumes than control twins; however, the ill twins from discordant pairs showed more hippocampal volume reduction than their healthy co-twin or concordant twins (van Haren et al., 2004). The same pattern has been reported in at least two other studies of discordant MZ twins (Baare et al., 2001; van Erp et al., 2004). These findings suggest that genetic risk for schizophrenia is associated with generalized reductions in brain volume, but that reductions in the hippocampus are most pronounced in association with the clinical syndrome of schizophrenia. This is consistent with the notion that the HPA axis-hippocampal system moderates the expression of genetically determined constitutional vulnerability for schizophrenia.

Extending this further, it has been shown that the intraclass correlation for hippocampal volume in healthy MZ twin pairs is larger than that for discordant MZ pairs, and the estimate for the magnitude of genetic effects on hippocampal volume is larger in healthy twins than in discordant twins (van Erp et al., 2004). Thus, hippocampal volume is largely affected by genetic factors in healthy twin pairs, and presumably other healthy individuals. But the smaller magnitude of genetic effects on hippocampal volume in discordant pairs indicates that environmental factors are having a greater impact; in other words, environmental factors may be adversely affecting size of the hippocampus in the ill twin, and reducing the similarity with the healthy co-twins. Similar findings have been reported for cortisol levels in healthy versus discordant MZ twin pairs; intraclass correlations for cortisol are high and significant for healthy twin pairs, but not for discordant twins (Walker, Bonsall, & Walder, 2002).

At the cellular level, there is evidence of reductions in hippocampal glucocorticoid receptors in schizophrenia (Ganguli, Singh, Brar, Carter, & Mintun, 2002). A postmortem study showed that GR mRNA levels were reduced in several regions of the hippocampus (dentate gyrus, CA4, CA3, and CA1) in schizophrenia patients, but not depressives (Webster, Knable, O'Grady, Orthmann, & Weickert, 2002). The dentate gyrus is a region that is especially sensitive to the affects of stress-induced corticosteroids (Sousa & Almeida, 2002; van der Beek et al., 2004), as well as exposure to alcohol and nicotine (Jang et al., 2002). A reduction in GR receptors in the hippocampus would be expected to compromise negative feedback to the HPA axis and thus contribute to HPA dysregulation (Heuser, Deuschle, Weber, Stalla, & Holsboer, 2000).

Adolescence Neurodevelopment: Hormones, Genes, and Brain

As noted, adolescent development is characterized by marked increases in neurohormone secretion. In addition to rising gonadal hormones, there is now mounting evidence of a pubertal increase in activity of the HPA axis. Cross-sectional studies of normal children reveal a gradual rise in salivary and urinary cortisol during middle childhood, then a marked increase that begins around 13 years of age and continues through adolescence (Kenny, Gancayo, Heald, & Hung, 1966; Kenny, Preeyasombat, & Migeon, 1966; Kiess et al., 1995; Lupien et al., 2002; Wingo, 2002). Recent longitudinal studies have also revealed increases in cortisol release during adolescence, with the most significant augmentation occurring at 13 years (Wajs-Kuto, De Beeck, Rooman, & Caju, 1999; Walker et al., 2002). Studies that have examined pubertal stage indicate that the changes are strongly linked with sexual maturation (Kenny, Gancayo, et al., 1966; Kiess et al., 1995; Tornhage, 2002).

It has been proposed that the HPA axis, in particular pituitary release of ACTH and adrenal release of cortisol, may be involved in triggering sexual maturation (Weber, Clark, Perry, Honour, & Savage, 1997). Consistent with this, Weber et al. (1997) found that individuals with familial glucocorticoid deficiency were more likely to manifest a lack of adrenarche. Conversely, children who have an early onset of adrenarche, as measured by the early (before age 8) appearance of Tanner stage II–III, show signs of heightened HPA activity (Dorn, Hitt, & Rotenstein, 1999). When compared to age-matched controls, girls with premature adrenarche show significantly higher concentrations of cortisol, as well as estradiol, thyroid-stimulating hormone, and adrenal androgens.

Changes in circulating steroid hormones are important for brain structure and function because they are transported through the bloodstream, then trigger cellular activity and regulate a range of physiological functions (Beach, 1975; Kawata, 1995; Keenan & Soleymani, 2001). Hormones affect the way neurons function because they modulate the response of neurons to neurotransmitters (Mesce, 2002). They do this by diffusing in the space surrounding neurons, and thereby influence individual neurons, as well as the structure and activity of neuronal circuits.

Two general classes of hormonal effects on brain have been described: activational and organizational (Arnold & Breedlove, 1985; Charmandari et al., 2003). Activational effects are conceptualized as transient inductions of time-limited, functional changes in neural circuitry. Hormones can have activational influences on sensory processes, autonomic nervous system activity, and enzyme systems (and thus, cellular permeability to electrolytes, water, and nutrients). In contrast, organizational effects are those that result in changes in the way the brain is organized—its structural characteristics (Buchanan, Eccles, & Becker, 1992).

Until recently, it was generally assumed that activational effects occur during adulthood, whereas organizational effects are restricted to the fetal neurodevelopment. But it now appears that some organizational effects of hormones occur later in life, including adolescence (Arnold & Breedlove, 1985; Charmandari et al., 2003). The magnitude of these effects is suggested by accumulating longitudinal studies of human adolescents that demonstrate that the brain undergoes significant organizational changes during this period. There are rapidly accumulating data on the postnatal development of the human brain, and they demonstrate that the maturational process extends through adolescence, and probably into early adulthood (Gogtay et al., 2004). Notable among these developments is an increase in the volume of the hippocampus (Suzuki, 2005). Using MRI, strong age-related increases are observed in the subiculum and CA1-CA3 (CAS) regions of the hippocampus (Saitoh, Karns, & Courchesne, 2001).

Adolescent Stress Sensitivity

Adolescence is a period of heightened stress sensitivity and vulnerability to the onset of major mental disorder (Arnsten & Shansky, 2004; Compas, Connor-Smith, & Jaser, 2004; Cunningham et al., 2002; Spear, 2000; Walker, 2002). Heightened stress sensitivity has been shown repeatedly in animal models of adolescent development, and recent studies of human subjects also suggest this (Chambers, Taylor, & Potenza, 2003). For example, rodents typically show hippocampal volume increases during the peri/postpubertal period (Isgor, Kabbaj, Akil, & Watson, 2004). But exposure to physical stress in early postpuberty reduces hippocampal growth, especially in the CA1 and CA3 pyramidal cell layers, and in the dentate gyrus. Exposure to chronic stress resulted in hippocampal volume deficits that were first observable 3 weeks later, but not 24 hours after exposure. Moreover, these volume deficits were associated with impairments in water-maze navigation, sustained downregulation in hippocampal GR gene expression, and greater acute stress-induced corticosterone. Thus, exposure of adolescents to chronic stress may lead to significant alterations in the HPA axis, as well as changes in hippocampal structure and cognitive function, that persist into adulthood. At the receptor level, there is evidence that glucocorticoids have differential effects on the regional expression of mRNA NMDA receptor subunits in the hippocampus, which would be expected to change the sensitivity of hippocampal neurons to the excitatory neurotransmitter, glutamate. Studies of rodents indicate that there may be window during adolescence in which the receptor genes are especially responsive to glucocorticoids (Lee, Brady, & Koenig, 2003).

In human adolescents, there are also data indicating increased sensitivity of the hippocampus. In subjects with a history of alcohol abuse, earlier age and longer duration of abuse was associated with reduced volume of the hippocampus (De Bellis et al., 2000). The volume of other brain regions was not associated with alcohol abuse. These findings were interpreted to suggest that during adolescence, the hippocampus may be particularly susceptible to the adverse effects of alcohol.

In summary, postpubertal neuromaturation entails significant changes in the HPA axis and the hippocampus. These changes may result in greater sensitivity of the HPA axis to external stress and increased sensitivity of the hippocampus to insult, including the damaging effects of glucocorticoid elevations. As described, the HPA-hippocampal system also appears to potentiate the behavioral expression of vulnerability for psychiatric symptoms. Thus, vulnerable individuals who experience dysregulation of, or damage to, this system may be at increased risk for developing the clinical syndrome. The fact that these systems are hypersensitive during adolescence may account for the rise in prodromal symptoms that has been observed in this developmental stage.

Psychopharmacology, HPA Activity, and Preventive Intervention

Interest in the possibility of preventing the onset of psychotic disorders has burgeoned in the past decade. To date, there is limited evidence that this may be feasible, in that antipsychotic drugs appear to delay or reduce the likelihood of transition to psychosis in vulnerable young adults who show prodromal or schizotypal signs (McGorry et al., 2002; McGlashan et al., 2003; Miller et al., 2003). The critical mechanisms of action responsible for such an effect are not understood. Although a reduction in dopaminergic activity figures prominently in theories about antipsychotic efficacy, these drugs have a myriad of other neurobiological effects, including a significant reduction in cortisol levels in adult patients (Walker & Diforio, 1997). The latter effect is of particular interest because it has potential implications for both neuromaturational processes and preventive mechanisms.

Several studies have shown that both typical antipsychotics, such as haloperidol (Wik, 1995), and atypical antipsychotics (i.e., olanzapine or risperidone) can decrease plasma cortisol in adult schizophrenia patients (Ryan, Flanagan, Kinsella, Keeling, & Thakore, 2004). Clozapine may have similar effects (Markianos, Hatzimanolis, & Lykouras, 1999), and it can also reduce the cortisol response to d-fenfluramine challenge in schizophrenia (Curtis, Wright, Reveley, Kerwin, & Lucey, 1995). The apparent dampening effects of antipsychotics on cortisol are consistent with dopamine antagonism. Given the evidence of more severe symptoms in patients with higher baseline and challenge-induced cortisol, it is possible that this effect also serves to reduce symptom severity. Moreover, cortisol reduction may be implicated in the prophylactic effects of antipsychotic drugs.

The effects of other psychotropics, especially antidepressants, on cortisol secretion have been of particular interest because the HPA axis is assumed to play a role in the etiology of mood disorders. In adults, some antidepressants have been shown to alter cortisol, although the direction of the effects varies (Pariante, Thomas, Lovestone, Makoff, & Kerwin, 2004). Discrepant findings can be attributed, at least in part, to the differential effects of certain subtypes of antidepressants. For example, at least one antidepressant, citalopram, a selective serotonin reuptake inhibitor (SSRI), appears to heighten cortisol secretion in normal controls and depressed patients (Bhagwagar, Hafizi, & Cowen, 2002; Harmer, Bhagwager, Shelley, & Cowen, 2003). In contrast, however, studies of other SSRIs reveal either no effect on cortisol (Deuschle et al., 2003; Inder, Prickett, Mulder, Donald, & Joyce, 2001; Muck-Seler, Pivac, Sagud, Jakovljevic, & Mihaljevic-Peles, 2002) or a decrease in cortisol secretion (Thakore, Barnes, Joyce, Medbak, & Dinan, 1997).

Findings from studies of tricyclics also vary, with some showing no change in cortisol (Inder et al., 2001; Sonntag et al., 1996), and others showing declines (Deuschle et al., 2003; Kunzel et al., 2003; Rodenbeck et al., 2003; Sonntag et al., 1996). Finally, the antidepressant mirtazapine, which does not inhibit the reuptake of norepinephrine or serotonin but is an antagonist of certain subtypes of presynaptic and postsynaptic receptors for serotonin, has been shown to produce a reduction in salivary cortisol in both responder and nonresponder depressed patients (Laakmann, Hennig, Baghai, & Schule, 2003), as well as healthy controls (Laakmann, Schule, Baghai, & Waldvogel, 1999). Taken together, the findings on antidepressants and cortisol suggest that the medication subtypes have varied effects. This, along with methodological factors, such as sampling method (plasma versus saliva) and subject characteristics, has probably contributed to divergent findings.

The few studies addressing stimulants and cortisol secretion, all conducted on adults, reveal either a drug-induced cortisol elevation in response to methylphenidate (Joyce, Donald, Nicholls, Livesey, & Abbott, 1986), or no change (W. A. Brown & Williams, 1976). Grady et al. (1996) found that plasma cortisol levels increased after intravenous d-amphetamine administration to healthy adults. A stimulant-induced cortisol increase would be predicted to result via the agonistic effect on dopamine.

The apparent effects of psychotropics (i.e., drugs that affect brain function) on HPA activity in adults raise important questions about their effects on cortisol secretion in adolescents, who are presumably in a critical period for hormonal maturation. Despite the rapid increase in the administration of psychotropics to adolescents, we are aware of no empirical reports concerning their effects on adrenal or gonadal hormones during the postpubertal period. It is important to understand how psychotropics affect cortisol secretion in youth at risk for mental disorder for two reasons: (1) there may be implications for normal maturational processes, and (2) there may be beneficial or detrimental effects on clinical progression. We are now examining this issue in our ongoing research on adolescents at risk for psychosis.

Adolescent Development and Risk for Psychosis

In our recent research, we have focused on adolescents who manifest personality disorders, especially schizotypal personality disorder, and who are therefore presumed to be at heightened risk for psychotic disorders. At this writing, 114 adolescents (mean age 14, $SD = 1.2$) have been recruited for participation in the study. A battery of diagnostic measures was administered, including the Structured Interview for DSM-IV Personality disorders (SIDP-IV; Pfohl, Blum, & Zimmerman, 1997), the Structured Clinical Interview for Axis I DSM-IV Disorders (SCID; First, Spitzer, Gibbon, & Williams, 1995), an interview with the parent, and the Child Behavior Checklist, a parent report measure. Of the total sample, 79 met diagnostic criteria for a DSM-IV Axis II disorder (39 for schizotypal personality disorder and 40 for other personality disorders) and 35 did not meet criteria for any DSM-IV disorder. About 30% were currently receiving one or more of three classes of medications: antidepressants, antipsychotics, or stimulants. All participants underwent a diagnostic assessment, and saliva samples for cortisol assay were obtained hourly, at least four times. Cortisol levels were examined as a function of current and past medication.

In the analyses described here, the relation between cortisol secretion and current and past psychotropic medication is examined in the mixed sample of healthy adolescents and adolescents with Axis II disorders. We considered the three most common classes of medication: antidepressants, stimulants, and antipsychotics. It should be noted that this is a naturalistic study, in that medication status was predetermined by the child's physician prior to enrollment in the research. Based on past findings, as well as the known actions of stimulants, it was predicted that those currently on stimulants would show elevations in cortisol. For antipsychotic medications, based on both empirical findings and their mechanisms of action, a reduction was predicted. Excluding citalopram, the extant empirical literature suggests a dampening effect of antidepressants on cortisol.

Mean cortisol levels (saliva samples 1–3) for the total sample ($n = 114$), by current medication status, are illustrated in figure 12-1. As described above, previous research findings indicate that the three classes of psychotropics differ in the direction of their relation with cortisol in adult populations. The mean values listed in figure 12-1 are generally consistent with earlier reports. The same pattern was found for the Axis II disorder group when examined separately. Given this pattern of results, as well as the high rate of coadministration, regression analyses were conducted so that the effect of each medication class was tested with statistical controls for the other medications. Further, the effects of age were controlled in the analyses.

Hierarchical regression analyses were conducted with mean cortisol as the dependent variable. Separate analyses were conducted to test the relation of cortisol with each of the three general classes of medication. For these regression equations, age and the "control" medication were entered in the first block. In the second block, the target medication was entered as a predictor variable, and the magnitude of R2 change was used to test for significance.

As shown in table 12-1, both antipsychotic and stimulant medication accounted for a significant proportion of the variance in cortisol level. For both of these classes

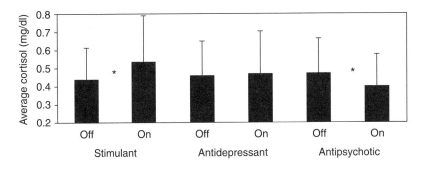

Figure 12-1 Mean (*SD*) cortisol levels by current medication status.

of medication, there was a significant increment in R2 for Block II. Again, the same pattern of findings held when children who did not meet clinical criteria were excluded. Because there is evidence that citalopram may be associated with an increase in cortisol, whereas other antidepressants decrease cortisol, data were also analyzed excluding subjects on citalopram. There was no significant relation between antidepressant use and cortisol, although the trend was toward lower cortisol in those on antidepressants. The same pattern held when data from the clinical subgroup (i.e., those with Axis II diagnosis) were analyzed separately.

In order to examine the effects of past medication, the same analytic procedure described above was employed. For these analyses there was no significant relation between past use of any of the three drug classes and cortisol.

In summary, controlling for age and other medications, current stimulant medication was associated with significantly higher mean cortisol. Antipsychotic medication was associated with significantly lower cortisol. There was no relation between antidepressant medication and cortisol level, although there was a trend toward lower cortisol in youth on antidepressants. This pattern mirrors the trends observed in studies of adult patients.

This is not a controlled experimental study, so we cannot conclude that the relation between cortisol and medication reflects a causal effect of the psychotropics. Instead, the differences may reflect characteristics of the adolescents that predated their medication. Nonetheless, there are several reasons for tentatively concluding that the relation reflects a medication effect. First, we find only a relation between the cortisol secretion and current medication; past psychotropic exposure is not linked with cortisol. Second, the pattern of findings is generally consistent with controlled studies on adults. Finally, the pattern of findings is consistent with what would be expected from the mechanisms of action of the drugs. Thus it is most plausible that the relations between cortisol and current medication observed in this study reflect the effects of the drugs on glucocorticoid secretion.

Conclusions

There is gradually accumulating evidence that the HPA-hippocampal system is impaired in patients with schizophrenia and other psychotic disorders. Two additional inferences can be drawn: (1) HPA-hippocampal impairment is at least partially due to environmental (i.e., nongenetic) factors, given findings from studies of discordant MZ twins, and (2) HPA-hippocampal impairment precedes the onset of the clinical disorder, in that hippocampal volumetric reduction and cortisol elevations are observed in young, first-episode patients who have never been treated. This pattern of findings is consistent with the assumption that the HPA-hippocampal system can moderate the expression of psychosis in vulnerable individuals. Although a review of the literature on HPA dysregulation in non-psychotic psychiatric syndromes is beyond the scope of this paper, it should be noted that there is extensive evidence implicating the HPA-hippocampal system in a range of mental illnesses, especially mood disorders.

With respect to normal maturational trends, it appears that adolescence is a sensitive period for the development of the HPA-hippocampal system, and that activity of the HPA axis is part of the biological chain of events that triggers the onset of puberty. In light of these observations, the apparent effects of psychotropics on cortisol secretion are noteworthy. The findings suggest mechanisms of action for both beneficial and detrimental effects. On the positive side, the suppression of cortisol by antipsychotics may be one component of the drug's therapeutic action. It has been suggested that the augmentation of dopamine activity produced by cortisol release may account for the apparent exacerbation of psychotic symptoms following stress exposure (Walker & Diforio, 1997). Recent studies of at-risk individuals have increased optimism that antipsychotics may have prophylactic effects with respect to the onset of psychosis (Miller et al., 2003). Assuming this prophylactic effect is confirmed in future research, it may be partially attributable to a dampening of the biological response to stress via cortisol reduction. On the other hand, there may be unforeseen adverse consequences; if developmental increases in cortisol secretion are triggering key maturational processes, suppressing secretion may interfere with these processes.

Conversely, augmentation of cortisol secretion by stimulants may also have both benefits and risks. The therapeutic effects of stimulant medication, with respect to both behavior and cognitive functioning, have been well-documented in youth. But the present findings suggest that stimulants could alter maturational processes or enhance stress sensitivity by augmenting cortisol release. Of equal concern is the prospect that stimulants may trigger the expression of psychosis in vulnerable individuals. It has long been recognized that stimulants, including prescription stimulants, can induce psychotic symptoms and episodes, and a recent review of the literature indicates that this effect may be especially pronounced for vulnerable individuals (Curran, Byrappa, & McBride, 2004). Future longitudinal investigations should address the impact of stimulants on at-risk youth.

Studies of the prodromal phase of psychosis have burgeoned, with the hope that they will shed light on the predictors of clinical psychosis. It is clear that psychotropic medications, as well as numerous other factors, have the potential to alter neurohormonal systems and thereby influence the expression of vulnerability. In light of the documented rise in psychotropic medication of youth, it is especially important to understand how these drugs affect all steroid hormones. There are obvious immediate and practical considerations with respect to treatment practices. At the same time, such research has the potential to shed light on the neurohormonal factors involved in the transition to psychosis, including the role of the HPA-hippocampal system.

References

Altamura, A. C., Boin, F., & Maes, M. (1999). HPA axis and cytokines dysregulation in schizophrenia: Potential implications for the antipsychotic treatment. *European Neuropsychopharmacology, 10*(1), 1–4.

Antonova, E., Sharma, T., Morris, R., & Kumari, V. (2004). The relationship between brain structure and neurocognition in schizophrenia: A selective review. *Schizophrenia Research, 70*(2–3), 117–145.

Arnold, A. P., & Breedlove, S. M. (1985). Organizational and activational effects of sex steroids on brain and behavior: A reanalysis. *Hormones and Behavior, 19*(4), 469–498.

Arnsten, A. F., & Shansky, R. M. (2004). Adolescence: Vulnerable period for stress-induced prefrontal cortical function? Introduction to part IV. *Annals of the New York Academy of Sciences, 1021,* 143–147.

Baare, W. F., van Oel, C. J., Hulshoff Pol, H. E., Schnack, H. G., Durston, S., Sitskoorn, M. M., & Kahn, R. S. (2001). Volumes of brain structures in twins discordant for schizophrenia. *Archives of General Psychiatry, 58*(1), 33–40.

Beach, F. A. (1975). Behavioral endocrinology: An emerging discipline. *American Scientist, 63*(2), 178–187.

Bhagwagar, Z., Hafizi, S., & Cowen, P. J. (2002). Acute citalopram administration produces correlated increases in plasma and salivary cortisol. *Psychopharmacology, 163,* 118–120.

Brown, E. S., Woolston, D., Frol, A., Bobadilla, L., Kahn, D. A., Hanczyc, M., Rush, A. J., Fleckenstein, J., Babcock, E., & Cullum, C. M. (2004). Hippocampal volume, spectroscopy, cognition, and mood in patients receiving corticosteroid therapy. *Biological Psychiatry, 55*(5), 538–545.

Brown, W. A., & Williams, B. W. (1976). Methylphenidate increases serum growth hormone concentrations. *Journal of Clinical Endocrinology and Metabolism, 43,* 937–939.

Buchanan, C. M., Eccles, J. S., & Becker, J. B. (1992). Are adolescents the victims of raging hormones? Evidence for activational effects of hormones on moods and behavior at adolescence. *Psychological Bulletin, 111*(1), 62–107.

Chambers, R. A., Taylor, J. R., & Potenza, M. N. (2003). Developmental neurocircuitry of motivation in adolescence: A critical period of addiction vulnerability. *American Journal of Psychiatry, 160*(6), 1041–1052.

Charmandari, E., Kino, T., Souvatzoglou, E., & Chrousos, G. P. (2003). Pediatric stress: Hormonal mediators and human development. *Hormone Research, 59*(4), 161–179.

Coe, C. L., Kramer, M., Czeh, B., Gould, E., Reeves, A. J., Kirschbaum, C., & Fuchs, E. (2003). Prenatal stress diminishes neurogenesis in the dentate gyrus of juvenile rhesus monkeys. *Biological Psychiatry, 54*(10), 1025–1034.

Compas, B. E., Connor-Smith, J., & Jaser, S. S. (2004). Temperament, stress reactivity, and coping: Implications for depression in childhood and adolescence. *Journal of Clinical Child and Adolescent Psychology, 33*(1), 21–31.

Cunningham, M. G., Bhattacharyya, S., & Benes, F. M. (2002). Amygdalo-cortical sprouting continues into early adulthood: Implications for the development of normal and abnormal function during adolescence. *Journal of Comparative Neurology, 453*(2), 116–130.

Curran, C., Byrappa, N., & McBride, A. (2004). Stimulant psychosis: Systemic review. *British Journal of Psychiatry, 185,* 196–204.

Curtis, V. A., Wright, P., Reveley, A., Kerwin, R., & Lucey, J. V. (1995). Effect of clozapine on d-fenfluramine-evoked neuroendocrine responses in schizophrenia and its relationship to clinical improvement. *British Journal of Psychiatry, 166,* 642–646.

De Bellis, M. D., Clark, D. B., Beers, S. R., Soloff, P. H., Boring, A. M., Hall, J., Kersch, A. K., & Matcheri, S. (2000). Hippocampal volume in adolescent-onset alcohol use disorders. *American Journal of Psychiatry, 157*(5), 737–744.

de Leon, M. J., McRae, T., Rusinek, H., Convit, A., De Santi, S., Tarshish, C., Golomb, J., Volkow, N., Daisley, K., Orentreich, N., & McEwen, B. (1997). Cortisol reduces hippocampal glucose metabolism in normal elderly, but not in Alzheimer's disease. *Journal of Clinical Endocrinology and Metabolism, 82*(10), 3251–3259.

Deuschle, M., Hamann, B., Meichel, C., Krumm, B., Lederbogen, F., Kniest, A., Colla, M., & Heuser, I. (2003). Antidepressive treatment with amitriptyline and paroxetine: Effects on saliva cortisol concentrations. *Journal of Clinical Psychopharmacology, 23,* 201–205.

Dorn, L. D., & Chrousos, G. P. (1997). The neurobiology of stress: Understanding regulation of affect during female biological transitions. *Seminars in Reproductive Endocrinology, 15*(1), 19–35.

Dorn, L. D., Hitt, S. F., & Rotenstein, D. (1999). Biopsychological and cognitive differences in children with premature vs. on-time adrenarche. *Archives of Pediatrics and Adolescent Medicine, 153,* 137–146.

Ferrari, E., Fioravanti, M., Magri, F., & Solerte, S. B. (2000). Variability of interactions between neuroendocrine and immunological functions in physiological aging and dementia of the Alzheimer's type. *Annals of the New York Academy of Sciences, 917,* 582–596.

First, M., Spitzer, R. L., Gibbon, M., & Williams, J. B. (1995). *Structured Clinical Interview for the DSM-IV Axis I Disorders (SCID-I), Patient Edition.* Washington, DC: American Psychiatric Press.

Ganguli, R., Singh, A., Brar, J., Carter, C., & Mintun, M. (2002). Hydrocortisone induced regional cerebral activity changes in schizophrenia: A PET scan study. *Schizophrenia Research, 56*(3), 241–247.

Gogtay, N., Giedd, J. N., Lusk, L., Hayashi, K. M., Greenstein, D., Vaituzis, A. C., Nugent, T. F., III, Herman, D. H., Clasen, L. S., Toga, A. W., Rapoport, J. L., & Thompson,

P. M. (2004). Dynamic mapping of human cortical development during childhood through early adulthood. *Proceedings of the National Academy of Science of the United States of America, 101*(21), 8174–8179.

Grady, T. A., Broocks, A., Canter, S. K., Pigott, T. A., Dubbert, B., Hill, J. L., & Murphy, D. L. (1996). Biological and behavioral responses to D-amphetamine, alone and in combination with serotonin3 receptor antagonist ondasterone, in healthy volunteers. *Psychiatry Research, 64,* 1–10.

Harmer, C. J., Bhagwagar, Z., Shelley, N., & Cowen, P. J. (2003). Contrasting effects of citalopram and reboxetine on waking salivary cortisol. *Psychopharmacology, 167,* 112–114.

Harrison, P. J. (2004). The hippocampus in schizophrenia: A review of the neuropathological evidence and its pathophysiological implications. *Psychopharmacology, 174*(1), 151–162.

Heuser, I., Deuschle, M., Weber, B., Stalla, G. K., & Holsboer, F. (2000). Increased activity of the hypothalamus-pituitary-adrenal system after treatment with mineralocorticoid receptor antagonist spironolactone. *Psychoneuroendocrinology, 25*(5), 513–518.

Hibberd, C., Yau, J. L., & Seckl, J. R. (2000). Glucocorticoids and the ageing hippocampus. *Journal of Anatomy, 197*(4), 553–562.

Inder, W. J., Prickett, T. C. R., Mulder, R. T., Donald, R. A., & Joyce, P. R. (2001). Reduction in basal afternoon plasma ACTH during early treatment of depression with fluoxetine. *Psychopharmacology, 156,* 73–78.

Irwin, C. E., Jr., Burg, S. J., & Uhler Cart, C. (2002). America's adolescents: Where have we been, where are we going? *Journal of Adolescent Health. 31*(6 Suppl.), 91–121.

Isgor, C., Kabbaj, M., Akil, H., & Watson, S. J. (2004). Delayed effects of chronic variable stress during peripubertal-juvenile period on hippocampal morphology and on cognitive and stress axis functions in rats. *Hippocampus, 14*(5), 636–648.

Jang, M., Shin, M., Jung, S., Lee, T., Bahn, G., Kwon, Y. K., Kim, E., & Kim, C. (2002). Alcohol and nicotine reduce cell proliferation and enhance apoptosis in dentate gyrus. *Neuroreport: For Rapid Communication of Neuroscience Research, 13*(12), 1509–1513.

Joyce, P. R., Donald, R. A., Nicholls, M. G., Livesey, J. H., & Abbott, R. M. (1986). Endocrine and behavioral responses to methylphenidate in normal subjects. *Biological Psychiatry, 21,* 1015–1023.

Kawata, M. (1995). Roles of steroid hormones and their receptors in structural organization in the nervous system. *Neuroscience Research, 24,* 1–46.

Keenan, P. A., & Soleymani, R. M. (2001). Gonadal steroids and cognition. In R. E. Tarter, M. Butters, et al. (Eds.), *Medical neuropsychology: Clinical issues in neuropsychology* (2nd ed., pp. 181–197). Dordrecht, Netherlands: Kluwer Academic.

Kenny, F. M., Gancayo, G. P., Heald, F. P., & Hung, W. (1966). Cortisol production rate in adolescent males in different stages of sexual maturation. *Journal of Clinical Endocrinology, 26,* 1232–1236.

Kenny, F. M., Preeyasombat, C., & Migeon, C. J. (1966). Cortisol production rate: II. Normal infants, children and adults. *Pediatrics, 37,* 34–42.

Kiess, W., Meidert, A., Dressendorfer, R. A., Scheiver, K., Kessler, U., & Konig, A. (1995). Salivary cortisol levels throughout childhood and adolescence: Relation with age, pubertal stage and weight. *Pediatric Research, 37,* 502–506.

Kunzel, H. E., Binder, E. B., Nickel, T., Ising, M., Fuchs, B., Majer, M., Pfennig, A., Ernst, G., Kern, N., Schmid, D. A., Uhr, M., Holsboer, F., & Modell, S. (2003). Pharmacological and nonpharmacological factors influencing hypothalamic-pituitary-adrenocortical axis reactivity in acutely depressed psychiatric in-patients, measured by the Dex-CRH test. *Neuropsychopharmacology, 28,* 2169–2178.

Laakmann, G., Hennig, J., Baghai, T., & Schule, C. (2003). Influence of mirtazapine on salivary cortisol in depressed patients. *Neuropsychobiology, 47*, 31–36.

Laakmann, G., Schule, C., Baghai, T., & Waldvogel, E. (1999). Effects of mirtazapine on growth hormone, prolactin, and cortisol secretion in healthy male subjects. *Psychoneuroendocrinology, 24*, 769–784.

Lee, P. R., Brady, D., & Koenig, J. I. (2003). Corticosterone alters N-methyl-D-aspartate receptor subunit mRNA expression before puberty. *Molecular Brain Research, 115*(1), 55–62.

Luna, B., & Sweeney, J. A. (2004). The emergence of collaborative brain function: FMRI studies of the development of response inhibition. *Annals of the New York Academy of Sciences, 1021*, 296–309.

Lupien, S. J., de Leon, M., de Santi, S., Convit, A., Tarshish, C., Nair, N. P., Thakur, M., McEwen, B. S., Hauger, R. L., & Meaney, M. J. (1998). Cortisol levels during human aging predict hippocampal atrophy and memory deficits. *Nature Neuroscience, 1*(1), 69–73.

Lupien, S. J., Wilkinson, C. W., Briere, S., Menard, C., Ng Ying Kin, N. M., & Nair, N. P. (2002). The modulatory effects of corticosteroids on cognition: Studies in young human populations. *Psychoneuroendocrinology, 27*, 401–416.

Markianos, M., Hatzimanolis, J., & Lykouras, L. (1999). Switch from neuroleptics to clozapine does not influence pituitary-gonadal axis hormone levels in male schizophrenic patients. *European Neuropsychopharmacology, 9*, 533–536.

McGlashan, T. H., Zipursky, R. B., Perkins, D., Addington, J., Miller, T. J., Woods, S. W., Hawkins, K. A., Hoffman, R., Lindborg, S., Tohen, M., & Breier, A. (2003). The PRIME North America randomized double-blind clinical trial of olanzapine versus placebo in patients at risk of being prodromally symptomatic for psychosis. I. Study rationale and design. *Schizophrenia Research, 61*(1), 7–18.

McGorry, P. D., Yung, A. R., Phillips, L. J., Yuen, H. P., Francey, S., Cosgrave, E. M., Germano, D., Bravin, J., McDonald, T., Blair, A., Adlard, S., & Jackson, H. (2002). Randomized controlled trial of interventions designed to reduce the risk of progression to first-episode psychosis in a clinical sample with subthreshold symptoms. *Archives of General Psychiatry, 59*(10), 921–928.

Meaney, M. J., Diorio, J., Francis, D., Widdowson, J., LaPlante, P., Caldji, C., Sharma, S., Seckl, J. R., & Plotsky, P. M. (1996). Early environmental regulation of forebrain glucocorticoid receptor gene expression: Implications for adrenocortical responses to stress. *Developmental Neuroscience, 18*(1–2), 49–72.

Meaney, M. J., O'Donnell, D., Rowe, W., Tannenbaum, B., Steverman, A., Walker, M., Nair, N. P., & Lupien, S. (1995). Individual differences in hypothalamic-pituitary-adrenal activity in later life and hippocampal aging. *Experimental Gerontology, 30*(3–4), 229–251.

Mesce, K. A. (2002). Metamodulation of the biogenic amines: second-order modulation by steroid hormones and amine cocktails. *Brain, Behavior and Evolution, 60*(6), 339–349.

Miller, T. J., Zipursky, R. B., Perkins, D., Addington, J., Woods, S. W., Hawkins, K. A., Hoffman, R., Preda, A., Epstein, I., Addington, D., Lindborg, S., Marquez E., Tohen, M., Breier, A., & McGlashan, T. H. (2003). The PRIME North America randomized double-blind clinical trial of olanzapine versus placebo in patients at risk of being prodromally symptomatic for psychosis. II. Baseline characteristics of the "prodromal" sample. *Schizophrenia Research, 61*(1), 19–30.

Muck-Seler D., Pivac, N., Mustapic, M., Crncevic, Z., Jokovljevic, M., & Sagud, M. (2004). Platelet serotonin and plasma prolactin and cortisol in healthy, depressed and schizophrenic women. *Psychiatry Research, 127*(3), 217–226.

Muck-Seler, D., Pivac, N., Sagud, M., Jakovljevic, M., & Mihaljevic-Peles, A. (2002). The effects of paroxetine and tianeptine on peripheral biochemical markers in major depression. *Progress in Neuropsychopharmacology and Biological Psychiatry, 26,* 1235–1423.

Neumann, C., & Walker, E. (1995). Developmental pathways to schizophrenia: Behavioral subtypes. *Journal of Abnormal Psychology, 104,* 1–9.

Ohl, F., Michaelis, T., Vollmann-Honsdorf, G. K., Kirschbaum, C., & Fuchs, E. (2000). Effect of chronic psychosocial stress and long-term cortisol treatment on hippocampus-mediated memory and hippocampal volume: a pilot-study in tree shrews. *Psychoneuroendocrinology, 25*(4), 357–363.

Pariante, C. M., Thomas, S. A., Lovestone, S., Makoff, A., & Kerwin, R. W. (2004). Do antidepressants regulate how cortisol affects the brain? *Psychoneuroendocrinology, 29,* 423–447.

Pfohl, B., Blum, N., & Zimmerman, M. (1997). *Structured Interview for DSM-IV Personality (SIDP-IV).* Washington, DC: American Psychiatric Press.

Ritsner, M., Maayan, R., Gibel, A., Strous, R. D., Modai, I., & Weizman, A. (2004). Elevation of the cortisol/dehydroepiandrosterone ratio in schizophrenia patients. *European Neuropsychopharmacology, 14*(4), 267–273.

Rodenbeck, A., Cohrs, S., Jordan, W., Huether, G., Ruther, E., & Hajak, G. (2003). The sleep-improving effects of doxepin are paralleled by a normalized plasma cortisol secretion in primary insomnia: a placebo-controlled, double-blind, randomized, cross-over study followed by an open treatment over 3 weeks. *Psychopharmacology, 170,* 423–428.

Ryan, M. C., Flanagan, S., Kinsella, U., Keeling, F., & Thakore, J. H. (2004). The effects of atypical antipsychotics on visceral fat distribution in first episode, drug-naive patients with schizophrenia. *Life Science, 74,* 1999–2008.

Ryan, M. C. M., Collins, P., & Thakore, J. H. (2003). Impaired fasting glucose tolerance in first-episode, drug-naive patients with schizophrenia. *American Journal of Psychiatry, 160*(2), 284–289.

Ryan, M. C. M., Sharifi, N., Condren, R., & Thakore, J. H. (2004). Evidence of basal pituitary-adrenal overactivity in first episode, drug naive patients with schizophrenia. *Psychoneuroendocrinology, 29*(8), 1065–1070.

Saitoh, O., Karns, C. M., & Courchesne, E. (2001). Development of the hippocampal formation from 2 to 42 years: MRI evidence of smaller area dentata in autism. *Brain, 124,* 1317–1324.

Sapolsky, R. M. (1994). *Why zebras don't get ulcers.* New York: Friedman.

Seidman, L. J., Pantelis, C., Keshavan, M. S., Faraone, S. V., Goldstein, J. M., Horton, N. J., Makris, N., Falkai, P., Caviness, V. S., & Tsuang, M. T. (2003). A review and new report of medial temporal lobe dysfunction as a vulnerability indicator for schizophrenia: A magnetic resonance imaging morphometric family study of the parahippocampal gyrus. *Schizophrenia Bulletin, 29*(4), 803–830.

Shenton, M. E., Dickey, C. C., Frumin, M., & McCarley, R. W. (2001). A review of MRI findings in schizophrenia. *Schizophrenia Research, 49*(1–2), 1–52.

Shirayama, Y., Hashimoto, K., Suzuki, Y., & Higuchi, T. (2002). Correlation of plasma neurosteroid levels to the severity of negative symptoms in male patients with schizophrenia. *Schizophrenia Research, 58*(1), 69–74.

Sonntag, A., Rothe, B., Guldner, J., Yassouridis, A., Holsboer, F., & Steiger, A. (1996). Trimipramine and imipramine exert different effects on the sleep EEG and on nocturnal hormone secretion during treatment of major depression. *Depression, 4,* 1–13.

Sousa, N., & Almeida, O. F. (2002). Corticosteroids: sculptors of the hippocampal formation. *Reviews in the Neurosciences, 13*(1), 59–84.

Spear, L. P. (2000). The adolescent brain and age-related behavioral manifestations. *Neuroscience and Biobehavioral Reviews, 24*(4), 417–463.

Starkman, M. N., Giordani, B., Gebarski, S. S., Berent, S., Schork, M. A., & Schteingart, D. E. (1999). Decrease in cortisol reverses human hippocampal atrophy following treatment of Cushing's disease. *Biological Psychiatry, 46*(12), 1595–1602.

Starkman, M. N., Giordani, B., Gebarski, S. S., & Schteingart, D. E. (2003). Improvement in learning associated with increase in hippocampal formation volume. *Biological Psychiatry, 53*(3), 233–238.

Suddath, R. L., Christison, G. W., Torrey, E. F., Casanova, M. F., & Weinberger, D. R. (1990). Anatomical abnormalities in the brains of monozygotic twins discordant for schizophrenia. *New England Journal of Medicine, 322*(12), 789–794.

Suzuki, M., Hagino, H., Nohara, S., Zhou, S. Y., Kawasaki, Y., Takahashi., T., Matsui., M., Seto, H., Ono, T., & Kurachi, M. (2005). Male-specific volume expansion of the human hippocampus during adolescence. *Cerebral Cortex, 15*(2), 187–193.

Tessner, K., Walker, E., Dhruv, S., Hamman, S., Hochman K. *Post-challenge cortisol levels are inversely associated with hippocampal volume.* Unpublished manuscript, 2006.

Thakore, J. H., Barnes, C., Joyce, J., Medbak, S., & Dinan, T. G. (1997). Effects of antidepressant treatment on corticotropin-induced cortisol responses in patients with melancholic depression. *Psychiatry Research, 73*, 27–32.

Tornhage, C. J. (2002). Reference values for morning salivary cortisol concentrations in healthy school-aged children. *Journal of Pediatric Endocrinology and Metabolism, 15,* 197–204.

van der Beek, E. M., Wiegant, V. M., Schouten, W. G., van Eerdenburg, F. J., Loijens, L. W., van der Plas, C., Benning, M. A., de Vries, H., de Kloet, E. R., & Lucassen, P. J. (2004). Neuronal number, volume, and apoptosis of the left dentate gyrus of chronically stressed pigs correlate negatively with basal saliva cortisol levels. *Hippocampus, 14*(6), 688–700.

van Erp, T. G., Saleh, P. A., Huttunen, M., Lonnqvist, J., Kaprio, J., Salonen, O., Valanne, L., Poutanen, V. P., Standertskjold-Nordenstam, C. G., & Cannon, T. D. (2004). Hippocampal volumes in schizophrenic twinsh. *Archives of General Psychiatry, 61*(4), 346–353.

van Haren, N. E., Picchioni, M. M., McDonald, C., Marshall, N., Davis, N., Ribchester, T., Hulshoff Pol, H. E., Sharma, T., Sham, P., Kahn, R. S., & Murray, R. (2004). A controlled study of brain structure in monozygotic twins concordant and discordant for schizophrenia. *Biological Psychiatry, 56*(6), 454–461.

Wajs-Kuto, E., De Beeck, L. O., Rooman, R. P., & Caju, M. V. (1999). Hormonal changes during the first year of oestrogen treatment in constitutionally tall girls. *European Journal of Endocrinology, 141,* 579–584.

Walder, D. J., Walker, E. F., & Lewine, R. J. (2000). Cognitive functioning, cortisol release, and symptom severity in patients with schizophrenia. *Biological Psychiatry, 48*(12), 1121–1132.

Walker, E., & Diforio, D. (1997). Schizophrenia: A neural diathesis-stress model. *Psychological Review, 104,* 1–19.

Walker, E. F. (2002). Adolescent neurodevelopment and psychopathology. *Current Directions in Psychological Science, 11*(1), 24–28.

Walker, E. F., Bonsall, R., & Walder, D. J. (2002). Plasma hormones and catecholamine metabolites in monozygotic twins discordant for psychosis. *Neuropsychiatry, Neuropsychology and Behavioral Neurology, 15*(1), 10–17.

Watzka, M., Beyenburg, S., Blumcke, I., Elger, C. E., Bidlingmaier, F., & Stoeffel-Wagner, B. (2000). Expression of mineralocorticoid and glucocorticoid receptor mRNA in the human hippocampus. *Neuroscience Letters, 290*(2), 121–124.

Weber, A., Clark, A. J., Perry, L. A., Honour, J. W., & Savage, M. O. (1997). Diminished adrenal androgen secretion in familial glucocorticoid deficiency implicates a significant role for ACTH in the induction of adrenarche. *Clinical Endocrinology, 46,* 431–437.

Webster, M. J., Knable, M. B., O'Grady, J., Orthmann, J., & Weickert, C. S. (2002). Regional specificity of brain glucocorticoid receptor mRNA alterations in subjects with schizophrenia and mood disorders. *Molecular Psychiatry, 7*(9), 985–994.

Wik, G. (1995). Effects of neuroleptic treatment on cortisol and 3-methoxy-4 hydroxyphenylethyl glycol levels in blood. *Journal of Endocrinology, 144,* 425–429.

Wingo, M. K. (2002). The adolescent stress response to a naturalistic driving stressor. *Dissertation Abstracts International: Section B: The Sciences & Engineering, 63,* 1082.

Wolf, O. T., Convit, A., de Leon, M. J., Caraos, C., & Qadri, S. F. (2002). Basal hypothalamo-pituitary-adrenal axis activity and corticotropin feedback in young and older men: Relationships to magnetic resonance imaging-derived hippocampus and cingulate gyrus volumes. *Neuroendocrinology, 75*(4), 241–249.

Zito, J. M., Safer, D. J., Dories, S., Gardner, J. F., Magder, L., Soeken, K., Boles, M., Lynch, F., & Riddle, M. A. (2003). Psychotropic practice patterns for youth: A 10-year perspective. *Archives of Pediatric and Adolescent Medicine, 157,* 17–25.

Chapter 13

The Adolescent Surge in Depression and
Emergence of Gender Differences

A Biocognitive Vulnerability-Stress Model in Developmental Context

Lauren B. Alloy and Lyn Y. Abramson

Depression is one of the most common forms of psychopathology (Kessler, 2002). Moreover, depression is highly recurrent (Judd, 1997) and associated with significant impairment (Greenberg et al., 1996; Gotlib & Hammen, 2002; Roy, Mitchell, & Wilhelm, 2001; Sullivan, LaCroix, Russo, & Walker, 2001). Indeed, due to depression's unique combination of high lifetime prevalence, early age of onset, high chronicity, and great role impairment (Kessler, 2000), the World Health Organization Global Burden of Disease Study ranked depression as the single most burdensome disease (Murray & Lopez, 1996).

Depression also is one of the most prevalent and serious problems faced by many adolescents. In contrast to the earlier belief that it could not occur in childhood or adolescence, it is now recognized that depression is a major mental health problem in adolescence (Compas, Connor, & Hinden, 1998; Kessler, Avenevoli, & Merikangas, 2001; Weissman et al., 1999). Not only is depression itself a major health problem for adolescents, it also is comorbid with and contributes to a wide range of other adolescent maladaptive outcomes and risk behaviors, including suicide, anxiety disorders, eating disorders, substance abuse, teen pregnancy and sexual risk-taking, and impairment in academic performance and family and social relationships (see Alloy, Zhu, & Abramson, 2003, for a review).

Surge in Depression and Emergence of Gender Differences in Adolescence

Adolescence, a transitional developmental period between childhood and adulthood, is characterized by more biological, psychological, and social role changes than any other stage of life except infancy (Holmbeck & Kendall, 2002). Developmental epidemiology has revealed two dramatic clinical phenomena of depression associated with adolescence that provide the point of departure for this chapter. First, whereas the rate of depression is low among children, there is a surge of depression during adolescence, with first episodes frequently occurring during this developmental period (Burke, Burke, Regier, & Rae, 1990). Prospective, longitudinal studies over the past decade (Hankin et al., 1998; Weissman et al., 1997) have shown that the rates of depression begin to increase dramatically in midadolescence, around age 13–14, and reach strikingly high levels by late adolescence, or age 18. Moreover, recent longitudinal studies have confirmed the continuity of depression from adolescence into adulthood (Lewinsohn, Rohde, Klein, & Seeley, 1999; Weissman et al. 1999), with formerly depressed adolescents showing very extensive impairment in young adulthood (Lewinsohn et al., 2003).

The second fact motivating this chapter is the robust finding of a gender difference in depression among adults. Twice as many adult women are depressed as adult men (Nolen-Hoeksema, 1990; Weissman & Klerman, 1977). Corroborating cross-sectional results (Nolen-Hoeksema & Girgus, 1994) with our prospective study, we (Hankin et al., 1998) found that the female preponderance in depression had clearly emerged by age 13–14. This gender gap in rates of depression widened dramatically between ages 14 and 18. By age 18, the sample exhibited the 2:1 ratio of greater female depression seen among adults. However, age may mask important developmental transitions (Rutter, 1989) that could more accurately pinpoint when the gender difference in depression emerges. In fact, pubertal development predicted the emergence of the gender difference better than age alone, as girls showed increased rates of depressive disorders after Tanner stage III (Angold, Costello, & Worthman, 1998).

Recent findings from two cross-sectional studies (Hayward, Gotlib, Schradley, & Litt, 1999; Siegel et al., 1998, 1999) suggest that ethnicity also must be considered in understanding the relation between puberty and the emergence of the female preponderance in depression. Specifically, gender differences in depression following puberty either do not occur or are weaker in African American and Latino adolescents. Two limitations of these studies, however, are that they were cross-sectional and assessed only depressive symptoms but not depressive episodes. Thus, it is not known whether ethnicity similarly would moderate the relationship between pubertal status and the emergence of gender differences in depression in longitudinal studies of onsets of depressive disorders.

Mechanisms Underlying the Surge of Depression and Emergence of Gender Differences in Adolescence

Why does depression surge so dramatically in adolescence, especially for females? Despite the public health and scientific significance of this question, the mechanisms underlying the adolescent surge and emergence of gender differences in depression are not understood well (Cyranowski, Frank, Young, & Shear, 2000; Hankin & Abramson, 2001; Nolen-Hoeksema & Girgus, 1994). It is puzzling that well corroborated theories of depression, when informed by adolescent development, have not as yet been applied to such core developmental depressive phenomena. In this regard, the cognitive vulnerability-stress model has been highly successful in elucidating the processes giving rise to depression, as well as generating powerful empirically supported therapies for it (Abramson et al., 2002). Thus, the overarching goal of this chapter is to examine the mechanisms underlying these developmental phenomena from the perspective of a biocognitive vulnerability-transactional stress model, embedded within a normative adolescent brain and cognitive development context.

A biocognitive vulnerability-transactional stress model of depression is especially plausible in explaining why many individuals become depressed for the first time during adolescence because some of the key etiological factors featured in the theory (e.g., Cognitive Vulnerability × Stress interaction, rumination, hopelessness) have just become developmentally operative during this period due to normative brain maturation and cognitive development (e.g., growth in attentional competence, working memory, hypothetical thinking, future orientation). Ironically, growth in cognitive competence during adolescence likely provides cognitive developmental "prerequisites" for the development of cognitive vulnerability to depression. Figure 13-1 provides an overview of the biocognitive vulnerability-transactional stress model that is developed throughout the remainder of this chapter.

Cognitive Vulnerability-Transactional Stress Model of Depression

The cognitive vulnerability-transactional stress model (Hankin & Abramson, 2001) is a developmentally sensitive elaboration of the two highly successful cognitive theories of depression, hopelessness theory (Abramson, Metalsky, & Alloy, 1989) and Beck's (1987) theory (see central portion of figure 13-1). The essence of this model is that individuals with cognitive vulnerability are more likely to become depressed than nonvulnerable individuals when they confront negative events and make negative inferences about the cause, consequences, or self-implications of the events (negative cognitive style). An individual exhibiting cognitive vulnerability who gets fired might attribute this negative event to stable, global causes (e.g., incompetence) and infer that she never will get another job and is worth-

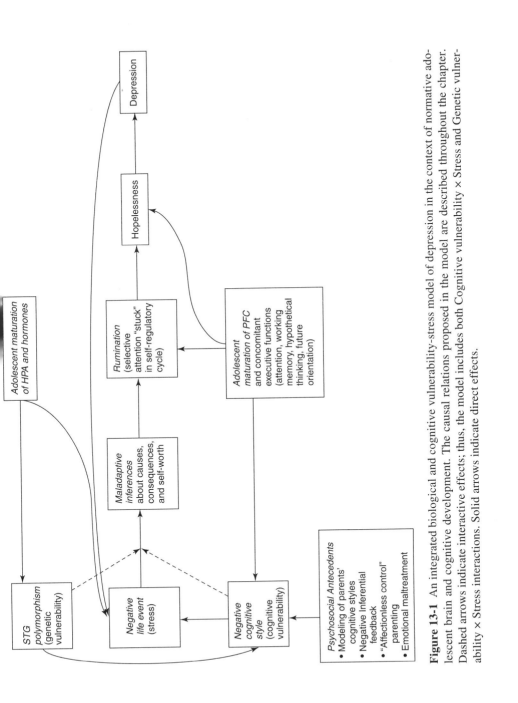

Figure 13-1 An integrated biological and cognitive vulnerability-stress model of depression in the context of normative adolescent brain and cognitive development. The causal relations proposed in the model are described throughout the chapter. Dashed arrows indicate interactive effects; thus, the model includes both Cognitive vulnerability × Stress and Genetic vulnerability × Stress interactions. Solid arrows indicate direct effects.

less. This model is a classic vulnerability-stress model because negative cognitive styles (the vulnerability) contribute only to the occurrence of depression in the presence, but not the absence, of a negative event (the stress). An additional feature of the model is that negative cognitions such as hopelessness mediate the link between the Cognitive Vulnerability × Stress component and the onset of depression. The model also features a transactional process in which increases in depression or cognitive vulnerability itself can contribute to the creation of further dependent, negative events.

We (Abramson et al., 2002; MacCoon, Abramson, Mezulis, Hankin, & Alloy, 2006) elaborated the model to emphasize selective attention in the causal chain and connect the concepts of cognitive vulnerability and rumination, another cognitive factor shown to be important in depression onset (Just & Alloy, 1997; Nolen-Hoeksema, 2000; Spasojevic & Alloy, 2001), duration (Nolen-Hoeksema, 1991), and severity (Just & Alloy, 1997), as well as in gender differences in depression among adults (Nolen-Hoeksema & Jackson, 2001). Self-regulation theorists (Carver & Scheier, 1998) emphasize that when faced with a negative event, it is adaptive to switch attention to this event, find a resolution, and then continue goal-directed behavior (i.e., the self-regulatory cycle). Selective attention often remains focused on the negative event until it is resolved or reduced. We highlighted three ways to exit this self-regulatory cycle: generate a solution to the problem, decrease the importance of the event, or distract attention away from the problem. Cognitively vulnerable individuals should have difficulty with all three exits due to their negative inferences.

For example, if a cognitively vulnerable adolescent attributes not getting a date to "ugliness," no solution is readily available. Instead, cognitively vulnerable individuals become "stuck" in the self-regulatory cycle with their attention focused on negative cognitive content because the inferences they generate in response to negative events lead only to yet further perceived problems (e.g., "no one will marry me because I am so ugly") rather than to resolutions. Such self-regulatory perseveration (Pyszczynski & Greenberg, 1987) constitutes rumination because selective attention remains focused on negative content, which, in turn, should result in the spiral into clinically significant depression. This self-regulatory perspective, then, highlights rumination as mediating the effects of cognitive vulnerability on depression.

Evidence for the Cognitive Vulnerability-Transactional Stress Model

The cognitive vulnerability-transactional stress model has garnered very considerable empirical support. Much of the most important evidence for the theory comes from the Temple–Wisconsin Cognitive Vulnerability to Depression (CVD) Project (Alloy & Abramson, 1999) and related studies. The CVD Project is a landmark, collaborative, two-site study that uses a behavioral high-risk design

(Alloy, Lipman, & Abramson, 1992) to test the cognitive vulnerability and other etiological hypotheses of the major cognitive theories of depression. More generally, the CVD Project examines the cognitive, psychosocial, and developmental risk factors and mechanisms in unipolar depression. We highlight the major findings here.

In the CVD Project, late adolescents ($n = 349$) at a major "age of risk" for depression and making the transition from late adolescence to early adulthood were followed for a total of 5.5 years. Ethnically diverse male and female university freshmen who were nondepressed and had no other Axis I psychiatric disorders at the outset of the study were selected to be at high risk (HR; $n = 173$) or low risk (LR; $n = 176$) for depression based on the presence versus absence of negative cognitive styles (negative inferential styles and dysfunctional attitudes).

Although nondepressed at the outset of the CVD Project, participants with past depression were retained in the final sample as long as they had remitted fully from any past depressive episode, to avoid having an unrepresentative group of HR participants. A powerful test of the cognitive vulnerability hypothesis is provided by our prospective findings. More than half of CVD Project participants entered college with no prior history of depression. These individuals potentially could experience their very first episode of depression during the follow-up. Consistent with the cognitive vulnerability hypothesis, Alloy et al. (1999, 2006) found that HR participants showed a greater likelihood than LR participants of a first onset of major depression (MD), minor depression (MiD), and hopelessness depression (HD; odds ratios = 5.6–11.7). These findings are especially important because they are based on a truly prospective test, uncontaminated by prior history of depression. Among participants with past depression, Alloy et al. (1999, 2006) found that HR participants were more likely than LR participants to develop recurrences of MD, MiD, and HD (odds ratios = 3.1–4.1). There were no risk group differences in prospective onsets of anxiety or other Axis I disorders in either the first onset or recurrence subsamples. However, in the full sample, the HR individuals did have a greater likelihood of an onset of anxiety disorder comorbid with depression, but not of anxiety disorders alone. In addition, Abramson et al. (1998) found that the HR group was more likely to exhibit suicidal ideation and attempts during the follow-up, mediated by hopelessness, than the LR group. These results are important because they provide the first demonstration that negative cognitive styles indeed appear to confer vulnerability to clinically significant depression and suicidality.

In elaborating our cognitive vulnerability-transactional stress model to place it in a self-regulatory context, we highlighted rumination as a form of self-regulatory perseveration that mediates the effects of cognitive vulnerability on depression. Consistent with this elaboration, Spasojevic and Alloy (2001) found that a ruminative response style mediated between cognitive risk and the development of prospective onsets of MD. Also, Robinson and Alloy (2003) extended the rumination hypothesis and suggested that cognitively HR individuals who tend to ruminate on their negative cognitions when stressful life events occur (stress-reactive rumination, SRR), and thereby recursively activate their negative cognitions, would be more likely to become depressed. Consistent with this proposed extension, HR participants who were also high in SRR were more likely to have a past history and prospective onsets of MD and HD than were HR participants low in SRR or LR participants regardless of their SRR (Alloy et al., 2000; Robinson & Alloy, 2003). These findings indicate that rumination may act as both a mediator and moderator of cognitive vulnerability.

In the cognitive vulnerability-transactional stress model, negative cognitive styles are hypothesized to confer vulnerability to depression when individuals confront negative life events and this Vulnerability × Stress interaction should be mediated by hopelessness. In studies of depressive symptoms, we found that negative cognitive styles interacted with negative life events to predict prospective increases in depressive symptoms, mediated by hopelessness (Alloy & Clements, 1998; Alloy, Just, & Panzarella, 1997; Metalsky, Joiner, Hardin, & Abramson, 1993). In addition, we found that HR participants who experienced high stress were about 2.5 times more likely to have an onset of MD/MiD and HD, mediated by hopelessness, than HR participants who experienced low stress or LR participants regardless of stress. We also tested the transactional part (stress-generation hypothesis) of the cognitive vulnerability-transactional stress model, which suggests that cognitively vulnerable participants generate stressful events in their lives. Safford, Alloy, Abramson, and Crossfield (in press) found that, controlling for current and past depression, HR participants, especially females, generated more controllable events dependent on their behavior, thereby increasing the likelihood that their vulnerability will be translated into depression. Thus, cognitively vulnerable individuals experience more negative events and then interpret them more negatively as well (i.e., a "two-hit" model).

In addition, according to the cognitive vulnerability-stress model, people with negative cognitive styles are vulnerable to depression in part because they tend to engage in negatively toned information processing about themselves when they encounter stressful events. Accordingly, Alloy et al. (1997) found that relative to LR participants, HR participants showed preferential processing of self-referent negative depression-relevant information (e.g., faster processing and better recall of content involving themes of incompetence, worthlessness, and low motivation). These findings provide converging evidence for information processing effects of cognitive styles on laboratory tasks adapted from cognitive science paradigms and, thus, support the construct validity of the cognitive style questionnaire measures.

Much evidence indicates that social support buffers against depression when people experience stress (Cohen & Wills, 1985). Panzarella, Alloy, and Whitehouse (2006) hypothesized that social support buffers against depression by preventing the development of hopelessness through two mechanisms and, in particular, by providing positive or "adaptive" inferential feedback (IF) that promotes benign inferences about the causes, consequences, and meaning of negative events, rather than depressogenic ones. In contrast, negative or maladaptive IF from others should promote depressogenic inferences. For example, a person may express the following depressogenic inference to a close friend: "Now, I'll never get promoted; I am so stupid, I always foul things up." The friend could offer an adaptive inferential alternative, e.g., "She will forget about it in no time, and you will still be promoted because most of your work is really good. You are not stupid; your boss is just very difficult to get along with, and you are doing better at it all the time," that would lead the affected individual to reevaluate her thinking, thereby modifying the original maladaptive inference or at least decreasing its certainty and thereby the likelihood of hopelessness.

Consistent with prediction, Panzarella et al. found that high levels of adaptive IF prospectively predicted less negative inferences for actual stressful events experienced and less negative inferential styles during the follow-up. Moreover, participants who were HR, who experienced a high number of stressful events, and who had more negative IF from others were more likely to become hopeless and depressed than participants with 0, 1, or 2 of these vulnerability factors (Risk × Stress × IF interaction). In addition, in an experimental design, we found that participants whose partners were taught to deliver positive IF showed reduced depressive symptoms and inferences following a laboratory failure compared to participants whose partners provided general or no social support (Dobkin, Panzarella, Nesbitt, & Alloy, 2004).

What are the developmental origins of cognitive vulnerability to depression? We highlight the most relevant developmental findings from the CVD Project here (but see Alloy et al., 2004, for a detailed review; see also the bottom left portion of figure 13-1).

In an examination of the familial origins of negative cognitive styles, Abramson et al. (2006) found that HR participants' mothers had greater lifetime histories of depression than LR participants' mothers (35% vs. 18%) based both on direct interviews of mothers and offspring reports. HR participants' fathers were marginally more likely to have a history of depression than LR participants' fathers (18% vs. 12%) based on offspring report only.

Individuals may develop negative cognitive styles through a variety of familial socialization practices. If modeling of parents' styles is a contributor to the development of cognitive vulnerability to depression, then offspring's cognitive styles should correlate with those of their parents. In addition to modeling, the inferential feedback (IF) parents provide to their children about causes and consequences of negative events in the child's life may contribute to the child's cognitive risk for depression, such that offspring's cognitive styles will be associated with their parents' IF styles. Finally, negative parenting practices, such as "affectionless control" (Parker, 1983), may also contribute to development of cognitive vulnerability to depression in offspring.

Alloy et al. (2001) examined the modeling, feedback, and parenting hypotheses. Consistent with modeling, mothers of HR participants had more negative cognitive styles, particularly dysfunctional attitudes, than mothers of LR participants. Supporting the feedback hypothesis, according to both child and parent reports on the Parental Attributions for Children's Events (PACE) Scale (Alloy et al., 2001), both mothers and fathers of HR participants provided more negative IF about causes and consequences of negative life events that happened to their child than did mothers and fathers of LR participants (see also Crossfield, Alloy, Abramson, & Gibb, 2002). Supporting the parenting hypothesis, according both to child and parent reports on the Children's Report of Parental Behavior Inventory (Schaefer, 1965), fathers of HR participants showed less warmth in raising their child than did fathers of LR participants (Alloy et al., 2001). Moreover, negative parental IF and fathers' low warmth predicted prospective onsets of depressive episodes in their offspring during the followup period, mediated by the offspring's cognitive risk status (Alloy et al., 2001).

Rose and Abramson (1992) hypothesized that a developmental history of maltreatment may contribute to the origins of cognitive vulnerability to depression. They hypothesized that emotional abuse should be especially likely to lead to development of negative cognitive styles because the depressive cognitions (e.g., "You're so stupid; you'll never amount to anything") are directly supplied to the child by the abuser. Consistent with the maltreatment hypothesis, we found that HR participants reported more emotional, but not physical or sexual, maltreatment than LR participants (Gibb et al., 2001a, 2001b). In addition, controlling for participants' initial depressive symptoms, a reported history of emotional maltreatment predicted onsets of MD, HD, and levels of suicidal ideation across the prospective follow-up, mediated totally or in part by their cognitive vulnerability and hopelessness (Gibb et al., 2001a, 2001b). Moreover, controlling for parental depression, parental cognitive styles, and parental abuse, peer victimization was also associated with cognitive HR status (Gibb, Abramson, & Alloy, 2004), suggesting that the association of emotional maltreatment with cognitive vulnerability is not entirely due to genetic effects or a negative family environment in general.

Application of the Cognitive Vulnerability-Stress Model to the Surge in Depression and Emergence of Gender Differences in Adolescence

The five constructs in the cognitive vulnerability-transactional stress model are negative life events (stress), cognitive vulnerability, rumination, Cognitive Vulnerability × Stress interaction, and hopelessness. If the model explains the adolescent surge in depression and the emergence of gender differences, then increases in levels or operation or "consolidation" of one or more of these variables should precede the occurrence of these developmental phenomena. Adolescence typically generates more turmoil than childhood or adulthood. A developmental rise in the number of negative life events occurs after age 13 for both boys and girls (Garber, Keiley, & Martin, 2002; but see Compas, Davis, & Forsyth, 1985), but especially for adolescent girls (Ge et al., 1994) and especially in the interpersonal domain (Hankin & Abramson, 2001). Finally, depressed adolescent females generate interpersonal, negative events at a high rate (transactional-stress component; Hankin & Abramson, 2001). To understand the role of stress in contributing to the surge in depression and emergence of gender differences in adolescence, it is crucial that future studies remedy problems associated with prior life events research (e.g., poor sensitivity in dating event and symptom onset, lack of uniformity in event definitions across participants) and examine the same children longitudinally, thereby permitting construction of individual trajectories of growth in stress across adolescence and comparison of such trajectories with those for hopelessness and depression. Because many depression theories feature negative life events, it is also important to see whether the cognitive factors unique to the cognitive vulnerability-stress model show relevant developmental changes that proximally precede the surge in depression and emergence of gender differences in adolescence.

Preliminary indications suggest that cognitive vulnerability may "consolidate" (relative stability over time and consistency across situations) by adolescence and, thus, be accessible for the Cognitive Vulnerability × Stress interaction (Abramson et al., 2002; Gibb et al., 2006). A longitudinal study of third–eighth graders showed that attributional style became more stable in the later grades and interacted with stress to predict depression in older but not younger children (Nolen-Hoeksema, Girgus, & Seligman, 1992; Turner & Cole, 1994). Also, due to achievement of formal operations and the ability to contemplate the future, beginning in early adolescence, children can experience hopelessness, the mediating link in the chain culminating in depression (Hankin, Abramson, & Siler, 2001; Kazdin et al., 1983). Moreover, work demonstrating decreases in attributional positivity and optimism as children transition into adolescence (Mezulis, Abramson, Hyde, & Hankin, 2004; Stipek & MacIver, 1989) suggests that cognitive vulnerability may increase during this transition and, in turn, contribute to the surge in depression (see also Garber et al., 2002; Gibb et al., 2006).

Developmental changes in cognitive vulnerability may contribute to the emergence of gender differences in depression in adolescence. Girls show greater rumination than boys postpuberty, but not before (Broderick, 1998; Smith, Floyd, Alloy, Hughes, & Neeren, 2006). Whereas prior research with psychometrically inadequate instruments typically has failed to reveal more negative cognitive styles among adolescent females than males, we recently developed a psychometrically superior measure of all three components of cognitive style for adolescents that did reveal more negative styles among adolescent females (Floyd, Alloy, Smith, Neeren & Thorell, 2006; Hankin & Abramson, 2002). Moreover, in three cross-sectional studies, adolescent females' more negative cognitive styles and rumination mediated the gender difference in depressive symptoms (Floyd et al., 2006; Hankin & Abramson, 2002; Smith et al., 2006). Thus, preliminary support exists for the hypothesis that adolescent females may exhibit greater cognitive vulnerability than adolescent males, which contributes to the gender difference in adolescent depression.

Whereas prior work focused on cognitive vulnerability in achievement and interpersonal domains, physical attractiveness and body satisfaction may be very motivationally significant for adolescent girls (Floyd et al., 2006; Hankin & Abramson, 2001), who may exhibit high levels of cognitive vulnerability in this domain, which may contribute to their greater depression. Accordingly, adolescent girls showed greater rumination (Mezulis, Abramson, & Hyde, 2002) and more negative cognitive styles in the physical attractiveness domain than did their counterpart males (Hankin & Abramson, 2002). Converging evidence suggests that body dissatisfaction contributes to the gender difference in depression among adolescents (Floyd et al., 2006; Hankin & Abramson, 2001; Smith et al., 2006). For many girls puberty is negative because the associated physical changes (weight gain and increased adiposity) move them away from the thin female ideal currently popularized in modern Western society (Floyd et al., 2006; Nolen-Hoeksema & Girgus, 1994; Rierdan, Koff, & Stubbs, 1989). In contrast, boys tend to view puberty as desired given its association with valued physical characteristics such as increased muscularity and lean body mass (O'Dea & Abraham, 1999; Petersen & Taylor, 1980).

Thus, in our model, bodily changes that accompany pubertal development are important to the surge in depression and emergence of gender differences, not just hormonal changes or other components of puberty per se. These considerations also have implications for understanding ethnicity effects on the puberty-gender differences in depression association. The increased body fat accumulated during puberty is more disappointing for Caucasian than for African American girls (Casper & Offer, 1990; Halpern, Udry, Campbell, & Suchindran, 1999; Parker et al., 1995). Thus, puberty may not initiate the causal chain to depression among African American girls (Floyd et al., 2006).

The cognitive vulnerability-stress model suggests that a history of maladaptive inferential feedback about the causes and consequences of stressful events from significant others should contribute to development of cognitive vulnerability. Accordingly, Alloy et al. (2001) found that a reported childhood history of negative inferential feedback from parents was associated with negative cognitive styles and vulnerability to depression in the adolescent offspring. Negative inferential feedback from others may represent the milder end of a continuum of negative emotional feedback with emotional abuse at the extreme end (Alloy et al., 2001). In a developmental extension of the hopelessness theory, Rose and Abramson (1992) hypothesized that recurrent childhood abuse, particularly emotional abuse, would lead to the development of cognitive vulnerability. We found preliminary support for this hypothesis with both retrospective (Gibb et al., 2004; Gibb et al., 2001a, 2001b; Spasojevic & Alloy, 2002) and prospective (Gibb et al., 2006) designs.

Negative inferential and emotional feedback from others may be especially likely to be internalized in early adolescence and contribute to the formation of cognitive vulnerability. Peers become increasingly important beginning in early adolescence (Harris, 1995; Steinberg, 2002), and rates of negative emotional feedback from peers, including teasing, harassment, rejection, and derogation (i.e., "relational aggression"; Crick & Grotpeter, 1996), rise at this time, especially among adolescent girls (e.g., Crick & Grotpeter, 1996). Thus, negative emotional feedback from peers, in particular, may contribute to both the adolescent surge in depression and emergence of gender differences (see Liu & Kaplan, 1999).

Placing the Cognitive Vulnerability-Stress Model in a Normative Adolescent Brain and Cognitive Development Context

Developmental psychopathologists (Cicchetti & Rogosch, 2002; Steinberg, 2002; Steinberg et al., 2004) and developmental neuroscientists (Casey, Tottenham, Liston, & Durston, 2005b; Walker, Sabuwalla, & Huot, 2004) emphasize that it is critical to apply knowledge of normative adolescent cognitive and brain development to the study of psychopathology in adolescence. On this view, an understanding of depression in adolescence from a cognitive vulnerability-transactional stress perspective must proceed with an explicit recognition of the brain maturation and concomitant cognitive capacities and attainments of the adolescent. It is well established that brain development and cognitive maturation occur concurrently in childhood and adolescence (Casey, Giedd, & Thomas, 2000; Sowell, Delis, Stiles, & Jernigan, 2001; Spear, 2000). Whereas prior work has tracked clinical phenomena as a function of age, little, if any, work has tracked changes in clinical phenomena as a function of cognitive development during adolescence (Steinberg, 2002). An important goal of this chapter is to embed the cognitive vulnerability-stress model in a normative adolescent brain and cognitive development context. Placed in such a context, some of the key etiological factors in the model (e.g., cognitive vulnerability, rumination, hopelessness) have just become developmentally operative during adolescence due to normative brain maturation and concomitant cognitive development (see bottom right portion of figure 13-1).

Contemporary noninvasive neuroimaging methods, such as magnetic resonance imaging (MRI) and diffusion tensor imaging (DTI), have provided evidence of changes in structural architecture and functional organization of the developing brain in vivo, as well as linkages between brain maturation and increases in cognitive competencies (Casey, Galvan, & Hare, 2005a; Casey et al., 2005b; Liston et al., 2003; Nagy, Westerberg, & Klingberg, 2004). Longitudinal MRI studies show that cognitive milestones in development parallel the sequence in which the cortex matures (Giedd, 2004; Gogtay et al., 2004; Sowell et al., 2003, 2004). Regions subserving primary functions such as motor and sensory systems mature earliest and higher-order association areas, such as the prefrontal cortex (PFC), that integrate sensorimotor processes and control "executive functions" such as self-regulation, attention, working memory, and decision making mature more slowly, and not completely, until early adulthood (Casey et al., 2005a, 2005b; Gogtay et al., 2004; Sowell et al., 2004).

During adolescence, frontal lobe gray matter volume, representing dense concentrations of neuronal cell bodies, begins to decline following a rise throughout childhood, peaking at about age 12 (around puberty; Casey et al., 2005a; Giedd, 2004; Gogtay et al., 2004; Sowell et al., 2003; 2004). Gray matter loss during adolescence is thought to involve synaptic pruning and the elimination of connections (Casey et al., 2005b; Giedd et al., 1996; Pfefferbaum et al., 1994). Concomitant with the loss of gray matter, PFC white matter volume increases throughout adolescence until young adulthood and may reflect ongoing myelination of axons, promoting neuronal conduction and signal transmission (Casey et al., 2005b; Giedd et al., 1999; Gogtay et al., 2004; Paus et al., 1999; Thompson et al., 2000). The gray matter volume loss and white matter volume increases occur in parallel, suggesting that connections are being fine-tuned with the elimination of extra synapses and the strengthening of the relevant connections (Casey et al., 2005b).

Moreover, there are sex differences in PFC maturation and function that begin in adolescence and continue into early adulthood. Males have been found to show greater loss of PFC gray matter volume and greater increase of PFC white matter volume compared with females as a function of age and pubertal status (De Bellis et al., 2001; Giedd et al., 1999). In addition, there are sex-specific patterns of development of PFC activation to emotionally salient stimuli (i.e., emotional faces; Killgore, & Yurgelun-Todd, 2004; McClure et al., 2004). Normal pubertal development is associated with large increases in sex hormones and glucocorticoids (Walker et al., 2004), which influence brain maturation (De Bellis et al., 2001; Walker et al., 2004), in part through their effects on gene expression (Walker et al., 2004). Thus, the maturational and functional changes in the adolescent brain may be linked to the surge in depression that occurs in adolescence, and the sex differences in adolescent brain development and function may be associated with the emerging gender differences in depression during this developmental period.

The developmental changes in cortical development have been found to correlate with cognitive performance measures (Casey, Trainor, Orendi et al., 1997b, 2005b; Sowell et al., 2001). The fine-tuning of PFC structural architecture during adolescence observed in MRI studies is associated functionally (fMRI) with a shift from diffuse recruitment of cortical regions by children performing cognitive tasks involving executive functions to more focal recruitment of PFC regions specifically implicated in cognitive control by adolescents (Brown et al., 2005; Casey et al., 2005a; Durston et al., 2005). Specifically, we hypothesize that four cognitive competencies (attentional executive functions, working memory, hypothetical thinking, and future orientation) attained during adolescence and linked to maturation of the PFC are cognitive developmental "prerequisites" for the Cognitive Vulnerability × Stress interaction to "pack its depressogenic punch." Ironically, adolescents' increased brain maturation and cognitive competence may come with a cost. It puts them at greater risk for depression than they were in childhood.

Earlier, we showed how attention is a self-regulatory mechanism in the causal chain of the cognitive vulnerability-stress model. Cognitively vulnerable individuals become stuck in the self-regulatory cycle with their attention focused on negative cognitive content (i.e., rumination; Abramson et al., 2002; MacCoon et al., 2006). An implication is that a cognitively vulnerable individual must have achieved substantial attentional executive functions in order for the Cognitive Vulnerability × Stress interaction to lead to full-blown depression. A cognitively vulnerable child who has not developed sufficient competence in selective and sustained attention may generate negative inferences when faced with a negative event but will not remain focused on such inferences and, thus, will not be as likely to suffer their depressogenic effects. We suggest that normative cognitive development of self-regulatory executive functions (i.e., sustained and selective attention and executive control over attentional switching) is a prerequisite for adolescents to fully engage in attempts to self-regulate negative affect and, thus, for full-blown rumination to occur (Abramson et al., 2002; Steinberg et al., 2004). Attentional processes are known to become more efficient with age and continue to develop through adolescence (Casey, Trainor, Giedd et al.et al., 1997a). Adolescent developmental maturation of the medial PFC and anterior cingulate cortex (ACC) is centrally involved in improved selective attention performance (Botvinik et al., 2001; Casey, Trainor, Giedd et al., 1997a). Thus, as attentional executive control develops during adolescence, rumination and the Cognitive Vulnerability × Stress interaction can fully "pack their punch" in contributing to the onset of and emergence of gender differences in depression.

Similarly, normative development of working memory is essential for maintaining information and the present context in mind (Cohen & Servan-Schreiber, 1992; Kimberg & Farah, 1993) and, thus, is also an important cognitive capacity underlying self-regulation. Thus, increases in working memory skills should also be a prerequisite for adolescents to fully engage in self-regulation and full-blown rumination. Working memory is most reliably associated with activation of the dorsolateral PFC (Owen, 2000).

With the advent of formal operations in adolescence comes the ability to think about possibilities rather than only concrete realities—in other words, abstract, hypothetical thinking. Adolescents develop greater competence in generating options, viewing situations from many perspectives, and anticipating potential consequences of decisions (Keating, 1990, 2004). Such increased competency in hypothetical thinking is also subserved by maturation of the PFC and should be a prerequisite for generating negative implications of stressful events and for experiencing hopelessness (Steinberg, 2002). In addition, in order to experience hopelessness, the proximal cause of depressive symptoms in the cognitive vulnerability-stress model (Abramson et al., 1989), children must develop the normative capacity to think about the future, also a likely outgrowth of PFC maturation in adolescence.

Our hypotheses regarding the dependence of the adolescent surge in depression and emergence of gender differences on the normative cognitive development of executive functions subserved by PFC maturation suggest important directions for future research. Specifically, prospective longitudinal studies are needed that track the trajectories of development of executive functions (attentional competence, working memory, abstract, hypothetical thinking, future orientation) during the transition to adolescence and relate these trajectories to the trajectories of development of negative cognitive styles, rumination, and hopelessness, and, in turn, depression.

Placing the Cognitive Vulnerability-Stress Model in a Genetic Context

Genetic Vulnerability-Stress Model of Depression

It has been well established that genetic factors contribute to depression (e.g., Kendler et al., 1992). However, much less is known about the processes by which genetic vulnerability culminates in depression. Shedding light on this issue, Kendler et al. (1995) demonstrated in an adult twin sample that genes, assessed in the aggregate, affected sensitivity to the depressogenic effects of negative life events. Genetically high risk individuals were more likely to become depressed following negative life events than were their low risk counterparts, whereas neither risk group was likely to become depressed in the absence of negative events (Genetic Vulnerability × Stress interaction). Similar results were obtained with adolescent twins (Silberg et al., 2001). But what specific genes are involved in this effect?

Exciting recent work by Caspi et al. (2003) has identified one such gene. Caspi et al. (2003) reasoned that the serotonin (5-HT) system provides a highly plausible source of candidate genes to participate in a Genetic Vulnerability × Stress interaction culminating in depression. In particular, the selective serotonin reuptake inhibitor (SSRI) drugs, highly effective in treating depression, target the serotonin transporter (5-HTT), which is involved in the reuptake of serotonin at brain synapses. The serotonin transporter gene has a well-studied functional polymorphism in the promotor region, commonly designated as 5-HTTLPR. There are two common functionally different alleles at the 5-HTTLPR site—the short (s) allele and the long (l) allele. The s allele is associated with reduced transcription and functional capacity of the serotonin transporter compared to the l allele (Lesch et al., 1996).

Although evidence for a direct association between the s allele at the 5-HTTLPR site and depression is inconclusive (Lesch, 2003), work with nonhuman primates (e.g., Bennett et al., 2002) and neuroimaging studies with humans (Hairi et al., 2002) suggest that the 5-HTTLPR genotype moderates the serotonergic response to stress and thus may interact with stressors to predict depression in humans. Accordingly, Caspi et al. (2003) reported a Gene × Environment interaction in which individuals with the s allele at the 5-HTTLPR site ("ss" and "sl") exhibited more depressive symptoms, diagnosable depression, and suicidality following stressful life events (including childhood maltreatment) than individuals homozygous for the long allele ("ll"); see top left portion of figure 13-1). The Caspi study has generated great excitement. To date, there are four published replications (Eley et al., 2004; Grabe et al., 2004; Kaufman et al., 2004; Kendler et al., 2005) and one failure to replicate (Gillespie et al., 2005).

The replications of Caspi et al. (2003) suggest important future directions for research on the 5-HTTLPR genotype in depression. First, whereas Caspi et al. (2003) found that major stressors interacted with the 5-HTTLPR genotype, Kendler et al. (2005) found this effect for *mild* stressors. Thus, future studies need to employ highly accurate measures of the full range of negative events, from mild to severe, especially because events triggering depression in adolescents often are mild to moderate (e.g., romantic breakup; Joyner & Udry, 2000). Second, it is important to determine whether the 5-HTTLPR Genotype × Stress interaction *specifically* predicts depression. Similar to our findings with cognitive vulnerability (Alloy et al., 2006; Hankin et al., 2004), Kendler et al. (2005) found that the 5-HTTLPR Genotype × Stress interaction showed specificity and predicted depression, but not anxiety. Third, Kaufman et al.'s (2004) finding that social support further moderates the 5-HTTLPR Genotype × Stress interaction (5-HTTLPR Genotype × Stress × Social Support interaction) reinforces the importance of examining whether maladaptive inferential and emotional feedback from parents and/or peers synergistically amplifies the effects of negative events on genetically (or cognitively) vulnerable adolescents (5-HTTLPR Genotype/Cognitive Vulnerability × Stress × Feedback interaction). Finally, in two of the replications (Eley et al., 2004; Grabe et al., 2004), the 5-HTTLPR Genotype × Stress interaction was obtained for females only. The moderation of this interaction by gender underscores the importance of examining whether the emergence of an operative 5-HTTLPR Genotype × Stress interaction mediates females' surge of depression in adolescence.

Of great importance, three studies have found ethnicity differences in 5-HTTLPR alleles and/or genotypes (Gelernter et al., 1997, 1998; Kaufman et al., 2004). African Americans are more likely to exhibit the "l" allele (or l/l genotype) and less likely to exhibit the "s" allele than Caucasians. These consistent findings suggest that, holding all other factors constant, African Americans should be less prone than Caucasians to develop depression when confronted with negative events. Consistent with this prediction, in the recently completed National Co-morbidity Survey Replication, with 9,282 English-speaking respondents aged 18 and older, non-Hispanic blacks showed a lower risk of mood disorders than non-Hispanic whites (Kessler et al., 2005). An important question for future research is whether African American girls' lower likelihood of showing a surge in depression during adolescence is partly due to a "protective" 5-HTTLPR genotype (and/or lesser cognitive vulnerability).

Placing the Genetic Vulnerability-Stress Model in a Neurodevelopment Context

To both understand and prevent depression, it is critical to know when the 5-HTTLPR Genotype × Stress interaction (and Cognitive Vulnerability × Stress interaction) becomes operative developmentally and contributes to clinically significant depression. Although some of the replications of the Caspi et al. (2003) study have included adolescents (e.g., Eley et al., 2004; Kaufman et al., 2004), none has examined whether the 5-HTTLPR Genotype × Stress interaction shows developmental changes. An important next step will be to employ a prospective design to construct a developmental timeline of the potency of the 5-HTTLPR Genotype × Stress interaction in predicting depression.

Work on developmental genetics and neurodevelopment suggests that this interaction may come "online" as children transition from late childhood to adolescence, age 10–15 years (see top right portion of figure 13-1). Investigators (e.g., Walker et al., 2004) have drawn on recent advances showing that hormones affect gene expression (e.g., Kawata, 1995) to suggest that pubertal hormonal changes may trigger the expression of genetic vulnerabilities for various disorders, including depression. This is consistent with the finding that the heritability estimate for depression increases significantly in adolescence, rising dramatically after puberty (Silberg et al., 1999). The expression of such genetic vulnerabilities (along with increased levels of cognitive vulnerability) may contribute to adolescents' increased "stress sensitivity" (Spear, 2000; Walker et al., 2004). Thus, the 5-HTTLPR Genotype × Stress interaction may exert an increasingly stronger effect on depression over the transition to adolescence and thus may contribute to the surge in depression, especially among females.

Further contributing to adolescents' stress sensitivity may be a pubertal increase in activity of the hypothalamic-pituitary-adrenal (HPA) axis (Walker et al., 2004), an important biological stress-response system. Thus, the combination of increased levels and operation of cognitive vulnerability, increased expression of genetic vulnerabilities, and increased activity of the HPA axis may make adolescents especially vulnerable to the effects of stress just at the time when they are experiencing a developmental rise in the number of stressors. This scenario suggests a "two-hit" model of the rise in depression during adolescence because both vulnerability to stress and stress itself are increasing.

Integrating the Cognitive Vulnerability-Stress and Genetic Vulnerability-Stress Models

To date, the cognitive and genetic approaches to depression have proceeded in parallel with little "cross-talk." Given the major success of each, it is time to integrate them. Providing a foundation for such an integration, two independent studies have shown that cognitive vulnerability has a genetic component (Lau, Rijsdijk, & Eley, in press; Schulman, Keith, & Seligman, 1993). In particular, higher concordances for cognitive vulnerability among monozygotic than dizygotic twins have been reported (Schulman et al., 1993). Similarly, in a study of over 1,300 adolescent twin and sibling pairs, model-fitting techniques revealed a genetic influence on cognitive vulnerability (attributional style; Lau et al., in press). For a number of reasons, it is highly plausible that the 5-HTTLPR genotype, in particular, is related to cognitive vulnerability. At a general level, cognitive vulnerability and 5-HTTLPR genotype vulnerability share some critical similarities. Both appear related to ethnicity, with African Americans less vulnerable than Caucasians. Moreover, both participate in vulnerability-stress interactions that moderate the effects of stress on the development of depression. At a more specific level, exciting recent work (Meyer et al., 2003, 2004) suggests that serotonin modulates dysfunctional attitudes, one type of cognitive vulnerability for depression. Finally, a link has been found between the 5-HTTLPR genotype and negative emotionality/neuroticism (e.g., Lesch et al., 1996, but for an exception, see Gelertner et al., 1998), which, in turn, interacts with negative life events to predict the development of cognitive vulnerability among children making the transition to adolescence (Mezulis, Hyde, & Abramson, in press).

Thus, a growing body of work suggests a link between cognitive vulnerability and the 5-HTTLPR genotype. Building on these findings, it will be important to determine whether cognitive vulnerability is related to the 5-HTTLPR genotype and whether cognitive vulnerability mediates, at least in part, the effects of this genotype on depression in response to the rise in adolescent stressors. The time is ripe to test such an integrated cognitive/genetic vulnerability-stress model as an explanation for the adolescent surge and emergence of gender differences in depression in a prospective study of children making the transition to adolescence.

Implications for Prevention

Insofar as depression has been ranked as the "single most burdensome disease" (Murray & Lopez, 1996) due to its unique combination of high lifetime prevalence, early age of onset, high chronicity, and great role impairment (Kessler, 2000), it is critical to develop effective programs to prevent this disorder. Moreover, as this chapter has shown, the period from late childhood to early adolescence may represent a "window of opportunity" to implement programs to prevent the adolescent surge in depression, especially among females. Knowledge of mechanisms underlying the adolescent surge in depression would suggest interventions for short-circuiting it and the recurrences and great impairment it portends for young adulthood (e.g., Lewinsohn et al., 1999, 2003; Weissman et al., 1999).

A recent meta-analysis (Horowitz & Garber, 2005) of prevention programs for depression in children and adolescents indicates small to moderate effect sizes, suggesting that such prevention programs may be premature and insufficiently informed by knowledge of risk factors and mechanisms underlying the development of these disorders in adolescence. In addition, this meta-analysis showed that selective prevention programs targeting high-risk individuals are more effective than universal programs.

Our application of the cognitive vulnerability-stress model to the adolescent surge in depression suggests that identifying youth with negative cognitive styles and teaching them more adaptive ways to interpret negative events may be an especially potent way to short-circuit the rise in depression during adolescence. Given adolescents' increased brain maturation and cognitive competence (e.g., selective attention), negative cognitive styles may become especially depressogenic during adolescence because they are likely to lead to ever-escalating rumination in the face of negative events. Thus, it also may be helpful to teach cognitively vulnerable youth how to exit from a ruminative cycle (e.g., better problem solving, distraction from the problem, decrease in the importance of the problem). Further, recall that individuals with negative cognitive styles not only interpret negative events more pessimistically than do their nonvulnerable counterparts, but they also experience more negative events (Safford et al., in press). Accordingly, cognitively vulnerable youth also should benefit from interventions designed to help them solve problems and increase their interpersonal skills in addition to decreasing the negativity of their event interpretations (see Jaycox, Reivich, Gillham, & Seligman, 1994, for a prevention program with a social problem-solving component). Indeed, given the developmental rise in negative life events after age 13 for both boys and girls (e.g., Garber et al., 2002), but especially for adolescent girls (Ge et al., 1994) in the interpersonal domain (Hankin & Abramson, 2001), teaching social problem solving skills should be an important component of preventive interventions with cognitively vulnerable youth.

An important issue in designing future programs to prevent the surge in depression in adolescence is the optimal age to intervene (e.g., high school vs. pre- or middle adolescence). In addition to cognitive vulnerability, 5-HTTLPR genotype may be an important identifier of youth most in need of interventions to prevent depression. An interesting possibility is that 5-HTTLPR genotype identifies individuals with cognitive vulnerability. Further, ethnicity and gender should be considered in designing optimal prevention programs. Finally, how broad should prevention programs for depression be? Will such programs also prevent the surge in adolescence of disorders comorbid with depression such as bulimia?

In contemplating interventions to prevent depression, we are reminded of a quote by Jonas Salk. On the 30th anniversary of the first Salk vaccine trials, Martin Seligman asked Jonas Salk what he would be doing today if he were a young scientist. Without hesitation, Salk replied, "I'd still do immunization, but I'd do it psychologically rather than biologically" (quoted in Buchanan & Seligman, 1995, p. 250). This chapter suggests that one way to immunize against depression in youth is to modify negative cognitive styles.

References

Abramson, L. Y., Alloy, L. B., Hankin, B. L., Haeffel, G. J., MacCoon, D. G., & Gibb, B. E. (2002). Cognitive vulnerability-stress models of depression in a self-regulatory and psychobiological context. In I. H. Gotlib & C. L. Hammen (Eds.), *Handbook of depression* (3rd ed., pp. 268–294). New York: Guilford.

Abramson, L. Y., Alloy, L. B., Hogan, M. E., Whitehouse, W. G., Cornette, M., Akhavan, S., & Chiara, A. (1998). Suicidality and cognitive vulnerability to depression among college students: A prospective study. *Journal of Adolescence, 21*, 473–487.

Abramson, L. Y., Alloy, L. B., Lever, N. T., Chiara, A., Whitehouse, W. G., & Hogan, M. E. (2006). *The Temple–Wisconsin Cognitive Vulnerability to Depression (CVD) Project: Psychopathology in the parents of individuals at high and low cognitive risk for depression.* Manuscript in preparation, University of Wisconsin–Madison.

Abramson, L. Y., Metalsky, G. I., & Alloy, L. B. (1989). Hopelessness depression: A theory-based subtype of depression. *Psychological Review, 96*, 358–372.

Alloy, L. B., & Abramson, L. Y. (1999). The Temple-Wisconsin Cognitive Vulnerability to Depression (CVD) Project: Conceptual background, design and methods. *Journal of Cognitive Psychotherapy: An International Quarterly, 13*, 227–262.

Alloy, L. B., Abramson, L. Y., Gibb, B. E., Crossfield, A. G., Pieracci, A. M., Spasojevic, J., & Steinberg, J. (2004). Developmental antecedents of cognitive vulnerability to depression: Review of findings from the Cognitive Vulnerability to Depression (CVD) Project. *Journal of Cognitive Psychotherapy: An International Quarterly, 18*, 115–133.

Alloy, L. B., Abramson, L. Y., Hogan, M. E., Whitehouse, W. G., Rose, D. T., Robinson, M. S., Kim, R. S., & Lapkin, J. B. (2000). The Temple-Wisconsin Cognitive Vulnerability to Depression (CVD) Project: Lifetime history of Axis I psychopathology in individuals at high and low cognitive risk for depression. *Journal of Abnormal Psychology, 109*, 403–418.

Alloy, L. B., Abramson, L. Y., Murray, L. A., Whitehouse, W. G., & Hogan, M. E. (1997). Self-referent information processing in individuals at high and low cognitive risk for depression. *Cognition and Emotion, 11*, 539–568.

Alloy, L. B., Abramson, L. Y., Tashman, N. A., Berrebbi, D. L., Hogan, M. E., Whitehouse, W. G., Crossfield, A. G., & Morocco, A. (2001). Developmental origins of cognitive vulnerability to depression: Parenting, cognitive, and inferential feedback styles of the parents of individuals at high and low cognitive risk for depression. *Cognitive Therapy and Research, 25*, 397–423.

Alloy, L. B., Abramson, L. Y., Whitehouse, W. G., Hogan, M. E., Panzarella, C., & Rose, D. T. (2006). Prospective incidence of first onsets and recurrences of depression in individuals at high and low cognitive risk for depression. *Journal of Abnormal Psychology, 115*, 145–156.

Alloy, L. B., Abramson, L. Y., Whitehouse, W. G., Hogan, M. E., Tashman, N. A., Steinberg, D. L., Rose, D. T., & Donovan, P. (1999). Depressogenic cognitive styles: Predictive validity, information processing and personality characteristics, and developmental origins. *Behaviour Research and Therapy, 37*, 503–531.

Alloy, L. B., & Clements, C. M. (1998). Hopelessness theory of depression: Tests of the symptom component. *Cognitive Therapy and Research, 22*, 303–335.

Alloy, L. B., Just, N., & Panzarella, C. (1997). Attributional style, daily life events, and hopelessness depression: Subtype validation by prospective variability and specificity of symptoms. *Cognitive Therapy and Research, 21*, 321–344.

Alloy, L. B., Lipman, A., & Abramson, L. Y. (1992). Attributional style as a vulnerability factor for depression: Validation by past history of mood disorders. *Cognitive Therapy and Research, 16*, 391–407.

Alloy, L. B., Zhu, L., & Abramson, L. Y. (2003). Cognitive vulnerability to depression: Implications for adolescent risk behavior in general. In D. Romer (Ed.), *Reducing adolescent risk: Toward and integrated approach* (pp. 171–182). Thousand Oaks, CA: Sage.

Angold, A., Costello, E. J., & Worthman, C. M. (1998). Puberty and depression: The roles of age, pubertal status and pubertal timing. *Psychological Medicine, 28*, 51–61.

Beck, A. T. (1987). Cognitive models of depression. *Journal of Cognitive Psychotherapy: An International Quarterly, 1*, 5–37.

Bennett, A. J., Lesch, K. P., Heils, A., Long, J. C., Lorenz, J. G., Shoaf, S. E., et al. (2002). Early experience and serotonin transporter gene variation interact to influence primate CNS function. *Molecular Psychiatry, 7*, 118–122.

Botvinik, M., Braver, T. S., Barch, S. M., Carter, C. S., & Cohen, J. D. (2001). Conflict monitoring and cognitive control. *Psychological Review, 108*, 624–652.

Braver, T. S., Barch, D. M., Gray, J. R., Molfese, D. L., & Snyder, A. (2001). Anterior cingulated cortex and response conflict: Effects of frequency, inhibition and errors. *Cerebral Cortex, 11*, 825–836.

Broderick, P. C. (1998). Early adolescent gender differences in the use of ruminative and distracting coping strategies. *Journal of Early Adolescence, 18*, 173–191.

Brown, T. T., Lugar, H. M., Coalson, R. S., Miezin, F. M., Persen, S. E., & Schlaggar, B. L. (2005). Developmental changes in human cerebral functional organization for word generation. *Cerebral Cortex, 15*, 275–290.

Buchanan, G. M., & Seligman, M. E. P. (1995). Afterword: The future of the field. In G. M. Buchanan & M. E. P. Seligman (Eds.), *Explanatory style* (pp. 247–252). Hillsdale, NJ: Erlbaum.

Burke, K. C., Burke, J. D., Regier, D. A., & Rae, D. S. (1990). Age at onset of selected mental disorders in five community populations. *Archives of General Psychiatry, 47*, 511–518.

Carver, C. S., & Scheier, M. F. (1998). *On the self-regulation of behavior.* Cambridge: Cambridge University Press.

Casey, B. J., Galvan, A., & Hare, T. A. (2005a). Changes in cerebral functional organization during cognitive development. *Current Opinion in Neurobiology, 15*, 239–244.

Casey, B. J., Giedd, J. N., & Thomas, K. M. (2000). Structural and functional brain development and its relation to cognitive development. *Biological Psychology, 54*, 241–257.

Casey, B. J., Tottenham, N., Liston, C., & Durston, S. (2005b). Imaging the developing brain: What have we learned about cognitive development? *Trends in Cognitive Sciences, 9,* 104–110.

Casey, B. J., Trainor, R., Giedd, J., Vauss, Y., Vaituzis, C. K., Hamburger, S., Kozuch, P., & Rapoport, J. L. (1997). The role of the anterior cingulated in automatic and controlled processes: A developmental neuroanatomical study. *Developmental Psychobiology, 30,* 61–69.

Casey, B. J., Trainor, R. J., Orendi, J. L., Schubert, A. B., Nystrom, L. E., Cohen, J. D., Noll, D. C., Giedd, J., Castellanos, X., Haxby, J., et al. (1997). A pediatric functional MRI study of prefrontal activation during performance of a Go-No-Go task. *Journal of Cognitive Neuroscience, 9,* 835–847.

Casper, R. C., & Offer, D. (1990). Weight and dieting concerns in adolescents, fashion or symptom? *Pediatrics, 86,* 384–390.

Caspi, A., Sugden, K., Moffitt, T. E., Taylor, A., Craig, I. W., Harrington, H., McClay, J., Mill, J., Martin, J.,Braithwaite, A., & Poulton, R. (2003). Influence of life stress on depression: Moderation by a polymorphism in the 5–HTT gene. *Science, 301,* 386–389.

Cicchetti, D., & Rogosch, F. A. (2002). A developmental psychopathology perspective on adolescence. *Journal of Consulting and Clinical Psychology, 70,* 6–20.

Cohen, J. D., & Servan-Schreiber, D. (1992). Context, cortex, and dopamine: A connectionist approach to behavior and biology in schizophrenia. *Psychological Review, 99,* 45–77.

Cohen, S., & Wills, T. A. (1985). Stress, social support, and the buffering hypothesis. *Psychological Bulletin, 98,* 310–357.

Compas, B. E., Connor, J. K., & Hinden, B. R. (1998). New perspectives on depression during adolescence. In R. Jessor (Ed.), *New perspectives on adolescent risk behavior* (pp. 319–364). Cambridge, UK: Cambridge University Press.

Compas, B. E., Davis, G. E., & Forsyth, C. J. (1985). Characteristics of life events during adolescence. *American Journal of Community Psychology, 13,* 677–691.

Crick, N. R., & Grotpeter, J. K. (1996). Children's treatment by peers: Victims of relational and overt aggression. *Development and Psychopathology, 8,* 367–380.

Crossfield, A. G., Alloy, L. B., Abramson, L. Y., & Gibb, B .E. (2002). The development of depressogenic cognitive styles: The role of negative childhood life events and parental inferential feedback. *Journal of Cognitive Psychotherapy: An International Quarterly, 16,* 487–502.

Cyranowski, J. M., Frank, E., Young, E., & Shear, K. (2000). Adolescent onset of the gender difference in lifetime rates of major depression: A theoretical model. *Archives of General Psychiatry, 57,* 21–27.

De Bellis, M. D., Keshavan, M. S., Beers, S. R., Hall, J., Frustaci, K., Masalehdan, A., Noll, J., & Boring, A. M. (2001). Sex differences in brain maturation during childhood and adolescence. *Cerebral Cortex,11,* 552–557.

Dobkin, R., Panzarella, C., Nesbitt, J., & Alloy, L. B. (2004). Adaptive inferential feedback depressogenic inferences, and depressed mood: A laboratory study of the expanded hopelessness theory of depression. *Cognitive Therapy and Research, 28,* 487–509.

Durston, S., Davison, M. C., Tottenham, N., Galvan, A., Spicer, J. A., Fossella, F., & Casey, B. J. (2005). A shift from diffuse to focal cortical activity with development. *Journal of Cognitive Neuroscience, 17,* S57–S58.

Eley, T. C., Sugden, K., Corsico, A., Gregory, A. M., Sham, P., Mcguffin, P., Plomin, R., & Craig, I. W. (2004). Gene-environment interaction analysis of serotonin system markers with adolescent depression. *Molecular Psychiatry, 9,* 908–915.

Floyd, T. D., Alloy, L. B., Smith, J., Neeren, A., & Thorell, G. (2006). *Puberty, ethnicity, and gender differences in depression: Role of cognitive vulnerability and the thin female ideal.* Manuscript in preparation, Temple University.

Garber, J., Keiley, M. K., & Martin, N. C. (2002). Developmental trajectories of adolescents' depressive symptoms: Predictors of change. *Journal of Consulting and Clinical Psychology, 70,* 79–95.

Ge, X., Lorenz, F. O., Conger, R. D., Elder, G. H., & Simons, R. L. (1994). Trajectories of stressful life events and depressive symptoms during adolescence. *Developmental Psychology, 30,* 467–483.

Gelernter, J., Kranzler, H., Coccaro, E. F., Siever, L. J., & New, A. S. (1998). Serotonin transporter protein gene polymorphism and personality measures in African American and European American subjects. *American Journal of Psychiatry, 155,* 1332–1338.

Gelernter, J., Kranzler, H., & Cubells, J. F. (1997). Serotonin transporter protein (SLC6A4) allele and haplotype frequencies and linkage disequilibria in African- and European-American and Japanese populations and in alcohol-dependent subjects. *Human Genetics, 101,* 243–246.

Gibb, B. E., Abramson, L. Y., & Alloy, L. B. (2004). Emotional maltreatment from parents, peer victimization, and cognitive vulnerability to depression. *Cognitive Therapy and Research, 28,* 1–21.

Gibb, B. E., Alloy, L. B., Abramson, L. Y., Rose, D. T., Whitehouse, W. G., Donovan, P., Hogan, M. E., Cronholm, J., & Tierney, S. (2001a). History of childhood maltreatment, negative cognitive styles, and episodes of depression in adulthood. *Cognitive Therapy and Research, 25,* 425–446.

Gibb, B. E., Alloy, L. B., Abramson, L. Y., Rose, D. T., Whitehouse, W. G., & Hogan, M. E. (2001b). Childhood maltreatment and college students' current suicidal ideation: A test of the hopelessness theory. *Suicide and Life-Threatening Behavior, 31,* 405–415.

Gibb, B. E., Alloy, L. B., Walshaw, P. D., Comer, J. S., Chang, G. H., & Villari, A. G. (2006). Predictors of negative attributional style change in children. *Journal of Abnormal Child Psychology 34,* 425–439.

Giedd, J. N. (2004). Structural magnetic resonance imaging of the adolescent brain. *Annals of the NY Academy of Science, 1021,* 77–85.

Giedd, J. N., Blumenthal, J., Jeffries, N. O., Castellanos, F. X., Lui, H., Zijdenbos, A., Paus, T., Evans, A. C., & Rapoport, J. L. (1999). Brain development during childhood and adolescence: A longitudinal MRI study. *Nature Neuroscience, 2,* 861–863.

Giedd, J. N., Snell, J. W., Lange, N., Rajapakse, J. C., Casey, B. J., Kozuch, P. L., Viatuzis, A. C., Vauss, Y. C., Hamburger, S. D., Kaysen, D., & Rapoport, J. L. (1996). Quantitative magnetic resonance imaging of human brain development: Ages 4–18. *Cerebral Cortex, 6,* 551–560.

Gillespie, N. A., Whitfield, J. B., Williams, D., Heath, A. C., & Martin, N. G. (2005). The relationship between stressful life events, the serotonin transporter (5-HTTLPR) genotype, and major depression. *Psychological Medicine, 35,* 101–111.

Gogtay, N., Giedd, J. N., Lusk, L., Hayashi, K. M., Greenstein, D., Vaituzis, A. C., Nugent, T. F., Herman, D. H., Clasen, L. S., Toga, A. W., Rapoport, J. L., & Thompson, P. M. (2004). Dynamic mapping of human cortical development during childhood through early adulthood. *Proceedings of the National Academy of Science, 101,* 8174–8179.

Gotlib, I. H., & Hammen, C. L. (2002). Introduction. In I. H. Gotlib & C. L. Hammen (Eds.), *Handbook of depression.* (3rd ed., pp. 1–20). New York: Guilford.

Grabe, H. J., Lange, M., Wolff, B., Votzke, H., Lucht, M., Freyberger, H. J., John, U., & Cascorbi, I. (2004). Mental and physical distress is modulated by a polymorphism in the 5-HT transporter gene interacting with social stressors and chronic disease burden. *Molecular Psychiatry, 10*, 220–224.

Greenberg, P., Kessler, R., Nells, T., Finkelstein, S., & Berndt, E. R. (1996). Depression in the workplace: An economic perspective. In J. P. Feighner & W. F. Boyer (Eds.), *Selective serotonin reuptake inhibitors: Advances in basic research and clinical practice* (pp. 327–363). New York: Wiley.

Halpern, C., Udry, J. R., Campbell, B., & Suchindran, C. (1999). Effects of body fat on weight concerns, dating, and sexual activity: A longitudinal analysis of black and white adolescent girls. *Developmental Psychology, 35*, 721–736.

Hankin, B. L., & Abramson, L. Y. (2001). Development of gender differences in depression: An elaborated cognitive vulnerability-transactional stress theory. *Psychological Bulletin, 127*, 773–796.

Hankin, B. L., & Abramson, L. Y. (2002). Measuring cognitive vulnerability to depression in adolescence: Reliability, validity, and gender differences. *Journal of Child and Adolescent Clinical Psychology, 31*, 491–504.

Hankin, B. L., Abramson, L. Y., Miller, N., & Haeffel, G. J. (2004). Cognitive vulnerability-stress theories of depression: Examining affective specificity in the prediction of depression versus anxiety in three prospective studies. *Cognitive Therapy and Research, 28*, 309–345.

Hankin, B. L., Abramson, L. Y., Moffitt, T. E., Silva, P. A., McGee, R., & Angell, K. E. (1998). Development of depression from preadolescence to young adulthood: Emerging gender differences in a 10–year longitudinal study. *Journal of Abnormal Psychology, 107*, 128–140.

Hankin, B. L., Abramson, L. Y., & Siler, M. (2001). A prospective test of the hopelessness theory of depression in adolescence. *Cognitive Therapy and Research, 25*, 607–632.

Hariri, A. R., Mattay, V. S., Tessitore, A., Kolachana, B., Fera, F., Goldman, D., et al. (2002). Serotonin transporter genetic variation and the response of the human amygdala. *Science, 297*, 400–403.

Harris, J. R. (1995). Where is the child's environment? A group socialization theory of development. *Psychological Review, 102*, 458–489.

Hayward, C., Gotlib, I. H., Schradley, P. K., & Litt, I. F. (1999). Ethnic differences in the association between pubertal status and symptoms of depression in adolescent girls. *Journal of Adolescent Health, 25*, 143–149.

Holmbeck, G. N., & Kendall, P. C. (2002). Introduction to the special section on clinical adolescent psychology: Developmental psychopathology and treatment. *Journal of Consulting and Clinical Psychology, 70*, 3–5.

Horowitz, J. S., & Garber, J. (2005). *The prevention of depression in children and adolescents: A meta-analytic review*. Manuscript under editorial review.

Jaycox, L. H., Reivich, K. J., Gillham, J., & Seligman, M. E. P. (1994). Prevention of depressive symptoms in school children. *Behaviour Research and Therapy, 32*, 801–816.

Joyner, K., & Udry, J. R. (2000). You don't bring me anything but down: Adolescent romance and depression. *Journal of Health and Social Behavior, 41*, 369–391.

Judd, L. L. (1997). The clinical course of unipolar major depressive disorders. *Archives of General Psychiatry, 54*, 989–991.

Just, N., & Alloy, L. B. (1997). The response styles theory of depression: Tests and an extension of the theory. *Journal of Abnormal Psychology, 106*, 221–229.

Kaufman, J., Yang, B. Z., Douglas-Palumberi, H., Houshyar, S., Lipschitz, D., Krystal, J. H., & Gelernter, J. (2004). Social supports and serotonin transporter gene moderate depression in maltreated children. *Proceedings of the National Academy of Science, 101*, 17316–17321.

Kawata, M. (1995). Roles of steroid hormones and their receptors in structural organization in the nervous system. *Neuroscience Research, 24*, 1–46.

Kazdin, A. E., French, N. H., Unis, A. S., Esveldt-Dawson, K., & Sherick, R. B. (1983). Hopelessness, depression, and suicidal intent among psychiatrically disturbed inpatient children. *Journal of Consulting and Clinical Psychology, 51*, 504–510.

Keating, D. P. (1990). Adolescent thinking. In S. Feldman & G. Elliott (Eds.), *At the threshold: The developing adolescent* (pp. 54–89). Cambridge, MA: Harvard University Press.

Keating, D. P. (2004). Cognitive and brain development. In R. J. Lerner & L. D. Steinberg (Eds.), *Handbook of adolescent psychology* (2nd ed.). New York: Wiley.

Kendler, K. S., Kessler, R. C., Walters, E. E., MacLean, C. J., Sham, P. C., Neale, M. C., Health, A. C., & Eaves, L. J. (1995). Stressful life events, genetic liability, and onset of an episode of major depression in women. *American Journal of Psychiatry, 152*, 833–842.

Kendler, K. S., Kuhn, J. W., Vittum, J., Prescott, C. A., & Riley, B. (2005). The interaction of stressful life events and a serotonin transporter polymorphism in the prediction of episodes of major depression: A replication. *Archives of General Psychiatry, 62*, 529–535.

Kendler, K. S., Neale, M. C., Kessler, R. C., Heath, A. C., & Eaves, L. J. (1992). A population-based study of major depression in women: The impact of varying definitions of illness. *Archives of General Psychiatry, 49*, 257–266.

Kessler, R. C. (2000). Burden of depression. In S. Kasper & A. Carlsson (Eds.), *Selective serotonin reuptake inhibitors 1990–2000: A decade of developments*. Copenhagen, Denmark: H. Lundbeck A/S.

Kessler, R. C. (2002). Epidemiology of depression. In I. H. Gotlib & C. L. Hammen (Eds.), *Handbook of depression*. (3rd ed., pp. 23–42). New York: Guilford.

Kessler, R. C., Avenevoli, S., & Merikangas, K. R. (2001). Mood disorders in children and adolescents: An epidemiologic perspective. *Biological Psychiatry, 49*, 1002–1014.

Kessler, R. C., Berglund, P., Demler, O., Jin, R., & Walters, E. E. (2005). Lifetime prevalence and age-of-onset distributions of DSM-IV disorders in the National Comorbidity Survey replication. *Archives of General Psychiatry, 62*, 593–602.

Killgore, W. D. S., & Yurgelun-Todd, D. A. (2004). Sex-related developmental differences in the lateralized activation of the prefrontal cortex and amygdala during perception of facial affect. *Perceptual and Motor Skills, 99*, 371–391.

Kimberg, D. Y., & Farah, M. J. (1993). A unified account of cognitive impairments following frontal lobe damage: The role of working memory in complex, organized behavior. *112*, 411–428.

Lau, J. Y. F., Rijsdijk, F., & Eley, T. C. (in press). I think, therefore I am: A twin study of attributional style in adolescents. *Journal of Clinical Psychology and Psychiatry.*

Lesch, K. P. (2003). Neuroticism and serotonin: A developmental genetic perspective. In R. Plomin, J. C. DeFries, I. W. Craig, & P. McGuffin (Eds.), *Behavioral genetics in the postgenomics era* (pp. 389–424). Washington, DC: American Psychological Association.

Lesch, K. P., Bengel, D., Heils, A., Sabol, S. Z., Greenberg, B. D., Petri, S., Benjamin, J., Muller, C. R., Hamer, D. H., & Murphy, D. L. (1996). Association of anxiety-related traits with a polymorphism in the serotonin transporter gene regulatory region. *Science, 274*, 1527–1531.

Lewinsohn, P. M., Rohde, P., Klein, D. N., & Seeley, J. R. (1999). Natural course of adolescent major depressive disorder: I. Continuity into young adulthood. *Journal of the American Academy of Child and Adolescent Psychiatry, 38*, 56–63.

Lewinsohn, P. M., Rohde, P., Seeley, J. R., Klein, D. N., & Gotlib, I. H. (2003). Psychosocial functioning of young adults who have experienced and recovered from major depressive disorder during adolescence. *Journal of Abnormal Psychology,112*, 353–362.

Liston, C., Watts, R., Tottenham, N., Davidson, M. C., Niogi, S., Ulug, A., & Casey, B. J. (2003). Developmental differences in diffusion measures of cortical fiber tracts. *Journal of Cognitive Neuroscience, 15*, S57–S58.

Liu, X., & Kaplan, H. B. (1999). Explaining gender differences in symptoms of subjective distress in young adolescents. *Stress Medicine, 15*, 41–51.

MacCoon, D. G., Abramson, L. Y., Mezulis, A. H., Hankin, B. L., & Alloy, L. B. (2006). *The attention mediated hopelessness (AMH) theory: The role of attention in connecting cognitive vulnerability to rumination in depression.* Manuscript under editorial review.

McClure, E. B., Monk, C. S., Nelson, E. E., Zarahn, E., Leibenluft, E., Bilder, R. M., Charney, D. S., Ernst, M., & Pine, D. S. (2004). A developmental examination of gender differences in brain engagement during evaluation of threat. *Biological Psychiatry, 55*, 1047–1055.

Metalsky, G. I., Joiner, T. E., Hardin, T. S., & Abramson, L. Y. (1993). Depressive reactions to failure in a naturalistic setting: A test of the hopelessness and self-esteem theories of depression. *Journal of Abnormal Psychology, 102*, 101–109.

Meyer, J. H., Houle, S., Sagrati, S., Carella, A., Hussey, D. F., Ginovart, N., Goulding, V., Kennedy, J., & Wilson, A. A. (2004). Brain serotonin transporter binding potential measured with carbon 11–labeled DASB positron emission tomography: Effects of major depressive episodes and severity of dysfunctional attitudes. *Archives of General Psychiatry, 61*, 1271–1279.

Meyer, J. H., McMain, S., Kennedy, S., Korman, L., Brown, G., DaSilva, J., Wilson, A., Blak, T., Eynan-Harvey, R., Goulding, V., Houle, S., & Links, P. (2003). Dysfunctional attitudes and serotonin$_2$ receptors during depression and self-harm. *American Journal of Psychiatry, 160*, 90–99.

Mezulis, A. H., Abramson, L. Y., & Hyde, J. S. (2002). Domain specificity of gender differences in rumination. *Journal of Cognitive Psychotherapy: An International Quarterly, 16*, 421–434.

Mezulis, A. H., Abramson, L. Y., Hyde, J. S., & Hankin, B. L. (2004). Is there a universal positivity bias in attributions: A meta-analytic review of individual, developmental, and cultural differences in the self-serving attributional bias. *Psychological Bulletin, 130*, 711–747.

Mezulis, A. H., Hyde, J. S., & Abramson, L. Y. (in press). The developmental origins of cognitive vulnerability to depression: Temperament, parenting, and negative life events as contributors to negative cognitive style. *Developmental Psychology.*

Murray, C. J. L., & Lopez, A. D. (Eds.). (1996). *The global burden of disease: A comprehensive assessment of mortality and disability from diseases, injuries, and risk factors in 1990 and projected to 2020.* Cambridge, MA: Harvard University Press.

Nagy, Z., Westerberg, H., & Klingberg, T. (2004). Maturation of white matter is associated with the development of cognitive functions during childhood. *Journal of Cognitive Neuroscience, 16*, 1227–1233.

Nolen-Hoeksema, A. (1990). *Sex differences in depression.* Stanford, CA: Stanford University Press.

Nolen-Hoeksema, S. (1991). Responses to depression and their effects on the duration of the depressive episode. *Journal of Abnormal Psychology, 100*, 569–582.

Nolen-Hoeksema, S. (2000). The role of rumination in depressive disorders and mixed anxiety/depressive symptoms. *Journal of Abnormal Psychology, 109*, 504–511.

Nolen-Hoeksema, S., & Girgus, J. S. (1994). The emergence of gender differences in depression during adolescence. *Psychological Bulletin, 115*, 424–443.

Nolen-Hoeksema, S., Girgus, J. S., & Seligman, M. E. P. (1992). Predictors and consequences of childhood depressive symptoms: A 5-year longitudinal study. Journal of Abnormal Psychology, 101, 405–422.

Nolen-Hoeksema, S., & Jackson, B. (2001). Mediators of the gender difference in rumination. *Psychology of Women Quarterly, 25*, 37–47.

O'Dea, J. A., & Abraham, S. (1999). Onset of disordered eating attitudes and behaviors in early adolescence: Interplay of pubertal status, gender, weight, and age. *Adolescence, 34*, 671–679.

Owen, A. M. (2000). The role of the lateral frontal cortex in mnemonic processing: The contribution of functional neuroimaging. *Experimental Brain Research, 133*, 33–43.

Panzarella, C., Alloy, L. B., & Whitehouse, W. G. (2006). Expanded hopelessness theory of depression: On the mechanisms by which social support protects against depression. *Cognitive Therapy and Research*, 30.

Parker, G. (1983). Parental "affectionless control" as an antecedent to adult depression. *Archives of General Psychiatry, 34*, 138–147.

Parker, S., Nichter, M., Nukovic, N., Sims, C., &Ritenbaugh, C. (1995). Body image and weight concerns among African American and White adolescent females: Differences that make a difference. *Human Organization, 54*, 103–114.

Paus, T., Zijdenbos, A., Worsley, K., Collins, D. L., Blumenthal, J., Giedd, J. N., Rapoport, J. L., & Evans, A. C. (1999). Structural maturation of neural pathways in children and adolescents: In vivo study. *Science, 283*, 1908–1911.

Petersen, A. C., & Taylor, B. (1980). The biological approach to adolescence: Biological change and psychological adaptation. In J. Adelson (Ed.), *Handbook of adolescent psychology*. New York: Wiley.

Pfefferbaum, A., Mathalon, D. H., Sullivan, E. V., Rawles, J. M., Zipursky, R. B., & Lim, K. O. (1994). A quantitative magnetic resonance imaging study of changes in brain morphology from infancy to late adulthood. *Archives of Neurology, 51*, 874–887.

Pyszczynski, T., & Greenberg, J. (1987). Self-regulatory perseveration and the depressive self-focusing style: A self-awareness theory of reactive depression. *Psychological Bulletin,102*, 122–138.

Rierdan, J., Koff, E., & Stubbs, M. L. (1989). A longitudinal analysis of body image as a predictor of the onset and persistence of adolescent girls' depression. *Journal of Early Adolescence, 9*, 454–466.

Robinson, M. S., & Alloy, L. B. (2003). Negative cognitive styles and stress-reactive rumination interact to predict depression: A prospective study. *Cognitive Therapy and Research, 27*, 275–291.

Robinson, N. S., Garber, J., & Hilsman, R. (1995). Cognitions and stress: Direct and moderating effects on depressive versus externalizing symptoms during the junior high transition. *Journal of Abnormal Psychology, 104*, 453–463.

Rose, D. T., & Abramson, L. Y. (1992). Developmental predictors of depressive cognitive style: Research and theory. In D. Cicchetti & S. Toth (Eds.), *Rochester symposium on developmental psychopathology* (Vol. IV). Rochester, NY: University of Rochester Press.

Roy, K., Mitchell, P., & Wilhelm, K. (2001). Depression and smoking: Examining correlates in a subset of depressed patients. *Australian and New Zealand Journal of Psychiatry, 35,* 329–335.

Rutter, M. (1989). Age as an ambiguous variable in developmental research: Some epidemiological considerations from developmental psychopathology. *International Journal of Behavioral Development, 12,* 1–34.

Safford, S. M., Alloy, L. B., Abramson, L. Y., & Crossfield, A. G. (in press). Negative cognitive style as a predictor of negative life events in depression-prone individuals: A test of the stress generation hypothesis. *Journal of Affective Disorders.*

Schaefer, E. S. (1965). Children's reports of parental behavior: An inventory. *Child Development, 36,* 413–424.

Schulman, P., Keith, D., & Seligman, M. E. P. (1993). Is optimism heritable: A study of twins. *Behaviour Research and Therapy, 31,* 569–574.

Siegel, J. M., Aneshensel, C. S., Taub., et al. (1998). Adolescent depressed mood in a multiethnic sample. *Journal of Youth and Adolescence, 27,* 413–427.

Siegel, J. M., Yancey, A. K., Aneshensel, C. S., & Schuler, R. (1999). Body image, perceived pubertal timing, and adolescent mental health. *Journal of Adolescent Health, 25,* 155–165.

Silberg, J. L., Pickles, A., Rutter, M., Hewitt, J., Simonoff, E., Maes, H., Carbonneau, R., Murrelle, L., Foley, D., & Eaves, L. (1999). The influence of genetic factors and life stress on depression among adolescent girls. *Archives of General Psychiatry, 56,* 225–232.

Silberg, J., Rutter, M., Neale, M., & Eaves, L. (2001). Genetic moderation of environmental risk for depression and anxiety in adolescent girls. *British Journal of Psychiatry, 179,* 114–121.

Smith, J. M., Floyd, T. D., Alloy, L. B., Hughes, M., & Neeren, A. M. (2006). *An integrated model of the gender difference in depression: Pubertal development, response style, and body dissatisfaction.* Manuscript under editorial review.

Sowell, E. R., Delis, D., Stiles, J., & Jernigan, T. L. (2001). Improved memory functioning and frontal lobe maturation between childhood and adolescence: A structural MRI study. *Journal of the International Neuropsychology Society, 7,* 312–322.

Sowell, E. R., Peterson, B. S., Thompson, P. M., Welcome, S. E., Henkenius, A. L., & Toga, A. W. (2003). Mapping cortical change across the human life span. *Nature Neuroscience, 6,* 309–315.

Sowell, E. R., Thompson, P. M., Leonard, C. M., Welcome, S. E., Kan, E., & Toga, A. W. (2004). Longitudinal mapping of cortical thickness and brain growth in normal children. *Journal of Neuroscience, 24,* 8223–8231.

Spasojevic, J., & Alloy, L. B. (2001). Rumination as a common mechanism relating depressive risk factors to depression. *Emotion,1,* 25–37.

Spasojevic, J., & Alloy, L. B. (2002). Who becomes a depressive ruminator?: Developmental antecedents of ruminative response style. *Journal of Cognitive Psychotherapy: An International Quarterly, 16,* 405–419.

Spear, L. P. (2000). The adolescent brain and age-related behavioral manifestations. *Neuroscience Biobehavioral Review, 24,* 417–463.

Steinberg, L. (2002). Clinical adolescent psychology: What it is, and what it needs to be. *Journal of Consulting and Clinical Psychology, 70,* 124–128.

Steinberg, L., Dahl, R., Keating, D., Kupfer, D. J., Masten, A. S., & Pine, D. (2004). The study of developmental psychopathology in adolescence: Integrating affective neuroscience with the study of context. In R. J. Lerner & L. D. Steinberg (Eds.), *Handbook of adolescent psychology* (2nd ed.). New York: Wiley.

Stipek, D., & MacIver, D. (1989). Developmental change in children's assessment of intellectual competence. *Child Development, 60,* 521–538.

Sullivan, M. D., LaCroix, A. Z., Russo, J. E., & Walker, E. A. (2001). Depression and self-reported physical health in patients with coronary disease: Mediating and moderating factors. *Psychosomatic Medicine, 63*, 248–256.

Thompson, P. M., Giedd, J. N., Woods, R. P., MacDonald, D., Evans, A. C., & Toga, A. W. (2000). Growth patterns in the developing brain detected by using continuum mechanical tensor maps. *Nature, 404*, 190–193.

Turner, J. E., Jr., & Cole, D. A. (1994). Developmental differences in cognitive diatheses for child depression. *Journal of Abnormal Child Psychology, 22*, 15–32.

Walker, E. F., Sabuwalla, Z., & Huot, R. (2004). Pubertal neuromaturation, stress sensitivity, and psychopathology. *Development and Psychopathology, 16*, 807–824.

Weissman, M. M., & Klerman, G. L. (1977). Sex differences in the epidemiology of depression. *Archives of General psychiatry, 34*, 98–111.

Weissman, M. M., Warner, V., Wickramaratne, P., Moreau, D., & Olfson, M. (1997). Offspring of depressed parents: 10 years later. *Archives of General Psychiatry, 54*, 932–942.

Weissman, M. M., Wolk, S., Goldstein, R. B., et al. (1999). Depressed adolescents grown up. *Journal of the American Medical Association, 281*, 1707–1713.

Part V

Reversible Disorders
of Brain Development

Chapter 14

Early Identification and Prevention of Early-Onset Bipolar Disorder

Kiki Chang, Kim Gallelli, and Meghan Howe

Bipolar disorder (BD) is a chronic, recurrent disorder carrying high morbidity and mortality, leading to annual health costs of $45 billion (Kleinman et al., 2003). Up to 4% of the U.S. population may be affected by bipolar spectrum disorders (Akiskal et al., 2000). Twenty-five to 50% of individuals with BD attempt suicide at least once, and 8.6–18.9% die due to completed suicide (Y. W. Chen & Dilsaver, 1996). Suicidal risk, along with increased substance use and comorbidity, is likely greatest in childhood compared to adult-onset BD (Bellivier, Golmard, Henry, Leboyer, & Schurhoff, 2001; Carter, Mundo, Parikh, & Kennedy, 2003).

In the last decade, there has been a flurry of research targeting more effective pharmaco- and psychotherapies to treat BD in children and adults. However, given the severe morbidity and mortality associated with BD, it seems imperative to develop interventions designed to *prevent* individuals from ever developing BD. Appropriate interventions early in the development of the illness may accomplish the following: (1) prevent inappropriate interventions that may worsen or hasten development of BD, (2) delay the onset of first depressive or manic episode, and/or (3) prevent development of full BD.

Prevent Inappropriate Treatments. Recent studies have reported an approximate 5- to 10-year lag between the onset of BD symptoms and appropriate diagnosis and treatment in individuals with BD (Egeland et al., 2000; Lish et al., 1994). Inappropriate or inadequate treatment early in the course of the illness may have potentially devastating effects. For example, if the first mood episode of a patient with BD is depression, misdiagnosis of unipolar depression may lead to treatment with SSRIs, which could trigger mania or cause suicidality in patients with BD (Faedda, Baldessarini, Glovinsky, & Austin, 2004), Baumer et al., in press). There is also some concern about the chronic use of stimulants in children with or before the onset of BD. Because attention deficit/hyperactivity disorder (ADHD) commonly precedes pediatric-onset BD (K. D. Chang, Steiner, & Ketter, 2000; Faraone, Biederman, Mennin, Wozniak, & Spencer, 1997), the risk of premorbid stimulant therapy is very real. Thus, as will be discussed in this chapter, more appropriate interventions, whether pharmacologic or psychotherapeutic, would obviate the possibility of this inappropriate treatment.

Delay or Ameliorate Severity of Mania. If total prevention may not be possible, at least delay of onset of first manic episode seems likely. In a cohort of 60 children with BD, who all had a parent with BD as well, age at onset (AAO) of mania was 2–3 years later in children with prior exposure to either valproate or carbamazepine ($p = .03$) or lithium ($p = .04$) compared to those without such exposure (Chang et al., 2006). This indirect evidence suggests that more appropriate early treatment could delay the first episode of mania. Amelioration might mean greater time between episodes, less severe mood symptoms, and prevention of suicidality and suicide.

Prevent Full Expression of BD. The theory of kindling is important to the concept of prevention. First applied to seizure disorders, the theory holds that with the combination of psychosocial stress and genetic vulnerability, greater destabilization occurs until a full mood episode occurs (figure 14-1; Post, 1992). Then, with each mood episode, the brain becomes sensitized, so that it becomes easier to have the next mood episode—until spontaneous episodes occur without the need for psychosocial stress. Thus, patients with BD not properly treated would develop episodes closer to one another, with more severity, leading to rapid cycling and more treatment resistance (Post & Weiss, 1996). This naturally progressive course has not been proven, as it is difficult and unethical to conduct such a long, controlled longitudinal study with one subset of participants receiving no treatment. Nevertheless, retrospective reporting from patient histories (Roy-Byrne, Post, Uhde, Porcu, & Davis, 1985) and research at the level of the cell (Post, 1992) support this hypothesis.

Interventions early in the course of kindling may reverse the illness course. For example, rats given repeated subseizure-level electrical stimulation to their amygdalae will eventually develop seizures, leading to a spontaneous seizure disorder. However, if the same rat is administered valproate early on, no seizure disorder will ever develop (Post, 2002). Thus, if similar interventions are performed early enough in bipolar illness development, it is possible that the full expression of BD could be completely averted.

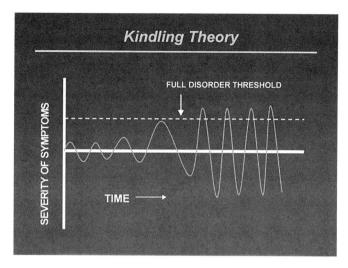

Figure 14-1 According to kindling theory, development of affective disorder begins with subthreshold symptoms that over time combined with psychosocial stress eventually develop to a fully syndromal disorder; without intervention, the disorder naturally worsens in severity and course.

Population for Intervention

Before early interventions can be studied or definitively recommended, a population that is most suitable for intervention should be identified. It is important that this population be at sufficient high risk for BD development to warrant intervention. For example, because intervention with medications have risks as well as potential benefits, the long-term adverse effects of most candidate psychotropics are either unknown or known to be problematic. As the benefit must clearly outweigh the risk, there should be a certain degree of certainty, or likelihood, of BD development if no intervention were taken. Less clear is, to what extent this likelihood should be—should it be 35%? 50%? 75%? 100%? Currently we do not have the necessary research data yet to assign such a specific numerical risk, but this should be the goal of research in this field.

Nevertheless, first it appears that a fairly young population should be targeted for early identification and preventative intervention, as the age at onset (AAO) of BD appears to be decreasing. Much different from the early to mid-20th century, when pediatric-onset BD was thought to be fairly rare (Goodwin & Jamison, 1990; Kraeplin, 1921), BD is now thought to usually begin in childhood and adolescence (Lish, Dime-Meenan, Whybrow, Price, & Hirschfeld, 1994; Perlis et al., 2004). In a recent survey of 983 adults with BD, two-thirds reported having had their first mood episode before age 18 and almost one-third before age 12 (Perlis et al., 2004). One reason for this decreasing AAO may be genetic anticipation. Anticipation refers to the phenomenon of a disease state occurring in successive generations with earlier ages of onset and/or higher severity. This phenomenon has been described in other neurological disorders (e.g., Huntington's, Fragile X, myotonic dystrophy), and in some cases it has been linked to genetic causes: that of trinucleotide repeat sequences expanding in number of repeats with each generation (for review, see Goossens, Del-Favero, & Van Broeckhoven, 2001). Although genetic repeat expansions have not been definitively linked to anticipation in BD, anticipation itself has been found to occur in cohorts of families with BD (Howe et al., 2004; McInnis et al., 1993). Studies of birth cohorts with BD in Pennsylvania found that patients born after 1940 experienced their first mood episode 4.5 years earlier in life than those born before 1940 (Chengappa et al., 2003). In a Northern California cohort of 57 families of parents with BD, the mean AAO of mania in the adults was 16.8 years, compared to 11.2 years for their offspring with BD, a difference of 5.6 years between generations (Howe et al., 2004). However, it is unclear whether this anticipation is solely due to genetic reasons. Other possible reasons include better diagnostic skills of clinicians, heightened public and professional awareness of the possibility of mood disorders in children, environmental effects such as growth hormone in milk leading to earlier onset of puberty, and other exogenous factors such as the recent increase in use of stimulants and antidepressants in youth (Reichart & Nolen, 2004). Whatever the cause, it now appears that most cases of BD begin in childhood or adolescence. Therefore early detection and intervention programs should be aimed at this age group.

During childhood, the early symptoms of BD are often difficult to diagnose because they often do not fulfill the required criteria for a full mood episode. Premorbid symptoms also may vary from child to child, depending on the subtype of BD, because BD is a fairly heterogeneous disorder with different subtypes included within the bipolar spectrum. For example, bipolar spectrum diagnoses in the DSM-IV include bipolar I and II disorder, cyclothymia, and bipolar disorder not otherwise specified (NOS). The classic form of manic-depressive illness, as described by Emil Kraeplin, is episodic in nature with periods of interepisode recovery (Goodwin & Jamison, 1990). In this "classic" form, there may be no premorbid symptoms before the first mood episode, often a first manic "break" occurring during late adolescence or early adulthood. Currently, this type of BD is thought to be less common than other more chronic and rapid-cycling forms, and forms that include irritability instead of euphoria as the primary manic mood (Akiskal, 1996). Adults with this type of BD commonly report that they experienced symptoms of depression, mania, suicidality, and so on, years before their first manic episode (Lish et al., 1994). Therefore, in the majority of cases there may be symptom complexes that predate the full expression of BD. Identification of these complexes may help in determining populations at high risk for BD development.

Reliable identification of these symptom complexes requires prospective studies of patients before their development of BD. Studying a high-risk population appears to be the best approach for this type of study. Currently, the clearest risk factor for BD is a family history of BD (Faraone & Tsuang, 2003). As twin and family studies have reported a 59–87% heritability of BD, it has become clear that first-degree relatives of probands with BD are at high risk of BD themselves (Smoller & Finn, 2003). Thus, a readily accessible population at high risk for BD development would be offspring of parents with BD.

Bipolar Offspring Are at High-Risk for Bipolar Disorder Development

Children of parents with BD ("bipolar offspring") may be the most relevant cohort to study in order to understand risk factors for BD. A meta-analysis of studies conducted before 1997 found bipolar offspring to be at 2.7 times higher risk for development of any psychiatric disorder and 4 times higher risk for developing a mood disorder than children of parents without psychiatric illness (Lapalme, Hodgins, & LaRoche, 1997). Recent studies have found that 50–60% of bipolar offspring have some type of psychiatric disorder (K. Chang, Steiner, Dienes, Adleman, & Ketter, 2003; K. D. Chang et al., 2000; Wals et al., 2001), especially mood, anxiety, and disruptive behavior disorders (Carlson & Weintraub, 1993; K. Chang et al., 2003; K. D. Chang et al., 2000; Wals et al., 2001). Rates of BD spectrum disorders in these offspring range from 14–50%, and rates of MDD range from 7–43% (K. D. Chang & Steiner, 2003).

Predictors of BD Among High-Risk Offspring—Putative Prodromal BD

From these studies of high-risk populations, symptom complexes predating first manic episode can be identified. Attention deficit/hyperactivity disorder (ADHD) has been proposed to be a common initial presentation of BD, especially early-onset BD. In studies conducted since 1988, approximately 27% of bipolar offspring have met criteria for ADHD or significant behavioral or attention problems (K. D. Chang & Steiner, 2003). This finding, in conjunction with the high comorbidity of ADHD and BD in childhood (Faraone, Biederman, Wozniak et al., 1997), has led to the suggestion that ADHD in children with strong family histories of BD may be the first sign of developing BD. Furthermore, family studies of probands with ADHD and BD have supported this comorbidity as representing a familial type of early-onset BD (Faraone, Biederman, Mennin et al., 1997; Faraone, Biederman, Wozniak et al., 1997). In one study of bipolar offspring, seven out of eight offspring with BD had met criteria for ADHD before obtaining a diagnosis of BD (K. D. Chang et al., 2000). Furthermore, parents with BD who had retrospectively reported a history of ADHD during their own childhood were more likely to have children diagnosed with BD as compared to bipolar parents without a history of ADHD (Sachs, Baldassano, Truman, & Guille, 2000), supporting the concept of ADHD as one initial presentation of a familial early-onset BD.

Another symptom complex commonly predating mania is depression. Prospective studies have found high rates (20–30%) of switching to mania in children who initially presented with prepubertal major depressive disorder (Geller, Fox, & Clark, 1994; Geller, Zimerman, Williams, Bolhofner, & Craney, 2001). The rate of conversion to BD in depressed children who are bipolar offspring would seem to be even greater, but no studies have yet specifically examined this cohort longitudinally.

Given the above epidemiological and phenomenological data, a specific subgroup at highest risk for developing BD can be identified. Clearly, there exists a high familial vulnerability in offspring with first-degree relatives with BD. However, in addition to this familial vulnerability, the above-cited literature suggests that offspring who also have a depressive disorder or ADHD are at even higher risk of developing BD. Moreover, it can be hypothesized that those offspring with both ADHD and significant mood symptoms would be at the highest risk of developing BD and may be experiencing a prodromal form of the illness (Carlson & Weintraub, 1993; K. Chang et al., 2003; Wozniak et al., 1995). Data from retrospective studies of adults (Egeland, Hostetter, Pauls, & Sussex, 2000; Lish et al., 1994; Perlis et al., 2004) and children with BD (Fergus et al., 2003) support that these children are at extremely high risk for eventual BD development.

The few longitudinal studies published also have been supportive of this hypothesis (Carlson & Weintraub, 1993; Egeland et al., 2003; Hodgins, Faucher, Zarax, & Ellenbogen, 2002). Carlson and Weintraub (1993) found that attentional and behavioral problems in childhood were specifically associated with the development of mood disorders in young adulthood for bipolar offspring and not offspring of parents with other psychiatric illness or offspring of healthy controls. Similarly, in another prospective longitudinal study of offspring of affectively ill mothers, having a mother with either BD or major depressive disorder as well as behavior problems in childhood greatly increased the risk of BD in offspring compared to control families (Hodgins et al., 2002). All but one of the offspring who developed BD by age 27 had a history of childhood disruptive behavior disorder. Finally, in a 7-year follow-up of Amish children, children of parents with BD showed significantly more mood, attentional, and behavioral problems, and those children were felt to be at significantly higher risk for BD than children of Amish parents without psychiatric illness (Egeland et al., 2003). These studies support that behavioral disorders and nonbipolar mood disorders in bipolar offspring are often a prodromal exhibition of BD. Additional prospective studies of children identified with these putative prodromal presentations are necessary to document illness progression and actual rates of conversion to fully developed BD.

A limitation of using these symptom complexes to identify children at high risk for BD is the relatively low specificity of this approach. That is, ADHD is one of the more common disorders of childhood, with an estimated prevalence in the

United States of 3–7% (K. D. Chang, 2000). In one academic child psychiatry clinic, cross-sectional assessment found only 12% of children with ADHD to also have BD (Biederman et al., 1996). Irritability is furthermore often associated with uncomplicated ADHD (American Psychiatric Association, 1994). Thus, it is unlikely that most children with ADHD, and just irritability, will develop BD, but clearly some of them do. Similarly, although rates of conversion from depression to BD during childhood are estimated to be 20–30% (Geller et al., 1994), 70–80% of children with depression will *not* experience a manic episode. Thus, the sensitivity of using these symptom complexes is high, but the specificity relatively low. Adding a family history of BD, for example, a first- or second-degree relative with BD would increase the specificity, but it is unclear by how much. Children of parents without BD can still develop BD, so inclusion of a first-degree relative with BD as a required risk factor overlooks these children.

Personality or temperament traits may add further clues. We found that bipolar offspring having both parents with a mood disorder, and thus believed to be at even higher familial risk for BD, had higher levels of rejection sensitivity, a lack of mood reactivity (self-soothing capability), and overall more severity of irritability and depressed mood (K. D. Chang et al., 2000). Offspring with psychiatric disorders were considered to have had less flexibility, less task orientation, and fewer periods of good mood compared to those without disorders (K. D. Chang, Blasey, Ketter, & Steiner, 2003). Other key symptoms that may appear before full mania include hyperactivity and hypersexuality (Geller & Luby, 1997).

Biological Markers of Risk for Bipolar Disorder Development

Despite these phenomenological findings, there is still significant uncertainty. Biological markers that are linked specifically to BD are needed to lessen doubt of risk for BD development. It is now widely agreed upon that numerous psychosocial factors, including life stress and family environment, act together with genetic predisposition to create BD (Post, Leverich, Xing, & Weiss, 2001). This genetic predisposition is likely reflected in brain characteristics, such as regional gray matter volume, local neurotransmitter receptor density and sensitivity, and preferential neural circuitry used in affective situations. Identification of the brain characteristics most highly associated with BD development, along with the genetic factors that affect their development, could lead to early identification of those at highest risk for BD development and a better understanding of the pathophysiology of BD.

Neuroimaging Findings in Bipolar Disorder

Magnetic resonance imaging (MRI) studies in adults with BD have found assorted global cortical abnormalities, including aberrant total brain volume, lobar volume, gray/white matter ratios, ventricular size, and number of white matter hyper-intensities (WMH; reviewed in Strakowski, DelBello, Adler, Cecil, & Sax, 2000). However, findings have not always been replicated, perhaps due to small sample sizes, differences in image acquisition, processing and analyses, and heterogeneity of subject samples. Neuroimaging studies have also indicated that subcortical structures are involved in the pathophysiology of this condition (Strakowski et al., 2000). Primarily, candidate regions have included the hippocampus, caudate, putamen, thalamus, and amygdala. These limbic and paralimbic structures have all been implicated in circuits of mood regulation (Blumberg, Charney, & Krystal, 2002; Mayberg, 1997), making them logical candidates for further study in BD. Thus, the prefrontal cortex, amygdala, and the circuits involving these two regions are particularly of interest regarding neurobiological characteristics of BD that may serve as markers.

Role of the Amygdala in Bipolar Disorder

The amygdala is particularly relevant to the pathophysiology of BD. In addition to having a prominent role in emotion perception and response, the amygdala demonstrates activation abnormalities during functional imaging studies of adults with BD (Drevets et al., 2002; Yurgelun-Todd et al., 2000). Volumetric findings in adults with BD have been equivocal, with reports of similar (Swayze, Andreasen, Alliger, Yuh, & Ehrhardt, 1992), decreased (Blumberg, Kaufman, et al., 2003; Pearlson et al., 1997), or increased (Altshuler et al., 2000; Strakowski et al., 1999) amygdalar volumes. Amygdalar findings in pediatric BD have been more consistent, as three studies of adolescents with BD found decreased amygdalar volumes in patients compared to healthy controls (Blumberg, Kaufman, et al., 2003; K. Chang, Karchemskiy, Barnea-Goraly, Garrett, et al., 2005; DelBello, Zimmerman, Mills, Getz, & Strakowski, 2004). Blumberg et al. (Blumberg, Kaufman et al., 2003) reported a decrease in amygdalar volume of 15.6% compared to controls in a combined group of adolescents and adults with BD. DelBello et al. (2004) reported a 10.9% decrease in overall amygdalar volume in children and adolescents with BD. We recently reported a similar 10.4% decrease in amygdalar volume in 20 bipolar offspring with BD compared to controls, a finding driven by reduction in gray matter volume (K. Chang, Karchemskiy, Barnea-Goraly, Garrett, et al., 2005). Furthermore, another study found a trend for decreased left amygdalar volume (mean decrease 13.6%) in adolescents and young adults with BD (B. K. Chen et al., 2004). The convergence of structural and functional amygdalar abnormalities in children and adults with BD point to likely involvement of the amygdala in the pathophysiology of BD. Because children with BD usually are temporally closer to their time of BD onset and thus have had less time than adults to accrue influence of external factors (medications, substances, or mood episodes) on brain morphometry and function, these abnormalities could represent trait markers, present before the onset of full BD, and thus may also serve as risk factors for BD development.

Role of Prefrontal Cortex in Bipolar Disorder

The human prefrontal cortex (PFC) is responsible for many higher functions, including regulation of mood/emotion and attention (Goethals, Audenaert, Van de Wiele, & Dierckx, 2004; Ramnani & Owen, 2004). Several analyses of cerebral lobes and subregions in BD suggest abnormalities of the PFC. These abnormalities include decreased neuronal and glial density in the dorsolateral PFC (DLPFC; Rajkowska, Halaris, & Selemon, 2001), decreased subgenual prefrontal gray matter (Drevets et al., 1997) and glial cells (Ongur, Drevets, & Price, 1998), and decreased prefrontal gray matter volumes bilaterally (Lopez-Larson, DelBello, Zimmerman, Schwiers, & Strakowski, 2002). Given this convergence of positive histopathological and morphometric findings, it is likely that prefrontal gray matter volume is abnormal in adults with BD, but it is less clear whether these abnormalities are present before the onset of mania.

We recently detected a trend toward decreased cortical gray matter volume in bipolar offspring with BD (K. Chang, Karchemskiy, Barnea-Goraly, Simeonova, et al., 2005). In this analysis, we found no statistically significant differences between bipolar participants and controls in ventricular to brain ratio (VBR) or number of participants with significant WMH. Due to these findings, we do not feel that variables such as VBR or WMH are good candidates for further study as biological markers of BD, as they may become relevant only after onset of BD. PFC gray matter volume may be a slightly better marker, as we did detect a trend for overall decreased gray matter in patients with BD compared to controls ($p = .09$; K. Chang, Karchemskiy, Barnea-Goraly, Simeonova, et al., 2005). This decrease in cortical gray matter (4.3%) was not as robust as the 9.4–16.8 % reported in adult samples with BD (Lim, Rosenbloom, Faustman, Sullivan, & Pfefferbaum, 1999; Lopez-Larson et al., 2002). Thus we feel in most cases PFC gray matter volume may begin to decrease more sharply only after years of bipolar illness (Gallelli et al., 2005). However, we did not account for genetic variation within our bipolar group. For example, it is possible that those with the val66met allele of the BDNF gene may have relatively decreased prefrontal gray matter volumes compared to those without this allele (see below).

Although prefrontal morphometric abnormalities may not be easily detected before the onset of BD, prefrontal *function* might be significantly different premorbidly. Functional imaging studies have supported PFC functional abnormalities in BD. Yurgulen-Todd et al. (2000) found adults with BD to have decreased DLPFC activation when viewing fearful faces. Importantly, during this task increased amygdalar activation also was found in patients with BD. Decreased activation in adults with BD was found in medial prefrontal cortex during a continuous performance task (Strakowski, Adler, Holland, Mills, & DelBello, 2004) and in ventral PFC independent of mood state during a color-word Stroop task (Blumberg, Leung, et al., 2003). There have been only two fMRI studies published in pediatric BD. The first found abnormalities in ventral PFC activation in adolescents with BD, as activation did not increase with age as it did in controls (Blumberg, Martin, et al., 2003). The second, our study, found increased DLPFC activation in bipolar offspring with BD when viewing negatively valenced stimuli or performing a visuospatial working memory task (K. Chang et al., 2004). We also detected subcortical limbic overactivation in these participants, primarily insular. We were not able to determine whether prefrontal overactivation was in regulatory response to subcortical/limbic overactivation. Nonetheless, it is clear that PFC is involved in BD, likely with overactivity in response to stress/affect in early stages of the disorder, progressively decreasing toward underactivation after sustained periods of continued mood episodes (K. Chang et al., 2004). The role of both PFC and amygdala are summarized in figure 14-2.

Again, one could presume that these patterns of prefrontal and limbic overactivation may be present before onset of first manic episode. Indeed, preliminary data on our prodromal offspring indicate that they have similar patterns of prefrontal-subcortical overactivation to affective stimuli (Chang et al., unpublished data). However, these participants need to be compared to other participants with similar disorders (ADHD, depression) before the specificity of these findings can be determined. Regardless, it is possible that decreased amygdalar gray matter, amygdalar hypersensitivity, and prefrontal overactivation could serve as components of a set of markers used to determine risk for BD development. Genes that

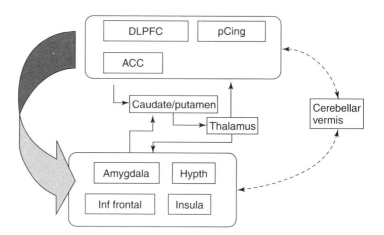

Figure 14-2 Corticolimbic model of mood regulation in bipolar disorder. Abnormally elevated activation of subcortical structures such as amygdala and insula require greater activation of prefrontal areas such as DLPFC and ACC to modulate subcortical signals and regulate emotion and mood. Neurodegeneration of prefrontal areas may lead to decreased ability to modulate subcortical signals, leading to mood episodes, rapid cycling, and treatment resistance (K. Chang et al., 2004). DLPFC = dorsolateral prefrontal cortex, pCing = posterior cingulate, ACC = anterior cingulate cortex, Hypth = hypothalamus, Inf frontal = inferior frontal cortex; areas in gray indicate other areas that likely have a modulatory role by communicating with both cortical and subcortical structures.

affect these neurobiological circuits or directly increase risk for BD could serve as other factors in this set.

Genetic Markers for Bipolar Disorder Risk

Two potential BD gene candidates code for the serotonin transporter (5-HTT) and for brain-derived neurotrophic growth factor (BDNF). Polymorphisms of these genes have been associated with depression and BD (Caspi et al., 2003; Geller et al., 2004; Neves-Pereira et al., 2002). However, because these polymorphisms are relatively common in the population, these genes likely lead to a gross effect on the brain (such as general changes in serotonergic functioning) and thus carry only a small effect by themselves in creating risk for BD. Perhaps due to these small effects and the complexity of human behavior, polymorphisms in genes such as these have not been well linked to behavioral outcomes such as BD on a consistent, replicated basis. As genes do not encode for behavior, a more direct effect of genes to study may be the effect on brain structure and function (Hariri & Weinberger, 2003). Here we will discuss the effects of these two candidate genes on increasing risk for mood disorders and on brain regions involved in BD.

Role of Serotonin Transporter Gene
Polymorphisms in Mood Disorders

The serotonin transporter protein is involved with regulating the concentration of available synaptic serotonin and thus may have widespread effect on mood and mood regulation (Smith et al., 2004). The serotonin transporter (5-HTT) gene contains a common polymorphism: a 44-base-pair (bp) insertion/deletion polymorphism in the promoter region (5-HTTLPR). This polymorphism results in two commonly found functional alleles at the 5-HTTPLR, a short (*s*)-allele and a long (*l*)–allele. The *s*-allele contains a shorter promoter segment and results in reduced transcription and functionality of the protein compared to the *l*-allele. This is a relatively common polymorphism, as the frequency of the *s*-allele in people of European descent is approximately 40% (Hariri & Weinberger, 2003). A recent meta-analysis of 14 studies investigating association of these polymorphisms with BD or major depressive disorder (MDD) found a significant association for BD with the 5-HTT *s*-allele (Lasky-Su, Faraone, Glatt, & Tsuang, 2004). The odds ratio (OR) was 1.13, indicating a small but significant effect. No associations were found between either polymorphism and MDD. However, presence of the *s*-allele may confer increased risk for depression when combined with stressful life events (Caspi et al., 2003). This finding has been replicated in children with histories of maltreatment (Kaufman et al., 2004). Therefore, the *s*-allele of 5-HTT may confer risk for development of mood disorders, including BD, particularly in the context of psychosocial stress.

Role of BDNF Gene Polymorphisms in Mood Disorders

Brain-derived neurotrophic growth factor (BDNF) appears to be critical for regulating neuronal survival during brain development (Poo, 2001) and may be involved in response to antidepressants (D'Sa & Duman, 2002) and lithium (Hashimoto et al., 2002). A common functional polymorphism exists for BDNF as a single nucleotide polymorphism (SNP) at codon 66 resulting in an amino acid change from val (val66) to met (val66met). Association studies have reported association of the val166 allele with BD (Neves-Pereira et al., 2002; Sklar et al., 2002), but another Japanese study was not able to replicate this finding (Nakata et al., 2003). However, linkage disequilibrium of the val166 allele recently was reported for a cohort of children with prepubertal-onset BD (Geller et al., 2004), the first positive genetic finding in a childhood-onset BD cohort. Thus, it is possible that the val66 polymorphism is also a gene of small but significant effect on BD development.

Gene Effects on Brain Structure and Function

The 44-bp insertion/deletion polymorphism of 5-HTT may also directly affect brain structure and function in regions thought to be involved in the pathophysiology of BD. Using voxel-based morphometry techniques to study 114 healthy volunteers, Pezewas et al. (2005) reported that those carrying the 5-HTT s-allele had reduced amygdalar and perigenual cingulate gray matter volume compared to l/l participants. Morphometric abnormalities do not necessarily imply functional changes. Nevertheless, amygdalar *volume* was found to be inversely correlated to amygdalar activation in one study of depressed adults (Siegle, Steinhauer, Thase, Stenger, & Carter, 2002). This finding supports the hypothesis that individuals at risk for BD with decreased amygdalar gray matter volume may also have amygdalar overactivation during affective situations.

Healthy carriers of the s-allele also have been found to have increased right amygdalar activation when viewing fearful or angry faces, compared to those without the s-allele (Hariri et al., 2005; Hariri et al., 2002). Negatively valenced stimuli (aversive pictures from the International Affective Pictures System, IAPS) caused greater amygdalar activation and greater coupling between amygdala and ventromedial prefrontal cortex in healthy volunteer carriers of the s-allele compared to noncarriers (Heinz et al., 2005). Furthermore, the number of s-alleles in each individual was correlated with amount of amygdalar activation when viewing negatively valenced pictures. In carriers of the s-allele, ventromedial PFC (vmPFC) activation was more strongly coupled to amygdalar activation and resulted in greater activation of vmPFC compared to those with the l/l genotype. These powerful findings suggest that modulations in serotonergic activity caused by 5-HTT gene polymorphisms affect degree of amygdalar and prefrontal activation in response to affective challenge. These findings imply that in individuals at risk for BD, the 5-HTT s-allele may have pronounced effects on amygdalar structure and direct or indirect effects on amygdalar activation (figure 14-3).

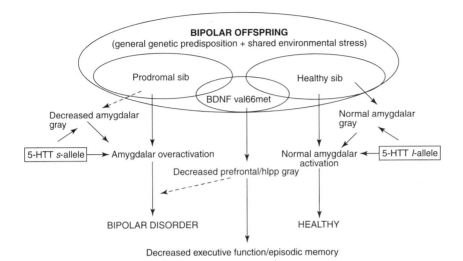

Figure 14-3 Schematic of bipolar disorder (BD) development in children of parents with BD. Offspring siblings share both general genetic predisposition to BD and general environmental stress. Those with increased genetic predisposition for BD are more likely to have decreased amygdalar gray matter and overactivation to affective stress. Presence of the 5–HTT *s*-allele further increases amygdalar overactivation and may further decrease amygdalar gray matter volume, which combined with the other risk factors above, leads to BD. Presence of the BDNF val66met allele, in all offspring, predisposes to decreased prefrontal and hippocampal ("hipp") gray matter volume, which leads to relatively decreased cognitive function (executive function and episodic memory). These deficits moderate course and severity of those offspring developing BD, possibly leading to earlier age at onset, more severe episodes, and worse course and outcome.

The val66met polymorphism of the BDNF gene may also affect brain structure and function in areas relevant to BD development. It is theorized that this polymorphism results in abnormal intracellular packaging and secretion of BDNF, particularly in hippocampal neurons, but perhaps in all areas where BDNF is secreted (Egan et al., 2003). Healthy volunteers with the BDNF vall66met allele were found to have poorer episodic memory and decreased hippocampal activation on fMRI (Egan et al., 2003; Hariri et al., 2003) and reduced hippocampal and prefrontal gray matter, especially bilateral DLPFC (Pezawas et al., 2004), compared to *val/val* carriers. This effect on prefrontal gray matter may be relevant to the course and severity of BD, as discussed above. For example, adults with BD who were carriers of the val66met allele had decreased performance on the Wisconsin card-sorting task compared to *val/val* carriers, implying reduced prefrontal cognitive function in BD patients with the val66met allele. Hippocampal effects of the BDNF polymorphism may also be relevant in BD. Although our group did not find hippocampal volumetric differences in children with BD (K. Chang,

Karchemskiy, Barnea-Goraly, Garrett, et al., 2005), one group did find decreased hippocampal volume in pediatric BD (Frazier et al., 2005).

However, these findings related to the val66met allele appear discrepant with association and linkage findings discussed above, which associate the *val66* allele with BD. The complexity of bipolar genetics may be underlying this discrepancy: for example, it may be that whereas the *val66* allele does confer broadly increased risk for BD, those who have BD but have the vall66*met* allele may actually be prone to hippocampal and PFC abnormalities that lead to worsened executive function and episodic memory, which might worsen the course and severity of their illness. An interaction with the 5-HTT *s*-allele may partially explain this discrepancy: Serotonin signaling appears to increase BDNF secretion (Coppell, Pei, & Zetterstrom, 2003; Nibuya, Nestler, & Duman, 1996), which then leads to modification of serotonergic innervation in the brain (Goggi, Pullar, Carney, & Bradford, 2002; Mamounas et al., 2000). Those with the vall66met allele may have impaired sensitivity to this serotonin signaling such that if these patients also are *s*-allele carriers, the increase in serotonergic signaling may be offset by a lack of responsivity in BDNF that would have otherwise reorganized serotonergic innervation to increase risk for mood disorder development. In this way, it is possible that although possession of the BDNF val66met allele can lead to cognitive dysfunction, when combined with the 5–HTT *s*-allele it becomes protective against mood disorders. Therefore, it is possible that whereas the val66met polymorphism is a *moderator* on the course and severity of bipolar illness, the val66 polymorphism is a *risk factor* for BD development (see figure 14-3), especially when combined with presence of the 5–HTT *s*-allele. It is this type of gene-gene-brain interaction that deserves further study for understanding the creation of risk factors for development of mood disorders, such as BD.

In summary, although we are still years away from creating a definitive set of biological markers to help predict risk for BD, these early findings suggest that abnormalities in prefrontal-amygdalar areas and polymorphisms in genes encoding for relevant neuronal substrates may be good candidates for inclusion in this set.

Early Intervention Strategies

Although we may eventually be able to more specifically target individuals for early intervention based on neurobiology and genes, it appears prudent to develop potential intervention strategies now. As for the treatment of all psychiatric illnesses, interventions would be either pharmacologic or psychosocial.

Pharmacologic Intervention
When considering type of medication, at first it would seem logical to use the class of medication that treats the disease that is trying to be averted. This approach has

been used for other psychiatric disorders: During times of trauma, SSRIs have been proposed to reduce or prevent symptoms of PTSD (Martenyi, Brown, Zhang, Prakash, & Koke, 2002), and antipsychotics have been used successfully to treat relatives of schizophrenic probands with subsyndromal symptomatology and adolescents with early signs of schizophrenia (Cannon et al., 2002; Tsuang, Stone, & Faraone, 2002). Therefore, one might consider mood stabilizers and atypical antipsychotics to be the class of medications to be used for prevention of BD. However, effects of medications on acute symptoms may differ from their potential to prevent worsening of pathology. Perhaps, then, medications proven useful in relapse prevention in BD (lithium, valproate, lamotrigine, olanzapine, and aripiprazole) would be good candidates. The term "neuroprotection" is often used when discussing such medications that could prevent worsening of BD, or in our case, development of first-episode mania.

Neuroprotection

Although psychotropic medications have been studied for their acute therapeutic properties and adverse effects profile, less is known about their neuroprotective characteristics. For this discussion, we will consider the concept of neuroprotection at four different levels: protection of brain tissue against injury or death (true neuroprotection), prevention of onset of a seizure disorder (antikindling properties), indirect promotion of neuronal survival or growth by activation of neurotrophic factors or inhibition of neurotoxic pathways at the cellular level, or detectable creation of new neurons (neurogenesis).

Anticonvulsants specifically have long been thought to have true neuroprotective qualities. Primarily, these qualities have been determined by animal studies in which animals given these medications have reduced areas of brain infarction following an induced stroke or other neurotoxic procedure. Typically, the infarction is caused by the resulting loss of tissue oxygenation, or "ischemia." Findings of this type of neuroprotection have been most positive for topiramate (Kudin, Debska-Vielhaber, Vielhaber, Elger, & Kunz, 2004; Yang, Shuaib, Li, & Siddiqui, 1998), lamotrigine (Calabresi et al., 2003; Shuaib et al., 1995), and tiagabine (Inglefield, Perry, & Schwartz, 1995; Yang, Li, Wang, Jeerakathil, & Shuaib, 2000). Weaker evidence has been found for felbamate, leviteracetam, tiagabine, and zonisamide (Leker & Neufeld, 2003). Barbituates, benzodiazepines, valproate, phenytoin, and carbamazepine do not appear to be good candidates for ischemia prevention due to lack of efficacy or negating effects of cerebral blood flow reduction (Leker & Neufeld, 2003). Of the atypical antipsychotics, which have been less studied for neuroprotection, olanzapine was found to protect neuronal cells from oxidation with hydrogen peroxide (Wei, Bai, Richardson, Mousseau, & Li, 2003). Although these findings are intriguing, this type of neuroprotection may be less relevant to diseases with non-ischemic models of neuronal insult, such as BD.

Antikindling properties of medications may be more relevant to BD development. The most common antikindling paradigm involves testing the medication for its efficacy in preventing amygdala-kindled seizures in rats. Anticonvulsants have not all been found to have the same antikindling potential, as they may differ by what stage they are most effective. For example, if valproate and diazepam are administered early in the course of kindling before seizures appear, then the animal will not develop a seizure disorder (Loscher, Fisher, Nau, & Honack, 1989). However, phenytoin and carbamazepine do not have this effect and can prevent recurrent seizures only after the seizure disorder has begun (R. L. Findling, Kowatch, & Post, 2003). Similar positive antikindling properties also have been described for lamotrigine and leviteracetam (Stratton, Large, Cox, Davies, & Hagan, 2003). Given the previous discussion of the amygdala's involvement in BD and natural progression of the illness, the kindling model appears appropriate to apply to BD. However, whether antikindling agents can have the same effects on BD development as they do in seizure disorder prevention remains to be seen.

Attempts have been made to study neuroprotective effects of psychotropic medications at the cellular level. Valproate is one of the best-studied medications in this regard. In animal studies, valproate has been shown to increase frontal cortex bcl-2 (G. Chen, Zeng, et al., 1999; Manji, Moore, & Chen, 2000a), a neurotrophic and neuroprotective protein that is a downstream agent of endogenous nerve growth factors. Valproate also activates protein kinases that mediate the effects of these neurotrophic factors to stimulate neural dendritic growth (Manji & Lenox, 1999). Lithium has similar effects as valproate on protein kinase C and bcl-2 (Manji & Lenox, 1994; Manji, Moore, & Chen, 2000b). Lithium also inhibits glycogen synthase kinase-3b (GSK-3b; Gould, Chen, & Manji, 2004), an enzyme that may be involved in activating proteins involved in neuronal death. Valproate may (G. Chen, Huang, Jiang, & Manji, 1999) or may not (Jin, Kovacs, Sui, Dewhurst, & Maggirwar, 2005) have similar effects on GSK-3b. These complex effects on neurotrophic pathways may eventually lead to neurogenesis. Both lithium and valproate have been found to have neurogenic effects in rat brains and neural stem cells (Hashimoto, Senatorov, Kanai, Leeds, & Chuang, 2003; Laeng et al., 2004). The concept of neurogenesis in humans is quite controversial, as only recently has it been discovered to occur (Eriksson et al., 1998). Nonetheless, lithium has potential in this regard: In 8 out of 10 patients with BD, overall gray matter increased by 3% after 4 weeks of lithium monotherapy (Moore, Bebchuk, Wilds, Chen, & Manji, 2000). Lithium treatment in BD and healthy adults has also been found to increase cortical levels of N-acetylaspartate, an indirect marker of neuronal density and integrity (Moore, Bebchuk, Hasanat et al., 2000). Although the implications from these findings are exciting to entertain, the question still remains whether or not such potential neurogenic effects of these medications are beneficial to the recipient.

Pharmacologic Early-Intervention Studies

It is clear that certain medications have neuroprotective qualities and therefore may be effective in reducing risk for development of BD in vulnerable populations. However, as yet there have been no true BD prevention studies, only early-intervention studies with eventual prevention in mind. In the first such study, Geller and colleagues (1998) studied children with major depression and a family history of affective disorder. Forty percent of participants had a parent with BD, 40% had a more distant relative (aunt, uncle, or cousin) with BD, and 20% had a family history of major depression only (without mania). Participants were randomized in a double-blind fashion to receive 6 weeks of lithium or placebo. No differences were found between the two groups in improvement in depressive symptoms. The final Clinical Global Assessment of Severity scores in both groups, although improved, were still below 60, indicating continuing clinical problems. However, there appeared to be a wide distribution of participants who responded well and participants who responded poorly, suggesting that some participants may have had unique factors associated with response. Whether these factors were related to increased family history of BD is unknown, as the authors did not report such a subanalysis of data grouped by family history. Furthermore, no longitudinal follow-up was done to investigate potential effects on bipolar outcome of these children, so the prophylactic qualities of lithium cannot be commented on.

In another early intervention study, we investigated the use of divalproex (a form of valproate) in 24 bipolar offspring with mood and/or disruptive behavioral disorders (K. D. Chang, Dienes et al., 2003). None of the participants, aged 7–17, had bipolar I or II disorder, but all had at least some mild affective symptoms as manifested by a minimum score of 12 on the Young Mania Rating Scale (YMRS) or Hamilton Rating Scale for Depression (HAM-D). Thus, as discussed earlier, they fit the criteria for offspring at the highest risk for BD development. Many participants had had previous trials of antidepressants and/or stimulants. Participants were tapered off of any current medications, and then begun on divalproex monotherapy, eventually reaching a mean final dose of 821 mg/day (serum level = 79.0 +/– 26.8 mg /mL). After 12 weeks, 78% of participants were considered responders, having general improvement in mood and functioning, with the majority showing improvement by Week 3. Although this study demonstrated the potential of divalproex in treating acute symptoms of children with putative prodromal BD, another similar, but placebo-controlled, study found that both divalproex and placebo led to equal improvement of affective symptoms in adolescents with cyclothymia or bipolar disorder not otherwise specified who were bipolar offspring. Notably, though, divalproex was superior to placebo in a subset of patients who had very strong family histories of bipolar disorder (R. L. Findling, 2002; R. L. Findling, Gracious, McNamara, & Calabrese, 2000). As these studies addressed acute improvement, longitudinal controlled studies are still needed to determine the efficacy of valproate in actual prevention of BD development.

Physiological Effects of Candidate Pharmacologic Agents

When considering pharmacologic intervention, risks versus benefits of treatment also need to be considered. For example, potential adverse effects of valproate therapy include sedation, weight gain, and potential neuroendocrine effects leading to polycystic ovarian syndrome or osteoporosis (K. Chang & Simeonova, 2004). Although these conditions are relatively manageable and reversible, these are fairly acute adverse effects, mostly occurring over weeks to a few years. As valproate has been used extensively since the 1980s in patients with epilepsy or BD, including children, researchers should have long-term adverse effects data. Yet currently there is little published in this regard (Rana et al., 2005). Therefore, it is not only difficult to quantify the risks of *not* receiving treatment for children at putative risk for BD, but also difficult to discern the long-term risks of receiving such treatment.

Furthermore, although behavioral effects of these medications may be largely positive, what are the direct effects on the brain? Six bipolar offspring with putative prodromal BD who participated in the previously discussed divalproex study (K. D. Chang, Dienes et al., 2003), were scanned pre- and postdivalproex treatment using functional magnetic resonance imaging (fMRI), performing a task involving watching affectively valenced pictures. participants had significantly greater prefrontal (DLPFC) activation after divalproex treatment compared to healthy controls also scanned at 12-week intervals. figure 14-4).

Thus, it appears that functional changes in the brain may be detected after medication treatment. These findings are consistent with the hypothesis that as symptoms and functioning improve in children at high risk for BD development, prefrontal- areas increase in activation in order to maintain relative euthymia (K. D. Chang, Chang, Garrett, Adleman, & Reiss, 2003).

Additional studies with control groups and larger cohorts need to be studied in this regard. Analysis of gray matter volumes pre- and posttreatment could also shed light on neurogenic effects of these medications, similar to such studies with lithium (Moore, Bebchuk, Wilds, Chen, Manji, et al., 2000). For example, in our group of bipolar offspring with BD with decreased amygdalar volume, those with prior exposure to lithium or valproate tended to have greater amygdalar gray matter volume than those who did not (K. Chang, Karchemskiy, Barnea-Goraly, Garrett, et al., 2005). However, we do not know whether administration of these medications led to new amygdalar neurons or instead protected existing neurons from death due to toxicity or apoptosis.

It is not clear whether these brain changes after medication treatment are safe and/or desirable, but when coupled with behavioral and symptomatic improvement, it would seem that these are positive effects on brain structure and func-

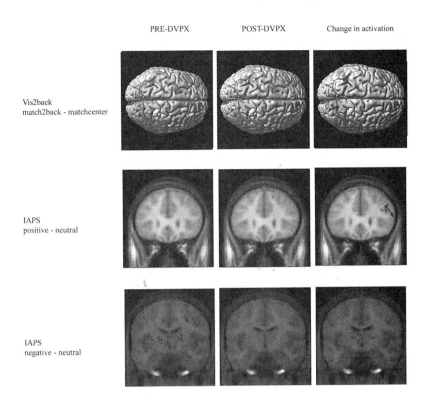

Figure 14-4 Areas of activation and deactivation in pediatric patients with putative pro-dromal BD before and after 12 weeks of divalproex monotherapy (red = areas of activation; blue = areas of decreases in activation compared to baseline). See color insert.

tion. The ability of the human brain to respond to pharmacologic or environmental stimuli with neurogenesis leads to the possibility of newly formed neuronal circuits "healing" brain abnormalities that would otherwise lead to full BD. The exciting potential of pharmacologic prevention of BD cannot be ignored and deserves further careful study.

Psychotherapeutic Interventions

As discussed earlier, it has been generally believed that psychosocial stressors such as dysfunctional family environments, stressful life events, and ineffective coping strategies interact with genetic predispositions to induce the full expression of BD (Post et al., 2001). Thus, specific psychotherapeutic interventions targeted at these psychosocial factors in high-risk individuals may help prevent or delay the onset of BD.

Psychotherapy can be less invasive than pharmacotherapy and may prove as or even more effective in illness prevention. Unlike treatment with medication, which may be accompanied by deleterious side effects and cannot specifically treat psychosocial stressors, psychotherapy is a safe modality that can be designed to address specific stressors such as unstable family environments and ineffective coping styles. Therefore, although requiring more time and conscious effort from both patients and clinicians, psychotherapy has the potential for precise, targeted intervention.

Utility of Psychotherapy in the Treatment of BD

One can infer the utility of psychotherapeutic interventions for the *prevention* of BD development from data supporting the efficacy of psychosocial interventions for the *treatment* and *prevention of relapse* of BD. It is currently recommended that all patients with BD receive both medication and adjunct psychotherapy (Keller, 2004; Kowatch et al., 2005). Thus, although extensive advances have been made in the pharmacological treatment of BD, it has become apparent that medication alone is not enough for the management of this chronic, recurrent illness. Medication noncompliance, lack of ability to recognize symptom exacerbation, and the inability to cope with stressors that precipitate illness episodes are problematic for many individuals with BD and are often related to illness relapse (Lam, Hayward, Watkins, Wright, & Sham, 2005; Miklowitz et al., 2000; Vieta & Colom, 2004).

Psychoeducation, cognitive behavioral therapy, family therapy, and interpersonal and social-rhythm therapy have all been demonstrated to decrease frequency of mood episodes, increase medication compliance, and improve overall functioning in adults with BD (Frank, Swartz, & Kupfer, 2000; Lam et al., 2005; Miklowitz et al., 2000; Perry, Tarrier, Morriss, McCarthy, & Limb, 1999). Although these treatments vary in theoretical approaches, they all share a focus on medication adherence, symptom recognition and management, social and family problem solving, and improvement of communication skills (Otto, Reilly-Harrington, & Sachs, 2003). More recently, researchers have begun to modify and test the efficacy of adjunctive psychosocial interventions for children and adolescents with BD. Though still under development, treatments such as Family Focused Therapy for Adolescents (FFT-A; Miklowitz et al., 2004), Multi-Family Psychoeducation Groups (Fristad, Gavazzi, & Mackinaw-Koons, 2003), and a modified cognitive behavior therapy combined with family therapy (Pavuluri et al., 2004) have shown initial success in decreasing symptom severity and preventing relapse in children with BD.

FFT-A is a modification of the adult version of FFT, addressing developmental issues and unique clinical presentations of adolescents with BD (Miklowitz et al., 2004). FFT has been shown to reduce relapse rates, enhance stabilization of mood symptoms, improve medication compliance, and decrease stressful family interactions in adults with BD (Miklowitz et al., 2000). In an open trial of this modified therapy, 21 sessions of FFT-A were administered to 20 adolescents with BD who had an exacerbation of manic, depressed, or mixed symptoms within the previous 3 months. In addition to an introductory session and a final, wrap-up session, the sessions were divided into 9 sessions of psychoeducation, 5 of enhancing communication skills, and 5 of learning problem solving skills. This open treatment trial found that FFT-A, in combination with standard pharmacotherapy, was associated with improvements in both depression and mania symptoms, as well as decreased behavioral problems over the course of 1 year. This efficacy of this intervention is currently being further studied in a multisite, randomized, controlled trial.

Psychotherapeutic Interventions for the Prevention of BD

Of the existing psychosocial interventions for children with BD, it appears evident that implementing a family therapy treatment model would be most effective for bipolar offspring at high risk for developing BD. Focusing on the family unit is essential given that children and adolescents typically live with their parents and are more dependent on their families than adults. Moreover, by definition, one or more of the parents of the at-risk bipolar offspring will have BD themselves. In general, family environmental factors are correlated with the course and occurrence of mood disorders (Miklowitz & Hooley, 1998) and when several individuals are struggling with mood regulation, the likelihood of a chaotic and potentially stressful family environment increases greatly. Several studies have found that adult bipolar patients who have parents or spouses who express high levels of criticism, hostility, or are emotionally overinvolved (or families with high expressed emotion) have poorer outcomes than BD patients with more healthy or low expressed emotion environments (Honig, Hofman, Rozendaal, & Dingemans, 1997; Miklowitz & Hooley, 1998). Also, many of the children at high risk for developing BD are already on complicated medication regimes that can be hard to maintain in a chaotic family environment. In order to prevent BD in high-risk children and adolescents it is important to treat the whole family, thus enabling all members to better understand the signs and symptoms of the illness, develop treatment plans, manage stressors, and promote an overall healthy family environment.

We are currently developing a study to test the efficacy of a modified version of FFT-A for symptomatic bipolar offspring. FFT-A currently consists of three phases: psychoeducation, communication enhancement, and problem-solving skills training. All three topics will be addressed, but a special emphasis will be placed on monitoring and prevention issues most salient to a high-risk population. Another unique aspect of the planned interventions is the inclusion of sessions designed to enhance mood stability in the bipolar parent as well as the child at high risk for developing the illness themselves. We will then be able to determine whether parental stability is linked to improved offspring outcome as well. We anticipate that early intervention with FFT-A will decrease mood and behavioral symptoms, improve the child's social and academic functioning, improve family interactions, and provide the child and the family with the overall skills to minimize as well as cope effectively with stressful events. Implementing such an intervention in this population may not only prove useful in preventing early-onset BD in at-risk children, but should also help the affected parent(s) better manage their own symptoms.

The exploration of the impact of these psychosocial interventions on high-risk populations is important. These interventions clearly target the "environment" portion of the "gene + environment = BD" equation. It is possible that psychotherapy also targets the "gene" portion. That is, development of more appropriate coping strategies and cognitive appraisal of self mood state and vigilance toward symptoms of relapse likely strengthens the ability of PFC to regulate abnormal subcortical/limbic activity (figure 14-1). There may even be actual neurobiological change resulting from psychotherapeutic intervention that counteracts and lessens the impact of the inborn genetic/brain characteristics that predispose to BD. This possibility argues for further neuroimaging studies measuring change following such interventions.

Conclusions

There is still much work to be done to discover both methods of BD risk detection and methods of early preventative intervention. We need more understanding of the developmental neuropathophysiology of BD and how gene-environment interactions lead to the beginning of kindling. We need controlled longitudinal studies of interventions, both psychosocial and pharmacologic, for periods at least 3 to 4 years. In order to counteract the natural course of BD development, we need to understand how to reduce exogenous stressors and increase internal stress buffers. The most appropriate psychosocial interventions still need to be determined. Pharmacologic candidates need further study to determine which carry the highest risk-to-benefit ratio and which have the most potential for neuroprotection.

Groups at highest risk for BD development deserve to be the first studied for such interventions, but as we continue to understand this area, then interventions could be gradually extended to populations at lower risk levels. Currently we believe that those in the highest-risk population are children and adolescents with a strong family history of BD who themselves have moderate mood disturbances. Biological markers will help to further delineate risk in the near future. Promising genetic markers include the 5-HTT and BDNF polymorphisms or evidence of trinucleotide repeat expansions in candidate gene areas. Abnormalities in prefrontal-subcortical areas and circuits, including decreased amygdalar gray matter and overactivation of these circuits in response to stress or affective stimuli, deserve further study as additional biological markers to be used. It is likely that in the next 5 to 10 years we will be able to use a set of 10 or so factors to quantify risk for BD development. Such a set could include current symptomatology, family history, and genetic and brain markers. Ideally, the degree of risk would then be correlated with degree of intervention needed—none, psychotherapy only, or psychotherapy combined with medications.

The most tantalizing aspect of prevention is that early intervention would lead to a change in trajectory of brain development, such that a normal trajectory would be achieved and the brain, which typically continues to develop through early adulthood, would "heal itself." Then such medication or psychosocial interventions could be removed, with the child/adolescent/adult continuing to function free of psychiatric symptomatology. This is a far cry from the current recommendations regarding the treatment of children and adolescents with fully developed BD: Most experts agree that such patients usually require lifelong treatment with medications and psychotherapy (Kowatch et al., 2005). This dire outcome highlights the significant need for further research geared toward preventing this debilitating and life-threatening disorder from ever reaching this irreversible state in at-risk individuals.

References

Akiskal, H. S. (1996). The prevalent clinical spectrum of bipolar disorders: Beyond DSM-IV. *Journal of Clinical Psychopharmacology, 16*(2 Suppl. 1), 4S–14S.

Akiskal, H. S., Bourgeois, M. L., Angst, J., Post, R., Moller, H., & Hirschfeld, R. (2000). Re-evaluating the prevalence of and diagnostic composition within the broad clinical spectrum of bipolar disorders. *Journal of Affective Disorders, 59 Suppl 1*, S5–S30.

Altshuler, L. L., Bartzokis, G., Grieder, T., Curran, J., Jimenez, T., Leight, K., et al. (2000). An MRI study of temporal lobe structures in men with bipolar disorder or schizophrenia. *Biological Psychiatry, 48*(2), 147–162.

American Psychiatric Association. (1994). *Diagnostic and statistical manual of mental disorders* (4th ed.). Washington, DC: Author.

Baumer, F., Howe, M., Gallelli, K., Chang, K.D. (2006). A Pilot Study of antidepressant-induced mania in pediatric bipolar disorder: characteristics, risk factors, and the serotonin transporter gene. *Biological Psychiatry, 60*, 1005–1012.

Bellivier, F., Golmard, J. L., Henry, C., Leboyer, M., & Schurhoff, F. (2001). Admixture analysis of age at onset in bipolar I affective disorder. *Archives of General Psychiatry, 58*(5), 510–512.

Biederman, J., Faraone, S., Mick, E., Wozniak, J., Chen, L., Ouellette, C., et al. (1996). Attention-deficit hyperactivity disorder and juvenile mania: An overlooked comorbidity? *Journal of the American Academy of Child and Adolescent Psychiatry, 35*(8), 997–1008.

Blumberg, H. P., Charney, D. S., & Krystal, J. H. (2002). Frontotemporal neural systems in bipolar disorder. *Seminars in Clinical Neuropsychiatry, 7*(4), 243–254.

Blumberg, H. P., Kaufman, J., Martin, A., Whiteman, R., Zhang, J. H., Gore, J. C., et al. (2003). Amygdala and hippocampal volumes in adolescents and adults with bipolar disorder. *Archives of General Psychiatry, 60*(12), 1201–1208.

Blumberg, H. P., Leung, H. C., Skudlarski, P., Lacadie, C. M., Fredericks, C. A., Harris,

B. C., et al. (2003). A functional magnetic resonance imaging study of bipolar disorder: State- and trait-related dysfunction in ventral prefrontal cortices. *Archives of General Psychiatry, 60*(6), 601–609.

Blumberg, H. P., Martin, A., Kaufman, J., Leung, H. C., Skudlarski, P., Lacadie, C., et al. (2003). Frontostriatal abnormalities in adolescents with bipolar disorder: Preliminary observations from functional MRI. *American Journal of Psychiatry, 160*(7), 1345–1347.

Calabresi, P., Marti, M., Picconi, B., Saulle, E., Costa, C., Centonze, D., et al. (2003). Lamotrigine and remacemide protect striatal neurons against in vitro ischemia: An electrophysiological study. *Experimental Neurology, 182*(2), 461–469.

Cannon, T. D., Huttunen, M. O., Dahlstrom, M., Larmo, I., Rasanen, P., & Juriloo, A. (2002). Antipsychotic drug treatment in the prodromal phase of schizophrenia. *American Journal of Psychiatry, 159*(7), 1230–1232.

Carlson, G. A., & Weintraub, S. (1993). Childhood behavior problems and bipolar disorder—relationship or coincidence? *Journal of Affective Disorders, 28*(3), 143–153.

Carter, T. D., Mundo, E., Parikh, S. V., & Kennedy, J. L. (2003). Early age at onset as a risk factor for poor outcome of bipolar disorder. *Journal of Psychiatric Research, 37*(4), 297–303.

Caspi, A., Sugden, K., Moffitt, T. E., Taylor, A., Craig, I. W., Harrington, H., et al. (2003). Influence of life stress on depression: Moderation by a polymorphism in the 5-HTT gene. *Science, 301*(5631), 386–389.

Chang, K., Adleman, N. E., Dienes, K., Simeonova, D. I., Menon, V., & Reiss, A. (2004). Anomalous prefrontal-subcortical activation in familial pediatric bipolar disorder: A functional magnetic resonance imaging investigation. *Archives of General Psychiatry, 61*(8), 781–792.

Chang, K., Karchemskiy, A., Barnea-Goraly, N., Garrett, A., Simeonova, D. I., & Reiss, A. (2005). Reduced amygdalar gray matter volume in familial pediatric bipolar disorder. *Journal of the American Academy of Child and Adolescent Psychiatry, 44*(6), 565–573.

Chang, K., Barnea-Goraly, N., Karchemskiy, A., Simeonova, D. I., Barnes, P., Ketter, T., Reiss, A.L. (2005). Cortical MRI findings in pediatric familial bipolar disorder. *Biological Psychiatry 58*, 197–203.

Chang, K.D., Saxena, K., Howe, M., Simeonova, D. (2006). Psychotropic medication exposure and age at onset of bipolar disorder in offspring of parents with bipolar disorder. (In review).

Chang, K., & Simeonova, D. (2004). Mood stabilizers: Use in pediatric psychopharmacology. In H. Steiner, K. Chang, J. Lock & J. Wilson (Eds.), *Handbook of mental health interventions in children and adolescents: An integrated developmental approach* (pp. 363–412). New York: Jossey-Bass.

Chang, K., Steiner, H., Dienes, K., Adleman, N., & Ketter, T. (2003). Bipolar offspring: A window into bipolar disorder evolution. *Biological Psychiatry, 53*(11), 945–951.

Chang, K. D. (2000). Attention-deficit hyperactivity disorder. In D. F. Darko (Ed.), *Medicine, ob/gyn, psychiatry, and surgery/psychiatry*. St. Petersburg, FL: eMedicine.com.

Chang, K. D., Blasey, C. M., Ketter, T. A., & Steiner, H. (2003). Temperament characteristics of child and adolescent bipolar offspring. *Journal of Affective Disorders, 77*(1), 11–19.

Chang, K. D., Chang, M., Garrett, A., Adleman, N., & Reiss, A. L. (2003, December 7-11). *Brain activation patterns correlating with positive response to divalproex in children at high risk for bipolar disorder.* Paper presented at the 42nd Annual Meeting of the American College of Neuropsychopharmacology, San Juan, Puerto Rico.

Chang, K. D., Dienes, K., Blasey, C., Adleman, N., Ketter, T., & Steiner, H. (2003). Divalproex monotherapy in the treatment of bipolar offspring with mood and behavioral disorders and at least mild affective symptoms. *Journal of Clinical Psychiatry, 64*(8), 936–942.

Chang, K. D., & Steiner, H. (2003). Offspring studies in child and early adolescent bipolar disorder. In B. Geller & M. DelBello (Eds.), *Bipolar disorder in childhood and early adolescence* (pp. 107–129). New York: The Guilford Press.

Chang, K. D., Steiner, H., & Ketter, T. A. (2000). Psychiatric phenomenology of child and adolescent bipolar offspring. *Journal of the American Academy of Child and Adolescent Psychiatry, 39*(4), 453–460.

Chen, B. K., Sassi, R., Axelson, D., Hatch, J. P., Sanches, M., Nicoletti, M., et al. (2004). Cross-sectional study of abnormal amygdala development in adolescents and young adults with bipolar disorder. *Biological Psychiatry, 56*(6), 399–405.

Chen, G., Huang, L. D., Jiang, Y. M., & Manji, H. K. (1999). The mood-stabilizing agent valproate inhibits the activity of glycogen synthase kinase-3. *Journal of Neurochemistry, 72*(3), 1327–1330.

Chen, G., Zeng, W. Z., Yuan, P. X., Huang, L. D., Jiang, Y. M., Zhao, Z. H., et al. (1999). The mood-stabilizing agents lithium and valproate robustly increase the levels of the neuroprotective protein bcl-2 in the CNS. *Journal of Neurochemistry, 72*(2), 879–882.

Chen, Y. W., & Dilsaver, S. C. (1996). Lifetime rates of suicide attempts among participants with bipolar and unipolar disorders relative to participants with other Axis I disorders. *Biological Psychiatry, 39*(10), 896–899.

Chengappa, K. N., Kupfer, D. J., Frank, E., Houck, P. R., Grochocinski, V. J., Cluss, P. A., et al. (2003). Relationship of birth cohort and early age at onset of illness in a bipolar disorder case registry. *American Journal of Psychiatry, 160*(9), 1636–1642.

Coppell, A. L., Pei, Q., & Zetterstrom, T. S. (2003). Bi-phasic change in BDNF gene expression following antidepressant drug treatment. *Neuropharmacology, 44*(7), 903–910.

D'Sa, C., & Duman, R. S. (2002). Antidepressants and neuroplasticity. *Bipolar Disorders, 4*(3), 183–194.

DelBello, M. P., Zimmerman, M. E., Mills, N. P., Getz, G. E., & Strakowski, S. M. (2004). Magnetic resonance imaging analysis of amygdala and other subcortical brain regions in adolescents with bipolar disorder. *Bipolar Disorders, 6*(1), 43–52.

Drevets, W. C., Price, J. L., Bardgett, M. E., Reich, T., Todd, R. D., & Raichle, M. E. (2002). Glucose metabolism in the amygdala in depression: Relationship to diagnostic subtype and plasma cortisol levels. *Pharmacology Biochemistry and Behavior, 71*(3), 431–447.

Drevets, W. C., Price, J. L., Simpson, J. R., Jr., Todd, R. D., Reich, T., Vannier, M., et al. (1997). Subgenual prefrontal cortex abnormalities in mood disorders. *Nature, 386*(6627), 824–827.

Egan, M. F., Kojima, M., Callicott, J. H., Goldberg, T. E., Kolachana, B. S., Bertolino, A., et al. (2003). The BDNF val66met polymorphism affects activity-dependent secretion of BDNF and human memory and hippocampal function. *Cell, 112*(2), 257–269.

Egeland, J. A., Hostetter, A. M., Pauls, D. L., & Sussex, J. N. (2000). Prodromal symptoms before onset of manic-depressive disorder suggested by first hospital admission histories. *Journal of the American Academy of Child and Adolescent Psychiatry, 39*(10), 1245–1252.

Egeland, J. A., Shaw, J. A., Endicott, J., Pauls, D. L., Allen, C. R., Hostetter, A. M., et al.

(2003). Prospective study of prodromal features for bipolarity in well Amish children. *Journal of the American Academy of Child and Adolescent Psychiatry, 42*(7), 786–796.

Eriksson, P. S., Perfilieva, E., Bjork-Eriksson, T., Alborn, A. M., Nordborg, C., Peterson, D. A., et al. (1998). Neurogenesis in the adult human hippocampus. *Nature Medicine, 4*(11), 1313–1317.

Faedda, G. L., Baldessarini, R. J., Glovinsky, I. P., & Austin, N. B. (2004). Treatment-emergent mania in pediatric bipolar disorder: A retrospective case review. *Journal of Affective Disorders, 82*(1), 149–158.

Faraone, S. V., Biederman, J., Mennin, D., Wozniak, J., & Spencer, T. (1997). Attention-deficit hyperactivity disorder with bipolar disorder: A familial subtype? *Journal of the American Academy of Child and Adolescent Psychiatry, 36*(10), 1378–1387, discussion 1387–1390.

Faraone, S. V., Biederman, J., Wozniak, J., Mundy, E., Mennin, D., & O'Donnell, D. (1997). Is comorbidity with ADHD a marker for juvenile-onset mania? *Journal of the American Academy of Child and Adolescent Psychiatry, 36*(8), 1046–1055.

Faraone, S. V., & Tsuang, M. T. (2003). Heterogeneity and the genetics of bipolar disorder. *American Journal of Medical Genetics Part C: Seminars in Medical Genetics, 123*(1), 1–9.

Fergus, E. L., Miller, R. B., Luckenbaugh, D. A., Leverich, G. S., Findling, R. L., Speer, A. M., et al. (2003). Is there progression from irritability/dyscontrol to major depressive and manic symptoms? A retrospective community survey of parents of bipolar children. *Journal of Affective Disorders, 77*(1), 71–78.

Findling, R. L. (2002). *Combination pharmacotherapy in pediatric bipolar disorders.* Paper presented at the Scientific Proceedings of the 49th Annual Meeting of the American Academy of Child and Adolescent Psychiatry, San Francisco, CA.

Findling, R. L., Gracious, B. L., McNamara, N. K., & Calabrese, J. R. (2000). The rationale, design, and progress of two novel maintenance treatment studies in pediatric bipolarity. *Acta Neuropsychiatrica, 12*, 136–138.

Findling, R. L., Kowatch, R. A., & Post, R. M. (2003). *Pediatric bipolar disorder: A handbook for clinicians.* London: Martin Dunitz.

Frank, E., Swartz, H. A., & Kupfer, D. J. (2000). Interpersonal and social rhythm therapy: Managing the chaos of bipolar disorder. *Biological Psychiatry, 48*(6), 593–604.

Frazier J.A., Chiu S., Breeze, J.L., Makris, N., Lange, N., Kennedy, D.N., Herbert, M.R., Bent, E.K., Koneru, V.K., Dieterich, M.E., Hodge, S.M., Rauch, S.L., Grant, P.E., Cohen, B.M., Seidman, L.J., Caviness, V.S., Biederman, J. (2005). Structural brain magnetic resonance imaging of limbic and thalamic volumes in pediatric bipolar disorder. *American Journal of Psychiatry 162*(7): 1256–1265.

Fristad, M. A., Gavazzi, S. M., & Mackinaw-Koons, B. (2003). Family psychoeducation: An adjunctive intervention for children with bipolar disorder. *Biological Psychiatry, 53*(11), 1000–1008.

Gallelli, K., Wagner, C., Karchemskiy, A., Howe, M., Spielman, D., Reiss, A., et al. (2005). N-acetylaspartate levels in bipolar offspring with and at high-risk for bipolar disorder. Bipolar *Disorders, 7*(6), 589–597.

Geller, B., Badner, J. A., Tillman, R., Christian, S. L., Bolhofner, K., & Cook, E. H., Jr. (2004). Linkage disequilibrium of the brain-derived neurotrophic factor Val66Met polymorphism in children with a prepubertal and early adolescent bipolar disorder phenotype. *American Journal of Psychiatry, 161*(9), 1698–1700.

Geller, B., Cooper, T. B., Zimerman, B., Frazier, J., Williams, M., Heath, J., et al. (1998).

Lithium for prepubertal depressed children with family history predictors of future bipolarity: A double-blind, placebo-controlled study. *Journal of Affective Disorders, 51*(2), 165–175.

Geller, B., Fox, L. W., & Clark, K. A. (1994). Rate and predictors of prepubertal bipolarity during follow-up of 6– to 12–year-old depressed children. *Journal of the American Academy of Child and Adolescent Psychiatry, 33*(4), 461–468.

Geller, B., & Luby, J. (1997). Child and adolescent bipolar disorder: A review of the past 10 years. *Journal of the American Academy of Child and Adolescent Psychiatry, 36*(9), 1168–1176.

Geller, B., Zimerman, B., Williams, M., Bolhofner, K., & Craney, J. L. (2001). Adult psychosocial outcome of prepubertal major depressive disorder. *Journal of the American Academy of Child and Adolescent Psychiatry, 40*(6), 673–677.

Goethals, I., Audenaert, K., Van de Wiele, C., & Dierckx, R. (2004). The prefrontal cortex: Insights from functional neuroimaging using cognitive activation tasks. *European Journal of Nuclear Medicine and Molecular Imagin, 31*(3), 408–416.

Goggi, J., Pullar, I. A., Carney, S. L., & Bradford, H. F. (2002). Modulation of neurotransmitter release induced by brain-derived neurotrophic factor in rat brain striatal slices in vitro. *Brain Research, 941*(1–2), 34–42.

Goodwin, F. K., & Jamison, K. R. (1990). *Manic-depressive illness.* New York: Oxford University Press.

Goossens, D., Del-Favero, J., & Van Broeckhoven, C. (2001). Trinucleotide repeat expansions: Do they contribute to bipolar disorder? *Brain Research Bulletin, 56*(3–4), 243–257.

Gould, T. D., Chen, G., & Manji, H. K. (2004). In vivo evidence in the brain for lithium inhibition of glycogen synthase kinase-3. *Neuropsychopharmacology, 29*(1), 32–38.

Hariri, A. R., Drabant, E. M., Munoz, K. E., Kolachana, B. S., Mattay, V. S., Egan, M. F., et al. (2005). A susceptibility gene for affective disorders and the response of the human amygdala. *Archives of General Psychiatry, 62*(2), 146–152.

Hariri, A. R., Goldberg, T. E., Mattay, V. S., Kolachana, B. S., Callicott, J. H., Egan, M. F., et al. (2003). Brain-derived neurotrophic factor val66met polymorphism affects human memory-related hippocampal activity and predicts memory performance. *Journal of Neuroscience, 23*(17), 6690–6694.

Hariri, A. R., Mattay, V. S., Tessitore, A., Kolachana, B., Fera, F., Goldman, D., et al. (2002). Serotonin transporter genetic variation and the response of the human amygdala. *Science, 297*(5580), 400–403.

Hariri, A. R., & Weinberger, D. R. (2003). Functional neuroimaging of genetic variation in serotonergic neurotransmission. *Genes, Brain and Behavior, 2*(6), 341–349.

Hashimoto, R., Senatorov, V., Kanai, H., Leeds, P., & Chuang, D. M. (2003). Lithium stimulates progenitor proliferation in cultured brain neurons. *Neuroscience, 117*(1), 55–61.

Hashimoto, R., Takei, N., Shimazu, K., Christ, L., Lu, B., & Chuang, D. M. (2002). Lithium induces brain-derived neurotrophic factor and activates TrkB in rodent cortical neurons: An essential step for neuroprotection against glutamate excitotoxicity. *Neuropharmacology, 43*(7), 1173–1179.

Heinz, A., Braus, D. F., Smolka, M. N., Wrase, J., Puls, I., Hermann, D., et al. (2005). Amygdala-prefrontal coupling depends on a genetic variation of the serotonin transporter. *Nature Neuroscience, 8*(1), 20–21.

Hodgins, S., Faucher, B., Zarax, A., & Ellenbogen, M. (2002). Children of parents with bipolar disorder: A population at high risk for major affective disorders. *Child and Adolescent Psychiatric Clinics of North America, 11*(3), 533–53, ix.

Honig, A., Hofman, A., Rozendaal, N., & Dingemans, P. (1997). Psycho-education in bipolar disorder: Effect on expressed emotion. *Psychiatry Research, 72*(1), 17–22.

Howe, M. G., Yee, J., Baumer, F., Simeonova, D., Hallmayer, J., & Chang, K. D. (2004, October). *Age at onset in familial bipolar disorder.* Poster session presented at the 51st Annual Meeting of the American Academy of Child and Adolescent Psychiatry, Washington, DC.

Inglefield, J. R., Perry, J. M., & Schwartz, R. D. (1995). Postischemic inhibition of GABA reuptake by tiagabine slows neuronal death in the gerbil hippocampus. *Hippocampus, 5*(5), 460–468.

Jin, N., Kovacs, A. D., Sui, Z., Dewhurst, S., & Maggirwar, S. B. (2005). Opposite effects of lithium and valproic acid on trophic factor deprivation-induced glycogen synthase kinase-3 activation, c-Jun expression and neuronal cell death. *Neuropharmacology, 48*(4), 576–583.

Kaufman, J., Yang, B. Z., Douglas-Palumberi, H., Houshyar, S., Lipschitz, D., Krystal, J. H., et al. (2004). Social supports and serotonin transporter gene moderate depression in maltreated children. *Proceedings of the National Academy of Sciences of the United States of America, 101*(49), 17316–17321.

Keller, M. B. (2004). Improving the course of illness and promoting continuation of treatment of bipolar disorder. *Journal of Clinical Psychiatry, 65 Suppl 15,* 10–14.

Kleinman, L., Lowin, A., Flood, E., Gandhi, G., Edgell, E., & Revicki, D. (2003). Costs of bipolar disorder. *Pharmacoeconomics, 21*(9), 601–622.

Kowatch, R. A., Fristad, M., Birmaher, B., Wagner, K. D., Findling, R. L., & Hellander, M. (2005). Treatment guidelines for children and adolescents with bipolar disorder. *Journal of the American Academy of Child and Adolescent Psychiatry, 44*(3), 213–235.

Kraeplin, E. (1921). *Manic-depressive insanity and paranoia.* Edinburgh: ES Livingstone.

Kudin, A. P., Debska-Vielhaber, G., Vielhaber, S., Elger, C. E., & Kunz, W. S. (2004). The mechanism of neuroprotection by topiramate in an animal model of epilepsy. *Epilepsia, 45*(12), 1478–1487.

Laeng, P., Pitts, R. L., Lemire, A. L., Drabik, C. E., Weiner, A., Tang, H., et al. (2004). The mood stabilizer valproic acid stimulates GABA neurogenesis from rat forebrain stem cells. *Journal of Neurochemistry, 91*(1), 238–251.

Lam, D. H., Hayward, P., Watkins, E. R., Wright, K., & Sham, P. (2005). Relapse prevention in patients with bipolar disorder: Cognitive therapy outcome after 2 years. *American Journal of Psychiatry, 162*(2), 324–329.

Lapalme, M., Hodgins, S., & LaRoche, C. (1997). Children of parents with bipolar disorder: A meta-analysis of risk for mental disorders. *Canadian Journal of Psychiatry, 42*(6), 623–631.

Lasky-Su, J. A., Faraone, S. V., Glatt, S. J., & Tsuang, M. T. (2004). Meta-analysis of the association between two polymorphisms in the serotonin transporter gene and affective disorders. *American Journal of Medical Genetics. Part B: Neuropsychiatric Genetics, 133B*(1), 110–115.

Leker, R. R., & Neufeld, M. Y. (2003). Anti-epileptic drugs as possible neuroprotectants in cerebral ischemia. *Brain Research: Brain Research Reviews, 42*(3), 187–203.

Lim, K. O., Rosenbloom, M. J., Faustman, W. O., Sullivan, E. V., & Pfefferbaum, A. (1999). Cortical gray matter deficit in patients with bipolar disorder. *Schizophrenia Research, 40*(3), 219–227.

Lish, J. D., Dime-Meenan, S., Whybrow, P. C., Price, R. A., & Hirschfeld, R. M. (1994). The National Depressive and Manic-depressive Association (DMDA) survey of bipolar members. *Journal of Affective Disorders, 31*(4), 281–294.

Lopez-Larson, M. P., DelBello, M. P., Zimmerman, M. E., Schwiers, M. L., & Strakowski, S. M. (2002). Regional prefrontal gray and white matter abnormalities in bipolar disorder. *Biological Psychiatry, 52*(2), 93–100.

Loscher, W., Fisher, J. E., Nau, H., & Honack, D. (1989). Valproic acid in amygdala-kindled rats: Alterations in anticonvulsant efficacy, adverse effects and drug and metabolite levels in various brain regions during chronic treatment. *The Journal of Pharmacology and Experimental Therapeutics, 250*(3), 1067–1078.

Mamounas, L. A., Altar, C. A., Blue, M. E., Kaplan, D. R., Tessarollo, L., & Lyons, W. E. (2000). BDNF promotes the regenerative sprouting, but not survival, of injured serotonergic axons in the adult rat brain. *Journal of Neuroscience, 20*(2), 771–782.

Manji, H. K., & Lenox, R. H. (1994). Long-term action of lithium: A role for transcriptional and posttranscriptional factors regulated by protein kinase C. *Synapse, 16*(1), 11–28.

Manji, H. K., & Lenox, R. H. (1999). Ziskind-Somerfeld Research Award. Protein kinase C signaling in the brain: Molecular transduction of mood stabilization in the treatment of manic-depressive illness. *Biological Psychiatry, 46*(10), 1328–1351.

Manji, H. K., Moore, G. J., & Chen, G. (2000a). Clinical and preclinical evidence for the neurotrophic effects of mood stabilizers: Implications for the pathophysiology and treatment of manic-depressive illness. *Biological Psychiatry, 48*(8), 740–754.

Manji, H. K., Moore, G. J., & Chen, G. (2000b). Lithium up-regulates the cytoprotective protein Bcl-2 in the CNS in vivo: A role for neurotrophic and neuroprotective effects in manic depressive illness. *Journal of Clinical Psychiatry, 61 Suppl 9*, 82–96.

Martenyi, F., Brown, E. B., Zhang, H., Prakash, A., & Koke, S. C. (2002, March). Fluoxetine versus placebo in posttraumatic stress disorder. *Journal of Clinical Psychiatry, 63*(3), 199–206.

Mayberg, H. S. (1997). Limbic-cortical dysregulation: A proposed model of depression. *Journal of Neuropsychiatry and Clinical Neurosciences, 9*(3), 471–481.

McInnis, M. G., McMahon, F. J., Chase, G. A., Simpson, S. G., Ross, C. A., & DePaulo, J. R., Jr. (1993). Anticipation in bipolar affective disorder [see comments]. *American Journal of Human Genetics, 53*(2), 385–390.

Miklowitz, D. J., George, E. L., Axelson, D. A., Kim, E. Y., Birmaher, B., Schneck, C., et al. (2004). Family-focused treatment for adolescents with bipolar disorder. *Journal of Affective Disorders, 82 Suppl 1*, S113–128.

Miklowitz, D. J., & Hooley, J. M. (1998). Developing family psychoeducational treatments for patients with bipolar and other severe psychiatric disorders. A pathway from basic research to clinical trials. *Journal of Marital and Family Therapy, 24*(4), 419–435.

Miklowitz, D. J., Simoneau, T. L., George, E. L., Richards, J. A., Kalbag, A., Sachs-Ericsson, N., et al. (2000). Family-focused treatment of bipolar disorder: 1-year effects of a psychoeducational program in conjunction with pharmacotherapy. *Biological Psychiatry, 48*(6), 582–592.

Moore, G. J., Bebchuk, J. M., Hasanat, K., Chen, G., Seraji-Bozorgzad, N., Wilds, I. B., et al. (2000). Lithium increases N-acetyl-aspartate in the human brain: In vivo evidence in support of bcl-2's neurotrophic effects? *Biological Psychiatry, 48*(1), 1–8.

Moore, G. J., Bebchuk, J. M., Wilds, I. B., Chen, G., & Manji, H. K. (2000). Lithium-induced increase in human brain grey matter. *Lancet, 356*(9237), 1241–1242.

Moore, G. J., Bebchuk, J. M., Wilds, I. B., Chen, G., Manji, H. K., & Menji, H. K. (2000). Lithium-induced increase in human brain grey matter. *Lancet, 356*(9237), 1241–1242.

Nakata, K., Ujike, H., Sakai, A., Uchida, N., Nomura, A., Imamura, T., et al. (2003). Association study of the brain-derived neurotrophic factor (BDNF) gene with bipolar disorder. *Neuroscience Letters, 337*(1), 17–20.

Neves-Pereira, M., Mundo, E., Muglia, P., King, N., Macciardi, F., & Kennedy, J. L. (2002). The brain-derived neurotrophic factor gene confers susceptibility to bipolar disorder: Evidence from a family-based association study. *American Journal of Human Genetics, 71*(3), 651–655.

Nibuya, M., Nestler, E. J., & Duman, R. S. (1996). Chronic antidepressant administration increases the expression of cAMP response element binding protein (CREB) in rat hippocampus. *Journal of Neuroscience, 16*(7), 2365–2372.

Ongur, D., Drevets, W. C., & Price, J. L. (1998). Glial reduction in the subgenual prefrontal cortex in mood disorders. *Proceedings of the National Academy of Sciences of the United States of America, 95*(22), 13290–13295.

Otto, M. W., Reilly-Harrington, N., & Sachs, G. S. (2003). Psychoeducational and cognitive-behavioral strategies in the management of bipolar disorder. *Journal of Affective Disorders, 73*(1–2), 171–181.

Pavuluri, M. N., Graczyk, P. A., Henry, D. B., Carbray, J. A., Heidenreich, J., & Miklowitz, D. J. (2004). Child- and family-focused cognitive-behavioral therapy for pediatric bipolar disorder: Development and preliminary results. *Journal of the American Academy of Child and Adolescent Psychiatry, 43*(5), 528–537.

Pearlson, G. D., Barta, P. E., Powers, R. E., Menon, R. R., Richards, S. S., Aylward, E. H., et al. (1997). Ziskind-Somerfeld Research Award 1996. Medial and superior temporal gyral volumes and cerebral asymmetry in schizophrenia versus bipolar disorder. *Biological Psychiatry, 41*(1), 1–14.

Perlis, R. H., Miyahara, S., Marangell, L. B., Wisniewski, S. R., Ostacher, M., DelBello, M. P., et al. (2004). Long-Term implications of early onset in bipolar disorder: Data from the first 1000 participants in the systematic treatment enhancement program for bipolar disorder (STEP-BD). *Biological Psychiatry, 55*(9), 875–881.

Perry, A., Tarrier, N., Morriss, R., McCarthy, E., & Limb, K. (1999). Randomised controlled trial of efficacy of teaching patients with bipolar disorder to identify early symptoms of relapse and obtain treatment. *British Medical Journal, 318*(7177), 149–153.

Pezawas, L., Meyer-Lindenberg, A., Drabant, E. M., Verchinski, B. A., Munoz, K. E., Kolachana, B. S., et al. (2005). 5-HTTLPR polymorphism impacts human cingulate-amygdala interactions: A genetic susceptibility mechanism for depression. *Nature Neuroscience, 8*(6), 828–834.

Pezawas, L., Verchinski, B. A., Mattay, V. S., Callicott, J. H., Kolachana, B. S., Straub, R. E., et al. (2004). The brain-derived neurotrophic factor val66met polymorphism and variation in human cortical morphology. *Journal of Neuroscience, 24*(45), 10099–10102.

Poo, M. M. (2001). Neurotrophins as synaptic modulators. *Nature Reviews Neuroscience, 2*(1), 24–32.

Post, R. M. (1992). Transduction of psychosocial stress into the neurobiology of recurrent affective disorder. *American Journal of Psychiatry, 149*(8), 999–1010.

Post, R. M. (2002). Do the epilepsies, pain syndromes, and affective disorders share common kindling-like mechanisms? *Epilepsy Research, 50*(1–2), 203–219.

Post, R. M., Leverich, G. S., Xing, G., & Weiss, R. B. (2001). Developmental vulnerabilities to the onset and course of bipolar disorder. *Development and Psychopathology, 13*(3), 581–598.

Post, R. M., & Weiss, S. R. (1996). A speculative model of affective illness cyclicity based on patterns of drug tolerance observed in amygdala-kindled seizures. *Molecular Neurobiology, 13*(1), 33–60.

Rajkowska, G., Halaris, A., & Selemon, L. D. (2001). Reductions in neuronal and glial density characterize the dorsolateral prefrontal cortex in bipolar disorder. *Biological Psychiatry, 49*(9), 741–752.

Ramnani, N., & Owen, A. M. (2004). Anterior prefrontal cortex: Insights into function from anatomy and neuroimaging. *Nature Reviews Neuroscience, 5*(3), 184–194.

Rana, M., Khanzode, L., Karnik, N., Saxena, K., Chang, K., & Steiner, H. (2005). Divalproex sodium in the treatment of pediatric psychiatric disorders. *Expert Review of Neurotherapeutics, 5*(2), 165–176.

Reichart, C. G., & Nolen, W. A. (2004). Earlier onset of bipolar disorder in children by antidepressants or stimulants? An hypothesis. *Journal of Affective Disorders, 78*(1), 81–84.

Roy-Byrne, P., Post, R. M., Uhde, T. W., Porcu, T., & Davis, D. (1985). The longitudinal course of recurrent affective illness: Life chart data from research patients at the NIMH. *ACTA Psychiatrica Scandinavica. Supplementum, 317*, 1–34.

Sachs, G. S., Baldassano, C. F., Truman, C. J., & Guille, C. (2000). Comorbidity of attention deficit hyperactivity disorder with early- and late-onset bipolar disorder. *American Journal of Psychiatry, 157*(3), 466–468.

Shuaib, A., Mahmood, R. H., Wishart, T., Kanthan, R., Murabit, M. A., Ijaz, S., et al. (1995). Neuroprotective effects of lamotrigine in global ischemia in gerbils. A histological, in vivo microdialysis and behavioral study. *Brain Research, 702*(1–2), 199–206.

Siegle, G. J., Steinhauer, S. R., Thase, M. E., Stenger, V. A., & Carter, C. S. (2002). Can't shake that feeling: Event-related fMRI assessment of sustained amygdala activity in response to emotional information in depressed individuals. *Biological Psychiatry, 51*(9), 693–707.

Sklar, P., Gabriel, S. B., McInnis, M. G., Bennett, P., Lim, Y. M., Tsan, G., et al. (2002). Family-based association study of 76 candidate genes in bipolar disorder: BDNF is a potential risk locus. Brain-derived neutrophic factor. *Molecular Psychiatry, 7*(6), 579–593.

Smith, G. S., Lotrich, F. E., Malhotra, A. K., Lee, A. T., Ma, Y., Kramer, E., et al. (2004). Effects of serotonin transporter promoter polymorphisms on serotonin function. *Neuropsychopharmacology, 29*(12), 2226–2234.

Smoller, J. W., & Finn, C. T. (2003). Family, twin, and adoption studies of bipolar disorder. *American Journal of Medical Genetics Part C: Seminars in Medical Genetics, 123*(1), 48–58.

Strakowski, S. M., Adler, C. M., Holland, S. K., Mills, N., & DelBello, M. P. (2004). A preliminary FMRI study of sustained attention in euthymic, unmedicated bipolar disorder. *Neuropsychopharmacology, 29*(9), 1734–1740.

Strakowski, S. M., DelBello, M. P., Adler, C., Cecil, D. M., & Sax, K. W. (2000). Neuroimaging in bipolar disorder. *Bipolar Disorders, 2*(3 Pt. 1), 148–164.

Strakowski, S. M., DelBello, M. P., Sax, K. W., Zimmerman, M. E., Shear, P. K., Hawkins, J. M., et al. (1999). Brain magnetic resonance imaging of structural abnormalities in bipolar disorder. *Archives of General Psychiatry, 56*(3), 254–260.

Stratton, S. C., Large, C. H., Cox, B., Davies, G., & Hagan, R. M. (2003). Effects of lamotrigine and levetiracetam on seizure development in a rat amygdala kindling model. *Epilepsy Research, 53*(1–2), 95–106.

Swayze, V. W., II, Andreasen, N. C., Alliger, R. J., Yuh, W. T., & Ehrhardt, J. C. (1992). Subcortical and temporal structures in affective disorder and schizophrenia: A magnetic resonance imaging study. *Biological Psychiatry, 31*(3), 221–240.

Tsuang, M. T., Stone, W. S., & Faraone, S. V. (2002). Understanding predisposition to schizophrenia: Toward intervention and prevention. *Canadian Journal of Psychiatry, 47*(6), 518–526.

Vieta, E., & Colom, F. (2004). Psychological interventions in bipolar disorder: From wishful thinking to an evidence-based approach. *ACTA Psychiatrica Scandinavica. Supplementum.*(422), 34–38.

Wals, M., Hillegers, M. H., Reichart, C. G., Ormel, J., Nolen, W. A., & Verhulst, F. C. (2001). Prevalence of psychopathology in children of a bipolar parent. *Journal of the American Academy of Child and Adolescent Psychiatry, 40*(9), 1094–1102.

Wei, Z., Bai, O., Richardson, J. S., Mousseau, D. D., & Li, X. M. (2003). Olanzapine protects PC12 cells from oxidative stress induced by hydrogen peroxide. *Journal of Neuroscience Research, 73*(3), 364–368.

Wozniak, J., Biederman, J., Kiely, K., Ablon, J. S., Faraone, S. V., Mundy, E., et al. (1995). Mania-like symptoms suggestive of childhood-onset bipolar disorder in clinically referred children. *Journal of the American Academy of Child and Adolescent Psychiatry, 34*(7), 867–876.

Yang, Y., Li, Q., Wang, C. X., Jeerakathil, T., & Shuaib, A. (2000). Dose-dependent neuroprotection with tiagabine in a focal cerebral ischemia model in rat. *Neuroreport, 11*(10), 2307–2311.

Yang, Y., Shuaib, A., Li, Q., & Siddiqui, M. M. (1998). Neuroprotection by delayed administration of topiramate in a rat model of middle cerebral artery embolization. *Brain Research, 804*(2), 169–176.

Yurgelun-Todd, D. A., Gruber, S. A., Kanayama, G., Killgore, W. D., Baird, A. A., & Young, A. D. (2000). fMRI during affect discrimination in bipolar affective disorder. *Bipolar Disorders, 2*(3 t. 2), 237–248.

Chapter 15

Resilience and Vulnerability to Trauma

Psychobiological Mechanisms

Nicole S. Cooper, Adriana Feder, Steven M. Southwick, and Dennis S. Charney

Trauma, Risk, and Resilience

Most people are exposed to at least one traumatic event during their lifetime (Bonanno, 2004; Ozer et al., 2003). Stressful life events appear to have a strong causal association with posttraumatic stress disorder (PTSD), depression (Caspi et al., 2003; Kaufman et al., 2004; Kendler et al., 2005), and other forms of psychopathology, placing people who have experienced traumatic events at a greater risk for developing stress-related mental health problems. However, not all people who have been exposed to trauma develop psychiatric problems. In fact, although the National Comorbidity Study (NCS) found that lifetime exposure to trauma was 60.7% in men and 51.2% in women (Kessler et al., 1995) in epidemiologic studies, lifetime prevalence rates of PTSD in the general population range from 7.8% to 12.3% (American Psychiatric Association, 1987; Breslau et al., 1991; Kessler et al., 1995; Resnick et al., 1993). Clearly then, psychopathology is not an inevitable consequence of trauma exposure. Why are some individuals resilient and others vulnerable?

Trauma-related factors contribute to the probability of developing PTSD and other forms of trauma-related psychopathology. For instance, NCS data indicates that certain types of trauma are associated with a much higher conditional probability of PTSD, such as rape (65.0%) and combat exposure (38.8%) for men, and rape (45.9%) and physical abuse (48.5%) for women (Kessler et al., 1995). Other factors related to the nature of the trauma itself or to the survivor's perception of his or her role in the trauma can also predict development of psychopathology. Some of these factors are trauma severity (Kessler et al., 1995), predictability, controllability and perceived threat, passive coping during and after trauma, loss (of a loved one or property), physical injury or pain, and exposure to gross body disfigurement (Jordan et al., 1991; Overmier & Murison, 2005; Yehuda, 2002, 2004). Other risk factors associated with development of posttraumatic emotional disturbance include preexisting psychiatric disorders, a family history of psycho-pathology, poor social support, and a history of childhood trauma (Breslau, 2002; Heim & Nemeroff, 2002). Furthermore, a study exploring the effects of trauma on adolescent girls indicated that in this population, psychological outcomes dif-fered depending on the type of trauma (e.g., traumatic bereavement, sexual as-sault, and physical assault) the adolescents experienced. However, cumulative effects of multiple trauma versus single trauma, and trauma versus nontrauma (i.e., individuals who have experienced no trauma), played a larger role than trauma type in differentiating groups' (grouped based on type and nature of trauma) re-sults on psychological outcome measures (Krupnick et al., 2004).

In the last decade, there has been increased interest in understanding and defin-ing the parameters of a complex construct referred to as resilience. According to Masten, resilience is a "common phenomenon that results . . . from the operation of basic human adaptational systems" (2001, p. 227) working optimally in the face of stress. Resilience describes the process of adapting well in the face of stress, adversity, trauma, or tragedy, and is characterized by the ability to bounce back quickly from negative experiences through flexible adaptation to the ever-changing demands of life. Depression and PTSD, on the other hand, may be understood in part as the result of a failure to adapt successfully to chronic emotional stress (Nemeroff et al., 2006).

Resilience/vulnerability to posttraumatic pathology is multidetermined, involv-ing an interconnected and synergistic mix of factors, such as peri- and posttrau-matic circumstances, the individual's own trauma history, psychological factors, availability of social support and biological factors such as genes and neurotrans-mitter systems (Charney, 2004; Southwick et al., 2005; Yehuda, 2004). When neurobiological systems are functioning optimally, they allow an organism to adapt to stressors or challenges and maintain homeostasis. The neurobiological compo-nent of this homeostasis is known as allostasis (McEwen, 1998). The concept of allostatic load (or more explicitly, allostatic overload), refers to a cumulative measure of physiological dysregulation across multiple biological systems (McEwen, 1998; McEwen & Stellar, 1993). Dysregulation occurs when systems are overstimulated or activated too frequently, when systems fail to return to baseline after exposure to a stressor, and when interconnected systems fail to re-spond to one another appropriately (McEwen, 1998). The effects of allostatic overload are measurable by neuroimaging, neurochemical assays and behavioral assessment. In short, stress promotes adaptation or allostasis. Prolonged stress can lead to allostatic load, which can damage brain structures, organ systems, and the delicate neurochemical balance that governs mood, emotion, cognition, and behavior (McEwen, 2004), thus increasing the risk for disease.

Like allostatic load, fear conditioning plays a significant role in the development of psychopathological responses to trauma,. Fear conditioning is a complex adaptational mechanism with psychological, behavioral, and neurobiological components, hardwired to protect an organism from reexposure to dangerous experiences; as such, conditioned fear responses are difficult to attenuate or extinguish. It is is a form of associative learning in which an organism comes to pair a neutral stimulus with an aversive event such that the neutral stimulus takes on frightening properties. The fear-conditioned organism may also generalize a feared stimulus to a broader category of stimuli. For instance, a woman who has been raped by a man may develop a fearful response to all men. Encoding, consolidation and reconsolidation of traumatic memory also play a role in this learning process (reviewed by LeDoux, 1994, 2000). The learned association takes place in the amygdala, which projects to areas of the hypothalamus and brainstem that mediate autonomic, behavioral, and endocrine responses that signal danger (Blair et al., 2001). Interactions among corticotropin releasing hormone (CRH), cortisol, and norepinephrine in the amygdala and hippocampus are involved in memory processing (McGaugh, 2002; Roozendaal et al., 2000). Conditioned fear is maintained by avoidance of feared situations, because avoidance inhibits the new learning necessary to extinguish the conditioned fear. When an organism can predict and respond appropriately to threat, it has an increased chance of survival. Furthermore, exposure to feared situations (via active coping style or exposure therapy, described below) can facilitate new adaptive association.

Early Life Environment

Much of what we know about resilience in the face of exposure to trauma comes from research with children and adolescents. Early life stress has a clearly established role in promoting future vulnerability or resilience to stress (Charney, 2004; Parker et al., 2004, 2005). The influence of childhood stress on future risk and resilience is at least bidirectional, if not multidirectional: Childhood stress that is masterable or manageable appears to carry protective properties and may contribute to the development of a more resilient adult psychological profile (Charney, 2004; Parker et al., 2004, 2005). On the other hand, early childhood deprivation, neglect, abuse, or unmanageable trauma can predispose an organism to dysregulation of fear-related neurobiological systems (reviewed in Heim & Nemeroff,

2002), maladaptive emotional, cognitive, and behavioral outcomes, and greater susceptibility to PTSD and other psychiatric disturbance (Southwick et al., 2005).

Severe Childhood Stress

Childhood adversity, in the form of trauma, neglect, deprivation, or abuse, may be especially harmful during critical periods in brain development. It is well known that external stressors impact the structure, organization, and activity of the CNS (e.g. Heim & Nemeroff, 2002). Early developmental stress is associated with both short- and long-term neurobiological changes (reviewed in Heim & Nemeroff, 2002) and related emotional, cognitive, and behavioral alterations.

Chronic stress created by an unstable childhood (e.g., maternal separation, deprivation, neglect, physical or sexual abuse, or other early trauma) can cause allostatic load, which results in neurobiological alterations that can be long-lasting. Studies investigating the effects of early social environment have shown that stress can promote potentially permanent alterations in brain regions and neurotransmitter systems related to the pathophysiology of depression and PTSD (reviewed in Heim & Nemeroff, 2002, and Kaufman & Charney, 2001). Furthermore, it is likely that the neurobiological alterations associated with early adverse experience confer vulnerability, or sensitize the organism to later development of stress-related mental disorders (Charney, 2004). Due in part to these neurobiological anomalies, childhood abuse is correlated with increased incidence of psychiatric illnesses such as major depression, PTSD, and other mood and anxiety disorders (Bremner et al., 1993; De Bellis, 2001; Kaufman et al., 1998). It is thought that these structural and functional neurobiological alterations can be reversed by an enriched caregiving environment, through pharmacological interventions (Kaufman et al., 1998), and possibly also through psychological or psychotherapeutic intervention.

Extensive rodent studies by Meaney and colleagues have explored the effects (both protective and deleterious) of early environment on neurobiological systems. They found that postnatal maternal separation in rat pups increases hypothalamic corticotropin-releasing factor (CRF) gene expression and hypothalamic-pituitary-adrenergic (HPA) axis response to stress, along with fear-related behavioral changes (e.g., exploration of environment, appetitive behavior, startle response). However, when rat pups were exposed to an enriched environment (i.e., increased handling), the neurobiological changes reversed (Francis et al., 2002). Meaney and colleagues also found that natural variations in maternal care of rat pups (i.e., high and low levels of licking/grooming and arched-back nursing) produced parallel differences in HPA axis functioning in their offspring. It is also known that early mothering impacts the development and function of the hippocampus (Liu et al., 2000). Rodent mothers who displayed increased caregiving behaviors (i.e., licking/grooming and arched-backed nursing) had offspring with increased hippocampal synaptogenesis and improved spatial learning and memory (Bredy et al.,

2003; Liu et al., 2000). Meaney and colleagues also found that maternally separated and nonhandled rat pups (in comparison to nonseparated, handled counterparts) displayed more hyperactive behavior in a novel setting, higher sensitivity to cocaine-induced locomotor activity, and greater increases in nucleus accumbens dopamine levels in the context of a mild stressor (tail-pinch; Brake et al., 2004).

Coplan and Mathew's studies (Coplan et al., 2005; Mathew et al., 2002) using bonnet macaque monkeys have interesting implications for the impact of early social environment on neurobiology. This set of studies, using a procedure called "variable foraging demand," demonstrated that in nonhuman primates, developmental stress can permanently alter the "set-point" of the HPA axis, therefore changing the output of stress-related neurochemicals (reviewed by Gorman et al., 2002). Mothers were presented with a stressor: unpredictability of food availability for 16 weeks within the first year of their offspring's lives. Cerebrospinal fluid (CSF) samples were obtained simultaneously on mothers and infants. Both mothers and infants demonstrated elevated concentrations of CRF in their CSF, in comparison to controls. Thus, early maternal stress without subsequent intervention permanently altered the output of the HPA axis (i.e., increased CRF), producing neurobiological changes associated with increased vulnerability to stress (Coplan et al., 2005; Mathew et al., 2002).

Similar findings are being reported in human children. A number of studies have demonstrated that childhood abuse is associated with a cascade of neurobiological changes that can alter the structure and function of the brain (reviewed by Bremner, 2003; Heim & Nemeroff, 2002; Teicher et al., 2003). Structural findings include decreased hippocampal volume (Vythilingam et al., 2002), smaller size of the corpus callosum, and abnormalities of the left neocortex and the amygdala (reviewed by Teicher et al., 2003). Abused children have also been found to have decreased cerebral volume compared to nonabused children (reviewed by Heim & Nemeroff., 2002). Functional abnormalities include HPA-axis dysregulation (DeBellis et al., 1994), along with elevated cortisol levels (reviewed in Heim & Nemeroff, 2002) and increased electrical sensitivity of the limbic structures, which govern emotional processing. Abused children also have been found to exhibit psychophysiological changes such as elevated heart rate, blood pressure changes, autonomic hyperactivity, and exaggerated startle response (reviewed in Heim & Nemeroff, 2002; Penza et al., 2003).

The literature on abused children is supplemented by recent studies on the psychoneuroendocrinology of Eastern European orphans. Research indicates that lack of proper care and nurturance in childhood can create long-lasting changes in oxytocin and arginine vasopressin, hormones that regulate the formation and maintenance of social bonds. Pollak's recent study (Wismer Fries et al., 2005) found that Eastern European orphans had deficiencies in oxytocin, which confers a sense of protection, trust, and security (Heinrichs et al., 2003; Kosfeld et al., 2005), and in vasopressin, which facilitates recognition of familiar people and social/pair bonding (reviewed by Young & Wang, 2004). These neuroendocrine deficits persisted even after the children were placed in nurturing families.

Preclinical and clinical evidence clearly demonstrates that young organisms exposed to maltreatment or other forms of extreme stress are likely to have elevated neurobiological risk factors, and in humans this can indicate an increased likelihood of developing psychiatric illnesses such as depression and PTSD. Currently it is not well understood which neurobiological changes are reversible or permanent, nor whether there are particular windows of opportunity for intervention.

Stress Inoculation

In contrast, recent research has indicated that exposure to mild to moderate stressors (particularly challenges that the young organism can successfully manage or master) can provide inoculation to subsequent stressors, creating a hardier or more resilient phenotype. Lyons et al. exposed young squirrel monkeys (postnatal 17–27 weeks) to mild early life stressors (short-term isolation by removal from contact with other monkeys). Upon subsequent evaluation of the monkeys' ability to cope with new challenges, the team found that the stress-inoculated monkeys had reduced production of potentially damaging stress hormones such as adrenocorticotropic hormone (ACTH) and cortisol. In addition, the group that was exposed to mild stress demonstrated better socioemotional functioning than the nonstressed group, evinced by fewer anxious behaviors, bolder exploration of the environs, and larger food consumption (Parker et al., 2004). Subsequent work by Lyons and colleagues indicated that young primates who were exposed to mild to moderate stressors demonstrated improved functioning of the prefrontal cortex (PFC), which may in turn enhance cognitive performance in areas that are reliant on the prefrontal cortex (Parker et al., 2005).

Research on U.S. Special Forces soldiers by Morgan, Southwick, and Charney (Morgan et al., 2000) has similar implications for stress inoculation. Special Forces (SF) troops are thought to be more "stress hardy" than most other soldiers, due in part to the rigorous stress inoculation training they receive in U.S. Army survival school and at the various challenging levels of military training that they must complete before entering the Special Forces training program. This study looked at levels of neuropeptide Y (NPY) concentration in SF and non-Special Forces soldiers under the stressful conditions of survival school. NPY is a 36-amino acid peptide that is released with norepinephrine when the sympathetic nervous system (SNS) is strongly activated. NPY regulates CRH-related activity at the amygdala, reduces locus coeruleus firing, and inhibits the continued release of norepinephrine so that the SNS does not "overshoot." NPY is also thought to confer neuroprotection and anxiolysis (Heilig et al., 1994; Heilig & Widerlov, 1990). It has also been negatively associated with dissociation during a stressor (Morgan et al., 2000), and is found in lower concentration in combat-traumatized veterans with PTSD as compared to healthy controls (Rasmusson et al., 2000). The results of the SF study (Morgan et al., 2000) indicated that specially trained soldiers, compared to non-SF subjects, demonstrated a more robust NPY response to stress and regained baseline NPY values within 24 hours after stress exposure. Thus, the SF troops had a more finely tuned SNS stress response that remained contained (in part by NPY) under pressure and returned rapidly to baseline after stress, reducing the likelihood of allostatic load.

This finding could be explained in various ways. One interpretation is that the SF soldiers inherited a more effective NPY system that made admission to elite SF group more likely. Alternatively, it is possible that the various challenging levels of military training that led up to their acceptance into the SF and survival school training program made them hardier and produced a more effective NPY system.

Selected Psychobiological Factors Associated With Resilience

Dynamically interrelated environmental, psychological, neurobiological, and genetic elements contribute to human resilience. Of particular interest in the resilience paradigm are a set of psychological factors including positive emotions, cognitive flexibility, moral compass, active coping style, and social support (Charney, 2004; Southwick et al., 2005). These psychological attributes are thought to have a buffering effect on chronic stress and may contribute to an individual's ability to stave off psychopathology in the aftermath of trauma.

Positive Emotions

Positive emotions, including positive attitude, optimism, and sense of humor are characteristic of resilient individuals. Optimism has been repeatedly correlated with increased psychological well-being and health (Affleck & Tennen, 1996; Goldman et al., 1996) and with greater life satisfaction (Klohnen, 1996). Also, positive emotions play a critical role in the capacity to tolerate stress; they are associated with decreased occurrences of stress-related illnesses, reduced use of medical services, and fewer mood disturbances in individuals exposed to missile attacks (Zeidner & Hammer, 1992), breast cancer (Carver et al., 1993), and open heart surgery (Scheier et al., 1989). Positive affect in the context of chronic stress is thought to be adaptive, replenishing depleted emotional resources, relieving suffering, and enhancing positive coping strategies (Folkman & Moskowitz, 2000).

Fredrickson (2001) proposes that positive emotions (e.g., joy, interest, contentment, pride, love) tend to broaden one's focus and enhance an individual's ability to draw on healthier cognitive resources such as creativity and cognitive flexibility (Folkman & Moskowitz, 2000; Isen et al., 1987). Over time, the cognitive/affective broadening that accompanies positive emotion serves to build enduring physical, psychological, and intellectual resources, and attracts social support

(Fredrickson, 2001). Additionally, it has been proposed that positive emotions decrease autonomic arousal (Folkman & Moskowitz, 2000; Isen et al., 1987), protecting the individual against the development of stress-related disorders and facilitating the maintenance of allostasis.

The field is beginning to elucidate the underlying neurobiology of optimism, a psychological attribute that is at least partially inherited. The neural circuitry of brain reward systems is complex and involves several regions, including meso-limbic dopamine pathways, the PFC, and the amygdala. Mesolimbic dopamine pathways play a critical role in reward, motivation, and pleasure (Charney, 2004). Dopaminergic neurons in the ventral tegmental area innervate the nucleus ac-cumbens, where increased dopamine activity has been associated with reward and reward expectations. It has been suggested that people who remain optimistic and hopeful in the context of trauma and other extremely stressful life events may have a dopaminergic reward system that is either hypersensitive to rewarding stimuli or resistant to dysregulation in the face of chronic stress (Charney, 2004). For example, research on U.S. Special Forces soldiers demonstrated enhanced acti-vation of brain regions that govern emotion and reward processing in reward-related situations, such as the anterior cingulate cortex, right caudate, and right midbrain, as compared to healthy civilians (Vythilingham et al., 2005).

The appreciation and use of humor characterizes many resilient individuals. Humor has been identified as a mature defense mechanism (Vaillant, 1977) and as a coping strategy that may decrease the probability of developing stress-induced depression (Deaner & McConatha, 1993; Thorson & Powell, 1994). In studies of resilient Vietnam veterans (Hendin & Haas, 1984), surgical patients (Carver et al., 1993), cancer patients (Culver et al., 2002), and at-risk children (Werner & Smith 1992; Wolin & Wolin, 1993), the ability to use humor to deal with adver-sity has been cited as a healthy coping mechanism. Humor is thought to diminish the threatening nature and negative emotional impact of stressful situations via cognitive reappraisal or reframing (Folkman, 1997), fostering a more positive perspective on challenging circumstances. Humor also relieves tension and dis-comfort (Vaillant, 1992) and attracts social support (Silver et al., 1990). For in-stance, Manne et al. (2003) found that humor was associated with reductions in maternal depressive symptoms in a study of mothers of children undergoing bone marrow transplantation. Additionally, Thorson and Powell (1994) and Deaner and McConatha (1993) found a negative relationship between sense of humor and depression.

Humor is thought to activate a network of subcortical regions that are critically involved in the dopaminergic reward system (Mobbs et al., 2003; Moran et al., 2004). In a functional magnetic resonance imaging study of healthy volunteers, Mobbs et al. (2003) found that funny cartoons, in contrast to nonfunny cartoons, activated the amygdala, ventral striatum/nucleus accumbens, ventral tegmental area, anterior thalamus, and subadjacent hypothalamus. A time-series analysis showed that nucleus accumbens activation increased with the intensity of humor. The nucleus accumbens is associated with psychologically and pharmacologically mediated rewards, and the amygdala has been linked with processing of positive emotions, laughter, and reward magnitude (Mobbs et al., 2003; Moran et al., 2004).

Cognitive Flexibility: Explanatory Style, Cognitive Reappraisal and Acceptance

Individuals who are able to think flexibly, come up with alternate explanations, reframe positively, and accept challenging situations or distressing events tend to be more psychologically resilient than inflexible thinkers. Seligman and colleagues have put forth two essential dimensions of explanatory style: permanence and pervasiveness (Seligman et al., 1998). Individuals who are depressed tend to blame themselves for negative events, and to interpret problems as permanent and pervasive. Resilient and optimistic individuals have a different explanatory style; they tend to view negative events more flexibly and realistically, seeing problems more often as temporary and manageable. They are less likely to impose self-blame automatically and more likely to see problems as limited in scope.

Cognitive reappraisal, or the ability to reframe and reevaluate experiences in a more positive light is another psychological capability often seen in resilient individuals (Southwick et al., 2005). It is the deliberate, conscious cognitive transformation of emotional experience or reinterpretation of adverse events so as to find meaning and opportunity in them. The ability to find meaning in adversity creates a more positive outcome and reverses negative affect (Schaefer & Moos, 1992, 1998). Resilient individuals tend to find more positive meaning in the stressors of daily life than nonresilient individuals (Tugade & Fredrickson, 2002). Survivors of many different kinds of trauma (war, disaster, medical conditions, divorce) have demonstrated psychological growth in the wake of trauma, deriving a wide variety of benefits, such as increased emotional endurance, enhanced spirituality, new value systems, and closer social ties (reviewed in Anderson & Anderson, 2003; Tedeschi et al., 1998).

In addition, recent brain-imaging research using healthy volunteers offered evidence that cognitive reappraisal impacts brain regions that govern emotional processing. When healthy individuals were shown aversive photographs and instructed to change their emotional responses to the images, reappraisal of the negatively charged images led to decreased negative affect, increased activity in lateral and medial prefrontal cortex, and decreased activation of the amygdala and medial orbitofrontal cortex (Ochsner et al., 2002). These results support the idea that the capacity to reappraise negative stimuli can change affect and brain activity.

Within the domain of cognitive flexibility, acceptance is an adaptive coping strategy among people who are able to tolerate extreme and uncontrollable stress (Manne et al., 2003; Siebert, 1996). Acceptance involves recognizing the uncontrollable aspects of certain stressors, reappraising the stressor in light of acceptance, changing expectations about outcome and control of outcome, and focusing on controllable aspects of the stressor. Acceptance is not to be confused with resignation, which is giving up or coping passively. Acceptance has been linked with better physical and psychological health and lower levels of distress in mothers coping with children who are undergoing bone marrow transplantation (Manne et al., 2003), in pediatric traumatic injury (Wade et al., 2001), and in women undergoing breast cancer treatment (Carver et al., 1993). Individuals who had an accepting coping style were also found to have fewer PTSD symptoms following the terrorist attacks of September 11, 2001 (Silver et al., 2002).

Moral Compass: Religion, Spirituality and Altruism
Another characteristic of resilient individuals is a strong moral compass. Developing and maintaining a framework of belief that few things can shatter is thought to enhance an individual's ability to find meaning in and cope adaptively with adversity (Southwick et al., 2005). This construct includes adherence to a religious or spiritual system and an altruistic outlook toward others.

Recent research has indicated that religion and spirituality may have a protective effect on physical and psychological well-being in healthy individuals and may help people cope with illness. A recent meta-analysis of 126,000 individuals in 42 independent samples indicated that religious practice or involvement had a robust relationship with higher probability of survival (lower risk of all-cause mortality; McCullough et al., 2000). In addition, higher levels of religious belief have been correlated with lower incidence of depression in numerous populations, including college students (Donahue, 1985), bereaved adults (Borestein et al., 1973), medically ill older patients (Koenig et al., 1998, 2004), and community-dwelling elderly people in the United States and Europe (Braam et al., 2001). Recent longitudinal studies have indicated that level of religiousness also predicts rate of remission from depression in medically hospitalized and nonhospitalized older adults (Braam et al., 1997; Koenig et al., 1998). Along the same lines, religious adolescents tend to have lower suicide rates than nonreligious adolescents (Donahue & Benson, 1995). Interestingly, the specific religious affiliation is not implicated in the overall relationship between religiousness and improved psychological and physical health.

There is some neurobiological evidence from PET studies to indicate that spiritual or self-transcendent experiences are associated with density of available serotonin 5-HT(1A) receptors, implicated in the pathophysiology of depression, (reviewed by Hasler et al., 2004) in the dorsal raphe nuclei, hippocampus, and neocortex in healthy adult males (Borg et al., 2003). The role of the serotonin system in spiritual experience is further supported by studies showing that drugs known to impact serotonin (e.g., LSD, mescaline, psilocybin) often produce spiritual awareness, a sense of insight, and religious ecstasy (Borg et al., 2003). Chronic stress has been shown to increase CRH and cortisol levels, which in a sequence of neurochemical events downregulate 5HT(1A) receptors, creating a lower threshold for tolerating stress and anxiety (Charney, 2004) and therefore an increased probability of developing stress-related psychopathology. Spiritual or religious experiences may enhance the functioning of the serotonin system, fostering resilience and helping to protect against the development of stress-related psychopathology.

Altruism is another important component of a moral compass that acts as a stress buffer. The capacity for finding meaning in contributing to community or society, the drive toward providing for others, pursuing meaningful work-related goals, or embracing a survivor mission are elements of a moral framework that often characterizes resilient individuals (Southwick et al., 2005). Some individuals are able to find meaning in tragedy by embracing a survivor mission as an outgrowth of personal trauma. Among numerous examples of this phenomenon are rape survivors who go public with their experience in the service of raising social awareness through events such as Take Back the Night, and mothers who founded Mothers Against Drunk Driving after their children were injured or killed in drunk driving accidents. Research on altruistic behavior of citizens during WWII elucidates the concept of "required helpfulness" (Rachman, 1979). Individuals who cared for others after bombing attacks suffered fewer trauma-related mood and anxiety symptoms than would be expected; individuals who were symptomatic preattack and performed personally satisfying acts experienced a meaningful decrease in psychological distress (Rachman, 1979). Thus, it is likely that individuals who decide and act based on a strong moral compass guided by religion, spirituality, and/or altruism are more likely to exhibit resilience in the face of stress and trauma.

Active Coping

A large body of literature exists on the myriad ways people cope with adversity and on how coping style impacts mental and physical well-being. Active coping, for the purposes of this discussion, means employing healthy strategies for the management of stress and the regulation of negative emotions that may arise in the aftermath of adverse events. Some examples of active coping are seeking social support, employing skills for effective self-soothing, adopting a fighting spirit, reframing stressors in a more positive light, facing fears, and exercising.

Active Coping Style

Active coping has been repeatedly associated with hardiness and psychological resilience in various populations (Moos & Schaefer, 1993) including: undergraduate students (Maddi, 1999a, 1999b; Valentiner et al., 1994), at-risk children (Werner & Smith, 1992), traumatized and depressed adults (Fondacaro & Moos, 1989), and patients with medical illnesses (Holahan et al., 1995). In contrast, passive coping, such as maladaptive management of negative affect or blunting of emotions through the use of alcohol/drugs, denial, disengagement or resignation, is associated with depression (e.g., Billings & Moos, 1984) and lower levels of hardiness (Maddi, 1999a, 1999b).

It has been proposed that active coping, both at the time of trauma and upon reexposure to trauma reminders, may impact the neural circuitry of fear conditioning. Active coping at the time of stress or trauma may inhibit the development of fear-conditioned responses to the trauma (reviewed in LeDoux & Gorman, 2001). Also, using rodent models, LeDoux and Gorman have proposed that active coping at the time of reexposure to fear-conditioned stimuli may decrease the intensity of fear-conditioned responses by redirecting activity in the lateral and central nuclei of the amygdala away from the brainstem and toward the motor circuits in the ventral striatum. This has the effect of reducing brain-stem-mediated responses to fear, such as freezing behavior and autonomic and endocrine responses. This redirection takes place only when the organism is active, not passive, in coping upon reexposure. Active coping reduces or attenuates fear conditioning, and may decrease the intensity of already conditioned associations, thereby reducing the likelihood of developing trauma-related psychopathology and functional impairments such as avoidance of feared situations (LeDoux & Gorman, 2001).

In addition, active coping can be seen as the inverse of learned helplessness. Animals and humans, in the face of inescapable stress, often develop a set of behaviors including passive withdrawal, resignation, and resistance to reversing a negative experience (Abramson et al., 1978; Seligman, 1972); in short, the organism stops trying to improve the situation or remove the stressor. The phenomenon of learned helplessness is a well-known animal model for depression and is thought to produce a dysregulation of serotonin in the dorsal raphe nuclei (Greenwood et al., 2003) and a reduction in hippocampal cell proliferation. Because serotonin has far-reaching effects in shaping and regulating the limbic system's circuitry, a dysregulation due to learned helplessness may have serious and pervasive effects on mood. Thus, active coping in the face of trauma can prevent the neurobiological disruptions associated with passive coping/learned helplessness and therefore contribute to a more resilient psychology.

Facing Fears

Facing fears is another component of the active coping paradigm. As discussed earlier, fear conditioning plays a major role in the development and maintenance of posttraumatic psychopathology. Individuals with PTSD avoid a wide variety of life's opportunities (people, places, events, etc.) that may serve as reminders of the trauma; thus conditioned fear is maintained rather than extinguished. Resilient individuals are more likely to use fear as a warning signal that danger may be imminent, to utilize fear as a guide to accurately appraise threat, and to direct appropriate and adaptive action. They learn and practice skills necessary to move through fear and thus extinguish or attenuate the conditioned fear.

Foa, Rothbaum, and colleagues at the University of Pennsylvania designed a psychotherapeutic treatment specifically for PTSD called prolonged exposure (PE) (Foa & Rothbaum, 1998). PE is a manualized, exposure-based cognitive-behavioral technique based on principles of learning theory (habituation and extinction). The core of the treatment is exposure therapy, including imaginal exposure to the traumatic memory (i.e., having the participant repeatedly retell the story of the trauma) and in vivo exposure (exposing the participant to previously avoided situations that may trigger the conditioned fear). The treatment also involves skill-based interventions, including psychoeducation about common reactions to trauma and breathing retraining. PE can thus be seen as a form of active coping and stress inoculation, in that it exposes the participant to traumatic memories and avoided situations within a manageable/masterable context. It requires the participant to face fear through repeated retelling of the traumatic story and engaging in feared (but not dangerous) activities. PE also assists the participant in addressing distorted cognitions (e.g., self-blame) and maladaptive behaviors (e.g., avoidance, passive coping) that perpetuate the symptoms of PTSD. In recent comparison studies, PE has been found to have longer-lasting symptom reduction than other modalities (e.g., Stress Inoculation Training, supportive counseling, and waiting list conditions; Foa et al., 1999a, 1999b).

Recent research indicates that extinction actually represents new learning, rather than the attenuation of the old fear-conditioned association. Facing fears through exposure ideally leads to extinction of the conditioned fear. Davis and Myers (Davis, 2002; Davis & Myers, 2002) have demonstrated in animal models that the neurotransmitters gamma-aminobutyric acid (GABA) and glutamate are critical components of this process. GABA may exert an inhibitory influence on the amygdala (central to fear leaning), and glutamate, acting at N-methyl-D-aspartate receptors (NMDA) may facilitate this GABA-mediated inhibition (Davis & Myers, 2002). These neurobiological findings have potentially meaningful implications for exposure therapy outcomes.

Physical Exercise
Attending to physical well-being is part of good self-care; exercising as a means of relieving stress and dealing with negative affect is part of an active coping style. Consistent physical exercise has consistently been shown to have positive effects on physical hardiness, mood, and self-esteem. Individuals who exercise regularly report lower depression scores than those who do not exercise (Brosse et al., 2002; Camacho et al., 1991). In addition, exercise is associated with a number of neurobiological effects that contribute to resilience. It is related to increases in plasma monoamines and tryptophan (precursor to serotonin) levels, and attenuates HPA activity in response to stress. Exercise also increases release of endorphins, which contributes to mood elevation. From a genetic perspective, physical exercise is thought to induce the expression of several genes related to neuroplasticity and

neurogenesis, such as hippocampal brain-derived neurotrophophic factor (BDNF) and other neurotrophic factors involved in plasticity, connectivity, cell life, and learning (Cotman & Berchtold, 2002). Thus, exercise as part of an active coping style has meaningful psychobiological impact on resilience.

Social Support
Social support has been widely studied and shown to buffer against stress and protect mental and physical well-being. Two essential components have been identified within this construct: structural (social network size and frequency of social interaction) and functional (emotional, instrumental; Wills & Fegan, 2001). Social isolation and lack of social support have been consistently associated with higher rates of mood and anxiety disorders, higher levels of stress, and higher levels of mortality and morbidity in a variety of medical illnesses, whereas higher levels of social support have been associated with better outcomes following a wide variety of stressors (Resick, 2001). Social support is thought to reduce the rate of high-risk behavior (Rozanski et al., 1999), foster adaptive coping (Holahan et al., 1995), and encourage less negative appraisals of threat (Fontana et al., 1989). It is also thought to counteract feelings of loneliness (Bisschop et al., 2004), increase a sense of self-efficacy, reduce functional impairment (Hays et al., 2001; Travis et al., 2004), and increase treatment compliance. Individuals who seek and nurture a supportive social network during times of stress will have a more resilient constitution than socially isolated individuals and will likely fare better in the face of stress or adversity.

In addition to a supportive social network, role models and mentors can change the course of an individual's development. Observation and imitation are powerful forms of learning throughout the life span, especially during childhood and adolescence when the nervous system is changing and habitual styles of thinking and behavior are being consolidated. Resilient role models can set a positive example and help an individual learn skills and attitudes that foster resilience, such as active coping, positive emotion, affect regulation, cognitive flexibility, and finding meaning in adversity (Southwick et al., 2005). As metastudies on psychotherapy efficacy have shown across therapeutic modalities, a salient ingredient in any psychotherapeutic treatment is the therapeutic alliance (reviewed in Martin et al., 2000). A healthy therapeutic alliance can be a positive addition to an individual's social network and a therapist can serve as a positive role model.

The neurobiology of social support is complex and involves many brain regions, biological pathways, and neurochemicals. The neuropeptide oxytocin is particularly important in social behavior. As described earlier, oxytocin plays an important role in social attachment, prosocial behavior, and maternal-style bonding and nurturance behaviors (Heinrichs et al., 2003). In addition, oxytocin has behavioral and physiological stress-attenuating and anxiolytic effects (Heinrichs et al.,

2003). Heinrichs and colleagues also found that stress-related release of oxytocin reduces secretion of ACTH, corticosterone, and catecholamines in rats and is thought to reduce HPA axis overactivity in women. Thus, social support and positive social interaction are psychologically and neurobiologically relevant to the resilience paradigm.

Resilience Interventions

Clinical intervention with survivors of trauma is a challenging endeavor, and various modalities of treatment are being explored in the field. Today, there is no single treatment identified as the optimal intervention for trauma survivors (or for individuals with a PTSD diagnosis), and in some cases a combination of different treatment modalities may provide the most symptom relief and improvement in psychological functioning. These approaches focus both on recovery in the aftermath of trauma, and resilience to future adverse events. The following section will briefly illustrate the state-of-science in treating trauma survivors.

In addition to identifying and bolstering the psychosocial factors described in earlier sections, a skilled clinician can facilitate a trauma survivor's recovery through careful intervention. Trauma expert Judith Herman, in *Trauma and Recovery* (1997), describes a three-phase model of recovery after trauma; this model serves as a good conceptual framework for thinking about the treatment of trauma survivors in any modality. The phases do not necessarily progress in a linear fashion and the process can be facilitated by a mental health professional in a variety of settings.

Establishing safety is the first phase; a trauma survivor, having lost a sense of safety and trust in the world must feel safe in the therapeutic setting in order to begin to recover. Telling the trauma story within the context of a safe environment is the second phase. Here, the survivor tells and retells the trauma story, consolidating memory and making meaning of the events; this phase is akin to the exposure element of other treatment approaches. Those who bear witness to the retelling (e.g., therapist, group members, peers) must work continually to provide a safe and supportive environment. The third phase is about connection and reconnection; the survivor begins to rebuild meaningful connections with individuals and the community that have been strained or lost in the aftermath of trauma. The survivor may also begin to establish new connections and to test and modify the boundaries of existing relationships, as well as work toward reconnecting with parts of him/herself that may have been fragmented due to trauma. The ultimate goal of this model is to help the survivor move from helplessness and shame to empowerment and personal agency.

Although most clinicians treating trauma survivors use psychodynamic or supportive therapies, there are no outcome data for these modalities (reviewed by

Nemeroff et al., 2006). The International Society for Traumatic Stress Studies' clinical practice guidelines (Foa et al., 2000) and other outcome studies (as reviewed in Keane, 1995; Marks et al., 1998) suggest that exposure-based therapies (such as PE) have the most efficacy for PTSD, but cognitive therapy (Resick et al., 2002) and interpersonal psychotherapy (Bleiberg & Markowitz, 2005) have also been shown to be effective for this disorder. As discussed earlier, exposure is a salient ingredient in therapy for PTSD and other anxiety disorders because it facilitates new associations and learning, and the extinction of the learned fear. Davis and colleagues have elucidated a gluatamergic/GABAergic underpinning for the extinction of fear conditioning (Davis & Myers, 2002), and further research will determine whether exposure-based therapies impact these and other neurotransmitter systems in a meaningful way.

Maladaptive thoughts (e.g., the world is unsafe, the traumatized individual is incompetent/at fault) are associated with the development and maintenance of mood and anxiety disorders, including PTSD (Foa & Jaycox, 1999). Nonexposure-based cognitive-behavioral therapies (CBT) generally address the maladaptive thought patterns that maintain psychopathological symptoms in depression and anxiety. CBT attempts to facilitate the participant's understanding of the connections between thoughts, feelings, and behaviors and the environment. Within this framework, CBT also strives to teach the participant to regulate emotions effectively, to extinguish fearful responses brought about by traumatic memories, and to cope adaptively and actively with life's challenges. Clearly, in order to benefit from any kind of cognitive therapy, the patient must have the neurocognitive ability and developed prefrontal cortex to comprehend the treatment. Adolescents with this capacity can participate in and benefit from CBT, which has been demonstrated to be more effective than wait-list or attention control in adolescents with anxiety disorders (reviewed by James et al., 2005).

In addition, psychotherapeutic interventions focused on affective regulation, such as meditation, EMDR (McNally, 1999; Shapiro, 1995) and dialectical behavior therapy (Linehan, 1993), and approaches focused on optimism/positive psychology (Seligman & Csikszentmihalyi, 2000) are also promising in their ability to promote psychological resilience in the aftermath of trauma. Research is currently underway to better understand the potential adjuvant effects of psychotherapies on the neurobiological underpinning and psychological manifestations of mental illnesses like PTSD and depression (Yehuda, 2002). Further, as the field advances its understanding of the psychological elements of stress-related psychopathology, clinicians can develop better tools for the assessment, diagnosis, and treatment of PTSD and other trauma-related illnesses.

Progress in understanding the neurobiology of resilience and vulnerability to stress-related illnesses, and the dynamic interactions between biological substrate and human experience will hopefully lead to improvements in the pharmacological treatment of trauma survivors. At present, medications such as antidepressants, anxiolytics and anticonvulsants, originally developed for other disorders, are currently being tested and used with some success in the treatment of PTSD (reviewed in Friedman, 2000). Antidepressants, including MAOIs, tricyclics, and SSRIs are considered effective pharmacotherapeutic treatments for PTSD. Among these drug classes, SSRIs such as Prozac, Paxil, and Zoloft are considered first-line agents for PTSD (reviewed in Albucher & Liberzon, 2002), though no particular SSRI has emerged the clear leader. Medication is particularly helpful in reducing distressing PTSD symptoms, associated depression, and functional impairments and disabilities (reviewed in Stein et al., 2006); thus medication may facilitate participation in psychotherapy. In addition, rats pretreated (treatment before exposure to a stressor, e.g., forced swim test) with a benzodiazepine or tricyclic antidepressant did not develop learned helplessness (Petty et al., 1992, 1997). Thus, it is possible that medication prior to trauma could increase resilience or raise the threshold for development of psychopathology.

Recent findings on the neurobiological correlates of PTSD have generated new interest in mechanisms that may have implications for PTSD and other stress-related illnesses. At this time, PTSD-specific drug trials are underway to evaluate the efficacy of new compounds that may have an impact on the unique pathophysiology of PTSD. Some of these include NPY enhancers, substance P antagonists, NMDA agonists, antiadrenergics, and compounds that downregulate glucocorticoid receptors (reviewed in Friedman, 2000). In addition, recent data suggest that D-cycloserine, an NMDA receptor partial agonist (widely available and safe) may be used in conjunction with exposure therapy to facilitate the acquisition of new learning, accelerate the formation of new associations, and thereby reduce symptoms of conditioned fear. In a study evaluating the combination of D-cycloserine and exposure therapy in acrophobic patients, the treatment was effective in significantly reducing symptoms of fear and anxiety (Ressler et al., 2004). This combination may hold promise for the treatment of PTSD, though no conclusive studies have ascertained this yet.

A coordinated approach is essential in any endeavor to promote resilience. Bolstering one resilience factor will have additive properties and synergistic effects on overall well-being. Considerations such as a healthy lifestyle (diet, exercise), social support, religion/spirituality, community membership, self-help/bibliotherapy, alternative healing practices, and psychotherapeutic or psychopharmacologic interventions are all of interest in creating a resilient psychological response to trauma. Furthermore, a deeper understanding of the complicated dynamics of genetics, biological substrate, and human experience of trauma will illuminate the future of psychiatric and psychological intervention.

References

Abramson, L. Y., Seligman, M. E., & Teasdale, J. D. (1978). Learned helplessness in humans: Critique and reformulation. *Journal of Abnormal Psychology, 87*, 49–74.

Affleck, G., & Tennen, H. (1996). Construing benefits from adversity: Adaptational significance and dispositional underpinnings. *Journal of Personality, 64*, 899–922.

Albucher, R. C., & Liberzon, I. (2002). Psychopharmacological treatment in PTSD: A critical review. *Journal of Psychiatric Research, 36*(6), 355–367.

American Psychiatric Association. (1987). *Diagnostic and statistical manual of mental disorders* (3rd ed., Rev.). Washington, DC: Author.

Anderson, N. B., & Anderson, P. E. (2003). *Emotional longevity: What really determines how long you live.* New York: Viking.

Billings, A. G., & Moos, R. H. (1984). Coping, stress and social resources among adults with unipolar depression. *Journal of Personality and Social Psychology, 46*, 877–891.

Bisschop, M. I., Kriegsman, D. M., Beekman, A. T., & Deeg, D. H. (2004). Chronic diseases and depression: The modifying role of psychosocial resources. *Social Science and Medicine, 59*(4), 721–733.

Blair, H. T., Schafe, G. E., Bauer, E. P., Rodrigues, S. M., & LeDoux, J. E. (2001). Synaptic plasticity in the lateral amygdala: A cellular hypothesis of fear conditioning. *Learning and Memory, 8*, 229–242.

Bleiberg, K. L., & Markowitz, J. C. (2005). A pilot study of interpersonal psychotherapy for posttraumatic stress disorder. *American Journal of Psychiatry, 162*, 181–183.

Bonanno, G. A. (2004). Loss, trauma and human resilience: Have we underestimated the human capacity to thrive after extremely aversive events? *American Psychologist, 59*(1), 20–28.

Borestein, P. E., Clayton, P. J., Halikas, J. A., Maurice, W. L., & Robins, E. (1973). The depression of widowhood after thirteen months. *British Journal of Psychiatry, 122*, 561–566.

Borg, J., Andree, B., Soderstrom, H., & Farde, L. (2003). The serotonin system and spiritual experiences. *American Journal of Psychiatry, 160*(11), 1965–1969.

Braam, A. W., Beekman, A. T., Deeg, D. J., Smit, J. H., & van Tilburg, W. (1997). Religiosity as a protective or prognostic factor of depression in later life: Results from a community survey in the Netherlands. *Acta Psychiatrica Scandinavica, 96*, 199–205.

Braam, A. W., Van den Eeden, P., Prince, M. J., Beekman, A. T., Kivela, S. L., Lawlor, B. A., Birkhofer, A., Fuhrer R., Lobo, A., Magnusson, H., Mann, A. H., Meller, I., Roelands, M., Skoog, I., Turrina, C., & Copeland, J. R. M. (2001). Religion as a cross-cultural determinant of depression in elderly Europeans: Results from the EURODEP collaboration. *Psychological Medicine, 31*, 803–814.

Brake, W. G., Zhang, T. Y., Diorio, J., Meaney, M. J., & Gratton, A. (2004). Influence of early postnatal rearing conditions on mesocorticolimbic dopamine and behavioral responses to psychostimulants and stressors in adult rats. *European Journal of Neuroscience, 19*(7), 1863–1874.

Bredy, T. W., Grant, R. J., Champagne, D. L., & Meaney, M. J. (2003). Maternal care influences neuronal survival in the hippocampus of the rat. *European Journal of Neuroscience, 18*(10), 2903–2909.

Bremner, J. D. (2003). Long-term effects of childhood abuse on brain and neurobiology. *Child and Adolescent Psychiatric Clinics of North America, 12*(2), 271–292.

Bremner, J. D., Southwick, S. M., Johnson, D. R., Yehuda, R., & Charney, D. S. (1993). Childhood physical abuse and combat-related posttraumatic stress disorder in Vietnam Veterans. *American Journal of Psychiatry, 150*, 235–239.

Breslau, N. (2002). Epidemiologic studies of trauma, posttraumatic stress disorder, and other psychiatric disorders. *Canadian Journal of Psychiatry, 47*(10), 923–929.

Breslau, N., Davis, G. C., Andreski, P., & Peterson, E. (1991). Traumatic events and posttraumatic stress disorder in an urban population of young adults. *Archives of General Psychiatry, 48,* 216–222.

Brosse, A. L., Sheets, E. S., Lett, H. S., & Blumenthal, J. A. (2002). Exercise and the treatment of clinical depression in adults: Recent findings and future directions. *Sports Medicine, 32,* 741–746.

Camacho, T. C., Roberts, R. E., Lazarus, N. B., Kaplan, G. A., & Cohen, R. D. (1991). Physical activity and depression: Evidence from the Alameda county study. *American Journal of Epidemiology, 134,* 220–231.

Carver, C. S., Pozo, C., Harris, S. D., Noriega, V., Scheier, M. F., Robinson, D. S., Ketcham, A. S., Moffat, F. L., Jr., & Clark, K. C. (1993). How coping mediates the effect of optimism on distress: A study of women with early stage breast cancer. *Journal of Personality and Social Psychology, 65*(2), 375–390.

Caspi, A., Sugden, K., Moffitt, T. E., Taylor, A., Craig, I. W., Harrington, H., McClay, J., Mill, J., Martin, J., Braithwaite, A., & Poulton, R. (2003). Influence of life stress on depression: Moderation by a polymorphism in the 5-HTT gene. *Science, 301*(5631), 386–389.

Charney, D. (2004). Psychobiological mechanisms of resilience and vulnerability: Implications for successful adaptation to extreme stress. *American Journal of Psychiatry, 161*(2), 195–216.

Charney, D. S., & Nestler, E. J. (Eds.). (2004). *Neurobiology of mental illness* (2nd ed.). New York: Oxford University Press.

Coplan, J. D., Altemus, M., Mathew, S. J., Smith, E. L., Sharf, B., Coplan, P. M., Kral, J. G., Gorman, J. M., Owen, M. J., Nemeroff, C. B., & Rosenblum, L. A. (2005). Synchronized maternal-infant elevations of primate CSF CRF concentrations in response to variable foraging demand. *CNS Spectrums, 10*(7), 530–536.

Cotman, C. W., & Berchtold, N. C. (2002). Exercise: A behavioral intervention to enhance brain health and plasticity. *Trends in Neuroscience, 25,* 295–301.

Culver, J. L., Arena, P. L., Antoni, M. H., & Carver, C. S. (2002). Coping and distress among women under treatment for early stage breast cancer: Comparing African Americans, Hispanics and Non-Hispanic whites. *Psycho-Oncology, 11,* 495–504.

Davis, M. (2002). Role of NMDA receptors and MAP kinase in the amygdala in extinction of fear: Clinical implications for exposure therapy. *The European Journal of Neuroscience, 16*(3), 395–398.

Davis, M., & Myers, K. M. (2002). The role of glutamate and gamma-aminobutyric acid in fear extinction: Clinical implications for exposure therapy. *Biological Psychiatry, 52*(10), 998–1007.

De Bellis, M. D. (2001). Developmental traumatology: The psychobiological development of maltreated children and its implications for research, treatment, and policy. *Developmental Psychopathology, 13*(3), 539–564.

De Bellis, M. D., Chrousos, G. P., Dorn, L. D., Burke, L., Helmers, K., Kling, M. A., Trickett, P. K., & Putnam, F. W. (1994). Hypothalamic-pituitary-adrenal axis dysregulation in sexually abused girls. *Journal of Clinical Endocrinology and Metabolism, 78*(2), 249–255.

Deaner, S. L., & McConatha, J. T. (1993). The relation of humor to depression and personality. *Psychological Reports, 72,* 755–763.

Donahue, M. J. (1985). Intrinsic and extrinsic religiousness: Review and meta-analysis. *Journal of Personality and Social Psychology, 48,* 400–419.

Donahue, M. J., & Benson, P. J. (1995). Religion and well-being in adolescents. *Journal for the Scientific Study of Religion, 15*, 29–45.

Foa, E., & Jaycox, L. H. (1999). Cognitive behavioral theory and treatment of post-traumatic stress disorder. In Spiegel, D. S. (Ed.), *Efficacy and cost-effectiveness of psychotherapy* (pp. 23–61). Washington DC: American Psychiatric Press.

Foa, E. B., Dancu, C. V., Hembree, E. A., Jaycox, L. H., Meadows, E. A., & Street, G. P. (1999a). A comparison of exposure therapy, stress inoculation training, and their combination for reducing posttraumatic stress disorder in female assault victims. *Journal of Consulting and Clinical Psychology, 67*, 194–200.

Foa, E. B., Ehlers, A., Clark, D., Tolin, D. F., & Orsillo, S. M. (1999b). Posttraumatic Cognitions Inventory (PTCI): Development and validation, *Psychological Assessment, 11*, 303–314.

Foa, E. B., Keane, T. M., & Friedman, M. J. (Eds.) (2000). *Effective treatments for PTSD: Practice guidelines from the International Society for Traumatic Stress Studies*. New York: Guilford Press.

Foa, E. B., & Rothbaum, B. O. (1998). *Treating the trauma of rape*. New York: Guilford Press.

Folkman, S. (1997). Positive psychological states and coping with severe stress. *Social Science and Medicine, 45*, 1207–1221.

Folkman, S., & Moskowitz, J. T. (2000). Positive affect and the other side of coping. *The American Psychologist, 55*, 647–654.

Fondacaro, M. R., & Moos, R. H. (1989). Life stressors and coping: A longitudinal analysis among depressed and nondepressed adults. *Journal of Community Psychology. 17*, 330–340.

Fontana, *A.F., Kerns R.D., Rosenberg R.L. & Colonese K.L.* (1989). Support, stress, and recovery from coronary heart disease: a longitudinal causal model. *Health Psychology, 8*(2), 175–93.

Francis, D. D., Diorio, J., Plotsky, P. M., & Meaney, M. J. (2002). Environmental enrichment reverses the effects of maternal separation on stress reactivity. *Journal of Neuroscience, 22*(18), 7840–7843.

Fredrickson, B. L. (2001). The role of positive emotions in positive psychology. The broaden-and-build theory of positive emotions. *The American Psychologist, 56*(3), 218–226.

Friedman, M. J. (2000). What might the psychobiology of posttraumatic stress disorder teach us about future approaches to pharmacotherapy? *Journal of Clinical Psychiatry, 61*(Suppl. 7), 44–51.

Goldman, S. L., Kraemer, D. T., & Salovey, P. (1996). Beliefs about mood moderate the relationship to illness and symptom reporting. *Journal of Psychosomatic Research, 41*, 115–128.

Gorman, J. M., Mathew, S., & Coplan, J. (2002). Neurobiology of early life stress: Nonhuman primate models. *Seminars in Clinical Neuropsychiatry, 7*(2), 96–103.

Greenwood, B. N., Foley, T. E., Day, H. E., Campisi, J., Hammack, S. H., Campeau, S., Maier, S. F., & Fleshner, M. (2003). Freewheel running prevents learned helplessness/behavioral depression: Role of dorsal raphe serotonergic neurons. *Journal of Neuroscience, 23*(7), 2889–2898.

Hasler, G., Drevets, W. C., Manji, H. K., & Charney, D. S. (2004). Discovering endophenotypes for major depression. *Neuropsychopharmacology, 29*(10), 1765–1781.

Hays, J. C., Steffens, D. C., Flint, E. P., Bosworth, H. B., & George, L. K. (2001). Does social support buffer functional decline in elderly patients with unipolar depression? *American Journal of Psychiatry, 158*, 1850–1855.

Heilig, M., Koob, G. F., Ekman, R., & Britton, K. T. (1994). Corticotropin-releasing factor and neuropeptide Y: Role in emotional integration. *Trends in Neurosciences, 17,* 80–88.

Heilig, M. & Widerlov, E. (1990). Neuropeptide Y: An overview of central distribution, functional aspects, and possible involvement in neuropsychiatric illnesses. *Acta Psychiatrica Scandinavica, 82*(2), 95–114.

Heim, C., & Nemeroff, C. B. (2002). Neurobiology of early life stress: Clinical studies. *Seminars in Clinical Neuropsychiatry, 7*(2), 147–159.

Heinrichs, M., Baumgartner, T., Kirschbaum, C., & Ehlert, U. (2003). Social support and oxytocin interact to suppress cortisol and subjective responses to psychosocial stress. *Biological Psychiatry, 54*(12), 1389–1398.

Hendin, H., & Haas, A. P. (1984). *Wounds of war: The psychological aftermath of combat in Vietnam.* New York: Basic Books.

Heresco-Levy, U., Kremer, I., Javitt, D. C., Goichman, R., Reshef, A., Blanaru, M., & Cohen, T. (2002). Pilot-controlled trial of D-cycloserine for the treatment of post-traumatic stress disorder. *International Journal of Neuropsychopharmacology, 5*(4), 301–307.

Herman, J. (1997). *Trauma and recovery: The aftermath of violence-from domestic abuse to political terror.* New York: Basic Books.

Holahan, C. J., Holahan, C. K., Moos, R. H., & Moos, P. L. (1995). Social support, coping and depressive symptoms in a late-middle-aged sample of patients reporting cardiac illness. *Health Psychology, 14,* 152–163.

Isen, A. M., Daubman, K. A., & Nowicki, G. P. (1987). Positive affect facilitates creative problem solving. *Journal of Personality and Social Psychology, 52,* 1122–1131.

James, A., Soler, A., & Weatherall, R. (2005). Cognitive behavioural therapy for anxiety disorders in children and adolescents. *Cochrane Database of Systematic Reviews,* (4), CD004690.

Jordan, B. K., Schlenger, W. E., Hough, R., Kulka, R. A., Weiss, D., Fairbank, J. A., & Marmar, C. R. (1991). Lifetime and current prevalence of specific psychiatric disorders among Vietnam veterans and controls. *Archives of General Psychiatry, 48*(3), 207–15.

Kaufman, J., Birmaher, B., Perel, J., Dahl, R. E., Stull, S., Brent, D., Trubnick, L., al-Shabbout, M., & Ryan, N. D. (1998). Serotonergic functioning in depressed abused children: Clinical and familial correlates. *Biological Psychiatry, 44*(10), 973–981.

Kaufman, J., & Charney, D. (2001). Effects of early stress on brain structure and function: Implications for understanding the relationship between child maltreatment and depression. *Developmental Psychopathology, 13*(3), 451–471.

Kaufman, J., Plotsky, P. M., Nemeroff, C. B., & Charney, D. S. (2000). Effects of early adverse experiences on brain structure and function: Clinical implications. *Biological Psychiatry, 48*(8), 778–790.

Kaufman, J., Yang, B. Z., Douglas-Palumberi, H., Houshyar, S., Lipschitz, D., Krystal, J. H., & Gelernter, J. (2004). Social supports and serotonin transporter gene moderate depression in maltreated children. *Proceedings of the National Academy of Sciences of the United States of America, 101*(49), 17316–17321.

Keane, T. (1995). The role of exposure therapy in the psychological treatment of PTSD. *NCP Quarterly 5*(4). Retrieved January 31, 2006, from www.ncpptsd.va.gov

Kendler, K. S., Kuhn, J. W., Vittum, J., Prescott, C. A., & Riley, B. (2005). The interaction of stressful life events and a serotonin transporter polymorphism in the prediction of episodes of major depression: A replication. *Archives of General Psychiatry, 62*(5), 529–535.

Kessler, R. C., Sonnega, A., Bromet, E., Hughes, M., & Nelson, C. B. (1995). Posttraumatic stress disorder in the National Comorbidity Survey. *Archives of General Psychiatry, 52,* 1048–1060.

Klohnen, E. C. (1996). Conceptual analysis and measurement of the construct of ego-resiliency. *Journal of Personality and Social Psychology, 70,* 1067–1079.

Koenig, H. G., George, L. K., & Peterson, B. L. (1998). Religious importance and remission of depression in medically ill older patients. *American Journal of Psychiatry, 155,* 536–542.

Koenig, H. G., George, L. K., & Titus, P. (2004). Religion, spirituality, and health in medically ill hospitalized older patients. *Journal of American Geriatrics Society, 52,* 554–562.

Kosfeld, M., Heinrichs, M., Zak, P. J., Fischbacher, U., & Fehr, E. (2005). Oxytocin increases trust in humans. *Nature, 435*(7042), 673–676.

Krupnick, J. L., Green, B. L., Stockton, P., Goodman, L., Corcoran, C., & Petty, R. (2004). Mental health effects of adolescent trauma exposure in a female college sample: exploring differential outcomes based on experiences of unique trauma types and dimensions. *Psychiatry, 67*(3), 264–279.

LeDoux, J. E. (1994). Emotion, memory and the brain. *Scientific American, 270*(6), 55–57.

LeDoux, J. E. (2000). Emotion circuits in the brain. *Annual Review of Neuroscience, 23,* 155–184.

LeDoux, J. E., & Gorman, J. M. (2001). A call to action: overcoming anxiety through active coping. *American Journal of Psychiatry, 158,* 1953–1955.

Linehan, M. (1993). *Cognitive-behavioral treatment of borderline personality disorder.* New York: Guilford Press.

Liu, D., Diorio, J., Day, J. C., Francis, D. D., & Meaney, M. J. (2000). Maternal care, hippocampal synaptogenesis and cognitive development in rats. *Nature Neuroscience, 3*(8), 799–806.

Maddi, S. R. (1999a). Hardiness and optimism as expressed in coping patterns. *Consulting Psychology Journal: Practice and Research, 51,* 95–105.

Maddi, S. R. (1999b). The personality construct of hardiness: Effects on experiences, coping and strain. *Consulting Psychology Journal: Practice and Research, 51,* 83–94.

Manne, S., Duhamel, K., Ostroff, J., Parsons, S., Martini, D. R., Williams, S. E., Mee, L., Sexson, S., Austin, J., Winkel, G., Boulad, F., & Redd, W. H. (2003). Coping and the course of mother's depressive symptoms during and after pediatric bone marrow transplantation. *Journal of the American Academy of Child and Adolescent Psychiatry, 42*(9), 1055–1068.

Marks, I., Lovell, K., Noshirvani, H., Livanou, M., & Thrasher, S. (1998). Treatment of posttraumatic stress disorder by exposure and/or cognitive restructuring: A controlled study. *Archives of General Psychiatry, 55,* 317–325.

Martin, D. J., Garske, J. P., & Davis, M. K. (2000). Relation of the therapeutic alliance with outcome and other variables: a meta-analytic review. *Journal of Consulting and Clinical Psychology, 68*(3), 438–450.

Masten, A. (2001). Ordinary magic: Resilience processes in development. *American Psychologist, 56*(3), 227–238.

Mathew, S. J., Coplan, J. D., Smith, E. L., Scharf, B. A., Owens, M. J., Nemeroff, C. B., Mann, J. J., Gorman, J. M., & Rosenblum, L. A. (2002). Cerebrospinal fluid concentrations of biogenic amines and corticotropin-releasing factor in adolescent non-human primates as a function of the timing of adverse early rearing. *Stress, 5*(3), 185–193.

McCullough, M. E., Hoyt, W. T., Larson, D. B., Koenig, H. G., & Thoresen, C. (2000). Religious involvement and mortality: A meta-analytic review. *Health Psychology, 19*(3), 211–222.

McEwen, B. S. (1998). Stress, adaptation, and disease: Allostasis and allostatic load. *Annals of the New York Academy of Sciences, 840,* 33–44.

McEwen, B. S. (2003). Early life influences on life-long patterns of behavior and health. *Mental Retardation and Developmental Disabilities Research Reviews, 9*(3), 149–154.

McEwen, B. S. (2004). Protection and damage from acute and chronic stress: Allostasis and allostatic overload and relevance to the pathophysiology of psychiatric disorders. *Annals of the New York Academy of Sciences, 1032,* 1–7.

McEwen, B. S., & Stellar, E. (1993). Stress and the individual. Mechanisms leading to disease. *Archives of Internal Medicine, 153*(18), 2093–2101.

McGaugh, J. L. (2002). Memory consolidation and the amygdala: A systems perspective. *Trends in Neurosciences, 25,* 456–461.

McNally, R. J. (1999). Research on eye movement desensitization and reprocessing (EMDR) as a treatment for PTSD. *PTSD Research Quarterly, 10*(1), 1–7.

Mobbs, D., Greicius, M. D., Eimanabdel-Azim, & Menon, V. (2003). Humor modulates the mesolimbic reward centers. *Neuron, 40,* 1041–1048.

Moos, R. H., & Schaefer, J. A. (1993). Coping resources and processes: Current concepts and measures. In L. Goldberger & S. Breznits (Eds.), *Handbook of stress: Theoretical and clinical aspects* (pp. 234–257). New York: The Free Press.

Moran, J. M., Wig, G. S., Adams, R. B., Jr., Janata, P., & Kelley, W. M. (2004). Neural correlates of humor detection and appreciation. *NeuroImage, 21*(3): 1055–1060.

Morgan, C. A., III, Wang, S., Southwick, S. M., Rasmusson, A., Hazlett, G., Hauger, R. L., & Charney, D. S. (2000). Plasma neuropeptide-Y concentrations in humans exposed to military survival training. *Biological Psychiatry, 47*(10), 902–909.

Nemeroff, C. B., Bremner, J. D., Foa, E. B., Mayberg, H. S., North, C. S., & Stein, M. B. (2006). Posttraumatic stress disorder: A state-of-the-science review. *Journal of Psychiatric Research, 40*(1), 1–21.

Ochsner, K. N., Bunge, S. A., Gross, J. J., & Gabrieli, J. D. (2002). Rethinking feelings: An fMRI study of the cognitive regulation of emotion. *Journal of Cognitive Neuroscience, 14,* 1215–1229.

Overmeier, J., & Murison, R. (2005). Trauma and resulting sensitization effects are modulated by psychological factors. *Psychoneuroendocrinology, 30,* 965–973.

Ozer, E. J., Best, S. R., Lipsey, T. L., & Weiss, D. S. (2003). Predictors of posttraumatic stress disorder and symptoms in adults: A meta-analysis. *Psychological Bulletin, 129,* 52–71.

Parker, K. J., Buckmaster, C. L., Justus, K. R., Schatzberg, A. F., & Lyons, D. M. (2005). Mild early life stress enhances prefrontal-dependent response inhibition in monkeys. *Biological Psychiatry, 57*(8), 848–855.

Parker, K. J., Buckmaster, C. L., Schatzberg, A. F., & Lyons, D. M. (2004). Prospective investigation of stress inoculation in young monkeys. *Archives of General Psychiatry, 61*(9), 933–941.

Penza, K. M., Heim, C., & Nemeroff, C. B. (2003). Neurobiological effects of childhood abuse: implications for the pathophysiology of depression and anxiety. *Archives of Women's Mental Health, 6*(1), 15–22.

Petty, F., Jordan, S., Kramer, G. L., Zukas, P. K., & Wu, J. (1997). Benzodiazepine prevention of swim stress-induced sensitization of cortical biogenic amines: An in vivo microdialysis study. *Neurochemical Research, 22*(9), 1101–1104.

Petty, F., Kramer, G., & Wilson, L. (1992). Prevention of learned helplessness: In vivo correlation with cortical serotonin. *Pharmacology, Biochemistry & Behavior, 43*(2), 361–367.

Rachman, S. (1979). The concept of required helpfulness. *Behavior Research and Therapy, 17*, 1–6.

Rasmusson, A. M., Hauger, R. L., Morgan, C. A., Bremner, J. D., Charney, D. S., & Southwick, S. M. (2000). Low baseline and yohimbine-stimulated plasma neuropeptide Y (NPY) levels in combat-related PTSD. *Biological Psychiatry, 47*(6), 526–539.

Resick, P. A. (2001). *Clinical psychology: A modular course.* Philadelphia, PA: Taylor & Francis.

Resick, P. A., Nishith, P., Weaver, T. L., Astin, M. C., & Feuer, C. A. (2002). A comparison of cognitive-processing therapy with prolonged exposure and a waiting condition for the treatment of chronic posttraumatic stress disorder in female rape victims. *Journal of Consulting and Clinical Psychology, 70*(4), 867–879.

Resnick, H. S., Kilpatrick, D. G., Dansky, B. S., Saunders, B. E., & Best, C. L. (1993). Prevalence of civilian trauma and posttraumatic stress disorder in a representative national sample of women. *Journal of Consulting and Clinical Psychology, 61*, 984–991.

Ressler, K. J., Rothbaum, B. O., Tannenbaum, L., Anderson, P., Graap, K., Zimand, E., Hodges, L., & Davis, M. (2004). Cognitive enhancers as adjuncts to psychotherapy: Use of D-cycloserine in phobic individuals to facilitate extinction of fear. *Archives of General Psychiatry, 61*(11), 1136–1144.

Roozendaal, B. (2000). Glucocorticoids and the regulation of memory consolidation. *Psychoneuroendocrinology, 25*, 213–238.

Rozanski, A., Blumenthal, J. A., & Kaplan, J. (1999). Impact of psychological factors on the pathogenesis of cardiovascular disease and implications for therapy. *Circulation, 99*, 2192–2217.

Schaefer, J. A., & Moos, R. H. (1992). Life crisis and personal growth. In B. N. Carpenter (Ed.), *Personal coping: Theory research and application* (pp. 149–170). Westport, CT: Praeger.

Schaefer, J. A., & Moos, R. H. (1998). The context for posttraumatic growth: Life crises, individual and social resources, and coping. In I. B. Weinger (Ed.), *Posttraumatic growth: Positive changes in the aftermath of crisis* (pp. 99–125). Mahwah, NJ: Erlbaum.

Scheier, M. F., Matthews, K. A., Owens, J. F., Magovern, G. L., Lefbvre, R. C., Abbott R. A., & Carver, C. S. (1989). Dispositional optimism and recovery from coronary artery bypass surgery: The beneficial effects of physical and psychological well-being. *Journal of Personality and Social Psychology, 57*(6), 1024–1040.

Seligman, M. E. (1972). Learned helplessness. *Annual Review of Medicine, 23*, 407–412.

Seligman, M. E., Castellon, C., Cacciola, J., Schulman, P., Luborsky, L., Ollove, M., & Downing, R. (1988). Explanatory style change during cognitive therapy for unipolar depression. *Journal of Abnormal Psychology, 97*(1): 13–18.

Seligman, M. E., & Csikszentmihalyi, M. (2000). Positive psychology. An introduction. *American Psychologist, 55*(1), 5–14.

Shapiro, F. (1995). *Eye movement desensitization and reprocessing: Basic principles, protocols and procedures.* New York: Guilford Press.

Siebert, A. (1996). *The survivor personality.* New York: Pedigree Books.

Silver, R., Wortman, C., & Crofton, C. (1990). The role of coping in support provision: The self-presentation dilemma of victims of life crises. In B. Sarason, I. Sarason & G. Pierce (Eds.), *Social support.* New York: Wiley.

Silver, R. C., Holman, E. A., McIntosh, D. N., Poulin, M., & Gil-Rivas, V. (2002). Nationwide longitudinal study of psychological responses to September 11. *Journal of the American Medical Association, 288*, 1235–1244.

Southwick, S. M., Charney, D. S., & Vythilingham, M. (2005). The psychobiology of depression and resilience to stress: Implications for prevention and treatment. *Annual review of Clinical Psychology, 1*, 255–291.

Southwick, S. M., Morgan, C. A., Vythilingham, M., Krystal J. H., & Charney, D. S. (2003). Emerging neurobiological factors in stress resilience. *PTSD Research Quarterly*. Retrieved January 15, 2006, from http://www.ncptsd.va.gov/publications/rq/rqpdf/V14N4.PDF

Stein, D. J., Ipser, J., & Seedat, S. (2006). Pharmacotherapy for posttraumatic stress disorder. *Cochrane Database of Systematic Reviews*, (1), CD002795.

Tedeschi, R. G., Park, C. L., & Calhoun, L. G. (1998). *Posttraumatic growth*. Mahwah, NJ: Erlbaum.

Teicher, M. H., Andersen, S. L., Polcari, A., Anderson, C. M., Navalta, C. P., & Kim, D. M. (2003). The neurobiological consequences of early stress and childhood maltreatment. *Neruoscience and Biobehavioral Reviews, 27*(1–2), 33–44.

Thorson, J. A., & Powell, F. C. (1994). Depression and sense of humor. *Psychological Reports, 75*, 1473–1474.

Travis, L. A., Lyness, J. M., Shields, C. G., King, D. A., & Cox, C. (2004). Social support, depression, and functional disability in older adult primary-care patients. *American Journal of Geriatric Psychiatry, 12*, 265–271.

Tugade, M. M., & Fredrickson, B. L. (2002). Positive emotions and emotional intelligence. In L. Feldman Barrett & P. Salovey (Eds.), *The wisdom of feelings: Psychological processes in emotional intelligence* (pp. 319–340). New York: Guilford Press.

Vaillant, G. E. (1977). *Adaptation to life*. Boston: Little Brown.

Vaillant, G. E. (1992). The historical origins and future potential of Sigmund Freud's concept of the mechanisms of defense. *International Review of Psychoanalysis, 19*, 35–50.

Valentiner, D. P., Holahan, C. J., & Moos, R. H. (1994). Social support, appraisals of event controllability, and coping: an integrative model. *Journal of Personality and Social Psychology, 66*, 1094–1102.

Vythilingam, M., Heim, C., Newport, J., Miller, A. H., Anderson, E., Bronen, R., Brummer, M., Staib, L., Vermetten, E., Charney, D. S., Nemeroff, C. B., & Bremner, J. D. (2002). Childhood trauma associated with smaller hippocampal volume in women with major depression. *American Journal of Psychiatry, 159*(12), 2072–2080.

Vythilingham, M., Scaramozzo, M., Nelson, E., Hazlett, G., Waldeck, T., Hadd, K., Agarwal, R., Drevets, W., Pine, D., Charney, D., & Ernst, M. (2005). Resilient Special Forces soldiers have enhanced activation of reward related circuits. *Biological Psychiatry, 57*, 103–104S.

Wade, S. L., Borawski, E. A., Taylor, H. G., Drotar, D., Yeates, K. O., & Stancin, T. (2001). The relationship of caregiver coping to family outcomes during the initial year following pediatric traumatic injury. *Journal of Consulting and Clinical Psychology, 69*(3), 406–415.

Werner, E., & Smith, R. (1992). *Overcoming the odds: High-risk children from birth to adulthood*. Ithaca, NY: Cornell University.

Wills, T. A., & Fegan, M. F. (2001). Social networks and social support. In A. Baum, T. A., Revenson, & J. E. Singer (Eds.), *Handbook of health psychology* (pp. 203–234). Mahwah, NJ: Erlbaum.

Wismer Fries, A. B., Ziegler, T. E., Kurian, J. R., Jacoris, S., & Pollak, S. D. (2005). Early experience in humans is associated with changes in neuropeptides critical for regulating social behavior. *Proceedings of the National Academy of Sciences of the United States of America, 102*(47), 17237–17240.

Wolin, S. J., & Wolin, S. (1993). *Bound and determined: growing up resilient in a troubled family.* New York: Villard.

Yehuda, R. (2002). Current concepts: post-traumatic stress disorder. *New England Journal of Medicine, 346,* 108–114.

Yehuda, R. (2004). Risk and resilience in posttraumatic stress disorder. *Journal of Clinical Psychiatry, 65*(Suppl. 1), 29–36.

Young, L. J., & Wang, Z. (2004). The neurobiology of pair bonding. *Nature Neuroscience, 7*(10), 1048–1054.

Zeidner, M., & Hammer, A. L. (1992). Coping with missile attack: Resources, strategies, and outcomes. *Journal of Personality, 60,* 709–746.

Chapter 16

The Developing Adolescent Brain
in Socioeconomic Context

Martha J. Farah, Kimberly G. Noble, and Hallam Hurt

Some of the most promising approaches to the study of adolescence focus on neurocognitive function. In addition to mapping developmental change in the brain systems responsible for cognitive abilities such as attention, memory, and inhibitory control (e.g., Sowell, Thompson, & Toga, this volume), it is possible to identify and intervene on risk factors for adolescent development in terms of individual differences in these systems (e.g., Greenberg, Riggs, & Blair, this volume; Rueda, Rothbart, Saccomanno, & Posner, this volume). This chapter is aimed at understanding the neurocognitive basis of a major influence on adolescent development, namely socioeconomic status (SES).

SES is typically measured by a combination of income, educational attainment, and occupation status, although it encompasses a large number of correlated factors such as neighborhood quality, family structure (e.g., one-parent versus two-parent families), and physical health. Adolescents of low SES are more likely than their middle-SES counterparts to drop out of school, suffer major psychiatric illness, become parents at an early age, and come under the control of the criminal justice system. Given the importance of SES for adolescent development, it is important to understand its neurocognitive basis, including the neurocognitive correlates of SES and the aspects of childhood experience that affect adolescent neurocognitive status.

The correlations between SES and children's performance on standardized tests such as IQ tell us that SES must be related to brain development, as cognitive ability is a function of the brain. Yet little is currently known about the relationship between SES and brain function, in terms of two key issues: the specific brain systems that correlate with SES and the mechanisms by which these correlations emerge. The goal of this chapter is to review some preliminary studies that address these issues.

We begin with the first issue: the characterization of the SES gap in children's neurocognitive development in terms that can be related to current cognitive neuroscience conceptions of mind and brain. One hypothesis is that SES correlates with all neurocognitive systems equally, across the board. Alternative hypotheses are that SES correlates with certain systems more than others. There is already reason to believe that the development of the brain systems underlying language system is associated with SES, as a number of relatively pure tests of language development have revealed a robust SES gap (Whitehurst, 1997). Would other systems that, like language, undergo prolonged postnatal development also show specific sensitivity to SES? Prefrontal cortex is a brain region that continues to mature throughout childhood, with pronounced cellular changes in the preschool and early childhood years (Johnson, 1997). It is also a region on which many of the cognitive achievements of early childhood depend (Case, 1992; Diamond, 1990; Diamond, Prevor, et al., 1997; Johnson, 1997; Posner & Rothbart, 1998). A disproportionate effect of SES on prefrontal function is therefore a hypothesis of particular interest.

Neurocognitive Correlates of SES

The first set of studies reviewed here was aimed at characterizing the neurocognitive profile of poverty. They take, as their starting point, the existence of an SES gap in cognitive achievement and ask, Is the SES gap uniform over different neurocognitive systems, or is the development of some systems more strongly correlated with SES than others? We have so far addressed this question in three different studies. The three are distinguished primarily by the ages of the children who participated and the specific neurocognitive tasks used to assess the children's brain development. In addition, two of the studies compared groups of low and middle SES children, whereas one analyzed children's task performance as a function of continuously varying SES.

In an initial study we compared the neurocognitive performance of 30 low and 30 middle SES African American Philadelphia public school kindergarteners (Noble, Norman, & Farah, 2005). SES was established on the basis of parental education, job status, and family income-to-needs ratio. The children were tested on a battery of tasks adapted from the cognitive neuroscience literature, designed to assess the functioning of five key neurocognitive systems. These systems are defined in anatomical and functional terms—that is, based on their brain localizations and the kinds of information processing for which they are used.

Two systems were the subject of a priori hypotheses, as described earlier. The "left perisylvian/language" system is a complex, distributed system encompassing semantic, syntactic, and phonological aspects of language and dependent predominantly on the temporal and frontal areas of the left hemisphere that surround the Sylvian fissure. The "prefrontal/executive" system enables flexible responding in situations in which the appropriate response may not be the most routine or attractive one, or in which it requires maintenance or updating of information concerning recent events. It is dependent on prefrontal cortex, a late-maturing brain region that is disproportionately developed in humans.

In addition, we assessed three other neurocognitive systems that play important roles in school and the real world. The "medial temporal/memory" system is responsible for one-trial learning, the ability to retain a representation of a stimulus after a single exposure to it (which contrasts with the ability to gradually strengthen a representation through conditioning-like mechanisms), and is dependent on the hippocampus and related structures of the medial temporal lobe. The "parietal/spatial cognition" system underlies our ability to mentally represent and manipulate the spatial relations among objects, and is primarily dependent on posterior parietal cortex. The "occipitotemporal/visual cognition" system is responsible for pattern recognition and visual mental imagery, translating image format visual representations into more abstract representations of object shape and identity, and reciprocally translating visual memory knowledge into image format representations (mental images).

The results of our first study replicated the well-known SES gap in cognitive test performance in general, with the middle-SES children performing better than the low SES children on the battery of tasks as a whole. As predicted for the left perisylvian/language system and the prefrontal/executive system, the disparity between low and middle SES kindergarteners was both large and statistically significant. Indeed, the groups differed by over a standard deviation in their performance composite on language tests, and by over two thirds of a standard deviation in the executive function composite. The other systems did not differ significantly between low and middle SES children, and differed significantly less than the first two.

In a subsequent study we attempted to replicate and extend these findings in a larger group of children, 150 first graders of varying ethnicities whose SES spanned a range from low through middle, as determined by parental education, job status and, when available, income-to-needs ratio (Noble, McCandliss & Farah, 2006). These children completed a different set of tests designed to tap the same neurocognitive systems as the previous study, with two main differences.

The first difference was an improvement in the medial temporal/memory system tests. In the previous study, the test phase had followed immediately after the initial exposure to the stimuli, making the tests more sensitive to immediate memory ability than the longer-term memory for which medial temporal structures are needed. The memory tasks of the second study included a longer delay between initial exposure to the stimuli to be remembered and later test.

A second difference between this and the previous study is that we subdivided prefrontal/executive function into subsystems and assessed each separately with its own tests. The three subsystems, again defined in anatomical and functional terms, are described here.

The "lateral prefrontal/working memory" system enables us to hold information "on line" to maintain it over an interval and manipulate it, and is primarily dependent on the lateral surface of the prefrontal lobes. (Note that this is distinct from the ability to commit information to long-term memory, which is dependent on the medial temporal cortex.) The "anterior cingulate/cognitive control" system is required when we must resist the most routine or easily available response in favor of a more task-appropriate response, and is dependent on a network of regions within prefrontal cortex including the anterior cingulate gyrus. The "ventromedial prefrontal/reward processing" system is responsible for regulating our responses in the face of rewarding stimuli, allowing us to resist the immediate pull of an attractive stimulus in order to maximize more long-term gains.

The results of this study confirmed the strong relationship between the left perisylvian/language system and SES found previously. Also as before, prefrontal/executive systems were correlated with SES. The design of this study allowed us to specify in greater detail the components of executive function that correlate with SES: Children's performance on the lateral prefrontal/working memory and anterior cingulate/cognitive control tasks were both significantly associated with their SES, although no such relation was observed for the ventromedial prefrontal/reward processing tasks. This study also revealed an association between SES and the parietal/spatial cognition system and, with the delay introduced between exposure and test in the memory tasks, with the medial temporal/memory system.

Finally, we assessed these same neurocognitive systems in older children, with yet a different battery of tasks. We tested 60 middle school students, half of low and half of middle SES, as determined by parental education and job status, matched for age, gender, and ethnicity (Farah et al., 2004, 2006). Again, sizeable and significant SES disparities were observed for language and the two executive subsystems, working memory and cognitive control, as well as for memory.

In sum, although the outcome of each study was different, there were also commonalities among them, despite different tasks and different children tested at different ages. The most robust neurocognitive correlates of SES appear to involve the left perisylvian/language system, the medial temporal/memory system (insofar as SES effects were found in both studies that tested memory with an adequate delay), and the prefrontal/executive system, in particular its lateral prefrontal/

working memory and anterior cingulate/cognitive control components. Children growing up in low SES environments perform less well on tests that tax the functioning of these specific systems.

The profile of SES disparities, with greatest disparity in systems needed for language, memory, working memory, and cognitive control, would be expected to affect children's life trajectories. The importance of language and memory is obvious, from the social sphere to the world of school and work. Less obvious is the impact of working memory and cognitive control on real-world success, but studies have linked individual differences in these systems to individual differences in children's behavioral self-regulation and adult intelligence and problem-solving ability (Davis et al., 2002; Duncan et al., 1995; Engle et al., 1999; Gray et al., 2003).

These studies suggest that one important prefrontal system, the ventromedial prefrontal/reward processing system, may not be affected by SES. The two studies that explicitly assessed this system found that low and middle SES children were equivalent in their ability to control their own responsivity to reward. This was demonstrated by four different tasks across the two studies: two different reversal learning tasks in which children must unlearn a series of initial associations between stimulus properties and reward value in order to maximize reward, and two in which they must delay responding in order to maximize reward. In addition, although the first study was not designed to distinguish among different prefrontal systems, one of the tasks provided a measure of reward processing, specifically the tendency to discount future reward. When the children were offered one sticker immediately or multiple stickers following a delay, and low and middle SES groups were identical in their preference for larger future rewards.

Some of the challenges of adolescence involve the ability to delay gratification and reappraise the value of objects and activities in the light of new information about their risks and rewards. Examples of such challenges include opportunities for illicit drug use and early sexual activity. The results of our research so far suggest that although adolescents of low SES generally face more life challenges than their higher SES counterparts, and although on average they must face these challenges with less well developed language, memory, and executive function systems, they may be equally well equipped to deal with them in one important respect. The ability to exercise restraint in the face of temptation by rewarding stimuli and to shift one's behavior from approach to avoidance of previously rewarding stimuli, which depend on ventromedial prefrontal cortex, appear to be unrelated to SES in our studies. One possible explanation for this comes from the timing of maturation within different regions of prefrontal cortex. Fuster (2002) had pointed out that ventromedial regions mature earlier than other regions of prefrontal cortex and might therefore be less sensitive to differences in childhood experience.

What Causes the SES Gap
in Neurocognitive Development?

From a scientific point of view, all we have done in the first three studies is to describe the SES gap in more physiologically meaningful terms than standardized test results. The question of mechanism—in other words, what causes the effects described here—has not yet been discussed. A complete scientific understanding of the effects of SES on neurocognitive development must include an account of the mechanisms by which different aspects of brain function come to be associated with SES. From a practical point of view, knowing which systems are most affected by SES has only indirect implications for intervention or prevention programs. Knowing how the effects come about would be far more useful in suggesting how to close the developmental gap between low and middle SES children.

To address this issue, the first question we must ask concerns the direction of causality: Do the associations discussed so far reflect the effects of SES on brain development, or the opposite direction of causality? Perhaps families with higher innate language, executive, and memory abilities tend to acquire and maintain a higher SES. Such a mechanism seems likely, a priori, as it would be surprising if genetic influences on cognitive ability did not, in the aggregate, contribute to individual and family SES. However, it also seems likely that causality operates in the opposite direction as well, with SES influencing cognitive ability through childhood environment and experience. Given that the direction of causality is an empirical issue, what data bear on the issue?

The methods of behavioral genetics research can, in principle, tell us about the direction of causality in the association between SES and the development of specific neurocognitive functions. However, these methods have yet to be applied to that question. They have been applied to a related question, namely the heritability of IQ and SES. Cross-fostering studies of within- and between-SES adoption suggest that roughly half the IQ disparity in children is experiential (Capron & Duyme, 1989; Schiff & Lewontin, 1986). If anything, these studies are likely to err in the direction of underestimating the influence of environment because the effects of prenatal and early postnatal environment are included in the estimates of genetic influences in adoption studies. Additional evidence comes from studies of when, in a child's life, poverty was experienced. Within a given family that experiences a period of poverty, the effects are greater on siblings who were young during that period (Duncan et al., 1994), an effect that cannot be explained by genetics. In sum, multiple sources of evidence indicate that SES does indeed have an effect on cognitive development, although its role in the specific types of neurocognitive system development investigated here is not yet known.

Physical and Psychological Determinants
of Neurocognitive Development

What aspects of childhood environment and experience might be responsible for the effects of SES on neurocognitive development? A large set of possibilities exist, some affecting brain development by their direct effects on the body and some by less direct psychological mechanisms. Three somatic factors have been identified as significant risk factors for low cognitive achievement by the Center for Children and Poverty (1997): inadequate nutrition, lead exposure, and substance abuse (particularly prenatal exposure).

Two nutritional factors, iron deficiency and mild-to-moderate protein-energy malnutrition (PEM; the shortage of both protein and calories), are more prevalent at lower levels of SES. Iron-deficiency anemia afflicts about one quarter of low-income children in the United States (Center on Hunger, Poverty and Nutrition Policy, 1998) and is known to impair brain development when severe. The neurocognitive impact mind-to-moderate PEM is not well established (see Ricciuti, 1993, and Sigman, 1995, for differing viewpoints). The Center on Hunger, Poverty and Nutrition Policy (1998) has suggested that it probably has little effect on its own.

The role of nutrition in SES disparities in brain development has been difficult to resolve because nutritional status is so strongly correlated with a host of other family and environmental variables likely to impact neurocognitive development, including all of the potential mechanisms of causation to be reviewed here. Although nutritional supplementation programs could in principle be used as an "experimental manipulation" of nutritional status alone, in practice these programs are often coupled with other, nonnutritional forms of enrichment or affect children's lives in nonnutritional ways that perpetuate the confound (e.g., children given school breakfast are absent and late less often). The consensus regarding the role of nutrition in the cognitive outcomes of poor children has shifted over the past few decades, from primary cause to a factor that contributes indirectly and through synergies with other environmental disadvantages (Center on Hunger, Poverty and Nutrition Policy, 1998).

Lead is a neurotoxin found in older house paint that accumulates in the bodies of low SES children who are more likely to live in old dwellings with peeling paint. A meta-analysis of low-level lead exposure on IQ indicates estimated that every 10 ug/dL increase in lead is associated with a 2.6 point decrease in IQ (Schwartz, 1994). As with nutrition, the effect of lead synergizes with other environmental factors and is more pronounced in low SES children (Bellinger et al., 1987). For example, low iron stores render children more susceptible to environmental lead (Center on Hunger, Poverty and Nutrition Policy, 1998).

Prenatal substance exposure is a third factor that affects children of all SES levels but is disproportionately experienced by the poor. Maternal use of alcohol, tobacco, marijuana, and other drugs of abuse have been associated with adverse cognitive outcomes in children (Chasnoff et al., 1998). Although the highly publicized phenomenon of "crack babies" led to dire predictions of an irreparably damaged generation of children growing up in the inner city, in retrospect this was overreaction. Indeed, epidemiological studies have found the effects on cognitive performance to be subtle (Hurt et al., 1999; Mayes, 2002; Vidaeff & Mastrobattista, 2003). For example, the low SES 4-year-olds of Hurt's cohort, whose average IQ was 81, served as control subjects for a cohort with prenatal cocaine exposure, whose average IQ was a statistically indistinguishable 79. This lack of difference contrasts with the substantial difference between both low SES groups' IQ scores and those of middle SES children, the majority of whom have IQs of 90 or above.

The set of potentially causative somatic factors just reviewed is far from complete. There are SES gradients in a wide variety of physical health measures, many of which could affect children's neurocognitive development through a variety of different mechanisms (Adler et al., 1997). Having briefly reviewed the most frequently discussed factors, we turn now to a consideration of the psychological differences between the experiences of low and middle SES children that could also affect neurocognitive development.

As with potential physical causes, the set of potential psychological causes for the SES gap in cognitive achievement is large, and the causes are likely to exert their effects synergistically. Here we will review research on differences in cognitive stimulation and stress.

One difference between low and middle SES families that seems predictable, even in the absence of any other information, is that low SES children are likely to receive less cognitive stimulation than middle SES children. Their economic status alone predicts that they will have fewer toys and books and less exposure to zoos, museums, and other cultural institutions because of the expense of such items and activities. This is indeed the case (Bradley et al., 2001) and has been identified as a mediator between SES and measures of cognitive achievement (Bradley & Corwyn, 1999; Brooks-Gunn & Duncan, 1997; McLoyd, 1998). Such a mediating role is consistent with the results of neuroscience research with animals. Starting many decades ago (e.g., Volkmar & Greenough, 1972), researchers began to observe the powerful effects of environmental stimulation on brain development. Animals reared in barren laboratory cages showed less well developed brains by a number of different anatomical and physiological measures, compared with those reared in more complex environments with opportunities to climb, burrow, and socialize (see van Praag et al., 2000, for a review).

Other types of cognitive stimulation, for example parental speech designed to engage the child in conversation, are also less common in low SES homes (B. N. Adams, 1998). The average number of hours of one-on-one picture book reading experienced by children prior to kindergarten entry has been estimated at 25 for low SES children and between 1,000 and 1,700 for middle SES children (M. J. Adams, 1990). Thus, in addition to material limitations, differing parental expectations and concerns also contribute to differences in the amount of cognitive stimulation experienced by low and middle SES children.

The lives of low SES individuals tend to be more stressful for a variety of reasons, some of which are obvious: concern about providing for basic family needs, dangerous neighborhoods, and little control over one's work life. Again, research bears out this intuition: Turner and Avison (2003) confirmed that lower SES is associated with more stressful life events by a number of different measures. The same appears to be true for children as well as adults, and is apparent in salivary levels of the stress hormone cortisol (Lupien et al., 2001).

Why is stress an important consideration for neurocognitive development? Psychological stress causes the secretion of cortisol and other stress hormones, which affect the brain in numerous ways (Gunnar, this volume; McEwen, 2000). The immature brain is particularly sensitive to these effects. In basic research studies of rat brain development, rat pups are subjected to the severe stress of prolonged separation from the mother and stress hormone levels predictably climb. The later anatomy and function of the brain is altered by this early neuroendocrine phenomenon. The brain area most affected is the medial temporal area needed for memory, although prefrontal systems involved in the regulation of the stress response are also impacted (Meaney et al., 1996).

Cognitive Stimulation and Social/Emotional Nurturance: Different Causal Roles

The three studies summarized earlier show an association between SES and the development of specific neurocognitive systems, most consistently in language, memory, and executive function. Whereas we previously knew that SES was associated with cognitive achievement as measured by broad-spectrum tests of cognitive ability such as IQ and school achievement tests, our results redescribe this relationship in terms of the theoretically more meaningful components of cognitive function specified by cognitive neuroscience. Appropriately describing a phenomenon can be a crucial step in understanding it. Explanations are facilitated when the phenomena to be explained are described in terms corresponding to the natural kinds involved in potential mechanisms.

Knowing that SES effects are manifest in IQ and high school graduation rates tells us little about the possible brain mechanisms of SES effects on cognitive achievement. In contrast, knowing that SES effects are found in specific neurocognitive systems enables us to harness what we know about the development of those systems to frame hypotheses about the origins of the effects. An important corollary of this point is that different mechanisms may be responsible for SES effects on different neurocognitive systems. By resolving the SES disparity into its multiple underlying components, we can disentangle multiple causal pathways and test hypotheses about each separately. This is important because such separation allows more selective, and hence more powerful, tests of mechanism.

Our current research is an attempt to make use of the description of the neuro-cognitive description of SES disparities to test hypotheses about the causal pathways. Drawing on our previous research that identified three neurocognitive systems as having the most robust differences as a function of SES, we are now testing hypotheses concerning the determinants of individual differences in the development of these systems in children of low SES. Specifically, we are investigating the role of childhood cognitive stimulation and social/emotional nurturance (Farah et al., 2005).

The participants in this research are 110 low SES children from a cohort enrolled at birth in a study of the effects of prenatal cocaine exposure (see Hurt et al., 1995). At the time of neurocognitive testing, the children were on the cusp of adolescence, between 10 and 14 years old. Approximately half of the children were exposed to cocaine prenatally, and half were not. Maternal use of cocaine, amphetamines, opiates, barbiturates, benzodiazepines, marijuana, alcohol, and tobacco are ascertained by interview and medical record review at time of birth and, for all but the last three substances, maternal and infant urine specimens.

As part of the ongoing study of these children, a research assistant visited the home of each child at ages 4 and 8 and administered the HOME inventory (Home Observation and Measurement of Environment; Caldwell & Bradley, 1984). HOME includes an interview with the mother about family life and observations of the interactions between mother and child. HOME has a number of different subscales relevant to different aspects of the child's experience. We combined a number of different subscales indicative of the amount of cognitive stimulation provided to the child to make a composite measure of cognitive stimulation, and a number of different subscales indicative of the amount of social/emotional nurturance provided to the child to make a composite measure of social/emotional nurturance. The subscales used for each composite, along with representative items, were as follows.

The Cognitive Stimulation composite for 4-year-olds was composed of the following: learning stimulation ("Child has toys that teach color," "At least 10 books are visible in the apartment"), language stimulation ("Child has toys that help teach the names of animals," "Mother uses correct grammar and pronunciation"), academic stimulation ("Child is encouraged to learn colors," "Child is encouraged to learn to read a few words"), modeling ("Some delay of food gratification is expected," "Parent introduces visitor to child"), and variety of experience ("Child has real or toy musical instrument," "Child's artwork is displayed someplace in house"). For 8-year-olds, the subscales used for the Cognitive Stimulation composite were as follows: growth-fostering materials and experiences ("Child has free access to at least 10 appropriate books," "House has at least two pictures of other type of artwork on the walls"), provision for active stimulation ("Family has a television, and it is used judiciously, not left on continuously," "Family member has taken child, or arranged for child to go, to a scientific, historical, or art museum within the past year"), and family participation in developmentally stimulating experiences ("Family visits or receives visits from relatives or friends at least once every other week," "Family member has taken child, or arranged for child to go, on a trip of more than 50 miles from his home").

The Social/Emotional Nurturance composite for 4-year-olds was composed of the following: warmth and affection ("Parent holds child close 10–15 minutes per day," "Parent converses with child at least twice during visit") and acceptance ("Parent does not scold or derogate child more than once," "parent neither slaps nor spanks child during visit"). For 8-year-olds, the subscales used for the Social/Emotional Nurturance composite were as follows: emotional and verbal responsivity ("Child has been praised at least twice during past week for doing something," "Parent responds to child's questions during interview"), encouragement of maturity ("Family requires child to carry out certain self-care routines," "Parents set limits for child and generally enforce them"), emotional climate ("Parent has not lost temper with child more than once during previous week," "Parent uses some term of endearment or some diminutive for child's name when talking about child at least twice during visit"), and paternal involvement ("Father [or father substitute] regularly engages in outdoor recreation with child," "Child eats at least one meal per day, on most days, with mother and father [or mother and father figures; one-parent families rate an automatic no]").

Two other variables with the potential to account for differences in neuro-cognitive development included in our analyses were maternal intelligence and prenatal substance exposure. The former was measured by the Weschler Adult Intelligence Scale–Revised (WAIS-R). Maternal IQ could influence child neuro-cognitive outcome by genetic mechanisms or by its effect on the environment and experiences provided by the mother for the child. Prenatal substance exposure was coded for analysis on an integer scale of 0 to 4, with 1 point for each of the following substances: tobacco, alcohol, marijuana, and cocaine. Use of other substances was an exclusionary criterion.

We used statistical regression to examine the relations between the neuro-cognitive outcome measures and the predictor variables cognitive stimulation, social/emotional nurturance, maternal IQ, and polysubstance use, as well as the child's gender and age at time of neurocognitive testing. Our results indicate that the development of different neurocognitive systems are affected by different variables. Children's performance on the tests of left perisylvian/language system function was predicted by age at testing and average cognitive stimulation. In contrast, performance on tests of medial temporal/memory ability was predicted by average social/emotional nurturance.

The relation between memory and early emotional experience is consistent with the animal research cited earlier, showing a deleterious effect of stress hormones on hippocampal development. Our analyses did not reveal any systematic relation of the predictor variables considered here to lateral prefrontal/working memory or anterior cingulate/cognitive control function. In conclusion, different aspects of early experience affect different systems of the developing brain. Cognitive stimulation influences the development of language, whereas social/emotional nurturance affects the development of memory but not language.

Conclusions

Many risk factors and protective factors have been identified for adolescence, some related to the psychological functioning of individuals themselves and some to their life circumstances. Strong executive function is a psychological trait that has a well-established protective role with respect to drug abuse, crime, and other negative life outcomes (e.g., Giancola, Martin, Tarter, Pelham, & Moss, 1996). It is also associated with reduced risk for major psychopathologies, many of which are likely to first appear in adolescence or young adulthood, including schizophrenia (see Chang et al., this volume). Language ability is also predictive of adolescent outcome (Beitchman et al., 2001). The research described in this chapter relates individual differences in these and other abilities to differences in socioeconomic status.

We used the framework of cognitive neuroscience to parse cognitive ability into a set of component systems, which we assessed behaviorally using tasks adapted from the cognitive neuroscience literature. Our findings indicate that both executive and language function vary with SES. By subdividing executive function into anatomically and functionally different systems, we found that working memory and cognitive control have the strongest relationship to SES. Although previous studies of executive function and adolescent risk did not discriminate among different systems of executive function, their measures included tasks that tax these systems, particularly cognitive control (Giancola et al., 1996). In contrast, we could find no detectable relationship between SES and reward processing, another form of executive function that is predictive of real-world life outcomes (Mischel, Shoda, & Rodriguez, 1989).

In addition to assessing the relationship between SES and neurocognitive function, we have begun to seek the specific causal factors responsible for this relationship. The results of our preliminary study suggest that the quality of cognitive stimulation and social/emotional nurturance early in childhood both affect neurocognitive function in middle school. Language ability seems particularly sensitive to cognitive stimulation, and memory ability seems particularly sensitive to social/emotional nurturance. Our measures of childhood experience did not account for variability in any of the prefrontal/executive systems.

The preliminary findings summarized here must be confirmed with additional research, using different study populations and different assessment methods. In the meantime, we can provisionally conclude that SES does bear a significant relationship with neurocognitive functions known to play a role in adolescent outcome, and that at least part of this relationship is probably mediated by child-hood experience. Better understanding of the causal connections among SES, childhood experience, and neurocognitive development may enable more ratio-nally designed intervention programs for at-risk children and adolescents.

Acknowledgments

The research described here was supported by the following grants from NIH: R21-DA01586, R01-HD043078, R01-DA14129, R01-DA18913, P30-HD269-04S2, and M01-RR00240.

References

Adams, B. N. (1998). *The family: A sociological interpretation.* New York: Harcourt Brace.

Adams, M. J. (1990). *Learning to read: Thinking and learning about print.* Cambridge, MA: MIT Press.

Adler, N. E., Boyce, T., Chesney, M. A., Cohen, S., Folkman, S., Kahn, R. L., & Syme, S. L. (1994). Socioeconomic status and health: The challenge of the gradient. *American Psychologist, 49,* 15–24.

Beitchman, J. H., Wilson, B., Johnson, C. J., et al. (2001, January). Fourteen-year follow-up of speech/language-impaired and control children: Psychiatric outcome. *Journal of the American Academy of Child and Adolescent Psychiatry, 40*(1), 75–82.

Bellinger, D., Leviton, A., Waternaux, C., Needleman, H., & Rabinowitz, C. (1987). Longitudinal analyses of prenatal and postnatal lead exposure and early cognitive de-velopment. *New England Journal of Medicine, 316,* 1037–1043.

Bradley, R. H., & Corwyn, R. F. (1999). Parenting. In C. L. B. Tamis-Lemonda (Ed.), *Child psychology: A handbook of contemporary Issues* (pp. 339–362). New York: Psychology Press.

Bradley, R. H., Corwyn, R. F., McAdoo, H. P., & Garcia Coll, C. (2001). "The home environments of children in the United States. Part 1: Variations by age, ethnicity, and poverty-status. *Child Development, 72,* 1844–1867.

Brooks-Gunn, J., & Duncan, G. J. (1997). The effects of poverty on children. *The Future of Children, 7,* 55–71.

Caldwell, B. M., & Bradley, R. H. (1984). *Home observation for measurement of the environment (HOME).* Little Rock: University of Arkansas.

Capron, C., & Duyme, M. (1989). Assessment of effects of socio-economic status on IQ in a full cross-fostering study. *Nature, 340,* 552–554.

Case, R. (1992). The role of the frontal lobes in the regulation of cognitive development. *Brain and Cognition, 20,* 51–73.

Chasnoff, I. J., Anson, A., Hatcher, R., Stenson, H., Iaukea, K., & Randolph, L. (1998). Prenatal exposure to cocaine and other drugs: Outcome at four to six years. *Annals of the New York Academy of Sciences, 846,* 314–328.

Davis, E. P., Bruce, J., & Gunnar, M. R. (2002). The anterior attention network: associa-tions with temperament and neuroendocrine activity in 6-year-old children. *Develop-mental Psychobiology, 40,* 43–56.

Diamond, A. (1990). The development and neural bases of memory functions as indexed by the A(not)B and delayed response tasks in human infants and infant monkeys. In A. Diamond (Ed.), *The development and neural bases of higher cognitive functions* (pp. 267–317). New York: Academy of Science.

Diamond, A., Prevor, M. B., et al. (1997). *Prefrontal cortex cognitive deficits in children treated early and continuously for PKU.* Chicago: The University of Chicago Press.

Duncan, J., Burgess, P., & Emslie, H. (2002). Fluid intelligence after frontal lobe lesions. *Neuropsychologia, 33,* 261–268.

Duncan, G. J., Brooks-Gunn, J., & Klebanov, P. K. (1994). Economic deprivation and early-childhood development. *Child Development, 65,* 296–318.

Duncan, G. J., Yeung, W. J., Brooks-Gunn, J., & Smirth, J. R. (1998). How much does childhood poverty affect the life chances of children? *American Sociological Review, 63,* 406–423.

Engle, R. W., Tuholski, S. W., Laughlin, J. E., & Conway, A. R. (1999). Working memory, short-term memory, and general fluid intelligence: A latent-variable approach. *Journal of Experimental Psychology: General, 128,* 309–331.

Farah, M. J., Savage, J., Brodsky, N. L., Shera, D., Malamud, E., Giannetta, J., & Hurt, H. (2004). Association of socioeconomic status with neurocognitive development. *Pediatric Research* (Suppl.).

Farah, M. J., Shera, D., Savage, J., Betancourt, L., Giannetta, J., Brodsky, N. L., Malamud, E., & Hurt, H. (2006). *Childhood poverty: Selective correlations with neurocognitive development.* Manuscript submitted for publication.

Fuster, J. M. (2002). Frontal lobe and cognitive development. *Journal of Neurocytology, 31,* 373–385.

Giancola, P. R., Martin, C. S., Tarter, R. E., Pelham, W. E., & Moss, H. B. (1996, July). Executive cognitive functioning and aggressive behavior in preadolescent boys at high risk for substance abuse/dependence. *Journal of Studies on Alcohol, 57*(4), 352–359.

Gray, J. R., Chabris, C. F., & Braver, T. S. (2003). Neural mechanisms of general fluid intelligence. *Nature Neuroscience, 6,* 316–322.

Hurt, H., Brodsky, N. L., Betancourt, L., Braitman, L., Malmud, E., & Giannetta, J. (1995). Cocaine exposed children: Follow-up at 30 months. *Developmental and Behavioral Pediatrics, 16,* 29–35.

Hurt, H., Malmud, E., Braitman, L., Betancourt, L. M., Brodsky, N. L., & Giannetta, J. M. (1998). Inner-city achievers: Who are they? *Archives of Pediatric and Adolescent Medicine, 152,* 993–997.

Johnson, M. H. (1997). *Developmental cognitive neuroscience.* Oxford: Blackwell's.

Lupien, S. J., King, S., et al. (2001). Can poverty get under your skin? Basal cortisol levels and cognitive function in children from low and high socioeconomic status. *Development and Psychopathology, 13,* 653–676.

Mayes, L. C. (2002). A behavioral teratogenic model of the impact of prenatal cocaine exposure on arousal regulatory systems. *Neurotoxicology and Teratology, 24,* 385–395.

McCloyd, V. C. (1998). Socioeconomic disadvantage and child development. *American Psychologist, 53,* 185–204.

McEwen, B. S. (2000). The neurobiology of stress: From serendipity to clinical relevance. *Brain Research, 886,* 172–189.

Meaney, M. J., Diorio, J., Francis, D., et al. (1996). Early environmental regulation of forebrain glucocoricoid receptor gene expression: Implications for adrenocortical responses to stress. *Developmental Neuroscience, 18,* 49–72.

Mischel, W., Shoda, Y., & Rodriguez, M. I. (1989). Delay of gratification in children. *Science, 244*, 933–938.

Noble, K. G., Norman, M. F., & Farah, M. J. (2005). Neurocognitive correlates of socio-economic status in kindergarten children. *Developmental Science, 8*, 74–87.

Noble, K. G., McCandliss, B. D. & Farah, M. J. (2006). *Socioeconomic gradients predict individual differences in neurocognitive abilities.* Manuscript submitted for publication.

Posner, M. I., & Rothbart, M. K. (1998). Attention, self-regulation, and consciousness. *Philosophical Transactions of the Royal Society of London, 353*(1377), 1915–1927.

Schiff, M., & Lewontin, R. (1986). *Education and class: The irrelevance of IQ genetic studies.* Oxford: Clarendon Press.

Turner, R. J., & Avison, W. R. (2003). Status variations in stress exposure: implications for the interpretation of research on race, socioeconomic status, and gender. *Journal of Health & Social Behavior, 44*, 488–505.

van Praag, H., Kempermann, G., & Gage, F. H. (2000). Neural consequences of environmental enrichment. *Nature Reviews Neuroscience, 1*, 191–198.

Vidaeff, A. C. & Mastrobattista, J. M. (2003). In utero cocaine exposure: A thorny mix of science and mythology. *American Journal of Perinatalogy, 20*, 165–172.

Volkmar, F. R., & Greenough, W. T. (1972). Rearing complexity affects branching of dendrites in the visual cortex of the rat. *Science, 176*, 1145–1447.

Whitehurst, G. J. (1997). Language process in context: Language learning in children reared in poverty. In L. B. Adamson & M. A. Romski (Eds.), *Research on communication and language disorders: Contribution to theories of language development* (pp. 233–266). Baltimore: Brookes.

Chapter 17

Brain Development as a Vulnerability
Factor in the Etiology of Substance
Abuse and Addiction

Charles P. O'Brien

Substance Abuse and Addiction

The concept of addiction as a brain disease has had a major impact on understanding and treating patients with this disorder. Abraham Wikler was the first to recognize that addiction was fundamentally a learned response. His pioneering animal experiments showed that removal of the drugs from the body did not eliminate the conditioned reflexes that had been developed over years of drug use (Wikler, 1965). Studies in human subjects demonstrated that the effects of drugs could be conditioned and that craving and withdrawal symptoms reported by drug free addicts when they were exposed to drug associated cues followed the laws of classical conditioning (C. P. O'Brien, Greenstein, Ternes, McLellan, & Grabowski, 1979; C. P. O'Brien, Testa, O'Brien, Brady, & Wells, 1977). More recently, these conditioned, involuntary responses were found to have consistent representation in the brain (Childress et al., 1999) and changes in brain receptors accompanied these long-term behavioral effects (Volkow, Fowler, & Wang, 2004).

The vast majority of substance abusers begin their drug use prior to the age of 25 and most prior to age 21 (figure 17-1; Wagner & Anthony, 2002). Thus adolescence is a critical period for the development of abuse and addiction. This applies both to legal drugs, such as nicotine and alcohol, and illegal drugs, such as marijuana, cocaine, heroin, and methamphetamine. The Monitoring the Future

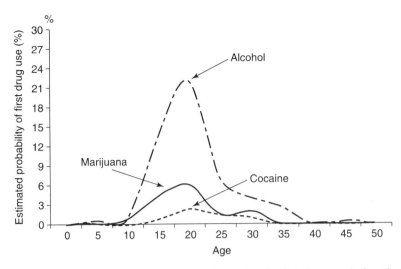

Figure 17-1 The vast majority of substance abusers begin their drug use before the age of 25 and most prior to age 21. (Wagner & Anthony, 2002).

study, initiated in 1975, has charted annually the extent of drug exposure in 8th, 10th and 12th graders in the United States using similar methodology (L. Johnston, 1996). This series of studies tracks the changes in drug usage over the years, and the prevalence of experimentation with various substances has remained consistently high among students since the studies began. The epidemiological data suggest that there may be factors in adolescents that encourage the initiation of substance abuse. Of course risk-taking behavior is a well-known characteristic of adolescence (Steinberg, 2004).

A neurodevelopmental perspective has been proposed by Chambers et al. (2003), who reviewed data from animal and human studies suggesting that adolescence is a period of change in brain organization and function. These changes are structural, involving synaptic pruning, and functional, with relative increases in promotivational dopamine function and relative reduction in inhibitory serotonin systems. The result tips the balance toward impulsivity and risk taking. Drugs of abuse, which are excitatory to dopamine systems, may be more effective during this period. Thus adolescents are more likely to take the risk of experimentation and, once exposed, are more susceptible to the seductive effects of these drugs.

Although exposure through drug experimentation is high, most of the adolescents exposed to drugs do not progress to abuse or addiction. Table 17-1 shows the proportion of American adults who were exposed and the percentage of these who progressed to addiction (Anthony, Warner, & Kessler, 1994). The first requirement for the development of substance abuse or addiction is drug exposure, taking the first dose. This depends on availability and willingness to take risks and may be influenced by drug prevention programs and supply reduction efforts by the government. Once exposure has occurred, however, other factors begin to play an increasingly important role. Research over the past 30 years has demonstrated vulnerability factors that influence the likelihood of progression once exposure has occurred. Thus it is likely that the development of an addictive disorder is influenced by multiple classes of variables as outlined in the medical model: *agent* (type of drug and availability), *host* (heredity, personality) and *environment* (peer group; C. O'Brien, 2005).

Note in table 17-1 that the "most addicting drug," because of the proportion of users who progress to dependence, is nicotine and that only 16% of those exposed to cocaine progress to dependence. The risk of addiction after exposure to heroin is 23%, whereas analgesics, which are also opiates, had only a 7.5% risk. This may be explained by differences in route of administration as heroin is generally injected, whereas analgesics are usually taken orally with slower onset of effect. Also the setting and motivation for taking analgesics is quite different from that of heroin. Thus, risk of addiction depends on more than the pharmacological potency of the drug, and one of the variables appears to be age of exposure.

Nicotine

Breslau et al. (1993) reported on the role of psychiatric comorbidity in smoking initiation. Both major depression and anxiety disorders have been associated with smoking (Breslau, 1995). The pharmacological effects of nicotine may suppress symptoms of these disorders; thus they would return when the smoker attempts to quit. Also, quitting is much more difficult for those smokers who began at a young

Table 17-1. Risk of addiction.

DRUG CATEGORIES	EVER USED (%)	DEPENDENCE (%)	RISK (%)
Tobacco	75.6	24.1	31.9
Alcohol	91.5	14.1	15.4
Other Drugs	51.0	7.5	14.7
Marijuana	46.3	4.2	9.1
Cocaine	16.2	2.7	16.7
Stimulant	15.3	1.7	11.2
Anxiolytics, etc.	12.7	1.2	9.2
Analgesics	9.7	0.7	7.5
Psychedelics	10.6	0.5	4.9
Heroin	1.5	0.4	23.1
Inhalants	6.8	0.3	3.7

Source: Anthony, Warner & Kessler, 1994

age. The available evidence suggests that delaying initiation of smoking would increase the likelihood of success when the smoker later engages in a nicotine dependence treatment program (Breslau & Peterson, 1996).

Genetic factors are thought to play a role in vulnerability to all addictions. In the case of nicotine, heredity is estimated to account for 70% of the variance in moving from initiation of smoking to nicotine addiction (Sullivan & Kendler, 1999). Relevant nicotine exposure may be as early as in utero exposure. Women whose mothers smoked during pregnancy had a four-fold increase in smoking rates as adults when compared to women whose mothers did not smoke during their pregnancy (Kandel, Wu, & Davies, 1994).

Stimulants

Animal models of adolescence may shed light on critical periods of drug exposure and the mechanisms by which this exposure could have effects far into the future. For example, Mague and colleagues (Mague, Andersen, & Carlezon, 2005) reported that exposure of rat pups to two injections of the stimulant methylphenidate during preadolescence (postnatal days 20–35, approximating ages 4–12 years in humans) resulted in lasting changes in the brain reward system as measured by sensitivity to the rewarding effects of cocaine tested during adulthood. Sensitivity was measured by changes in the threshold for intracranial self-stimulation produced by cocaine. The early stimulant exposure rendered the rats less sensitive to cocaine when they became adults. These findings are an interesting contrast to the opposite finding in adult rats in which stimulant exposure sensitizes the animal to subsequent doses of stimulant (Meririnne, Kankaanpaa, & Seppala, 2001). They may also help to explain the lack of severe problems in babies born to cocaine using mothers when compared to appropriate controls (Hurt, Brodsky, Roth, Malmud, & Giannetta, 2005).

Other studies in animal models have shown that early methylphenidate treatment also reduces the effects of cocaine in adulthood as measured by place preference (Carlezon, Mague, & Andersen, 2003). These findings are important because of the large number of children who receive methylphenidate as effective treatment for attention deficit/hyperactivity disorder (ADHD). Concern has been expressed because of the possibility that exposing children to a drug that has a mechanism of action similar to cocaine could lead to later stimulant abuse. Actual studies of children with carefully diagnosed ADHD have found that untreated ADHD is indeed associated with an increased probability of substance abuse, but in those who have been treated with methylphenidate, the risk of substance abuse is significantly lower (Wilens, Faraone, Biederman, & Gunawardene, 2003). Thus the clinical findings are consistent with the report in adolescent rats showing reduced stimulant effects after adolescent exposure. It should be noted, however, that stimulant treatment in adolescents could have adverse effects. A history of methylphenidate has been associated with severity of subsequent bipolar disorder in a sample of 80 adolescent bipolar patients (Soutullo et al., 2002), and there is a concern about the rare association of methylphenidate with cardiac arrhythmias (Chernoff, Wallen, & Muller, 1962; Lucas, Gardner, Wolkowitz, Tucker, & Cowdry, 1986).

Alcohol

Exposure to alcohol begins at an early age in the United States, with 44% of 8th graders already reporting alcohol use, increasing to 77% by the 12th grade in 2004 (L. Johnston, O'Malley, Bachman, & Schulenberg, 2005). Binge drinking, defined as five or more drinks at a single occasion, is reported by 11% of 8th graders and 29% of 12th graders. Binge drinking in college has been reported for several years to be in the 44% range (Knight et al., 2002; Wechsler, Lee, Kuo, & Lee, 2000) and is associated with significant health and accident problems. Although stress has been found to be a powerful predictor of alcohol and other drug abuse (Spear, 2000), binge-type drinking behavior is so widespread among college students that some might consider it to be a cultural norm even for nonstressed individuals (Shedler & Block, 1990).

Because so many adolescents are exposed to alcohol, is there any evidence that this produces lasting effects? Correlational studies in human populations suggest that this might occur. Just as was found with nicotine exposure, early exposure to alcohol increases the risk of abuse and dependence in adulthood. In one large sample, the rate of lifetime alcoholism was 40% when drinking was started at age 14 or younger, but only 10% when drinking was initiated at age 20 or older (Fergusson, Lynskey, & Horwood, 1994).

There is also evidence for the role of heredity in the sensitivity to alcohol and the risk of developing alcoholism. Young men with a family history of alcoholism show less sensitivity (i.e., more tolerance) to graded doses of alcohol in the laboratory than men of similar age and drinking experience with a negative family history for alcoholism (Schuckit & Smith, 2004). The researchers continued the testing longitudinally and found a significant increase in sensitivity to alcohol with increasing age among light drinkers, but little change among heavy drinkers.

Alcohol acts as a sedative on the brain. The annual toll of alcohol overdose deaths among college students is testimonial to the sedating effects of a drug that many adolescents consider to be a stimulant. Among heavy drinkers during adolescence, neuropsychological deficits have been reported. Heavy drinking adolescents tested 3 weeks after detoxification from alcohol showed deficits in visuospatial functioning and in retrieval of verbal and nonverbal information (Brown, Tapert, Granholm, & Delis, 2000). What is not clear is the degree to which neurocognitive defects evident during adolescence at a time when the brain is developing are reversible after long-term abstinence. There is evidence that substantial recovery of short-term but not long-term memory can occur in adults (Brandt, Butters, Ryan, & Bayog, 1983). Individuals who experienced heavy alcohol exposure during adolescence could have more or less recovery than adults depending on the long-term effects of alcohol on the developing brain, but appropriate longitudinal studies have not yet been done (Brown & Tapert, 2004).

Animal experiments tend to support the implications of the correlational studies in clinical populations. Early exposure to alcohol involves exposing the developing brain to a neurotoxin that could produce effects beyond simply abuse or dependence in the future (Brown & Tapert, 2004). There is abundant evidence from animal models that shows changes in response to alcohol during development. Spear (2004) points out that rodent models of adolescence show a combination of reduced sensitivity to cues that would tend to moderate alcohol intake, such as motor impairment and sedation, but increased sensitivity to other effects, such as social facilitation. One of the major structures affected by alcohol is the hippocampus (White & Swartzwelder, 2004), which plays a key role in learning and memory. Adolescent rats are more sensitive to the effects of alcohol on NMDA receptor-mediated synaptic potentials (Swartzwelder, Wilson, & Tayyeb, 1995a). Long-term potentiation (LTP), which is believed to be part of the underlying mechanism of memory, is more affected by alcohol in adolescent than in adult rats (Swartzwelder, Wilson, & Tayyeb, 1995b).

Marijuana

Marijuana is the most commonly used illegal drug. Its use peaked in 1979 among high school students and has fluctuated over the years in inverse proportion to the perception of harm (figure 17-2). As perception of risk goes up, experimentation with marijuana goes down. There is controversy over the dangers of marijuana. Clearly it has a direct effect on attention, learning, and memory. Thus it would be expected to diminish school performance if taken during class or homework time. This concept is supported by studies showing a correlation between marijuana use and poor school performance (Bergen, Martin, Roeger, & Allison, 2005). But such findings may not imply a causal relationship.

There is good evidence that cognitive impairment persists beyond the period of the marijuana "high," but it is unclear whether these residual effects last longer than a day or two (Pope & Yurgelun-Todd, 1996). Heavy marijuana use has also been associated with an "amotivational syndrome" in adolescents. This name was given to adolescents who seem to lose ambition, but it doesn't fit the classical pattern of major depression (Kolansky & Moore, 1975). Laboratory experiments with humans have been conducted to determine whether marijuana has a specific

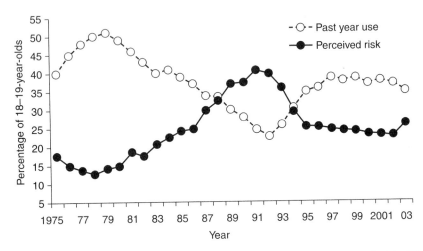

Figure 17-2 Marijuana is the most commonly used illegal drug. Its use peaked in 1979 among high school students and has fluctuated over the years in inverse proportion to the perception of harm. As perception of risk goes up, experimentation with marijuana goes down.

effect on motivation. Although some have shown this effect, it is difficult to extrapolate this finding to behavior outside the laboratory (Lane, Cherek, Pietras, & Steinberg, 2005).

The risk of developing marijuana addiction among users is in the range of the risk for alcoholism among those exposed to alcohol and is related to the frequency and duration of use. Adolescents become dependent at a lower frequency and quantity of use than adults, thus fitting the pattern of adolescent vulnerability noted for nicotine and alcohol (Chen, Kandel, & Davies, 1997).

Opiates

Opiates are the fastest growing form of adolescent substance abuse. Nonmedical use of prescription opioids (e.g., Vicodin, Oxycontin) obtained from various sources, including the parents' medicine cabinet, has been growing in national surveys. Nonprescription Vicodin use was reported by 10% of high school seniors and Oxycontin by 5% in recent years (Johnston et al., 2005). Although it is probable that adolescents are more vulnerable to the development of opiate addiction than adults, no relevant data are available. Because opiates (derived from opium) and opioids (synthetic opiates) act on the same receptors as do endogenous opioids (endorphins), they mimic the effects of the endogenous substances. Most opiates and opioids are not neurotoxic, although they can be taken in overdose that could fatally suppress respiration. Chronic opiate use has not been associated with a decrease in IQ, and the main risk, apart from overdose, is infection from nonsterile needles (McLellan, Woody, & O'Brien, 1979).

Treatment

Studies of treatment for addictive disorders among adolescents are scarce. There are ethical issues concerning how to obtain consent from a minor and how to involve parents. There is also the difficulty in getting adolescents to accept the need for treatment and to volunteer for a study. Currently the first randomized clinical trial of a medication for opiate addiction (buprenorphine) among adolescent opiate addicts is underway, but recruitment of volunteers has been difficult (G. Woody, personal communication, May 2006). Most treatment programs tailored to the needs of adolescents use the same psychotherapeutic approaches and medications that have been found effective in adults. We know, however, that psychoactive medications as well as drugs of abuse have different effects on the adolescent brain as compared to the adult. Thus randomized controlled clinical trials in the adolescent population will be necessary. A review of the literature concerning treatments for substance abuse in adolescents has recently been published (O'Brien et al., 2005).

Prevention

Some degree of risk taking and thrill seeking is normal in adolescence. (Steinberg, 2004). School-based programs aimed at primary prevention of substance abuse have had variable success. Evaluations of drug education programs such as DARE have generally found them to be ineffective (Becker, Agopian, & Yeh, 1992; Ennett, Tobler, Ringwalt, & Flewelling, 1994). In contrast, there have been well-designed programs teaching social resistance skills in junior high school that have produced significant results. In well-controlled outcome studies using similar comparison groups, the adolescents exposed to the training and 2 years of booster sessions showed significant reductions in nicotine, alcohol, and marijuana use at follow-up (Botvin, Baker, Dusenbury, Botvin, & Diaz, 1995; Griffin, Botvin, Nichols, & Doyle, 2003). For an extensive review of adolescent substance abuse prevention programs See O'Brien et al, 2005.

Conclusions

Adolescence is a vulnerable period for initiating substance abuse. Progression from use to abuse to addiction is influenced by multiple, simultaneous variables categorized in the medical model as agent, host, and environment. Happily, the majority of adolescents who experiment with drugs do not progress to addiction, although they could experience harm or fatalities from acute effects and accidents. Those beginning at a younger age have the highest risk of developing an addiction and the poorest results when they later seek treatment as adults. Few controlled studies of the treatment of adolescent substance abusers have been conducted, and thus little is known about the efficacy of psychotherapy and medications in adolescent populations.

References

Anthony, J. C., Warner, L. A., & Kessler, R. C. (1994). Comparative epidemiology of dependence on tobacco, alcohol, controlled substances, and inhalants: Basic findings from the National Comorbidity Survey. *Experimental and Clinical Psychopharmacology, 2*, 244–268.

Becker, H. K., Agopian, M. W., & Yeh, S. (1992). Impact evaluation of drug abuse resistance education (DARE). *Journal of Drug Education, 22*(4), 283–291.

Bergen, H. A., Martin, G., Roeger, L., & Allison, S. (2005). Perceived academic performance and alcohol, tobacco and marijuana use: Longitudinal relationships in young community adolescents. *Addictive Behaviors, 30*(8), 1563–1573.

Botvin, G. J., Baker, E., Dusenbury, L., Botvin, E. M., & Diaz, T. (1995). Long-term follow-up results of a randomized drug abuse prevention trial in a white middle-class population. *Journal of the American Medical Association, 273*(14), 1106–1112.

Brandt, J., Butters, N., Ryan, C., & Bayog, R. (1983). Cognitive loss and recovery in long-term alcohol abusers. *Archives of General Psychiatry, 40*(4), 435–442.

Breslau, N. (1995). Psychiatric comorbidity of smoking and nicotine dependence. *Behavior Genetics, 25*(2), 95–101.

Breslau, N., Fenn, N., & Peterson, E. L. (1993). Early smoking initiation and nicotine dependence in a cohort of young adults. *Drug and Alcohol Dependence, 33*(2), 129–137.

Breslau, N., & Peterson, E. L. (1996). Smoking cessation in young adults: age at initiation of cigarette smoking and other suspected influences. *American Journal of Public Health, 86*(2), 214–220.

Brown, S. A., & Tapert, S. F. (2004). Adolescence and the trajectory of alcohol use: basic to clinical studies. *Annals of the New York Academy of Sciences, 1021*, 234–244.

Brown, S. A., Tapert, S. F., Granholm, E., & Delis, D. C. (2000). Neurocognitive functioning of adolescents: effects of protracted alcohol use. *Alcoholism: Clinical and Experimental Research, 24*(2), 164–171.

Carlezon, W. A., Mague, S. D., & Andersen, S. L. (2003). Enduring behavioral effects of early exposure to methylphenidate in rats. *Biological Psychiatry, 54*(12), 1330–1337.

Chambers, R. A., Taylor, J. R., & Potenza, M. N. (2003). Development neurocircuitry of motivation in adolescence: A critical period of addiction vulnerability. *American Journal of Psychiatry, 160*, 1041–1052.

Chen, K., Kandel, D. B., & Davies, M. (1997). Relationships between frequency and quantity of marijuana use and last year proxy dependence among adolescents and adults in the United States. *Drug and Alcohol Dependence, 46*(1–2), 53–67.

Chernoff, R. W., Wallen, M. H., & Muller, O. F. (1962). Cardiac toxicity of methylphenidate. Report of two cases. *Nord Hyg T, 266*, 400–401.

Childress, A. R., Mozley, P. D., McElgin, W., Fitzgerald, J., Reivich, M., & O'Brien, C. P. (1999). Limbic activation during cue-induced cocaine craving. *American Journal of Psychiatry, 156(1)*, 11–18.

Ennett, S. T., Tobler, N. S., Ringwalt, C. L., & Flewelling, R. L. (1994). How effective is drug abuse resistance education? A meta-analysis of Project DARE outcome evaluations [see comments]. *American Journal of Public Health, 84*(9), 1394–1401.

Fergusson, D. M., Lynskey, M. T., & Horwood, L. J. (1994). Childhood exposure to alcohol and adolescent drinking patterns. *Addiction, 89*(8), 1007–1016.

Griffin, K. W., Botvin, G. J., Nichols, T. R., & Doyle, M. M. (2003). Effectiveness of a universal drug abuse prevention approach for youth at high risk for substance use initiation. *Preventive Medicine, 36*(1), 1–7.

Hurt, H., Brodsky, N. L., Roth, H., Malmud, E., & Giannetta, J. M. (2005). School performance of children with gestational cocaine exposure. *Neurotoxicology and Teratology, 27*(2), 203–211.

Johnston, L.D., O'Malley, P.M., & Bachman, J.G. (1996). *National survey results on drug use from the Monitoring the Future study, 1975–1995.*. Volume I: Secondary school students. (NIH Publication No. 96–4139). Rockville, MD: National Institute on Drug Abuse.

Johnston, L., O'Malley, P., Bachman, J., & Schulenberg, J. (2005). *Monitoring the Future national survey results on drug use, 1975–2004. Vol. 1: Secondary school students.* (NIH Publication No. 05–5727). Bethesda: National Institute on Drug Abuse.

Kandel, D. B., Wu, P., & Davies, M. (1994). Maternal smoking during pregnancy and smoking by adolescent daughters. *American Journal of Public Health, 84(9)*, 1407–1413.

Knight, J. R., Wechsler, H., Kuo, M., Seibring, M., Weitzman, E. R., & Schuckit, M. A. (2002). Alcohol abuse and dependence among U.S. college students. *Journal of Studies on Alcohol, 63*(3), 263–270.

Kolansky, H., & Moore, W. T. (1975). Marihuana. Can it hurt you? *Journal of the American Medical Association, 232*(9), 923–924.

Lane, S. D., Cherek, D. R., Pietras, C. J., & Steinberg, J. L. (2005). Performance of heavy marijuana-smoking adolescents on a laboratory measure of motivation. *Addictive Behaviors, 30*(4), 815–828.

Lucas, P. B., Gardner, D. L., Wolkowitz, O. M., Tucker, E. E., & Cowdry, R. W. (1986). Methylphenidate-induced cardiac arrhythmias [letter]. *New England Journal of Medicine, 315*(23), 1485.

Mague, S. D., Andersen, S. L., & Carlezon, W. A. (2005). Early developmental exposure to methylphenidate reduces cocaine-induced potentiation of brain stimulation reward in rats. *Biol Psychiatry, 57*(2), 120–125.

McLellan, A. T., Woody, G. E., & O'Brien, C. P. (1979). Development of psychiatric illness in drug abusers. *New England Journal of Medicine, 301*, 1310–1314.

Meririnne, E., Kankaanpaa, A., & Seppala, T. (2001). Rewarding properties of methylphenidate: sensitization by prior exposure to the drug and effects of dopamine D1- and D2-receptor antagonists. *Journal of Pharmacology and Experimental Therapeutics, 298*(2), 539–550.

O'Brien, C. P. (2005). Drug addiction and drug abuse. In L. Brunton (Ed.), *Goodman & Gilman's the pharmacological basis of therapeutics* (11th ed., pp. 607–627). New York: McGraw-Hill.

O'Brien, C. P., Greenstein, R., Ternes, J., McLellan, A. T., & Grabowski, J. (1979). Unreinforced self-injections: Effects on rituals and outcome in heroin addicts. *National Institute on Drug Abuse Research Monograph, 27*, 275–281.

O'Brien, C. P., Testa, T., O'Brien, T. J., Brady, J. P., & Wells, B. (1977). Conditioned narcotic withdrawal in humans. *Science, 195*(4282), 1000–1002.

O'Brien C. P., , J. C., Carroll, K., Childress, A. R., Dackis, C., Diamond, G., Hornik, R., Johnston, L. D., Jones, R., Koob, G. F., Kosten, T., Lerman, C., McLellan, A. T., Moss, H., Pettinati, H., & Spoth, R. (2005). *Treating and preventing adolescent mental health disorders.* New York: Oxford University Press: 335–430.

Pope, H. G., & Yurgelun-Todd, D. (1996). The residual cognitive effects of heavy marijuana use in college students. *Journal of the American Medical Association, 275(7)*, 521–527.

Schuckit, M. A., & Smith, T. L. (2004). Changes over time in the self-reported level of response to alcohol. *Alcohol and Alcoholism, 39*(5), 433–438.

Shedler, J., & Block, J. (1990). Adolescent drug use and psychological health: A longitudinal inquiry. *Am Psychol, 45*(5), 612–630.

Soutullo, C. A., DelBello, M. P., Ochsner, J. E., McElroy, S. L., Taylor, S. A., Strakowski, S. M., et al. (2002). Severity of bipolarity in hospitalized manic adolescents with history of stimulant or antidepressant treatment. *Journal of Affective Disorders, 70*(3), 323–327.

Spear, L. P. (2000). The adolescent brain and age-related behavioral manifestations. *Neuroscience Biobehavioral Reviews, 24*(4), 417–463.

Spear, L. P. (2004). Adolescence and the trajectory of alcohol use: Introduction to part VI. *Annals of the New York Academy of Sciences, 1021*, 202–205.

Steinberg, L. (2004). Risk taking in adolescence: What changes, and why? *Annals of the New York Academy of Sciences, 1021*, 51–58.

Sullivan, P. F., & Kendler, K. S. (1999). The genetic epidemiology of smoking. *Nicotine & Tobacco Research, 1 Suppl 2*, S51–57; discussion, S69–70.

Swartzwelder, H. S., Wilson, W. A., & Tayyeb, M. I. (1995a). Age-dependent inhibition of long-term potentiation by ethanol in immature versus mature hippocampus. *Alcoholism: Clinical Experimental Research, 19*(6), 1480–1485.

Swartzwelder, H. S., Wilson, W. A., & Tayyeb, M. I. (1995b). Differential sensitivity of NMDA receptor-mediated synaptic potentials to ethanol in immature versus mature hippocampus. *Alcoholism: Clinical Experimental Research, 19*(2), 320–323.

Volkow, N. D., Fowler, J. S., & Wang, G. J. (2004). The addicted human brain viewed in the light of imaging studies: brain circuits and treatment strategies. *Neuropharmacology, 47*(Suppl. 1), 3–13.

Wagner, F. A., & Anthony, J. C. (2002). From first drug use to drug dependence; developmental periods of risk for dependence upon marijuana, cocaine, and alcohol. *Neuropsychopharmacology, 26*(4), 479–488.

Wechsler, H., Lee, J. E., Kuo, M., & Lee, H. (2000). College binge drinking in the 1990s: A continuing problem. Results of the Harvard School of Public Health 1999 College Alcohol Study. *Journal of American College Health, 48*(5), 199–210.

White, A. M., & Swartzwelder, H. (2004). Hippocampal function during adolescence: A unique target of ethanol effects. *Annals of the New York Academy of Sciences, 1021*, 206–220.

Wikler, A. (1965). Conditioning factors in opiate addiction and relapse. In D. M. Wilner & G. G. Kassebaum (Eds.), *Narcotics* (pp. 85–100). New York: McGraw-Hill.

Wilens, T. E., Faraone, S. V., Biederman, J., & Gunawardene, S. (2003). Does stimulant therapy of attention-deficit/hyperactivity disorder beget later substance abuse? A meta-analytic review of the literature. *Pediatrics, 111*(1), 179–185.

Part VI

Educational Interventions
for Enhanced Neurocognitive
Development

Chapter 18

Modifying Brain Networks
Underlying Self-Regulation

M. Rosario Rueda, Mary K. Rothbart, Lisa Saccomanno,
and Michael I. Posner

In the invitation to contribute to this volume, the editor raised two issues on which we were invited to comment: (1) What neurodevelopmental processes in children and adolescents could be altered so that mental disorders might be prevented? (2) What interventions or life experiences might be able to introduce such changes? In our work, we have examined attentional networks related to pathologies that influence the ability to regulate emotions and actions, and we have developed an intervention that holds some promise in improving attention in young children and perhaps mitigating the effects of these pathologies. Our work is largely with young children. We believe, however, that both the methods used and some of the results described in this chapter could be important in answering the two questions posed by the organizers.

In this chapter we briefly review the anatomy and function of attentional networks, with special emphasis on the executive network, the one most clearly related to self-regulation. Next, we present evidence from our work and others showing that various pathologies are related to the functioning of this network. This section clearly establishes that there is an association between pathologies and deficits in the executive attentional network, although it does not show that the deficits of attention cause these pathologies. Finally, we introduce an intervention that has been shown to improve the function of the executive attention network in young children. We consider the possibility that such interventions could be an important part of education preventing mental illnesses related to deficits of self-regulation.

Attentional Networks

During the past several years we have examined the development of brain networks involved in three attentional functions: obtaining and maintaining the alert state, orienting to sensory stimuli, and regulating responses, thoughts, and feelings. These networks, common to all people, involve different brain areas (Fan, McCandliss, Fossella, Flombaum, & Posner, 2005) and exhibit different time courses of development during childhood (Rueda, Fan, McCandliss, Halparin, Gruber, et al., 2004a).

The three networks are illustrated in table 18-1, showing the brain areas that serve as the sources of the attentional effects and the neuromodulators that affect their functioning. Although the neuroanatomy of attention is well defined, given its regulatory function, the sites at which attention operates are numerous. In fact, many studies have suggested that the regulatory effects of attention are common to most areas of the brain. Attention has been shown to modulate the function of sensory systems; for example, orienting to visual stimuli activates visual areas of the occipital cortex, whereas orienting to auditory stimuli activates primary and secondary auditory areas. However, this regulatory function applies just as well to brain systems involved in the processing of language, memorization of information, and generation of emotions (Posner & Raichle, 1994).

Measuring Individual Differences on Attention

In the past years, we have developed the Attention Network Test (ANT) to examine individual differences in the efficiency of the brain networks of alerting, orienting, and executive attention discussed above (Fan, McCandliss, Sommer, Raz, & Posner, 2002; Rueda, Fan, et al., 2004a). The ANT uses differences in reaction time (RT) between conditions to measure the efficiency of each network. Each trial begins with a cue (or a blank interval, in the no-cue condition) that informs the participant that a target will be occurring soon, where it will occur, or both. The target always occurs either above or below fixation, and it consists of a central arrow, surrounded by flanking arrows that can either point in the same direction (congruent) or in the opposite direction (incongruent). Subtracting RTs for congruent from incongruent target trials provides a measure of conflict resolution and assesses the efficiency of the executive attention network. Subtracting RTs obtained in the double-cue condition from RT in the no-cue condition gives a measure of alerting due to the presence of a warning signal. Subtracting RTs to

Table 18-1 Brain Areas and Neuromodulators Involved in Attention Networks

FUNCTION	STRUCTURES	MODULATOR
Orient	Superior parietal Temporal parietal junction Frontal eye fields Superior colliculus	Acetylcholine
Alert	Locus Coeruleus Right frontal and parietal cortex	Norepinephrine
Executive Attention	Anterior cingulate Lateral ventral prefrontal Basal ganglia	Dopamine

targets at the cued location (spatial cue condition) from trials using a central cue gives a measure of orienting, because the spatial cue, but not the central cue, provides valid information on where a target will occur.

In previous work, we found that children work best when their actions are related to a story and when there is clear feedback on their performance (Berger, Jones, Rothbart, & Posner, 2000). In the child version of the ANT (see figure 18-1), five colorful fish replace the arrows that typically appear in the adult flanker task. Children are invited to "make the middle fish happy" or "feed the middle fish" by pressing a button corresponding to the direction in which it is pointing. Visual feedback (the middle fish smiles and bubbles come out of its mouth) and auditory feedback (a "Woohoo!" sound) is provided when the response has been successful.

The ANT has some useful properties as a measure of attentional efficiency. It does not use language stimuli, so it can be used with children, speakers of any language, patients unable to read, and other special populations. The test provides within 20 minutes a measure of the efficiency of the alerting, orienting, and conflict networks, in addition to the overall RT and error rate. Using the adult ANT with a sample of 40 normal adults, the network efficiency scores were found to be reliable over two successive presentations (Fan et al., 2002). In addition, the scores provided by the task are independent, as no correlation was found among them.

Using the Child ANT, the developmental course of the attentional networks from 4 years of age to adulthood has been studied (Rueda et al., 2004a; Rueda, Posner, & Rothbart, 2005). Despite a steady decline in overall reaction time from 4 years of age to adulthood, each network also showed a different developmental course. Significant improvement in conflict resolution was found up until age 7, but a remarkable stability in both RT and accuracy of conflict scores was found from

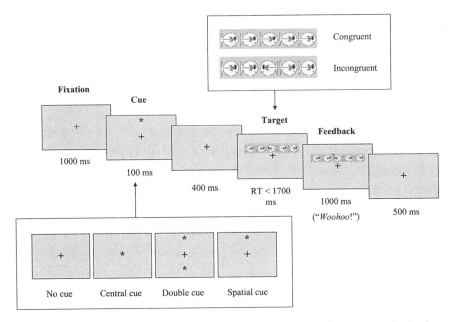

Figure 18-1 A schematic of the Child ANT. The various network scores are obtained as follows. Alert: No Cue RT–Double Cue RT; Orient: Central Cue RT–Spatial Cue RT; Executive Attention (conflict): Incongruent RT–Congruent RT. The top box displays the two types of target. The middle shows the time line of events in each trial starting with a cue, then a target and feedback following the target. The four types of cue conditions are shown in the bottom box (after Rueda et al., 2004a).

age 7 to adulthood. The development of conflict resolution is illustrated in table 18-2. Alerting scores showed some improvement up to age 10 and continued development between age 10 and adulthood. Finally, the orienting score was similar to adult levels even at the youngest age studied.

Executive Attention, Temperament, and Externalizing Behavior Problems

Parents can report on the ability of their children to self-regulate behavior using measures such as the Child Behavior Questionnaire (CBQ; Rothbart, Ahadi, Hershey, & Fisher, 2001). Their answers can be summarized in a higher-order factor called effortful control, which is defined as the ability to inhibit a dominant response to perform a subdominant response, to detect errors, and to engage in planning (Rothbart & Rueda, 2005). We have repeatedly found that executive attention, as measured in cognitive conflict tasks such as the ANT, is correlated with effortful control throughout childhood (Berger, Jones, Rothbart, & Posner, 2000; Chang & Burns, 2005; Gerardi-Caulton, 2000). On the basis of this evidence, we have argued that the executive attention network provides the biological basis for self-regulation of thoughts and behavior (Rueda, Posner & Rothbart, 2004b).

Table 18-2 The conflict score is calculated subtracting the RT for congruent flankers trials from the RT for incongruent flankers trials. The 4.5 year old children were run in a separate study from the others. The 6 year old to adult data are presented in Rueda et al, 2004a.

AGE (YRS)	OVERALL RT	% ERROR	CONFLICT SCORE
4.5	1614	16.7	424
6	931	15.8	115
7	833	5.7	63
8	805	4.9	71
9	734	2.7	67
10	640	2.2	69
Adults	483	1.2	61

Effortful control is also related to crucial aspects of children's socialization such as the development of conscience (Kochanska, 1995), empathy (Rothbart, Ahadi, & Hershey, 1994), ability to delay gratification (Mischel, Shoda, & Peake, 1988), and development of theory of mind (Carlson & Moses, 2001).

The CBQ also constitutes a reliable tool for studying the relation between effortful control and actual behavior in natural settings. A recent study of 220 three-year-olds examined the relation between effortful control and difficulties in behavior, as reported by parents and teachers (Olson, Sameroff, Kerr, Lopez, & Wellman, 2005). The study revealed a substantial negative relationship between the two, even when other factors were controlled, and when multiple measures of externalizing factors (e.g., aggression, impulsivity, rule breaking) in different environments were used. Effortful control and executive attention as measured by cognitive tasks continue to be related to antisocial behavior into adolescence (Ellis, Rothbart, & Posner, 2004).

Genes and Executive Attention

Effortful control and executive attention result from the influence of the child's genes and environment (Rothbart & Posner, 2005). It is our goal to understand how the joint operation of genes and specific environmental experience guides the development of executive attention, and produces the wide range of outcomes that can be observed in the self-regulation of children and adolescents.

ANT scores have been used as a phenotype to assess the heritability of each of the attentional functions with a sample of 26 adult pairs of MZ and DZ twins (Fan, Wu, Fossella, & Posner, 2001). In accordance with their neuroanatomical independence, the three attentional networks showed different heritability indexes. Despite the small scale of the study, the executive network scores showed a high heritability coefficient. Heritability was also significant, although weaker, for alerting scores, whereas the orienting network showed no evidence of heritability.

Moreover, several genes that influence the amount of dopamine in limbic and frontal brain areas have been shown to relate to individual differences in the ability to resolve conflict (Blasi, Mattay, Bertolino, Elevag, Callicott, et al., 2005; Diamond, Briand, Fosella, & Gehlbach, 2004; Fan et al., 2003b; Fossella et al., 2002). In addition, the alerting and orienting networks have been found to be influenced by genes related to the noradrenergic and cholinergic systems respectively (Fossella et al., 2002; Parasuraman, Greenwood, Kumar, & Fossella, 2005).

In the next section of this chapter we deal with development and pathologies related to executive attention. We examine some forms of pathology that have been documented as involving deficits in conflict scores from the ANT.

Disorders Involving Executive Attention

The attention network test has been applied to a number of forms of pathology in children, adolescents, and adults. In this chapter we deal with several pathologies that involve executive attention (see table 18-3), but a fuller account including disorders involving other aspects of attention, is provided in a review by Rothbart & Posner (2006).

Alzheimer's Disease

A recent study by Fernandez-Duque & Black (2006) used the ANT to study patients with Alzheimer's disease in comparison to normal elderly and young adults. Table 18-3 shows the conflict scores for patients in comparison with age-matched adults, indicating a significant deficit in the patients. Non-Alzheimer age-matched controls and younger adults exhibited similar conflict scores, suggesting that the poor executive attention in patients resulted from the disease and was not the result of normal aging.

Table 18-3 Conflict scores for a number of disorders compared to controls.

DISORDER	PATIENTS	CONTROLS
Alzheimers Disease *	149	96
Schizophrenia **	150	99
Borderline Personality ***	140	110

All differences between patients and controls are statistically significant.

Conflict scores are expressed in ms. Data from: *Fernandez-Duque & Black, 2006; **Wang et al., 2005; ***Posner et al., 2002.

Schizophrenia

A number of years ago, never-medicated schizophrenic patients were tested both by imaging and by a cued detection task similar to the orienting part of the ANT. At rest, these patients in comparison with normals showed a focal decrease in cerebral blood flow in the left globus pallidus, a part of the basal ganglia with close ties to the anterior cingulate (Early, Posner, Reiman, & Raichle, 1989). They also showed a deficit in orienting similar to what had been found for left-parietal patients. When their visual attention was engaged, they had difficulty in shifting attention to the right visual field, and they also showed deficits in conflict tasks, particularly when they had to rely on a language cue (Early et al., 1989). It was concluded that the overall pattern of their behavior was most consistent with a deficit in the anterior cingulate and basal ganglia, parts of a frontally based executive attention system (see table 18-1 for the relation of these brain areas to executive attention).

The deficit in orienting rightward has been replicated in schizophrenics who are undergoing their first episode of the disorder, but it does not seem to be true later when the disorder becomes chronic (Maruff, Currie, Hay, McArthur-Jackson, & Malone, 1995), nor does the pattern appear to be part of the genetic predisposition for schizophrenia (Pardo, Knesevich, Vogler, Pardo, Towne, et al., 2000). Schizophrenic participants undergoing their first episode have often been shown to have left hemisphere deficits, and there have been many reports of anterior cingulate and basal ganglia deficits in patients with schizophrenia (Benes, 1999). The anterior cingulate may be part of a much larger network of frontal and temporal structures that operate abnormally in schizophrenia (Benes, 1999).

A recent study using the ANT (Wang, Fan, Dong, Wang, Lee, et al., 2005) casts some light on these results. In this study, the schizophrenic patients were chronic and they were compared with a control group matched by age. The schizophrenic patients had a much greater difficulty resolving conflict than did the normal controls. There was nevertheless a great deal of overlap between the patients and normal subjects, indicating that ANT results are not sufficient for making a differential diagnosis. The data showed a much smaller orienting deficit in schizophrenic patients. These findings suggest a strong executive deficit in chronic schizophrenia, as would be anticipated by Benes's (1999) theory. It remains to be determined whether this deficit exists prior to the initial symptoms, or whether it develops with the disorder.

Chromosome 22q11 Deletion Syndrome

This syndrome is a complex one that involves a number of abnormalities, including facial and heart structure, but also mental retardation due to deletion of a number of genes. Children with the deletion are at a high risk for developing schizophrenia. Among the genes deleted in this syndrome is the COMT gene, which has been associated with performance in a conflict task (Blasi et al., 2005; Diamond et al., 2004) and with schizophrenia (Egan, Goldberg, Kolachana, Callicott, Mazzanti, et al., 2001). In light of these findings, it was to be expected that the disorder would produce a large executive attention deficit, and results confirmed this expectation (Simon, Bish, Bearden, Ding, Ferrante, et al., 2005; Sobin, Kiley-Brabeck, Daniels, Blundell, Anyane-Yeboa, et al., 2004). Sobin et al. also found that the deficit in resolving conflict is associated with inhibition of the startle pattern to a loud noise when a cue warns that the noise will be presented (prepulse inhibition). Prepulse inhibition has been widely studied in animal models and has a well-known anatomy. The association of executive attention and prepulse inhibition deficit suggests a pathway that includes both the basal ganglia and the anterior cingulate (Sobin, Kiley-Brabeck, & Karayiorgou, 2005).

Borderline Personality
Borderline personality disorder is characterized by very great lability of affect and problems in interpersonal relations. In some cases, patients are suicidal or carry out self-mutilation. Because this diagnosis has been seen as a personality disorder, it might at first be thought of as a poor candidate for a specific pathophysiology involving attentional networks. However, we studied a number of patients who had been diagnosed by psychiatrists as having borderline disorder following extensive interviews (Posner, Rothbart, Vizueta, Thomas, Levy, et al., 2003). Our research focused on the temperamentally based core symptoms of high negative emotionality and low effortful control (difficulty in self-regulation). We found that the diagnosed patients were, as expected, very high in negative emotion and relatively low in effortful control, and we also defined a temperamentally matched control group of persons without personality disorder who were equivalent in scores on these two dimensions.

Our study with the ANT found a deficit specific to the executive attention network in borderline patients (Posner et al., 2003). A study using neuroimaging of these patients identified reduced responding in the anterior cingulate and related midline frontal areas when negative words related to the deficit of the patients were presented. This suggested a difficulty in regulating negative affect. Patients with higher levels of effortful control and better conflict scores on the ANT were also more likely to show improvement due to therapy (Clarkin & Posner, 2005; Posner et al., 2003).

Summary
These results show that executive attention provides a basis for the ability of children to regulate their behavior through the use of effortful control, that is to say, voluntarily controlling their motivational and emotional impulses. Executive attention has a well-defined neuroanatomy (see table 18-1), and something is known about the role of genes in modulating its efficiency. As we have reviewed in this section, difficulties in effortful control may be symptomatic of problems in child

socialization and in a number of disorders of children and adults. Executive attention represents a neurodevelopmental process that extends over childhood and adolescence. Data reviewed above suggest that the alteration of this process could affect the propensity for the development of a number of disorders.

Attention Training

The second issue to which this volume is addressed is the question of possible interventions that might influence the neurodevelopmental processes related to pathology. The impact of genetic and temperamental factors on the functioning of the executive attention system could lead to the conclusion that the system is not subject to the influence of experience. However, several training-oriented programs have been successful in improving attention in patients suffering from different pathologies. For example, the use of attention process training (APT) has led to specific improvements in executive attention in patients with specific brain injury (Sohlberg, McLaughlin, Pavese, Heidrich, & Posner, 2000) as well as in children with attention deficit/hyperactivity disorder (ADHD; Kerns, Esso, & Thompson, 1999). With normal adults, training with video games produce better performance on a range of visual attention tasks (Green & Bavelier, 2003).

To examine the role of experience on the development of the executive attention network, we have developed a number of training exercises. Our intention was to test the effect of training during the period of major development of executive attention, which takes place between 4 to 7 years of age according to our data (see table 18-2). Therefore, we designed a number of computer tasks appropriate for young children, hoping to observe in trained children an improvement in conflict resolution, as measured by the ANT, that would generalize to other aspects of cognition.

The exercises were divided in different categories depending on the aspect of attention being trained. A list of the categories and exercises included in the training program is shown in table 18-4. The first category (Tracking) consisted of a set of exercises in which the child was trained to focus attention by controlling the movement of an on-screen cartoon cat using a joystick. The Anticipation exercises were directed to teach the child to predict where an object would move, given its initial trajectory, by tracking two objects simultaneously on the screen (see figure 18-2). Stimulus Discrimination exercises required the child to pay close attention to specific features of cartoon portraits of animals for a matching-to-sample task and then emphasized the use of working memory to retain information about those features. Finally, Conflict Resolution and Inhibitory Control exercises consisted of versions of the number Stroop and Go–No-Go tasks, requiring the resolution of conflict and inhibition of response respectively (see figure 18-3). Our tasks were graded in difficulty, leading the children toward experience in aspects more closely related to executive attention.

Table 18-4 Training exercises.

CATEGORY	EXERCISE	NO. OF LEVELS	MINIMUM NO. OF TRIALS
Tracking	Side	7	21
	Chase	7	21
	Maze	6	6
Anticipation	Hole visible	7	21
	Hole invisible	7	21
Stimulus Discrimination	Portrait	7	21
	Portrait delay	7	21
Conflict Resolution	Numbers	5	45
	Stroop	6	18
Inhibitory control	Farmer	7	66

In order to advance from one level to the next children ought to perform three correct trials in a row. The minimum number of trials refers to the trials needed to complete all the levels of each particular exercise; however, given the criteria to advance from level to level, most of the children needed more trials to complete the games. The inhibitory control exercise was added for the six year olds study.

We tested the efficacy of a very brief five days of attention training with groups of 4- and 6-year-old children. The children were brought to the laboratory for 7 days for sessions lasting about 45 minutes. These sessions were conducted over a 2- to 3-week period. The first and last days were used to assess the effects of the training by children's performance on the ANT, a general test of intelligence (the K-BIT; Kaufman & Kaufman, 1990), and a temperament scale (the CBQ; Rothbart et al., 2001).

During administration of the ANT, we recorded brain activity with a 128-channel EEG system in order to determine whether the status of the executive attention network following training had become more similar to that of normal adults in its time course and strength of activation. Of particular importance was the mid-frontal negativity that arises around 200 milliseconds following the target (N2). In adults, the N2 component is shown to be larger in incongruent compared to congruent conditions. In addition, this negativity has been shown to arise in the anterior cingulate and thus is thought to be related to the resolution of conflict (van Veen & Carter, 2002). In young children the electrophysiological effect of conflict appears later in time, around 500 milliseconds posttarget, and has a more prefrontal distribution (Rueda et al., 2004c).

We ran a series of experiments with our training program. During our first experiment, we compared twelve 4-year-old children who underwent our training procedure with twelve who were randomly selected and took no training, but came in twice for assessment. In our second experiment, we again used 4-year-olds, but

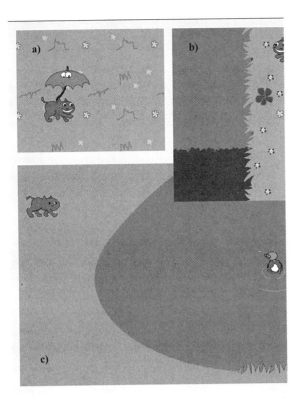

Figure 18-2 Pictures of the screen during attention training exercises. Tracking exercises: *A*, the child's task is to move the cat under a moving umbrella to avoid the rain; *B*, the child moves the cat to the grass to avoid the mud. Over trials, the amount of grass is reduced and the mud increased until considerable concentration is required of the child to move the cat to a grassy section. *C*, the child moves the cat to intercept the duck as it exits the pond. As the duck always swims in a straight line, in this exercise, the child can learn to predict where it will come out of the pond.

the nontrained group performed a "control activity" instead of the training program for the same number of sessions. The control activity consisted of watching videos that required an occasional response to keep the video moving forward. A third experiment was identical to the second, except that children were 6 years old. All of the children seemed to enjoy the experience, and their caregivers were quite supportive of the effort.

Five days seems a very brief period of training to influence the development of networks that develop for many years. Our goal was to see whether the influence of this small amount of training could be shown in performance on the ANT, and whether it would generalize to a measure of intelligence. We also wished to determine whether the training had any influence on the underlying networks as measured by electrical activity on the scalp.

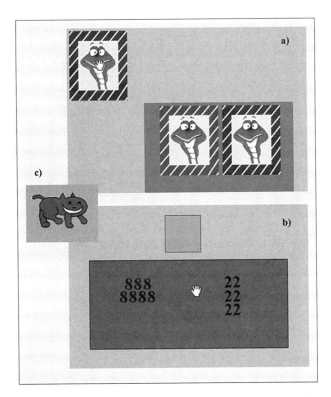

Figure 18-3 Pictures on the screen during attention training exercises. Visual attention and conflict resolution exercises. *A,* matching-to-sample exercise: The child must select the picture on the brown board that matches the sample on the upper left corner. Matching to sample difficulty is increased over the trials by making the competing pictures more similar. At advanced levels, the sample picture is removed from the screen and the child has to memorize it in order to select the correct matching picture. *B,* conflict resolution exercise: The child has to select the group with the most numbers in it. In congruent trials, like the one illustrated, the more numerous group is made up of numbers larger in value. In incongruent trials, the more numerous group is made up of numbers smaller in value. *C,* illustration of the visual feedback for completing a set of trials of equal difficulty. See also color insert.

We present here a brief overview of our initial results. A complete account is given in Rueda, Rothbart, McCandliss, Saccomanno and Posner (2005). For the child ANT, both 4- and 6-year old children showed better ability to resolve conflict after training than children in the control group. However, the difference between groups did not reach statistical significance, reflecting the high variability in children's performance at these ages. As we will discuss later, we have now shown that a portion of that variability is likely due to genetic differences.

We also found a significantly greater improvement in intelligence as measured by the K-BIT in the experimental group compared to the control children. This finding suggested that training effects had generalized to a measure of cognitive processing that is far removed from the training exercises. We did not observe changes in temperament over the course of the training, but this was expected, due to the short time elapsing between assessment sessions.

Analysis of the EEG data showed clear evidence of improvements due to training. As described above, the N2 is a component of the scalp-recorded ERP that has been shown to arise in the anterior cingulate and is related to the resolution of conflict (Rueda et al., 2004c; van Veen & Carter, 2002). In figure 18-4 we show the event-related potentials (ERPs) of adults and trained and nontrained 6-year-old children performing the child ANT. Results are shown for a central electrode (Cz) and a more frontal midline electrode. As in previous studies, adults show a larger N2 for incongruent than for congruent trials (shown at the bottom left-hand column of figure 18-4 marked by arrow). The 6-year-old children without training showed no evidence of larger N2 activity for the incongruent trials in this electrode's location (see figure 18-4, bottom right-hand panel). However, after training children in the experimental group showed the same pattern as the adults (see figure 18-4, bottom center panel, marked by arrow). There is some evidence that a similar greater negativity for incongruent trials emerges somewhat later and at more prefrontal channels in nontrained 6-year-olds (see figure 18-4 Fz top right marked by arrow) and also in trained 4-year-olds (not shown in the figure). These data suggest that the training has altered the network in a more adultlike direction.

There is further evidence in the literature with older children who suffer from attention deficit/hyperactivity disorder (ADHD) that using attention training methods can produce improvement in the ability to concentrate and in tests of general intelligence (Kerns, Esso, & Thompson, 1999; Klingberg, Forssberg, & Westerberg, 2002; Shavlev, Tsal, & Mevorach, 2003). As a result, we are working with other groups carrying out these exercises in children with learning-related problems such as ADHD and autism. These projects will test whether the programs are efficacious with children who have special difficulties with attention as part of their disorder. We also hope to have preschools adopt attention training as a specific part of their curriculum. Viewing the attentional system as central for the successful development of cognitive and emotional regulation of behavior, it is expected that a more extensive training of attention will result in improving self-regulatory capacities.

Gene-Environment Interaction

The existence of gene by environment interaction is not controversial, and it is well known that gene expression can be influenced by the microenvironment of the brain area where it is expressed. There is also ample evidence that in primates, gene expression can be influenced by events, which, like maternal separation, can be a part of human development (Soumi, 2003).

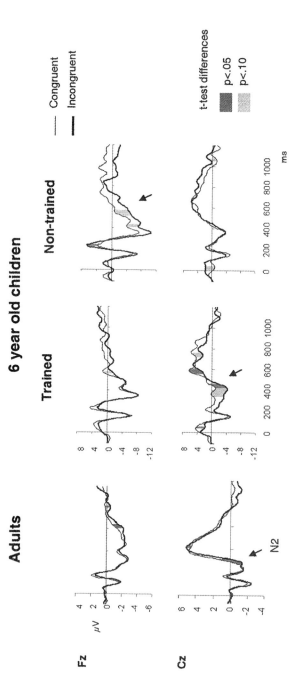

Figure 18-4 Pattern of brain activations for trained and nontrained children compared to adults during performance of the Child ANT. Target-locked event-related potentials (ERPs) at prefrontal (Fz) and frontoparietal (Cz) leads. The arrows points to the areas of significant differences between conditions. These effects appear at the N2 component in adults and trained children, but emerge some later and at more prefrontal channels in nontrained children.

Not all children need or benefit from attention training. This may be why variability is so high. In some of our studies we found that those children with the most initial difficulty in resolving conflict showed the greatest overall improvement due to training. Our research has also suggested a genetic marker of difference in attention among children. A dopamine-related gene, the dopamine transporter 1 (DAT1) gene, has been shown to be related to the efficiency of the executive attention network (Fossella et al., 2002). We were able to genotype most of the 6-year-old children who participated in our training study. Children were divided into two groups according to their particular form of the DAT1 gene, those carrying the pure long form and those carrying the pure short or mixed short/long forms of the gene. Because our sample was small, we combined 6-year-olds who had attention training with those in the control condition. Performance was examined on the first and second ANT. Although there were only seven children in the pure long allele group and eight in the mixed long/short group, we found a significant advantage in conflict scores for the pure long allele group.

Several features of our data supported the relation between the DAT1 polymorphism and individual differences in the efficiency of executive attention. Children in the two groups differed in their conflict scores as well as in the effortful control scores obtained with the parent-reported temperament questionnaires even before any training. In particular, the short/long mixed group showed higher conflict scores and lower effortful control than those in the pure long group. The two groups also differed in their EEG data. In the first session, the children with the pure long allele showed the effect of flankers in the expected direction (more negative N2 for incongruent condition, as shown in figure 18-4), whereas children in the mixed alleles group did not show such an effect. This difference corresponds to the trend we found for development between 4 and 6 years of age and to the effect of training, and suggests that the pure long form is associated with more mature executive attention.

The DAT1 gene has also been associated with ADHD; however, the exact relation between executive attention efficiency in normals and the presence of attention deficits in ADHD is not clear (Swanson, Oosterlaan, Murias, Moyzis, Schuck, et al., 2000).

Given the wide range of differences among individuals in the efficiency of attention, it is expected that attention training could be especially beneficial for those children with poorer initial efficiency. These could be children with pathologies that involve attentional networks, children with particular genetic backgrounds associated with poorer attentional performance, or children raised in different degrees of deprivation.

Summary

In this part of our paper, we have summarized evidence that attention training at 4 and 6 years of age can modify the functioning of networks involved in self-regulation.

Although our work is more a demonstration than an actual educational trial, it has the virtue of being computerized, so that it can and has been made accessible to researchers and users over the web (http://www.teach-the-brain.org). This allows it to be tried by researchers, teachers, parents, and children. It is probably best to view it as a demonstration that could form part of an organized curriculum to develop better attentional control. In addition, we are encouraged that it will be possible to determine from genetics and temperament the children most likely to profit from training.

Conclusions

In the first part of this chapter we sought to answer the question asked by the organizers: What neurodevelopmental processes in children and adolescents could be altered so that mental disorders might be prevented? We have summarized data that show that deficits in the executive attention system are a critical part of a number of mental disorders in children and adults. Although executive attention deficits are not necessarily the defining characteristic of any of these disorders, there is evidence that improved effortful control may help people overcome them.

In the second part of the chapter, we discussed a specific educational intervention that we have used to improve the executive attention of children. Our data provide support for the idea that training of executive attention during its development can improve performance and generalize to cognitive challenges far removed from the training. In addition, we found evidence that attention training moves the underlying network toward adult levels and that differences in genes related to dopamine function might help us choose which children are most likely to benefit from attention training.

The organizers also asked, What interventions or life experiences might be able to produce such changes? We do not argue that the particular intervention we have used is the correct one, or that an intervention rather than improved parenting is a better way to develop executive attention. There is already evidence that other forms of training can improve attention in children with disorders (Klingberg et al., 2002). Instead, we believe that various methods of improving attention of preschool children would be useful both in promoting success in schools and in helping to overcome the propensity toward attention problems. Only sustained research will improve these methods and provide the best help for the world's children.

Acknowledgments

This chapter was presented as a paper at the conference on Adolescent Psychopathology and the Developing Brain held June 17–18, 2005, at the University of Pennsylvania.

This work was supported by NIH grants MH 43361 and HD 38051, by a 21st Century grant from the James S. McDonnell Foundation and the Dana Foundation Arts initiative. The first author is now at the Department of Psychology, University of Granada, Spain, and can be reached at rorueda@ugr.es.

References

Benes, F. M. (1999). Model generation and testing to probe neural circuitry in the cingulate cortex of postmortem schizophrenic brains. *Schizophrenia Bulletin, 24,* 219–229.

Berger, A., Jones, L., Rothbart, M. K., & Posner, M. I. (2000). Computerized games to study the development of attention in childhood. *Behavioral Research Methods and Instrumentation, 32,* 297–303.

Blasi, G., Mattay, G. S., Bertolino, A., Elvevåg, B., Callicott, J. H., Das, S., Kolachana, B. S., Egan, M. F., Goldberg, T. E., & Weinberger, D. R. (2005). Effect of Catechol-*O*-Methyltransferase *val* [158] *met* genotype on attentional control. *Journal of Neuroscience, 25*(20), 5038–5045.

Carlson, S. M., & Moses, L. J. (2001). Individual differences in inhibitory control and children's theory of mind. *Child Development, 72,* 1032–1053.

Chang, F., & Burns, B. M. (2005). Attention in preschoolers: Associations with effortful control and motivation. *Child Development, 76,* 247–263.

Clarkin, J. F., & Posner, M. I. (2005). Defining the mechanisms of borderline personality disorder. *Psychopathology, 38,* 56–63.

Diamond, A., Briand, L., Fossella, J., & Gehlbach, L. (2004). Genetic and neurochemical modulation of prefrontal cognitive functions in children. *American Journal of Psychiatry, 161,* 125–132.

Early, T. S., Posner, M. I., Reiman, E. M., & Raichle, M. E. (1989). Left striato-pallidal hyperactivity in schizophrenia part II. Phenomenology and thought disorder. *Psychiatric Developments, 2,* 85–121.

Egan, M. F., Goldberg, T. E., Kolachana, B. S., Callicott, J. H., Mazzanti, C. M., Straub, R. E., Goldman, D., & Weinberger, D. R. (2001). Effect of COMT Val108/158 Met genotype on frontal lobe function and risk for schizophrenia. *Proceedings of the National Academy of Sciences of the USA, 98,* 6917–6922.

Ellis, E., Rothbart, M. K., & Posner, M. I. (2004). Individual differences in executive attention predict self-regulation and adolescent psychosocial behaviors. *Annals of New York Academy of Sciences, 1031,* 337–340.

Fan, J., Fossella, J. A., Summer, T., & Posner, M. I. (2003). Mapping the genetic variation of executive attention onto brain activity. *Proceedings of the National Academy of Science USA, 100,* 7406–7411.

Fan, J., McCandliss, B. D., Fossella, J., Flombaum, J. I., & Posner, M. I. (2005). The activation of attentional networks. *Neuroimage, 26,* 471–479.

Fan, J., McCandliss, B. D., Sommer, T., Raz, M., & Posner, M. I. (2002). Testing the efficiency and independence of attentional networks. *Journal of Cognitive Neuroscience, 3,* 340–347.

Fan, J., Wu, Y., Fossella, J., & Posner, M. I. (2001). Assessing the heritability of attentional networks. *BioMed Central Neuroscience, 2,* 14.

Fernandez-Duque, D., & Black, S. (2006). Attentional networks in normal aging and Alzheimer's disease. *Neuropsychology, 20,133–143.*

Fossella, J., Sommer, T., Fan, J., Wu, Y., Swanson, J. M., Pfaff, D. W., & Posner, M. I.

(2002). Assessing the molecular genetics of attention networks. *BMC Neuroscience, 3,* 14.

Gerardi-Caulton, G. (2000). Sensitivity to spatial conflict and the development of self-regulation in children 24–36 months of age. *Developmental Science, 3,* 397–404.

Green, C. S., & Bavelier, D. (2003). Action video game modifies visual selective attention. *Nature, 423,* 534–537.

Kaufman, A. S., & Kaufman, N. L. (1990). *Kaufman Brief Intelligence Test–Manual.* Circle Pines, MN: American Guidance Service.

Kerns, K. A., Esso, K., & Thompson, J. (1999). Investigation of a direct intervention for improving attention in young children with ADHD. *Developmental Neuropsychology, 16,* 273–295.

Klingberg, T., Forssberg, H., & Westerberg, H. (2002). Training of working memory in children with ADHD. *Journal of Clinical and Experimental Neuropsychology, 24,* 781–791.

Kochanska, G. (1995). Children's temperament, mothers' discipline, and security of attachment: Multiple pathways to emerging internalization. *Child Development, 66,* 597–615.

Maruff, P., Currie, J., Hay, D., McArthur-Jackson, C., & Malone, V. (1995). Asymmetries in the covert orienting of visual spatial attention in schizophrenia. *Neuropsychologia, 31,* 1205–1223.

Mischel, W., Shoda, Y., & Peake, P. K. (1988). The nature of adolescent competencies predicted by preschool delay of gratification. *Journal of Personality and Social Psychology, 54,* 687–696.

Olson, S. L., Sameroff, A. J., Kerr, D. C. R., Lopez, N. L., & Wellman, H. M. (2005). Development of foundations of externalizing problems in young children: The role of effortful control. *Development and Psychopathology, 17,* 25–46.

Parasuraman, R., Greenwood, P. M., Kumar, R., & Fossella, J. (2005). Beyond heritability—Neurotransmitter genes differentially modulate visuospatial attention and working memory. *Psychological Science, 16,* 200–207.

Pardo, P. J., Knesevich, M. A., Vogler, G. P, Pardo J. V., Towne, B., Cloninger, C. R., & Posner, M. I. (2000). Genetic and state variables of neurocognitive dysfunction in schizophrenia: A twin study. *Schizophrenia Bulletin, 26,* 459–477.

Posner, M. I., & Raichle, M. E. (1994). *Images of mind.* New York: Scientific American Books.

Posner, M. I., Rothbart, M. K., Vizueta, N., Thomas, K. M., Levy, K., Fossella, J., Silbersweig, D. A., Stern, E., Clarkin, J., & Kernberg, O. (2003). An approach to the psychobiology of personality disorders. *Development and Psychopathology, 15,* 1093–1106.

Rothbart, M. K., Ahadi, S. A., & Hershey, K. L. (1994). Temperament and social behavior in childhood. *Merrill-Palmer Quarterly, 40,* 21–39.

Rothbart, M. K., Ahadi, S. A., Hershey, K. L., & Fisher, P. (2001). Investigations of temperament at three to seven years: The Children's Behavior Questionnaire. *Child Development, 72,* 1394–1408.

Rothbart, M. K., & Posner, M. I. (2005). Genes and experience in the development of executive attention and effortful control. In L. A. Jensen & R. W. Larson (Eds.), *New horizons in developmental theory and research* (pp. 101–108). San Francisco: Jossey-Bass.

Rothbart, M. K., & Posner, M. I. (2006). Temperament, attention, and developmental psychopathology. In D. Cicchetti & D. J. Cohen (Eds.), *Handbook of developmental psychopathology* (pp. 465–501). New York: Wiley.

Rothbart, M. K., & Rueda, M. R. (2005). The development of effortful control. In U. Mayr, E.

Awh, & S. W. Keele (Eds.), *Developing individuality in the human brain: A tribute to Michael I. Posner* (pp. 167–188). Washington, DC: American Psychological Association.

Rueda, M. R., Fan, J., McCandliss, B. D., Halparin, J., Gruber, D., Lercari, L. P., & Posner, M. I. (2004a). Development of attention networks during childhood. *Neuropsychologia, 42,* 1029–1040.

Rueda, M. R., Posner, M. I., & Rothbart, M. K. (2004b). Attentional control and self regulation. In R. F. Baumeister & K. D. Vohs (Eds.), *Handbook of self-regulation: Research, theory, and applications* (pp. 283–300). New York: Guilford Press.

Rueda, M. R., Posner, M. I., & Rothbart, M. K. (2005). The development of executive attention: Contributions to the emergence of self-regulation. *Developmental Neuropsychology, 28*(2), 573–594.

Rueda, M. R., Posner, M. I., Rothbart, M. K., & Davis-Stober, C. P. (2004c). Development of the time course for processing conflict: An event-related potentials study with 4-year-olds and adults. *BMC Neuroscience, 5,* 39.

Rueda, M. R., Rothbart, M. K., McCandliss, B. D., Saccommano, L., & Posner, M. I. (2005). Training, maturation and genetic influences on the development of executive attention. *Proceedings of the National Academy of Sciences, USA, 102,* 14931–14936.

Rumbaugh, D. M., & Washburn, D. A. (1995). Attention and memory in relation to learning: A comparative adaptation perspective. In G. R. Lyon & N. A. Krasnegor (Eds.), *Attention, memory and executive function* (pp. 199–219). Baltimore, MD: Brookes.

Shavlev, L., Tsal, Y., & Mevorach, C. (2003). Progressive attentional training program: Effective direct intervention for children with ADHD. *Proceedings of the Cognitive Neuroscience Society, New York,* pp. 55–56.

Simon, T. J., Bish, J. P., Bearden, C. E., Ding, L., Ferrante, S., Nguyen, V., Gee, J., McDonald-McGinn, D., Zackai, E. H., & Emanuel, B. S. (2005). A multi-level analysis of cognitive dysfunction and psychopathology associated with chromosome 22q11.2 deletion syndrome in children development and psychopathology. *Developmental Psychopathology, 17,* 753–784.

Sobin, C., Kiley-Brabeck, K., Daniels, S., Blundell, M., Anyane-Yeboa, K., & Karayiorgou, M. (2004). Networks of attention in children with the 22q11 deletion syndrome. *Developmental Neuropsychology, 26*(2), 611–626.

Sobin, C., Kiley-Brabeck, K., & Karayiorgou, M. (2005). Association between prepulse inhibition and executive visual attention in children with 22q11 deletion syndrome. *Molecular Psychiatry, 10,* 553–562.

Sohlberg, M. M., McLaughlin, K. A., Pavese, A., Heidrich, A., & Posner, M. I. (2000). Evaluation of attention process therapy training in persons with acquired brain injury. *Journal of Clinical and Experimental Neuropsychology, 22,* 656–676.

Soumi, S. J. (2003). Gene-environment interactions and the neurobiology of social conflict. *Annals of the New York Academy of Sciences, 1008,* 132–139.

Swanson, J., Oosterlaan, J., Murias, M., Moyzis, R., Schuck, S., Mann, M., Feldman, P., Spence, M. A., Sergeant, J., Smith, M., Kennedy, J., & Posner, M. I. (2000). ADHD children with 7-repeat allele of the DRD4 gene have extreme behavior but normal performance on critical neuropsychological tests of attention. *Proceedings of the National Academy of Sciences, USA, 97,* 4754–4759.

van Veen, V., & Carter, C. S. (2002). The timing of action-monitoring processes in the anterior cingulate cortex. *Journal of Cognitive Neuroscience, 14,* 593–602.

Wang, K. J., Fan, J., Dong, Y., Wang C., Lee, T. M. C., & Posner, M. I. (2005). Selective impairment of attentional networks of orienting and executive control in schizophrenia. *Schizophrenia Research.*78, 235–241.

Chapter 19

The BrainWise Curriculum

Neurocognitive Development Intervention Program

Patricia Gorman Barry and Marilyn Welsh

Searching for "the Green"

David[1] is a slightly built 18-year-old who looks younger than his age. He has an IQ of 50 and attends an urban high school that has contained classrooms for disabled students. He is friends with Ed, another student with disabilities.

Pat Austin, a special education expert and social worker, teaches both boys in a thinking skills course called BrainWise. The BrainWise curriculum provides basic information on the brain and uses this as a framework to teach a series of skills called the "10 Wise Ways." Each wise way builds on another, merging knowledge about the brain with cognitive concepts. When students practice and learn the concepts, they develop problem-solving behaviors.

BrainWise material can be taught in 20 to 30 hours, with an additional 30 or more hours spent reinforcing the skills. However, special needs students require many more hours of instruction and often take the course for consecutive years. David and Ed were completing their second year and had received an estimated 300 contact hours of materials and practice. Still, Mrs. Austin wondered how much they had learned. "It was all I could do to get them to understand the basics," she said.

A few months before the school year ended, David started exhibiting signs of schizophrenia, saying he was hearing voices. This was not surprising as his parents were diagnosed with paranoid schizophrenia. One day, David said that he not only heard voices, but saw flying clocks and feared that the voices were going to steal the clocks—and his brain. This happened when David was in the school hallway with Ed.

"Where is the green? Help me find the green," he cried over and over, hitting his forehead with his fist. Students stared as Ed guided his friend through the crowded hallway to Mrs. Austin's office. David entered her office, twisting his body, pounding his forehead, and crying, "I need the green! I can't find the green!"

Mrs. Austin tried to calm him. "You're safe, David. Take some deep breaths."

He wailed, "Where is the green? I can't find the green."

"What is 'the green'?" asked Mrs. Austin.

David did not answer, but moaned, "I can't find the green," and kept hitting his forehead.

Ed answered, "Mrs. Austin, you know! The green's his Wizard Brain. That's why we came to you."

Now Mrs. Austin knew what David was saying. In the BrainWise program, each student receives a picture of the brain, which they label and color as they learn about its different parts. They learn that their senses send signals to the thalamus (also called the brain's relay center), and they color it blue.

The limbic system contains the amygdala (emotions) and the hypothalamus, which houses the fight-or-flight reaction, a response also found in reptiles. Because of this, it is called the Lizard Brain. They learn that the thalamus and limbic system are close to each other and connected, helping the brain send signals to the body so that it responds quickly to protect it from harm. The brain interprets any intense emotion as a threat and will always react without thinking. Because of this, students color the limbic system red.

The prefrontal cortex, or Wizard Brain, is behind the forehead and houses executive functions. Students color it green. Unlike the Lizard Brain, which is connected to the thalamus at birth, connections to the Wizard Brain must be learned. Each time students learn a thinking skill, they draw a line on their picture of the brain showing how the skill connects the thalamus with the Wizard Brain. They learn that thinking skills' connections intercept signals to the Lizard Brain, helping them stop and think before they react.

Mrs. Austin assured David that he had found "the green"—he had used his Wizard Brain to stay low on his emotions elevator and had come with Ed to her office for help. She contacted his parents and helped them make arrangements to get David to his doctor. He was hospitalized and put on new medications.

When David returned to school, Mrs. Austin praised the boys for their use of thinking skills. Ed smiled and said, "I used my Wizard Brain."

David nodded in agreement and pointed to his forehead. "It's here."

The BrainWise Program

How do you help students of all ages and academic abilities understand the brain and how their thinking affects their feelings and behaviors? Helping young people learn how to make good choices is what BrainWise is all about. If David and Ed had not learned skills that underlie the thinking process, this scenario would have been very different. We have found that using mnemonics, drawings, and colors to teach BrainWise concepts engages people of all ages and abilities. Depending on the ages and capability of the students, teachers have the option of adding more information on the brain and explaining the complex relationship between the ventromedial and dorsolateral divisions of the prefrontal cortex, the hippocampus, the amygdala, and the HPA axis and its components, the hypothalamus, the pituitary, and the adrenal-cortex (Bremner, 2003; Davidson et al., 2000; Davidson et al., 2003; Goldsmith & Davidson, 2004; Gunnar, this volume; Teicher et al., 2003). However, the Wizard Brain/Lizard Brain explanation helps students grasp abstract concepts of thinking, emotion, and impulse. The result is a method that helps children and adolescents acquire developmental skills normally found in more mature youth and adults.

Scientifically demonstrating the outcomes of intervention programs is difficult, especially with at-risk populations. In this chapter, we present the theoretical underpinnings of the BrainWise program, as well as research we are conducting using measures of executive function to demonstrate that the program's design and approach help individuals learn and develop thinking skills. Although students may not have much control over what happens to them, we want to teach them that they do have control over how they react.

During the past 15 years, numerous character education, social and emotional learning, and positive youth development programs have been introduced to schools to help students prevent or manage the problems they face (Barry, 1996, 1998, 1999; Benson et al., 1993; Eggert et al., 1995; Elias et al., 1997; Kusché & Greenberg, 1994; Nichols, 1996; Romer, 2003; Shure, 1992; Steinberg, 1996; Zins et al., 2004). In addition, a growing number of programs are available that address specific problems including, but not limited to, AIDS education, anger management, smoking cessation, and prevention of bullying, drug and alcohol abuse, suicide, and teen pregnancy.

All of these programs compete for classroom time, creating a difficult balancing act for teachers who are increasingly under pressure to raise test scores. In addition, many interventions have come and gone, yielding little in the way of positive and lasting change (U.S. Department of Education, 2003). To promote greater success, organizations like the Center for Social and Emotional Education, the Collaborative to Advance Social and Emotional Learning (CASEL), the Center for the Study and Prevention of Violence, the U.S. Department of Education's Institute of Educational Sciences, and the U.S. Department of Health and

Human Services are establishing lists and registries that identify evidence-based prevention and intervention programs. However, these lists are meaningless if the curricula are not taught as designed. A random sample of 1,905 middle school teachers found that only 25 percent of the lead staff who taught substance abuse prevention used an evidence-based curriculum and less than one third of them taught the curriculum using best practice standards (Ennett et al., 2003).

Aware of these challenges, BrainWise was designed as a universal program that addresses academic standards and can easily be integrated into the classroom. Its 10 skills teach problem-solving strategies that students use to assess and analyze their own problems as well as the problems of others. And because instructors choose to teach BrainWise, there is an increased likelihood that they will closely follow the curriculum.

Originally developed to help high-risk middle and high school students learn to make responsible choices, the program now is taught to children in grades K–12 and to adults. Many schools and agencies use the program solely with risk populations, but it also has been applied universally—for example, integrated into regular classrooms, used in after-school programs, and taught to college students. Girl Scouts can earn a BrainWise badge. Illiterate girls in China are taught thinking skills to resist sex traffickers. Some high school students even wrote a play performed for classes throughout their district that includes a rap song titled "You Gotta Stop and Think." More than 2,000 instructors have been trained to teach BrainWise, including 400 educators in China and representatives from Alaska's seven native reservations. Countless other instructors are self-taught and use the program's scripted lesson plans and online and telephone support for guidance.

Theoretical Foundations of BrainWise

The theoretical foundation of BrainWise is based on research from several disciplines, including neuroscience, the social sciences, and education. Aspects from all of these approaches are integrated into the content and delivery of an intervention used to teach children and youth how to stop and think.

Neuroscience

The brain and body are designed for survival. The body's senses (sound, sight, taste, and touch) act as sentinels, sending signals that warn the brain of danger. These signals trigger fear and the fight/flight/freeze response in the hypothalamic region, releasing glucocorticoids that bring about increased blood pressure, heart rate, and body metabolism (H. Benson, 1975; Cozolino, 2002; van der Kolk, 2003). This reaction places the body in a state of heightened alert, a response that is necessary if someone must jump out of the path of an oncoming car, but that creates problems if someone becomes violent after being accidentally bumped. The brain perceives both the car and the bump as threats, triggering nonthinking emotional and impulsive reactions (Jenson, 2000; LeDoux, 1996).

Goldsmith and Davidson (2004) suggest that chronic exposure to stressful life events that results in elevated cortisol levels may, over time, impair emotion-relevant contextual processing and inhibition. Streeck-Fischer and van der Kolk (cited in Scott et al., 2003) agree, indicating that chronic traumatic experiences affect children's capacity for emotional regulation, causing a negative sense of self, poor impulse control, and distrust of others. Even isolated traumatic incidents tend to produce discrete, conditioned behavioral and biologic responses to reminders of trauma, and chronic incidents (e.g., ongoing abuse or exposure to repeated medical procedures) have a wide range of effects on neurobiological developments (van der Kolk, 2003). Prolonged alarm reactions alter limbic, midbrain, and brainstem functions through "use-dependent" changes (van der Kolk, 2003), which change the degree to which cortical structures help modulate the brain's response to danger (Teicher et al., 2003).

What effect does this have on the large number of children and youth who daily are exposed to stress? At every BrainWise training, we ask teachers, counselors, and social workers to examine a list of 20 risk factors, ranging from "no consistent mealtime or bedtime" to "lives in a constant state of fear or threat," and check which ones their students have. Their responses are the same: "I would check all of them," or "It would be easier to check the ones they don't have." In an era of school violence (Columbine), terrorist attacks (World Trade Center, 9/11), bioterrorism threats (anthrax), random sniper shootings, and natural disasters (Hurricane Katrina), more children fear that they or someone close to them will be harmed.

The media's extensive coverage of terrifying events and the resulting aftermath—school lockdowns, security officers, routine weapon checks, false alarms—contribute to stressful physiological reactions. Research on youth exposed to war and terrorism found that they had difficulty concentrating, were irritable, and were described by teachers as oscillating between apathy and aggressive behaviors in the classroom (Saltzman et al., 2003). Posttraumatic stress research shows that participants have baseline autonomic hyperarousal states and greater resting heart rate variability compared with controls (Cohen et al., 2002), an outcome exemplified by abnormally high resting heart rates recorded in traumatized children (Perry, 1994; Perry & Pollard, 1998).

Unfortunately, many school personnel and youth workers blame the child or youth rather than considering that these young people may not know any other way to react and that their behaviors may be secondary responses to stress, grief, and depression (Saltzman et al., 2003). This is why it is important to teach young people skills that will give them control over how they respond to problems and that show them how to overcome habitual fight/flight/freeze reactions.

Experiences interpreted as traumatic will, during development, determine the functional capacity of the human brain. The same molecular characteristics of nerve tissue that allow the mature brain to store new information are also those for organizing the brain during development (Goelet & Kandel, 1986; Kandel & Schwartz, cited in Perry, 1994.) These findings emphasize how important it is to understand the effect that the external world has on the brain and the body and the impact this has on learning. They also help explain why it is important to teach children skills that will give them control over how they respond to problems.

NEURODEVELOPMENT OF COGNITIVE SKILLS.   The ability to learn new skills is the subject of Eric Kandel's research. The regulation of gene expression by social factors makes all bodily functions, including the brain, susceptible to social influences (Kandel, 1998). All functions of the mind reflect workings of the brain. Thinking must be learned, and the brain does this by forming new synaptic connections. If thinking skills are never learned, not used, or used infrequently, neural connections to the Wizard Brain (prefrontal cortex) are nonexistent or weak, and the brain resorts to its hardwired survival response—responding without thinking.

Kandel won the 2000 Nobel Prize in Medicine for his research showing how this happens. He studied changes that occur in the brain with learning and how that information is retained in memory. By examining nerve cells in the sea snail *Aplysia*, he was able to observe the molecular process of learning.[2] "You can see in front of your eyes that the connections change. When the animal remembers something for the long term, it grows new synaptic connections" (cited in Mirskey, 2000, p. 2).

BrainWise teaches students that new synaptic connections to the prefrontal cortex must be formed in order to regulate the Lizard Brain's strong survival instinct. It ties in the biological explanation of learning by having students draw lines on a picture of the brain, showing how each time they learn a concept, they are building new neural connections. When the skills are used and practiced, the connections are solidified and an "Aha!" experience takes place. They learn the "use it or lose it" mantra of learning—that being aware of these connections is not enough; practice is necessary for thinking skills to be retained.

Learning to modify behaviors is the feature that distinguishes an animal's behavior and reaches its highest form in humans (Kandel, 2000). What better way to demonstrate this feat than to incorporate findings from neurobiology into a curriculum used to teach thinking skills? By breaking down and simplifying key information about learning, the BrainWise program provides a method that works for people of all ages and abilities.[3] Research is beginning to examine the interaction of genes and environment, showing that neural networks underlie thoughts and emotions (Rothbart & Posner, 2005). These findings suggest that training may guide the development of reactive and self-regulatory behavior in children (Reuda et al., this volume).

NEURAL MEDIATION OF EXECUTIVE FUNCTION.   The prefrontal cortex integrates sensory information and links it to planned movement. Because of these functions, it is thought to be one of the anatomical substrates of goal-directed action in long-term planning and judgment (Kandel, 1999). These abilities are called executive functions by some researchers (e.g., Welsh & Pennington, 1988), and they do not develop automatically, but must be learned (Greenberg, Kusché, & Riggs, 2004). These skills appear to be substantially influenced by environmental input throughout childhood, although more empirical research on this issue is needed (Welsh, Friedman, & Spieker, in press).

There is general agreement that executive function refers to the cognitive processes that are necessary for purposeful, future-oriented behavior. These include, but are not limited to, regulation of attention; perception; language; inhibition of inappropriate responses; coordination of working memory; and capacities to organize, sequence, and plan adaptive behavior. These skills are necessary for efficient and effective future-oriented behavior, whether that behavior is an infant retrieving a toy or an attorney planning the perfect closing argument (Welsh, 2002). Executive functions are defined in terms of their problem-solving outcomes (Zelazo & Mueller, 2002). BrainWise's 10 Wise Ways (described below) teaches skills that are characteristic of executive functions.

Based on clinical studies with adults who have suffered various forms of brain damage (e.g., Eslinger, 1996; Luria, 1973; Stuss & Benson, 1984; Teuber, 1964), the mediation of executive function processes by the frontal cortex has gained general acceptance (e.g., Tranel, Anderson, & Benton, 1995). It is important to note here that the frontal cortex comprises over one third of human cortical tissue and is composed of a variety of anatomical components, each with specialized cortical and subcortical connections (Damasio & Anderson, 1993). Rather than linking executive function to the frontal lobe en masse, neuroscientific research suggests that it is more accurate to attribute executive processes to the prefrontal cortex and, even more specifically, to two regions within the prefrontal cortex: the dorsolateral and orbital-frontal areas (Iversen & Dunnett, as cited in Barkley, 1997). More recently, the underlying neural mediation of executive functions has been viewed from a "systems perspective," implicating the involvement of entire fronto-subcortical circuits (Banfield et al., 2004; Heyder, Suchan, & Daum, 2004; Roth & Syakin, 2004). For example, Banfield et al. (2004) suggest that the connections between the dorsolateral prefrontal cortex and subcortical structures, such as the basal ganglia and thalamus, mediate the so-called "cold" executive functions, such as planning, conceptual reasoning, strategic behavior, flexibility, and working memory. In contrast, the circuit that involves the ventromedial/orbito-frontal prefrontal cortex and basal ganglia and thalamic structures underlies what might be called "hot" executive functions, such as self-monitoring and regulation of emotion processing and emotional response. This new direction for research in executive function and its neural correlates has direct relevance to goals of the BrainWise program given that this curriculum focuses on improving both "cold" executive functions (e.g., planning, effective communication) and "hot" executive functions (e.g., controlling one's emotions, recognizing "red flags" in one's environment).

As discussed above, the notion that learning new skills and information results in the development of new synaptic connections in the brain is generally well accepted (e.g., Kandel, 2000). However, it has also been proposed by Changeux and colleagues (Changeux & Danchin, 1976; Changeux, Heidmann, & Patte, 1984) that during development, millions of excess, redundant connections are created between neurons in the brain and, through interactions with one's environment, these excess connections are "pruned down" to more manageable and efficient levels. That is, repetitive stimulation from and interactions with the environment should functionally stabilize networks of neuronal connections that are necessary for adaptive behavior, whereas unnecessary connections are eliminated. Examinations of the synaptic density in the prefrontal cortex suggest that there are a tremendous number of excess synaptic connections, referred to as "exuberant connectivity" by Chugani (1994), in the brains of children from about 3 years of age through adolescence and, in fact, this synaptic density far exceeds that of adults (Huttenlocher & Dabholker, 1997). The sharp increase and high point in synaptic contacts occurs at an age when executive function processes are only just beginning to manifest in a child's behavior. In contrast, the protracted period of improvement in executive processes that is apparent across the school age and adolescent years actually parallels a gradual *decline* in synaptic density in the prefrontal region. It may be precisely this *decrease* in synaptic number that reflects the stabilization of the functional networks underlying advances in cognitive processing, as proposed in Changeux's theory of stabilization. Therefore, as early as age 5 and as late as age 16, the prefrontal cortex may be particularly "primed" and ready to be exposed to the BrainWise lessons that are taught, repeated, and reinforced over time, potentially creating functional networks of connections not only within the prefrontal cortex, but between the prefrontal cortex and critical subcortical structures, such as the limbic system.

Social Science

BrainWise adopts many of the premises that define cognitive restructuring. Cognitive models include teaching specific techniques designed to help people change distorted patterns of thinking (Beck et al., 1979; Ellis, 1985; Ellis & Harper, 1975). Cognitive restructuring has successfully been used to promote optimism, enhance personal control, increase performance, and boost self-esteem (Burns, 1980; Seligman, 1991). The theory of learned optimism has grown, helping launch a movement toward positive psychology devoted to fostering factors that allow individuals to flourish as decision makers with choices, preferences, and the possibility of becoming masterful (Seligman & Csikszenmihalyi, 2000). In BrainWise, mastery of thinking occurs when individuals are able not only to apply the 10 Wise Ways to themselves and to others, but to apply them to themselves and others simultaneously.

Bandura's (1977a, 1977b, 1986) social learning theory addresses how children learn appropriate responses through the observation of others' behavior and the subsequent consequences (outcome and efficacy). This theory is at the center of entertainment education programs designed to promote literacy, empower women, prevent pregnancy, and halt the spread of HIV. Offered in developing countries, social learning programs reach millions around the world, helping people learn from role models whose behavior they wish to emulate (Smith, 2002). By fostering the belief that individuals have control over their choices and decisions, they increase their self-efficacy. BrainWise applies this concept by having students use the 10 Wise Ways to analyze popular television shows, movies, and song lyrics. They may learn how to teach thinking skills to members of dysfunctional families found in television shows like *The Simpsons,* analyze the bad and good choices of celebrities, or discuss the thinking skills behind sports figures who use talent, not drugs, to advance their performance.

Education

The theory of multiple intelligences says that intelligence entails the ability to solve problems and that problem-solving skills allow one to approach a situation in which a goal is to be obtained and to identify the appropriate route to that goal (Gardner, 1993). Certain habits of thought, such as taking one's time, considering alternatives, sharing one's work with others, and assuming the perspective of another person, are habits of the mind—characteristics that should be cultivated early and widely (Gardner, 1993). BrainWise was designed to develop good habits in students by helping them learn how to use the Wise Ways to solve problems.

Sternberg's (2001) balance theory of wisdom complements the preceding theories, including Kandel's research on learning and memory. To make wise judgments requires combining explicit knowledge (the knowledge one learns directly in school and life) with implicit knowledge (informal knowledge more likely to be picked up through life experience than through formal classroom teaching). He sees educators as providing learning experiences that will help the individual make his or her own wise decisions (Sternberg, 2001). BrainWise does this and more—it provides specific tools, the 10 Wise Ways, to guide young people to make wise choices.

Optimal learning occurs in predictable sequences, and BrainWise incorporates its five stages: preparation (prime and preexpose); acquisition (use teaching strategies that involve direct and indirect learning); elaboration (give students opportunities for experimentation and feedback); memory formation (encode learning); and functional integration (extend usage of materials; Jenson, 2000).

The BrainWise curriculum integrates characteristics found in successful programs: Instructors provide students with 50 or more contact hours, use multiple teaching techniques, and address both risk and protective factors. Additionally, the program can be replicated at multiple sites with demonstrated effects. It involves parents, and its instructors receive ongoing support and training (Bartlett, 1985; Elliot, 2001; Hawkins et al., 1992; Payton et al., 2000; Steinberg, 1996).

Description of the BrainWise Intervention

The BrainWise curriculum consists of an instructor's manual that contains 17 scripted lessons and a set of reproducible student worksheets, a poster set of the 10 Wise Ways, bookmarks, supplemental lessons, and a companion book for parents. To address teacher resistance to "another new program," it is taught by instructors who want to teach it. Although the program's lesson plans contain many examples, instructors are encouraged to customize the lessons to fit the age, sex, culture, ability, and specific needs of their students or clients. The program's language and terminology make it easy to integrate and generalize its 10 lessons into activities inside and outside the classroom.

The intervention involves a series of skills called the 10 Wise Ways (as displayed in table 19-1). These skills are designed to help young people to cope with problems, especially those that create stress and heightened emotional reactions. The following example demonstrates this aspect of the curriculum:

Table 19-1 The 10 Wise Ways to Stop and Think

Wise Way #1: Use your Wizard Brain over your Lizard Brain.
Wise Way #2: Use your Constellation of Support.
Wise Way #3: Recognize Internal and External Red Flags.
Wise Way #4: Exit your Emotions Elevator. (In BrainWise, emotions are compared to a ten-story elevator. The higher up you are, the more likely you are to use your Lizard Brain. Techniques to lower the elevator include taking deep breaths, using control self-talk, redirecting your emotions, and using relaxation techniques.)
Wise Way #5: Separate Fact from Opinion.
Wise Way #6: Ask Questions and Gather Information.
Wise Way #7: Identify your Choices (IDC).
Wise Way #8: Consequences of Choices.
   Consequences Now and Later (CNL).
   Consequences Affecting Others (CAO).
Wise Way #9: Set Goals and Plans for Action.
Wise Way #10: Communicate Effectively.
  1. Nonverbal communication.
  2. Verbal communication.
    a. I messages.
    b. Recognizing differences.
    c. Avoid using double messages.
  3. Assertive communication
    a. Aggressive communication
    b. Passive communication
    c. Passive aggressive communication
    d. Assertive communication

A Denver kindergarten teacher described how her 5-year-olds used skills they learned in BrainWise after the killings at nearby Columbine High School. The children talked about how Eric Harris and Dylan Klebold used their Lizard Brain, did not use their constellation of support, were high on their emotions elevators, and made bad choices that had consequences for many people. The children pointed out that the grownups did not recognize the boys' red flags and didn't ask the right questions to find out about their problems and talk with them. The teacher said what others have said about BrainWise: It gives words to talk about problems, and the concepts help them understand what happened and how to react to the events calmly, not with fear. "I get goose bumps when I tell the story," she said.

BrainWise skills also help inhibit the emotional and impulsive behaviors of teenagers, the population for whom the curriculum was originally developed. When talking about BrainWise, their conversations are filled with terms they learned in the curriculum—for example, "I used to be a Lizard Brain," "My new friends help me solve problems and my old friends created problems," "Being aware of red flags helps me stay low on my emotions elevator," "Now I think about my choices and the consequences," "I know what it means to set goals," "I try to separate fact from opinion," "It helps when I take other people's points of view," "*I messages* have helped me solve problems," and "I notice who is being aggressive, passive, and passive aggressive and use my thinking skills to be assertive." Statements like these are consistent across all program sites, even programs in China.

Evidence of Program Effectiveness: Research on Program Outcomes

Study of Urban Middle School Students

This study evaluated the effects of the BrainWise curriculum in a sample of 113 middle school students in regular classrooms at posttest (51 intervention and 62 comparison students). Two schools participated in the study; seventh graders from School A received the intervention, and those in School B did not. The sample included 65% Hispanic, 27% Caucasian, 4% American Indian, 2% African American, 1% Asian American, and 1% children from other ethnic minority populations (OMNI Research and Training, Inc., 2001).

Students at both schools were administered pretests and posttests containing several scales predicted to measure BrainWise outcomes. The central research question addressed was whether changes in the attitudes and behaviors of seventh-grade students could be observed after they completed the BrainWise course.

In addition, 42 students participated in three focus groups conducted at the experimental and comparison schools at the beginning of the spring semester and again at the end of the semester. The students were shown a video clip with four brief scenarios of typical situations they face—stealing, rumors, not turning in homework, and relationships. Discussion questions were designed to probe their understanding and use of the concepts behind the 10 Wise Ways. Students in School A were also asked to describe key BrainWise concepts.

At posttest, students who had received BrainWise demonstrated significant improvements on three of the scales: decreased physical aggression, reduced negative affect (feelings of loneliness, sadness, and being upset), and increased peer acceptance. Two other scales, social skills and belief in moral order, also showed differences. Students at the comparison school showed no change and scored worse on the belief in moral order scale.

Results from pre- and postprogram focus groups indicated that intervention students improved in communication and information gathering, assertiveness, honesty, deescalation of emotions, and recognizing consequences; and they showed decreased lying, fighting, and disrespecting others. In describing BrainWise, one student summarized the program by saying, "It doesn't change the person, it changes how the person thinks."

Study of Elementary, Middle, and High School Students

The evolving study of executive function provides what may be a more comprehensive way to measure the neurocognitive changes that occur with the BrainWise intervention. Two instruments, the Tower of London-Revised (Schnirman, Welsh, Retzlaff, 1998) and the Stroop Test (Stroop, 1935), were selected to measure executive function in BrainWise students. Because it was a pilot study, no control group was used. The sample included 36 elementary, middle school, and high school students living in a metropolitan area. The students were almost evenly divided between Caucasians and Hispanics, and one third was boys and two thirds were girls. All students were in regular classrooms except a class of special education students at one of the high school sites.[4]

In High School A, BrainWise was taught to regular students for two semesters, 45 minutes one day a week. At High School B, BrainWise was integrated into a special education classroom, where it was taught for two semesters, 50 minutes twice a week. The two elementary schools taught BrainWise to regular students for two semesters, pulling selected students out of other classes, 30 minutes one day a week. Middle school students in the after-school program were taught BrainWise for 24 weeks, one hour one day a week. Teachers, school social workers, and parents selected participating students as youth who would benefit from the skills taught in BrainWise.

Typical of schools, the study participants received a wide range of the intervention in both quality and amount. The BrainWise curriculum's 10 concepts, lesson plans, order of skill presentation, and ongoing reinforcement provided consistency across the sites. The pilot study gave us information on the feasibility of this format as well as on the instruments we can use to measure executive function among students taking BrainWise.

Two outcome measures of executive functions were included in this preliminary study. The Tower of London–Revised (TOL–R) measures executive function
skills such as planning, working memory, and inhibition (Schnirman et al., 1988).
The Stroop test measures executive processes such as interference control, inhibition, and cognitive flexibility and, according to the test authors, performance
reflects an individual's ability to cope with cognitive stress and process complex
input (Western Psychological Services, 2004). Both tests were administered to
male and female students in fifth grade, middle school, and high school who participated in the BrainWise intervention during the 2004–2005 academic year.
Thirty-four students were tested twice on the TOL–R, and 36 students were tested
twice on the Stroop. The pretests took place during October and November 2004,
and the posttests were administered during April and May 2005.

During the pretest phase, both the TOL–R and Stroop test scores were positively
correlated with age, and neither test exhibited gender differences. On the TOL–R,
the high school students outperformed the middle school and elementary school
students, and these latter two groups did not differ from each other. Regarding the
Stroop test score, both the high school and elementary school students exhibited
inhibition scores that were superior to those of the middle school students.

During the posttest phase, the scores on the TOL–R and Stroop tests again correlated in the expected direction with age of the student. Consistent with the pretest phase, the average TOL–R score of the high school students was superior to
that of the middle school and elementary school students, and these groups did
not differ from each other. With regard to the Stroop test, the high school students demonstrated better inhibition scores than the middle school and elementary school students, who did not differ from each other.

In terms of the change in the scores on the two tests, the data from 34 students
who had pretest and posttest scores for both tests were analyzed, and these mean
scores and standard deviations are presented in table 19-2. Regarding the TOL–R,
there was a significant increase from pretest (mean of 17.91 out of 30 points) to
posttest (mean of 19.12). There was also a significant effect of Age Group with the
mean performance of each age group as follows: elementary school, 14.5; middle
school, 17.75; high school, 21.93. Pairwise comparisons indicated that the high
school group was superior to both the middle school and elementary school groups,
which did not differ. The Intervention by Age Group interaction was not significant; thus, the age groups demonstrated similar improvement from the pretest to
posttest sessions. However, an inspection of the means demonstrates that, as a group,
the high school students did not change in the TOL–R mean score. This unexpected
results appears to be the consequence of a few outlier participants, who either scored
at ceiling at both test sessions or who went down dramatically from pretest to posttest.
Seven of fourteen students improved their score on the test, and four of fourteen
remained the same. The TOL–R scores were highly positively correlated ($r = .81$)
from the pretest to the posttest sessions, indicating good test–retest reliability.

Table 19-2 Means and Standard Deviations for Performance on the TOL-R and Stroop Tests for Three Age Groups and for the Pre-Intervention and Post-Intervention Sessions.

AGE GROUP	PRETEST TOL–R	POSTTEST TOL–R	PRETEST STROOP	POSTTEST STROOP
5th Grade	13.60	15.40	–.56	1.31
n = 10	(4.72)	(5.02)	(7.44)	(4.26)
Middle School	16.60	18.90	–2.98	1.35
n = 10	(5.85)	(6.57)	(7.80)	(4.25)
High School	21.93	21.93	4.65	7.42
n = 14	(4.43)	(4.80)	(5.72)	(6.75)

Note: The TOL–R score is number correct out of possible 30 points. The Stroop score reflects the degree to which the individual can inhibit the reading response in order to make the color naming response. As the score increases in a negative direction, this indicates increasingly poor inhibition (a longer time than would be predicted by reading and naming speeds alone). As the score increases in a positive direction, this indicates increasingly effective inhibition.

With regard to the Stroop test, a positive score indicates better inhibition during the conflict task, and a negative score indicates poor inhibition. There was a significant increase from the pretest (mean of .369) to the posttest (mean of 3.36). There was also a significant effect of Age Group, with the mean performance of each age group as follows: elementary school, .376; middle school, –.813; high school, 6.032. Again, the high school group's inhibition was superior to that of both the middle school and elementary school groups, which did not differ. The Intervention by Age Group interaction was not significant, consistent with the results for the TOL–R test. The Stroop scores were also positively correlated from the pre- to posttest sessions ($r = .60$), indicating adequate test–retest reliability.

Given the wide individual differences in performance, both across and within age groups, a preliminary examination of within-person change in scores was conducted. An improvement in number correct on the TOL–R and a change in a more positive direction in the Stroop inhibition score were examined for each student. Of the entire sample of 34 students, 16 showed improvement on both tests; 6 showed improvement in the TOL–R only; 6 showed improvement in Stroop only; 2 showed decline in the Stroop only; and 4 showed decline in both tests. Therefore, 28 of 34 (82%) demonstrated improved performance on at least one of the measures, and 16 of 34 (47%) showed improvement on both measures.

It is important to point out that all or some portion of this improvement may be due to maturation and cognitive development that occurred during the 6 months that elapsed between the pretests and posttests. In light of the absence of a matched control group in this preliminary study, the degree to which maturation accounted for the significant changes in performance could not be examined directly. However, an estimate of the change that might be expected to occur in 6 months was calculated by regressing age onto the pretest score of each measure and determining the slope of each line. The slope provides an estimate of the change in the TOL–R and Stroop preintervention scores with an increase of one year in the cross-sectional data. One-half of this number would provide an estimate of the increase in performance on these two tests in a 6-month time period (the time between the preintervention score and the postintervention score).

For the TOL–R test, the expected increase in the score for 6 months was .70 points, and this can be compared to an actual increase of 1.40 points from pretest to posttest in the entire sample. A statistical comparison of the actual difference scores and the expected difference scores was not significant, paired samples $t(33) = .803, p > .05$. For the Stroop test, the expected improvement in the inhibition score was .48, and this can be compared to an actual increase in the inhibition score of 2.9 from pretest to posttest. The paired t-test between the actual and expected difference scores was significant, $t(35) = 2.4, p = .022$. It's important to note that these rough estimates of expected "change" in the scores over a period of six months are derived from cross-sectional data, which informs us about developmental differences and not developmental change. However, if these estimates are relatively close to what would be expected to occur with maturation alone, the observed improvements in executive function performance over the course of a 6-month exposure to the BrainWise program appear to exceed these levels (see figure 19-1). In this preliminary study, a significant change was only observed in the Stroop interference score, which presumably reflects improvements in impulse control.

The study showed that the Stroop in particular, and potentially the TOL–R, may capture cognitive and behavioral characteristics that are targeted for change in the course of the BrainWise intervention. We plan to conduct follow-up research with a larger sample and a matched control group to see to what extent this improvement is due to maturation, the BrainWise intervention, or some combination of the two factors. Our current research is based on the assumption that some individuals have relatively weak executive skills and the BrainWise intervention is designed to bolster executive functions in general. Although this may be true for a subset of individuals, others may have adequate executive functions under "normal circumstances," but they have difficulty recruiting and executing these skills under conditions of high stress. Many of the lessons included in the BrainWise curriculum involve making good decisions, controlling emotions, and communicating effectively in situations that are characterized by high levels of stress and tension (e.g., peer pressure, bullying). Therefore, another interesting avenue for research will be to examine the degree to which the BrainWise intervention is particularly effective in helping children and adolescents exercise their executive function skills while under stress. That is, it

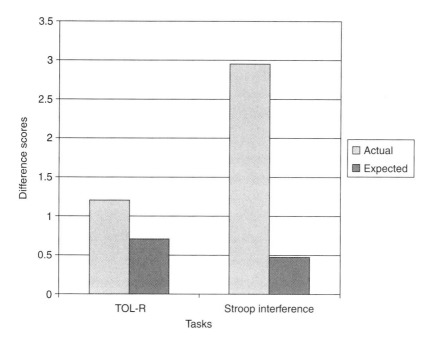

Figure 19-1 A comparison of actual and expected difference scores for Tower of London–Revised (TOL-R) accuracy and Stroop interference.

may be the case that the more sensitive test of the effectiveness of BrainWise is not in terms of changes in executive functions as seen under "normal" testing conditions, but in terms of changes in executive skills under "stressful" testing conditions (e.g., conditions more stressful than the time limits required by the Stroop).

Future research involves evaluating BrainWise as a school- and family-based intervention to improve school adaptation, performance, and achievement in low-income children. Evidence suggests that programs designed to alter parenting attitudes and practices result in improved school readiness, literacy, and academic achievement (Brooks-Gunn & Markman, 2005; Olds et al., 2004). The target children will receive BrainWise at school, and their caregivers will be taught BrainWise at home. Outcomes of this group will be compared with matched groups who receive BrainWise only in school and not at home, and children and parents who do not receive BrainWise. This "double dose" of the BrainWise intervention will allow pairwise comparisons to determine whether enhancing cognitive stimulation at school or the school and home is sufficient to produce improvements in child outcomes, as well as the attendant effects of teaching caregivers new thinking skills.

Conclusion

The classroom is not a scientific laboratory. It is difficult to control the quality and amount of BrainWise material that students receive, just as it is difficult to control other variables that can jeopardize the effective delivery of a program or a study's internal and external validity. We are beginning to gather data that show how teaching children about the brain helps them learn skills to make good decisions.

As we gain a better understanding of the neurodevelopment of the frontal cortex and how it complements skills that are called executive function, we will be able to integrate brain research into helping individuals learn how to replace impulse and emotions with a thinking process. The BrainWise curriculum uses a simple explanation of this process to help students understand that how they think affects how they act, and provides a framework to teach skills that promote positive youth development.

Educators, psychologists, and sociologists need to work closely with scientists studying the biology of learning so their discoveries can be applied to programs taught in schools, communities, and homes. Emotion and cognition once were considered independent and separate, but now can be understood as intricately bound and inseparable (Bell & Wolfe, 2004). We are getting closer to the day when scientific evidence will explain how the *Aha!* of learning takes place in everyone, including at-risk adolescents, kindergartners, and developmentally disabled youth like David and Ed.

Acknowledgments

We thank Nicole Sperekas, Marilyn Anderson, Christina McFadden, Nancy Zook, and James Holland for their help testing students; instructors Marsha Harman, Barbara Lamana, Brenda Knoop, Virginia Grogan, and Elizabeth Long for teaching BrainWise to the study's participants; and our anonymous reviewers for their helpful comments.

Notes

1. The students' names have been changed.
2. Nerve cells of the sea snail were easier to study than those of a mammalian brain, as *Aplysia* has 20,000 central nerve cells clustered around 10 ganglia, each of which contains 2,000 cells, versus a "million-million" nerve cells in a human (Kandel, 2000).
3. Kindergartners and developmentally disabled children take longer to learn the concepts. It's important not to equate knowing the BrainWise terminology (e.g., Wizard Brain, Lizard Brain, emotions elevator, and so on) with understanding the concepts. That is like expecting a child who knows the alphabet to be able to read. Demonstrating knowledge of the skills through behavior indicates that the skills have been learned.
4. These were high performing special education students, different from David and Ed's class for profoundly disabled students.

References

Bandura, A. (1977a). *Social learning theory.* Englewood Cliffs, NJ: Prentice Hall.

Bandura, A. (1977b). Self-efficacy: Toward a unifying theory of behavioral change. *Psychological Review, 84*(2), 191–215.

Bandura, A. (1986). *Social foundations of thought and action: A social cognitive theory.* Englewood Cliffs, NJ: Prentice Hall.

Banfield, J. F., Wyland, C. L., Macrae, C. N., Munte, T. F., & Heatherton, T. F. (2004). The cognitive neuroscience of self-regulation. In R. F. Baumeister & K. D. Vohs (Eds.), *Handbook of self-regulation: Research, theory, and applications* (pp. 62–83). New York: Guilford Press.

Barkley, R. A. (1997). Behavioral inhibition, sustained attention, and executive functions: Constructing a unified theory of ADHD. *Psychological Bulletin, 121,* 65–94.

Barry, P. G. (1996). *BrainWise for grades 6–12.* Denver, CO: Innisfree Press.

Barry, P. G. (1998). *BrainWise for grades K–5.* Denver, CO: Innisfree Press.

Barry, P. G. (1999). *BrainWise one-on-one for counselors, social workers and others who work individually with children and youth.* Denver, CO: Innisfree Press.

Bartlett, E. E. (1985). Summary of findings of the school health education evaluation: Health promotion, effectiveness and implementation. *Journal of School Health, 55*(8), 316–22.

Beck, A., Rush, A., Shaw, B., & Emery, G. (1979). *Cognitive therapy for depression.* New York: Guilford Press.

Bell, M. A., & Wolfe, C. (2004). Emotion and cognition: An intricately bound developmental process. *Child Development, 75,* 366–370.

Benson, H. (1975). *The relaxation response.* New York: Avon Books.

Benson, P., Galbraith, J., & Espeland, P. (1993). *What teens need to succeed.* Minneapolis, MN: Free Spirit.

Bremner, J. (2003). Long-term effects of childhood abuse on brain and neurobiology. *Child and Adolescent Psychiatric Clinics of North America, 12,* 271–292.

Brooks-Gunn, J., & Markman, L. (2005). The contribution of parenting and ethnic and racial gaps in school readiness. *The Future of Children, 15,* 139–168.

Burns, D. (1980). *Feeling good: The new mood therapy.* New York: New American Library.

Changeux, J.-P., & Danchin, A. (1976). Selective stabilization of developing synapses as a mechanism for the specification of neuronal networks. *Nature, 264,* 705–712.

Changeux, J.-P., Heidmann, T., & Patte, P. (1984). Learning by selection. In P. Marler & H. S. Terrace (Eds.), *The biology of learning* (pp. 115–137). New York: Springer-Verlag.

Chugani, H. T. (1994). Development of regional brain glucose metabolism in relation to behavior and plasticity. In G. Dawson & K. W. Fischer (Eds.), *Human behavior and the developing brain* (pp. 153–175). New York: Guilford Press.

Cohen, J., Perel, J., DeBellis, M., Friedman, M., & Putnam, F. (2002). Treating traumatized children: Clinical implications of the psychobiology of post-traumatic stress disorder. *Trauma Violence and Abuse, 3,* 91–108.

Cozolino, L. (2002). *The neuroscience of psychotherapy.* New York: Norton.

Damasio, A. R., & Anderson, S. W. (1993). The frontal lobes. In K. M. Heilman, & E. Valenstein (Eds.), *Clinical neuropsychology* (3rd ed., pp. 409–460). New York: Oxford University Press.

Davidson, R. J., Jackson, D. C., & Kalin, N. H. (2000). Emotion, plasticity, context and regulation: Perspectives from affective neuroscience. *Psychological Bulletin, 126,* 890–906.

Davidson, R. J., Pizzagalli, D. Nitschke, J. B., & Katlin, N. H. (2003). Parsing the sub-components of emotion and disorders of emotion: Perspectives from affective neuroscience. In R. J. Davidson, K. Scherer, & H. H. Goldsmith (Eds.), *Handbook of effective sciences* (pp. 8–24). New York: Oxford University Press.

Eggert, L, Nicholas, L., & Owen, L. (1995). *Reconnecting youth: A peer group approach to building life skills.* Indiana: National Education Service.

Elias, M., Zins, J., Weissberg, R., Frey, K., Greenberg, M., Haynes, N., Kessler, R., Schwab-Stone, M., & Shriver, T. (1997). *Promoting social and emotional learning: Guidelines for educators.* Alexandria, VA: Association for Supervision and Curriculum Development.

Elliott, D. (2001). Ensuring program success. *Blueprints News, 2*(3), 1–3.

Ellis, A. (1985). Expanding the ABC's of rational emotive therapy. In M. Mahoney & A. Freeman (Eds.), *Cognition and psychotherapy.* New York: Stuart.

Ellis, A. & Harper, A. (1975). *A new guide to rational living.* Hollywood, CA: Wilshire.

Ennett, S. T., Ringwalt, C. L., Thorne, J., Rohrbach, L., Vincus, A., Simons-Rudolph, A., & Jones, S. (2003). A comparison of current practice in school-based substance abuse use prevention programs with meta-analysis findings. *Prevention Science, 4,* 1–14.

Eslinger, P. J. (1996). Conceptualizing, describing, and measuring components of executive function: A summary. In G. R. Lyon & N. A. Krasnagor (Eds.), *Attention, memory, and executive function* (pp. 367–395). Baltimore: Brookes.

Gardner, H. (1993). *Multiple intelligences: The theory in practice.* New York: Basic Books.

Goelet, P., & Kandel, E. (1986). Tracking the flow of learned information from membrane receptors to genome. *Trends in Neuroscience, 9,* 492–499.

Goldsmith, H. H. & Davidson, R. J. (2004). Disambiguating the components of emotion regulation. *Child Development, 75,* 361–365.

Greenberg, M., Kusché, C., & Riggs, N. (2004). The PATHS curriculum: Theory and research on neurocognitive development and school success. In J. Zins et al. (Eds.), *Building academic success on social and emotional learning.* New York: Teachers College Press.

Hawkins, J., Catalano, R., & Miller, J. (1992). Risk and protective factors for alcohol and other drug problems in adolescence and early adulthood: Implications for substance abuse. *Psychological Bulletin, 112,* 64–105.

Heyder, K., Suchan, B., & Daum, I. (2004). Cortico-subcortical contributions to executive control. *Acta Psychologica, 115,* 271–289.

Huttenlocher, P. R., & Dabholker, A. S. (1997). Developmental anatomy of prefrontal cortex. In N. Krasnegor, G. R. Lyon, & P. S. Goldman-Rakic (Eds.), *Development of the prefrontal cortex: Evolution, neurobiology, and behavior* (pp. 69–83). Baltimore: Brookes.

Jenson, E. (2000). *Brain-based learning.* San Diego, CA: The Brain Store.

Kandel, E. (1998). A new intellectual framework for psychiatry. *American Journal of Psychiatry, 155*(4), 457–469.

Kandel, E. (1999). Biology and the future of psychoanalysis: A new intellectual framework for psychiatry revisited. *American Journal of Psychiatry, 156*(4), 505–524.

Kandel, E. (2000, December 8). *The molecular biology of memory storage: A dialog between genes and synapses.* Nobel Lecture, Howard Hughes Medical Institute, Columbia University, New York.

Kandel, E., & Schwartz, J. (1982). Molecular biology of an elementary form of learning: Modulation of transmitter release by cyclic AMP. *Science, 218,* 433–443.

Kusché, C., & Greenberg, M. (1994). *The PATHS curriculum.* Seattle: Developmental Research and Programs.

LeDoux, J. (1996). *The emotional brain.* New York: Simon & Schuster.

Luria, A. R. (1973). *The working brain.* New York: Basic Books.

Mirskey, S. (2000). *The future of psychiatry: Eric Kandel says it lies with biology.* Retrieved June 27, 2006, from http://www.hhmi.org/bulletin/kandel/

Nichols, P. (1996). *Clear thinking: A program for teachers and counseling professionals.* Iowa City, Iowa: River Lights.

Olds, D. L., Kitzman, H., Cole, R., Robinson, J., Sidora, K., Luckey, D. W., Henderson, C. R., Hanks, C., Bondy, J., and Holmberg, J. (2004). Effects of home-visiting on maternal life course and child development: Age 6 follow-up results of a randomized trial. *Pediatrics, 114,* 1550–1559.

OMNI Research and Training, Inc. (2001). *BrainWise final evaluation report.* Denver, Colorado: Author.

Payton, J., Wardlaw, D., Gracyzk, P., Bloodworth, M., Tompsett, C., & Weissberg, R. (2000). Social and emotional learning: A framework for promoting health and reducing risk behavior in children and youth. *Journal of School Health, 70*(5), 179–185.

Perry, B. (1994). Neurobiological sequelae of childhood trauma: PTSD in children. In Murburg, M. (Ed.), *Catecholamine function in post-traumatic stress disorder: Emerging concepts* (pp. 233–254). Washington, DC: American Psychiatric Press.

Perry, B., & Pollard, R. (1998). Homeostasis, stress, trauma and adaptation. *Child and Adolescent Psychiatry Clinics of North America, 7,* 33–51.

Romer, D. (2003). *Reducing adolescent risk: Toward an integrated approach.* Thousand Oaks, CA: Sage.

Roth, R. M., & Syakin, A. J. (2004). Executive dysfunction in attention-deficit/hyperactivity disorder: Cognitive and neuroimaging findings. *Psychiatric Clinics of North America, 27,* 83–96.

Rothbart, M., & Posner, M. (2005). Genes and experience in the development of executive function and effortful control. *New Directions for Child and Adolescent Development, 106,* 101–107.

Saltzman, W. R., Layne, C. M., Steinberg, A. M., Arslanagic, B., & Pynoos, R. S. (2003). Developing a culturally and ecologically sound intervention program for youth exposed to war and terrorism. *Child and Adolescent Psychiatric Clinics of North America, 12,* 319–342.

Schnirman, G., Welsh, M., & Retzlof, P. (1998). Development of the Tower of London–Revised. *Assessment, 54,* 355–360.

Scott, K. L., Wolfe, D. A., & Wekerle, C. (2003). Maltreatment and trauma: Tracking the connections in adolescence. *Child and Adolescent Psychiatric Clinics of North America, 12,* 211–230.

Seligman, M. (1991). *Learned optimism.* New York: Alfred Knopf.

Seligman, M., & Csiksentmihalyi, M. (2000). Positive psychology: An introduction. *American Psychologist. 55*(1), 5–14.

Shure, M. (1992). *I can problem solve (ICPS): An interpersonal cognitive problem solving program for children (intermediate elementary grades).* Champaign, IL: Research Press.

Smith, D. (2002). The theory heard 'round the world. *Monitor on Psychology, 33*(9), 30–32.

Steinberg, L. (1996). *Beyond the classroom: Why school reform has failed and what parents need to do.* New York: Simon & Schuster.

Sternberg, R. (2001). Why schools should teach wisdom: The balance theory of wisdom in educational settings. *Educational Psychologist, 36*(4), 227–245.

Stroop, J. (1935). Studies of interference in serial verbal reactions. *Journal of Experimental Psychology, 18*, 643–661.

Stuss, D. T., & Benson, D. F. (1984). Neuropsychological studies of frontal lobes. *Psychological Bulletin, 95*, 3–28.

Teicher, M. H., Andersen, S. L., Polcari, A., Anderson, C. M., Navalta, C. P., & Kim, D. M. (2003). The neurological consequences of early stress and childhood maltreatment. *Neuroscience and Biobehavioral Reviews, 27*, 33–44.

Tranel, D., Anderson, S. W., & Benton, A. L. (1995). Development of the concept of executive function and its relationship to the frontal lobes. In F. Boller & J. Grafman (Eds.), *Handbook of neuropsychology* (Vol. 9, pp. 126–148). Amsterdam: Elsevier.

Tueber, H. L. (1964). The riddle of frontal lobe function in man. In. J. Warren & K. Akert (Eds.), *The frontal granular cortex and behavior* (pp. 410–440). New York: McGraw-Hill.

U.S. Department of Education. (2003). *Identifying and implementing educational practices supported by rigorous evidence.* Washington, DC: Institute for Educational Sciences, National Center for Educational Evaluation and Regional Assistance.

van der Kolk, (2003). The neurobiology of childhood trauma and abuse. *Child and Adolescent Psychiatric Clinics of North America, 12*, 293–317.

Welsh, M. (2002). Developmental and clinical variations in executive functions. In U. Kirk & D. Molfese (Eds.), *Developmental variations in language and learning* (pp. 139–185). Hillsdale, NJ: Erlbaum.

Welsh, M., Friedman, S., & Spieker, S. (in press). Executive functions in developing children: Current conceptualizations and questions for the future. In D. Phillips & K. McCartney (Eds.), *Handbook of early childhood development.* New York: Blackwell.

Welsh, M., & Pennington, B. (1998). Assessing frontal lobe functioning in children: Views from developmental psychology. *Developmental Neuropsychology, 4*, 199–230.

Western Psychological Services. (2004). *Tests, books, software, therapy materials* [Catalog]. Los Angeles, CA: Author.

Zelazo, P., & Mueller, U. (2002). Executive function in typical and atypical development. In U. Goswasmi (Ed.), *Handbook of childhood cognitive development* (pp. 445–469). Oxford: Blackwell.

Zins, J., Weissberg, R., Wang, M., & Walburg, R. (2004). *Building academic success: What does the research say?* New York: Teachers College Press.

Chapter 20

The Role of Preventive Interventions in Enhancing Neurocognitive Functioning and Promoting Competence in Adolescence

Mark T. Greenberg, Nathaniel R. Riggs, and Clancy Blair

Serious physical, psychological, and social costs accompany the development of child conduct problems including increased risk for social and educational failure (Lahey, Loeber, Quay, Frick, & Grimm, 1997), adolescent depression and suicidality (Anderson & Smith, 2003), as well as early alcohol, illegal drug, and tobacco use (Galaif, Hser, Grella, & Joshi; 2001; White, Xie, Thompson, Loeber, Stouthamer-Loeber, 2001). Consequently, preventive interventions have been developed as one strategy to decrease the incidence of childhood and adolescent mental health problems and early substance initiation (Drug Strategies, 1998; Greenberg, Domitrovich, & Bumbarger, 1999; U.S. Department of Health and Human Services, 1999).

Researchers' capacities to develop interventions that can decrease the incidence of problem behavior and increase positive functioning are dependent, at least in part, on an understanding of the multiple, interacting processes that promote healthy adolescence development. Developmental processes, at both the behavioral and neurobiological level, are further embedded in influences (Bronfenbrenner, 1977) that reside at the levels of individuals, peers, families, schools, and communities (Hawkins & Catalano, 1992; Masten, 2004; Steinberg et al., in press). Understanding these transactional processes between youth capacities and family, school, and community contexts during the prolonged period of adolescence can assist prevention scientists in constructing and implementing prevention and treatment programs that strengthen the social and behavioral trajectories of children (Dodge, 2001).

There are four primary goals for this chapter. The first is to briefly consider aspects of the developing adolescent for understanding the development of competence, risk, and psychopathology. Second, we review research on the potential influence of neurocognitive abilities and changes in neurobiological systems on social and emotional competence. Here we utilize the term neurocognitive to denote executive functions including inhibitory control, set shifting, planning, and maintaining information in working memory, as well as the role of language in guiding behavior. Third, we review research indicating the potential mediating role of changes in neurocognitive function in the prevention of problem behaviors in childhood. Finally, we discuss the implications and future directions of this research for the linkage of prevention science and developmental neuroscience during adolescence.

A central question in modern psychology is the reciprocal relationship between emotion, arousal and motivation, and cognition (Bandura, 1986; Blair, Granger, & Razza, 2005; Cicchetti & Schneider-Rosen, 1984; Gray et al., 2005; Luria, 1973). The developmental processes involved and the contextual forces that shape the integration of cognition and emotion have become one of the most exciting aspects of research in development from infancy through adolescence (Steinberg et al., in press). Central to the nascent integrative understanding of these changes is the emergence and integration of developmental neuroscience. This research has altered our understanding of the flexibility and malleability of the brain in relation to environmental stimulation and deprivation (Bush, Luu, & Posner; 2000; Gunnar & Vazquez, 2001; Ochsner, Bunge, Gross, & Gabrieli, 2002).

An exciting result of these new integrations across brain, behavior, and context are conceptual models of development that begin to fully embrace the complexity of person-environment interactions at different developmental stages (Blair, 2002; Greenberg & Kusche, 1993; Steinberg et al., 2006). In addition, a number of more specific models that integrate neurocognitive and biological factors have been conceptualized for the development of aggression and delinquency in adolescence (Moffitt, 1993) and substance abuse (Fishbein, Hyde, Coe, & Paschal, 2004).

The complexity of understanding necessary to fully characterize adolescence surely includes a model that includes both pubertal/hormonal changes, developments and integrations at the neurological level (especially in the prefrontal area), changes in roles and identity, along with the increasing striving for autonomy, as well as the decreased monitoring by adults that was present in childhood. The challenges of adolescence present the combination of increasing autonomy and risk taking and, a central struggle of this period is the management of impulsivity in the context of high emotionality. As a result, similarly to other periods in childhood, youth's social and cognitive competencies in hypothetical situations or in "cool" situations of low emotional arousal are not strong predictors of their behavior in risky contexts in which emotions run high (potential to shoplift when with friends at the mall, to drink with peers at an unsupervised party, etc.).

Given the central importance of the development of self-reflection and mindfulness (metacognition) in middle childhood and adolescence in regulating strong emotions, the field of neuropsychology holds promise in the construction of comprehensive, developmental models of problem behavior (Greenberg, Kusche, & Riggs, 2004). As such, models that incorporate a focus on neural maturation in social contexts can help researchers better design and implement programs aimed at preventing the development of adolescent problem behavior.

Development of Neural Systems and Pathways Related to Social, Cognitive, and Emotional Competence

Neural development is a product of the complex interaction between the genotype (the full complement of genes inherited by parents) and environmental conditions surrounding individuals (Greenough, Black, & Christopher, 1987). Genetic mechanisms combine with environmental influences to impact each aspect of neural development from neurogenesis, migration, synapse formation and density, pruning, myelination, to degeneration (see Grossman, Churchill, McKinney, Kodish, Otte, & Greenough, 2003). However, there is a great deal of heterogeneity in the time course of development in different areas of the brain with the longest period of development occurring in the frontal area (Giedd et al., 1999; Giedd, Castellanos, Casey, & Kozuch, 1994). During childhood and into adolescence, the areas of the brain responsible for behavioral control and self-regulation are rapidly proceeding through genetically influenced phases of structural organization. However, although genes play an important role in neural development, neural organization is malleable and can be shaped by both shared and unique experience in determining ultimate neural structure and functioning. Findings at the molecular level indicate the role of gene-environment interactions in adolescent development (Caspi, Moffitt, Cannon, McClay, Murray, et al., 2005).

The Limbic System and Frontal Cortex

The limbic system, which is situated in the middle of the brain, is often referred to as the brain's "emotion center." It controls the automatic processing of multiple aspects of emotion and behavior, such as the recognition of emotional expression in faces, action tendencies, and the storage of emotional memories (Aggleton, 1992). Although the limbic system is functionally immature at birth, children who receive an appropriate level of environmental stimuli (see Greenough, et al., 1987) achieve relative mastery in these "limbic" tasks by toddlerhood. However, children at this age are especially prone to impulsive, emotional, and behavioral reactions due, in part, to an underdeveloped frontal cortex.

The frontal cortex, situated in the anterior region of the brain, provides secondary processing of emotions at a more sophisticated level than does the limbic system. Specifically, emotion information, processed in the limbic system, travels through ascending neurons to the frontal cortex, which is the only neocortical site in which this information is represented (Damasio, 1994). The frontal cortex then transmits information back to the limbic system to modify emotion signals and to the sensory-motor cortex to influence potential behaviors (LeDoux, 1996).

Executive Function and the Development of Vertical Control in Childhood

The developmental achievement of higher-order cognitive processes exerting control over lower-level limbic impulses is known as "vertical control." Children and young adolescents are not capable of exercising full vertical control until the frontal cortex itself, and the neural pathways connecting the frontal cortex to the limbic system, have fully developed. Frontal-cortical development progresses quickly from birth to the second year of life, and then is followed by another growth spurt from about 4 to 7 years of age (Luria, 1973). After this, there are less dramatic increases in the growth of frontal lobe volume. However, early in adolescence (around 10–11 years of age), the pruning process begins to sculpt and mold the frontal lobes, and continues to do so at least into early adulthood (Gogtay, Giedd, Rapoport, 2002; Sowell et al., 2003). This time course of morphological development distinguishes the frontal cortex as one of the last brain regions to achieve functional maturity (Dempster & Corkill, 1999; Diamond, 1990) and thus the most likely to be influenced by environmental input. Compared to adults, teens also show less consistency in suppressing prepotent responses, a central function of the prefrontal cortex (Luna & Sweeny, 2004). As a result, they show more risk-taking behavior and may be more susceptible to impulsive decisions when highly emotionally aroused.

With the development of the frontal lobes comes the development of "executive function" (Pennington & Ozonoff, 1996; Welsh, Pennington, & Groisser, 1991). Executive function (EF) generally refers to the psychological processes that are involved in the conscious control of thought and that have been linked to prefrontal cortex (PFC). Examples of processes believed to be involved in conscious control of thought are inhibition, future time orientation, consequential thinking, and the planning, initiation, and regulation of goal-directed behavior (Luria, 1972).

Developmental delays and/or damage to the frontal cortex can have substantial implications for the development of EF, and consequently children's behavioral development (Raine, 2002). For example, variations in EF functions have been related to difficulties in such behavioral domains as distractibility, impulsivity, inattention, language processing, and foresight necessary for behavior regulation, and recognition of the consequences of actions from early childhood through adolescence (Brophy, Taylor, & Hughes, 2002; Kusche, Cook, & Greenberg, 1993; Morgan & Lilenfeld, 2000; Stuss & Benson, 1984). In turn, some aspects of executive dysfunction may interfere with children's ability to regulate behavior, thus setting the stage for the development of antisocial behavior (Moffitt, 1993). Thus, at a neurological level, mature decision making is a reflection of increasing frontal executive control over the limbic activity of the brain.

Verbal Ability and the Development of Horizontal Communication

In addition to greater frontal control, language plays an important role. Research suggests hemispheric asymmetry in the processing of particular types of emotion-related information (de Hann, Nelson, Gunnar, & Tout, 1998). Specifically, the left hemisphere of the brain is responsible for processing receptive and expressive language, as well as the expression of positive affect. The right hemisphere specializes in processing both the recognition of comfortable and uncomfortable emotions, as well as expression of uncomfortable affect (Bryden & Ley, 1983). Therefore, in order to become aware of and verbally label emotional experiences, it is hypothesized that unconscious information must be transmitted via the corpus callosum from the right to the left hemisphere. This process is known as "horizontal communication."

With the development of horizontal control comes the ability to verbally represent emotion and behavior. As children develop throughout early childhood, self-control becomes increasingly regulated via internal forms of mediation such as internal verbal representation (Kopp, 1982). Thompson, Giedd, Woods, MacDonald, Evans, and Toga (2000) have found that an increased ability to internally regulate behavior is accompanied by commensurate growth in the tissue of fiber systems of the corpus callosum known to mediate language function and associative thinking. In their study, peak growth occurred between 6 and 13 years of age and attenuated shortly thereafter, which the authors argue coincides with the end of a "critical period" for learning language. Interestingly, Giedd et al. (1999) conjecture that because previous studies have found no evidence of postnatal development of callosal axons (Lamantia& Rakic, 1984), the increase in callosal volume may be due to increases in the amount of neural myelination.

Because verbal labeling can aid in the accurate perception of emotional experiences, children's verbal abilities have been hypothesized to play a key role in their behavioral development. Specifically, the ability to verbally represent and assess behavior allows children to analyze the consequences of their behavior for self and other and to gain greater control over their behavior (Dewey, 1933; Luria, 1973). An inability to perform these verbal tasks may preclude children from being able to plan and perform prosocial objectives, leaving them at risk for problem behaviors.

In sum, two interrelated aspects of neurocognitive development are clearly implicated in the children's development of social and emotional competence:

executive function and verbal communication. First, verbal ability can be used as a tool for internal representation (self-talk), which in turn serves as one mechanism for inhibiting behavior (Luria, 1966). Second, internal representation allows children to plan and sequence goal-directed behavior in response to challenging social situations. Therefore, although executive function and verbal skills are distinctive abilities, it is likely that they are strongly associated (Kusche & Greenberg, in press).

The Link Between Neurocognition and Adolescent Social and Emotional Development

Considerable evidence suggests that deficits in neurocognitive abilities during childhood and adolescence are linked with the development of problem and risky behavior. Much of this research involves concurrent negative associations between adolescents' neurocognitive abilities and conduct problems (Hill, 2002; Lahey, Loeber, Hart, Frick, et al., 1995; Lynam & Henry, 2001), delinquency (Brickman, McManus, Grapentine, & Alessi, 1984; Lynam, Moffitt, & Stouthamer-Loeber, 1995; Spellacy, 1977; Moffitt & Henry, 1989; White, Moffitt, Caspi, Jeglum-Bartusch, Needles, & Stouthamer-Loeber, 1994), and substance abuse (Deckel & Hesselbrock, 1996; Giancola, Martin, Tarter, Pelham, & Moss, 1996; Giancola, Mezzich, & Tarter, 1998; Giancola & Tarter, 1999). Relations between neurocognitive abilities and aspects of problem behavior have also been found in younger children (Cole, Usher, & Cargo, 1993; Speltz, DeKlyen, Calderon, Greenberg, & Fisher, 1999). There has been little research on the relation between neurocognitive abilities and depression in adolescence.

Moffitt (1993) has argued that delinquent children exhibit deficits in a number of executive abilities (i.e., abstract reasoning, concept-formation, inhibitory control, problem-solving behavior, planning, and sustained attention). White et al. (1994) found empirical support for this argument in demonstrating a link between impulsivity and delinquency in 10-, 12-, and 13-year-old children. Their study established that undercontrolled, restless, impatient, and impulsive children were significantly more delinquent than children who were less impulsive. Furthermore, Spellacy (1977) found that among delinquent individuals, those considered to be violent offenders have been shown to score even worse on presumed measures of neurocognitive functioning. Cauffman, Steinberg, and Piquero (2004) reported that both spatial span (which assesses an aspect of working memory) and difficulties in self-control predict adolescent offender status. Others have demonstrated that deficient neurocognitive function may also be associated with increased risk for alcohol and other substance abuse (Giancola, et al., 1996; Giancola, et al., 1998; Giancola & Tarter, 1999).

A link also has been consistently demonstrated between youth verbal deficits and behavior problems (Kusche, Cook, & Greenberg, 1993; Lynam & Henry, 2001; Lynam et al., 1993; Moffitt, 1990; Moffitt & Lynam, 1994). In addition, Lahey et al. (1995) found that verbal abilities predicted improvements in conduct disorder (CD) over a period of 4 years. At the neurological level, it is hypothesized that the ability to internally regulate behavior is accompanied by commensurate growth and myelination of the neuronal pathways in the corpus callosum that are known to mediate language function and associative thinking (Giedd et al., 1999; Thompson et al., 2000).

Although the above studies demonstrate an association between deficient neurocognitive abilities and substance abuse or other adolescent problem behavior, a major limitation of these studies is that most are cross-sectional; neurocognitive deficits and antisocial behavior may have occurred as a result of a third process (i.e., being reared in a family with an alcoholic parent or from chronic physical abuse, or other prenatal or postnatal trauma). In such cases, environmental events may have both shaped neurocognitive growth as well as antisocial behavior with no necessary causal link involved between the two processes.

Models of Neurocognitive Development

To date, studies linking neurocognitive dysfunction to adolescent problem outcomes shed valuable light on developmental processes and highlight the potential of neurocognitive models in formulating and assessing models of prevention and treatment during childhood and adolescence. However, clearer conceptual, multilevel models of both adolescent development and neurological growth will be necessary to move to the next level of understanding.

Moffitt (1993) provides one conceptual model that distinguishes between life-course-persistent (LCP) and adolescent-limited (AL) antisocial behavior. She has suggested that AL antisocial behavior is considered to be normative, tends to desist in early adulthood, and is not considered to involve neurocognitive deficit but is likely related to peer associations and other contextual factors linked to minor adolescent delinquency and risk taking. However, children demonstrating LCP antisocial behavior are those exhibiting early, continuous, severe, and frequent antisocial behavior across situations and stages of development that may involve deficits. Although Moffitt contends that environmental risks exacerbate the neurocognitive deficits, thus leading to the development of persistent antisocial behavior, she contends that neurocognitive deficit is the *necessary* component for the development of LCP antisocial behavior.

This model has been generative, but only partially supported by longitudinal studies. Aguilar, Sroufe, Egeland, and Carlson (2000) take issue with Moffitt's contention of neurocognitive primacy in the development of antisocial behavior. Their findings support Moffitt's distinction between the two groups of antisocial children, which they label early-onset/persistent (EOP) and adolescent-onset (AO) antisocial behavior. However, they found little evidence for the assertion that early neurocognitive deficit was the principal factor in distinguishing between the two groups of children, and instead found support for links between psychosocial variables and later persistent antisocial behavior.

Blair (2002) provides a model of children's social development in which neurocognitive function and neurophysiology interact with environmental contexts in the development of social competence and behavior regulation. He proposes that children who are emotionally reactive and poorly regulated, and are also developing in environments that cannot optimize and support their regulatory deficits, will likely be at risk for atypical neurocognitive and social-emotional trajectories. However, if these same children were raised in environments in which adults supported their language development and regulatory skills (emergent executive functions), they would be less likely to exhibit a propensity toward reactive forms of regulation and aggression.

In the early childhood period, high levels of negative emotionality and poor regulation of this emotionality within an unsupportive environment are thought to establish patterns of behavioral, physiological, and neurological response to stimulation that serve to enhance reactive rather than self-regulatory types of responding. High levels of reactive responding feed back on neural structures important for the effortful cognitive regulation of behavior and regulation of negative emotionality and the physiological response to stress. Such reactive responding also feeds forward on parent-child interactions and on peer relations to further establish patterns of interaction and social relationships that work to further maintain trajectories and behavior patterns characterized by high levels of reactivity and poor self-regulation. As with the early childhood period, adolescence may be a time in the life course in which the biosocial system is particularly plastic and open to influence. However, perhaps even more so than in the early childhood period, adolescence is characterized by an emerging sense of self and conception of self efficacy that works to influence patterns of reactivity and self-regulation. Also, the relative influence of peer and parental influences on trajectories of reactivity and regulation may be unique in adolescence, creating a specific set of social influences that combine with neurobiology to reinforce a low level of neurocognitive functioning and problems with the regulation of behavior.

In sum, neurocognitive function may not be a necessary component in *all* problem behaviors. However, it is likely that neurocognitive ability is linked to the development of behavior problems at least in some children, and theoretical models can lead to testable hypotheses with respect to neurocognition's relation to antisocial behavior. Furthermore, both Blair's and Moffitt's models have important implications for early prevention and intervention in that children may be developing under the dual risks of neurocognitive deficit and unsupportive environments that are at highest risk for the development of later difficulties. As a result, they may have the greatest need for preventive interventions targeting the enhancement of behavioral trajectories.

Longitudinal Research: Understanding the Influence of Neurocognitive Development

Two types of research findings can help to clarify the role of neurocognitive development on the quality of adaptation in childhood and adolescence (McCall, 1977). The first type involves longitudinal data that can examine whether early neurocognitive deficit's influence later outcomes. The second type of research is experimental—that is, research that demonstrates alterations in neurocognitive development as a result of an intervention and then examines how these changes may be related to other associated outcomes (the potential mediating role of neurocognitive change on further developmental outcomes). Both forms of research have been relatively uncommon; most research has been cross-sectional, comparing differing populations.

Our laboratory has been involved in both types of research involving middle childhood, and we believe that such research has implications for innovative research in adolescence. Two studies will illustrate the potential contribution of neurocognitive models to our understanding of relationships discussed here. The first study longitudinally followed 60 regular education children. At Time 1, the students were in first and second grade (Riggs, Blair, & Greenberg, 2003). We assessed IQ and two aspects of executive function, inhibitory control (using the Stroop Test and WISC–R Coding) and sequencing using the Trails test. These tests generally assess competency in inhibiting incorrect responses and sequencing relevant information, which requires keeping information in working memory. In addition, their teachers and parents completed rating scales on internalizing and externalizing problems. We longitudinally followed these children and examined teacher and parent ratings again 2 years later at the end of third and fourth grades. The central question we addressed was, after accounting for early behavior and IQ, did inhibitory control and/or sequencing predict the growth or change in behavior problems across this 2-year period? The findings indicated that even after accounting for academic skills and verbal abilities, both sequencing abilities and inhibitory control accounted for significant variance in both teacher and parent reports of changes in externalizing problems. In addition, both inhibitory control and sequencing predicted changes in the parent but not the teacher report of internalizing problems. Taken in concert, these findings provide evidence that children's ability to perform well on tasks of executive ability during the first and second grades predicts change in their behavior over a 2-year period. The combination of inhibitory control and sequencing ability predicted 15% of the variance in 2-year change in teacher-reported externalizing problems, 13% in parent-reported externalizing problems, and 13% and parent-reported internalizing symptoms. In a second study with a larger sample, we found that similar variables (Trails and the Stroop test) also predicted teacher rating of positive social competency across the same 2-year period (Nigg, Quamma, Greenberg, & Kusche, 1999).

One implication of these findings is that relative deficits in neurocognitive abilities may place young children at risk for developing behavior problems. If this is the case, it may behoove those interested in children's behavioral development to intervene with early-school-aged children who demonstrate weak neurocognitive functioning. By doing so, researchers can either apply a new component to, or a more intensive version of, intervention with the hope that enhancing children's neurocognitive skills may reduce their future behavior problems. Researchers may also consider placing children with poor executive skills in environments that promote the development of executive ability. For example, smaller classrooms and/or environments with fewer distractions may enhance children's ability to focus their attention on tasks, thus aiding in their ability to inhibit and sequence behavior.

In sum, research implicates children's neurocognitive abilities as one factor to be considered in the developmental process of both competence and psychopathology during childhood. Generally, this research suggests that dysfunction in domains of neurocognition, such as EF and verbal abilities, are associated with increased problem behaviors.

The Potential Roles of Neurocognitive Function in Prevention Research

A central research question in the prevention of problem behavior is the extent to which neurocognitive ability mediates the relation between preventive intervention and behavioral outcomes. With few exceptions, children's neurocognitive abilities have not been considered as an important component in models of the prevention of adolescent problem behavior. However, researchers are beginning to conceptualize the role of change in neurocognitive abilities following preventive interventions (Fishbein, 2001; Raine, 2002). In a recent paper, we review the use of neurocognitive measures as moderators and mediators of behavioral outcomes, or as an outcome itself following preventive efforts (Riggs & Greenberg, 2004). Here we illustrate the role of neurocognitive function as a mediator of behavioral outcomes.

Although few preventive interventions intend to explicitly promote the development of neurocognitive abilities (Greenberg & Kusche, 1998), some (Botvin et al., 1995; Frey, Hirschstein & Guzzo, 2002; Shure & Spivack, 1982; Yung &

Hammond, 1998) promote skills such as conscious strategies for self-control, attention, concentration, and problem-solving that may ultimately aid in the development of children's neurocognitive capabilities. Therefore, preventive interventions such as those that teach children developmentally appropriate social skills and conflict resolution strategies may also strengthen children's neurocognitive abilities. In turn, the strengthening of neurocognitive abilities may be related to further decreases in children's problem behaviors. However, more complete tests of models of change that incorporate neurocognitive development, as well as more direct measures of brain activity (Aguilar et al., 2000; Blair, 2002; Moffitt, 1993), are needed to test this possibility.

At present, there is little research investigating neurocognition's mediational role in prevention trials. However, we have been involved in a preventive intervention that explicitly intends to promote neurocognitive development known as the Promoting Alternative THinking Strategies (PATHS; Kusche & Greenberg 1994) curriculum. PATHS is a social-emotional learning curriculum that explicitly attends to models of frontal lobe organization that take into account vertical control and horizontal communication (Kusche, Riggs, &Greenberg, 1999). The PATHS curriculum includes lessons focusing on readiness and self-control, feelings and relationships, and interpersonal cognitive problem solving. Previous studies indicate that PATHS was effective for both low- and high-risk children in improving the vocabulary and fluency necessary in discussing emotional experiences, efficacy beliefs regarding the management of emotions, and developmental understanding of emotions. Results also indicate that in some cases, greater improvement was shown in children with higher teacher ratings of psychopathology (Greenberg, Kusche, Cook, & Quamma, 1995). Finally, there were also significant reductions in both internalizing and externalizing problems in grades 4 and 5 up to 2 years after PATHS was implemented in special education populations (Kam, Greenberg, & Kusche, 2003).

One study directly tested the mediational model on which PATHS was developed (Riggs, Greenberg, Kusche, & Pentz, in press). This study confirmed direct program effects on both externalizing and internalizing behaviors in grades 3 and 4 at 1-year follow-up. In addition, children in the PATHS program demonstrated significantly greater inhibitory control and verbal fluency at 9-months posttest. This finding is one of few that have demonstrated the ability of preventive intervention to promote neurocognitive functioning in youth. In turn, inhibitory control at 9-months posttest was negatively related to both externalizing and internalizing behavior, and verbal fluency was negatively related to internalizing behavior. These results add to previous findings reviewed earlier demonstrating links between neurocognitive function and problem behavior. Finally, tests of indirect effects verified that these two neurocognitive variables significantly mediated the relations between program condition and both domains of behavior problems, with inhibitory control demonstrating the greatest indirect effects of the two. Figure 20-1 illustrates these relations.

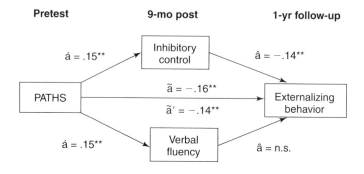

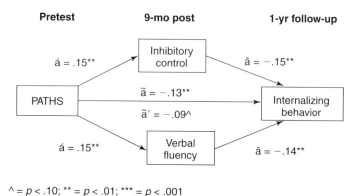

$^\wedge = p < .10; ^{**} = p < .01; ^{***} = p < .001$

Figure 20-1 PATH mediation models of externalizing and internalizing behavior. $^\wedge = p < .10; ^{**} = p < .01; ^{***} = p < .001$.

A second study that indicates the potential for enhanced neurocognitive function resulting from preventive intervention is that of Dowsett and Livesey (2000). This training study focused expressly on improving executive skills associated with antisocial behavior. Their trial demonstrated that repeated exposure to tasks requiring both the manipulation of visual representations and response control enhanced children's inhibitory control to a greater extent than for nonexposed comparison groups. The authors contend that experience with these tasks increased the acquisition of complex rules via demands placed on executive processes.

Although no studies that examine brain activation as a mediator or outcome could be found in the literature on prevention of behavior or emotional problems, Shaywitz et al. (2004) illustrate such a model by demonstrating that a reading intervention both improved reading outcomes as well as demonstrated changes in brain activation.

The Potential Role of Neurocognitive Function in Preventive Interventions in Adolescence

In sum, preventive interventions such as PATHS can take advantage of the time course in the morphological development of the frontal lobes. During childhood, the frontal lobes are malleable and proceed through a stage of rapid structural organization (Grossman et al., 2003). Thus, there is great potential for preventive interventions implemented in the preschool and elementary years to impact the neural substrates controlling such development. However, important changes continue into adolescence. For example, Luna and Sweeny (2004) reported that adolescents are as able as adults to suppress a prepotent response, but they are less reliable or consistent at doing so. The implication is that adolescents may not be as efficient at utilizing frontal skills and likely require greater vigilance for success. Thus, as Keating (2004) has pointed out, context, emotional arousal, and attention are likely to influence the use of frontal abilities such as inhibition and planning in adolescence. The primary question is not one of cognitive reasoning, nor of estimation of risk; it is using complex executive function in context of high emotional arousal (Steinberg et al., 2006). Given the rapidly changing nature of adolescent development, a central challenge for prevention science is to conceptualize what types of interventions may be successful in reducing the risk for serious adolescent problems.

Steinberg (2004; Steinberg et al., 2006) aptly characterizes the dilemma of early and middle adolescence as one in which the individuating youth is pubertally driven to engage in new levels of emotional stimulation and risk taking, while still having a less-than-fully developed set of executive functions for regulating responses to affective experiences. In light of this knowledge, Steinberg suggests that it is unlikely that teaching young teens skills will be successful in preventing early problem behaviors such as initiation of substance use, minor delinquency, or teen intercourse. Instead, he promotes the concept of creating environments that limit risk or reduce harm, such as parental monitoring, curfews, and increased taxes on cigarettes to limit their attractiveness (Liang & Chaloupka, 2002). Other such environmental interventions that have shown effectiveness include new state laws regulating the nature of driving and driving with peers at certain hours (Oregon Department of Transportation, 2004). In addition, building effective parent-child communication and norms regarding substance use has shown to be an effective strategy (Spoth, Redmond, & Chin, 2001).

Although we strongly agree that environmental/ecological interventions that help to externally regulate adolescent behavior are likely to be protective, we also believe that teaching skills, including those associated with emotional awareness and executive functions, have a viable role in the adolescent prevention portfolio. We believe that the mediating role of executive functions in childhood, presented earlier, provides a model for such research. Further, although not directly examining executive functions, Epstein, Griffin, and Botvin (2002) found that self-reported changes in decision-making skills served as a mediator for the delay in substance abuse initiation in the teen years. One of the problems heretofore is the lack of integrated theory and study design that includes both theoretical models and data collection that encompasses both neurocognitive and traditional measures.

Given the central role of emotion regulation in problem behaviors, one approach would be to teach and model social and emotional skills and decision making in the context of hot emotions. From our standpoint, it would be hard to imagine an applicable theory of action that does not take as important the ability to monitor, recognize, and label one's affect as a central step in the process of interrupting an impulsive, risk-seeking chain of actions. Although it is not possible to actually teach these skills at the mall or a late-night party, more effective prevention curricula utilize role-playing of such contexts as a central component (Tobler Research Associates, 1998). However, in most of these models, there is very little focus on the value of being mindful or self-reflective, or on the recognition and labeling of one's emotional state.

Recently, there has been considerable interest in the concept of mindfulness. Mindfulness can be defined as paying attention moment to moment without judgment to whatever is going on in the mind and in the body—including thoughts, physical sensations, and emotions. In other words, mindfulness means being aware without judgment (Segal, Williams, & Teasdale, 2001). With the considerable and growing interest in mindfulness research and intervention with adults (Davidson et al., 2003; Teasdale, 2004), we believe that careful clinical trials of interventions focused on mindfulness training or the "potentiation of cognitive control" (Keating, 2004) are warranted. Carefully controlled research on mindfulness, as well as some martial arts traditions and yoga, would create an exciting agenda that would provide a theory-based prevention model that would naturally lead to examination of neural mediation.

By actively promoting social-emotional and behavioral competence and mindfulness at a time in children's lives when their neurocognitive abilities are rapidly developing and most influenced by environmental input, participation in preventive interventions might lead to commensurate increases in neurocognitive abilities, and in turn greatly influence the long-term prevention of adolescent risk and the promotion of health and competence. Preventive interventions that may alter neural structure or function can best be seen as one of type of environmental manipulation that may influence socioemotional and cognitive competence (Greenough, Black, & Christopher, 1987).

Although there is little research linking change in neurocognitive abilities specifically to participation in prevention programs, some (Raine, 2002) argue that preventive interventions that target or attempt to reverse neurocognitive deficits may the most effective way to improve behavioral outcomes. There is a great deal of research linking children's social experience to both temporary and permanent alterations in the structure and function of the brain (Beers & De Bellis, 2002; Cicchetti, 2002; De Bellis, Keshavan, Spencer, & Hall, 2000; Ito, Teicher, Glod, & Ackerman, 1998; Landry, Miller-Loncar, Smith, & Swank, 2002; McEwen, 1997; Sapolsky, 1996; Stein, Koverola, Hanna, Torchia, & McClarty, 1997). Some of this research examines the effects of stressful experiences and its potentially deleterious effects on executive function. Cortisol, a glucocorticoid hormone produced by the hypothalamic-pituitary-adrenal (HPA) axis in response to stress, is linked to the modulation of long-term neuronal changes in cognition and behavior occurring in response to psychological stress. Chronic elevations in cortisol are associated with hippocampal atrophy and with learning and memory deficits both in humans and nonhuman animal models (McEwen & Sapolsky, 1995). It is likely that chronic stress throughout childhood and adolescence impacts brain development in ways that interfere with the normal development of executive function. Research has shown that children with posttraumatic stress disorder exhibit lower neural integrity in the anterior cingulate (De Bellis, Keshavan, Spencer, & Hall, 2000) and poorer executive function (Beers & De Bellis, 2002).

Effective regulation of the physiological response to stress, in other words, moderate increase followed by downregulation, is important for cognitive functions associated with the prefrontal cortex (Erickson, Drevets, & Schulkin, 2003). As shown in adults, indicators of effective regulation of stress associated with not only HPA axis function (Lupien & McEwen, 1997) but also with sympathetic-adrenal medullary (SAM) function have been shown to significantly correlate with attentional processes (Skosnik, Chatterton, & Swisher, 2000). Similarly, effective regulation of the HPA axis response to stress has been associated with executive function and behavioral self-regulation abilities as early as the preschool years (Blair, Granger, & Razza, 2005). To the extent that preventive interventions can help teens reduce the incidence of stress exposure, develop greater awareness of their level of stress, and learn skills (mindfulness, relaxation or emotion regulation techniques) that reduce such stress, impacts may be shown on both brain and behavior.

Implications and Future Directions

Although a comprehensive model for the development of adolescent problem behavior does not exist, research is beginning to elucidate the importance of neurocognitive function as one component in an integrated, developmental model. The time course in the morphological development of the frontal lobes suggests the importance of timing in preventive interventions throughout childhood and early adolescence. It is now evident that the frontal lobes and the networks connecting them to the limbic system maintain an ability to restructure throughout the entire life span. However, the most rapid advances in the structural organization of the networks probably occur during childhood. There is clearly reorganization and further myelination of the prefrontal areas and their coordination with other brain areas throughout adolescence, but it is not yet clear whether interventions in adolescence may have the same influence that such intervention might have in childhood.

Given the high risks for psychopathology in adolescence, we suggest that there is a need to develop a substantial research agenda that integrates current knowledge of adolescent neuroscience with innovative intervention models. These interventions should focus on the goal of improving the management of emotional arousal and using executive functioning in this critical period of development. Such integrated research will further broaden our understanding of the influence of environments and self-development on adolescent outcomes.

References

Aggleton, J. P. (1992). *The amygdala: Neurobiological aspects of emotion, memory, and mental dysfunction.* New York: Wiley-Liss.

Aguilar, B., Sroufe, L. A., Egeland, B., & Carlson, E. (2000). Distinguishing the early-onset antisocial behavior types: From birth to 16 years. *Development and Psychopathology, 12,* 109–132.

Anderson, R. N., & Smith, B. L. (2003). Deaths: Leading causes for 2001. *National Vital Statistics Reports, 52*(9). Hyattsville, MD: National Center for Health Statistics.

Bandura, A. (1986). *Social foundations of thought and action.* Englewood Cliffs, NJ: Prentice Hall.

Beers, S. R., & De Bellis, M. D. (2002). Neuropsychological function in children with maltreatment-related posttraumatic stress disorder. *American Journal of Psychiatry, 159,* 483–486.

Blair, C. (2002). School readiness: Integrating cognition and emotion in a neurobiological conceptualization of children's functioning at school entry. *American Psychologist, 57,* 111–127.

Blair, C., Granger, D., & Razza, R. P. (2005). Cortisol reactivity is positively related to executive function in preschool children attending Head Start. *Child Development, 76,* 554–567.

Botvin, G. J., Baker, E., Dusenbury, L., Botvin, E. M., & Diaz, T. (1995). Long-term follow-up results of a randomized drug abuse prevention trial in a White middle-class population. *Journal of American Medical Association, 273,* 1106–1112.

Brickman, A. S., McManus, M., Grapentine, W. L., & Alessi, N. (1984). Neuropsychological assessment of seriously delinquent adolescents. *Journal of the American Academy of Child Psychiatry, 23,* 453–457.

Bronfenbrenner, U. (1977). Toward an experimental ecology of human development. *American Psychologist, 32,* 513–531.

Brophy, M., Taylor, E., & Hughes, C. (2002). To go or not to go: Inhibitory control in "hard to manage" children. *Infant and Child Development, 11,* 125–140.

Bryden, M. P., & Ley, R. G. (1983). Right-hemispheric involvement in the perception and expression of emotion in normal humans. In K. M. Heilman & P. Satz (Eds.), *Neuropsychology of human emotion* (pp. 6–44). New York: Guilford Press.

Bush, G., Luu, P., & Posner, M. I. (2000). Cognitive and emotional influences in the anterior cingulate cortex. *Trends in Cognitive Sciences, 4,* 215–222.

Caspi, A., Moffitt, T. E., Cannon, M., McClay, J., Murray, R., et al. (2005). Moderation of the effect of adolescent onset cannibus use on adult psychosis by a functional polymorphism in the Catechol-O-Methyltransferase gene: Longitudinal evidence of a gene X environment interaction. *Biological Psychiatry, 57,* 1117–1127.

Cauffman, E., Steinberg, L., & Piquero, A. R. (2004). Psychological, neuropsychological, and physiological correlates of serious anti-social behavior in adolescence: The role of self-control. *Criminology, 43,* 133–175.

Cicchetti, D. (2002). The impact of social experience on neurobiological systems: Illustration from a constructivist view of child maltreatment. *Cognitive Development, 17,* 1407–1428.

Cicchetti, D., & Schneider-Rosen, K. (1984). Theoretical and empirical considerations in the investigation of the relationship between affect and cognition in atypical populations of infants. In C. Izard, J. Kagan, & R. Zajonc (Eds.) *Emotions, cognition, and behavior* (pp. 366–406). New York: Cambridge.

Cole, P. M., Usher, B. A., & Cargo, A. P. (1993). Cognitive risk and its association with risk for disruptive behavior disorders in preschoolers. *Journal of Clinical Child Psychology, 22,* 154–164.

Damasio, A. R. (1994). *Descartes' error: Emotion, reason, and the human brain.* New York: Grosset/Putnam.

Davidson R. J., Kabat-Zinn, J., Schumacher, J., Rosenkranz, M., Muller, D., et al. (2003). Alterations in brain and immune function produced by mindfulness meditation. *Psychosomatic Medicine, 65,* 564–570.

De Bellis, M. D., Keshavan, M. S., Spencer, S., & Hall, J. H. (2000). N-Acetylaspartate concentration in the anterior cingulate of maltreated children and adolescents with PTSD. *American Journal of Psychiatry, 157,* 1175–1177.

Deckel, A. W., Hesselbrock, V. (1996). Behavioral and cognitive measurements predict scores on the MAST: A 3–year prospective study. *Alcoholism: Clinical and Experimental Research, 20,* 1173–1178.

Dempster, F. N., & Corkill, A. J. (1999). Interference and inhibition in cognition and behavior: Unifying themes for educational psychology. *Educational Psychology Review, 11,* 1–88.

Dewey, J. (1933). *How we think.* Boston: Heath.

Diamond, A. (1990). Developmental time course in human infants and infant monkeys, and the neural bases of inhibitory control in reaching. *Annals of the New York Academy of Sciences, 608,* 637–704.

Dodge, K. A. (2001). The science of youth violence prevention: Progressing from developmental epidemiology to efficacy to effectiveness to public policy. *American Journal of Preventive Medicine, 2,* 63–70.

Dowsett, S. M., & Livesey, D. J. (2000). The development of inhibitory control in preschool children: Effects of "executive skills" training. *Developmental Psychobiology, 36,* 161–174.

Drug Strategies. (1998). *Safe schools, safe students: A guide to violence prevention strategies.* Washington, DC: Drug Strategies.

Epstein, J. A.. Griffin, K. W., & Botvin, G. J. (2002). Positive impact of competence skills and psychological wellness in protecting inner-city adolescents from alcohol use. *Prevention Science, 3,* 95–104.

Erickson, K., Drevets, W., & Schulkin, J. (2003). Glucocorticoid regulation of diverse cognitive functions in normal and pathological emotional states. *Neuroscience and Biobehavioral Reviews, 27,* 233–246.

Fishbein, D. (2001). The importance of neurobiological research to the prevention of psychopathology. *Prevention Science, 1,* 89–106.

Fishbein, D., Hyde, C., Coe, B., & Paschall, M. J. (2004). Neurocognitive and physiological prerequisite for prevention of adolescent substance abuse. *Journal of Primary Prevention, 24,* 471–493.

Frey, K. S., Hirschstein, M. K., & Guzzo, B. A. (2000). Second step: Preventing aggression by promoting social competence. *Journal of Emotional & Behavioral Disorders, 8*(2), 102–112.

Galaif, E. R., Hser, Y. I., Grella, C. E., & Joshi, V. (2001). Prospective risk factors and treatment outcomes among adolescents in DATOS-A. *Journal of Adolescent Research, 16,* 661–678.

Giancola, P., Martin, C., Tarter, R., Pelham, W., & Moss, H. (1996). Executive cognitive functioning and aggressive behavior in preadolescent boys at high risk for substance abuse/dependence. *Journal of Studies on Alcohol, 59,* 352–359.

Giancola, P., Mezzich, A., & Tarter, R. (1998). Disruptive, delinquent and aggressive behavior in adolescent female substance abusers: Relation to executive cognitive functioning. *Journal of Studies on Alcohol, 59,* 560–567.

Giancola, P., & Tarter, R. (1999). Executive cognitive functioning and risk for substance abuse. *Psychological Science, 10,* 203–205.

Giedd, J. N., Blumenthal, J., Jeffries, N. O., Rajapakse, J. C., Vaituzis, A. C., Liu, H., Berry, Y. C., Tobin, M., Nelson, J., Castellanos, F. X. (1999). Development of the human corpus callosum during childhood and adolescence: A longitudinal MRI study. *Progress in Neuro-Psychopharmacology and Biological Psychiatry, 23,* 571–588.

Giedd, J. N., Castellanos, F. X., Casey, B. J., & Kozuch, P. (1994). Quantitative morphology of the corpus callosum in attention deficit hyperactivity disorder. *American Journal of Psychiatry, 151,* 665–669.

Gogtay, N., Giedd, J., & Rapoport, J. L. (2002). Brain development in healthy, hyperactive, and psychotic children. *Archives of Neurology, 59,* 1244–1248.

Gray, J., Burgess, G., Schaefer, A., Yarkoni, T., Larsen, R., & Braver, T. (2005). Affective personality differences in neural processing efficiency confirmed using fMRI. *Cognitive, Affective, and Behavioral Neuroscience, 5,* 182–191.

Greenberg, M. T., Domitrovich, C., & Bumbarger, B. (1999). *Preventing mental disorder in school-aged children: A review of the effectiveness of prevention programs.* Report submitted to the Center for Mental Health Services (SAMHSA), Prevention Research Center, Pennsylvania State University. Retrieved June 28, 2006, from http://www.prevention.psu.edu/pubs/CMHS.html

Greenberg, M. T., & Kusche, C. A. (1993). *Promoting social and emotional development in deaf children: The PATHS project.* Seattle: University of Washington Press.

Greenberg, M. T., & Kusche, C. A. (1998). *Promoting alternative thinking strategies, Book 10: Blueprint for violence prevention.* University of Colorado: Institute of Behavioral Sciences.

Greenberg, M. T., Kusche, C. A., Cook, E. T., & Quamma, J. P. (1995). Promoting emotional competence in school-aged children: The effects of the PATHS curriculum. *Development and Psychology, 7,* 117–136.

Greenberg, M. T., Kusche, C. A., & Riggs, N. (2004). The PATHS curriculum: Theory and research on neuro-cognitive development and school success. In J. Zins, R. Weissberg, & H. Walber (Eds.), *Building school success on social and emotional learning.* New York: Teachers College Press.

Greenough, W. T., Black, J. E., & Christopher, S. W. (1987). Experience and brain development. *Child Development, 58*, 539–559.

Grossman, A. W., Churchill, J. D., McKinney, B. C., Kodish, I. M., Otte, S. L., & Greenough, W. T. (2003). Experience effects on brain development: Possible contributions to psychopathology. *Journal of Child Psychology and Psychiatry, 44*, 33–63.

Gunnar, M. R., & Vazquez, D. M. (2001). Low cortisol and a flattening of expected daytime rhythm: Potential indices of risk in human development. *Development and Psychopathology, 13*, 515–538.

de Hann, M., Nelson, C. A., Gunnar, M. R., & Tout, K. A. (1998). Hemispheric differences in brain activity related to the recognition of emotional expressions by 5-year-old children. *Developmental Neuropsychology, 14*, 495–518.

Hawkins, J. D., & Catalano, R. F., Jr. (1992). *Communities that care: Action for drug abuse prevention.* San Francisco: Jossey-Bass.

Hill, J. (2002). Biological, psychological and social processes in the conduct disorders. *Journal of Child Psychology and Psychiatry, 43*, 134–164.

Ito, Y., Teicher, M. H., Glod, C. A., & Ackerman, E. (1998). Preliminary evidence for aberrant cortical development in abused children: A quantitative EEG study. *Journal of Neuropsychiatry and Clinical Neuroscience, 10*, 298–307.

Kam, C., Greenberg, M. T., & Kusché, C. A. (2003). Sustained effects of the PATHS curriculum on the social and psychological adjustment of children in special education. *Journal of Emotional and Behavioral Disorders, 12*, 66–78.

Keating, D. P. (2004). Cognitive and brain development. In R. J. Lerner & L. D. Steinberg (Eds.), *Handbook of adolescent psychology* (2nd ed.) New York: Wiley.

Kopp, C. B. (1982). Antecedents of self-regulation. *Developmental Psychology, 18*, 199–214.

Kusche, C. A., Cook, E. T., & Greenberg, M. T. (1993). Neuropsychological and cognitive functioning in children with anxiety, externalizing, and comorbid psychopathology. *Journal of Clinical Child Psychology, 22*, 172–195.

Kusche, C. A., & Greenberg, M. T. (1994). *The PATHS curriculum: Promoting alternative thinking strategies.* Seattle: Developmental Research and Programs.

Kusché, C. A., & Greenberg, M. T. (2006). Brain development and social emotional learning: An introduction for educators. In M. Elias & H. Arnold (Eds.), *The Educators Guide to Emotional Intelligence and Academic achievement: Social Emotional Learning in the Classroom* (15–34). Thousand Oaks, CA: Corwin.

Kusche, C. A., Riggs, R. S., & Greenberg, M. T. (1999). PATHS: Using analytic knowledge to teach emotional literacy. *The American Psychoanalyst, 33, 1.*

Lahey, B. B., Loeber, R., Quay, H. C., Frick, P. J., & Grimm, J. (1997). Oppositional defiant disorder and conduct disorder. In T. A. Widiger, A. J. Frances, H. A. Pincus, R. Ross, M. B. First, & W. Davis (Eds.), *DSM-IV sourcebook* (Vol. 3, pp. 189–209). Washington DC: American Psychiatric Association.

Lahey, B. B., Loeber, R., Hart, E. L., Frick, P. J., et al. (1995). Four-year longitudinal study of conduct disorder in boys: Patterns and predictors of persistence. *Journal of Abnormal Psychology, 104*, 83–93.

Lamantia, A. S., & Rakic, P. (1984). The number, size, myelination, and regional variation of axons in the corpus callosum and anterior commissure of the developing rhesus monkey. *Society for Neuroscience Abstracts, 10*, 1081.

Landry, S. H., Miller-Loncar, C. L., Smith, K. E., & Swank, P. R. (2002). The role of early parenting in children's development of executive process. *Developmental Neuropsychology, 21*, 15–41.

LeDoux, J. E. (1996). *The emotional brain: The mysterious underpinnings of emotional life.* New York: Simon & Schuster.

Liang, L., & Chaloupka, F. J. (2002). Differential effects of cigarette price on youth smoking intensity. *Nicotine and Tobacco Research, 4*, 109–114.

Luna, B., & Sweeney, J. A. (2004). The emergence of collaborative brain function: FMRI studies of the development of response inhibition. *Annals of the New York Academy of Sciences, 1021*, 296–309.

Lupien. S. J., & McEwen, B. S. (1997). The acute effects of corticosteroids on cognitions: Integration of human and animal model studies. *Brain Research Reviews, 24*, 1–27.

Luria, A. R. (1966). *Higher cortical functions in man.* New York: Basic Books.

Luria, A. R. (1973). *The working brain: An introduction for neuropsychology.* New York: Basic Books.

Lynam, D. R., & Henry, V. (2001). The role of neuropsychological deficits in conduct disorders. In J. Hill & B. Maughan (Eds.), *Conduct disorders in childhood and adolescence.* Cambridge: Cambridge University Press.

Lynam, D. R., Moffitt, T., & Stouthamer-Loeber, M. (1993). Explaining the relation between IQ and delinquency: Class, race, test motivation, school failure, or self-control? *Journal of Abnormal Psychology, 102*, 187–196.

Masten, A. S. (2004). Regulatory processes, risk and resilience in adolescent development. *Annals of the New York Academy of Sciences, 1021*, 310–319.

McCall, R. (1977). Challenges to a science of developmental psychology. *Child Development, 48*, 333–344.

McEwen, B. S. (1997). Possible mechanisms for atrophy of the human hippocampus. *Molecular Psychiatry, 2*, 255–262.

McEwen, B. S., & Sapolsky, R. M. (1995). Stress and cognition. *Current Opinion in Neurobiology, 5*, 205–216.

Moffitt, T. E. (1990). The neuropsychology of delinquency: A critical review of theory and research. In N. Morris & M. Tonry (Eds.), *Crime and justice: An annual review of research* (Vol.12, pp. 99–169). Chicago: University of Chicago Press.

Moffitt, T. E. (1993). Adolescence-limited and life-course persistent antisocial behaviour: A developmental taxonomy. *Psychological Review, 100*, 674–701.

Moffitt, T. E., & Henry, B. (1989). Neuropsychological assessment of executive function in self-reported delinquents. *Development and Psychopathology, 1*, 105–118.

Moffitt, T. E., & Lynam, D. R. (1994). The neuropsychology of conduct disorder and delinquency: Implications for understanding antisocial behaviour. In D. Fowles, P. Sutker, & S. Goodman (Eds.), *Progress in experimental personality and psychopathology research: Vol. 18. Psychopathy and antisocial personality: A developmental perspective* (pp. 233–262). New York: Springer.

Morgan, A. B., & Lilienfeld, S. O. (2000). A meta-analytic review of the relation between antisocial behavior and neuropsychological measures of executive function. *Clinical Psychology Review, 20*, 113–136.

Nigg, J. T., Quamma, J. P., Greenberg, M. T., & Kusche C. A. (1998). A two-year longitudinal study of neuropsychological and cognitive performance in relation to behavioral problems and competencies in elementary school children. *Journal of Abnormal Psychology, 27*, 51–63.

Ochsner, K. N., Bunge, S. A., Gross, J. J., & Gabrieli, J. D. E. (2002). Rethinking feelings: An fMRI study of the cognitive regulation of emotion. *Journal of Cognitive Neuroscience, 14*, 1215–1229.

Oregon Department of Transportation. (2004). Oregon teen driving laws saves lives. Retrieved June 3, 2005, from http://www.oregon.gov/ODOT/COMM/NR05032101.shtml

Pennington, B. F., & Ozonoff, S. (1996). Executive function and developmental psychopathology. *Journal of Child Psychology and Psychiatry, 1,* 51–87.

Raine, A. (2002). Annotation: The role of prefrontal deficits, low autonomic arousal, and early health factors in the development of antisocial and aggressive behavior in children. *Journal of Child Psychology and Psychiatry, 43,* 417–434.

Riggs, N. R., Blair, C. B., & Greenberg, M. T. (2003). Concurrent and 2-year longitudinal relations between executive function and the behavior of 1st and 2nd grade children. *Child Neuropsychology, 9,* 267–276.

Riggs, N. R., & Greenberg, M. T. (2004). The role of neuro-cognitive models in prevention research. In D. Fishbein (Ed.), *The science, treatment, and prevention of antisocial behaviors* (Vol. 2). Kingston, NJ: Civic Research Institute.

Riggs, N. R., Greenberg, M. T., Kusché, C. A., & Pentz, M. A. (2006). The mediational role of neurocognition in the behavioral outcomes of a social-emotional prevention program in elementary school students: Effects of the PATHS Curriculum. *Prevention Science, 7,* 91–102.

Sapolsky, R. M. (1996). Why stress is bad for your brain. *Science, 273,* 749–750.

Segal, Z., Williams, J. M., & Teasdale, J. (2001). *Mindfulness-based cognitive therapy for depression: A new approach for preventing relapse.* New York: Guilford.

Shaywitz, B. A., Shawitz, S. E., Blachman, B. A, Pugh, K. R., Fulbright, R. K., et al. (2004). Development of left occipitotemporal systems for skilled reading in children after a phonologically-based intervention. *Biological Psychiatry, 55,* 926–933.

Shure, M. B., & Spivack, G. (1982). Interpersonal problem-solving in young children: A cognitive approach to prevention. *American Journal of Community Psychology, 104,* 614–624.

Skosnik, P. D., Chatterton, R. T. Jr., & Swisher, S. P. (2000). Modulation of attentional inhibition by norepinephrine and cortisol after psychological stress. *International Journal of Psychophysiology, 36,* 59–68.

Sowell, E. R., Peterson, B. S., Thompson, P. M., Welcome, S. E., Henkenius, A., L., et al. (2003). Mapping cortical change across the human lifespan. *Nature Neuroscience, 6,* 309–315.

Spellacy, F. (1977). Neuropsychological differences between violent and nonviolent adolescents. *Journal of Clinical Psychology, 33,* 966–969.

Speltz, M. L., DeKylen, M., Calderon, R., Greenberg, M. T., & Fisher, P. A. (1999). Neuropsychological characteristics and test behaviors of boys with early onset conduct problems. *Journal of Abnormal Psychology, 108,* 315–325.

Spoth, R., Redmond, C., & Shin, C. (2001). Randomized trial of brief family interventions for general populations: Adolescent substance use outcomes four years following baseline. *Journal of Consulting and Clinical Psychology, 69*(4), 627–642.

Stein, M. B., Koverola, C., Hanna, C., Torchia, M. C., & McClarty, B. (1997). Hippocampal volume in women victimized by childhood sexual abuse. *Psychological Medicine, 27,* 951–959.

Steinberg, L. (2004). Risk-taking in adolescence. *Annals of the New York Academy of Sciences, 1021,* 1–8.

Steinberg, L., Dahl, R., Keating, D., Kupfer, D. J., Masten, A. S., Pine, D. (2006). The study of developmental psychopathology in adolescence: Integrating affective neuroscience with the study of context. In D. Cicchetti & D. Cohen (Eds.), *Handbook of developmental psychopathology* (2nd ed.) (pp. 710–741). Hoboken, NJ: Wiley.

Stuss, D. T., & Benson, D. F. (1984). Neuropsychological studies of the frontal lobes. *Psychological Bulletin, 95*, 3–28.

Teasdale, J. (2004). Mindfulness-based cognitive therapy. In J. Yiend (Ed.), *Cognition, emotion and psychopathology: Theoretical, clinical and empirical directions* (pp. 270–289). New York: Cambridge University Press.

Thompson, P. M., Giedd, J. N., Woods, R. P., MacDonald, D., Evans, A. C., & Toga, A. (2000). Growth patterns in the developing brain detected by using continuum mechanical tensor maps. *Nature, 404,* 190–193.

Tobler Research Associates, LLC. (1988). *School-based drug prevention programs: Technical report.* Washington, DC: National Committee for Abuse Prevention.

U.S. Department of Health and Human Services. (1999). *Mental health: A report of the Surgeon General.* Rockville, MD: Author.

Welsh, M. C., Pennington, B. F., & Groisser, D. B. (1991). A normative-developmental study of executive function: A window of prefrontal function in children. *Developmental Neuropsychology, 7,* 131–149.

White, H. R., Xie, M., Thompson, W., Loeber. R., & Stouthamer-Loeber, M. (2001). Psychopathology as a predictor of adolescent drug use trajectories. *Psychology of Addictive Behaviors, 15,* 210–218.

White, J. L., Moffitt, T. E. Caspi, A., Jeglum Bartusch, D., Needles, D. J., & Stouthamer-Loeber, M. (1994). Measuring impulsivity and examining its relationship to delinquency. *Journal of Abnormal Psychology, 103,* 192–205.

Yung, B. R., & Hammond, R. W. (1998). Breaking the cycle: A culturally sensitive violence prevention program for African-American children and adolescents. In J. R. Lutzker (Ed.). *Handbook of child abuse research and treatment: Issues in clinical child psychology* (pp. 319–340). New York: Plenum Press.

Conclusions

Elaine F. Walker and Daniel Romer

In this volume, we see evidence of tremendous progress in understanding the nature and developmental origins of behavioral dysfunction, especially the syndromes that typically emerge during adolescence. The chapters highlight the ways in which environmental and genetic factors act in concert to modulate the course of brain development and thereby confer vulnerabilities, as well as resilience, to mental disorders. They also describe new research findings that shed light on the developmental processes giving rise to functional impairment and some of the promising opportunities for intervention suggested by these models.

Developmental Models

There is rapidly accumulating evidence that adolescence is a critical developmental period for the expression of vulnerabilities for behavioral symptoms and syndromes, ranging from substance use to major mental illnesses. Why is adolescence a critical period for the onset of such a broad range of disorders? In addressing this question, it is of interest to consider the developmental models offered by the investigators featured in this volume. These models represent the major trends in conceptualizing the nature of adolescent development and risk for mental disorders.

Normal Brain Maturation

The contributors to this volume have posited models of adolescent vulnerability that vary with respect to their assumptions about the origins of brain dysfunction. Normal maturational processes figure prominently in several of these models. Drawing on seminal research findings from Elizabeth Sowell, Paul Thompson, and Arthur Toga (chapter 3) and others, these authors highlight the structural and functional changes that characterize the adolescent brain, then demonstrate how these changes can heighten the individual's sensitivity to environmental challenges.

For example, in chapter 10, Erin McClure and Daniel Pine draw on a model recently proposed by their research group to account for the emergence of mood and anxiety disorders in adolescence (Nelson, Leibenluft, McClure & Pine, 2004). The authors hypothesize that normative changes in adolescent social behavior reflect developmental changes in the brain circuitry involved in the social information processing network (SIPN). The SIPN is assumed to involve three nodes: the detection node, the affective node, and the cognitive-regulatory node. The *detection node* serves to categorize and process the properties of social stimuli, and includes regions of the occipital cortex, temporal cortex, and the fusiform face area. Once the social properties of the stimulus have been identified, the *affective node* is engaged. This node includes the amygdala, nucleus accumbens, and the hypothalamus. Finally, the *cognitive-regulatory node* then engages in more complex processing of the stimuli, and it enables the individual to reflect on the mental state and intentions of others, to inhibit prepotent responses, and to generate goal-directed behavioral options. These cognitive processes are subserved by the prefrontal cortex (PFC).

As described in several chapters, there is evidence that the brain regions subsumed in these nodes differ in their developmental trajectories. The areas comprising the detection node reach maturity in early childhood. In contrast, the regions that comprise the affective and cognitive-regulatory nodes undergo significant change during adolescence, and these changes are assumed to be linked with the alterations in cognitive and social behaviors that occur during this period. Because the cognitive-regulatory regions undergo the most protracted developmental course, the gradual increase in the capacity to regulate emotional expressions and social behavior extends into young adulthood.

Taken together, the temporal pattern of maturational changes in the affective and cognitive-regulatory nodes is presumed to play a role in the emergence of mood disorders in adolescence. Specifically, the authors propose that the increased intensity of emotional responses to social stimuli can result in heightened sensitivity to negative social events and thereby increase risk for mood disorders. Because the cognitive-regulatory functions subserved by the PFC are not fully mature in adolescence, the individual does not yet have the capability to reflect on social experiences and modulate responses. When the social environment is especially stressful, as is often the case in adolescence, the individual succumbs to symptoms of mood disorder.

The above model assumes that adolescence is a risk period for the emergence of mood disorder because the neural circuits that subserve socioemotional reactions come "online" following puberty. In other words, a normal neuromaturational process, interacting with environmental factors, sets the stage for the expression of anxiety and depression. Focusing on the cognitive manifestations of adolescent brain development, Lauren Alloy and Lyn Abramson (chapter 13) make this assumption in their biocognitive vulnerability-transactional stress model of depression, and posit that growth in cognitive competence during adolescence can set the stage for cognitive vulnerability to depression.

Other contributors to this volume make similar assumptions about adolescent-onset substance abuse (O'Brien, chapter 17), interpersonal problems (Tucker & Moller, chapter 4), and conduct problems (Greenberg, Riggs, & Blair, chapter 20). Along the same lines, in chapter 1, Linda Spear reviews evidence to suggest that adolescence is a period of increased risk taking and stress sensitivity because neural pathways that subserve responses to both reward and stress are undergoing maturation. For this reason, the postpubertal developmental period is associated with heightened risk for sensation-seeking behaviors, such as substance abuse.

Abnormal Adolescent Brain Development

In contrast to the focus on normative processes, some models posit that, for certain disorders, adolescence is a period of increased risk when neuromaturational processes go awry. Again, Sowell, Thompson, and Toga (chapter 3) elegantly describe several adolescent neuromaturational processes that could deviate, in nature or timing, from the normal trajectory. The notion of adolescent neuromaturational abnormalities has played a central role in the literature on psychotic disorders. Several authors have suggested that disturbances in the processes associated with normal adolescent brain maturation may be associated with schizophrenia. Other authors have pointed out that some of the neural processes occurring during adolescence involve a reduction in neuronal interconnections, referred to as synaptic pruning, which is presumed to make brain function more efficient. Based on this evidence, it has been suggested that the prodromal signs of schizophrenia tend to have their origins during adolescence because the pruning process exceeds normal levels and results in an aberrant pattern of interconnections that disrupts brain function (Keshavan & Hogarty, 1999).

The Interaction Between Constitutional Vulnerability and Adolescent Brain Maturation

Of course, many disorders that typically begin in adolescence are known to be linked with earlier indicators of behavioral dysfunction. Retrospective and prospective studies have shown that individuals who succumb to affective and psychotic disorders in late adolescence/young adulthood often manifest developmental delays and behavioral problems in early childhood. These abnormalities are apparent in the domains of cognitive, social, and motor function. Kiki Chang, Kim Gallelli, and Meghan Howe (chapter 14) describe how the epigenesis of bipolar disorder in late adolescence is often preceded by signs of cognitive dysfunction. The evidence of early abnormalities, coupled with genetic data showing a heritable component to these disorders, demonstrates that neural vulnerability can be congenital (i.e., present at birth) or acquired by exposure to nonoptimal postnatal experiences, even though the clinical expression may not be apparent until after puberty.

Assuming that there is a congenital or early acquired neural abnormality, some have proposed that adolescent neuromaturational processes interact with preexisting brain abnormality in the epigenesis of certain clinical disorders. For example, in the case of schizophrenia, it has been suggested that there may be a localized congenital brain abnormality that interacts with normal neuromaturational events following puberty. These postpubertal changes in neural circuitry set the stage for the expression of the prodromal stages of psychotic disorders. Such a model is described by Anthony Grace in chapter 11, where it is posited that developmentally triggered changes in limbic circuitry "unmask" a previously latent frontal abnormality. Others, attempting to account for the changing behavioral manifestations of vulnerability from infancy through adolescence, propose that the congenital lesion is not silent, but rather affects different behavioral domains as development proceeds. More specifically, Walker (1994) suggests that abnormalities in dopamine neurotransmission and receptors in the striatum give rise to different kinds of behavioral expressions as the various neural circuits that include this subcortical region come online. During adolescence, as the limbic-striatal and frontal-striatal circuitry mature, the preexisting striatal abnormality results in circuitry malfunction and affective and cognitive signs of psychosis.

Several of the chapters document evidence for psychobiological vulnerabilities that are acquired during infancy and early childhood. Megan Gunnar (chapter 6), Michael Meaney (chapter 7) and Nicole Cooper et al. (chapter 15) describe research findings that highlight the interplay between early exposure to stress and subsequent brain development. The generalized and sometimes persistent adverse effects of early childhood deprivation are clearly illustrated by the work of Charles Nelson, Charles Zeanah, and Nathan Fox (chapter 9). At the same time, their work suggests the possibilities for interrupting this cycle by environmental interventions. Farah and colleagues (chapter 16) find evidence for early stress effects on brain development brought about by chronic poverty conditions. They also find some evidence that deficits in cognitive stimulation during early childhood are related to the functioning of language centers in the developing brain.

The Onset of Brain Dysfunction in Adolescence

Finally, it is possible that the neuropathology underlying disorders that arise during adolescence does not involve either a congenital brain abnormality or aberrant neuromaturational processes. Instead, the brain dysfunction presumed to be associated with mental disorders may arise more gradually following the onset of puberty, and hormones may be implicated (Karen Bales & Sue Carter, chapter 8). A mechanism for this is suggested by the increasing evidence that gene expression changes with development and experience, and that hormones play a role in the expression of genes (Scott Hemby & Joann O'Connor, chapter 5). It has been suggested that the rise in risk for various mental disorders during adolescence may be a consequence of the effects of gonadal and adrenal hormones on the expression of genes that confer vulnerability for these disorders (Walker, McMillan, & Mittal, chapter 12). Thus, hormonal surges during puberty may trigger the expression of a gene, or more likely, multiple genes, that code for an abnormality in brain function.

In summary, the models that have attempted to account for the emergence of psychiatric symptoms and syndromes during adolescence vary with respect to whether they assume that postpubertal neuromaturational process are intact versus disrupted, and whether they assume the existence of a congenital versus gradually developing brain abnormality. It is likely that all of the above models have validity for at least some disorders. It may be that substance abuse and mood disorders, for example, are less likely to involve congenital vulnerability and more likely to entail an interaction between environmental factors and normal brain maturation. For schizophrenia and major mood disorders, however, both congenital vulnerability and abnormal adolescent brain development may be key etiologic factors.

The Neural Mechanisms in Vulnerability

Moving to the level of specific neural mechanisms, the chapters in this volume highlight both specific and nonspecific associations between various brain regions and disorders. It is clear that the prefrontal cortex (PFC), especially the dorsolateral prefrontal cortex, is prominent in many of the discussions. It shows a protracted course of development and may be the last region to come fully online. The "executive functions" subserved by the PFC appear to play an important role in a range of disorders. It is a focal point of developmental models of disorders of behavioral inhibition that often first emerges in the postpubertal period. For some behavioral problems that involve deficits in impulse control, such as attention, substance abuse, and conduct disorders, the PFC may indeed be the key region. For other disorders, such as the psychoses, the PFC may play a secondary role, in that it determines how vulnerabilities in other regions are behaviorally expressed. Given the ability of the PFC to modulate the response of other brain regions, it is often the target of interventions designed to enable coping with stressors and other challenges to mental health.

The limbic system, typically assumed to include the amygdala, hippocampus, and limbic regions of the cortex (cingulate gyrus and entorhinal cortex), plays a central role in emotional responses. Evidence suggests that the developmental course is not as protracted as the PFC. It is not surprising that dysfunction in these regions is posited to subserve symptoms of mood disorder and sociointerpersonal deficits that arise in adolescence.

The striatum (caudate, putamen, and nucleus accumbens) may be among the earlier maturing brain regions. It is most often cited in relation to the etiology of serious, often chronic, disorders that are assumed to involve congenital origins, including genetic factors and prenatal insults. Schizophrenia and mood disorders with psychotic features fall in this category, and often entail signs of risk in early childhood. This region may also play a role in the onset of sensation-seeking needs that are hypothesized to underlie the onset of risky behavior in adolescence such as drug use, sex, gambling, and self-injurious behavior.

Preventive Intervention: Time Is of the Essence!

The developmental models and theories of neural mechanisms discussed above have provided a foundation for the authors in this volume to speculate on promising preventive interventions. It is clear that past assumptions about the unidirectional relation between biology and behavior are not valid. The individual's biological constitution is not fixed by genetics and does not have immutable effects on behavior. Instead, we see that the relation between biology and behavior is complex and bidirectional. Environmental factors, including the psychosocial environment, influence brain structure, function, and development. In part, this is mediated by the effects of the environment on the expression of genes. Further, both the environment and the brain affect behavior.

These new insights in developmental neuroscience have changed our views of the opportunities for preventive intervention. First, we now realize that we can enhance brain functioning by reducing stress and improving the quality of the psychosocial environment, not only by the administration of drugs. Second, we have a greater appreciation for the importance of timing these interventions to optimize neuromaturation.

Early Childhood Stress and Trauma

Effects of stress during pregnancy and early development suggest that this period can have lasting effects on later development of mental disorder. High levels of stress can sensitize the HPA system (see Gunnar, chapter 6) and influence genetic expression of various stress responses, including impaired cognitive functioning under stressful conditions (see Meaney, chapter 7). Meaney's research suggests that these effects are mediated by the nurturing behavior of the primary caregiver, which in his animal models is the female rat. Neglectful and nonnuturing parenting in this model produces genetic effects that influence the parenting behavior of female offspring. This altered parenting behavior can then influence subsequent generations of offspring producing intergenerational effects on stress responses and parenting behavior. His work using cross-fostering designs indicates that these effects can be reversed when a nurturing mother raises the offspring of a non-nurturant mother. His work also suggests that stressful environments can unleash nonnurturant patterns of parenting and that these environments influence genetic expressions that control behavior into adolescence and adulthood. Although this pattern of gene expression may be adaptive for offspring born into high stress environments, it is likely to predispose offspring to later affective disorders and hyperreactivity to stressors (see also Teicher et al., 2003).

Meaney's research with an animal model may not translate completely to humans; however, the parallels are quite striking. Child abuse appears to have a strong inter-generational pattern that has been subject to either a genetic or modeling interpreta-tion (Buchanan, 1996; Thompson, 1995). In addition, chronic poverty and stress are strong predictors of abusive and neglectful parenting (Repetti, Taylor, & Seeman, 2002). Meaney's research suggests that chronic stress may unleash genetic effects in offspring mediated by nonnurturing parental behavior. He terms this a "nongenomic" effect because the neglectful behavior of the parent initiates it, and a nurturant parent can reverse it. Virtually the same effects of maternal behavior have been observed in Suomi's (1997) studies of rhesus monkeys who share many more social and behav-ioral characteristics with humans than rats. Suomi's research has also examined the effects of nonnurturant rearing on male development. His studies suggest that males raised by nonnurturant females are more likely to exhibit impulsive and aggressive behavior than males raised by normal or highly nurturant females.

Even if the animal models developed by Meaney and Suomi do not translate completely to humans, their outcomes explain the beneficial effects that have been observed for interventions designed to provide support during the pre- and post-natal period to mothers in high-risk (low-SES, single-parent) households (Olds, Henderson, Cole, Eckenrode, Kitzman, Luckey, et al., 1998). This home visita-tion program by public health nurses has been found to reduce maladaptive and abusive parenting, decrease the incidence of externalizing disorders in adolescence, and increase the adaptive functioning of mothers well beyond the early years of childbearing (Izzo et al., 2005). Gunnar (chapter 6) also finds evidence for the reversibility of early unresponsive parenting in human infants. Research she cites that examines the effects of nurturant foster care on previously institutionalized children suggests that HPA functioning can return to more normal levels of func-tioning if the intervention occurs during the preschool years. Research by Nelson and colleagues (chapter 9), with more seriously neglected children left in Roma-nian institutions, suggests that even such severely disrupted development can be partially reversed by appropriate foster care placement.

The evidence now accumulating from research with lower animals suggests that parenting interventions have the ability to prevent genetic effects that predispose children to mental disorders during childhood and adolescence. Much more research is needed, however, to understand how these processes unfold in humans. Although the benefits are already evident in the elegant work of Olds and colleagues, home visitation effects are not always robust and depend on the skills of the intervener (Gomby, Culross, & Behrman, 1999; Olds, Henderson, Kitzman, Eckenrode, Cole, & Tatlebaum, 1999). Future research using neurobehavioral assessments may help to identify the crucial elements of home visitation programs so that their beneficial effects can be targeted more precisely in intervention protocols.

It is sobering to contemplate the number of children currently being raised in households in which the debilitating effects of early parental stress are transferred with lasting consequence to children. National surveys conducted under the auspices of the Child Abuse Prevention, Adoption, and Family Services Act of 1988 (Sedlak & Broadhurst, 1996) indicate that more than 4% of children (ages birth to 17) are reported to be raised in settings with harmful or neglectful parenting. This estimate does not include children who do not come to attention of authorities. Furthermore, most of the children in this category were detected after age 5 when they first attended schools. Animal and human models of nonnurturant parenting suggest that the effects of neglect will already have been passed on to children well before they reach school age. Current federally funded intervention programs for children from disadvantaged homes (e.g., Head Start) do not begin until after the effects of early rearing have left their mark. The work of Farah and colleagues (chapter 16) suggests that early experiences of chronic poverty may also leave cumulative effects on areas of the brain that can influence intelligence and adaptive functioning. They suggest that development of the frontal lobes, hippocampus, and language centers is particularly sensitive to effects of chronic poverty, but may nevertheless be malleable, based on environmental interventions tested in both animal models and research with humans. More targeted interventions to prevent or reverse these adverse effects on brain development are greatly needed. A privately funded program titled Healthy Families America has attempted to replicate the home-visitation model on a national basis (Gomby, Culross, & Behrman, 1999). However, it does not reach all states and localities and should be expanded, potentially with federal funds.

In addition to exploring vulnerabilities, several of the contributors to this volume also examine childhood characteristics associated with resilience when the individual is later faced with the normative stresses of adolescence. Ann Masten (chapter 2), for example, proposes that the child's ability to negotiate the psychosocial challenges of adolescent transitions is greater if she has previously acquired effective systems for learning and regulating behavior, and has had positive relationships with supportive parents and peers. Masten also emphasizes the important role of social supports that can help the child to negotiate difficult transitions during adolescence.

In chapter 18, M. Rosario Rueda and colleagues address the question of intervention; specifically, what neurodevelopmental processes could be altered in childhood so that adolescent mental disorders might be prevented? They point to the broad evidence indicating that a number of mental disorders depend critically on disorganization of an executive attention system subserved by neural circuits that include the frontal lobes, as well as the anterior cingulate and basal ganglia. Although executive attention deficit is not necessarily the defining characteristic of adolescent-onset disorders, there is evidence that improved effortful control may help people overcome vulnerability to a range of disorders. Along these same lines, Mark Greenberg and colleagues (chapter 20) and Patricia Gorman Barry and Marilyn Welsh (chapter 19) conclude that the temporal course of the development of the frontal lobes underscores the importance of childhood preventive interventions aimed at enhancing cognitive abilities that can increase resilience. Although the frontal lobes and the networks connecting them to the limbic system maintain an ability to restructure throughout the entire life span, the most rapid advances in the structural organization of the networks probably occur during childhood.

Stressors During Adolescence

Research reviewed in this volume also underscores the critical role of stress during adolescence in the emergence of psychopathology. Various authors have delineated mechanisms whereby a preexisting genetic or other vulnerability leads to abnormal brain development that is made more vulnerable to disorder under conditions of stress. Grace (chapter 11), Walker et al. (chapter 12), Alloy and Abramson (chapter 13), and Chang et al. (chapter 14) note how this can lead to psychosis or mood disorder in those with the preexisting vulnerability. Alloy and Abramson note how cognitive processes that are quite normal in development can make female adolescents more vulnerable to depression under conditions of stress. Adolescents' increased sensitivity to stress suggests that interventions to help increase the ability to cope with stress during adolescence may be a useful strategy among those with the critical vulnerabilities. If adolescents with predisposition to depression or psychosis and their families (who often also exhibit the same symptoms) were given skills to cope with their stressful environments, the likelihood of transition to disorder may be reduced. Cooper and colleagues (chapter 15) review several of these strategies for increasing resilience following trauma. This recommendation echoes the conclusions derived from the Annenberg Sunnylands Commissions that examined intervention strategies for preventing further progression of disorder once the early signs were present (Evans et al., 2005).

Universal Training of Executive Coping Skills

In addition to selective interventions for those with signs of disorder, universal training programs for children in the early years of school may also produce beneficial preventive effects. The programs developed by Greenberg and Gorman Barry may have long-term effects on the maturation of the prefrontal cortex and enable adolescents to cope more adaptively with the natural stressors experienced during the adolescent years. Definitive support for this outcome awaits further research; however, the evidence in favor of the beneficial effects of these competence-enhancing programs is already available (cf. Romer, 2003), and existing evidence of more adaptive executive functioning is supportive. Given the predisposition to risky behavior in adolescents (Spear, chapter 1) and in particular the susceptibility to drug use (O'Brien, chapter 17), these interventions have the capability of reducing the ill effects of these risky behaviors. The newly emerging study of educational neuroscience is an exciting development that will hopefully bring greater understanding to the effects of school-based behavioral interventions and to education in general.

Skill-Based Prevention as an Alternative to Medication

Skill-based treatments such as cognitive behavior therapy and educational interventions such as developed by Posner and colleagues can influence brain function and possibly structure as much as medications. This exciting possibility is underrecognized among both scientists and the lay public. The potential use of such interventions should be studied to determine whether they can substitute for the use of medications. For example, if the Rueda et al. training program were successful in reducing attentional deficits typically diagnosed and treated as ADHD, then the use of stimulants to treat this disorder may decline. The Rueda et al. program can be administered easily and in a short duration with what appear to be powerful effects on the attention system. It remains to be seen if this intervention alone can undo the effects of all the attention deficits associated with ADHD, but the possibility deserves further research. Because medications are powerful agents with effects on brain development of their own, it would be desirable to identify experiential therapies that do not have untoward effects on the brain.

At the same time, it is possible that the optimal approach to the prevention of some disorders will require a combination of medication and psychotherapeutic intervention. Kiki Chang, Kim Gallelli, and Meghan Howe (chapter 14) highlight the potential for both pharmacologic and psychotherapeutic interventions for preventing or ameliorating the onset of bipolar disorder in children at risk. Moreover, their discussion of these strategies could easily generalize to other disorders, such as major depression and schizophrenia.

Societal Understanding of the Genetic Basis of Mental Disorder

Genetic effects on brain development are sizable. However, the research regarding these effects on mental health suggests that the environment has a powerful role to play in how these effects unfold. In some cases, the environment surrounding the newborn selects which genes will be expressed. In other cases, genes that predispose to disorder must be present for an environmental insult to produce adverse effects (e.g., in schizophrenia). In either case, the emergence of disorder is contingent on the environmental experience of the individual. This more nuanced understanding of the role of genetic influences has not been fully absorbed by either the scientific or lay community. Efforts to increase the understanding of these processes in secondary and undergraduate education should be a high priority. Public education regarding the reversibility of disorders in brain development should also be pursued. Neuroscience programs at the undergraduate and graduate levels are expanding rapidly, and these courses of study are ideal venues for examining the role of genetic and environmental influences on brain development and its consequences for mental health. Ultimately, the appreciation of this fundamental reality should help to reduce stigma associated with mental disorder and increase our ability to treat and prevent such disorders in the future.

Kandel (1998) called for new approaches to the study and treatment of mental disorder that would transform several of the basic oppositions that have defined scientific and lay understandings for decades. We see in this collection that two of these defining dichotomies, "nature versus nurture" and "biology versus behavior," are giving way to a more nuanced appreciation of development, in which nature is interwoven with nurture and behavior influences biology. In this most exciting time, we look forward to continued progress in our ability to apply this understanding to the prevention and treatment of mental disorder during childhood and adolescence and to increased opportunities for healthy development into adulthood.

References

Buchanan, A. (1996). *Cycles of child maltreatment: Facts, fallacies and interventions.* New York: Wiley.

Evans, D. L., Foa, E. B., Gur, R. E., Hendin, H., O'Brien, C. P., Seligman, M. E. P., & Walsh, B. T. (2005). *Treating and preventing adolescent mental health disorders: What we know and what we don't know.* New York: Oxford University Press.

Gomby, D., Culross, P. L., & Behrman, R. E. (1999). Home visiting: Recent program evaluations—analysis and recommendations. *The Future of Children, 9*(1), 4–26.

Izzo, C. V., Eckenrode, J. J., Smith, E. G., Henderson, C. R., Cole, R. E., Kitzman, H. J., & Olds, D. (2005). Reducing the impact of uncontrollable stressful life events through a program of nurse home visitation for new parents. *Prevention Science, 6*(4), 269–274.

Kandel, E. R. (1998). A new intellectual framework for psychiatry. *American Journal of Psychiatry, 155*, 457–469.

Keshavan, M. S., & Hogarty, G. E. (1999). Brain maturational processes and delayed onset in schizophrenia. *Development & Psychopathology, 11*(3), 525–543.

Olds, D., Henderson, C. R., Cole, R. E., Eckenrode, J. J., Kitzman, H. J., Luckey, D., et al. (1998). Long-term effects of nurse home visitation on children's criminal and antisocial behavior: 15–year follow-up of a randomized trial. *Journal of the American Medical Association, 280*(14), 1238–1244.

Olds, D., Henderson, C. R., Kitzman, H. J., Eckenrode, J. J., Cole, R. E., & Tatlebaum, R. C. (1999). Prenatal and infancy home visitation by nurses: Recent findings. *The Future of Children, 9*(1), 44–65.

Repetti, R. L., Taylor, S. E., & Seeman, T. E. (2002). Risky families: Social environments and the mental and physical health of offspring. *Psychological Bulletin, 128*(2), 330–366.

Romer, D. (Ed.). (2003). *Reducing adolescent risk: Toward an integrated approach.* Thousand Oaks, CA: Sage.

Sedlak, A. J., & Broadhurst, D. D. (1996). *The third national incidence study of child abuse and neglect (NIS-3).* Washington, DC: U.S. Department of Health and Human Services.

Suomi, S. J. (1997). Early determinants of behavior: evidence from primate studies. *British Medical Bulletin, 53*(1), 170–184.

Teicher, M. H., Andersen, S. L., Polcari, A., Anderson, C. M., Navalta, C. P., & Kim, D. M. (2003). The neurobiological consequences of early stress and childhood maltreatment. *Neuroscience and Biobehavioral Reviews, 27,* 33–44.

Thompson, R. A. (1995). *Preventing child maltreatment through social support: A critical analysis.* Thousand Oaks, CA: Sage.

Walker, E. (1994). Developmentally moderated expressions of the neuropathology underlying schizophrenia. *Schizophrenia Bulletin. 20*, 453–480.

Appendix A

Glossary

Shivali Dhruv

Acetylation A process that introduces an acetyl radical (CH3CO) to an organic compound, occurring as a modification of proteins as part of the regulation of gene expression.

ACTH (adrenocorticotropic hormone) A protein hormone of the anterior lobe of the pituitary gland that is part of the HPA stress response system, secreted in response to corticotropic releasing hormone (CRH), that stimulates the adrenal cortex to synthesize and release corticosteroids.

Afferents Neurons or pathways that send signals to the CNS from the periphery or a higher processing system.

Alpha 2 adrenergic receptor A postsynaptic, excitatory receptor that responds to binding of norepinephrine and epinephrine; activation causes various physiological reactions, including the stimulation of associated muscles and the constriction of blood vessels.

Amphetamine An amine (organic compound with a nitrogen containing functional group) frequently abused as a stimulant of the central nervous system but used clinically, especially in the form of its sulfate, to treat attention deficit disorder and narcolepsy and formerly as a short-term appetite suppressant.

Amygdala   A bilateral brain structure comprised of several nuclei that are specifically concerned with emotion, especially anxiety, and that coordinate the autonomic and endocrine responses to such emotional arousal. For anatomical localization, *see* Figure B1.

Amygdalofugal neurons   Neurons in one of the two major bundles of fibers connecting the amygdala with other areas of the brain; the two bundles of fibers are the stria terminalis and the ventral amygdalofugal pathway. The centromedial amygdala projects primarily to the lateral hypothalamus and brain stem through the ventral amygdalofugal tract, where it can influence hormonal and somatomotor aspects of behavior and emotional states.

Analgesic   A drug used to relieve pain, without the loss of consciousness.

Anterior cingulated cortex   The frontal part of the cingulated cortex that forms around the corpus collosum and plays a role in regulating heart rate and blood pressure, reward anticipation, decision making, empathy, and emotion.

Anterior commisure   A band of nerve fibers connecting the two hemispheres.

Anterior pituitary   An integral part of the endocrine system, under the influence of the hypothalamus, that produces and secretes peptide hormones that regulate physiological responses such as stress, growth, and reproduction. For brain localization, *see* Figure B1.

Antidromic   A nerve impulse or fiber conducting in a direction opposite to the norm in the local neural region.

Appetitive (response)   A response to a positively reinforcing stimulus.

Apoptosis   Programmed cell death that is a genetically determined normal physiological process of cell self-destruction to eliminate damaged or unwanted cells, marked by the fragmentation of nuclear DNA and activated by the presence or removal of a stimulus or suppressing agent. When halted, may result in uncontrolled cell growth and tumor formation.

Arcuate fasciculus   Thought to connect Broca's area, involved in language processing, speech production, and comprehension, to Wernicke's area, crucial to understanding and comprehending spoken language.

Atypical antipsychotics   Medications typically used as the first line of treatment for schizophrenia, favored over the typical antipsychotics for their decreased propensity to cause extrapyramidal side (EPS) effects, various movement abnormalities as a consequence of dopamine antagonism, and an absence of sustained prolactin elevation (*see* D FENFLURAMINE). These agents may also be used for acute mania, bipolar mania, and psychotic agitation.

Barbiturates   A class of hypnotic drugs that increases chloride current by binding to postsynaptic GABA A receptors, thereby enhancing inhibitory synaptic transmission. They can function as sedatives and anticonvulsants and are often used recreationally for their state of intoxication, very similar to alcohol-induced intoxication. Although many individuals have safely taken barbiturates, concern about the addiction potential and fatalities associated with them led to the therapeutic use of alternative medications, mainly BENZODIAZEPINES.

Basal ganglia   A brain region that includes the caudate, putamen, globus pallidus and substantia nigra, all bilateral structures that together participate in the regulation of motor function. For brain localization, *see* Figure B2.

Benzodiazepines   A class of muscle relaxants, hypnotics, anticonvulsants, and antianxiety drugs that increases chloride conductance via binding to the GABA A receptor, thereby enhancing synaptic activity. Because of the high degree of negative side effects with barbiturates, benzodiazepines (BZDs) are used more commonly for clinical application. The advantages of BZDs are that there is a greater dose margin between anxioloysis (a state of minimal sedation) and full sedation, lower tolerance and dependence, and less potential for abuse.

Binding   Referring to the process of a LIGAND connecting to its RECEPTOR.

Brainstem   A stalk of the brain below the cerebral hemispheres, comprised of the medulla oblongata, pons, and midbrain. The brainstem serves as a major communication route between the forebrain, spinal cord, and peripheral nerves and is responsible for processing sensation, such as hearing and taste, and controlling balance. For anatomical localization, *see* Figure B1.

Catecholamines   Any of various water-soluble amines that are derived from tyrosine and that function as hormones, neurotransmitters, or both. The most abundant catecholamines are epinephrine (adrenaline), NOREPINEPHRINE (noradrenaline), and DOPAMINE. High catecholamine levels are generally associated with stress and cause physiological changes in the body in preparation for the fight or flight response.

Caudate nucleus   A C-shaped structure in each cerebral hemisphere that comprises a mass of GRAY MATTER in the corpus striatum and is involved in the control of voluntary movement. For anatomical localization, *see* Figure B2.

cDNA array (complementary DNA array)   A procedure used to identify DNA samples in gene expression analyses; complementary DNA is synthesized from and complementary to a given RNA strand. A microarray uses a glass or plastic solid structure, onto which single-stranded cDNA fragments attach and serve as probes.

Cerebellum   A brain structure that plays an important role in the integration of sensory input and motor output, specifically involved in the learning of motor skills and modulating force and range of movement.

Cholinergic transmission   Synaptic transmission produced by a neuron that releases acetylcholine.

Chromatin   A complex of nucleic acid and basic proteins (HISTONES) in the nucleus of cells that is condensed into chromosomes. Packaging into a chromatin structure constrains the size of the DNA molecule and allows the cell to control the expression of genes.

Commisurotomy   A surgical procedure used in epilepsy, severing the corpus collosum and anterior commisure, to prevent spread of epilepsy to the unaffected hemisphere.

Consolidation   The process by which recent memories are crystallized into long-term memory; can refer to molecular consolidation, requiring protein synthesis, or network consolidation, as initial memory storage in the hippocampus is slowly moved into the neocortex.

Corpus collosum   The largest commissure and white matter structure in the brain, connecting the two cerebral hemispheres; serves as the main communication route between the left and right halves of the brain.

Corticotrophin releasing hormone/factor (CRH/CRF)   A polypeptide hormone and neurotransmitter secreted by the paraventricular nucleus of the hypothalamus that regulates the release of ACTH by the anterior lobe of the pituitary gland.

Cortisol   A GLUCOCORTICOID hormone produced by the adrenal cortex upon stimulation by ACTH that mediates various metabolic processes, has antiinflammatory and immunosuppressive properties, and is most importantly involved in the stress response in human and nonhuman primates (in subprimates, the main glucocorticoid hormone is corticosterone).

CSF (cerebrospinal fluid)   A clear bodily fluid that is secreted from blood into the lateral ventricles of the brain and spinal chord; is involved in the mechanical protection of the brain, distribution of neuroendocrine factors, the facilitation of pulsatile cerebral blood flow, and the maintenance of uniform pressure within the brain and spinal cord.

Cyclothymia   A chronic, low-level form of bipolar disorder that consists of short periods of mild depression alternating with short periods of hypomania.

Declarative memory   The aspect of memory that stores facts, objects, and events and can be divided into two types: episodic, or knowledge about events in a person's past, and semantic, or knowledge of the meaning of words. Can be contrasted with procedural memory, which stores skills and operations.

Decussation   The crossing of a neuronal pathway from one side of the body to the contralateral side.

Depolarization   Excitation or decrease in the membrane potential of the POSTSYN-APTIC cell increasing the likelihood that a neuron will generate an action potential.

Dexamethasone challenge   A procedure designed to assess function of the hypothalamic pituitary adrenal axis; involves the administration of the synthetic steroid, dexamethasone, followed by measurement of cortisol levels to obtain the test results.

d fenfluramine challenge   A procedure in which d fenfluramine stimulates the release of SEROTONIN and acts as a potent inhibitor of the reuptake of serotonin into the nerve terminal. The prolactin response to d fenfluramine challenge has been used to assess serotonergic function and appears to be blunted in depressed patients.

Diffusion tensor imaging   An MRI based technique that allows the visualization of location, orientation, and the anisotropy (being directionally dependent or having different characteristics depending on the specific direction) of the brain's WHITE MATTER tracts.

Dopamine   A catecholamine neurotransmitter found abundantly in the brain; is thought to play a role in Parkinson's disease and has important functions in the learning of novel stimuli, the experience of pleasure, the development of substance abuse and in the neural functioning of psychosis.

Dopamine receptors   A class of metabotropic G protein-coupled receptors with dopamine as their endogenous LIGAND.

D1-like receptor   Members of this family include the D1 and D5 dopamine receptors that tend to have excitatory actions.

D2-like receptor   Members of this family include the D2, D3, and D4 dopamine receptors that tend to have inhibitory actions.

EEG (electroencephalography)   The neurophysiologic, often diagnostic, measurement of the electrical activity of the brain using recording equipment attached to the scalp by electrodes.

Efferents   Neurons or pathways that send signals from the central nervous system to the periphery or a lower processing system.

Electrophysiology   A branch of physiology pertaining to the relationship between ion flow and its regulation; when speaking specifically of the brain, it includes measurements of the electrical activity of neurons, specifically action potentials.

Encoding   The process of transforming or recoding initial information into the memory system for later retrieval.

Epigenesis   Theory that an individual is developed by successive differentiation of an unstructured egg and that the embryo is not preformed. This definition has been expanded to other fields of medicine, and in psychiatry, generally refers to the occurrence of secondary symptoms as a result of disease. In genetics, epigenetic effects refer to the interaction between environmental and genetic factors in gene expression.

Executive function   A theorized cognitive system that mediates processes such as abstract thinking, cognitive flexibility, the planning of complex behaviors, rule acquisition, and personality expression, and that moderates social behavior by inhibiting inappropriate actions and irrelevant sensory information.

Extinction   The process by which learned associations are actively lost.

fMRI (functional magnetic resonance imaging)   The use of magnetic resonance imaging (MRI) to learn which regions of the brain are active during a specific function by measuring the haemodynamic (blood flow) response related to neural activity.

Frontal cortex or lobe   A brain region present in the front of each hemisphere in all vertebrates; controls movements of specific body parts and is involved in impulse control, judgment, language, memory, problem solving, sexual behavior, socialization, spontaneity and planning, and coordinating and controlling executive function. For subregions, *see* ORBITOFRONTAL CORTEX and PREFRONTAL CORTEX.

GABA   (gamma-aminobutyric acid) The major inhibitory neurotransmitter that tends to have relaxing, antianxiety and anticonvulsive effects.

GABA A receptor   A type of GABA receptor that is found ubiquitously in the CNS.

Glial cells   Commonly referred to as neuroglia, or just glia, the nonneouronal cells in the nervous system that maintain homeostasis, form the myelin sheath around neurons, provide support and nutrition, and have important developmental roles. Recent findings indicate that they are active participants in synaptic transmission, and may be more crucial then previously thought.

Glucocorticoid   A hormone that affects the metabolism of carbohydrates, fats, and proteins, regulates cardiovascular and homeostatic functions, acts as an anti-inflammatory, immunosuppressive agent that is crucial to the stress response. Glucocorticoids are made in the adrenal gland and chemically classified as steroids; cortisol is the major natural glucocorticoid in primates.

Glutamate   The major excitatory neurotransmitter and a common amino acid.

Gray matter   One of two main solid components of the CNS, consisting of nerve cell bodies and the nonmylelinated sections of axons and dendrites, crucial for information processing.

Habituation   A form of nonassociative learning in which there is a gradual attenuation of the behavioral response with repetition of an innocuous stimulus.

Hippocampus   A bilateral brain structure located in the temporal lobe and an integral part of the limbic system that plays an important role in aspects of declarative memory. It is also implicated in disorders such as amnesia, Alzheimer's disease, schizophrenia, and various mood disorders. For localization, *see* Figure B1.

Histone   Small, basic proteins found in the nuclei of the cells of most organisms, other than viruses and bacteria (eukaryotic cells); the chief proteins of CHROMATIN, playing a role in gene regulation and acting as spools around which DNA winds.

Homologous   A likeness because of shared ancestry.

HPA (hypothalamic pituitary adrenal) axis   A neural system activated by stress that governs a neurohormonal cascade that has pervasive effects on brain function. Activation of the HPA axis leads to subsequent release of CORTICOTROPHIN RELEASING HORMONE (CRH) from the HYPOTHALAMUS, ADENOCORTICOTROPIC HORMONE (ACTH) from the pituitary, and GLUCOCORTICOIDES from the adrenals.

The HPA axis also modulates cardiovascular function, immunity, fluid retention, and metabolism.

Hypophyseal portal system   The system of blood vessels that supplies blood to part of the hypothalamus and the anterior pituitary, allowing endocrine communication between the two structures.

Hypoplasia   Underdevelopment or incomplete development of a tissue or organ. Hypoplasia is less drastic than aplasia, in which there is no development at all.

Hypothalamus   The ventral region of the diencephalon that regulates autonomic, endocrine, and visceral functions. For anatomical localization, *see* Figure B1.

Internal capsule   A massive layer (8- to 10-mm thick) of WHITE MATTER that serves as a major route by which the cerebral cortex is connected with the brainstem and spinal cord. It is a V-shaped structure, divided into the genu, anterior limb, posterior limb, and retrolenticular and sublenticular portions.

Interneuron   One of the major functional types of neurons; these relay neurons communicate only with other neurons and provide inhibitory connections between sensory and motor neurons, as well as between themselves.

Intracerebroventricular (ICV)   For research purposes, describing injection into the cerebral ventricles of the brain.

Intracranial self-stimulation   A procedure in which electrodes are implanted into an animal's brain that are activated by the animal's voluntary pressing of a lever. This demonstrated that although stimulation in most sites of the brain is not reinforcing, when DOPAMINE is involved, presumably in reward pathways, reinforcement of the behavior occurred.

Ligand   An extracellular substance, typically referring to a transmitter, drug, or hormone, that binds to an ion channel or a POSTSYNAPTIC receptor. This binding leads to a conformational change, or change in the physical structure, that subsequently alters the cell's response.

Limbic system   A collective term for the structures involved in learning, memory, motivation, and emotion. These brain regions include the amygdala, cingulate gyrus, fornicate gyrus, hippocampus, hypothalamus, mammillary body, nucleus accumbens, orbitofrontal cortex, and parahippocampal gyrus. For brain localizations, *see* Figure B1.

LTP (long-term potentiation)   The long-lasting strengthening of a connection between two nerve cells.

Medial preoptic area (MPOA)   Region of the brain that is situated immediately below the anterior commissure, above the optic chiasma, and anterior to the hypothalamus, and that regulates certain autonomic activities often with the hypothalamus.

Mediators   Processes that act as an intermediary agent; used to describe variables that mediate the effect of one factor on another.

Mesencephalic reticular activating system   Situated at the core of the brain stem, the reticular activating system is believed to be the center of arousal and motivation in animals, involved in circadian rhythm, and affected by psychotropic drugs and anesthetics.

Methylation   The enzymatic introduction of a methyl group (CH3) in a chemical compound; involved in the regulation of gene expression, regulation of protein function, epigenetic inheritance, embryonic development, and RNA metabolism.

Methylphenidate   A mild stimulant of the central nervous system that is administered orally to treat narcolepsy and hyperactivity disorders.

Microcephaly   A condition in which the circumference of the head is abnormally small, usually associated with mental retardation.

Microgenesis   A theory of mind and brain based on a process approach to anatomy in relation to patterns of symptom formation in patients with disturbances of language, action, and perception. A model of the organization of cognition in the normal brain that is inferred from the symptoms of brain damage, their change over time, and their relation to pathology in specific brain areas.

Midbrain   Region including the inferior and superior colliculi, the cerebral peduncles, internal capsule, cerebral aqueduct, and substantia nigra; controls many sensory and motor functions.

Moderator   In statistics, a variable that changes the direction or strength of the association between two other variables.

Monoamines   Amines, specifically neurotransmitters and neuromodulators, that are functionally important in neural transmission, that have one organic substituent attached to the nitrogen atom. These include catecholamines (dopamine, norephine-phrine, and epinephrine), serotonin, histamine, thyronamines, tryptamine, tyramine, and β-Phenylethylamine.

mRNA (messenger RNA)   An RNA, produced by transcription, that encodes and carries genetic information from nuclear DNA to ribosomes, the site of protein synthesis.

Myelin sheath   An electrically insulating phospholipid layer surrounding the axons of neurons performed by glial cells; helps to speed transmission of information.

Neocortex   The large six-layered dorsal region of the cerebral cortex that is unique to mammals.

Neurogenesis   The process by which neurons are created and therefore extremely prominent during prenatal development to populate the growing brain. Recent findings show that this early developmental phenomenon also occurs in certain regions (dentate gyrus and olfactory bulb) in adulthood.

Neuropeptides   Endogenous peptides (as endorphins or enkephalins) that serve as a chemical signal to influence neural activity or functioning.

Neuroplasticity   The brain's ability to physically change in response to stimuli and activity; thought to be the neural mechanism of learning.

Neurotoxin   A protein complex that is specifically poisonous to neurons, usually by interacting with membrane proteins and ion channels.

Neurotransmitter   Any of several chemical substances released by PRESYNAPTIC neurons that relay, modulate, and amplify electrical signals by binding to POSTSYNAPTIC receptors. A neurotransmitter must be synthesized endogenously (originating from within the neuron) and be available in amounts sufficient to exert effects on POSTSYNAPTIC neurons. A biochemical mechanism for its inactivation must also be present, as the neurotransmitter must be physically inactivated after it exerts its effects. The final defining factor of a neurotransmitter is that systemic administration (superficially adding it) should mimic the endogenous effects. Examples include: (1) amino acids (primarily glutamic acid, GABA, aspartic acid, and glycine), (2) peptides (vasopressin, somatostatin, neurotensin, etc.), and (3) monoamines (norepinephrine, dopamine, and serotonin) plus acetylcholine.

NMDA receptor   A type of GLUTAMATE receptor that is activated by NMDA (N-methyl-D-aspartate) and is thought to play a critical role in synaptic plasticity, the cellular mechanism for learning and memory.

Noradrenergic transmission   Synaptic transmission produced by a neuron that releases norepinephrine.

Norepinephrine   A CATECHOLAMINE that is the chemical means of transmission across synapses in postganglionic neurons of the sympathetic nervous system and in some parts of the central nervous system. It is a vasopressor hormone of the adrenal medulla, has a prominent role in the stress response, is important in attention, and is a precursor of epinephrine in its major biosynthetic pathway.

Nucleotides   Basic structural units of DNA and RNA consisting of a ribose or deoxyribose sugar joined to a heterocyclic base and to a phosphate group that play important roles in energy production, metabolism, and signaling.

Nucleus accumbens   A collection of neurons that are part of the ventral striatum and thought to play an important role in reward, pleasure, and addiction. For localization see Figure B1.

Ontogenetic   The development or course of development of an individual organism.

Opiate   A drug derived from opium, tending to induce sleep and to work as an analgesic.

Orbitofrontal cortex (OFC)   A region of the medial PFC above the eyes important in decision making, emotion, and in the regulation of planning behavior associated with reward and punishment.

Oxytocin   A hormone that also acts as a neurotransmitter, secreted by the anterior lobe of the pituitary gland, that stimulates the contraction of uterine muscle and the secretion of milk, is released during orgasm, and is involved in social recognition and pair bonding.

Parietal lobe   The middle division of each cerebral hemisphere that is situated behind the central sulcus, above the sylvian fissure, and in front of the parieto-occipital sulcus and is crucial in the integration of sensory information and in the manipulation of objects.

Parvocellular   Characterized by relatively small cell bodies.

Phencyclidine (PCP)   A former medical and veterinary anesthetic, now often used illicitly as a psychedelic drug to induce hallucinogenic effects.

Polymorphism   The existence of a gene or molecule in two or more forms in a single species.

Postsynaptic cell A neuron whose excitability is affected by chemical or electrical signals in the synapse sent from a presynaptic cell.

Prefrontal cortex (PFC)   The gray matter of the anterior part of the frontal lobe that is highly developed in humans and plays a role in the regulation of complex cognitive, emotional, and behavioral functioning (executive function), including personality expression and moderating social behavior. The PFC includes the medial PFC and dorsolateral PFC. For anatomical localization, *see* Figure B1.

Presynaptic cell   The communicating cell that secretes the neurotransmitter, which binds to receptors on the postsynaptic cell.

Promoter   A regulatory region of DNA sequence, usually immediately upstream from the coding region, that enables the gene to be transcribed.

Propagule   The seed in sexual reproduction.

Prophylactic   A preventative, such as a drug, to impede the spread or incidence of a disease or infection.

Pruning   Elimination of axons to eradicate projections to inappropriate targets and to enhance the specificity of axonal projections.

Putamen   A portion of the basal ganglia that forms the outermost part of the lenticular nucleus that plays an important role in reinforcement learning. For anatomical localization, *see* Figure B2.

PVN (paraventricular nucleus)   A discrete band of nerve cells in the anterior part of the hypothalamus that contain centrally projecting peptide neurons and both magnocellular (that produce vasopressin and oxytocin) and parvocellular (that produce CRH, vasopressin, and TRH) neurosecretory cells.

Pyramidal neuron   A multipolar neuron located in the hippocampus and cerebral cortex that has a triangular-shaped soma, with both apical and basal dendrites. These neurons use GLUTAMATE as the neurotransmitter and make excitatory connections, as opposed to the inhibitory INTERNEURONS that use GABA.

Receptor   A protein on the cell membrane or within the cytoplasm or cell nucleus, characterized by the specific, high affinity binding of a LIGAND in a lock-and-key fashion. BINDING transmits the extracellular signal and triggers specific physiological events within the POSTSYNAPTIC cell.

Reversal potential   The membrane voltage at which there is no net flow of ions from one side of the membrane to the other.

Serotonin (5 hydroxytryptamine)   A monoamine neurotransmitter that is a powerful vasoconstrictor and is found in the brain, blood serum, and gastric mucous membrane of mammals. In the CNS, serotonin is thought to play a major role in regulation of mood, sleep, emesis, sexuality, and appetite, and is implicated in the pathophysiology of many disorders, such as depression, migraines, bipolar disorder, and anxiety.

5 HT (serotonin) receptor   A receptor of serotonin, as well as a broad range of pharmaceutical and hallucinogenic drugs such as antidepressants, anxiolytics, and antoemetics. There are many subtypes (5 HT_{1A}, 5 HT_{1B}, 5 HT_{1D}, 5 HT_{2A}, 5 HT_{2B}, 5 HT_{2C}, 5 HT_3, 5 HT_4, 5 HT_5, 5 HT_6, 5 HT_7) of this receptor that all have different actions, agonists, and antagonists.

Serotonin transporter   A MONOAMINE TRANSPORTER protein that regulates the serotonin concentration in the synapse by recycling serotonin back into the neuron. SSRIs (selective serotonin reuptake inhibitors) reduce binding of serotonin to the transporter, increasing its time and therefore effect in the synaptic cleft, and are used to treat depression and OCD.

Signal transduction   Any process, taking a millisecond or as long as a few seconds, by which a cell converts one kind of signal or stimulus into another, often involving a sequence of biochemical reactions inside the cell that are carried out by enzymes and linked through second messengers.

Spatial resolution   The ability to sharply and clearly define the extent or shape of features within an image, describing how close two features can be and still be resolved as unique.

Steroid hormones   Any of numerous hormones (such as glucocorticoids, mineralocorticoids, androgens, estrogens, and progestogens) having the characteristic ring structure of steroids and formed in the body from cholesterol.

Striatum   A subcortical brain structure, consisting of the caudate nucleus and the putamen, that plays important roles in planning and modulating movement pathways and other cognitive processes involving executive function. *See* Figure B2.

Substance P   A neuropeptide and neurotransmitter that is widely distributed in the brain, spinal cord, and peripheral nervous system that acts across nerve synapses to produce prolonged postsynaptic excitation. In the CNS, substance P is important in regulating mood disorders, anxiety, stress, reinforcement, neurogenesis, neurotoxicity, emesis, and pain.

Subunit   A single protein molecule that assembles with other protein molecules to form a multimeric (formed with many different subunits) or oligomeric (composed of many identical subunits) protein. A subunit is made up of one polypeptide chain, the sequence specifics of which are stored in the code of genes.

Sulcus   A groove between two gyri in the cerebral cortex.

Sympathetic adrenal medullary (SAM)   The adrenal medulla, the principal site of catecholamine synthesis, is actually a ganglion, a tissue mass that contains the dendrites and cell bodies of neurons, of the sympathetic nervous system.

Synaptogenesis   The formation of nerve synapses.

Telencephalon   The anterior-most embryological region of the brain that gives rise to the cerebral hemispheres and other, smaller structures within the brain.

Thalamus   Located in the center of the brain, serves as a relay station for nerve impulses carrying sensory information into the central nervous system and processes most of the information reaching the cerebral cortex. For localization, *see* Figures B1 and B2.

Transcription   The process of using a DNA molecule as a template to enzymatically construct a complementary messenger RNA molecule, thereby transferring genetic information.

Transcription factors   Any of various proteins that bind to DNA at specific promoter or enhancer regions to regulate gene expression by enhancing transcription.

Transporter   A protein that mediates the active transport of ions, nutrients, and other molecules into a cell against their electrochemical gradient by using energy from ATP hydrolysis, a reaction in which chemical energy stored in the form of phosphate bonds in ATP (adenosine triphosphate) is released.

Trinucleotide repeat sequences   Stretches of DNA in a gene that contain the same trinucleotide sequence repeated many times and occur throughout all genomic sequences. However, if the repeat is present in a gene, an expansion of the repeats may result in a defective gene product that can often lead to disease states.

Typical antipsychotics   Medications used to treat psychosis, especially schizophrenia, acute mania, and agitation; are thought to work by blocking dopamine receptors and are now being replaced by atypical antipsychotic drugs.

Vasopressin (arginine)   A polypeptide hormone, also known as antidiuretic hormone (ADH), that is secreted by the posterior lobe of the pituitary gland, increases blood pressure, and exerts an antidiuretic effect. Like OXYTOCIN, vasopressin is thought to play a role is social behaviors, such as pair bonding.

Ventricle   A cavernous system within the brain that produces cerebrospinal fluid (CSF), used to bathe and cushion the brain and spinal cord.

White matter   One of the two main solid components of the CNS, composed of myelinated axons that connect gray matter systems and carry nerve impulses between neurons; plays a crucial role in speeding information transmission.

Appendix B

Brain Locations

Eian More

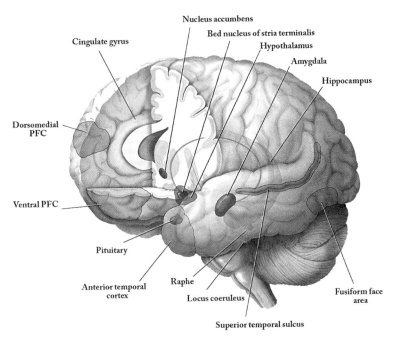

Figure B-1 Human brain structures relevant to psychopathology and mental health. Raphe and Locus coeruleus are in the brain stem. PFC refers to the prefrontal cortex.

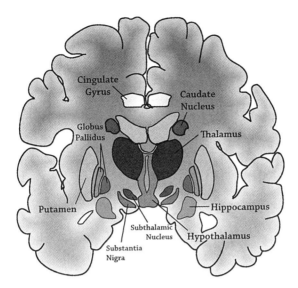

Figure B-2 Horizontal slice of the human brain showing internal view of brain structures relevant to psychopathology and mental health. The caudate nucleus and putamen are termed the corpus striatum; the basal ganglia are composed of the striatum and the globus pallidus.

Appendix C

Author Biographies

Lyn Abramson, Ph.D., is Professor of Psychology in the Department of Psychology, University of Wisconsin. Her research focuses on vulnerability and invulnerability to depression, with particular interest in the developmental, cognitive, motivational, and cultural determinants of information processing about the self. She has begun to explore the effects of early psychological, physical, and sexual maltreatment on the development of cognitive styles and vulnerability to depression in adulthood.

Lauren B. Alloy, Ph.D., is Professor and Joseph Wolpe Distinguished Faculty Fellow in the Department of Psychology, Temple University. Her research focuses on cognitive, psychosocial, and, recently, biological processes in the onset and course of depression and bipolar disorder. She studies the role of cognitive, psychosocial, and biological vulnerabilities in the context of developmental processes as precursors of mood disorders.

Karen L. Bales, Ph.D., is Assistant Professor in the Department of Psychology at the University of California, Davis, and an Affiliate Scientist at the California National Primate Research Center. She studies the physiology, neurobiology, and development of social bonding in monogamous species, including prairie voles, titi monkeys, and golden lion tamarins. She is particularly interested in the roles of the hormones oxytocin and vasopressin, as well as the effects of early experience on subsequent social bonding.

Clancy Blair, Ph.D., M.PH., is Associate Professor in the Department of Human Development and Family Studies at Penn State University. His work focuses on the ways in which neurobiology and experience interact to shape the development of self-regulation in early childhood.

C. Sue Carter, Ph.D., is Professor of Psychiatry and Co-Director of the Brain Body Center at the University of Illinois at Chicago. She is best known for her work on prairie voles, which led to a novel understanding of the neurobiology of monogamy and social bonding. Her research program continues to describe new roles for neuropeptide hormones, including oxytocin, vasopressin, and corticotropin-releasing hormone in social behavior and emotional regulation.

Kiki Chang, M.D., is Assistant Professor of Psychiatry and Behavioral Sciences at the Stanford University School of Medicine, Division of Child Psychiatry. He is Director of the Pediatric Bipolar Disorders Clinic, where he specializes in pediatric psychopharmacology and treatment of depression and bipolar disorder in children and adolescents. He is currently conducting phenomenologic, biologic, pharmacologic, and genetic studies of bipolar disorder in adults and children with the aim of detecting prodromal bipolar disorder in children who might then be treated to prevent the development of the full disorder.

Dennis S. Charney, M.D., is Dean for Academic and Scientific Affairs for Mount Sinai School of Medicine, and Senior Vice President for Health Sciences of the Mount Sinai Medical Center. From 2000 to 2004, he was Chief of the Mood and Anxiety Disorder Research Program and the Experimental Therapeutics and Pathophysiology Branch at the National Institute of Mental Health. His research focuses on the greater fundamental understanding of neural circuits, neurochemistry, and functional neuroanatomy of the regulation of mood and anxiety and the psychobiological mechanisms of human resilience to stress.

Nicole Cooper, Ph.D., is Assistant Professor in the Department of Psychiatry at the Mount Sinai School of Medicine and Chief Psychologist of the Mood and Anxiety Disorders Program. She specializes in the study and treatment of post-traumatic stress disorder and other mood and anxiety disorders. She has just launched two studies investigating trauma and resilience in medical students and in adolescents.

Shivali H. Dhruv, M.A., is a graduate student in the Emory Neuroscience Program interested in clinical research on the etiology of major mental disorders. She is particularly interested in the role of stress in triggering adverse neurohormonal processes that can lead to the expression of psychiatric symptoms in vulnerable individuals.

Martha Farah, Ph.D., is Professor of Psychology and Director of the Center for Cognitive Neuroscience at the University of Pennsylvania, where she does research on the neural bases of human cognition. In recent years she has undertaken a program of research on the neurocognitive correlates of socioeconomic status.

Adriana Feder, M.D., is Assistant Professor in the Department of Psychiatry at the Mount Sinai School of Medicine and an attending physician in the Mood and Anxiety Disorders Program. Her primary areas of research include the transmission of depression in families, biological markers of risk for depression, and vulnerability and resilience after psychological trauma.

Nathan A. Fox, Ph.D., is Professor of Human Development at the University of Maryland. His interests lie in the development of emotion, the effects of early experience on brain and social behavior, and the emergence of psychopathology in children. He is the recipient of a MERIT award from the National Institute of Child Health and Human Development for his work on infant temperament.

Kim Gallelli, Ph.D., is completing her postdoctoral fellowship in the Division of Child and Adolescent Psychiatry at Stanford University School of Medicine. Her research interests focus on the neurobiological correlates of bipolar disorder, as well as the development and implementation of psychosocial interventions for children with and at high risk for bipolar disorder.

Anthony Grace, Ph.D., is Professor of Neuroscience, Psychiatry, and Psychology at the University of Pittsburgh. His research interests lie at the interface of neurobiology and psychiatry. Experiments conducted in his laboratory combine in vivo and in vitro electrophysiological recordings of identified neurons with behavioral and neuroanatomical techniques to study central dopaminergic systems, with the ultimate goal of determining the neurobiological correlates of mental disorders and the modes of action of psychotherapeutic drugs.

Mark Greenberg, Ph.D., holds the Bennett Endowed Chair in Prevention Research in Penn State's College of Health and Human Development. He is currently Director of the Prevention Research Center for the Promotion of Human Development and Associate Director for the Penn State Consortium on Children, Youth and Families. Since 1981, he has been examining the effectiveness of school-based programs (e.g., the PATHS Curriculum) to improve the social, emotional, and cognitive competence of elementary-aged children.

Patricia Gorman Barry, Ph.D., is founding director of the Positive Life Choices® nonprofit agency in Denver, Colorado, and developer of the BrainWise program. Since 1995, the agency has provided BrainWise materials and training to improve the thinking skills of children, teens, and adults. BrainWise is taught by more than 2,000 teachers, social workers, counselors, visiting nurses, and other advocates throughout the world, and has been translated into Spanish and Chinese.

Megan R. Gunnar, Ph.D., is a Distinguished McKnight Professor of Child Development at the Institute of Child Development, University of Minnesota. She has documented the powerful role of close relationships in regulating stress biology in young children. She directs an NIH-sponsored research network on early experience, stress, and prevention science and is a member of both the Experience-Based Brain Development program of the Canadian Institute for Advanced Research and the National Scientific Council on the Developing Child.

Scott Hemby, Ph.D., is Associate Professor of Physiology and Pharmacology at Wake Forest University School of Medicine. His research focuses on the molecular neuropathology of schizophrenia and drug addiction.

Meghan Howe, M. SW., is the Laboratory Manager of the Pediatric Bipolar Disorders Program at Stanford University School of Medicine, Division of Child Psychiatry. Her research focuses on the development of therapeutic, educational, and advocacy programs for child and adolescent populations, with particular attention to bipolar disorder.

Hallam Hurt, M.D., is a neonatologist at the Children's Hospital of Philadelphia and the Hospital of the University of Pennsylvania. She has a long-standing interest in the outcomes of inner-city children. This interest stems, in part, from her investigations regarding effects of gestational substance exposure and poverty on child outcome. She currently is exploring precursors of substance use in 10- to 12-year-old youths.

Ann S. Masten, Ph.D., is Distinguished McKnight University Professor at the Institute of Child Development, University of Minnesota, serving as department chair 1999–2005. Masten is a licensed psychologist and Director of the Project Competence studies of risk and resilience in development. She is currently President of Division 7 (Developmental) of the American Psychological Association and serves on the Governing Council of the Society for Research in Child Development.

Erin McClure, Ph.D., is Assistant Professor of Psychology at Georgia State University. Previously, she served as a Research Fellow in the Emotional Development and Affective Neuroscience Branch in the Mood and Anxiety Disorders Program of the National Institute of Mental Health Intramural Research Program. Her research focuses on mood and anxiety disorders in children and adolescents, with particular interest in relationships among gender, social impairment, and neurobiological functioning.

Amanda McMillan, B.A., is a medical student who plans to specialize in child psychiatry. Prior to entering medical school, she coordinated research programs at Emory University for Dr. Elaine Walker in studies with adolescents at risk for psychotic disorders.

Michael J. Meaney, Ph.D., is a James McGill Professor of Medicine at Douglas Hospital Research Centre of McGill University. He is the Director of the Maternal Adversity, Vulnerability and Neurodevelopment Project and of the Developmental Neuroendocrinology Laboratory of McGill University. His primary research interest is on the effects of early experience on gene expression and development. His research is multidisciplinary and includes studies of behavior and physiology, molecular biology, and genetics. The primary objective of these studies is to define the processes that govern gene-environment interactions.

Vijay Mittal, M.A., is a graduate student in the Clinical Psychology program at Emory University. His dissertation research examines the longitudinal progression of motor abnormalities and prodromal symptomatology in adolescents at risk for psychotic disorders. He is particularly interested in research designed to elucidate the neurocorrelates of nonverbal deficits.

Lyda Moller, Ph.D., is a clinical psychologist in private practice. Her research has surveyed clinical psychology, developmental psychology, neuroscience, and evolution for common origins within these disciplines. Building on this framework, her theoretical work has proposed dual interpersonal motivations, based on left- and right-hemisphere contributions, that form the basis for the chapter with Tucker in the present volume.

Charles Nelson, III, Ph.D., holds the Richard David Scott Chair in Pediatric Developmental Medicine Research at Children's Hospital, Harvard Medical School. He chaired the John D. and Catherine T. MacArthur Foundation Research Network on Early Experience and Brain Development. His interests concern the effects of early experience on brain and behavioral development, and he studies both typically developing children and children at risk for neurodevelopmental disorders.

Kimberly Noble, Ph.D., is a recent graduate of the Neuroscience Program at the University of Pennsylvania. Her research has examined how socioeconomic background influences neurocognitive development in children, with an emphasis on reading development. She is also pursuing an M.D. from Penn and plans to pursue an academic career in pediatrics.

Charles P. O'Brien, M.D., Ph.D., is Kenneth Appel Professor and Vice-Chair of Psychiatry at the University of Pennsylvania, Vice Director of the Institute of Neurological Sciences, and Director of the Center for Studies of Addiction. His work involves discovery of CNS changes involved in relapse, new medications, behavioral treatments, and instruments for measuring the severity of addictive disorders. Many of these discoveries are now utilized in common practice for the treatment of addictive disorders throughout the world.

Daniel Pine, M.D., is Chief of the Emotional Development and Affective Neuroscience Branch and Chief of Child and Adolescent Research in the Mood and Anxiety Disorders Program of the National Institute of Mental Health Intramural Research Program. He has been engaged continuously in research focusing on the epidemiology, biology, and treatment of psychiatric disorders in children and adolescents. He is currently examining the degree to which mood and anxiety disorders in children and adolescents are associated with underlying abnormalities in the amygdala, prefrontal cortex, and other brain regions that modulate activity in these structures.

Michael Posner, Ph.D., is Professor Emeritus at the University of Oregon and Adjunct Professor of Psychology in Psychiatry at the Weill Medical College of Cornell, where he served as founding director of the Sackler Institute. He has worked on the anatomy, circuitry, development, and genetics of three attentional networks underlying maintaining alertness, orienting to sensory events, and voluntary control of thoughts and ideas. His current research involves understanding the interaction of specific experience and genes in shaping attention.

Nathaniel R. Riggs, Ph.D., is a Postdoctoral Research Fellow in the Institute for Prevention Research at the University of Southern California. Among his research interests are determining the role of neurocognition in models of prevention and translating evidence-based prevention programs for youth violence and substance use to programs focusing on the prevention of youth obesity.

Daniel Romer, Ph.D., is Director of the Adolescent Risk Communication Institute in the Annenberg Public Policy Center at the University of Pennsylvania. At the Institute, he promotes the synthesis of research on adolescent mental and behavioral health to educate the public, scholarly community, and policy makers about effective strategies to enhance adolescent development. He also conducts the annual National Annenberg Risk Survey of Youth, a national probability sample of young people ages 14 to 22, to assess trends in risks to health and their correlates and predictors.

Mary Rothbart, Ph.D., is a Distinguished Professor Emerita at the University of Oregon. She studies temperament and emotional and social development, and for the last 25 years has worked with Michael Posner studying the development of attention and its relation to temperamental effortful control. She has also made contributions to the education and support of new parents through Eugene, Oregon's Birth to Three organization.

M. Rosario Rueda, Ph.D., is Research Associate in the Cognitive Neuroscience Laboratory at the Department of Experimental Psychology, University of Granada (Spain). Her work has focused on studying the development of attention in children using cognitive and brain function assessments. Her current research involves exploring the appropriate methods to train attention in young children, as well as understanding the contribution of individual differences in attention to emotional regulation and social and school competency in children and adolescents.

Lisa Saccomanno, Ph.D., is a Postdoctoral Fellow with Bruce Bowerman at the University of Oregon. Prior to joining the Bowerman lab, Lisa was Director of the Genomics Facility at the University of Oregon, where she began a collaborative project with Michael Posner from the Institute of Neuroscience to examine the molecular basis for the neural network that underlies self-regulation of cognition and affect.

Steven Southwick, M.D., is Professor of Psychiatry at the Yale Medical School and at the Yale Child Study Center, Adjunct Professor of Psychiatry at the Mt. Sinai School of Medicine, and Deputy Director of the Clinical Neurosciences Division of the National Center for Posttraumatic Stress Disorder. His research focuses on the phenomenology and neurobiology of PTSD, the longitudinal course of trauma-related psychological symptoms, memory for traumatic events, treatment of PTSD, and neurobiological and psychological factors associated with resilience to stress.

Elizabeth Sowell, Ph.D., is Associate Professor in the Department of Neurology at the University of California, Los Angeles. Her research has focused on normative brain development and brain morphologic abnormalities in children with various neurodevelopmental disorders such as fetal alcohol syndrome and attention deficit/ hyperactivity disorder. She is currently conducting longitudinal studies of children with prenatal methamphetamine exposure using functional and structural neuroimaging.

Linda Spear, Ph.D., is a Distinguished Professor in Psychology at Binghamton University. Her current research interests focus on use of animal models to characterize age-specific neurobehavioral features of adolescence as contributors to the initiation, progression, and potential long-term consequences of alcohol, drug use, and other problem behaviors during adolescence.

Arthur W. Toga, Ph.D., is Professor of Neurology at the University of California, Los Angeles. His research focuses on neuroimaging, mapping brain structure and function, and brain atlasing. He directs the Laboratory of Neuro Imaging, is Co-Director of the Division of Brain Mapping, and is Founding Editor of the journal *NeuroImage*.

Don Tucker, Ph.D., is Professor of Psychology and Director of the Brain Electrophysiology Laboratory in the Department of Psychology, University of Oregon. His basic research examines motivational and emotional mechanisms of the human brain. His applied research focuses on technology for imaging human brain activity with dense array (256–channel) electroencephalographic recordings.

Elaine Walker, Ph.D., is the Samuel Candler Dobbs Professor of Psychology and Neuroscience in the Department of Psychology at Emory University. Her research focuses on the precursors and neurodevelopmental aspects of psychopathology, especially schizophrenia, with emphasis on the role of stress hormones in triggering behavioral disorders and cognitive dysfunction. Her research is also concerned with neuropsychological and motor deficits and their implications for the origins and course of mental illness.

Marilyn C. Welsh, Ph.D., is Professor of Psychology at the University of Northern Colorado. Her current research program examines the nature of executive function and the cognitive processes mediated by the prefrontal cortex. She has conducted studies that focus on understanding the development of executive processes in typical and atypical populations, the construction and validation of new assessment tools, and the degree to which interventions can facilitate executive functions in children and adults.

Charles H. Zeanah, Jr., M.D., is Professor of Psychiatry and Pediatrics and Director of Child and Adolescent Psychiatry at the Tulane University School of Medicine, where he holds the Sellars-Polchow Chair in Psychiatry. He has a long-standing interest in infant mental health, and his research and clinical interests concern the effects of abuse and serious deprivation on young children's development, developmental and clinical aspects of attachment, psychopathology in early childhood, and infant-parent relationships.

Index

Page numbers followed by an *f* or *t* indicate figures and tables. Page numbers followed by an "n" and another number indicate notes.